A SOURCEBOOK ON DOMESTIC
AND
INTERNATIONAL TERRORISM

Second Edition

A SOURCEBOOK ON DOMESTIC AND INTERNATIONAL TERRORISM

An Analysis of Issues, Organizations, Tactics and Responses

By

WAYMAN C. MULLINS, Ph.D.

Department of Criminal Justice
Southwest Texas State University
San Marcos, Texas

With a Foreword by

Michael J. McMains, Ph.D.

San Antonio Police Department

CHARLES C THOMAS • PUBLISHER, LTD.
Springfield • Illinois • U.S.A.

Published and Distributed Throughout the World by

CHARLES C THOMAS • PUBLISHER, LTD.
2600 South First Street
Springfield, Illinois 62794-9265

© *1997 by* CHARLES C THOMAS • PUBLISHER, LTD.
ISBN 0-398-06722-8 (cloth)
ISBN 0-398-06723-6 (paper)

Library of Congress Catalog Card Number: 96-30404

First Edition, 1988
Second Edition, 1997

With THOMAS BOOKS *careful attention is given to all details of manufacturing and design. It is the Publisher's desire to present books that are satisfactory as to their physical qualities and artistic possibilities and appropriate for their particular use.* THOMAS BOOKS *will be true to those laws of quality that assure a good name and good will.*

Printed in the United States of America
SC-R-3

Library of Congress Cataloging-in-Publication Data

Mullins, Wayman C.
  A sourcebook on domestic and international terrorism : an analysis
of issues, organizations, tactics, and responses / by Wayman C.
Mullins ; with a foreword by Michael J. McMains. — 2nd ed.
     p.   cm.
  Rev. ed. of: Terrorist organizations in the United States. c1988.
  Includes bibliographical references (p.   ) and index.
  ISBN 0-398-06722-8 (cloth). — ISBN 0-398-06723-6 (paper)
  1. Terrorism—United States.   2. Terrorism—United States—
Prevention.   3. Terrorists—United States.   I. Mullins, Wayman C.
Terrorist organizations in the United States.   II. Title.
HV6432.M86   1996
303.6'25'0973—dc20   96-30404
                                                                      CIP

This book is fondly dedicated to those who brung me to the dance:

William and Mary Anna Mullins
Louis, Ruth, and Rachael
Wilson Kimbrough

FOREWORD

S ince the publishing of the First Edition of Terrorist Organizations in the United States in 1988, terrorism has moved from fantasy to reality, from possible to probable in the thinking of law enforcement in the United States. The bombing of the World Trade Center in New York City made reality of a fear lurking in the back of the minds of some and denied completely by many. The bombing of the Federal Building in Oklahoma City demonstrated that it was not just the large metropolitan areas of the East and West coasts that needed to fear terrorists, but that mid-America, the heartland could be devastated as well. Oklahoma City taught us that it is not just foreign-based terrorists that are of concern, but home grown terrorists of the far right, a possibility to which Dr. Mullins pointed to in the first edition of this book.

In addition, these experiences have served to bring to the general public an awareness of "the true believers" of both the radical left and the reactionary right. However, with awareness has not necessarily come new knowledge. The awareness of the reality of terrorist acts in the U.S. has served to sensitize the public to the point that the first thing one thinks of is terrorism when an Oklahoma City type bombing occurs. However, it is also the first thing that occurs to us when an airliner explodes over the Atlantic, even when there is no evidence of terrorist activity. Such thinking is based on a lack of knowledge of the extent, methods and goals of terrorist groups in the U.S.

The degree to which terrorism is the first idea that occurs to the public is an indirect measure of the success of terrorism. It is evidence that terrorist goals of preying on fear and uncertainty are being achieved and it multiplies the effectiveness of terrorism. As long as it is believed that terrorists are behind such bombing, it matters little that they are not actually behind them. The thought that terrorists are the source of violence, even when there is no evidence that they are involved, is terrifying in itself, perhaps even more so than if there is evidence of their involvement. If there is evidence of who was involved in a bombing, it is sadly reassuring for most of us, because it is not a shadowy figure in our imagination with which we are dealing; it is a real organization.

However, when there is no evidence, one of two things happens: (1) the uncertainty around the incident keeps it in our awareness and keeps our anxiety high because of our lack of closure on the incident, or (2) our imagination fills our thoughts with answers and imagination is always more powerful than facts: we create a more powerful enemy than really exists.

As I said in the Foreword of the First Edition of Terrorist Organizations, an antidote to imagination is knowledge. If law enforcement and the general public know as much as is known about terrorism, terrorist groups in the U.S. terrorist organization, terrorists' preferred methods of operating, and the consequences of their acts, it reduces the uncertainty, narrows the scope of the problem, and makes planning and intervention easier. It reduces uncertainty and terror. It is analogous to a person having a pain in the stomach. He may have general knowledge about sources of pain in the stomach: it may be an ulcer, an appendicitis attack, or, perhaps, cancer. Beyond these possibilities, the person may know little. He may not know what the symptoms of these medical problems are. As a consequence, he may jump to the conclusion that he has terminal cancer and refuse to go to a doctor because he does not want to confirm his worst suspicion. He engages in self-defeating behavior that increases fear and reduces his ability to act. It is a kind of terror that builds from his imagination. The solution is to prepare the person by educating him to the symptoms of ulcers, appendicitis and stomach cancer as well as to the treatment options and survival rates for each disease. Then a better decision can be reached and a plan developed. Knowledge helps narrow the diagnosis and focus the treatment for terrorism in the same way it does for stomach problems. It takes away the power of uncertainty on which terrorism flourishes, reduces fear, and increases positive planning and action.

Dr. Mullins' expanded Second Edition gives law enforcement the most up-to-date available knowledge about terrorism. It brings together all important aspects of terrorism that law enforcement can use for planning its own response when confronted with the reality of terrorism. In addition, it provides a solid source of the information that law enforcement needs to develop a public awareness and education program to combat the fear of the unknown that is basic to terrorism. His expansion makes this reference the single most complete source available in the field.

Finally, such knowledge will help us develop legislation and techniques that will help discourage the pursuit of terrorism. For instance, the proposal that a chemical marker be added to the ingredients that are used to make bombs, making them easier to trace, is likely to be preventative if it is instituted and becomes widely advertised. It is based on the knowledge of what the current popular bombing technology includes. Many other counterterrorist measures will flow from an understanding of terrorism and its technology, psychology, and organization.

Several chapters are particularly useful in planning, politicking, and public education. They include Chapter 3, Terrorist Motivation and Psychology; Chapter 4, An Organizational Perspective; Chapter 5, United States Terrorist Organizations; Chapter 6, Terrorist Targets; Chapter 8, Nuclear, Biological and Chemical Terrorism; Chapter 9, Counter-Terrorism and Legal Issues.

Chapter 3 is a particularly useful chapter, because a clear understanding of terrorists' motivation helps Law Enforcement anticipate, plan for, and manage terrorist actions. For instance, one point that is well made by Dr. Mullins is that even though there are similarities between terrorists, there are significant differences. The motivation for state-sponsored terrorism may be considerably different than the motivation for the disenfranchised. The former may use terrorism to eliminate opposition or to eliminate dissent, while the latter may use terrorism to undermine faith in the current government. These goals dictate different targets, different strategies, and different tactics; all of which needs to be taken into consideration while planning, education, management and political responses to terrorism.

Chapter 4 is valuable in that it highlights the organizational structure that terrorists use which makes them difficult to deal with and it updates the list of terrorist organizations that are extant in the U.S. The former is a valuable resource in that it explains why it is difficult to gain intelligence of terrorist activities and at the same time it highlights the need for a different and more comprehensive approach to intelligence gathering. One of the implications is that more resources need to be expended on infiltrating terrorist groups before incidents occur. The public needs to be aware of this issue because it will require legislative action in balancing the need for intelligence and the civil rights of individuals and groups, as well as financial support for increased intelligence efforts in the U.S.

The separation of Chapters 6 and 5 is helpful in emphasizing the risk and easy availability of NBC weapons in the currently unstable world. The break-up of the Soviet Union and the subsequent loss of Russian control over its nuclear arsenal is but one source of sophisticated or simple and powerful weaponry that will increase terrorists' ability to raise the stakes and consequently the terror they are able to generate.

The addition of Chapter 9, Counter-Terrorism and Legal Issues, focuses not only on the balance between safety and security of citizens on the one hand and constitutional rights of citizens on the other; it also clarifies the different responses to terrorism that are available at the international level versus the domestic level of planning. For instance, Dr. Mullins rightly points out that preemptive military action is an option available in the prevention of terrorism at the international level, while preemptive law enforcement strikes are not currently an option domestically. Considerable debate would be necessary and appropriate before a change in domestic policy would be appropriate. Information about the constitutional implications of such policy changes needs to be available to the public in its consideration of the costs and gains in any response option. Dr. Mullins' book serves a valuable resource in educating a fairly informed public. Education is basic to a democratic republic and Dr. Mullins' book helps provide that education. It reduces doubt, fear, terror, and provides a base for educated decision making. It is a major asset to law enforcement, political action, and the public education.

MICHAEL J. MCMAINS, PH.D.

INTRODUCTION

In Hawaii is a cemetery containing over 31,000 young men violently struck down in the prime of life. This cemetery, called Punchbowl, sits high on a hill overlooking a simple, white oblong concrete structure in the harbor at Pearl Harbor. This memorial marks the site where the *USS Arizona* lies beneath the quiet waves of a calm Pacific ocean, cemetery for 1,177 other young sailors killed on 7 December 1941. These two testimonials of remembrance are but two of the thousands scattered throughout the world that call for reflection on the greatest conflagration the world has ever seen. Between 1931–1945, World War II cost the lives of over 20 million people, seriously injured almost another 50 million, and made over 100 million others homeless and destitute.

Today, over 50 years following the end of that war, few are alive who witnessed the events of that period. More tragically, few study and learn from the lessons taught during that time of world history. Today, few care what transpired around the globe during that period. Chapters in the book of the dead from that war fill huge volumes with vague names from a distance past: Auschwitz, Treblinka, Chelmno, Tobruk, Dresden, Ardennes, Tarawa, Boin and Gona (New Guinea), Peking, Pelileu, Okinawa, Hiroshima, and Nagasaki, to list a few. With each passing day, the contrast fades a little more, the memories a little less bright, the awareness less brilliant.

While it is important to remember, one must ask what the significance is of this memory to terrorism in the 1990s. World War II is significant in two respects. One, it was a war of terrorism unlike any war that preceded it. Two despots, each striving for the glory of power, turned a tool used by the disenfranchised and malcontent into a hammer-like weapon they used to shatter the globe. Hitler and Tojo personified terrorism at its very worst. Individually and together, they changed terrorism from its earlier art form into a calculated science of murder, destruction, and political ideology. Two, World War II ushered in a new era of terrorism. Prior to WWII, terrorism was primarily individual acts of assassination, isolated bombing incidents, and poorly organized rulers attempting to control a population. Hitler and Tojo demonstrated just how effective a tool terrorism could be if used correctly. Since 1945, hundreds of governments and thousands of individuals have practiced this science of terrorism with varying degrees of success.

Success cannot be measured by political outcomes, government change or overthrow, or legal remedies, although these are the ultimate goal of the terrorist. Success is instead measured by the amount of human suffering, misery, fear, anxiety, paranoia, change in life-style, and other psychological distress caused by the terrorist. From the inside looking out, success can only mean acceptance of a political ideology. The terrorist does not measure success by the human variables. He measures success by the amount of political change his violence produces. From the outside looking in, however, success is measured by the human dimension. It matters little to the citizen victimized by the terrorist whether or not the government changes a law, policy, doctrine, or even a political system. All the citizen sees is what the terrorist has done to people.

This can be clearly evidenced by the public reaction in the aftermath of the Alfred Murrah Federal Building bombing in Oklahoma City. People witnessing the horror cared little about the political ideology of the bomber. All they saw, thought about, or were concerned about were the bodies being carried away from the rubble. The focus of the world turned to the human dimensions and tragedy of the story, not the motivation of the terrorists. For months following the incident, the media devoted a significant amount of coverage to the disaster. The vast majority of this coverage was devoted to the human element in the story, not the political ideology of the bomber or the militia movement he was involved with.

But the reality is that violence is but a tool in the terrorist arsenal. The end product of terrorism is not violence; rather violence is only part of the terrorist process and one component of goal-directed behavior. The terrorist wants political change and believes the only way to bring about this political change is through violence directed at the public. The innocent public is caught up in terrorist events much like pawns are sacrificed on a chessboard. The terrorist is not performing violence to harm any particular member of the public. He is harming the public to force a government to change. To the terrorist, the public is a tool to be used and discarded. The terrorist is willing to use whatever means necessary to force political change, even if this means the death of hundreds of innocents. If these deaths do not produce political change, the terrorist will kill more and more until political change is made.

Another tool of the terrorist, and one more valuable and more effective than violence, is ignorance. Very few people understand terrorism.

Fewer still understand the terrorist. This may seem like a semantic difference rooted in academic terminology, but it is a significant difference. Terrorism is a technique designed to produce political change. Terrorists are individuals who are willing to do whatever is necessary to bring about that change. Terrorism is a concept that defines a particular category of criminal behavior. Terrorists operate outside the realm of normative and acceptable behavior. Few people, including law enforcement officials, understand this important difference. Calling the bombing of the World Trade Center terrorism carries little empirical meaning other than to classify the bombing as a specific criminal act. Failure to understand the difference between terrorism and terrorists leads to labeling persons who engage in terrorism as "fanatics," "nuts," "crazies," and mentally disturbed.

This labeling comes from a basic ignorance of what terrorism and terrorists are. Terrorists are certainly fanatic. They are not, however, crazy. They are violent, but unlike many criminals, their violence is goal directed. The purpose of this book is to take that most valuable tool away from the terrorist: ignorance. By understanding terrorism and the terrorist, their motives, strategies, tactics, and dynamics at work in the shadowy underworld of terrorism, ignorance becomes knowledge, knowledge becomes the tool in the fight against terrorism, and the terrorist can then be defeated.

This book first addresses the most difficult of all issues in understanding terrorism: what is terrorism? Well over a hundred definitions of terrorism have been posited. Definitions range from the ridiculously simplistic to the overly complex. One of the most significant detriments in our ability to combat terrorism is our inability to define exactly what it is we are attempting to combat. Even those government and law enforcement agencies designed to fight terrorism cannot agree on a common definition. To make any inroads against terrorism, we must first be able to clearly elucidate and agree on what we are talking about.

The next chapter is devoted to history. We must understand the historical precedents of today's terrorists to gain a better understanding of where they are going. Without knowing the historical roots of modern terrorism, we cannot hope to learn and predict terrorist behavior.

Chapter III explores the reasons why people become terrorists, what motivates them to work outside acceptable guidelines of behavior, why they freely engage in violence, and the psychological characteristics of both terrorists and terrorist leaders. One common misunderstanding people have concerning terrorists is that they are fanatical to the extreme. While this is true for some, the majority are just the opposite. Most terrorists are insecure, looking for acceptance, and have an overwhelming need to be accepted by somebody. These people are not drawn into terrorism because of some deep-seated political ideology, but only because they have found somebody who will accept them as people. It is likely that Timothy McVeigh, suspected bomber of the Oklahoma City Federal Building, fits this category of individual. Understanding the enemy is to know his weakness.

Chapter IV examines another of the more misunderstood aspects of terrorism, that of the terrorist organization. One of the difficulties in combating terrorism is a lack of understanding of the organizational culture and dynamics of terrorism. Many counter-terrorist activities deal with the terrorist as if the terrorist were working within the classical pyramidal bureaucracy. Again, this is not an artificial distinction designed to provide an additional chapter in an already crowded book. An understanding of the organizational structure and dynamics of the terrorist world is crucial to our ability to fight the terrorist. The terrorist organizational structure is responsible for many law enforcement failures to prevent terrorism.

Chapter V takes an in-depth look at the terrorist organizations operating in the United States. A theme repeated throughout this book is that law enforcement and the government have the perception that terrorism is on the decline. Many of the 1960 and 1970 radicals have been arrested or have graciously come to accept middle age. The far right has been repeatedly compromised and arrested and is once a shell of what they were. America is safe for democracy, mom, apple pie, and 75 mph speed limits—or at least that is what the public is led to believe. As will be shown, terrorism is not on the decline, the radical movements of the 1960s and 1970s have not disappeared into the ether of history, and the Rambos of the 1980s have not become an historical antecedent. All are alive and well and more dangerous than ever before.

Chapter VI deals with the strategy and tactics of terrorism. What types of operations do terrorists employ and what are the intended outcomes of these activities? Terrorists follow defined scripts in attempting to achieve their political goals. By knowing these scripts, law enforcement can change the story line. Many people believe terrorists indiscriminately run around killing and causing mayhem. In fact, just the opposite is true. Terrorists employ well-planned and well-designed operations. The Iranian embassy siege, the downing of Pan Am 103, the takeover of the *Achille Lauro,* and the bombings of the World Trade Center and Oklahoma City Federal Building were not random activities decided on the spur of the moment. They were well-planned and well-conducted military style operations. It is essential we understand how and why terrorists employ the types of operations they do and what purpose these operations are designed to accomplish if we are to prevent terrorism. This chapter also discusses an activity not usually perceived to be terroristic: hate crimes, and a new realm of terrorist involvement: drugs. Hate crimes are one of the oldest of all terrorist activities, yet they are not usually associated with terrorism. Recently, terrorists have become major players in the drug business. Terrorist involvement in both of these activities will be discussed. Also discussed is the role of the media in terrorism. Those who study terrorism are fond of saying that without the media there would be no terrorism. This overused adage is trite but true. Media influence on terrorism is presented, along with suggestions for reducing media influence.

Chapters VII and VIII examine the weapons terrorists employ. Chapter VII focuses on conventional weapons, while Chapter VIII discusses the more esoteric and lethal weapons of terrorism: nuclear, biological, and chemical. The conventional weapons of terrorism are guns and explosives. Almost 99 percent of all terrorist activities involve the use of one or both of these types of weapons. Chapter VII provides an overview of the more common convention weapons of terrorism, including a discussion of how they are obtained, made, and used. Chapter VIII provides an overview of the newest and deadliest weapons in the terrorist arsenal, the weapons of mass destruction. The thought of terrorists using nuclear weapons can produce an almost paralyzing fear just by thinking about the possibility of one of these weapons in the hands of the terrorist. Little recognized, however, is that there are even more potent, deadly, and fearsome weapons more readily available to the terrorist. Biological "creepy crawlies" and chemical means of mass destruction are now part of the terrorist arsenal and have moved terrorism into the twenty-first century. These weapons have the potential to completely change the face of terrorism and may have finally given the terrorist the upper hand.

Chapter IX discusses counter-terrorist options. Here the reader may be disappointed. People generally associate counter-terrorism with their well-defined Hollywood concept of counter-terrorism: Chuck Norris flinging people around like paper, Steven Segal blowing up large portions of the Arctic, and Clint Eastwood "making our day." The reality is that there is no John Wayne. Never has been, never will. Counter-terrorism is the development of appropriate non-violent strategies to prevent the occurrence of terrorism. It is true that military intervention has been used to prevent or stop terrorism, as evidenced by Reagan's bombing of Libya or Desert Storm. Most often, however, terrorism is fought in stuffy meeting rooms by the "suits" of the world. This chapter explains the available and realistic options open to fight terrorism, the effectiveness of those options, and suggestions for improving those available options.

Chapter X deals with the victims of terrorism. Although the goals of the terrorist are to bring about political change, the victims of terrorists are individuals caught in circumstances beyond their control. There are many ramifications to being victimized by terrorism. This chapter explains the effects of being victimized, the psychological outcomes of being victimized, and what can be done to assist the victims.

Chapter XI discusses the only terrorist operation law enforcement has the opportunity to intercede in: the hostage situation. One of the favored tactics of the terrorist (behind bombing) is to take hostages. Contrary to popular belief, propagated by the silver screen, hostage situations are not resolved by black-suited ninjas with blazing guns. They are resolved by talking, by discussing issues, and by long and complex negotiations. This chapter explains the negotiation process, the requirements for negotiating the hostage incident, handling demand issues, and how to make the negotiation process work against the terrorist. Part of this chapter is devoted to the most valuable asset of the negotiator, communications. By understanding the importance, value, and process of negotiations law enforcement has the advantage over the terrorist.

The final chapter provides a best guess for the future of terrorism. There is no crystal ball that allows us to look into the future and predict with absolute certainty what the future holds in regards to terrorism. Based upon what has brought us to this point, however, we can make some educated guesses about the future of terrorism. These observations are presented. Circumstances can change, resulting in significant changes in these predictions. For example, several years ago I predicted that the Mideast would see some stability. When these predictions seemed to come true following the precedent-setting accords between Israel and the PLO, I began feeling somewhat invulnerable and a prognosticator any Vegas bettor would be glad to pay large sums of money. Then the tragedy of assassination reared its ugly head when Israel's Prime Minister Rabin was killed. In that instant, all of my carefully predicated academic premonitions rushed down the proverbial toilet. With that in mind, future trends are offered as a template for prediction and planning. Barring unforeseen and catastrophic occurrences, this chapter will provide a general model for the future that can be used for planning purposes.

ACKNOWLEDGMENTS

I would like to take the opportunity to thank all of those who have assisted in this work. Thomas Martinez spent countless hours assisting in the research for this book, as did Alan Thompson. Kevin Foster provided necessary computer expertise, especially in graphics development. Jim Turner (J.T. to all who know him), Michael McMains, Mike Aamodt, Tomas Mijares, and Warren Zerr provided many of the original ideas. All are dear friends we all need more of. Wilson Kimbrough needs special mention. For almost 20 years, he has kept me moving forward when there were many reasons to do something else. Many people assisted who requested that their names be omitted from this roll. To all of those unnamed sources, my sincere thanks and appreciation. Finally, heartfelt thanks are extended to Mr. Payne Thomas, who initially rolled the dice and took the chance on an unknown.

CONTENTS

LIST OF FIGURES

LIST OF TABLES

A SOURCEBOOK ON DOMESTIC
AND
INTERNATIONAL TERRORISM

Chapter 1

TERRORISM—DEFINITIONS, TYPOLOGY, AND PROCESS

There is no question but that terrorism is a significant problem facing the United States. As this book will demonstrate, terrorism is an indiscriminate plague upon American society, an insidious form of violence that respects no ethnicity, social strata, geographical locale, nor particular demographic characteristics such as sex, age, race, or occupation. Even mention of the very word "terrorism" sends a chill through the majority of citizens.

Recent events, such as the World Trade Center and Oklahoma Federal Building bombings, have made terrorism the *nouveau cause celeb* of post-Cold War America. And in the paranoia of these events, terrorism has come to parallel crime, poverty, homelessness, juvenile gangs, and the weakening of the moral fabric of the country as an omnipotent sign to the "beginning of the end" of life as we know it. The media treats terrorism as if it were a well-defined and completely understood phenomenon; held up to the light to be seen, weighted, and measured on a balance scale. Most Americans readily subscribe to this concreteness. The quantification of a phenomenon reduces fear. If it can be defined, recognized and dissected, at least perceptually, the threat is reduced and security is returned to one's world. Unpredictability is fear, predictability is security. Terrorism is unpredictable violence. Introducing a measure of predictability introduces a measure of safety. Orderliness in the world provides a sense of control and the ability to forestall, plan for, and prevent.

While the overused and trite adage, "I can't define it, but I know it when I see it," certainly eases the public consciousness of safety and security, it does nothing to help us explain, define, and prevent terrorism from occurring. In reality, to those entrusted with combating terrorism, attempts to simply define terrorism have become the "Holy Grail." Law enforcement experts, political philosophizers, academicians, and others who study terrorism have great difficulty in being able to define what they are attempting to analyze, combat, and stop.

What is terrorism? Who are terrorists? Why do people turn to terrorism?

3

These questions are, on the surface, seemingly innocuous and straightforward questions that suggest simple answers. The national security forces of one country the author works with consider terrorists to be persons who believe in communism and place explosive devices in various locations. Any person or group who does not fit this paradigm are not terrorists and their activities are not terroristic. There are many who would not consider the individuals associated with the Oklahoma City Federal Building bombing to be terrorists. At the other end of the spectrum are those who consider any form of criminal activity to be terrorism.

The truth is that terrorism lies somewhere between the two ends of this continuum. The location on this continuum is the issue in question. In the social sciences, criminal justice, political science, psychology, sociology, and even history, attempts to define terrorism has been one of the more elusive concepts of inquiry. Whether a government official, law enforcement professional, academician, or citizen looking for stability and security in an unstable and insecure world, the attempt to define terrorism has been one of personal biases, subjective impressions, and unqualified guesswork.

In general, as the twentieth century has progressed, terrorism has kept pace and increased over the century. Terrorism does wax and wane with each year. A year-by-year examination of the terrorist incident curve will show a waveform, with a series of ups and downs. A decade-by-decade examination of the terrorist incident curve, however, will indicate an overall and general upward trend. But does such an examination accurately reflect changes in the form and function of terrorism?

Simon (1994) argued: "Statistics tend to mark the endless nature of terrorism by presenting it in a way that leaves the impression that terrorism is on the rise or decline, when in fact the volume of terrorist activity has little bearing upon its present and future course or its impact upon governments and societies." At their very best, statistics can only indicate the number of terrorist activities which occurred in a given period of time. They do not indicate how terrorism affects the citizen, nor do they help us understand the form or seriousness of terrorism. The 856 recorded terrorist events of 1988 do not show the tragic bombing of Pan Am 103 over Lockerbee, Scotland. The 800 incidents of terrorism in 1985 do not demonstrate the severity of the *Achille Lauro* cruise ship incident nor the Rome and Vienna airport massacres. Nor do the 455 terrorist incidents of 1990 reflect Saddam Hussein's barbarism in Kuwait and against the Iraqi Kurds.

Not only has terrorism increased as the twentieth century has progressed, the form and function of terrorism has changed. Various factors have been instrumental in these changes. One change in the form of terrorism has been the result of technological progression (Alexander & Finger, 1977). America has become highly dependent upon large dams, co-generation plants, nuclear facilities, regional power centers, centralized communication facilities, transportation networks, etc. Many of these systems have only minimal security protection and this protection is designed to only deter the casual criminal, not to stop the dedicated terrorist. An attack on any one of these facilities could paralyze a large segment of society. People travel in airplanes capable of carrying 300 passengers. An attack on one of these planes benefits the terrorist much more than an attack on a transportation vehicle which could carry only 25 people. Technology has resulted in targets which affect more people and to a larger degree than ever before. Furthermore, each year brings targets more attractive to the terrorist than the year before.

Advances in weapons technology has benefited the terrorist. In terms of conventional weapons, terrorists have employed rocket-propelled grenade launchers (Anable, 1978) and surface-to-air Strela missiles (SAM-7s; Jenkins, 1978). Conventional weapons are available which are easily concealable and can be operated by a single individual (Yeager, 1986). Nuclear, biological, and chemical weapons are now part of the terrorist arsenal. Nuclear warheads are readily available on the open market. Terrorists have already used chemical weapons in a number of instances, the most recent and memorable being the nerve gas attack on the Tokyo subway system in 1995. Biological weapons have been found in the possession of numerous terrorist groups. These weapons give the terrorist an awesome level of power and an advantage of unprecedented terror.

The advancement of communication systems has helped change the form and function of terrorism (Singh, 1977). In addition to an immediate worldwide audience, it is now an easy proposition for terrorists to communicate on a worldwide communications network (Alexander, 1977). Computer networks and satellite television technology are used by numerous terrorists. Most damaging, however, is the instantaneous media coverage terrorists can obtain. A terrorist incident anywhere in the world can be broadcast within seconds by the news media. Because of increased media coverage, it is necessary for the terrorist to turn to larger-scale events in order to receive the necessary media coverage. Airplane hijackings no longer make headline news. Instead, it is necessary to bring the airplane out of the sky. The burning of a government building, or small-scale bombing would hardly make the local news, much less be reported nationally or internationally. It is now necessary for the terrorist to completely destroy a multi-level, heavily populated building to receive media coverage.

The rise of third-world supportive states has contributed to changes in terrorism. Iraq, Libya, Cuba and other such countries cannot compete in the world economically, politically, or militarily. The only way for these countries to make a political statement or induce political change is through the use of terrorism (Shagmar, 1986). In many of these countries, the only way for a despot to remain in power is through the use of terrorism. Additionally, any terrorist organization which may help further the political agendas of these third-world countries will receive support, materials, finances, manpower, and safe havens from these governments.

Most governments cannot respond effectively to terrorism. Free societies will not allow a government to react with a policy of violence or legal restrictions. The government must operate within the dictates of the law, while the terrorist is under no such constraint. The terrorist can commit an act in one country and then flee to another for sanctuary, and the victimized government is powerless to pursue the terrorist. One of the major problems the United States has had in combating terrorism, and one of the reasons U.S. citizens are prime targets of terrorists, is the very constraints our legal system places upon our ability to pursue terrorists on the international battlefield. To pursue terrorists internationally and unilaterally violates the laws of both the U.S. and the world. To protect U.S. citizens would require the suspension or repeal of basic guarantees of the Constitution, a trade-off the government and people are not willing to make.

TERRORISM AS WARFARE

One of the more significant changes in terrorism in the twentieth century is that terrorism has become an acceptable form of warfare (Fromkin, 1978). Begun by Nazi Germany and Nationalist Japan in the 1930s and 1940s, nations have used terrorism, at least in their eyes, as a legitimate form of warfare. The conflicts of the later twentieth century are mixtures of conventional warfare, classic guerrilla warfare, and campaigns of terrorism conducted by regular and irregular armies (Jenkins, 1978, 1983; Thompson, 1989; Wilkinson, 1986). Terrorism no longer is limited to the basic formula of small groups of individuals or governments operating a country (Kren & Rapoport, 1977). Terrorism now includes insurgents, guerrillas, commandos, freedom fighters, rebels, social revolutionaries, and armies of national liberation (Poland, 1988).

Nazi Germany and Japan showed how effective terrorism could be used as a form of warfare. These two countries elevated terrorism to an unprecedented level, one that clearly demonstrated the international effectiveness of terrorism when used on a mass scale (Mullins, 1994). Since the end of WWII, terrorism has become widely accepted as a form of warfare. The Israelis used terrorism to force Britain to grant their independence, as did Algeria against the French. In Indochina, the Vietnamese effectively used terrorism to defeat first the French and then the United States. Iraq, Iran, Cuba, Korea, Yugoslavia, and in Africa, South America, and Asia, terrorism has been used to fight unconventional wars and defeat superior powers.

There are several reasons why terrorism has become an acceptable form of warfare. First, full-scale warfare has become too costly. The proliferation of nuclear weapons and other sophisticated weapons of mass destruction have made total warfare too costly. The great fear of the Cold War was a full-scale nuclear launch by both Russia and the U.S. The major factor in the prevention of a war of this nature was the fear of self-immolation. The collapse of the Eastern European bloc did little to ally fears of a worldwide "nuclear winter." The spread of nuclear technology, along with the development and sale of powerful conventional weapons, potent biological agents, and readily available chemical agents, have done nothing to lessen the fear of worldwide destruction. Even limited warfare, such as that conducted by Iraq and Iran in the 1980s, can get out of control and cost hundreds of thousands of lives within a matter of days.

Second, terrorism is relatively cost-effective as compared to full-scale warfare. The world has learned that political change can be effected rather easily without massive military expenditures. While the U.S. was spending billions of dollars to fight Communist Vietnam, the Russians (supporting Ho Chi Minh) were spending pennies. Many countries which desire to conquer and control cannot afford the costs required to support a full-scale military operation. Instead, they turn to terrorism to get the most "bang for the bucks."

Third, sponsoring nations can remain anonymous when using terrorism. Very few people, for example, realize the large Cuban presence in Vietnam during the 1960s and 1970s, or the Cuban presence in Nicaragua, Argentina, and Rwanda. Even the Soviets and East Germans had "advisors" in most of the world's hot spots during these decades. In Korea, Chinese intervention almost led to WWIII when they underestimated the U.S. resolve to bring that conflict to a democratic conclusion. If not for the determination of President Bush in the Persian Gulf, Kuwait would now be a province of Saddam Hussein and Iraq.

States which have used terrorism in an attempt to advance a political agenda are far spread. In addition to the obvious countries of China, Cuba, East Germany, Iran, Iraq, Libya, North Korea, the Soviet Union, and Sudan, the nations of Bulgaria, Israel, South Africa, Yugoslavia, and the United States have also sponsored terrorism (Alexander, 1985; Asa, 1985; Bar-Zohar & Haber, 1983; Cline & Alexander, 1985; Dobson, 1974; Francis, 1985; Jonas, 1984; Kuperman, 1986; Livingstone & Arnold, 1986; Motley, 1986; Nidal, 1986; Parry, 1976; Pluchinsky, 1982; Wilkinson, 1986a, 1986b; Vetter & Perlstein, 1991).

Fourth, in addition to achieving a primary goal of replacing a government, terrorism can be used to achieve secondary gains. Terrorism can be used to provoke an international incident which can open a war. Few Americans will ever forget the Japanese attack on Pearl Harbor on 7 December 1941. Terrorism can be used to destroy an enemy's morale and create fear and alarm in the adversary's country. This, in fact, was one of the aims of Japan in conducting the Pearl Harbor attack. One of the purposes of Hitler's Blitzkrieg was to produce international fear so no country dare oppose his regime. Terrorism can cause a country to divert needed military resources to protect itself internally during a war. During the Persian Gulf War, many U.S. military units were deployed in non-combat zones (U.S. and overseas) to protect American interests from potential Iraqi terrorist attacks. Had the Gulf War escalated, not having these units available could have had serious consequences. Terrorism can be used to conduct surgical strikes on an enemy. In Vietnam, Operation Phoenix was designed to specifically attack leaders of the People's Army and North Vietnamese regulars. As another example, rather than indiscriminately strike PLO targets following the 1972 Munich Olympic Games massacre, Israel directly attacked those responsible for the massacre.

There is a trite saying among those who study and operationally deal with terrorism: "one man's terrorist is another man's freedom fighter." Philosophically this dictum may have some meaning, but when discussing terrorism it is inaccurate. Terrorism is terrorism. Semantics do not make terrorism something different. Nor do semantics morally justify terrorism. Morality, political expediency, and philosophical justification may depend upon one's perspective, but they do not change terrorism into something it is not.

Urban guerrilla warfare and guerrilla warfare are terrorism. Some, such as Mallin (1978), argue urban guerrilla warfare encompasses more than just terrorist activity, such as ambushes, assaults, and street battles, and are confined to urban areas. Netanyahu (1986) argues guerrillas are soldiers (irregulars) who conduct warfare against other soldiers, while terrorists are not soldiers who conduct warfare against civilians. Both are incorrect. Urban guerrilla warfare is but one form of terrorism. Urban guerrillas conform, in form and function, to acceptable definitions of terrorism, including the one to be used in this book. They hope to achieve the same goals as other forms of terrorism and use the same techniques. Guerrilla warfare may be conducted on a larger scale than most terrorist acts (Miller, 1977), but size alone does not define terrorism. Urban guerrillas, like terrorists, do not fit within the 1949 Third Geneva Convention Articles (4A2) of legitimate combatants in war. According to the convention, combatants have to wear distinctive clothing, carry their weapons openly, have a recognized commander, and behave according to the laws and customs of war (Shagmar, 1986). Terrorists and urban guerrillas (as well as freedom fighters, commandos, rebels, social revolutionaries, and armies of national liberation) do none of the above.

TERROR OF TERRORISM

Before defining terrorism, it is necessary to define the terror of terrorism, for without the terror induced by the terrorist, there can be no terrorism. Terror is "the fear evoked by the individuals or the small groups of individuals whose capacity to constrain the behavior of others resides not in reason, in numerical preponderance, or in any legitimate exercise of authority, but only in their perception that they are able and willing to use violence unless their demands are satisfied" (Smart, 1978).

The public must believe the terrorist will use violence if required. The terrorist must lack moral sanctions against killing others and needs to be able to display a ruthlessness beyond the capabilities of most people (Neale, 1973). Should the public believe the terrorist will back down or not act upon their threats, then there can be no terror.

Second, the perception of the public must be that the terrorist will go to any length to see their actions completed, including their own death. Should the terrorist back down on any operation, the terror aspect will be lost, along with the future effectiveness of the terrorist. Many people, for example, criticize Israel and most European nations for their hard line toward terrorism. In a hostage situation, for instance, these countries only negotiate with terrorists to prepare for a tactical assault. The reason these countries have this philosophy concerning the use of tactical operations is the knowledge the terrorist will not negotiate and will kill innocents during the negotiation process.

Third, the public must believe that not only is the terrorist capable of committing any violence necessary to achieve a political goal, but any single member of the terrorist organization will do whatever is necessary to insure their goals are achieved. Very seldom do arrests of terrorist leaders end terroristic activity from a particular organization. Almost all grand dragons of the various Ku Klux Klan chapters have been arrested and jailed. Not one arrest has deterred or slowed Klan activity. Members continue Klan activities even in the absence of leadership.

Fourth, the terrorist is able and willing to engage in violence in the face of overwhelming odds. There is no recorded instance of the terrorist outnumbering his opponent. Many terrorists, in fact, are more than willing to face an opponent who has numerical superiority. In part, assuming the role of the underdog reinforces the concept of martyrdom and further ennobles the cognition of being a savior. Even to terrorist governments, this belief of martyrdom is an important concept in controlling the population. In Cuba, for example, Castro constantly stresses to the Cubans that deviation from his programs and disloyalty to the government will guarantee Cuban collapse at the hands of the U.S. imperialists.

Fifth, terrorist employ illegitimate means to achieve a goal. Vetter and Perlstein (1991) have indicated violence can be legitimate or illegitimate. Legitimate violence would be that violence used by police officers to stop a criminal in the commission of a crime, or a government stopping aggression by another government. Illegitimate violence, or the violence of a terrorist, would include assassination, bombing a cafe full of innocents, attacking a government official, killing a minority, or using a secret police to control a population. Illegitimate violence, whether by an individual, autonomous organization, or government, is terror. At the international level, estimates suggest between 1970–1980, the secret police of various governments killed over 30,000 people. In August 1980, in Caracoles, Bolivia, Bolivian government troops murdered over 900 people (Amnesty International, 1980). In Brazil, with government sanction, the Esquadrao de Morte (Death Squad), while "officially" off-duty, executed over 1,000 citizens as an object lesson (Rosenbaum & Sederberg, 1976).

Sixth, and most importantly, rationality has no place on the terrorist's agenda nor in the selection of targets. In war, targets are selected for their military value. An unfortunate by-product of target selection may be civilian deaths. The terrorist purposely selects innocents as victims of violence. There was no reason for David Koresh at the Branch Davidian compound in Waco, Texas, to not release the children in the compound. The children and infants had no concept of the danger in which they were placed, the ideology of Koresh, nor the politics that defined the situation. Instead, Koresh purposely sacrificed the lives of children, hoping this would rally the public to his cause. The passengers on Pan Am Flight 103 over Lockerbee, Scotland died because they were unfortunate enough to be "in the wrong place at the wrong time."

Terror is the cornerstone of terrorism. If the terrorist is not able to fulfill the conditions of terror, he will not be able to engage in terrorism.

To the terrorist, however, terror has become his last resort. In a sense, a terrorist is a person whose desperation has overcome his fear. Desperation leads to extreme violence, a willingness to sacrifice, extreme acts, standing alone for a belief, and being a messiah, acting outside of established structures, and willingness to sacrifice innocents to achieve a political goal. In all respects, the terrorist is like the cornered animal. With bared fangs, they are ready to challenge the world and legitimate authority.

DEFINITIONS OF TERRORISM

Terrorism is an extremely difficult concept to define. Terrorism is an ethereal philosophy, and terrorist actors engage in terrorism for a variety of purposes, motivations, and ideologies. Terrorists operate on a set of general and specific assumptions about the state of the world, the moral order of societies, and validity of political systems. Terrorist belief structures have strong emotional components which result in specific behaviors designed to reduce the terrorist's emotional upheaval. These emotions are why people become terrorists. Some have suggested that understanding the source of these emotions helps explain terrorist behavior. Vetter and Perlstein (1991) classified terrorists on a continuum from the radical far left to the reactionary far right, as shown in Figure 1.1. For the far left, the predominant value system is that involving justice, fair and equitable distribution of power, wealth, prestige, and privilege, while for the far right, the most important emotional values are based on order and a binding and pervasive morality (Smith, 1982).

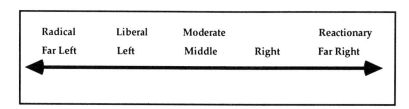

Figure 1.1. Terrorist continuum as identified by Vetter and Perlstein (1991).

The result of these differing ideologies is that terrorists use violence for different purposes (Van den Haag, 1972). One, some merely want to acquire power. Two, some terrorists merely like to exercise their power to satisfy internal need states. For many terrorists, the sense of control and power over others is a motivation in itself. Three, some terrorists want to challenge authority. To these individuals, terrorism is nothing more than a display meant to rebel against social, moral, and political controls. Four, terrorists may turn to violence in order to enforce authority (Mullins, 1990b). The classic examples of this type of terrorism would be despot governments who use terrorism to control a country.

These different ideologies have made it almost impossible to arrive at a single definition of terrorism (Bassiouni, 1975; Dugard, 1973; Franck & Lockwood, 1974; Hannay, 1974). Schmid (1983) examined over 100 definitions of terrorism. An analysis of these definitions led him to conclude that: (1) terrorism was an abstract concept with no essence. Terrorists are nothing more than criminals who rationalize criminal behavior behind the guise of working for the people. (2) A single definition of terrorism cannot account for all possible uses of the term. It would be almost impossible to arrive at a single definition that would include right-wing racial/religious separatists and left-wing revolutionaries. (3) Many different definitions share common elements as will be shown. (4) The meaning of terrorism derives from the victim or target, not necessarily from the terrorist's political agenda.

Definitions of terrorism have attempted to define the morality (or immorality) of terrorism, motivation of terrorists, persons involved in terrorism, political agendas, and even legalistic concepts of terrorist activity. Rapoport (1977) defined terrorism according to moral distinctions of terrorist activity. To him, terrorism involved persons who had no moral constraints committing acts of violence that caused injury. Bell (1975) believed terrorists could be defined by their motivation. Many attempts have been made to define terrorism legally. As a legal definition, for example, the Texas Penal Code, Section 22.07 (1985 revision), defines terrorism as, "A person commits an offense if he threatens to commit any offense involving violence to any person or property with intent to (1) cause a reaction of any type to his threat by an official or volunteer agency organized to deal with emergencies; (2) place any person in fear of imminent serious bodily injury; or (3) prevent or interrupt the occupation of use of a building, room, place of assembly, place to which the public has access, place of conveyance, or other public place; or (4) cause impairment or interruption of public communications, public transportation, public water, gas or power supply or other public service." Legalistic definitions of this nature try to legislate the event of terrorism, not the outcome of the activity.

Many definitions are overly simplistic. Wolfe (1978) defined terrorism as "the threat or use of deliberate violence, indiscriminately or selectively, against either enemies or allies to achieve a political end." The FBI defined terrorism as "the unlawful use of force or violence against persons or property to intimidate or coerce a government, civilian population, or any segment thereof, in furtherance of political or social objectives (Pomerantz, 1987; Smith, 1994). Krieger (1977) defined terrorism as "non-government public violence or its threat performed by an independent or small group and aimed at achieving social or political goals that may be subnational, national or international."

These definitions tend to focus on the act being unlawful and examine the motivation of the activity. Terrorism is outside the boundaries of legitimate behavior and legal attempts to alter government activity. These definitions emphasize the actual use of violence of terrorists; terrorism is not present unless a violent act is committed. No consideration is given to the threat of violence.

Other definitions emphasize violence, political ends, and the fear of terrorism. Schmid (1983) defined terrorism as a "method of combat in which the victims serve as a symbolic target. Violent actors are able to produce a chronic state of fear by using violence outside the realms of normative behavior. This produces an audience beyond the immediate victim and results in a change of public attitudes and actions." Lodge (1981) characterized terrorism as "an organized pattern of violent behavior designed to influence government policy or intimidate the population for the purpose of influencing government policy." Jenkins (1975) said terrorism was "a strategy whereby violence is used to produce certain effects in a group of people so as to attain some political end or ends."

These definitions emphasize that terrorism is used to produce fear or other emotions. Terrorist acts are committed so that normal citizens react emotionally and then work to force government change. These changes will be urged by the citizens to reduce or alleviate these emotional states. Once the terrorist uses violence and produces an emotional reaction, the terrorist then steps out of the political loop and watches the public force change.

Other definitions include the use of violence, the production of fear, and then add some other element. Netanyahu (1986) defined terrorism as "the deliberate and systematic murder, maiming and menacing of the innocent to inspire fear for political ends." This definition includes fear, political purposes, and violence for the audience watching, but ignores the threat of violence. His definition might be more accurate if it had said, "deliberate and systematic murder, maiming *or* menacing of the innocent to inspire fear for political ends."

In 1972, the Secretary General defined terrorism as: "(1) an act which had a terror outcome, (2) an act which had instrumental or immediate victims, (3) an act which had primary targets, whether populations, broad groups of people, or small groups of people, (4) acts of violence, and (5) acts with a political purpose." This definition included fear of civilians, political purposes, and terror purpose. It does, however, imply that violence is required for an act to be considered as terroristic. Covering the same points, Friedlander (1981) offered a similar, if shorter, definition: "Terrorism is the use of force, violence, or threats thereof to attain political goals through fear, intimidation or coercion." His definition, unlike the secretary general's, indicates that violence only has to be threatened.

In defining extremism, which is another term for terrorism, Scruton (1982) offered a similar definition when he offered the definition: "(1) taking a political idea to its limits, regardless of the unfortunate repercussions, impracticalities, arguments and feelings to the contrary, and with the intention not only to confront, but to eliminate opposition. (2) Intolerance toward all views other than one's own. (3) Adoption of means to political ends which show disregard for the life, liberty and human rights of others." This definition includes fear created in a civilian population, violence for an audience, and political purpose. It, like the definitions above, however, implies violence is an outcome measure.

Even more complex definitions include four elements of terrorism. For example, the International Convention on Terrorism (1937) defined terrorism as: "(1) a willful or intentional act, (2) an act with a terror purpose, (3) an act with an outcome of death, grievous bodily harm or loss of liberty to a set of instrumental targets, (4) an outcome of damage to or destruction of public property as instrumental targets, and (5) acts calculated to endanger the lives of the members of the public" (Paust, 1977). This definition included only the threat of violence, reliance on creating fear, violence of the terrorist as a means to an end, and acts having a political purpose. The definition, however, limits itself by considering terrorist acts as only those directed against public property. This definition would exclude terrorism directed toward groups of people, such as Ku Klux Klan activities against minorities, or environmental terrorism against a logging firm's interests.

In 1985, the United States Air Force defined terrorism as being the "culturally unacceptable use of or threat of violence directed toward symbolic targets to influence political behavior either directly through fear, intimidation, or coercion, or indirectly by affecting attitudes, emotions or opinions." A similar definition, which covered the same factors of terrorism as the U.S.A.F. definition, was one offered by Poland (1988): "Terrorism is the premeditated, deliberate, systematic murder, mayhem, and threatening of the innocent to create fear and intimidation in order to gain a political or tactical advantage, usually to influence an audience." Finally, a third definition recognizing that terrorism involves only threatened violence, fear, violence for the watching public, and political outcome is the that offered by Wardlaw (1989): "Political terrorism is the use, or threat of use, violence by an individual or a group, whether acting for or in opposition to established authority, when such action is designed to create extreme anxiety and/or fear-inducing effects in a target group larger than the immediate victims with the purpose of coercing that group into acceding to the political demands of the perpetrator."

Most of the preceding definitions use concepts familiar to most when discussing terrorism; illegal acts, violence for a political purpose, clandestine groups, and fear as the intent of violence. These definitions generally formalize the average citizen's conception of what terrorism is (Sobel, 1975) and recognize terrorism is a complex and difficult phenomenon to understand and clarify.

The very complexity of the problem often leads to misinterpretations of terrorism. For example, the National Advisory Commission on Criminal Justice Standards and Goals, in its 1976 *Report of the Task Force on Disorders and Terrorism,* said, "there is an area of true terroristic activity that clearly cannot be termed political, notably that ascribed to the present-day operations of organized crime. This is true terrorism, exhibiting conscious design to create and maintain a high degree of fear for coercive purposes, but the end is individual or collective gain rather than the achievement of a political objective." It seems a far stretch of the imagination to consider organized crime as a legitimate form of terrorism, much less that organized criminal activity has a political outcome.

To adequately define terrorism, a definition must have five components (Mullins, 1988). One, the definition has to recognize that terrorism uses violence as merely a tool. Violence is not the end product of terrorism, only a means to an end. Two, the definition has to recognize that violence only needs to be threatened. The terrorist does not have to use violence if the mere threat will suffice. Three, the production of fear is the political change agent of the terrorist. Producing fear in a civilian population produces political change, not violence directed against a government. Acts of terrorism have to produce an emotional response (Gerstein, 1983; Walter, 1969) Four, the definition has to realize that when violence is used by the terrorist, the violence is not directed at the victims but at the civilians who are not victims. Finally, the definition has to clearly specify that the outcome or goal has a political purpose. Regardless of the rubric of the terrorist, the core of terrorism is political change and nothing else.

The only definition that satisfies the above conditions was proffered by Jenkins (1975, reprinted in Milbank, 1978), who defined terrorism as "the threat of violence, individual acts of violence, or a campaign of violence designed primarily to instill fear—to terrorize—may be called terrorism. Terrorism is violence for effect; not only, and sometimes not at all, for the effect on the actual victims of the terrorists. In fact, the victim may be totally unrelated to the terrorist's cause. Terrorism is violence aimed at the people watching. Fear is the intended effect, not the by-product of terrorism." This definition clearly delineates the five points presented above as necessary to adequately define terrorism. Furthermore, this definition is specific enough to exclude non-terrorist criminal acts, such as organized crime and/or drug trafficking. For the purposes of this volume, this definition will be used to define terrorism.

TERRORIST TYPOLOGIES

Some scholars have argued it is not necessary to define terrorism but only to identify the type of terrorist being confronted (White, 1991). These attempts to classify terrorism relys on the use of predictive patterns of behavior to produce models of terrorism (Nelson, 1986). The Defense Intelligence Agency (DIA), for example, relies on typologies in an attempt to understand and explain terrorism.

There are several strengths typology schema's offer that definitions ignore. One, a typology identifies the type of terrorist problem. Considering terrorists to be anarchists, nationalists, religious supremacists, etc. allows one to understand the enemy. Knowing the far-right racial supremacists in the U.S. will concentrate their attacks on minorities helps plan response strategy and tactics to combat these individuals. Two, a typology allows for a given level of protection to be introduced. Knowing the tactics and goals of a terrorist organization allows planning to combat the threat. Three, an appropriate level of response can be administered. Security measures and anti-terrorist efforts can concentrate resources against the threat. Four, the public's understanding of an event or campaign can lessen the effects of the terrorist. Knowing terrorist tactics can help prepare the public and turn fear into anger. The response of the public after the Oklahoma City Federal Building explosion typifies this point. Once it was understood who was responsible for this atrocity, the public's fear turned to anger and outrage.

There are several weaknesses of typologies. One, the typology may break down and not be specific enough for a classification schema. Herman (1983), in one of the most simple classifications, developed a typology that classified terrorism as being either retail, consisting of isolated and independent small groups, or wholesale, or that terrorism used by governments. This classification, while parsimonious, does nothing for even a simple description of terrorism. It has long been recognized the primary targets of the far right have been minorities. Classifying the far right as retail terrorists does not explain some of their attacks on government structures and persons. Two, typologies do not recognize that terrorism constantly changes. The focus of the far-left's attacks in the 1960s and 1970s are not the focus of attacks in the 1990s. Three, typologies reflect the biases of those who develop the models. Four, they do not completely obviate the necessity for an adequate definition of the terrorist phenomenon. Typologies do not allow us to clearly explain terrorism, they only allow us to describe terrorism. Nor do typologies allow for an understanding of the political and social basis of terrorism (Flemming, Stohl & Schmidt, 1988). Five, typologies describe terrorism only in general terms and do not adequately describe the details. Knowing the far right attacks minorities does not offer insight into specifically why these individuals and organizations have turned to terrorism to further their political agenda.

One of the earliest attempts to provide a typology of terrorism was offered by Thornton (1964). According to Thornton, terrorism could be categorized as either enforcement terrorism or agitational terrorism. Enforcement terrorism was that used by governments against its own citizens or citizens of another nation to remove threats to their power and authority, and agitational terrorism was that of an organized group to change government structure. While most terrorist organizations could be placed in one category or another, this typology does little to explain and describe terrorists. It is overly general and does nothing to help understand the phenomenon.

Bell (1975) believed terrorists fit into one of six categories. Psychotic terrorists commit acts purely for psychological self-gratification. These persons have no political agenda, or the political agenda is secondary to self-satisfaction. These terrorists commit acts for no higher social good. Charles Manson's criminal activities would fit into this category. According to the acceptable understanding of what terrorism is, however, these individuals are not terrorists but criminals who use terrorist tactics, regardless of the magnitude of the act.

The second type of terrorists according to Bell (1975) are criminal terrorists, who commit acts of terror for profit and personal financial gain. An individual or group of individuals who kidnap a business executive and demand a ransom for his release may offer some political agenda, and there are certainly true terrorists who engage in this activity, but their intrinsic motivation is only to gain personal profit. The goal is not political but personal. As with the psychotics, these individuals are criminals who use terrorist tactics or disguise their activities in the hope of misleading authorities. They are not terrorists.

Third are vigilante terrorists. These terrorists engage in violence for retaliation against some slight or perceived injustice. Once again, though, individuals who engage in these tactics do not necessarily have a political agenda, may not want to produce fear in a population or engage in violence as a means to an end. Often, retaliation is the end objective or the goal.

Fourth, endemic terrorists are engaged in an internal struggle. These terrorists use terrorism against their own government (or another specific government) to produce political change in that government. Irish Republican Army (IRA) activities are only directed against British government interests, they do not attack the government of France, Germany, Japan, etc.

Fifth in Bell's (1975) classification are authorized terrorists. This is terrorism conducted by a government against its own people. The government uses terrorism as a form of political power and control and is normalized as an acceptable form of behavior. The governments of Stalin, Mao Tse Tung, Castro, Idi Amin, and Saddam Hussein are examples of authorized terrorism.

Sixth are revolutionary terrorists. These are the most dangerous terrorists and their only purpose for existence is to destroy existing power. Bell (1975) has identified six types of revolutionary terrorism. (1) Organizational terror is used by the terrorist to maintain discipline within the organization. (2) Allegiance terrorism are those acts designed to garner public support for the organization. (3) Functional terrorism involve acts designed to directly accomplish the goals and missions of the organization. Actions may involve the assassination of a key government leader or destruction of certain governmental structures. The Medellin Cartel's assassination of the judges of the Colombian Supreme Court in 1985 is an example of functional terrorism (Mullins, 1990c). (4) Provocative terrorism is that terrorism designed to force governments into repressive actions that will cause dissatisfaction in citizens and thereby result in citizen uprising against the government. (5) Manipulative terrorism is that designed to obtain demands through dramatic confrontation between the terrorists and the government. (6) Symbolic terrorism is that terrorism which strikes targets purely for their psychological impact on citizens.

In general, Bell's (1975) typology is a good typology. It does have several weaknesses that make it less than ideal. One weakness is that some categories are not designed for terrorists. Criminals fit into several categories. For another, many terrorist organizations, depending upon their activities, transcend categories and fit within several. This makes it difficult to describe terrorism. Also, several terrorist organizations fit no category. For example, animal rights terrorists have no place in Bell's typology. It could be argued that they fit within the category of functional terrorism, but they do not fit within this category's more encompassing concept of revolutionary change.

Hacker (1977) classified terrorism as either violence from above or from below. Terrorism from above was that designed to exercise power and enforce authority. This type of terrorism is primarily used by governments to control a population. Terrorism from below was that designed to remedy injustice and provide a basic motivation for terrorists. To the terrorist, poverty, oppression, and economic exploitation all are seen as legitimate redress and are conditions which can be altered by the use of terrorism.

In addition to classifying terrorism as from above or below, Hacker (1977) also subcategorized terrorists as either crusaders, criminals, or crazies. Crusaders use political violence to gain prestige and power in the service of a higher cause and commit terrorist acts to achieve a collective goal. Crusaders can consist of nationalistic groups or ideologues. Nationalistic groups have a political goal of self-determination and can be either internal or external to their own country. Examples would include the IRA, PLO, Popular Front for the Liberation of Palestine (PFLP), Abu Nidal, Basque ETA in Spain, FALN in Puerto Rico, and the Front Liberation in Algeria. Ideologues have as a goal the changing of a social, economic, or political system and can include anarchist organizations. Examples of ideologues include the Baader-Meinhof Gang (Red Army Faction) in Germany, Red Brigades in Italy, and the Red Army (Sekigen) in Japan. Crusaders represent terrorism from below.

The second subcategory Hacker (1977) identified are criminals, who can represent terrorism from above or below. Criminals are terrorists who engage in activities for personal gain or as part of a pattern of intimidation and coercion practiced by syndicated crime cartels. A criminal terrorist from above would include General Rafael Trujillo of the Dominican Republic and General Manuel Noriega of Panama. Criminals terrorists from below would be criminals caught in the act of committing another crime and turning to terrorism to avoid capture. Hostage taking is an example of the latter.

The third typology of Hacker (1977) are crazies. These are mentally and/or emotionally disturbed individuals whose terrorist targets are related to their psychopathology. Crazies commit acts that are unusual even by terrorist standards, acts that are unforeseen and unpredictable and incomprehensible, and can commit terrorism from above and below.

An example of a crazy from above would include Idi Amin from Uganda. Crazies from below are paranoids who suffer persecutory delusions and see themselves as a target of harassment from their perceived enemies. A crazy from below would be typified by the individual or individuals who bombed PanAm 103 over Lockerbee, Scotland.

Two immediate problems with Hacker's (1977) typology are the inclusion of criminals who engage in terroristic-like activities and paranoids and paranoid schizophrenics. While both of these types of person may use terror tactics, they are not terrorists. Also, as did the definition of terrorism by the National Advisory Committee on Criminal Justice Standards and Goals, Hacker includes organized crime as a form of terrorism. What is lacking from criminals and crazies is political motivation. In general, Hacker's typology is overly general and too nonspecific in describing terrorism.

Gregor (1983) developed a four-category schema to describe terrorism. One identified terrorist category was instrumental terrorism, or that terrorism designed to impair the functioning of a system or institution, either governmental or private. Tupemaro kidnappings of American executives in South America are instrumental terrorism, just as are IRA attacks on the British government. Gregor's second category of terrorism was demonstrative terrorism. This form of terrorism is designed to change the attitude of a population to the purposes and goals of the terrorist organization. Any activity conducted by terrorists to influence public attitudes toward a government would fit this category. The Castro-led Cuban revolution against the Batista government would be an example of demonstrative terrorism. The third category of terrorism was prophylactic terrorism, or terrorism employed in anticipation of resistance or rebellion. For example, Randy Weaver's standoff in Idaho in 1992 against federal law enforcement officials would be considered prophylactic terrorism. Fourth was the category of incidental terrorism, or criminal activities that impact on innocent victims by persons with psychological pathology, or persons committing acts for personal profit or personal advantage. Basically, this category involves criminal activity of a terroristic nature.

Gregor's (1983) typology, like those above, tends to be too general to help explain the dynamics of terrorism that help make some sense of an elusive phenomenon. The inclusion of criminal activity, psychological pathology, and personal gain include non-terroristic activity and make the categorization too inclusive. While all active terrorists are criminals, not all criminals are terrorists.

Schmid and de Graaf (1982) proposed a typology that included the categories of insurgent terrorism, state or repressive terrorism, and vigilante terrorism. Insurgent terrorism was that conducted against a particular state and included the subcategories of (a) social revolutionaries, (b) separatists, nationalists, or ethnics and (c) and single issue. Social revolutionaries engage in terrorism to bring about a worldwide revolution, separatists and nationalists want to change only one part of a governmental system, and single-issue terrorism is that designed to grant some special privileges to some group.

State or repressive terrorism is that used by a government or individuals against some less powerful segment of a society or population. The terrorism of Idi Amin and Fidel Castro, according to Schmid and de Graaf's (1982) classification, is the same as that of the Aryan Nations and skinheads against minorities. It is difficult to equate Amin's mass extermination of thousands of Ugandans with isolated attacks on minorities by a racist organization.

Vigilante terrorism is not directed against a state nor on behalf of the state. This is terrorism conducted by criminals, the pathological, and terrorists attacking private companies. This is a "catchall" category for any type of terrorism that does not fit into the above categories. As such, it does not help understand the form or function of terrorism and serves to further confuse an already confusing phenomenon.

Schmid and De Graaf's (1982) typology does not address several forms of terrorism (i.e., international and transnational terrorism; Poland 1988) and places several distinct forms of terrorism into the same category. Further, it includes acts by non-terrorist individuals. Expanding upon and clarifying Schmid and De Graaf's typology, Poland proposed five categories of terrorism: (1) political, (2) criminal, (3) pathological, (4) labor and (5) war. Political, criminal, and pathological terrorism are similar to that described by Schmid and De Graaf's classification. Labor terrorism is that conducted by workers to effect changes in a political system, and war terrorism is that terrorism used during wartime. While Poland does clarify and separate some forms of terrorism, his schema still leaves an unclear state of affairs.

Wilkinson (1974, 1977, 1986) developed a typology that relies upon five categories. First is criminal terrorism, or the planned use of terrorism for financial or material gain. His second category is psychic terrorism, or terrorism based upon magic beliefs, myths, and expectations induced by fanatical religious beliefs. Right-wing religious supremacists would be psychic terrorists. Wilkinson's third category is war terrorism, or that terrorism designed to annihilate an enemy through whatever means possible. This category would include acts of war that are not terroristic, such as two warring nations resorting to atomic weapons. State-sponsored terrorism, the fourth category, is the terrorist tactic used in international conflict.

The fifth category in Wilkinson's (1974, 1977, 1986) typology is political terrorism, or the use of violence to create fear and achieve a political objective. Within this category are four subcategories: (a) revolutionary terrorism, systematic tactics of violence to bring about a political revolution. Characteristics of political revolution include it being a group activity, having a moral justification in revolutionary ideology, having an organized group infrastructure, an established code of conduct with a policymaking committee, and a structured leadership for recruitment. (b) Subrevolutionary terrorism is that which is designed to force a government to change policy or laws, address and change controversial political issues, serve as a warning to government officials, or to retaliate against a government. (c) Repressive terrorism is used by government forces against their own people. (d) Nationalistic terrorism is that committed to gain political independence from a colonial power or to change the ethnic composition of an existing government without changing its ideological structure.

Political terrorism, regardless of subtype, has certain characteristics that help identify that terrorism: (1) it involves the systematic use of murder, injury, or threats to achieve a political objective of revolution or repression, (2) it creates an atmosphere of fear, coercion, and intimidation; (3) it involves indiscriminate attacks on innocent civilians; (4) it is unpredictable; (5) it does not use the rules and conventions of warfare; (6) it employs savage methods of destruction; and (7) it has a moral justification within a broader political philosophy.

Wilkinson's typology (1974, 1977, 1986), like other schema, identifies regular criminal behavior as being terroristic. It also considers wartime activities as terroristic. While this is certainly true of some wartime activity, as will be shown, it is not true of all military action during a conflict. His typology differentiates among forms of political terrorism and categorizes political terrorism as changing a government, altering a government, or the government terrorizing its citizens. However, it does allow for the overlapping of various terrorist organizations and activities into two or more categories. The Aryan Nations, for example, wish to change the policies of the government concerning minorities (nationalistic), but they also see the removal of the current government necessary to insure survival of the United States (revolutionary; Mullins, 1993). Finally, Wilkinson's typology assumes a developed and formalized organizational structure for terrorism. This is not always true, as numerous terrorist organizations have demonstrated over the years.

White (1991) developed a five-category typology of terrorism. His first category is criminal terrorism, or terrorism for profit and gain. Second is ideological terrorism, or the use of terrorism to change an ideological framework of political power. White's third category is nationalistic terrorism, that used to support the interests of an ethnic or nationalistic group irrespective of political ideology. The fourth category is state-sponsored terrorism, or the use or threat of violence in international relations outside the scope of normal diplomatic protocols. Fifth is guerrilla terrorism, or terrorism used as a technique of guerrilla warfare. Guerrilla terrorism ranges from being a state police of a despot government to strictly military operations conducted by an army in the course of war.

In addition to the problems of the typologies presented above, White's (1991) categorization includes military intervention during war as a form of terrorism. Further, he equates military actions during warfare as similar to a secret police being used to control the behavior of citizens. His category of state-sponsored terrorism would include international and transnational terrorism, making no distinction between why the terrorist activity is conducted or who sponsored the activity.

The typologies presented above are summarized in Table 1.1.

A typology developed by Crozier (1975) and based upon a continuum ranging from the far left to the far right is presented in Figure 1.2. At the extreme left are minority nationalists. This form of terrorism is conducted by ethnic factions who wish to replace a government with one composed of their own ethnic group. Next are Marxist revolutionaries, who wish to gain control of social and economic systems to change them from capitalist to socialist systems. Third are anarchists, revolutionaries who use terrorism to destroy an established social order and reduce government control and structure. Ideological mercenaries are individuals and organizations who engage in terrorism to help whatever current political movement is in vogue. These terrorists are mercenaries in the sense they shift alliances and engage in terrorism for the sake of terrorism. Pathological individuals and organizations are similar to anarchists, but their terroristic activities are criminal and are for personal gain or psychological gratification. Finally, Crozier classifies the far right as neo-fascists, or those with some racial or religious political destiny.

Most typologies, including Crozier's (1975), equate anarchist terrorism with a leftist political ideology and neo-fascism with purely rightist political philosophy. A terrorist ideology does not equate that way to political philosophy. Additionally, the terrorist motivation must be examined within the framework of the terrorist's capacity for violence. A more accurate and complete typology would examine terrorism along a three-dimensional representation rather than the one-dimensional typologies previously presented. The dimensions of this typology would represent

Table 1.1.
Summary of terrorist typologies.

Thornton (1964)
  Enforcement
  Agitational

Bell (1975)
  Psychotic
  Criminal
  Vigilante
  Endemic
  Authorized
  Revolutionary
    Organizational
    Allegiance
    Functional
    Provocative
    Manipulative
    Symbolic

Hacker (1977)

Above	Below
	Crusaders
	Nationalists
	Ideologues
Criminals	Criminals
Crazies	Crazies

Gregor (1983)
  Instrumental
  Demonstrative
  Prophylactic
  Incidental

Schmid & de Graaf (1982)
  Insurgent
    Social Revolutionary
    Separatist
    Single Issue
  State
  Vigilante

Poland (1988)
  Political
  Criminal
  Pathological
  Labor
  War

Table 1.1. Continued.

Wilkinson (1974)
  Criminal
  Psychic
  War
  State Sponsored
  Political
    Revolutionary
    Subrevolutionary
    Repressive
    Nationalistic

White (1991)
  Criminal
  Ideological
  Nationalistic
  State Sponsored
  Guerrilla

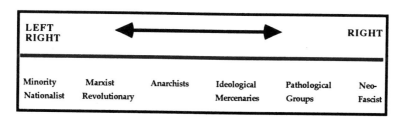

Figure 1.2. Crozier's (1975) continuum of terrorist typology.

terrorist belief structures, political philosophy, and the potential for violence and is presented in Figure 1.3.

Terrorist belief structures range from Marxist revolutionaries on one end of the continuum to neo-fascist supremacists on the other extreme. Marxist revolutionaries employ terrorism to attempt to introduce a specific socialist economic, social, and/or political system. Next on the continuum are anarchists, who use terrorism to destroy social structures and governments. Third are ideological revolutionaries, who employ terrorism much like the anarchists, with the difference being they wish to introduce a form of government controlled by themselves. Fourth are the nationalists, who engage in terrorism to change other governments and bring other nations into their sphere of influence. Last, and defining the opposite end of the continuum, are the neo-fascist supremacists, who

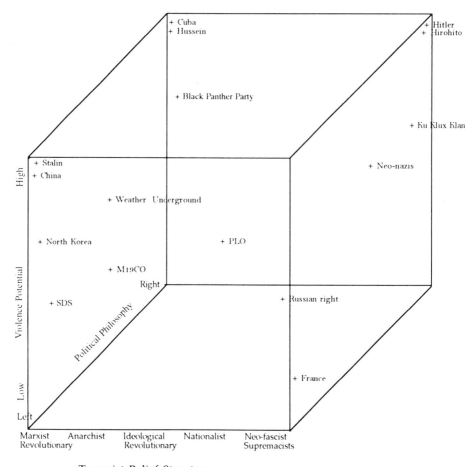

Figure 1.3. Multidimensional representation of terrorist typologies.

use terrorism to bring about racial or religious political supremacy and have government dedicated to those objectives.

Political philosophy is sometimes, but not always, correlated with belief structure. On this dimension, pure Marxist-Leninist regimes would be represented at the left extreme of the continuum and racial/religious/ethnic nationalists regimes at the other end. In the middle of this dimension are the moderate democracies. The third dimension, violence potential, represents future activity in terrorism based upon historical antecedents of violence, current geo-political conditions, and anticipated political, economic, and social conditions. This dimension is necessary as it separates the true terrorist from the rhetorical terrorist. Many pseudo-terrorists and terrorist-like regimes speak openly about conducting campaigns of terror against the United States or other governments, but they do not have the violence potential to actually become terrorists. The true terrorist must have a legitimate potential to use violence. The violence potential of the PLO, for example, has been elevated because of the assassination of Israel's Prime Minister Rabin in October 1995. Prior to that assassination, the PLO's violence potential was much lower. Figure 1.3 also illustrates the spatial location of several other well-known terrorist organizations and terrorist regimes.

It is realized there are several overlapping categories of terrorist in this schema. It does, however, avoid several of the major shortcomings of the other classification systems discussed. One, non-terrorist activity is not considered nor are terrorists engaging in purely criminal activity included. Two, personal motivations, except as they apply to controlling a government, are excluded. Criminals, the psychologically deranged, and organized criminal activity is excluded. Three, distinctions between guerrilla warfare, insurgency, rebels, commandos, and freedom fighters are not made. Four, a distinction is made between terrorism used in warfare and as part of warfare, and military actions during war. Five, no organizational structure is assumed for terrorists. Disorganized individuals as terrorists can be just as effective as highly structured and well-defined terrorist organizations. Six, political motivations can be identified. One of the objectives of a classification, and one objective missing from most typologies presented above, is to identify motivations of terrorists, an important component of describing and understanding the form and function of terrorism. This typology considers motivations. Finally, this typology introduces some specificity in the classification of terrorism.

If combined with the accepted definition of terrorism, this typology identifies the strategy, tactics, motivations, political outcome, and activity level of terrorists and can be used for intelligence purposes, prediction, and planning counter-terrorist activities.

PROCESS OF TERRORISM

In addition to trying to explain terrorism through definitions or typologies, the reasons persons engage in terrorism may be examined. Trying to understand the purposes and process of terrorism may assist in explaining terrorism. For example, Poland (1988) explained the terrorist process as involving: (1) the production of terror or paralyzing fear, (2) attracting attention and gaining sympathy, and (3) provoking a government to commit counter-atrocities. Poland has identified the components of terrorism in terms of the atrocities committed by terrorists, but says nothing of the other purposes of terrorism, such as being national or international in scope, the political purpose of government change, targets of the terrorist organization, strategies and tactics, etc.

Hutchison (1972) identified the components of terrorism as being: (1) international conduct, (2) terror purpose, (3) political purpose, (4) violence, (5) outcome of panic, (6) reliable patterns of behavior, (7) immoral acts, (8) shock value of the acts, (9) target selection, (10) random patterns of target selection, and (11) unpredictable behavior. There are several problems with Hutchinson's identification of terrorist purposes. First, he assumes terrorism must be international in scope. This would exclude domestic and state acts of terrorism. Second, he assumes terrorism requires violence. This excludes threats of violence. Third, outcome of panic (5) and shock value of the acts (8) essentially describe the same process. Fourth, unpredictable behavior is true only as it applies to target selection. Terrorist behavior is predictable in terms of the types of activities a particular organization engages in.

Paust (1977) defined the terrorist process as including: (1) types of terrorists, (2) objectives of the terrorist, (3) areas of action, (4) available resources, (5) particular strategies of the terrorist, (6) outcomes, and (7) legal effects of the acts. By knowing the typology, objectives, geographical regions, strategies and tactics, outcome measures, and legal effects, one could predict terrorist activity. Paust's terroristic process is designed to predict terrorist behavior more than the other processes presented in this section. Unfortunately, Paust does not focus on political change and the political purpose of terrorism, objectives of fear, nor use of threats.

Jenkins (1975) considered the terrorist process to consist of the following: (1) provoke government overreaction, especially indiscriminant reactions, (2) overthrow of oppressive regimes, (3) cause isolation and demoralization of individuals, creating an atmosphere of anxiety and insecurity, (4) release of prisoners and publish manifestos, (5) immobilize security forces, and (6) obtain finances to purchase weapons. To this process, Crenshaw (1981) added: (7) seizure of political power, (8) affect public attention and seize media, (9) maintain discipline and enforce obedience and conformity within the terrorist organization, (10) discredit and disrupt functioning of government, (11) win new recruits, and (12) project an image of strength that exceeds their numbers. The major weakness of this delineation is that it is a combination of description and prediction. Additionally, it is overspecific, including several corollary activities to the primary goals of the organization.

The above theories of the terrorist process are summarized in Table 1.2.

Like the definitions and typologies of terrorism, a delineation of the terrorist process should not only assist in understanding terrorism but

Table 1.2.
Terrorist process theories.

Poland (1988)
Production of terror or paralyzing fear
Attract attention and gain sympathy
Provoke government to commit counter—
  atrocities
	Paust (1977)
	Types of terrorists
	  Objectives of the terrorist
	Areas of action
	  Available resources
	  Particular strategies
	  Outcomes
	Legal effects

Hutchinson (1972)
International conduct
Terror purpose
Political purpose
Violence
Outcome of panic
Reliable patterns of behavior
Immoral acts
Shock value of the acts
Target selection
Random patterns of target selection
Unpredictable behavior
	Jenkins (1975)
	  Provoke government overreaction
	  Overthrow oppressive regime
	  Isolation and demoralization of individuals
	Release prisoners and publish manifestos
	Immoilize security forces
	  Obtain finances
	Added by Crenshaw (1981)
	  Seizure of political power
	  Affect public attention and media
	  Maintain internal discipline
	  Discredit and disrupt government
	  Win new recruits
	  Project an image of strength

should also help predict terrorist organization development and activity. The ability to understand terrorism without the ability to predict and foresee the terrorism future is not much help in combating terrorism. Thus, the identification of a terrorist process has to combine both concepts. A description of the terrorist process which does both would include:

1. Potential for violence and threats. A terrorist act does not have to involve actual violence, only the perception that violence could occur. If the target audience believes the terrorist organization is capable of performing violent acts, then the terrorist is well on his way toward achieving his objectives. Night cross-burnings by the Ku Klux Klan do not cause any physical harm but provide a forewarning of possible physical violence.

For terrorist threats to be effective, the organization has to show that it is capable of violence. Often, new organizations will engage in violent activity merely to demonstrate they have the capacity for violence. This behavior is not necessarily goal-directed but only a demonstration of ability. Additionally, if threats are not taken seriously, the terrorist may turn to violence to reinforce the attitudes and beliefs of the public.

Knowing the types of violence terrorists engage in and the types of threats they make help in predicting future terrorist behavior. Swastikas and racist slogans painted on Jewish synagogues are almost always indicative of skinhead activity (Mullins, 1990a). Establishing a pattern of skinhead activity helps predict future locations and forms of this activity.

2. **Availability of Resources.** The materials accessible by terrorists may help to explain and predict activity. Materials, manpower, money, equipment, and supplies will determine the capacity for potential activity for the terrorist organization. Many researchers concern themselves over the threat of nuclear terrorism. Nuclear terrorism is a low-probability event, as the terrorists lack the resources (nuclear mass, expertise, etc.) necessary to construct and/or detonate such a device (Mullins, 1992). One likely reason foreign organizations have not conducted more activities within the United States is because they do not have the resources in this country necessary for conducting operations. The United States far right has exponentially increased its available resources by networking and sharing resources among organizations.

Knowing what is available to the terrorist enables the prediction of future activity. One reason the government is concerned with the breakup of Russia and East Germany (as well as technical advances in the Mideast) is that the availability of expertise to assist with weapons of mass destruction (nuclear, biological and chemical weapons) have become suddenly accessible to the highest bidder. It is likely terrorists will make use of these assets (Mullins, 1991; Mullins & Becker, 1992).

3. **Internal Organizational Activities.** Some terrorist activities are designed to promote intergroup unity, increase conformity, recruit new members, gain the release of imprisoned members, obtain finances or supplies, and publish propaganda. If internal stress becomes severe, a terrorist activity may be conducted to relieve this stress. Activities may be conducted to improve group morale, provide practice for group members, or to improve other group dynamics. Knowing the infrastructure of the terrorist organization can help predict future activities. Monitoring of group processes can often lead to accurate assumptions about future activity.

4. **Geographical Areas of Operation.** Knowledge of physical locations of terrorist activity helps promote an understanding of a particular organization. Most Americans have the perception that the Ku Klux Klan is a predominantly southern organization, operating in the deep

south states of Louisiana, Mississippi, Alabama, Georgia, etc. In reality, the Klan is as strong in the North and West as it is in the South.

Knowledge of areas of operation is necessary to predict future activity. Geographical regions and geopolitical activity are both vital ingredients in the operation of terrorists. If a particular state is planning legislation to make abortions easier to obtain, it is likely that state will have a significant increase in the number of anti-abortion terrorist activities. Terrorism does not occur in a vacuum. It is dependent upon the specific social, economic, and legal activities of any given region (Mullins & Mijares, 1995).

5. **Strategy and Tactics.** Like any other criminal, the terrorist organization employs certain patterns of behavior which become a *modus operandi* of that organization. Cross-burnings exemplify the Klan, the FALN operates against military targets, and Al Fatah prefers attacks against airlines. Both strategy and tactics become a trademark of any terrorist organization. Each organization has its own preferred tactical methodology and strategic capability. The predictability of terrorists are one of the most important tools law enforcement can have in stopping the organization.

6. **Purpose of the Activity.** It is vital to determine exactly why a terrorist engages in a particular activity of violence or threatens violence. Activities may be engaged in for a variety of reasons, including internal organizational factors, audience or media reactions, government reactions, or to achieve a political goal. The reason for any particular activity is a vital key in understanding the organization. The purpose behind a Klan cross-burning, for example, can be for a Klan ritual and initiation, to force a minority family to leave a particular neighborhood, to send a message to the entire minority community, or to protest some government activity.

Understanding why a terrorist organization engages in an activity enables the prediction of future activity. A Klan cross-burning designed to force a minority family to leave a particular neighborhood will likely be followed by more serious activity directed against that family or similar activities directed against other minorities in the neighborhood. Misunderstanding the purpose of an activity will lead to false predictions and help promote future activity. This misunderstanding may also assist in directing citizen and media attention and sympathy to the terrorists, for now the government is "prosecuting" these individuals.

7. **Audience and Media Reaction.** Terrorist activity may be designed to produce fear in the public, gain attention to a particular cause, promote sympathy and anti-government reaction, gain attention of the media, and discredit or disrupt a government function. One major

problem posed by terrorism is that the media has become somewhat immune to terrorism. Without the media, there is no terrorism. Unfortunately, small-scale terrorist activities no longer gain the media's attention. It requires large-scale activities on a scale unimaginable even ten years ago. The nighttime bombing of a federal office building does not gain media attention, it takes the daylight bombing of epic proportions to garner media coverage. Advances in media technology have also served to make Americans more vulnerable to terrorism. In the past, attacks on Americans in remote areas of the world were not worthwhile activities because the attack was "old news" by the time it could be reported in the U.S. Today, the media can instantaneously televise any terrorist activity anywhere in the world. These advancements in media communications have literally spread terrorism to the four corners of the world.

Audience reaction and media attention can help predict future terrorist activity. An activity designed to gain public support and sympathy will be followed by similar acts. Activities designed to promote fear and anxiety will likewise be followed by similar activities. The Oklahoma City Federal Building bombing, for instance, crossed the line between producing fear and producing anger. It is doubtful the far right will attempt any similar activity in the near future. Instead, they are likely to return to smaller-scale activities such as murder, assassination, hate crimes, and similar activities.

8. Government Reaction. The terrorist wants governments to react to terrorist events in certain ways. They may want the government to begin engaging in unpredictable ways, to begin a program of counter-atrocities, to overreact and enact measures the public will revolt against, or to immobilize government security forces. It is important to realize these government reactions are not necessarily part of the terrorist organization's political goals. The government overreacting is serving to influence citizen attitudes toward that government. Understanding how a government body might react to a terrorist activity assists in predicting future activity. If a government overreacts by establishing an unwieldy series of roadblocks and checkpoints, the terrorist will engage in activities that will further tighten travel, not only on roads, but by air, rail, and ship. A continuation of similar activities will provoke the same government reaction and, in turn, citizen counter-reaction.

9. Political Outcomes. The goal of terrorism is to produce political change. Terrorism may be designed to change specific laws (such as eco-terrorism), disrupt the functioning of a government, seize political power, or overthrow an oppressive government. Terrorists may operate at the local, state, or federal level to change governments. Regardless of the public manifesto of the terrorist, such as racial or religious supremacy, the core of terrorism is to influence or change political systems. There is no other reason for terrorism.

Table 1.3.
The terrorist process for the prediction of activity and
the planning of the terrorist responses.

Potential for violence and threats
Availability of resources
Internal organizational activities
Geographical areas of operations
Strategy and tactics
Purpose of the activity
Audience and media reaction
Government reaction
Political outcomes

Understanding the political goals of the terrorist help predict terrorist activity. If a terrorist organization wants racial separation, they will attack those government structures that either help prevent racial separation or promote racial separation. In the latter case, the organization will want to speed government action to help achieve the terrorist's goals.

TYPES OF TERRORISM

Just as it is difficult to define terrorism, arrive at a common typology of terrorism, or produce a process of terrorism, there is disagreement concerning the types of terrorism (Mickolus, 1977). The accepted typology of terrorism presented in this chapter assists in defining the types of terrorism to the extent it identifies left-wing and right-wing terrorism. Left-wing terrorism is that terrorism intended to change a government to socialism, communism, or anarchism. Socialist governments would likely include the introduction of a democratic system of government as left-wing. Right-wing terrorism is based upon ideologies of racial or religious supremacy. Somewhere on the continuum between the two would be terrorism characterized as "specialized" terrorism. This would include the eco-terrorists, animal rights terrorists, and abortion terrorists. Specialized terrorism has a goal to only change a portion of government or set of laws to benefit their particular cause. The abortion movement, for example, has individuals and organizations dedicated to eliminating abortion and others dedicated to pro-abortion. It would be a stretch of the imagination to consider either side as left or right wing.

On a more specific scale, it is necessary to consider the type of terrorism in the context of purposes and operations. The Attorney General Guidelines on terrorism (1983), which guide FBI investigations of terrorism, type terrorists as being international or domestic. International terrorism, according to *The Attorney General Guidelines for FBI Foreign Intelligence Collection and Counterintelligence Investigations,* includes terrorist acts by groups or individuals that are foreign-based and/or directed by countries or groups outside the U.S. or which transcend national boundaries. Domestic terrorism, according to the *Attorney General's Guidelines on General Crimes, Racketeering Enterprise and Domestic Security/ Terrorism Investigations,* identifies groups that use force or violence for political motivation. The group does not have to commit actual violence and the focus is on group activity, not on individuals. Finally, the group has to claim responsibility for the acts.

By this typing, there are many overlapping areas. Would neo-Nazis in Europe who came to the U.S. be international or domestic terrorists? What if only one came to the U.S.? Is the IRA the same type of terrorist organization as is the PLO? This simple typing by the attorney general does not provide enough specificity and allows for multiple classification.

Simon (1994) types terrorism into six categories. One are religious terrorists. These terrorists commit terrorism as a result of moral justification of a religious belief, provide a solution to poverty, oppression and misery of a society, hope to achieve martyrdom, and will not be pacified by political agreements. Category two is ethnic-nationalist terrorism. This is terrorism necessary for achieving political and social objectives, gaining and keeping power for a particular ethnic-nationalist group, and providing support in communities. Simon believes ethnic-nationalist terror will be the fastest-growing terrorism in the coming years due to the worldwide rise in self-determination, independence, tribalism, the collapse of the USSR and eastern European bloc, and changes in the geopolitical changes in the Pacific Rim. Third, is political-ideological terrorism. This is terrorism intended to influence governments to change economic and environmental policies and law. This type of terrorism can be considered as either left- or right-wing and is the hardest type of terrorism for an individual to engage in. The public will not readily support political-ideological terrorism because it is less image conscious than ethnic-nationalist terrorism (Hewitt, 1990). The fourth type of terrorism is state-sponsored terrorism, or that which implements foreign-policy objectives. State-sponsored terrorism is rooted in self-interest and support for the terrorist is on a continuum of passive acceptance. State-sponsored terrorism can be conducted by a government against its own people or foreigners. Fifth is drug-related terrorism, that terrorism sponsored, supported, or conducted by drug interests. The purpose of drug-related terrorism is to produce fear, intimidation, and change specific laws. For example, in 1985, the Medellin cartel employed M-19, a left-wing terrorist organization, to kill 12 supreme court justices in the Palace of Justice, Bogota, Colombia. The purpose of this act was to send a message to other law enforcement personnel in Colombia. The sixth type of terrorism defined by Simon was criminal terrorism, or that terrorism conducted for individual gain. The 1982 Tylenol poisonings are an example of criminal terrorism.

Simon's (1994) typing tends to be fairly specific, but it can lead to overlap. U.S. far-right terrorists could fit within religious, ethnic-nationalist, political-ideological, and criminal terrorism. M-19 in Colombia, in addition to being drug-related terrorists, could also be ethnic-nationalist or political-ideological terrorists. By its complexity, this typing of terrorists leads to misunderstanding.

Terrorists can be sorted into four distinct, non-overlapping types that allow a clear understanding of the nature of the terrorist organization operating or being confronted. The categories of terrorism include transnational, international, domestic, and state terrorism. These categories are mutually exclusive and comprehensive in sorting terrorists.

Transnational Terrorism

Transnational terrorism involves actions conducted by non-state-supported actors, regardless of whether or not they receive any support from governments sympathetic to their cause (Milbank, 1978), and transcends national boundaries (Elliot & Gibson, 1978). The victims of the transnational terrorist are not necessarily citizens of one nation, although the victims could be one nationality. As defined by Mickolus (1980), Transnational terrorism is, "The use, or threat of use, of anxiety-inducing extranormal violence for political purposes by any individual or group, whether acting for or in opposition to established governmental authority, when such action is intended to influence the attitudes and behavior of a target group wider than the immediate victims, and when, through the nationality or foreign ties of its perpetrators, its location, the nature of its institutional or human victims, or the mechanics of its resolution, its ramifications transcend national boundaries." For an act to be considered Transnational terrorism, it must: (1) be an act committed against the nationals of one country (whether outside or inside the borders of that country), (2) be a political act, and (3) be an act designed to damage a government, an international organization and/or a national organization, either which would influence government action or policy (Evans, 1979).

Transnational terrorism has grown through three evolutionary phases.

In the first phase, governments provided logistical support to terrorists, such as weapons, transportation, finances, and training. In the second phase, terrorist organizations began cooperating with and assisting each other in terrorist operations. In the third phase, sympathetic governments began assisting the terrorist organizations. Cuba, for example, has committed troops to revolutionary movements in Central America, South America, and Africa. The Cubans not only serve as military advisers, provide military training, and material support but they actually fight alongside the revolutionaries or government troops (as the case may be). Many Near East countries, leading supporters of transnational terrorism, see this form of terrorism as a way to weaken the West and as a form of indirect warfare against the West.

Most airline hijackings and the takeover of the cruise ship, *Achille Lauro,* fit the definition of transnational terrorism. On the *Achille Lauro,* the terrorists were not working for a specific government, the victims came from several different nations, and demands were made of no one nation. Even if a country sympathetic to the terrorists had offered sanctuary, this act would still have satisfied the definition of transnational terrorism.

International Terrorism

International terrorism (also referred to at times as state-sponsored terrorism) is when terrorist acts are conducted by individuals or organizations controlled by a sovereign nation (Milbank, 1978) and is the natural extension of transnational terrorism. The sympathetic government first assists the terrorist organization and then, little by little, gains more and more control of the organization until the government finally controls the operations of the organization.

For an act to be considered international terrorism, the act must first be carried out against the citizens of a specific country, whether inside or outside that country's boundaries (Pierre, 1978). Two, the act must be political. Three, the terrorist operation must be planned to damage the interest of, or to gain concessions from, a particular government. Examples of international terrorism would include the Iranian takeover of the American Embassy in Tehran and the kidnapping of U.S. Army General Dozier in Europe by the Baader-Meinhof Gang.

Domestic Terrorism

Domestic terrorism is very similar to transnational terrorism. The major difference between the two is that domestic terrorists direct their actions against the citizens of one nation. As with transnational terrorism, domestic terrorism is not directly supported by any one government, although they may receive indirect or covert support from a government. The Irish Republic Army, the Ku Klux Klan, and the Aryan Nations are all domestic terrorist organizations.

State Terrorism

State terrorism consists of acts conducted by a government against its own citizens and within its own borders (Stohl, 1985). Maximilien Robespierre (France, 1789–1792), Vladimir Lenin, Joseph Stalin, Mao Tse Tung, and Adolph Hitler were all state terrorists. In recent years, there has been an increase in state terrorism. This increase cannot be solely attributed to the increase in numbers of third world nations but instead is primarily a function of the changed perceptions of the third world nations who rely on governmental control by a military response instead of a political response (Ayoob, 1984). Since Lenin, Stalin, Hitler, Tojo, and Mao taught the technique, governments have not seen it amoral to rule by military terror, nor as a crime against humanity to rule by elimination of the masses (Rubenstein, 1981).

Once the government begins to rule by force, the next logical step for that government becomes genocide (Horowitz, 1976). As has been demonstrated time and again, once the state begins to rule by force, it becomes a runaway train, gaining momentum until overthrown. Recent examples of state terrorism include Vietnam (after the pullout of American troops), Cambodia, Brazil (during the Peron era), Libya, Iran, Iraq, Nicaragua, and Cuba. It is important to note the right-wing extremist groups in the United States have professed that terrorism is the only way to rule a nation, and that should they gain control of the government, the acts of Stalin, Hitler, and Mao will pale in comparison. Table 1.4 summarizes the differences in the four types of terrorism.

Table 1.4.
The identification of the four types of terrorism in the world.

		Direct involvement of nationals of more than one state?	
		Yes	*No*
Government controlled	Yes	International	State
or Directed?	No	Transnational	Domestic

GROWTH OF TRANSNATIONAL TERRORISM

Of the four types of terrorism, transnational terrorism is rapidly outpacing the others. Milbank (1978) has identified several reasons for the rapid growth of transnational terrorism.

One, transnational terrorism is rapidly growing because of new technology. Technological advances in weapons, methods of mobility, technological industry, and advances in communications technology have benefited the transnational terrorist. Of these, satellite communications have had the greatest impact on transnational terrorism. Satellite communications have not only created new targets for the terrorist, they have also provided instantaneous media coverage. Today, the terrorist can take American hostages in outer Mongolia and within minutes Americans at home can watch live, up-to-the second developments on television (Lasky, 1975; Cooper, 1977; Johnpoll, 1977).

There are several other advantages to the terrorist using the mass media (O'Sullivan, 1986). The terrorist can spread fear and anxiety to entire populations. This was evidenced by the decrease in U.S. tourism to Europe in 1986, when President Reagan struck terrorist training centers in Libya. Kaddafi threatened retaliation against Americans, and this threat was enough to change the vacation plans of millions of Americans. Americans in 1986 did not travel abroad because they believed governments would be unable to stop Kaddafi from following through on his threats. The aftermath of the Oklahoma City Federal Building bombing produced similar effects. In addition to a belief of susceptibility to terrorist attack, a perception of moral decay and chaos can be spread.

The terrorist can gain respectability in the media. Many times, the media does not portray the terrorist as criminal, injuring and killing innocent people, but as political activists fighting for a cause. Following the Branch Davidian siege in Waco, Texas, many reporters portrayed David Koresh as a victim of government oppression. Few portrayed him as a paranoid schizophrenic who was deliberately planning for an Armageddon standoff with the government.

Communications within the terrorist organization are also enhanced by satellite communications, allowing an organization to conduct several simultaneous acts in different parts of the world. A single organization, at one time, could take hostages on several different continents and keep each other appraised of situational developments. Terrorists have recently begun using computer networks to share information, resources, and plans with other terrorists. Some terrorist organizations use computer bulletin boards, the Internet, and/or modum links with other organizations. Computers have provided the terrorist an easy and convenient method of rapidly sharing information. Using satellite television, terrorist organizations are producing and airing their own television broadcasts to spread their message and recruit new members. Right-wing extremists in the United States have taken full advantage of this technology.

Two, the increased number of world immigrants have made the task of the transnational terrorist easier. While most immigrants are hardworking members of their new society, many are political exiles, undesirables, and criminals. These émigrés provide the transnational terrorist cover, operational support, and even recruits. Some of these émigrés may even be members of the terrorist organization deliberately planted in a country.

Three, there has been a "revolutionary turn in the overall political environment" of the world (Milbank, 1978). This is an event which occurs every two to three hundred years. The superpowers which emerged from World War II have come under attack from many developing nations, from dissatisfied second-rate world powers, from upstart communist regimes, and from a broad range of social forces inspired by a new sense of social conscience. Algeria expelled the French regime in the 1960s, Great Britain has been ousted from most of its colonies, Vietnam fought and beat both the French and the United States, and developing nations in the Near East, Africa, South America, and Asia are looking to establish their credibility. All of this has benefited the terrorist. Milbank has indicated that this change in the world's political environment has "accorded an aura of legitimacy to the acts of any terrorist group claiming leftist revolutionary liberation movement status; frustrated efforts to develop more effective international countermeasures; facilitated transnational contact and cooperation among terrorist groups; fostered a significant increase in the number of national, transnational, and international organizations providing national liberation movements and other 'progressive' dissident formations with the various forms of direct and indirect support." This social consciousness has forced the United States, England, Japan, Russia, and China to withdraw from several politically explosive situations in the global community, affected foreign relations, and presented an increase in terrorism against the U.S.

Four, there has been a dramatic increase in the number of governments supportive of terrorism. These governments provide support, from verbal agreement to providing the transnational terrorist with money, weapons, training facilities, forged documents, and other forms of operational support (Netanyahu, 1986). Some countries even provide members of their armed forces to the terrorist cause. Cuba has provided all of the above to terrorists in Central and South America, Africa, and Asia. Many of these states not only sponsor terrorism, they actively conduct campaigns of terrorism (Schultz, 1986). Kaddafi, a leader of state-conducted transnational terrorism, has formed the "holy alliance," whereby the countries of Libya, Syria, and Iran not only share resources but also jointly participate in terrorist operations. A leader in government-supported terrorism has been the Soviet Union, which, even though losing its superpower status, has in some manner supported almost every major terrorist movement in the world. China, Iraq, Sudan, Chad, North Korea, and Cuba have also played a significant role in assisting terrorists.

Five, the global economic movement of the world has made the job easier for the transnational terrorist. An area of the world experiencing economic prosperity makes the movements of terrorists easier in that area, as large groups of émigrés are attracted to the area. As mentioned earlier, these émigré workers make it easier for the terrorist to operate and avoid detection. The economy of the 1990s is truly a world economy. Money can be instantly transferred anywhere in the world and in local currency. This has made the financial needs of the terrorist simple to achieve.

Six, nations of the West have made the terrorist's task easier by the very nature of their open societies. The lack of strong deterrence or response policies also contribute, as do the refusals of victimized nations to increase trade restrictions or place other embargoes on supportive states. In the early 1980s, two Libyan terrorists, firing from a window in the Libyan mission building in London (at a group of anti-Kaddafi protesters), killed Yvonne Fletcher, a British constable (Goldberg, 1986). The terrorists, who were identified by hundreds of onlookers, were allowed to leave England under the guise of "diplomatic immunity." Furthermore, the Libyan Embassy continued to operate in London. Only by taking strong sanctions against nations supportive of terrorism can the West begin to control terrorism.

SUMMARY

Democracies are especially vulnerable to terroristic operations. Democratic societies strive for non-violence, not only from its citizens, but also from its law enforcement agencies and military. The people will not condone an aggressive, violent response to terrorism. These societies are seen by the terrorist as the proverbial "ducks on the pond," for their response is weak rhetoric, not forceful reaction. Further, the terrorist realizes the democratic society will not reach out across foreign shores to strike at the heart of the terrorist organization. In 1986, when President

Reagan bombed terrorist training facilities in Libya, not only did the Eastern bloc countries rally to the unjustness of his actions, so also did many of the world's democracies of the world. England, Spain, and France, for example, led the international outcry against Reagan's actions. France threatened to withdraw from NATO as a result of U.S. strikes in Libya.

The highly industrialized democracies are the preferred targets of the terrorist (Smart, 1978). Urbanization offers easily accessible human targets with high economic value, service-oriented businesses and public utilities are especially vulnerable and provide attractive targets which can disable a wide segment of society with a single blow, and industry offers targets with low security and easy access. Finally, communication systems in democracies provide the essential ingredient for the terrorist— instant recognition by the public. Within minutes of conducting an operation, the terrorist can become known to an entire society. The media becomes the showcase for the terrorist, the tool for the terrorist to spread fear, and provides an open forum for propaganda. Most people had never heard of the island of Molucca until a group of South Moluccan terrorists took control of a Dutch passenger train in 1975. Immediately, everyone knew of Molucca and its fight for independence from Dutch control.

In the United States, the law enforcement community has to be concerned with all types of terrorism, except state terrorism. There are foreign agents in place in this country awaiting the signal from their organizations and/or sponsoring governments to begin operations. These terrorists have been and are a concern to law enforcement personnel. The FBI, for example, keeps extensive lists of most foreign university students, as some fit the demographic profile of the terrorist. These students are not nearly as much of a concern, however, as the home-grown terrorist. Even in light of recent international events, the domestic terrorist still presents the greatest threat to the safety and security of American citizens.

Until a common definition to terrorism can be agreed upon, terrorists will continue to exploit the public and government. Only by establishing a common definition of what terrorism is and what it is not can effective measures be taken to reduce and prevent terrorism. Understanding who the terrorists are, which can only be accomplished through unity of terms, is the necessary first step in preventing terrorism. Once that definition is agreed upon, then other counter-terrorist measures of prediction, interdiction, and prevention can be successfully used to prevent terrorism.

Chapter 2

THE HISTORY OF TERRORISM*

M any people perceived terrorism as a late twentieth century phenomenon, a post-World War II alternative to open, mass conflict. World War II demonstrated the futility of a dictatorship attempting to force its will on the world. In the wake of lessons learned in the 1940s, nations turned to terrorism as an alternative to declaring war on a much superior force. The Irgun and Stern gangs drove Britain from the Middle East and were the driving force behind the formation of Israel, but were so ruthless and violent the Israeli government outlawed them in September 1948 (Evans, 1979). Algeria gained independence from France using terrorist tactics. India, Vietnam, Cuba, and other colonial states employed terrorism to gain their independence.

Additionally, according to the perception of most people, by learning from nations who gained their independence from colonial powers, individuals formed small groups to apply the same lessons against any nation these "dissatisfied" groups did not like. The example most people will present is the actions of despots such as Kaddafi, Komeini, and Hussein against the United States, the IRA against Britain, and the PLO and Hezbollah against any Western powers. Others may remember and remark on Germany's Baader-Meinhof gang, Italy's Red Brigades, or Japan's Red Army Faction.

If Americans stayed home and avoided international travel, they were safe from terrorism. In the 1980s, according to the belief of most people, terrorism occurred to U.S. citizens who traveled or ventured overseas. The Beirut Marine barracks bombing, PanAm 103 over Lockerbee, the *Achille Lauro* cruise ship incident, and TWA flight 847 were not only unfortunate incidents but the unfortunate cost of going overseas. As long as you stayed home (in the contiguous United States), you were safe from terrorism.

If asked, the majority of the public will express their dismay over how terrorism has finally found its way to the United States. In the 1990s, according to the vast majority of the public, foreign terrorists entered the

---

*This chapter was coauthored by Lisa K. Zottarelli.

U.S. and bombed the World Trade Center. At approximately the same time, Americans learned lessons from the foreign terrorists as evidenced by the bombing of the Oklahoma City Federal Building and the rise of the militia movement. If queried, few could identify Robert Mathews and the Order, nor identify their activities in the 1980s. They would admit, if told, that Mathews and Order members were "probably terrorists."

To be blunt, these perceptions of terrorism are not only wrong, they are "dead wrong." Terrorism has been part of the world order since the earliest recorded times and part of the American collective since before there was an United States of America. A theme already expressed, and to be emphasized throughout this book, is that ignorance is one of the weapons of the terrorist. An ignorance of the history of terrorism is just as deadly as failing to understand what terrorism is, what motivates and drives terrorists, how terrorist organizations function, who are the terrorists, and what strategies and tactics terrorists employ.

Historians are fond of repeating the oft-used cliché, "those who fail to understand history are doomed to repeat it." While overused, that cliché is true concerning terrorism. Failure to understand where we are and how we got here provides a significant advantage to the terrorist. The lessons of the past are the lessons of the future. To know the danger confronting us in the years ahead, we must understand the terrorist past. Mideastern extremists did not suddenly awake one day, decide to become terrorists, and then embark on an untested operational methodology. The Oklahoma City Federal Building bomber did not "suddenly" decide his action could bring about the downfall of the federal government.

Like governments, social structures, warfare, and science, terrorists have a rich and varied past that have taught them the lessons needed to be an effective, efficient, skilled, and deadly enemy. This chapter and the next will identify and describe the history of terrorism, particularly as it affects the United States in the 1990s. This chapter will present a global overview of the people and events that have shaped terrorism as practiced today. Certain persons and events who played a significant role in developing and shaping the practice of modern terrorism will be presented. To present an historical world chronology of terrorism would fill several encyclopedia-sized volumes. To present a chronology of United States terrorism would fill an encyclopedia. Instead, this chapter will select persons and events that were significant in shaping this insidious form of political warfare into what we see today.

FOUNDATIONS OF TERRORISM

The earliest recorded instances of terrorism in the world were in the first century A.D., when the Sicarri, a group of Jewish zealots, used assassination against Roman rule. The name Sicarri came from the short sword, called a sica, they used in assassinating members of the Roman ruling class (Rapoport & Alexander, 1983). Their intent was to begin a revolution against the Roman government in Palestine. A favored tactic of the Sicarri was to conduct the assassinations in broad daylight, when the Romans were among friends and allies. This tactic was designed to send a message to the Romans that no Roman was safe anytime or anyplace. It was also a tactic designed to produce fear, which it did.

The Sicarri also attacked Jewish priests considered by the group to be "Hellenistic," or who had pledged alliance to the Roman rulers in Palestine. Many of the assassinations against the Jewish priests were carried out on holy days, which again was designed to send a message of fear through the Jewish priesthood community (Rapoport, 1988).

When the Roman army finally trapped the Sicarri at Massada in 73 A.D., over 900 Sicarri decided to commit suicide rather than surrender to the Romans (Simon, 1994). The mass suicide of the Sicarri set a precedent of self-sacrifice rather than surrender, succumb, or fall prey to the opposed ruling party. The tradition of self-sacrifice established by the Sicarri was later emulated by Hassan ben Sabbah and is still today a standard used by many Mideast terrorists.

Hassan ben Sabbah and the Thuggees

Many consider the roots of modern political terrorism to have begun with the "Old Man of the Mountain," Hassan ben Sabbah (Kedourie, 1986). Born in Qom, Iran (near Tehran), in 1007 A.D., ben Sabbah was an Ishmaili Muslim, fervently opposed to the Shia and Sunni Muslim sects. Differences between the three sects revolved around the Accession of the Imam, the religious leader sent to earth by Ali, the Prophet Mohammed's son-in-law. Traveling throughout Iran, Iraq, and Syria, ben Sabbah attempted to convert Muslims to the Ishmaili sect.

In 1057 A.D., according to legend, ben Sabbah moved to the Alamut Valley (Caspian Sea region) and constructed a palace containing virtually every pleasure known to man. Selecting goat-herders who lived in nearby caves, ben Sabbah would carefully select his potential assassin, drug this person, and then transport them to his secret palace. The chosen goat-herder would then awaken in "paradise" and be left to sample the pleasures of the palace for several days. After this time, the goat-herder would again be drugged and returned to his cave. After a short period of time, ben Sabbah would visit this goat-herder, claiming to be a representative of Allah, and graphically describe the goat-herder's adventures. If the goat-herder would do what ben Sabbah wanted, then Allah would guarantee an eternity of the same riches upon death. The overwhelmed goat-herder, accustomed to a life of loneliness and poverty, could hardly wait to join forces with ben Sabbah.

Ben Sabbah was recruiting and training a cadre of terrorists to spread the Ishmaili religious philosophy. His recruits were used to assassinate religious leaders, dignitaries, commanders of fortresses, governors of cities, and emirs. Most assassins embarked on suicide missions, conducting the assassination in locations and at times they were sure to themselves be killed. Because of this devotion to self-sacrifice, ben Sabbah's terrorists acquired the name Fedai, or Fedayeen (plural); Men of Sacrifice (Dobson, 1974). Also known as Hashishim, or Hashashin (hashish eaters; Lewis, 1967), or in the English translation, assassins, these political killers led to ben Sabbah being called the First Grand Master of the Order of Assassins.

Even after his death in 1091, the Ishmaili sect remained the dominant Muslim sect, stretching from the Persian Gulf to the Mediterranean Sea. Ben Sabbah's empire lasted until the Mongol invasion of Iran in 1256, when led by Hulagu, grandson of Genghis Khan, the Mongols destroyed Ishmaili strongholds. In 1258, the Mongols captured Baghdad, killed all inhabitants, and erected 120 towers built with the skulls of the city's residents.

Ben Sabbah's legacy continues to be a motivational force for Mideast terrorists. Many Mideast terrorists still refer to themselves as Fedayeen and find it honorable and glorifying to engage in self-sacrifice to defeat Allah's enemies. The concept of the Fedayeen is described in the *Koran* and is a standard of religious practice in the Muslim faith.

In India in the eleventh century, the Thuggee began almost eight centuries of terror. The Thugs operated in isolated areas of India, attacking, robbing, and murdering travelers. They engaged in ritual murder of their victims, strangling them with trademark silk scarves. After death, the Thugs would drain the blood of their victims and offer it as a show of allegiance to the goddess Kali (Simon, 1994). The Thugs were successful, in large part, because they only operated in isolated areas. By the time an attack was discovered and a counterterrorist operation mounted, the Thugs would have long since disappeared into the wilderness. In the nineteenth century, the Thugs were finally defeated by the British, primarily because of the coming of the telegraph and railroad, which ended the terrorist's isolation.

During the crusades, the concept of political genocide became a terrorist tool (Chalk & Jonassohn, 1993). In Japan in the seventeenth century, the Japanese Tokugawa court mass-executed Western Christians (primarily Spanish and Portuguese). The Japanese believed Western thought and ideas would corrupt their culture, end the traditional values of the social order, and usurp established trading patterns. Attempts were made by the Japanese to completely eliminate Westerners from the island nation. About the same time, in Europe, the period of the great witch hunts had begun. People by the thousands were accused of "conspiring with the devil" and executed in the most torturous manners. The Grand Inquisitor Torquemada of Spain was one of the most notorious of the executioners, developing and inventing insidious methods to elicit a confession from the "heretics" before killing them, often by burning at the stake. Many of the devices we now associate with the dungeons of the Inquisition, such as the Rack, Iron Skull, Coffin of Nails, etc. were invented by Torquemada.

From the Tokugawa court and the inquisitors of the Inquisition, genocide has today become a widespread form of state terrorism. Throughout the twentieth century, nations have used genocide to eliminate "unworthies," including the Turkish killings of Armenians in the early 1900s, the extermination program of Nazi Germany in the 1940s, Stalin's purges of Russia throughout the century, the Khmer Rouge massacres of over 1.3 million in Cambodia (Rummel, 1990), and the tribal slaughters in Rwanda in the 1990s.

Maximilien Robespierre and the Reign of Terror

Most scholars are in agreement that Robespierre was the father of modern terrorism, and that the reign of terror conducted by Robespierre in France ushered in the era of modern terrorism. There are two main reasons as to why the French Revolution is considered the beginning of modern terrorism. First, the French Revolution provided the model for the writings of Karl Marx and Frederick Engels, the fathers of communism, and for the form of government practiced by Vladimir Lenin in twentieth century Russia. Second, the French Revolution was the first time in history a group of revolutionaries seized control of a nation or government and legalized murder and torture using a formalized set of laws (LeFebvre, 1965).

There were many causes for the French Revolution, but three played a significant role in bringing about the revolution. One, France was engaged in a series of foreign wars throughout Europe that were not popular among the French citizens. Two, and related to these wars, France had developed a new economic class of citizens during the 1700s: the middle class. France had industrialized and thousands of peasants had left the life of poverty to form this new economic class. The Bourbon wars, combined with rampant government corruption, resulted in continual and harsh tax increases. Taxation was hitting the middle class the hardest, threatening to destroy their newfound financial independence. Three, the world of academia had opened the ivory tower, making available to the general public the philosophies of science, economics, business, law, and political science. Intellectually, the citizens of France were exposed to new ideas, thoughts, and theories concerning the world around them. They were learning that man had the right to self-determination and did not have to be subjugated by a monarchy.

The French Revolution began on 14 July 1789 (the Day of the Bastille). Rioters stormed the Paris prison to release all political prisoners, which to the rioters meant all prisoners (Parry, 1976). In July 1789, the revolutionaries took Paris and by September 1791, had taken control of the government, deposing the Bourbon king. In April 1792, the Legislative Assembly was formed and declared war against Austria, which was the beginning of the Revolutionary Wars. In August 1792, King Louis XVI and his wife, Marie Antoinette, were imprisoned in the Paris prison. Louis XVI was killed by the guillotine on 21 January 1793, and Marie Antoinette met the same fate on 16 October. In August 1973, the Legislative Assembly was abolished and the National Convention formed.

The National Convention consisted of two parties, the Girondins and Jacobins. The Jacobin party was the more radical and powerful of the two and was led by Maximilien Robespierre. While otherwise unassuming, Robespierre was a dynamic and convincing public speaker. A disciple of the philosopher Rousseau, Robespierre argued there were only two types of government: a revolutionary government which led the people in open warfare against the "people's" adversaries and a constitutional government that was charged with writing a constitution and preserving the peace. According to Robespierre, France was at a state of war from within. Dissident factions were intent on destroying the nation and all means necessary must be used to protect the citizens. Like Rousseau, Robespierre believed man was basically good but had been corrupted by civilization and that by embarking on a Reign of Terror he was performing a service for mankind by returning him to purity—the unborn state of perfection—via the guillotine.

To conduct his reign of terror, Robespierre formed the Committee of Public Safety. The Committee of Public Safety had its own police force, network of spies, and "revolutionary committees" throughout France. It was responsible for three functions: finding "enemies of the people," trying these enemies, and executing them for the security of France.

After arrest, the accused were often tried in groups of up to 150, sentenced to death, and executed the same day. Some fortunate citizens were granted temporary reprieve by being sentenced to prison. This was only a stay of execution until they could die from starvation or disease inside the squalid death factories of incarceration.

As is the case with almost all dictators, Robespierre's egomania and unquenchable thirst for absolute power led to his ultimate downfall. Robespierre developed a paranoia that the Girondin party was out to eliminate him, so he had the Committee of Public Safety arrest and execute Girondin party leaders. On 19 October 1793, Robespierre gave complete government authority to the Committee of Public Safety so they could, on their own authority, eliminate any other enemies of the state. In April 1794, Robespierre abolished all governmental ministries (comparable to U.S. cabinet positions), thus making himself dictator of France. Fearing for their own lives as Robespierre's paranoia worsened, the Committee of Public Safety conspired against Robespierre and on 28 July 1794, arrested and executed Robespierre by guillotine.

Approximately 42,000 people were executed during the French Revolution and 400,000 died in prison, one-fifth of the total population of France. Approximately 17,000 met their death at the guillotine. Others were hung, executed by firing squad, or killed in mob violence. One Jacobin, Carrier, developed a particularly gruesome method of mass murder. He had the secret police herd citizens aboard ship, lock them in the holds, then floated the ship to sea and set it afire (Simon, 1994).

Upon the death of Robespierre, the Jacobins were overthrown and France ruled by the Men of the Directory. This period of government was characterized by greed, corruption, and incompetence. The Directory, in 1804, fell under its own weight of bureaucratic incompetence and France was subjected to rule by Napoleon Bonaparte, a not so benevolent dictator who continued the terroristic policies of Robespierre. Reaching their limit of terrorist rule in 1814, the citizens of France brought back the Bourbon monarchy.

Robespierre and the Reign of Terror demonstrated that terrorists could organize and use the tools of terrorism to gain and control an entire country. Of greater significance, Robespierre developed and refined the model of government that would later be used by Lenin, Stalin, Mao Tse-tung, and countless other tyrants. Robespierre demonstrated the necessity of a dictator having a legitimized organization of state terror control the population and maintain a high level of fear.

Vladimir Lenin and Joseph Stalin

Vladimir Lenin ruled Russia from 1917–1924 and was replaced by Joseph Stalin, who ruled until 1953. They were responsible for some of the worst terrorist atrocities of the twentieth century. Lenin's political philosophy was heavily influenced by three men. The most influential was Karl Marx, the father of modern communism and author of *Das Kapital.* Marx believed socialism was the only form of government that could truly serve the citizens and that the ruling economic class must be disposed of for a proletarian government to be formed. The second person who impacted Lenin was the philosopher Nikolai Chernyshevsky, who believed an agrarian society was necessary to begin the Socialist movement. The third influence on Lenin came from Friedrich Engels, a colleague of Marx. Engels believed violence was a necessary ingredient in overthrowing the existing regime and also necessary to ensure obedience to the new regime (Wolfe, 1965).

Between 1913–1916, the Russian Revolution, led by Kerensky and middle-class liberal socialists, overthrew the tsars and established a new government. The new government was inefficient, financially bankrupt, and lacked the support of the populace. In the October Revolution of 1917, Lenin and the Bolshevik party wrested control from Kerensky and on 7 November 1917, Lenin emerged before the Congress of the Soviets as the new ruler of Russia. The Bolsheviks renamed themselves Communists. One of Lenin's first acts was to form Cheka, the official arm of state enforcement. Cheka was modeled after Robespierre's Committee of State Security and their primary job was to find and execute enemies of the state. Cheka (Ch.K., Extraordinary Commission for Combating Counterrevolution and Sabotage) was headed by Feliks Dzerzhinsky, who hired psychopaths, criminals, killers, and other unsavory characters to man the agency.

The terrorism administered by Cheka was called the Red Terror. First singled out for arrest and execution were the upper class and intelligentsia. As Lenin consolidated his power, other "undesirables" were added to the "wanted list": military officers, priests, government officials from prior regimes, peasants, industrial workers, and prostitutes. Not all state enemies were executed. Hundreds of thousands were sent to concentration camps and insane asylums (one of Lenin's legacies). Camps were used for slave labor and medical research. Much of the medical research was in pharmacology, and inmates were given reserpine (neural atrophy), aminazin (memory loss and loss of control of muscular movements), and sulfozin (Staff, 1972, in Parry, 1976). Internment in either facility was a death sentence. Inmates were brutalized, overworked, starved, and died by the thousands of disease and infection.

Lenin was wounded by an assassin's bullet in 1922 and died in 1924. During his rule, agents of Cheka killed more than one and one-half million Russians, and hundreds of thousands were imprisoned in concentration camps or admitted to insane asylums.

Born Iosif Dzhugashvili, Joseph Stalin took over the rule of Russia upon Lenin's death. At 18, Stalin began working for the Russian Social Democratic Party (Tucker, 1974), joined the Bolshevik party in 1904, and became editor of *Pravda,* the official Bolshevik newspaper in 1917 (Ulam, 1973). Stalin rose to power on Lenin's coattails, bringing his handpicked underlings with him. When he finally assumed control of Russia, there was no internal party opposition for him to contend with. Once he assumed control, Stalin quickly intensified the campaign of terror begun by Lenin.

One of Stalin's innovations to state terrorism were public show trials. During the 1930s, hundreds of thousands of Russians were placed on public trial to confess their sins against the state. At the public display, the accused confessed to whatever crimes the government decreed, were then found guilty, and promptly sentenced. The trials were nothing more than a form of behavioral control.

Stalin also specialized the concentration camps in Russia. Expanding the scope and function of these camps, Stalin was able to provide for the needs of Russia by using slave labor. Each camp performed a specialized function. Some camps mined coal, others cut and sawed lumber, some manufactured goods, others built railroads, etc. Without the concentration camps, the Russian industrial system would never have gotten started, there would have been no military machine, and Russia would not have made the scientific progress necessary to keep pace with the West. The nuclear research program of the Soviets was conducted at a concentration camp, from the mining of the ore to the actual building of the bomb.

Stalin reformed Cheka as the NKVD (Narodny Komissariate Vnutrenikh Del—People's Commissariate of the Interior). In addition to state terrorism, the NKVD was charged with developing an international network of spies for intelligence gathering. The NKVD did not become effective at state terrorism until 1938, when Levernty Beria was named director. Beria formed the KGB (Komitet Gosudarstvennoi Beopasnosti—Committee for State Security; Barron, 1974), the agency responsible for internal intelligence in Russia. In carrying out their mission, the KGB became one of the cruelest state police forces in history, rivaled and surpassed only by Adolph Hitler's Gestapo, SD, and SS. Mass rapes of female prisoners, sadistic beatings of the prisoner's families in the prisoner's presence, crushing limbs, pulling out fingernails, crushing of testicles, urinating into prisoner's mouths, and other exotic torture of prisoners were commonplace. Under Beria, the KGB added foreign intrigue to its duties, becoming the most powerful intelligence and espionage organization in the world.

On 5 March 1953, Stalin died a natural death. His 29-year reign of terror was responsible for between 15–35 million Russian deaths and imprisonments. At the concentration camps, the fatality rate ranged between 20%–50% of the inmate population per year. Ninety percent of the population of those camps were men and women of working age, an estimated 25% of the Russian population of that age group. In all, between 5%–8% of the total Russian population was killed by Stalin's agents.

Mao Tse-tung

In the East, while Stalin was conducting his show trials, one of the most ruthless, dictatorial, and efficient state terrorists in history was rising to power, Mao Tse-tung of China. Mao did not attempt to refine the political concepts or theories of any particular philosophy, nor introduce any new form of government. Mao knew only one form of government: absolute and total dictatorial control. Mao's rule of China was characterized by complete submission of the people to his control. Many modern terrorist organizations proclaim themselves Maoists, erroneously espousing a political rhetoric of socialism they attribute to "Chairman Mao." Typically, these organizations will argue a bastardized version of Marxism-Leninism and attribute these "improvements" and refinements to Mao.

Mao was not a political theoretician, philosophizer, idealist, or politician. Mao was a terrorist and a man in search of the perfect form of terrorism. He was an innovator in state-sponsored terrorism. His contributions were not to the political arena but to the terrorist arena. Mao did make several contributions to terrorism, and they were contributions which changed the form of state-sponsored terrorism and made it more effective, more powerful, and more frightening than ever before. Mao's influence on terrorism essentially opened the door for today's dictators and showed them how to more effectively operate in the world community.

The most significant innovation Mao brought to terrorism was the splitting of the family unit. It was his belief that a person could not serve two masters. The reason most terrorist despots ban religion is because it provides a resource of hope to the people. Mao also realized this and eliminated religion in Chinese life. He also realized the family unit was a more powerful moral and psychological resource than even religion. If a person was loyal to the family, they could not be loyal to the state. Thus, one of the primary goals of Mao was to break the centuries-old Asian tradition of family loyalty. To destroy family loyalty, Mao undertook massive campaigns designed to encourage people to report disloyal family members to the state. The closer the relation, the better. Children reporting parents and parents reporting children was the ideal. The offense was secondary to the reporting. As with Robespierre, Lenin, and Stalin, the charges could be embellished to suit the needs of the state. If a person reported a disloyal family member, that person was often rewarded with a parcel of land or some other valuable commodity. By abolishing the family unit, Mao also accomplished the goal of destroying religion. Religion was closely tied in with the family unit, and by destroying the family, generations of religious training rapidly broke down. All that was left was guidance and direction from the state, and the state could now not only dictate loyalty but also morality, a crucial component of total loyalty and devotion.

Mao's second innovation to the world of terrorism were the public show trials conducted throughout the country. Terrorist dictators using public trials to serve the purposes of the state were not new. Robespierre, Lenin, and Stalin had all used them successfully. What made the public show trials of Mao unique was the use of the audience to pass sentence and, in many cases, conduct the executions. The show trials in China were conducted in outdoor arenas. People from that town, neighboring cities, villages, and local rural areas would be invited to attend. The accused would be brought before the crowd in large groups (as many as 200–300 in some cases) and the state-appointed judge would exhort the crowd as to sentencing. At the urging of the judge, the crowds would scream out the guilt of the victim and then rabidly urge immediate death for the "traitors." The judge would agree and then carry out the execution on the spot. In many instances, the crowd was allowed to perform the execution by stoning or beating the accused to death. After the executions, the crowd would remain, chanting and singing praises to the state. So great was his reliance on these trials to control China, Mao had some broadcast on the radio for the rest of the nation to hear.

The public show trials were designed to fulfill two objectives. The first purpose was to scare the people into submissiveness, a fear tactic used by all terrorist states. The second purpose was to get the public actively involved in state-sponsored terrorism. By making the people accomplices to terrorism, Mao built loyalty among the Chinese. By passing sentence and, in some cases, being part of the execution of sentence, citizens were not supporters of the government in word alone, they were active participants and would pledge greater support to Mao.

The third terrorist innovation brought about by Mao was his bragging to the world about the killings. Unlike Lenin, Stalin, and even Hitler, who attempted to hide internal terrorism from the world's prying eyes, Mao would publicize the executions in the printed news and the electronic media. Western journalists were often invited in to witness the public trials and were kept current on the number of people executed. Many of the public show trials were broadcast live on European and Asian radio. No other terrorist in the world had Mao's audacity when it came to "bragging rights."

Walker (1971) summarized the legacy of terror wrought by Mao on the Chinese. Chinese death estimates attributable to Mao include 250,000–500,000 deaths during the First civil war (1927–1936), 1,250,000 during the Second civil war (1945–1949), 500,000–1,000,000 during the land reform campaign, 5–13 million by political liquidation, 1–3 million in the Drive for Communes (1958–1960), 500,000–1,000,000 in Mao's campaigns against minorities, 250,000–500,000 in the Cultural Revolution (1965–1969), and 15–25 million in labor camps. All told, somewhere between 38,250,000 and 61,250,000 Chinese were victims of the terrorism perpetrated by Mao Tse-tung. Rummel (1990) provided a figure of 45 million. These figures do not include those Chinese killed in the Sino-Japanese War (1937–1945), nor the 500,000–1,234,000 Chinese killed in the Korean War (1950–1953).

WORLD WAR II AND TERRORISM

Adolph Hitler and Nazi Germany

In March 1933, the National Socialist German Worker's Party (NSDAP—Nationalsozialist Deutsche Arbeiterpartei), or Nazi Party came to power in Germany. Led by an avowed Aryan supremacist, Adolph Hitler was to lead the world into the greatest terrorist conflagration in all of history. Using subterfuge, strong-arm tactics, and the paranoia of the German people, Hitler successfully replaced the Weimar Constitution with the murderous Third Reich (Stanley, 1989). By August 1934, Hitler had consolidated the power of the President and Chancellor, naming himself Fuehrer of Germany. From the day he consolidated government power, Hitler attempted to use terrorism to purify Germany.

One of his first acts was to pass the Enabling Act (Law to Remove the Distress of People and State), a law taking legislative power from the

Reichstag, banned all political parties except the NSDAP, disbanded trade unions, and placed Nazi governors in control of all German states. By fall 1934, Hitler had opened the first concentration camp at Dachau. That same year, Hitler established the Nuremburg Laws (Ghetto Laws), depriving all persons of "non-German blood" citizenship rights. Jews were excluded from professional positions, banned from schools, courts, and hospitals, and their property taken by the state. In 1935, Hitler declared the Treaty of Versailles illegal, stated that Germany would follow its own destiny, and increased the size of the military to 36 divisions and over one-half million men (Snyder, 1989). In November 1937, he convened the Hossbach Conference, where he announced his plans to annex Europe to provide space for Germany. In 1938, he annexed Austria and Czechoslovakia. On 1 September 1939, Hitler invaded Poland and began WWII.

At the heart of Hitler's politics and military campaign was the concept of racial purity. Nazi's believed that through the course of history, Aryan blood had become mixed with that of other races and Germans were a "culture-stained race." To return Germany to purity, two courses of action were embarked upon. One, it was necessary to reintroduce Germans of racial purity into the population by a program of selective breeding. Two, it was necessary to rid Germany and Europe of all non-Aryan races. For the breeding program, "perfect" peasant women were paired with members of Heinrich Himmler's SS corps and Josef Sep Dietrich's Waffen SS (as per the Procreation Order of 1941) at Lebensborn (special farms for breeding and caring for the offspring; Gilbert, 1989).

"Impaired" Aryans had to be removed from society and was to be accomplished by a five-stage euthanasia program (Lifton, 1986). One, coercive sterilization was mandated for the "hereditarily sick": mentally deficient, schizophrenics, manic-depressives, insane, epileptic, Huntington's chorea, hereditary blindness and deafness, malformed, and the alcoholic. The program was later expanded to include other physical and mental conditions, including congenital defects, clubfoot, harelip, cleft palate, and "carriers" (relatives including brothers and sisters, parents, cousins, and other relatives). Two and three, "impaired" children and adults were to be euthanized in special hospitals. Over 20 institutions were built and used for euthenasia programs. Four, "impaired" inmates in prisons and camps were to be euthanized. Finally, all camp inmates were to be killed, especially Jews. Hitler's advancing armies were also to kill all non-Aryans in their march across the world (Gilbert, 1989).

Four units of the Nazi party were responsible for helping purify Germany. The Storm Detachment (Sturmabteilung—SA) was responsible for the preservation of internal order and policing. The SA was tasked with identifying opponents of the NSDAP, arresting those individuals, and identifying people for arrest by other NSDAP units.

The Security Service (Sicherheitsdienst—SD) was the intelligence arm of the Nazi Party. Led by Reinhard Heidrich, the SD had the power to arrest, prosecute, send to concentration camps, or execute any person believed working in interests opposed to the state. In occupied territories, the SD was responsible for weeding out partisan groups, resistance movements, political dissidents, and other undesirables. SD functionaries operated some of the concentration camps in Poland and other territories.

The Elite Guard (Schutzstaffel—SS), led by Heinrich Himmler, was the largest unit responsible for state security. The SS was symbolized by the double lighting bolt insignia. The SS operated the concentration and extermination camps in Europe (Discovery, 1994). A military branch of the SS, the Waffen SS (Josef Sep Dietrich) often spearheaded German blitzkriegs. A third SS unit, the Death's Head Formation (SSTV, SS–Totenkopfverbande), commanded by Theodor Eicke, performed duties as camp guards, state police in occupied territories, and "cleaned up" civilian problems.

The Gestapo (Geheime Staatspolize—Secret State Police) was the most feared police force in history. It was a force designed to protect the politics, policies, and programs of the Third Reich. Led by Heinrich Muller, the Gestapo was completely independent and autonomous from any authority except Hitler's. It established its own laws, legal system, court system, and prisons. The Gestapo had free reign to conduct executions and imprison any person it wished.

The worst of Hitler's terror programs were conducted at the vast array of concentration and extermination camps established in Europe. From the opening of the first camps in 1933 to the end of the war in 1945, Hitler executed somewhere between 8–10 million people in these camps of death. Figure 2.1 shows the locations of the primary concentration and extermination camps operated by the Nazi Party in the 1930s and 1940s.

Each camp became identified with a particular atrocity. Auschwitz-Birkenau, opened in 1940 and commanded by SS Hauptsturmfueher Rudolf Franz Hoess, became the main camp for the Final Solution and primary site of medical experimentation. Bathhouses (badeanstalten) were constructed for mass executions and corpse cellars (leichenkeller) held the dead awaiting cremation. Over four million people were murdered at Auschwitz-Birkenau. Belzec was the first camp to test Zyklon-B as a mass gas agent. Bergen-Belsen became the site of mass cannibalism among inmates. Buchenwald inmates were systematically exterminated

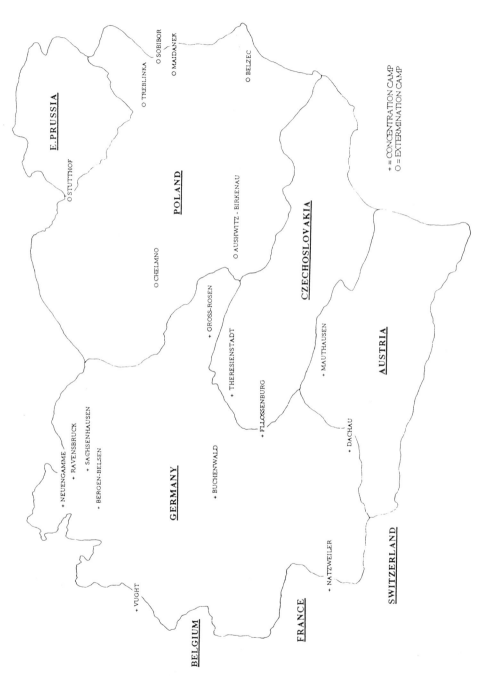

Figure 2.1. Locations and sites of Nazi concentration and extermination camps.

by starvation, torture, and overwork. Chelmno experimented with a bone-crushing machine (knockenmuhle). Dachau was host to a variety of medical experiments, including some conducted on American POWs. Maidanek counted over 1.5 million dead. Mauthausen was a labor camp for granite mining. Neuengamme was a site of medical experimentation. Ravensbruck housed female inmates for medical experimentation. Sobibor was an extermination camp. Theresienstadt was a transport stop for Auschwitz. Treblinka was one of the main extermination camps for Polish Jews.

At these and other camps throughout Nazi Europe, people met their deaths by the thousands per day. The Nazi killing machine continued uninterrupted, day in and day out, every day of the year. It was not until the Allied armies marched across Europe and into the camps that the full scope of Hitler's reign of terror became known. The loss of life was not staggering, it was beyond comprehension. Battle-hardened combat troops, upon seeing the conditions in the camps and amount of death wrought by the Nazi machine, broke down and wept.

Following the defeat of Germany, those responsible for the terrorism were made to stand accountable. At Nuremberg, between November 1945–October 1946, a military tribunal from the U.S., Britain, France, and the Soviet Union tried 22 leading members of the Nazi Party on four counts: conspiracy to commit crimes alleged in other counts, crimes against peace, war crimes, and crimes against humanity. All members of the SD, SS, and Gestapo were also found guilty. The American Military Tribunal Number 1 tried the doctors who worked at the camps. Charges included common design or conspiracy, war crimes, crimes against humanity, membership in criminal organizations, and individual crimes for medical experiments (Snyder, 1989). Between 1963–1965, the Frankfurt Trial was conducted in Germany where 21 SS officers from Auschwitz were brought to trial for murder, complicity in murder, and joint murder. Tables 2.1, 2.2, and 2.3 list the results of these trials.

Japan and the Pacific War

On the other side of the world, following a mass wave of extreme right-wing nationalism, Japan invaded China. On 13 December 1937, General Iwane Mastsui led the Japanese Kwantung Army into Nanking. Within a month, the Japanese military had brutally murdered over 250,000 Chinese (Costello, 1981). By 1941, over two million Chinese had been killed. By December 1941, the Japanese had decided to place all of Asia under its control. On 7 December 1941, in an attempt to paralyze America and prevent the U.S. from entering the war, Japan attacked

Table 2.1.
**Accused, verdict, and punishment of defendants at
the Nuremberg Trial following World War II.**

Accused	Verdict by Count	Punishment
Bormann, Martin	3, 4	Death
Doenitz, Karl	2, 3	Ten years
Frank, Hans	3, 4	Death
Frick, Wilhelm	2, 3, 4	Death
Fritzsche, Hans	Not guilty	Acquitted
Funk, Walther	2, 3, 4	Life
Goering, Hermann	1, 2, 3, 4	Death
Hess, Rudolph	1, 2	Life
Jodl, Alfred	1, 2, 3, 4	Death
Kaltenbrunner, Ernst	3, 4	Death
Keitel	1, 2, 3, 4	Death
von Neurath, Constantin	1, 2, 3, 4	15 years
von Papen, Franz	Not guilty	Acquitted
Raeder, Erich	2, 3, 4	Life
von Ribbentrop, Joachim	1, 2, 3, 4	Death
Rosenberg, Alfred	1, 2, 3, 4	Death
Sauckel, Fritz	2, 4	Death
Schacht, Hjalmar	Not guilty	Acquitted
von Schirach, Baldur	4	20 years
Seyss-Inquart, Artur	2, 3, 4	Death
Speer, Albert	3, 4	20 years
Streicher, Julius	4	Death

FROM: Snyder, L.L. (1989). *Encyclopedia of the Third Reich*. New York: Paragon Press.

Hawaii (Rostow, 1991). Using midget submarines and aircraft from carriers, Japan attempted to produce enough fear into the American public that America would refuse to intervene with Japan's Pacific intentions. The attackers struck Wheeler Field, Kaneohe Naval Air Station, Bellows Field, Ewa Field, Ford Island, Hickam Field, John Rodgers Field, and Pearl Harbor. In just over two hours time, the American Pacific fleet lay a shattered wreck (see Burlingame, 1992; DiVirgilio, 1991; Martinez, 1991; Prange, Goldstein, & Dillon, 1981 and 1988). Table 2.4 lists the U.S. Pacific Fleet damage from this attack. Almost simultaneously, the Japanese struck the American outposts in the Philippines, Guam, and Wake Island, the British at Singpore, Shanghai, and French and Dutch interests throughout the South Pacific.

Japan's intent to produce overwhelming fear in the American public failed. Instead, their audacity and verve produced anger and a unity unmatched in American history. Unlike in Europe, where the U.S. was fighting the Nazis, the Pacific became a race war. The Japanese were

Table 2.2.
**Accused, role in the Nazi Party, and sentence given to
leading medical doctors of the Third Reich.**

Name	Professional Role	Verdict
Becker, Freysing, Hermann	MD, aviation medicine	20 years
Beigelbock, Wilhelm	MD, professor, University of Vienna Clinic	15 years
Blome, Kurt	Professor, Deputy Reich Health leader and Deputy Chief, Reich Chamber of Medicine	Acquitted
Brack, Victor	Chief administrative officer, Reich Chancellery	Death
Brandt, Karl	MD, Hitler's physician, Health & Sanitation Comm.	Death
Brandt, Rudolf	LLD, chief of Ministerial Office, Ministry of Interior	Death
Fischer, Fritz	MD, assistant surgeon Hohenlychen	Life
Gebhardt, Karl	MD, Himmler's physician, chief surgeon to Reich Physician of SS	Death
Genzken, Karl	MD, chief of Medical Service for Waffen SS	Life
Handloser, Siegried	MD, chief of medical services of armed forces	Life
Hoven, Waldemar	MD, camp physician at Buchenwald	Death
Mrugowsky, Joachim	MD, chief of Institute of Hygiene, Waffen SS	Death
Oberheuser, Herta	MD, assistant surgeon Hohenlychen	20 years
Pokorny, Adolf	Urologist and dermatologist	Acquitted
Poppendick, Helmut	MD, chief surgeon for Office of Race and Resettlement	10 years
Romberg, Hans Wolfgang	MD, German Experimental Institute for Aviation	Acquitted
Rose, Gerhart	MD, chief of Division for Tropical Medicine at Koch Institute	Life
Rostock, Paul	MD, chief of Berlin University Clinic, chief of medical science and research	Acquitted
Ruff, Siegfried	MD, chief of Institute of Aviation Medicine	Acquitted
Schafer, Konrad	MD, chemotherapy labs at Schering Corporation	Acquitted
Schroder, Oskar	MD, chief of Air Force Medical Service	Life
Sievers, Wolfram	Chief of Institute for Military Scientific Research	Death
Welz, Georg August	MD, chief of Institute of Aviation Medicine	Acquitted

FROM: Snyder, L.L. (1989). *Encyclopedia of the Third Reich.* New York: Paragon Press.

depicted in a variety of negative caricatures: bucktoothed and nearsighted, descendants of monkeys, short in stature and unskilled, lacking intelligence and technical ability, and afraid to fight face-to-face. The Japanese likewise promoted their own racist images of America. The U.S. was the "Great Satan," and Anglos had horns, tails, and the trident of Satan. Children were hatched from eggs. Americans were lazy, promiscuous, gangsters, violent, and immoral. The American soldier would brutalize and rape civilians and cannibalize the dead.

From the earliest days, these images dictated the intensity of the war. On Tarawa, the U.S. lost 1,300 men. Of a Japanese garrison of over 4,500 men, only 17 surrendered (Sherrod, 1993). On Saipan, 3,500 U.S. troops

Table 2.3.
Outcome of the Frankfurt Trial listing names, Auschwitz duty, major charges, and verdict.

Name	Duty	Major Charges	Verdict
Baretzski, Stefan	Blockleader	5 murders, 11 joint murders	Life + 5 years
Bednarek, Emil	Prisoner	14 murders	Life
Boger, Wilhelm	Camp Gestapo	144 murders, 10 joint murders	Life + 5 years
Breitwieser, Johan	Disinfection Section	22 joint murders	Acquitted
Broad, Percy	Camp Gestapo	22 joint murders	4 years
Capesius, Dr. Victor	Head, camp pharmacy	Complicity 4 joint murders of 2,000 deaths each	9 years
Dylewski, Klaus	Guard unit	Complicity in joint murder on 32 occasions	5 years
Frank, Dr. Willi	Chief, dental station	Complicity in joint murder on 6 occasions	7 years
Hantl, Emil	Medical section	Complicity in joint murder on 40 occasions	3 years, 6 months
Hocker, Karl	Adjutant to commander	Complicity in joint murder on 3 occasions	7 years
Hofmann, Franz	Officer in charge	1 murder, 30 joint murders	Life
Kaduk, Oswald	Roll-call leader	10 murders, joint murder of 1,000	Life
Klehr, Joseph	Medical section	475 murders	Life + 15 years
Lucas, Dr. Franz	Camp medical officer	Complicity in 1,000 murders	3 years, 3 months
Mulka, Robert Karl	Adjutant to commander		14 years
Schatz, Dr. Willi	Dental station	Complicity in 700 murders	Acquitted
Scherpe, Herbert	Medical section	Complicity in joint murder on 8 occasions	4 years, 6 months
Schlage, Bruno	Prison bunker guard	Complicity in joint murder on 8 occasions	6 years
Schoberth, Johann			Acquitted
Stark, Hans	Camp Gestapo	Joint murder on 44 occasions	10 years

FROM: Snyder, L.L. (1989). *Encyclopedia of the Third Reich.* New York: Paragon Press.

died and 13,000 were wounded (Wheal, Pope, & Taylor, 1989). Over 22,000 Micronesians were killed by the Japanese, and over 30,000 Japanese died (Polmar & Allen, 1991). On Okinawa, over 107,000 Japanese and civilians were killed, 7,163 U.S. troops died, another 31,807 were wounded, and 9,731 Naval personnel were killed by Kamikaze attacks. There were over 25,000 U.S. casualties due to post-traumatic stress syndrome, or "battle fatigue" as it was then called (see Feifer, 1992; Leckie, 1995). All through the Pacific, the Japanese and Allies fought to the death, the civilians usually killed by retreating Japanese.

Some of the worst terrorist atrocities of the war were inflicted by the

Table 2.4.
U.S. Navy fleet losses at Pearl Harbor on 7 December 1941.

Ship	Class*	Disposition	Torpedoes	Damage Bombs 800 kg	Bombs 250 kg
Arizona**	BB	Sunk	2	2	
California	BB	Sunk, Salvaged	2		1
Maryland	BB	Damaged			2
Nevada	BB	Sunk, Salvaged	1	3	5
Oklahoma	BB	Sunk	12		
Pennsylvania	BB	Damaged			1
Tennessee	BB	Damaged	2	2	
Utah**	BB	Sunk	2		
West Virginia	BB	Sunk, Salvaged	9	2	
Cassin	DD	Sunk, Salvaged			1
Downes	DD	Sunk, Salvaged			1
Monaghan***	DD	Damaged			
Shaw	DD	Damaged			1
Oglala	Minelayer	Sunk, Salvaged	1		
Helena	Cruiser	Damaged	1		
Honolulu	Cruiser	Damaged			1
Raleigh	Cruiser	Damaged	1		
Curtis***	Seaplane Tender	Damaged			
Vestal	Repair Ship	Damaged			2

*BB = Battleship
DD = Destroyer
**Never raised
***Monaghan and Curtiss hit a Japanese midget submarine and sustained damage

Japanese upon POWs. Over 40% of U.S. POWs of the Japanese died at the hands of their captors, as compared to less than 1% of POWs held by the Nazis (Bird, 1992). Of all Japanese POWs (British, Australian, French, Dutch, and Asian), between five and eight million POWs were killed. POWs were held throughout the Pacific. Some of the most notorious sites were the camps in Burma and Thailand along the infamous Death Railway, where it is estimated that one Allied POW died for every railroad tie laid along the 250-kilometer railroad (Daws, 1995; Mullins, 1994). One camp along the route was designated specifically as a "camp for the dead" (LaForte & Marcello, 1993; LaForte, Marcello, & Himmel, 1994). Lifespans were measured in days. At all camps, POWs were killed by malnutrition, disease, abuse, mistreatment, brutality, and for sport. Psychological torture was as common as physical (Mullins, 1995).

The severity of POW treatment can be expressed by one simple fact. No POW of the Japanese experienced the Stockholm syndrome, the case where a captive and captor develop positive feelings and affect toward one another. POWs of the Germans, and later the Koreans and Vietnamese, report the development and use of the Stockholm syndrome. This phenomenon is completely missing from POWs of the Japanese.

The Japanese also killed tens of thousands of people by using them as subjects in biological and chemical warfare experiments. Under the specialized biological and chemical Unit 731, Unit 100, and Unit 1644, Chinese, Asians, and Allied POWs were killed in experiments to test pathogens and gases (Harris, 1994). Not only were prisoners of these units subject to various pathogens and gases, most of these same substances were tested by free release among cities and towns in China. Water in Harbin was contaminated with typhoid bacilli; cholera was released in Changchun, Manchukuon; cholera and typhoid were released in Ning Bo; plague fleas were released over Chang Teh, Hunan and Non Gan, Jilin; and typhoid and paratyphoid were released in Nanking. Children were given anthrax-infected chocolate, dumplings, and sweet cakes. In 1942 alone, field tests killed over 100,000 people. Over two million Chinese were killed in these experiments. Even after the war, the deaths continued. Ping Fan experienced rampant plague epidemics between 1946–1948, 30,000 died from the plague in 1947, and 6,000 died in 1948. Over two million chemical weapons, containing over 120 tons of CB material, were buried in the Chinese and Manchurian countryside by the retreating Japanese. These weapons and epidemics are still being discovered and experienced by the Chinese.

The U.S. engaged in terrorism during the Pacific War. Two notable examples are the B-29 firebomb raids and atomic bombings of Japan. B-29s flying from the Marianas Islands of Guam, Tinian, and Saipan conducted a series of incendiary firebomb raids over the Japanese homeland in the spring of 1945. On 10 March, 279 B-29s released 1,665 tons of incendiaries over Tokyo. The resulting firestorms killed over 83,000, destroyed 55 square miles, and burned 250,000 buildings. One million were homeless and 60% of Tokyo's commercial district was destroyed (Costello, 1981; Polmar & Allen, 1991). On 10 March, 300 B-29s flew over Nagoya, burning over three square miles. Other raids were flown against Osaka, Kobe, Nagoya, and other major cities. In all, over 10,000 tons of incendiaries were dropped and over 200,000 killed.

On 6 August 1945, the first atomic bomb ever used was dropped on Hiroshima. Within one year 140,000 civilians in that city had died as a result of the bomb, named Little Boy. Three days later, the Fat Man bomb was dropped on Nagasaki, killing 70,000. For both bombs, civilian targets had been purposely selected, the hope being the Japanese would become fearful enough to force the government to end the war.

The firebombings over Japan and use of nuclear weapons raise several issues concerning the use of terrorism as a government tool. It should be clearly stated that the author agrees with the decisions made by the political and military leaders of 1945 in the use of these weapons. Based on the information available to them at the time, these individuals made a difficult decision to hasten the end of a terrible war and save millions of lives. Nevertheless, several questions must be posed concerning the use of terrorism as a legitimate political tool (Woodruff, 1991, in the context of the American mission to shootdown Admiral Yamamoto).

One, was the activity directed against any specific person(s)? Two, was the motive punishment or revenge? Three, was the use of the weapons personal punishment or revenge? Four, was the use of these weapons a legitimate act of war? Five, was the use of these weapons a deliberate use of terror tactics? Six, was the use of these weapons forward-looking and designed to weaken the enemy? Seven, were less drastic measures available? A corollary is: would less drastic measures have worked? Eight, were non-terrorist tactics available and would they have been less costly? Finally, was the use of terrorism the most viable alternative? Each situation requires an examination of the total of these questions. In regards to the U.S. use of terrorism against Japan in 1945, all answers lead to one conclusion: terrorism was justifiable.

A planned Allied invasion of Japan was expected to cost over two million lives (Polmar, 1995). Japan had no intention of surrendering, even though some have suggested the marine blockade and Soviet entry into the war would have led to Japan's surrender (Bird, 1995; Bernstein, 1995). The data suggest either of these would have led to Japan's surrender (see Allen, 1995). Edwin Teller (1995), one of the designers of the atomic bomb, suggested the U.S. could have exploded a nuclear device at high altitude to demonstrate the power of the bomb and this may have forced the Japanese to surrender. The evidence indicates otherwise. It took two atomic bombs before Japan would surrender, and even then, the emperor averted a last-minute military coup to prevent the surrender.

In all, WWII cost 30–50 million deaths and introduced forms of terrorism that continue to be used today. The terrorism practiced by Hitler and Japan continue to provide the model for terrorists in the 1990s. The far right in the U.S., for example, sees Hitler as the savior of the Aryan race. The extreme nationalism of 1930s and 1940s Japan provide the model for the militia movement of the 1990s.

TERRORISM IN THE UNITED STATES

Terrorism in the United States is older than the nation. Throughout our history, the United States has experienced acts of international, transnational, domestic, and state terrorism. Since the first settlers arrived from Europe, there has not been a year when the peoples of America have not been exposed to or victimized by acts of terrorism. United States citizens have been subjected to more forms of terrorism than anywhere else in the world. The remainder of this chapter will provide an overview of some of the significant terrorist activities in the history of the United States.

Pre- and 1700s

As early as the 1600s, America experienced terrorism. The earliest recorded incident of terrorism in the New World occurred in 1622 when the settlers of Jamestown were massacred by Indians. This opened a long series of terrorist activities between settlers from the old world and native Americans that continues even today.

The Indian nations committed acts of terrorism against the intruders in an attempt to keep from losing their freedom, territory, and tribal traditions. The armies of the British and French, the two largest populations of colonists, waged campaigns of terrorism against the Indians in order to acquire territory for the increasing European population and to bring the Indians under colonial control. Both sides committed terrorist atrocities and the other side would retaliate in kind. Homes of settlers would be burned and families massacred, and in retaliation, tribal encampments raided, warriors beheaded, women raped and brutalized, and children tortured and killed. Some of the more notable atrocities were the Pontiac Conspiracy against the British, Little Turtle's War, the Blackhawk War, the Seminole War, and the revolt against colonial rule by the Creeks and Cherokees (George & Wilcox, 1992). One aspect of the terrorist activities committed by the settlers was the deliberate and first use in America of biological terrorism. Blankets infested with smallpox were distributed to the Indians to introduce the deadly disease into the Indian populations, who had no natural immunity (Harvey, 1991).

In the 1760s, the first United States' vigilantes appeared in the Carolinas. The government did not have the manpower or resources to protect the citizens from roving bands of bandits, so rural citizens took the law into their own hands. These citizens called themselves Regulators and upheld the law as it suited their needs or own personal interests. In 1769, sheriff's offices and district courts were introduced and this greatly reduced the number of vigilantes. By the 1780s, however, vigilante organizations began to reappear, this time to oppose the English Crown and Tory rule. Between 1800–1900, over 300 vigilante organizations operated in the United States, and from these vigilantes came the American tradition dictating that communities have the right to act in collective self-defense when threatened by outside sources (Brown, 1975).

Prior to the Revolutionary War, the English loyalists were subjected to campaigns of terrorism by American patriots. The homes of loyalists were burned, their crops destroyed, livestock killed, and families massacred. Many loyalists were tortured and systematically mutilated. Most loyalists, fearing for their lives, fled to Canada, which provided a safe haven.

The Revolutionary War was in large part brought about by terrorists. As stated by George and Wilcox (1992), "If one were to describe the American Revolution as a seditious conspiracy fomented by a band of extremists, misfits, malcontents, and troublemakers dedicated to the overthrow of recognized authority, one might well be right on the mark." The leaders of the revolution were traitors to the Crown, subversives, seditious propagandists, and radical pamphleteers. One group, called the Sons of Liberty, initially began as an anti-taxation organization, staged protests, and organized demonstrations against British rulers (Gelb, 1984). At one of these protests in Boston in 1770, the British fired into the crowd, killing five Americans. This action led to the Boston Tea Party, an act of protest where members of the Sons of Liberty stormed British merchant ships, throwing goods and supplies into the harbor. The Boston port was closed and British soldiers were sent to Boston to arrest the conspirators and regain control of the demonstrations (Dawson, 1969; Griswold, 1972; Zobel, 1970). King George III and the British Parliament at the same time implemented other repressive measures that ultimately led to war.

During the Revolutionary War, Americans used tactics of terrorists and guerrilla warfare to defeat the British. In the early days of the war, the Minutemen were formed as a military force to defeat the British. Not only did the Minutemen declare open warfare on the British, they also engaged in acts of intimidation, torture, tarring and feathering soldiers and loyalists alike, and beatings and murder. Additionally, according to Gelb (1984), freebooter organizations formed. These organizations claimed themselves to be patriots, but only used that justification to wander the countryside pillaging homes, destroying property, and engaging in wanton and indiscriminate killings.

Following the Revolutionary War, a long series of Indian wars began, lasting over a century until they finally culminated at Wounded Knee,

South Dakota, in 1890 (Brown, 1972). Terrorism against the Indians was sanctioned by the government in order to allow westward expansion of the growing European population in the newly formed United States. Random attacks, rape, torture, murder, and genocide were routinely practiced against the Indian nations. One example is the Trail of Tears of the Cherokee, an act where the United States forced the Cherokee to leave their homeland in the southern U.S. and relocate in Florida. During the march south and internment in the southern swamps, over 25% of the Cherokee Nation was killed or died from disease and starvation (Wald, 1985). Biological terrorism was routinely used against Indian tribes. The Sioux, Pawnee, Cheyenne, Arapahoe, Mandan, Cree, Blackfoot, and Assiniboin were infected with smallpox. Connell (1984) estimates that before 1843, over 100,000 Indians east of and in Missouri were killed by smallpox.

In 1789, the Barbary pirates began attacking American merchant shipping in the Mediterranean, stealing the cargoes, assigning the ships to Barbary pirates and imprisoning and enslaving the crews. The leaders of Algiers (called deys), Morocco (emperors), Tripoli (bashaws), and Tunis (beys) demanded ransom payments for the release of the crews and regular payment to themselves to assure future safe passage of American ships in the Mediterranean (Beach, 1986). In one instance, the *George Washington* delivered the tribute to the dey of Algiers and was then forced to carry the annual payment from Algiers to the sultan of Turkey under the Algerian flag. Upon returning to Washington D.C., the naval commander of the *George Washington,* William Bainbridge, forcefully wrote, "The next time I am directed to deliver tribute, I hope it will be through the mouths of cannon!" (Beach, 1986). At one point, the United States was paying over $1 million annual in tribute. The Barbary states had established set ransoms for American crewmen. Passengers cost $4,000, regular sailors $1,500, mates $4,000, and masters and officers $6,000 (Simon, 1994).

In May 1801, President Jefferson declared the American strategy in the Mediterranean would be to blockade ports, followed by seizure or destruction of privateers and enemy ships. In the summer of 1801, U.S. warships blockaded the port of Tripoli and in 1802, the U.S. declared war on Tripoli. In 1803, the *USS Philadelphia* ran around at Tripoli and was surrendered with all crew. On the night of 16–17 February 1804, Stephen Decatur, Jr., commanding the 12-gun *Enterprise,* snuck into the harbor and sank the *Philadelphia.* Throughout 1804, naval gunships ventured intermittently into Tripoli and captured pirate gunboats and raiders.

Because of impending war with Britain (War of 1812), Jefferson removed American warships from the Mediterranean in 1807. In 1812, the dey of

Algiers declared war on the United States and in February 1815, President Madison sent two squadrons of naval warships to the Mediterranean. In June, three frigates captured the Algerian *Mashuda*, taking the ship and over 400 crewmen prisoner. Later that summer, Commander William Bainbridge, aboard the 74-gun *Independence*, entered the Mediterranean. Faced by a hostile and overwhelming U.S. Navy, the dey signed a peace treaty on 20 June 1815, thus ending the Barbary terrorism against U.S. merchantmen (Hagan, 1991). The terrorism of the Barbary pirates involved the first United States incidents of arms for hostages.

1800–1900

In addition to terrorism against the Indians and Hispanics as the U.S. expanded west, the early half of the nineteenth century was characterized by numerous assassinations and mob actions. Many of these activities were religious and nationalist terrorism. In 1834, in Boston, a Protestant mob burned the Ursuline Catholic Convent in a wave of anti-Catholic fervor. In 1837, in Alton, Illinois, the noted writer Alton P. Lovejoy was killed by a political mob after a speech of inflammatory oratory. In 1844, a Protestant religious mob killed the Mormon leaders Joseph and Hiram Smith in Carthage, Illinois. In 1853 and 1854, many eastern cities were subjected to anti-Catholic and anti-Irish riots. Hundreds of Catholics and Irish were beaten, stoned, and killed in waves of Protestant righteousness.

On 14 April 1865, John Wilkes Booth assassinated President Abraham Lincoln. Booth killed Lincoln as a form of political and social protest, believing his death would result in the American people revolting against the current government.

In 1867, in Pulaski, Tennessee, Civil War General Nathaniel Bedford Forrest formed the Ku Klux Klan and was elected its first Grand Dragon at a Klan convention held in Nashville (Cook, 1980; Holden, 1985). The Klan was a terrorist organization who targeted blacks, sympathetic whites, and carpetbaggers. Victims were beaten to death, flogged, hung, and burned at the stake (Vetter & Perlstein, 1991). Between 1867 and 1871, the Ku Klux Klan had active chapters in Georgia, North Carolina, and Tennessee and grew to about 500,000 members (Fogelson & Rubenstein, 1969). In 1871, the Ku Klux Klan Act was passed in South Carolina, which suspended the writ of habeas corpus, and under the law, over 1,000 Klansmen were arrested and imprisoned (George & Wilcox, 1992). In 1872, the Klan was disbanded, only to officially reappear in 1915.

During the same time period (approximately 1860–1880), terrorism against the Indians and Hispanics greatly increased as the United States pushed toward the West Coast. America experienced the Range Wars, terrorist atrocities between cattlemen and sheep ranchers, each attempting to secure land and water for their animal herds. Each side destroyed herds, burned grazing land, poisoned water supplies, destroyed buildings, and hung, brutalized, and otherwise murdered ranchers. On the West Coast, the white settlers were engaged in the Coolies Must Go Campaign against the Chinese workers brought to the U.S. to work on railroad expansion.

Between 1860 and 1870, the Molly Maguires, Irish coal miners in Pennsylvania, were conducting terrorist campaigns against police, mine bosses, and company supervisors. The Molly Maguires were based upon the ancient Irish fraternity of the Ancient Order of Hibernians and worked for the Philadelphia Reading Coal and Iron Company, a subsidiary of the Philadelphia and Reading Railroad. In 1973, the company hired Pinkerton Detectives to infiltrate the Molly Maguires and gather evidence on their terrorist activities. At the end of the investigation, and between 1877–1879, 19 members of the Molly Maguires were arrested, convicted, and hung.

In 1874, New York experienced the Tomkins Square riot. The East Coast was in a deep recession and unemployment was rampant. In a riot begun by the homeless and unemployed, hundreds of rioters and police were killed in a violent clash. In 1877, largely as a result of the recession, railroad workers formed an anarchist society, the Railroadmen. They embarked upon a short-lived campaign of terrorism designed to improve working conditions and better pay. Thousands of dollars worth of property was destroyed and several dozen lives lost.

Between 1867–1877, 32 public officials were targets of assassination attempts. Political officials that were subject of these attacks included a U.S. senator, two congressional representatives, three state governors, ten state legislative representatives, 16 judges, and other office holders. Twenty-three of these attacks were fatal (Ford, 1985).

In 1882, the socialist movement in this country became formalized when Johannes Most, Albert R. Parsons, and August Spies formed the International Working People's Association in Chicago (Parry, 1976). In the late 1970s, Johannes Most had become an anarchist and had published *Revolutionary (Urban) Warfare: A Handbook of Instruction Regarding the Use and Manufacture of Nitroglycerine, Dynamite, Guncotton, Fulminating Mercury, Bombs, Arson, Poisons, etc.* Often considered the father of the letter bomb, Most believed that killing "pigs" was morally okay because murder only applied to humans and the police were not human (Vetter & Perlstein, 1991).

Most of the ideas of Most, Parsons, and Spies were formulated by the

International Congress of Anarchists, who met in London in July 1881 and put forth a manifesto which argued that revolution against the government could only be achieved through illegal means (Fleming, 1982; Ivianski, 1985). For their party manifesto, Serge Nachaeyev wrote the Revolutionary Catechism, which said in part: "The revolutionary is a dedicated man. He has no personal inclinations, no business affairs, no emotions, no attachments, no property, and no name. Everything in him is subordinated towards a single exclusive attachment, a single thought, and a single passion—the revolution.... The object is the same: the prompt destruction of this filthy order" (from Vetter & Perlstein, 1991).

In Chicago, on 3 May 1886, the International Working People's Association held a demonstration to assist the striking workers of the McCormick Harvester plant (Symes & Clemet, 1972). Only several hundred protesters showed up, and in an attempt to disperse the crowd, the police fired into the mob, killing two persons. August Spies called for another protest rally the next day. Approximately 500 protesters showed up at Haymarket Square. Police strikebreakers were dispatched to break up the mob. Some unknown individual threw a bomb into the 180-man police contingent, killing and wounding several. The police confronted the angry mob and a brief gunbattle ensued. When the shooting ended, seven police lay dead and over 60 had been wounded. Several members of the crowd were killed and dozens injured.

In the aftermath of the Haymarket Square riots, Albert Parsons, August Spies, and two other leaders of the demonstration were hung. One committed suicide before sentencing and three were given life sentences. Johannes Most was not at the Haymarket Square riot, being in prison already for inciting violence. He eventually was deported back to his native Germany. The Chicago riots ended the International Working People's Association.

In the 1890s, eleven Italians were hung in New Orleans in a wave of anti-Irish hatred. In 1894, the militia and federal troops were called upon to quell the Pullman strike. In Wilmington, North Carolina, in 1898, mobs of whites killed dozens of blacks to protest blacks who had been given political positions (Hofstadter & Wallace, 1971).

1900 to Present

Terrorism in the new century began almost immediately. In Buffalo, New York, on 6 September 1901, President McKinley was assassinated by Leon Czolgosz, a socialist and anarchist committed to political revolution. McKinley was at the Pan American Exposition to dedicate the exhibit and was greeting the crowd when Czolgosz approached with a pistol wrapped in a handkerchief. After shooting McKinley, Czolgosz proclaimed the president was "an enemy of the good working people" (Vetter & Perlstein, 1991).

Because of activities such as the Railroadmen's strikes, the Haymarket Square riots, and the assassination of President McKinley, in 1903 Congress passed federal law to ban foreign anarchists from the United States and to deport any foreign nationals suspected of being anarchists. This law remained in the federal books until 1952. During the law's tenure, thousands of innocent people were denied immigration rights or visitation rights, hundreds were deported, and dozens of convicted criminals executed because of their suspected anarchist political beliefs. The most famous of these were Nicola Sacco and Bartolomeo Vanzetti, who were executed on 23 August 1927, for killing a store clerk. Popular opinion of the day, and most historians tend to concur, was that Sacco and Vanzetti received the death penalty because of their anarchist political ideology and not because of killing the clerk (Jackson, 1981; Russell, 1986).

In Los Angeles on 1 October 1910, John and James McNamara of the International Association of Bridge and Structural Iron Workers Union, detonated a bomb in the *Los Angeles Times* building. That same day, two bombs were discovered at the home of Harrison Otis, owner of the *Times.* The bombs were planted because of Otis's anti-union editorials. John was arrested shortly after the Times building explosion and James the following April in Indiana. John was sentenced to 15 years in prison, while the younger James got life.

In Ludlow, Colorado, in 1913–1914, workers of the Colorado Fuel and Iron Company went on strike for better working conditions and higher pay (Poland, 1988). In the first five weeks of the strike, 18 people were killed in strike violence. The governor of Colorado called in the state militia to quell the demonstrations and riots. On 20 April 1914, strikers confronted the militia in a 15-hour gun, knife, and hand battle. The militia gained the upper hand and the miners retreated back into their tent city. The militia pursued, firing into the tents. Two women and 11 children were killed, causing the miners to go on a ten-day rampage that covered over 250 square miles. They destroyed property, fences, killed livestock herds, beat and murdered any who got in their way, and burned forests. Federal troops had to be called in to forcefully drive the miners back to the "Black Hole of Ludlow" (Papanikolas, 1982).

In Atlanta, Georgia, William J. Simmons founded the second Ku Klux Klan in 1915 (Randell, 1965). By 1920, the Klan claimed over 100,000 members. Simmons hired Edward Clarke and Elizabeth Tyler to operate promotions for the Klan. In the wake of a public sex scandal between Clarke (who was married) and Tyler, Simmons was forced to resign.

Hiram Wesley Evans, a dentist from Texas, assumed control of the Klan. As in the 1860s, the Klan targeted blacks, Catholics, Jews and foreign immigrants, claiming they were responsible for America's woes. The primary targets of the second Klan, however, were those individuals, regardless of race, nationality or religion, who were deemed "immoral" by the Klan. Their targets were people who did not abide by the morality of the Bible and who violated the norms of small-town and rural America. To spread their message of hate, the Klan published *The Firey Cross, The Courier* and *The Imperial Hawk.* In 1925, Klan headquarters was moved from Atlanta to Washington D.C., David C. Stephenson was named Grand Dragon, and Klan membership numbered between four–five million. In 1926, Stephenson was charged with the murder and rape of Madge Oberholtzer and the downfall of the second Klan had begun. By 1928, Klan membership numbered only several hundred in the deep south of Alabama and Georgia. By 1944, the Klan had been disbanded.

In April 1919, 37 mail bombs were sent to various senators, congressmen, and industry leaders. Through sheer luck, only two people were injured. Although no organization claimed responsibility, federal investigators believed members of the Communist Party of America were responsible for the letter bombs. Two acid letters were sent to Senators Hardwick (Georgia) and Averman (North Carolina), both avowed anti-communists. Neither were injured.

In 1920, 34 people were killed and over 200 injured in New York City when a bomb destroyed the J.P. Morgan Bank building. The U.S. Attorney General blamed the Communist Party of America for the attack (Mickolus, 1980). As a result of the letter bomb campaign and bombing of the J.P. Morgan Bank, the great Red Scare began. The paranoia against communists was almost as fevered as in the McCarthyism of the 1950s. Federal and state agents rounded up thousands of suspected communists, radicals, and leftists and had them imprisoned or deported.

In 1933, the first of two attempts were made on the life of Franklin D. Roosevelt. In Miami, Florida, Guiseppe Zangare attempted to assassinate FDR. The assassin's bullet missed and instead killed Chicago Mayor Anton Cermak. The second attempt was a letter bomb mailed to Roosevelt. It was discovered and disarmed.

The 1930s also saw general increases in radical political ideology and philosophy. Communist, socialist, anarchist, and fascist organizations sprang up all across the United States in response to events in Europe and Asia. Nationalist and isolationist organizations also joined the radical mix. Other organizations rallied and protested to get America involved in the war. When America did enter the war at the end of 1941, both sides and most political dissidents coalesced and worked together to end the war. All in all, the 1940s (with the exception of war-related terrorist activity) was the most peaceful period in United States history as regards to terrorism.

When World War II ended, terrorism in the United States resumed. On 1 November 1950, Griselio Torresola and Oscar Collazo, Puerto Rican nationalists and terrorists, attempted to assassinate President Harry Truman at Blair House in Washington D.C. Their attack was a continuation of a terrorist attack on a police headquarters in Puerto Rico committed by Pedro Albiza Campos in 1936. Campos, leader of the National Party of Puerto Rico, was a separatist, wanting independence for Puerto Rico from U.S. intervention. After killing a police commander in the 1936 attack, Campos and seven other members of the terrorist organization were brought to the United States and convicted for plotting to overthrow the government of the United States. He served seven years and was returned to Puerto Rico.

Torresola and Collazo, carrying a support letter from Campos, were discovered by a security guard attempting to enter Blair House, where President Truman was meeting with senators and congressmen. When hailed by the guard to stop, the terrorists pulled weapons and a brief gunbattle ensued. Torresola and one security guard were killed and Collazo wounded. A federal court sentenced Collazo to death, but Truman commuted the sentence to life in prison.

On 1 March 1954, another Puerto Rican separatist terrorist attack shocked the nation's capital. Four Puerto Rican nationalists, waving a Puerto Rican flag and shouting "viva Puerto Rico" from the house gallery, fired numerous rounds from pistols onto the floor of the House of Representatives. Five congressmen were wounded in the attack. Their attack was timed to coincide with the opening of the Inter-American Conference in Caracas, Venezuela, and the purpose was to embarrass the United States in front of its southern neighbors in Latin America. The terrorists were caught at the time of the attack and authorities discovered evidence indicating other members of the organization were planning to assassinate President Eisenhower and other government officials.

On 28 June 1958, Raul Castro took 29 servicemen stationed at Guantanamo Bay, Cuba, hostage while they were riding on a military bus outside the camp. His intent was to bring attention to the revolutionary's plight and force world opinion to convince the United States to quit supplying arms and weapons to the Batista regime. The American public and many members of Congress wanted immediate military retaliation against the Cuban rebels, including New York Senator Victor Anfuso, who suggested to Alan Dulles, Secretary of State, that the U.S. give an ultimatum to the terrorists to release the hostages within 48 hours or suffer the consequences (Simon, 1994). President Eisenhower, however, set a precedent all future presidents would follow when he ordered negotiations to be opened with the terrorists. Before the situation became critical, Fidel Castro decided the hostages would hurt rather than help the Cuban revolution and had them released.

The 1950s also saw state terrorism in the form of Senator Joseph McCarthy's communist inquisition. Russia had risen to superpower status and had developed nuclear weapons. The American public was becoming paranoid about the "red menace," and backyard bomb shelters were appearing in neighborhoods all over the country. Himself rabidly anti-communist, McCarthy fed off this paranoia, searching out communists under every rock and tree. He was particularly ruthless with the art and entertainment industry, calling hundreds of members of that community in front of Congress to testify as to their Americanism. If the witnesses did not pass McCarthy's test, he branded them as communist. The art, film, and newly developing television community, fearing massive loss of profits, "blackballed" McCarthy's communists, some of whom did not work in the industry for a decade or more later. Federal, state, and local law enforcement officials relentlessly pursued suspected communists, arresting thousands under "trumped up" charges. The "blacklists" were officially maintained until 1960.

As the 1960s began, no one could have predicted the next two decades would be the most violent terroristic decades in the nation's history. The 1960s changed the face of U.S. terrorism. Beginning in the 1960s, with few exceptions, international, transnational, and domestic terrorism all became intent on only one goal: overthrowing the government of the United States (Laqueur, 1977). In 1960, little did anyone realize that national and international events were to lead to a continuing siege on the American political system and American citizens that still lasts today.

The 1960s actually began with the 1954 school desegregation riots in Little Rock, Arkansas, and the 1955 and 1956 Montgomery bus boycott by Martin Luther King, Jr. and other blacks wanting equal rights. By the early 1960s, blacks were still second-class citizens and were demanding equality. Blacks were subjected to rampant discrimination in businesses, housing, education, and the criminal justice system. Although the government had promised to end discrimination and was in the process of enacting laws to eliminate racial discrimination, in many parts of the country blacks were still required to use separate water fountains, black restrooms, and denied basic human rights.

By the mid-1960s, in spite of government regulation, laws, and intervention, little had changed for blacks. The 1963 march on Selma demonstrated to many blacks that peaceful demonstration would not produce change. Frustrated and angered by continued repression and unfulfilled promises, American cities erupted in waves of violence (National Advisory Commission on Civil Disorders, 1968). Blacks began the series of riots in the Watts ghetto, Los Angeles, in 1964. In 1966, there were 43 riots across the nation and 164 in 1967 (Vetter & Perlstein, 1991).

Meanwhile, the Vietnam War was building, the youth of America were rebelling against established authority and traditional values, and social controls were weakening (Silberman, 1980). As early as 1961, Vietnam was polarizing the country: left versus right, liberal versus conservative, democrat versus republican, young versus old, white versus black, South versus North, East versus West, rich versus poor, etc. Vietnam divided the country like no other event ever has, either before or since. All of the movements of the 1960s, including the black struggle for civil rights, were given an added urgency and added measure of violence by the Vietnam War.

Led by men such as Stokely Carmichael, Eldridge Cleaver, Huey P. Newton, H. Rap Brown, David Hilliard, George Jackson, and Bobby Seale, the Black Panther Party formed on the West Coast. The Black Panther Party had a political agenda for the rights of blacks based upon violence and revolution. The party's agenda included: (1) the release of all black political prisoners in the United States, which was directed at all black prisoners in the U.S.; (2) total military exemption for all black males and blacks taken out of the military draft; (3) federal and state government payments to all blacks for "past sins" against blacks; and (4) creation of a separate black nation on the West Coast. Their message was lost among their violence. The Black Panthers targeted police officers and white businesses for death and destruction. A favored Panther tactic was to ambush and murder police officers. Throughout the country, the Panthers bombed white businesses and military establishments during their short-lived existence.

In the Midwest, the Students for a Democratic Society (SDS) were organizing. The SDS was a leftist organization formed to change the government from democracy to socialism and to protest America's involvement in Vietnam. Led by college youth, the left movement was urban, middle-class, disciplined, trained, and used sophisticated tactics in their activities of violence (Strentz, 1988). Throughout the 1960s and early 1970s, the SDS demonstrated, protested, marched, destroyed property, burned ROTC and other university buildings, seized university administration offices, and attempted, in general, to interrupt government and societal functions.

One splinter faction of the SDS did not believe the organization was moving fast enough or violently enough to overthrow the government.

Leaders of this splinter movement were Bernardine Dohr, Mark Rudd, Jane Alpert, Kathy Boudin, Cathlyn Wilkerson, and Esther Persons. In the late 1960s, they split from the SDS and formed their own organization, the Weathermen, often referring to themselves as the "grandpersons of the American revolutionary organizations" (Trick, 1976). This name was soon changed to the Weather Underground because of the sexist connotation of the old name. One of the more violent terrorist organizations in the history of the United States, the Weather Underground first came to the attention of the American public for the "four days of rage" in Chicago at the Democratic National Convention in 1968. Members desecrated the statue dedicated to the police officers killed at the Haymarket Square riots, which touched off a four-day-long riot between police and protesters. Running rampant through the riots, members of the Weather Underground attempted to enter a military induction center, destroyed storefronts, and jumped bail.

The Weather Underground was responsible for numerous bombings on college campuses, including ROTC military units, biology labs, history departments, and English departments. In 1970, the organization bombed the New York City Police Department headquarters building, and shortly after, three members were killed in a brownstone in New York when a bomb under construction detonated. In 1971, the Weather Underground bombed the U.S. Capital and in 1975, the U.S. State Department building. In 1974, they published *Prairie Fire,* which said in part: "We believe that carrying out armed struggle will affect the people's consciousness of the nature of the struggle against the state.... Action teaches the lessons of fighting and demonstrates that armed struggle is possible" (Simon, 1994). The Weather Underground became so violent that even some members of the Black Panthers and SDS denounced them (Parry, 1976).

Another revolutionary party with its roots in the social protest movement of the 1960s was the Yippie Party, led by Abby Hoffman and Jerry Rubin. Preaching peace, the Yippie Party practiced violence and perfected "street theater," acts designed to draw media and public attention to their cause. The Yippie Party also played a predominant role in the 1968 Chicago Democratic National Convention riots and the "street theater" trial that followed. The trial of the Chicago 7 for civil disorder in Chicago during 1968 rapidly became an absurdity. The defendants shouted-down witnesses, would not respond to the judge's instructions, and goaded the media. At one point, Judge Hoffman ordered the defendants tied to their chairs and gagged.

In San Francisco in 1970, the New World Liberation Front published Carlos Marighella's *Minimanual of the Urban Guerrilla,* a monograph that rapidly became the "bible" of the far left. The *Minimanual,* in some detail, described how to bring about and conduct a revolution. The tactics discussed by Marighella quickly became the *modus operandi* of the far-left movement. The New World Liberation Front also served as an umbrella organization for other left-wing organizations, such as the Chicano Liberation Front and the Red Guerrilla Family.

On 27 October 1970, the United States experienced its first nuclear terroristic threat when the city of Orlando, Florida received a written demand for $1 million, media coverage, and passage out of the country for the perpetrators (Mullins, 1992). If these demands were not met, a nuclear device would be exploded within the city. Examination of the accompanying drawings led authorities to conclude the device was workable and there was a possibility of an actual nuclear bomb in the city. The investigation soon revealed that a 14-year-old boy was responsible for the threat.

In Vietnam, the United States government began a specific campaign of terrorism in the Vietnam War. Operation Phoenix was a CIA operation and, on paper, designed to arrest leading Viet Cong and North Vietnamese Army leaders and officers from the villages and hamlets in South Vietnam. Village elders and leaders were identified by the CIA as being enemy cadre members or sympathizers and gave orders to various U.S. special forces units to "eliminate this person with extreme prejudice." The selected military unit would then infiltrate the village and assassinate the suspect. Many other terrorist atrocities in Vietnam were committed by both sides, many more by North Vietnam than by U.S. forces (for example, members of the U.S. Army had committed the My Lai massacre, where approximately 200 civilians were lined up and shot in retaliation for assisting the North Vietnamese). Operation Phoenix was the first officially sanctioned and conducted campaign designed to specifically target civilians since the 1800s.

In September 1992, terrorism exploded onto the conscious of the world public with the Munich Olympic games massacre. Thirteen Arab Black September terrorists broke into the Israeli athlete living complex at Conolly Street #13, killed two Israeli participants and took 13 others hostage. They demanded the release of approximately 200 Arab prisoners in Israeli prisons and transportation to the airport (Schreiber, 1973). The Israeli government refused to release the prisoners and Egypt refused the terrorist's request to land on Egyptian soil. German authorities prepared a tactical plan that would end the hostage situation at the Munich airport. The terrorists and hostages were allowed to travel to the airport on helicopters. At the airport, as the terrorists and hostages were moving back and forth between their helicopter and the airplane, the police began the tactical assault. In a 15-minute firefight, ten hostage takers were killed, 11 Israelis died from a grenade terrorists threw into the helicopter holding the hostages, and one police officer was killed by gunfire (McMains & Mullins, 1995). Terrorism had reached international and epidemic proportions.

In San Francisco in October 1973, a religious cult calling themselves the Death Angels committed 14 "Zebra" murders of whites. The Death Angels were a splinter organization of the Nation of Islam and believed that whites were devils who should be eliminated. All of their victims were whites who had been randomly selected.

In 1973–1974, the Symbionese Liberation Army in Los Angeles gained national notoriety by kidnapping Patty Hearst, heiress to the Randolph Hearst newspaper fortune. The SLA received more recognition for their demise than for their actions. The Los Angeles Police Department cornered the SLA in a small house in Los Angeles, and rather than surrender, the SLA died in a shootout with the police when their house caught fire and burned around them. The only surviving members of the SLA were not in the house at the time.

In Washington D.C., on 9 March 1977, Hanafi Muslims, a sect of the American Black Muslim movement, took hostages in three locations in the city: B'nai B'rith national headquarters, the Islamic Center, and the Washington D.C. City Council officers. Hamaas Khaahlis, leader of the Hanafi's, was committing the act as revenge for the murder of a woman and child by a rival Muslim group. Although the perpetrator had been caught, Khaahlis believed he did not receive his punishment followed the dictates of the *Koran*. Additionally, Khaahlis wanted a theater movie depicting the Muslim faith removed from theaters, $750 reimbursed to him from the courts he had paid as a fine for contempt of court, and all Moslem countries notified he intended to kill Moslems to create an international incident (McMains & Mullins, 1995). One hostage was killed and several others beaten. After over 40 hours, Khaahlis released the hostages and surrendered after a district court judge agreed to allow Khaalis to remain free on bond until trial (American Justice, 1994; Miron & Goldstein, 1979).

On 4 November 1979, the nation was shocked when 63 U.S. citizens were taken hostage at the American embassy in Tehran, Iran. Initially, the hostage takers took the embassy hostage to protest the ex-Shah of Iran's asylum in the United States. Before the incident ended 444 days later, however, the action became a rallying point for the Islamic revolution. Islamic terrorists unified in their cause to bring about the downfall of the U.S. The incident was responsible for bringing an end to the Carter presidential administration and became such a media sensation, it spawned the nightly television show *Nightline,* originally called *Nightline: America Held Hostage.*

After various diplomatic efforts to free the hostages had failed, the Carter administration decided upon a military solution. The U.S. Army Delta force, a newly created special operations team, was tasked with the rescue. In late 1980, eight RH-53D helicopters departed from the aircraft carrier *USS Nimitz* in the Sea of Oman, headed for the Iranian desert, where they were to be joined by six C-130s and three EC-130s carrying fuel from Egypt. The forces were to rendezvous near Tabas, approximately 100 miles south of Tehran. The helicopters were to be refueled in the desert and the rescue team to fly to Tehran and wait for nightfall, when Delta would attack the embassy and a 13-man contingent free three hostages held in the foreign ministry building. All the hostages would be taken to an abandoned airfield near Tehran, where Air Force C-141s would be waiting to fly the hostages out of the country.

The rescue mission, code-named Eagle Claw, was plagued from the beginning. Only the minimum amount of equipment necessary was allocated to the mission and no backup equipment was available. The secrecy surrounding the mission was too great and even some of the peripheral military participants did not know the mission plan. In many respects, the mission was overly complex for its size and scope. When the rescue team landed at Desert One, the helicopters had been delayed for over an hour and one-half because of a desert sandstorm. A passing bus full of Iranian civilians was taken captive and a fuel truck using a nearby road was destroyed with a rocket. Two of the helicopters did not even make it to Desert One as a result of mechanical failures due to the weather (one had engine trouble and other had its fuel system clogged by the sandstorm). A third helicopter made the landing at Desert One but experienced partial hydraulic failure. With only five operational helicopters, it was decided to cancel the mission. As the rescue forces were leaving the scene, a helicopter hit one of the fuel-laden C-130s, exploding both and killing eight servicemen.

Following the aborted rescue attempt, diplomatic negotiations resumed and the United States finally secured the release of the hostages after agreeing to pay ransom and release Iranian assets frozen in the United States of $7.97 billion. In sum, the Iranian hostage incident had given unlimited power to a loose-knit group of militant terrorists and had brought the United States government to its knees, a lesson terrorists of the 1980s would not soon forget.

In the early 1980s, remnants of the Weather Underground and Black Panther Party formed the United Freedom Front (UFF; Harris, 1987). An extremely small organization totaling only seven members, the UFF embarked upon an almost decade-long campaign of terrorism against the United States. The UFF was a Marxist/Leninist organization intent on overthrowing the government of the United States, eliminating capitalist-inspired racism and oppression of the workers, and to create a reserve army from blue-collar labor (Berkman, 1979). The UFF believed the capitalist system was designed to purposely keep races opposing each other so they could not unify to overthrow the system, and it was the duty of the UFF to bring about the collapse of the system and unify the races (Irwin, 1980). Many scholars, however, believed the rhetoric of the UFF was simply a disguise to cover their true motivation, which was to cause death and destruction for personal gain (see, for example, Gurr, 1988).

In Verona, Italy, on 17 December 1981, the Red Brigades kidnapped U.S. Army General James Dozier from his residence. Dozier was an assistant commander of NATO forces in Europe, and his kidnapping was an attempt to get NATO disbanded and the American military removed from Europe. Before negotiations progressed, the Italian Nucleo Operativeo di Sicurezza (NOCS), a paramilitary rescue force, freed Dozier from his kidnappers. All five kidnappers were arrested with no injuries (Simon, 1994).

On 23 October 1983, 241 United States Marines were killed in Beirut when Islamic extremists drove a dynamite-laden truck containing over 1,200 pounds of TNT into their barracks. The same day, terrorists from the same organization killed 47 French MNF U.N. peacekeepers in a similar attack. The organization responsible has never been totally identified, but most authorities believe the attacks were conducted by terrorists sponsored by the Iranian government. It is believed Shiite Hezbollah terrorists were recruited in Baalbek, Iran, and trained at the Iranian embassy in Damascus. Again, the terrorists won, forcing the U.N. forces to withdraw from Beirut.

On 7 October 1985, the *Achille Lauro* cruise ship was taken by members of the Palestine Liberation Front off the coast of Egypt. The original plan devised by Abu Abbas, leader of the organization, was that the terrorists would strike the Israeli port of Ashdod. Instead, when discovered by a crewmember of the *Achille Lauro,* they hijacked the ship. Only 97 passengers and 344 crew members were aboard the ship at the time, the rest of the passenger complement being ashore on a tour of Egypt. The terrorist demands were that 50 Palestinians be released from Israeli prisons. The ship sailed to Tartus, Syria, but was denied entry into the port. After sailing to Port Said, Egypt, the terrorists surrendered after being guaranteed safe passage out of Egypt. On 10 October, Navy F-14s intercepted the civilian airliner carrying the terrorists and Abu Abbas and forced it to land at the United States-Italian NATO base in Sicily. The Italians commandeered the plane and arrested the terrorists, but allowed Abu Abbas to flee to Belgrade, Yugoslavia. The terrorists were convicted of hijacking and the murder of one American, wheelchair bound Leon Klinghoffer. Abu Abbas was sentenced to life imprisonment in absentia (Simon, 1994).

On 5 April 1986, the LaBelle discotheque in West Berlin was destroyed by a bomb. One U.S. soldier was killed and over 230 other customers injured. In retaliation for this act of Mideast-sponsored terrorism, on 14 April, President Reagan ordered 24 F-111 fighter-bombers, five EF-111 electronic jamming planes, 15 A-6 and A-7 Navy fighter-bombers and 28 KC-135 air-to-air refuelers to strike at one of the hearts of Mideast terrorism, Libya. The military airfield at Tripoli was bombed, along with the Libyan terrorist training center at Sid Bilal, military bases near Benghazi, and the el-Azzizya military barracks. Libyan leader Mohammar Kaddafi was injured in the attack.

At home in the United States, the form of terrorism began to change. Left-wing terrorism deceased, while right-wing terrorism significantly increased. Left-wing terrorist activity did continue to plague Americans, however. In January 1980, Omega 7, an anti-Castro Cuban organization, planted a homemade bomb in the Padron Handmade Cigar and Pilota Cigar store in Little Havana, Miami, Florida. On 15 March 1980, the Puerto Rican separatist organization, Armed Forces of National Liberation, took over the Carter-Mondale campaign headquarters in Chicago and the Bush campaign headquarters in New York City. Although no one was harmed, significant amounts of property was destroyed and defaced with pro-Puerto Rican spray-painted slogans.

In November 1981, the Justice Commandos of the Armenian Genocide bombed the Turkish consulate in Los Angeles (Mickolus, 1989a). In 1983 and early 1984, another Puerto Rican separatist movement, the Armed Resistance Unit, placed three bombs in the U.S. Capital, the National War College, and the Naval Yard Officers Club in Washington D.C. Between 1980–1984, the United Freedom Front had claimed responsibility for 14 bombs throughout the East Coast. In 1985, an organization calling itself the Red Guerrilla Defence, an alias for the UFF, bombed the Police Benevolent Association building in New York City (Mickolus, 1989b).

In May 1988, Omega 7 was suspected of placing a bomb in the Cuban Museum of Art and Culture in Miami (Mickolus, 1993). By the end of the 1980s, most left-wing organizations had been disbanded and their members arrested. Leading members of the UFF and the Armed Forces of National Liberation had been arrested for the murder of a police officer and armored truck robberies in Connecticut. Other left-wing terrorists had simply given up the fight for a more peaceful and less stressful existence.

Foreign terrorists also conducted a series of operations in the United States during the 1980s. On 20 July 1988, the FBI arrested two Libyan intelligence officer and four terrorists for plotting to kill Oliver North, former national security aide, in retaliation for the 1986 attacks on Libya. In 1989, several bookstores carrying Salmon Rushdie's *Satanic Verses* were bombed, most by Muslims protesting the book. On 10 March 1989, the van of Sharon Rogers was bombed, wife of Captain Will Rogers III who, while commanding the *USS Vincennes,* accidentally destroyed an Iranian jetliner in June of the previous year. She was not injured. The Islamic Revolution claimed credit (Mickolus, 1993).

The 1980s also saw the rise of single or special interest terrorism. Animal, environmental, and abortion rights advocates, in some instances, turned to terrorism to bring about political change. In November 1988, Fran Stephanie Trutt attempted to bomb Leo Hirsch, director and founder of the U.S. Surgical Corporation in Norwalk, Connecticut, because of his use of animals in research. In December 1988, the Brazilian Consulate in New York was bombed and four people killed, including the suspected bomber, a leader of the animal rights movement. On 3 April 1989, the Animal Liberation Front destroyed two research laboratories and burned a research center and off-campus office at the University of Arizona (Hueston, 1990). Abortion rights activists stepped up their activity, turning to bombs, harassment, and physical confrontations at abortion clinics. Physicians were harassed, threatened with death, and sent hate literature. One doctor and his wife were kidnapped and held for eight days in Illinois (Kort, 1987). Between 1982–1986, over 40 abortion clinics were bombed (Hoffman, 1987). Primarily in the Northwest, environmental rights organizations began violent activity, driving large metal spikes into trees to prevent loggers from cutting them. Several dozen loggers were injured, several seriously, when their chainsaw blades hit the spikes and broke, kicking back and hitting the logger using the saw.

In the 1980s, the far right turned from isolated attacks on minorities to concerted attacks designed to overthrow the government of the United States. Organizations that ranged from neo-Nazi, to paramilitary/survivalist, to the Christian Identity movement, joined forces and organized and increased their level of activity. Organizations with names like the American Nazi Party, Aryan Nations, Order, Church of Jesus Christ Christian, Posse Comitatus, and Ku Klux Klan worked together to bring terrorism to the United States. Thousands of Americans joined this far-right movement. Although no exact estimates are available, probably about 60–75,000 people were members of these organizations at their height of popularity. David Duke, while serving as a state senator in Louisiana, published an anti-Semitic newspaper with over 30,000 subscribers (Cohler, 1989; Magnuson, 1989).

Hundreds of incidents of violence occurred in the 1980s attributable to the far right, from typical Klan-type assaults on minorities, to the murder of federal agents, to bank and armored truck robbery, to bombings of minority churches and synagogues, to murder (Mullins, 1993). The full range of terrorist activity was perpetrated by the far right, including detailed plots to cause mass destruction by the destruction of public utilities, the poisoning of municipal water supplies, to the explosion of a liquid natural gas ship in Puget Sound, Washington. Violent confrontations between law enforcement authorities and the far right were every-year occurrences. Gordon W. Kahl, founder of the Posse Comitatus, killed two U.S. marshals and wounded three others in Median, North Dakota (ADL, 1995). Robert Mathews of the Order was killed on Whidby Island, Washington in a confrontation with FBI agents attempting to arrest him (Mullins, 1986, 1990, 1991). The activities of the far right will be covered in detail in the chapter on "U.S. Organizations" and so will not be covered in detail here.

In the 1990s, terrorism did not abate in the United States. Although the far right declined in size, their activities increased in scope (Klanwatch, 1993; Mullins, 1989; 1991). Some far-right organizations increased in size, notably the skinhead movement and militia organizations (ADL, 1995; Klanwatch, 1995). The skinheads are seen as the next wave of far-right terrorists and have been indoctrinated and trained by elders of the far-right movement (ADL, 1993; Mullins & Mijares, 1993). The militia movement is comprised mostly of loose-knit organizations that are rural or semi-rural and want to reduce government interference in the lives of citizens.

Additionally, special-interest terrorism continued to grow. Anti-abortionist terrorists, in particular, increased their terrorism. In February 1993, a Corpus Christi, Texas abortion clinic was firebombed. On 10 March 1993, Michael F. Griffin, founder and director of the Defensive Action anti-abortion organization, killed Dr. David Gunn of the Women's Medical Services clinic in Florida. On 29 July 1994, Paul J. Hill shot and killed an abortion clinic doctor in Pensacola, Florida. Hill believed he had a moral responsibility to kill abortion doctors.

On 26 February 1993, the nation was shocked when the World Trade Center in New York City was bombed. Twelve hundred pounds of ammonium nitrate fertilizer was detonated in the basement parking garage of the building. Six people were killed and hundreds injured.

Nine Sudanese Muslims were arrested and ultimately convicted for being responsible, including Ibrahim Siddig Ala, Mohammed Salamel, and Nidal Ayyad, who mailed the letter claiming the Liberation Army Fifth Battalion was responsible. The mastermind of the attack was Sheik Omar Abdel Rahman, a Muslim cleric who had previously been involved and acquitted for issuing the Fatwa (religious blessing) for Anwar Sadat's death. He was leader of the al-Gama'a al-Islamiyya faction in Egypt and was deported to Sudan in 1990, only to return to the U.S. in 1991, when he called for a Jihad (holy war) against the United States.

Mohammed Salamel was arrested the day following the blast when he returned to the New Jersey rental car agency to retrieve his deposit on the vehicle used to hold the explosives. As other members of the organization were arrested, law enforcement authorities discovered plans for bombing the U.N., Holland Tunnel, Lincoln Tunnel, and Federal Building in Manhattan. All nine terrorists were given 240-year prison sentences.

The nation thought it had seen the worst of the worst in regards to terrorism until 19 April 1995. At shortly before 9:00 A.M., suspected bomber Timothy McVeigh parked a nondescript panel van in front of the Alfred P. Murrah Federal Building in Oklahoma City and walked away. At 9:05, approximately 1,200 pounds of ammonium nitrate detonated, collapsing and completely destroying the building. Over 260 people died and hundreds more injured. McVeigh was a member of the Michigan Militia and planted the bomb as reprisal against the federal government (his motivation is only suspected). Shortly after the bombing, the militia movement experienced a significant increase in membership.

Airline Hijacking

At the turn of the century, Wilbur and Orville Wright invented the airplane, a mode of transportation that would revolutionize the world. It also provided the perfect vehicle for terrorists to advance a political cause. On 10 October 1933, the first airplane bomb incident occurred, when a United Airlines transcontinental airplane exploded near Chesterton, Indiana. Seven people were killed in the explosion and crash. Since that time, airplanes have been destroyed by terrorists and other crazies, and passengers on planes taken hostage for political goals. The airplane became a convenient, easy-to-hit target where the terrorist could terrorize dozens or even hundreds of citizens at one stroke.

The early airplane incidents were mostly caused by individuals with personal grudges against one or more of the passengers. For example, on 7 May 1949, a Philippines Airline exploded, killing all 13 on board. A female wanted to kill her husband and gain his inheritance. On 9 September 1949, Albert Guay placed a bomb aboard an aircraft, and the subsequent explosion at Sault Au Cochon, Canada, 40 miles from Quebec, killed 23. Guay wanted to win back a girlfriend and collect insurance on his wife. On 1 November 1955, John Graham bombed a United Airlines DC-6 near Denver so he could collect on an insurance policy on his mother. Forty-four passengers were killed and the FBI and Civil Aeronautic Association opened an office to research bomb damage. In 1956, a federal law was enacted providing for the death penalty for causing loss of life by damaging an airplane (Simon, 1994).

While occasional bombing continued, the airplane became a tool for hostage taking in the 1960s. On 1 May 1961, the first airplane was hijacked to Cuba. A National Airlines Convair, flying from Marathon to Key West, Florida, was hijacked by a single male and ordered to fly to Cuba. Castro provided asylum to the hijacker but returned the airplane the same day. On 24 July 1961, an Eastern Airlines Electra flying from Miami to Tampa was hijacked to Cuba by Alfredo Equendo. Castro released the passengers but kept the airplane. On 3 August 1961, three males ordered a Continental B-707 en route from Phoenix to El Paso to fly to Cuba. While refueling at El Paso, FBI and police sharpshooters shot out the plane's tires, ending the incident.

This rash of hijacking prompted the federal government to pass new laws increasing the sentence for hijacking, improve airport security, design better metal detectors, offer a $10,000 reward for hijackers, bolt cockpit doors and arm crews with pistols, enact laws prohibiting the interference with crews, and place INS agents on board. Some federal senators suggested providing crews with secret codes for military interception of hijacked planes and to give stewardesses "knockout" drugs to give hijackers. A new term also entered popular lexicon to describe airline hijacking: skyjacking.

These new rules and suggestions, however, did not prevent hijacking for long. On 9 August 1961, Albert Charles Cadon hijacked a Pan Am World Airways DC-8 flying between Mexico City and Guatamala City to Cuba. Castro released the plane and passengers the next day. Hijacking continued, with over 200 terrorist incidents occurring against aircraft in the 1960s and 1970s. A chronology compiled by Mickolus (1980) showed that over 100 airline incidents involved individuals who skyjacked or attempted to skyjack aircraft to Cuba. Skyjackers also selected other esoteric locales, such as Arkansas, Detroit, Las Vegas, New Jersey, Algeria, Israel, Italy, Mexico, North Korea, North Vietnam, South Africa, Sweden, and Switzerland. In one of the most celebrated aircraft ransom episodes ever, a person calling himself D.B. Cooper successfully skyjacked a Northwest Airlines B-272, obtained $200,000 in ransom money, and parachuted out over the forests of Oregon and Washington. Cooper was never heard from again, becoming a folk hero among many people. Over 30 years later, speculation still runs rampant concerning Cooper's fate.

In the late 1960s, international terrorists turned to skyjacking to achieve political goals. In July 1968, George Habash of the Popular Front for the Liberation of Palestine, skyjacked an El Al airliners at Athens, killing one passenger. On 29 August 1969, terrorists skyjacked a TWA Boeing 707 to Damascus. On 21 February 1970, a Swissair Transport Company airplane was bombed near Frankfurt, with 47 people killed. The same day, an Austrian Airlines plane was bombed in approximately the same location, but the pilot was able to land the seriously damaged airplane. The investigation revealed the Baader-Meinhof Gang to be responsible.

On 6 September 1970, the Popular Front for the Liberation of Palestine pulled off a well-coordinated attack, skyjacking several airplanes at one time. Four airplanes bound for New York were skyjacked with over 600 passengers taken hostage. A Pan Am from Amsterdam was skyjacked, along with two TransWorld and Swissair airliners from Frankfurt and Zurich. The Pan Am was flown to Beirut and then Cairo, Egypt, where the plane was destroyed. The other planes were flown to Dawson Field near Amman, Jordan. Also, one El Al airplane was subjected to an attempted skyjacking, but guards killed one of the skyjackers and captured the other in London. On 9 September 1970, the PFLP skyjacked another plane and flew it to Dawson Field (by now renamed Revolution Airport). On 12 September, the passengers were removed and the planes destroyed. Several hundred hostages were released at the International Hotel in Amman. Between 26–29 September, the remaining passengers were released in exchange for the release of Palestinian prisoners in Switzerland, West Germany, and England (Simon, 1994).

On 14 June 1985, TWA flight 847 was skyjacked from Athens Airport by two members of Hezbollah and taken to Beirut and on to Algiers. Over 150 persons were taken hostage, including 135 Americans. At Algiers, the plane was refueled and the driver of the fuel truck demanded payment before he would allow the airplane to leave. A stewardess, Uli Derickson, paid the fuel bill with a Shell Oil credit card. Before leaving, several hostages were released. The plane then returned to Beirut, where the terrorists killed U.S. Navy diver Robert Stethem and threw him out of the airplane (televised internationally). The airplane then returned to Algiers where several more hostages were released. On the fourth day of the incident, the airplane returned to Beirut one final time. The terrorists then demanded all Shiite terrorists be released from Israeli prisons. Over the next several days, the United States and Great Britain attempted to negotiate with the terrorists. After 17 days, the Syrian government was able to resolve the incident by getting the skyjackers to agree that the United States would respect the sovereignty of Lebanon.

On 21 December 1988, the world witnessed the worst terrorist air incident in history, when Pan Am flight 103, flying to New York, was blown up over Lockerbee, Scotland. All 259 passengers and crew and eleven people on the ground were killed in the explosion. Czechoslovakian Semtex plastic explosives were used and were in the forward baggage carrier #14-Left, above the wing. The radio bomb used to bring down Pan Am 103 was first placed on an Air Malta flight as unaccompanied baggage, transferred to a Pan Am connecting flight from Frankfurt to London's Heathrow airport, and placed aboard Pan Am 103. The timer had been set so the plane would explode over the Atlantic ocean, thus defeating any possible evidence-gathering efforts. The plan would have worked to perfection, except that Flight 103 was delayed for almost 15 minutes at Heathrow.

The investigation first identified Ahmed Jabril, leader of the Popular Front for the Liberation of Palestine—General Committee, as being the mastermind behind the attack. When the West German police raided the Frankfurt safe house of the PFLP–GC, they found a Toshiba radio rigged with plastic explosives that was similar to the one aboard Pan Am 103. In 1990, investigators discovered another piece of plastic in a shirt that was a fragment from the circuit board of a digital electric timer different than the timer found at the PFLP–GC safe house. About the same time, customs inspectors in Senegal confiscated a similar timer from Libyan agents. The investigation revealed similar timers had been sold by the Libyan government to Togo shortly before the explosion. The timer used was then tracked to a Swiss manufacturer that had sold 20 twin devices to Libya in the mid-1980s.

With the evidence at hand, authorities now believe Iran, Libya, and Syria all conspired to bring down Pan Am 103 as retaliation for the U.S. Navy warship *USS Vincennes* downing an Iranian airliner in the Persian Gulf on 3 July 1988, an incident that killed 290 Iranians. The actual persons who built and placed the bomb that exploded aboard Pan Am 103 have never been positively identified.

SUMMARY

The United States has a long, varied, and bloody history of being victimized by terrorism and of using terrorism against enemies. Throughout the country's history, left- and right-wing terrorists have attacked citizens and the government in the cause of political change. In the late 1800s and all through the 1900s, foreign terrorists have operated in the U.S., hoping to destroy the U.S. way of life. Their terrorism has been couched in terms of the body politic of the "great white Satan," but it is likely part of the motivation of these foreign terrorists is jealousy of the American freedoms and rights the citizens enjoy.

From the outset of our existence in the New World, our government has used terrorism against citizens and non-citizens alike. The morality of governmental terrorism in defending our liberties is oft and long debated. Chapter 3 contains a discussion of the ethical and moral issues that must be considered concerning government terrorism. The morality of this terrorism is largely a function of the times we live in. In the mid-1800s, few settlers would have argued the illegitimacy of government terrorism against the Indian nations. The citizens moving westward were themselves often the victims of terrorism. Did the government conduct campaigns of terror against the Indians to protect its citizens, or were these acts deliberate genocide? Even political and military leaders of the time would argue that point.

In the foreseeable future, the United States will continue to be subjected to terrorist atrocities. Although the far left is virtually dead, it will, like the Phoenix, arise from the ashes. The far right may be smaller now than in the 1980s. It will not stay that way. Foreign-based terrorism will continue to be a pox upon the citizenry, both external and internal to the U.S. Special interest or special issue terrorism will continue to grow in terms of both scope and issues. Terrorism will continue to employ larger and more deadly attacks. The Pandora's box of large-scale mass destruction has been opened with the Marine barracks in Beirut, Pan Am 103 over Lockerbee, Scotland, the bombing of the World Trade Center and the destruction of property and lives at the Oklahoma City Federal Building.

Later in this book, the complex and interrelated factors resulting in mass-scale attacks will be discussed. Those factors include improvements in weapons and explosives, media attention and motivations of the terrorist, to name just three. In the 1990s, the U.S. faces the distinct possibility of nuclear, biological and chemical terrorism, weapons that elevate terrorism into another realm (Mullins, 1992; Mullins & Becker, 1992). Prior limited use of those weapons in warfare, and in very limited circumstances, terrorism, has shown just how deadly those weapons can be in the wrong hands.

While the future is not bright, it is not entirely bleak. The more the public is educated concerning terrorism, the safer the public will be. The terrorist's greatest enemy is education. The more we know about terrorists, the more we understand their motivations, operations, weapons, and organizations, the better prepared we are to defeat the terrorist.

Chapter 3

TERRORIST MOTIVATION AND PSYCHOLOGY

Robespierre was well-educated and upper-class. Lenin came from a religious, middle-class background. Hitler was born into a lower-middle-class family with an alcoholic and abusive father and religious mother. Che Guevera was a medical doctor. Members of the Weather Underground and United Freedom Front were either college graduates or had some college education. Members of the Black Panther Party did not have much formal education, but instead received their education in the ghettos and streets of inner-city America. Richard Butler of the Aryan Nations was an engineer for Lockheed. Robert Mathews of the Order was a high school graduate. Many terrorist members of the far left in the United States have college educations and relatively high IQs. Many in the far right are from middle America, have relatively little formal education, and have conservative roots.

Terrorists are as diverse as any cross section of America (or the world). They are of all races and both sexes, come from a multitude of backgrounds, have diverse educations, and have worked in a variety of occupations. What makes people turn to terrorism? There are obviously no easy or simplistic answers to this question, nor is there a simple motivational, psychological, or behavioral explanation that can be applied to all terrorists. Terrorists become terrorists for the same reasons people become police officers, lawyers, doctors, construction workers, mechanics, etc. People become terrorists for a multitude of reasons and have a range of motivations for engaging in terrorist activities.

There is no "typical" terrorist. One common misperception people in the United States have of Mideastern terrorists is that all Muslims and Islams are either terrorists or support terrorists. That is as absurd as believing all fundamentalist Christians are far-right extremists or that all Jews are members of the Jewish Defense League. Only a very few people become disenchanted enough to become terrorists. Most extremists, whether liberal or conservative, ever resort to terrorism to address political ills. It is even difficult to consider terrorists at the extremes of political discord. What of terrorists who work to overthrow a repressive regime? In their case, the repressive regime is at the extreme of the political spectrum and the terrorists are more moderate in their political philosophy.

This illustrates that even a simple perception that all terrorists are at the fringes of acceptable behavior is a misleading perception. The terrorist may be at the fringe of the continuum in relation to a particular political system, but that system may be an extreme itself. For example, many Cubans opposed Castro's regime in Cuba and resort to terrorism to attempt to overthrow his government. Are these terrorists extremists? They may be considered political extremists, but their political beliefs are not extreme. Their political beliefs may be considered "mainstream." This illustrates that even in political ideology, there may be wide variances in political motivations for the terrorist.

There are, however, some commonalities among terrorists—in motivation, psychological characteristics, and demographics. This chapter will explore those similarities, discuss dissimilarities, and examine the demographic characteristics of terrorists. There is very little research that empirically examines the motivations, psychological characteristics, or demographics of terrorists. That minimal amount of research will be presented, along with the available observational data. This data, both empirical and observational, generally describes the terrorist. Not every terrorist will conform to these findings, for in any given population of people, there is a great deal of variability present. This data does describe the vast majority of terrorists and begins the process of profiling the individual as terrorist.

MOTIVATION FOR TERRORISM

Before examining the individual as terrorist, it is important to examine the reasons persons engage in terrorist activities. That is, what factors in the government, society, ethnic culture, or religious group would lead persons either as individuals or collectively to engage in violent activity? What are the reasons for this discontent, what factors serve to channel this discontent into political avenues, why do those discontented individuals turn to violence, and what factors increase or decrease the levels of political violence (Sederberg, 1994)? As with individual motivations, there are no simple answers as to why collective social or government groups turn to terrorism.

At the government level, Slann (1993) has indicated states may use terrorism against their own people or other nations for several reasons. One, states may wish to force their message of ideology, politics, or religion upon people or other nations. Castro, after overthrowing the corrupt Batista regime, used state terrorism to force Cubans to accept communism and reject capitalism. His use of Cuban troops throughout Latin America and Africa is an attempt to establish communism in the Western Hemisphere and become the self-proclaimed leader of world communism now that the Soviet Union and eastern Europe has collapsed.

Two, states may use terrorism to eliminate dissent among the population. A government that rules by force is required to force compliance. Robespierre, Lenin, Stalin, and Idi Amin are all examples of state terrorism to force compliance to the political regime. After the tsars in Russia were overthrown by the Bolsheviks, one of the first acts of Lenin was to kill or imprison all Russian military officers in case they were still loyal to the tsars. After the military was brought under control, Lenin's secret police then turned their attention to the general population, murdering or imprisoning any who were suspected of being disloyal to his government.

Three, governments may resort to terrorism to eliminate normal political systems or because of fear of another system developing and being embraced by citizens. Most nations, if given the choice, will vote to eliminate dictatorships or strong-arm rulers. Terrorism can prevent the rise of competing political movements within a country. When Manuel Noriega came under attack in Panama by competing political factions, he eliminated elections and used the military to crush opposing political parties and influence the outcome of elections. Eventually, he suspended elections and declared himself "ruler for life." It took U.S. military intervention to return Panama to a democracy.

Four, the government may use terror to harass, control, or eliminate political, religious, or racial minorities. Once in power, Adolph Hitler used the government to build a pure Nordic-Aryan race by exterminating non-Aryans in Germany and occupied countries. Ethnic and social cleansing has been a major force behind dictatorial governments in the twentieth century. The Turks against the Armenians, Germany and Japan in the forties, Pol Pot in Cambodia, Hussein against the Kurds, tribal cleansing throughout Africa, and the current conflict in Bosnia are all examples of governments "purifying" a population.

Five, the government may see itself as the self-designated enforcer of the "truth." In this case, the government sees itself as not only the protector of the people but also the educator for the uninformed and ignorant masses. The "truth," of course, is political violence to control a population for the goals of the government. The "truth" in South Africa, for example, was the government educating the people in the ways of apartheid. Until Mandela was elected president, the South African government perceived themselves as being one of the last defenders of white rights in the world.

Six, the government may be in constant conflict with external enemies. This provides a convenient excuse to not only commit terrorism against foreign governments but to extend that policy to the citizens of their own country. Kaddafi, Khomeni, and Hussein use terrorism to fight the "satanic" West. They also terrorize their own nations in the name of "righteousness." Hussein has vowed to eliminate the Kurds from Iraq because they are part of the Western "satanic" conspiracy to eliminate Islam.

Seven, the government may be in business purely for itself and for what it can get without regard to the welfare of its citizens. The purpose of the government becomes to fill its pockets. The government getting wealthy comes at the expense of the people, however. Citizens are used for giving to the government, and when they have no more to give, they are discarded. In Nicaragua, the government lives comfortably while the people starve.

The motivations for state terrorism are not necessarily mutually exclusive. Many terrorist regimes will engage in state-sponsored terrorism for a multiplicity of the above-listed motivations. The government will undergo a learning curve as they establish and begin to use their terrorist policies. A government who begins using terrorism as a tool for ethnic cleansing will eventually expand its campaign of terrorism to fulfill other needs, such as the elimination of rising dissident parties, become rich, expand its global sphere of political influence, etc. As government terrorism expands, the government rationalizes the increase in violent action, legitimizing the necessity for using violence (Ross, 1993).

The motivations for collectives of individuals to use terrorism for political redress are more complex. Schechterman (1990) suggested terrorists are produced by the "technetronic age." The rapid advances of technology and societies making quantum and qualitative leaps forward in technology produces fear. Persons cannot deal with the rapid and significant societal requirements produced by improved technology and become scared. The economic and political transformations produced by technological advancements leave people with a sense of insecurity and dread of the future. Some, to maintain the status quo of their society, turn to terrorism to resist this change.

Schechterman (1990) argues the trauma produced by change is greatest in the developing nations and is the most significant threat faced by that population. The societal norms, established over generations, become disrupted and unacceptable to the people of that culture. The threats come from an elite class of rulers who make new demands on society to keep up with technological developments. The ruling elite increases taxes, produces and distributes goods and materials, and demands new and unaccustomed services from the people. These new demands disrupt the social order people have become familiar with and lead to fear, which in turn leads to reactionary political beliefs. With some people, these reactionary beliefs lead them into a life of terrorism.

Related to these changes are changes produced in government by technology, where the government fails to include the people in technological change. The government progresses and moves forward into the technological age and refuses to help the people do the same. The citizens then become resentful of the government for "abandoning" them in their time of need. Fear of change is combined with resentment toward the government for changing.

Schechterman (1990) also argues many cultures are threatened by the intervention of the United States and its technology into the culture's life-style. America's intervention threatens the mores and values of that culture, and the culture, in turn, rebels against America. Many of the Middle East, Latin American, and African states are examples of this. The oil boom of the latter part of the twentieth century has made millionaires out of many Arabs, introduced a new life-style, brought different religious and political beliefs to a long-established culture, and brought many into the twentieth century technological era. The United States is responsible for destroying the established culture and is the enemy. To many, it is not sufficient that the United States merely be forced to remove its presence from the Mideast: America must be destroyed so it cannot in the future return and disrupt the culture.

Kelly and Cook (1995) also argue modern society is largely responsible for terrorism as a form of political redress. Kelly and Cook believe rapid social mobility affects the familiar and traditional institutions of society, such as family, class, ethnic identity, community, and caste. As a result of this mobility, the values of the culture and community lose their anchors and cannot be reestablished. As the society continues to progress, cultural norms are lost and people are left "free-floating." As a result, people long for the past and the way life used to be. As disenchantment grows, people turn to terrorism to force a return to the past.

A return to past cultural values also helps explain why there has been a significant growth of religious extremism in the world (Kelly & Cook, 1995). Religion is an available and convenient system for people to use to reestablish a past life-style. It is simple, easily understood, self-contained, can stand alone without other belief structures, and produces an inspiration for people to fall back on. Additionally, religion requires no other moral or individual responsibility for terrorism. The morality of terrorism is self-contained within the religion.

Religion simplifies a complex life. The Bible provides universal truth and takes the complexity from a forward-moving society. The world is polarized into good and evil. The past is good, the future evil. Static society is good, change is evil. Simplicity is good, technology is evil. With religion, there is no compromise nor are there gray areas. Religion can become the new culture of the society and provides the rational for violence. Religion teaches evil must be eliminated and all that is involved in change is evil. Thus, there is no other basis needed to justify terrorism. In the Mideast, the catch-phrase for everything the West stands for is summed up in "the great white Satan." Without the West, the world will be pure, life simple, culture preserved, and societies once again in control of their own destiny.

Religions also embellish the concept of man being basically bad and impure. The individual is corrupt and will destroy himself if not protected. People need authority, the arm of obedience, and a government to subjugate them and keep people from becoming evil. Religion becomes nationalism and the basis for government control. If the government rejects the religion as the controlling factor over society, people will resort to violence to make religion the governing body. The religion, in fact, demands that religion become the guiding political philosophy for the culture. All means necessary must be used to overcome "evil," and violence is a justifiable course of action to eliminate "evil."

Burton (1975) and Laqueur (1977) identified seven variables which were conducive for potential terrorism. One, ethnic, cultural, or religious minorities who were both segregated from the mainstream of society and who were self-conscious of both their minority status and cultural/social isolation were prone to terrorism. The minority culture wants equal treatment and respect from the majority and government and may turn to terrorism to achieve those goals. The Black Panthers of the 1960s and 1970s exemplified this type of terrorist. Their primary political agenda was for equality for blacks in the United States.

Two, minorities that are economically or politically repressed with poor job opportunities are prone to terrorism, especially if change is promised and not delivered. Many of the urban riots of the 1960s, 1970s, 1980s, and 1990s were the result of economic and political oppression. The minority populations of the ghettos finally got tired of hearing empty promises, broken assurances of improvements in educational and job opportunities, and government inaction.

Three, rising unemployment and inflation can result in people turning to terrorism in an attempt to force improvements in economic and workforce conditions. In the United States, the recession has hit farmers and the lower middle class particularly hard. The far right has provided a potential solution to these people by promising to overthrow the Zionist Occupational Government, a government of moneyed Jews only interested in the welfare of minorities. Those who join the far-right movement believe there is no other recourse to improve economic conditions and bring the economy back under control.

Four, some people may become terrorists through external encouragement. People who are not happy or satisfied with the government, but who are willing to work inside society structures to bring about change, may become terrorists through the influence of foreigners engaged in terrorism. If a foreign terrorist conducts an activity that is successful, that success may demonstrate a technique to use for political change. Alternatively, a foreign agitator (or terrorist) may provide a unique and new solution through the use of terrorism. The neo-Nazi movement in the United States has formed alliances with the neo-Nazi movement in Europe. Both provide motivation for the other to bring about the rise of the Fourth Reich.

Five, there may be an historical "them" that leads people into terrorism. People may perceive the current regime to be nothing more than an extension of an older, more repressive regime. These people may not recognize that new brings differences and the present government bears little relationship to old administrations. This motivation is somewhat similar, for example, of blacks demanding payment from the government for past sins of slavery. Even though slavery was abolished over a century ago, some blacks believe the government of today, built on the foundation of government of the past, is still responsible for nineteenth century injustices. The only thing that will absolve the government of these past injustices is the overthrow of the government and replacement with an entirely different form of government.

Six, frustrated ideologicals may arise and provide a "leader-figure" whom the fringe element will follow. This person would be a strong enough motivation to get people to overcome resistances to violence and so persuasive that moral sanctions against violence would become secondary to the emotional need to produce change. The classic example of this "being in the right place at the right time" was the rise to power of Adolph Hitler and German willingness to either assist or silently accept the slaughter of over ten million Europeans. Recently, Charles Manson was a strong, charismatic leader-figure for a small sect of violent criminals. Prior to Manson's influence, none of his followers had engaged in any serious criminal activity.

Seven, merely living in a society that is democratic and upwardly mobile may be motivation enough, in and of itself, to lead people into terrorism. Democracies tend to produce attitudes of "more and more" and "get what I can while I can." The psychological ethos of the democratic society is sufficient in and of itself to lead some people into terrorism. This motivation is evident in the U.S. society of the 1990s. People are not satisfied to maintain the status quo, nor are they willing to accept personal responsibility for their troubles. Someone else is responsible for the nation's shortcomings, the government is at fault for every injustice, and personal failure is the fault of society. Nothing is ever good enough, fast enough, or equal enough to satisfy people. Only by taking drastic action can these injustices be rectified.

Ross (1995) developed a structural model of motivation for terrorism with ten rationales. According to Ross, motivations for terrorism include: (1) Modernization level, which is related to technological change and the disruption of society and cultural values. (2) Geographical location. Some areas of the globe are more conducive to terrorism than others for a variety of reasons. Some geographical areas have a history of terrorism as the norm for political change. Third-world areas are particularly vulnerable to terrorism, both internally or externally. (3) Type of political system. Some political systems are more conducive to terrorism than others. Political systems that rule by terrorism teach its citizens that terrorism is a legitimate form of redress against other governments and peoples. Iraqi citizens have little regards for the human rights of the Kurds, nor do Iraqis have moral concerns over using violence to bring down the United States. Terrorism is the political system they know. (4) Presence of other forms of political unrest. Normal political dissonance will lead to increases in terrorism. (5) Historical and cultural history of terrorism. A history of using terrorism within a society will promote terrorism. (6) Failure of counter-terrorist operations or groups. The ineffectiveness or failure of anti- or counter-terrorist units to stop acts of terrorism or apprehend terrorists will increase levels of terrorism. (7) Organizational split and development. Political, religious, and social organizations that fragment will result in increased terrorism. (8) Availability of weapons and explosives. The more the availability of weapons, the greater the potential for terrorism. (9) Support for terrorism. The general public condoning terrorism will lead to increases in people involved in terrorist activity. (10) Grievances against a government. The more dissatisfied people are with the functioning or policies of a government, the more people will resort to terrorism.

MOTIVATIONS FOR ENGAGING
IN TERRORIST ATROCITIES

A willingness to engage in terrorism and actually engaging in terrorism are two different matters. Just because a person believes in using terrorism to address political wrongs does not mean the person will actually engage in terrorism. In the United States, tens of thousands of people are dissatisfied with the government and want to see it significantly changed or overthrown. The vast majority are not willing to engage in the violence necessary to bring about that change. Why do a small minority turn to senseless violence as a method of political change? Pierre (1978) has suggested several reasons as to why people actually engage in terrorist activity.

One, the terrorist is both committed to a political goal and is dedicated to achieving that goal. Terrorist activities are designed with the intent to make a government appear oppressive and repressive. By making a government appear oppressive, the terrorist believes the people will turn against the government and at the same time adopt the terrorist's agenda. If the people can be attuned to the terrorist agenda, they will then engage in terrorist activity.

Two, the terrorist conducts operations designed to undermine the authority of the government. By destroying normal life-styles, creating uncertainty, producing fear in the populace, and creating economic uncertainty, the terrorist hopes to polarize citizens against the government (Eckstein, 1984). Repeated terrorist operations against the XYZ Corporation in Peru may cause that company to cease operations in that country, which could cause widespread unemployment, disrupt the economy, and cause nationwide unrest and dissatisfaction. The people would turn their frustrations against the government and open the door for the terrorist.

On a more personal level, incidents such as the 1980 Tylenol poisonings serve the same purpose. The people came to believe the government, including law enforcement, could not protect them and became resentful and distrustful of the government. Left unchecked, this resentment and distrust will become fear and anger. In the Tylenol poisonings, the fear of the people caused the government to enact new legislation and corporations to change the way they conducted business. Stricter government controls were placed upon food and drug manufacturers and the companies themselves spent millions to more adequately seal bottles, cans, and jars.

The terrorist's purpose is even better served if the government takes repressive measures to try and halt terrorism. As the government becomes more aggressive, the citizens will become more angry and frustrated and, as hoped by the terrorist, eventually turn against the government. Scott (1970) suggested Batista's repression of Cubans in response to Castro's guerrilla operations led more to his downfall than did actual terrorist operations conducted by Castro. In the U.S. in 1994 and 1995, national and world events led to ever-increasing and tighter airport security. Airport security interferes with convenience of air travel. The American public will not stand long for increased waits and disruption of their travel routines. If airport security restrictions do not ease after a reasonable time, the discontent of the public will turn into anger and possibly violence against the government to relax the travel restrictions.

Three, the terrorist may commit acts of terrorism as a justification for religious beliefs. Members of the Christian Identity movement believe that the Second Coming of Christ is destined to occur in the United States, but that the Second Coming will not take place until the country is "purified." For Christ to return, racial and religious minority groups have to be eliminated, either by killing them or deporting them.

The terrorist also believes acts of terror committed against minority groups will convince other minorities to voluntarily leave a geographical area or neighborhood. If enough hate activities are perpetrated against a black family in a neighborhood, other minority members in that neighborhood might move.

Four, the terrorist may be trying to attract publicity and attention for their cause. Klan rallies, neo-Nazi demonstrations, hate graffiti painted on synagogues, and other such activities are designed to produce public awareness, support, and sympathy for the terrorist's cause. Acts designated to attract publicity and attention are the most risky type of activities the terrorist can engage in. Acts of attention are on a very narrow fence. They can easily generate as much anger as they do support. Many skinhead acts, such as racial beatings, which are designed to draw attention and support to their movement, produce community anger and a sense of revenge to bring the guilty to justice.

Five, the terrorist may believe the only way to express a grievance is by the commission of acts of terror. The terrorist may believe the government is unsympathetic to the demands of the people, and that the only way to gain the ear of the government is to resort to terrorist activities. Many revolutionaries realize the futility of conducting large-scale operations against a government, so they resort to terrorism. The Puerto Rican separatists such as the FALN and Macheteros believe the U.S. government to be unsympathetic to the cause of independence for Puerto Rico, and that the only way to get the government to acquiesce and make Puerto Rico a free nation is through acts of terrorism.

Six, the terrorist may want to free colleagues from prison. The terrorist may resort to kidnapping or hostage taking for bargaining power in getting other terrorists released from prison. At times, the "jailed" colleagues may be an entire nation. In 1975, the Free South Moluccan Youth Movement took Dutch hostages as barter for the release of the island of Molucca from Dutch control.

Seven, the terrorist may need money to purchase weapons, supplies, and/or equipment. The terrorist may engage in crimes not normally associated with terrorism such as bank robberies, armored truck robberies, thefts from police and military armories, and kidnapping. The Order has been involved in the robberies of several armored cars on the West Coast to finance their organization. On the East Coast, the United Freedom Front and FALN have used robbery to finance their terrorist activities.

Mallin (1971) indicated that the terrorist activity may also be directed at recruiting new members and/or improving the morale within the organization. In the 1960s and 1970s, many college-age youth joined the SDS, Yippie Party, and Weather Underground for the sense of excitement and adventure these organizations provided. As discussed in the chapter on terrorist organizations, terrorist organizations are particularly vulnerable to the internal stressors of living in a closed environment. Sometimes it is necessary for the organization to engage in activities to reduce these internal stressors.

THE TERRORIST INDIVIDUAL

Political, religious, philosophical, moral, ethical, and other belief structures are arranged on a continuum. Any one of these belief systems can be arranged along a normal curve, with the majority of the population towards the middle of the continuum, and terrorists, extremists, and radicals towards the extremes of the continuum. These belief structures can be imagined as fitting in a bell curve function. Figure 3.1 illustrates how this continuum might appear for a social system, national population, or class of people within a population. Whether talking about political, religious, philosophical, or other beliefs, all fit the same general function.

Taking United States political beliefs as an example, the vast majority of Americans would fit in the middle of the curve, as most Americans believe in the present political system, although no one believes 100 percent in everything about the present system. Any person on the continuum would like to see something in the system changed. Toward one extreme of the continuum would be left-wing beliefs. These individuals are socialists, communists, and anarchists. Toward the other end of the continuum are the right-wing political beliefs, the fascists, and

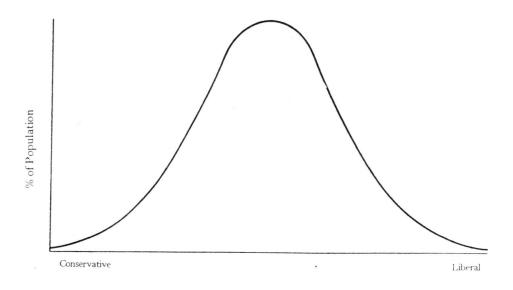

Belief Structure

Figure 3.1. Political, religious, philosophical, moral, ethical, and other belief structures of a given population.

nationalists. At the very extremes of the continuum are the terrorists. Not only are they the smallest in number, but they are also the most vocal in their beliefs.

The belief structures of terrorists, unlike most of the other people who fit along the continuum, tend to be based on distortions of reality and on what the terrorists want to believe to be true. As George and Wilcox (1992) described them, "the a priori thinker who believes what he 'must' believe, regardless of evidence to the contrary." Leon Festinger (1957) described the psychological concept of cognitive dissonance, which helps to explain the radicalism of terrorists. According to the theory of cognitive dissonance, if two or more things are not psychologically consistent, the person will attempt to make those things consistent. The person may change their behavior, opinion, or perception of the world. Furthermore, the person will change whichever is easiest and produces the most consistency in life. For example, in the gasoline crisis of the 1970s, many people changed their behavior by buying small, fuel-efficient automobiles. Others kept their large "Detroit-mobile" gas guzzlers and rationalized their small amount of driving made would make no difference in the level of world oil reserves. Most terrorists change their perceptions of the world to fit their beliefs and behavior. Terrorists are more prone than most people to resort to violence, so to fit their behavior patterns of aggression, they alter their cognitions and attitudes about the world.

Wilcox (1992) identified 22 characteristics in the style of individual terrorists. These are listed in Table 3.1. George (1992) also points out that these characteristics are not unique to one particular form or type of terrorism. These characteristics are shared by most terrorists. In fact, in comparing the far left and far right, George illustrates the commonalities among the two extremes of political thought. One, both are absolutely convinced they have the only political truth, even though for each that is a totally different political system. The left is convinced socialism, communism, or anarchy is the only pure form of politics, while the right's political belief system is based upon nationalism and supremacy.

Two, they both avowed a deep-rooted hatred for any who oppose them. To both ends of the spectrum, the federal government is the enemy. To the left, the government wants to destroy the only pure political system available. To the right, the government is involved in a conspiracy to prevent Aryans from achieving their rightful greatness and prevent a Constitution based upon Christianity.

Three, neither extreme has any faith in the democratic process. To the left, if the government was truly a democracy, they would let the people vote to change the system. To the right, the government should disband itself and let nationalism and supremacy run its natural course. The people are not a part of this conspiracy but have been brainwashed by the existing government to believe that democracy is now pure and just.

Four, America is controlled by a conspiratorial group. To the left, the conspiracy is against the establishment of world communism and socialism. The government is an avowed enemy of Marxism. To the right, the conspiracy is led by the government-dominated Jewish conspiracy and international banking system (which is Jewish led).

Five, both sides believe that to produce change, basic civil liberties must be denied to certain groups of citizens. To the left, all citizens must be denied civil liberties and placed into the proletariat for the collective good. All citizens are equal, share in the rewards and punishments equally, and must suffer the consequences of change equally. To get political change, however, some must suffer more than others. To the far right, the only citizens deserving of equal and fair treatment under the law are true Aryans. All others are perceived as non-citizens and to be used to serve the needs of Aryans.

Six, both extremes engage in character assassination and irresponsible accusations. The far left coined the phrase "pigs" for law enforcement officers and deliberately taunt any who oppose them. The far right considers enemies part of the "ZOG conspiracy." Neither side will allow

Table 3.1.
Characteristics of terrorists as identified by Wilcox (1992).

Character Assassination. Attack opponents at personal level, not facts of opponent's belief system. Terrorists attack motives, qualifications, personality, personal characteristics, and mental state of enemies.

Labeling and Name Calling. Do not use legitimate debate or discourse but use shouting, yelling, racial and ethnic slurs, and profanity to ignore real issues.

Sweeping Generalizations. Confuse similarity with sameness. If political structure is wrong in one respect, they must be wrong in all.

Motivated by Feelings, Not Facts. Make irrational assertions without proof. Logical fallacy is common.

Live in a System of Double Standards. Opposition is illegal, morally corrupt, and unenlightened because they lack "proof."

Opponents are Evil. Opponents are dishonest, immoral, prejudiced, and satanic.

Manichaean World View. World is absolute, good versus evil, and morality versus immorality. Applies to all terrorist beliefs, not just political.

Control Opponents. Opposition must be censored, repressed, controlled, and isolated because they are evil, immoral, and corrupt.

Attribute Attributes to Opposition They are Guilty of. Traits, motivations, attributes, and psychological characteristics of the terrorist are ones the terrorist uses to characterize enemy.

Argue by Intimidation. Opponents are judged by who they are as much as by what they believe.

Rely on Slogans, Buzzwords, Cliches. Do not use logical thought. No attempt to persuade or explain position. Slogan should be enough to convince.

Morally Superior to Others. Superiority based on political philosophy and leads to willingness for self-sacrifice.

Engage in Doomsday Thinking. Not changing system will lead to end of mankind.

Harm is Okay if Used to Produce Good. Anything necessary to defeat opponents is legitimate.

Emphasize Emotional Behavior and De-emphasize Reason and Logic. Propaganda is education and symbolism necessary to get emotional response from audience.

Hypersensitive and Overly Vigilant. Terrorists highly paranoid and everyone is potential enemy.

Political Agenda Becomes Religious. Politics become a religious obsession land rational for beliefs assumes supernatural reality.

Cannot Tolerate Ambiguity and Uncertainty. Wants security and to eliminate unpredictableness. Necessary to establish special laws and rules for enemy.

Engages in Group Think. Independent thought among members is discouraged.

Hostility Becomes Personalized. Individuals within opposition system are enemies. Enemies "deserve" what they get.

Political System is Corrupt Because Terrorists Lost. System unjustly prosecutes terrorists, and citizens have been brainwashed.

Accept and Foster Wide-Ranging Conspiracy Theories. Terrorists leap to conclusions, ignore evidence, and rely on far-reaching theories and facts to support their position.

anyone to debate their beliefs in a normal manner or engage them in open dialogue.

Motivation of the Individual

The reasons for the collective to engage in terrorism has been explored, along with the various characteristics of terrorists. Most of the above discusses the individual within the framework of the group. The dynamics of the group in intense conflict with society, being outside the normal support channels of society, and group pressures help reinforce motivations and characteristics at the group level. Peer pressure serves as a reinforcing function to keep group members headed in the same direction and same path. If a member of the group is resistant to engage in an activity, the other group members can usually force that individual to conform and participate.

That still leaves the question of individual motivation and psychology of the person who joins the organization to begin with. What compels an individual to initially become a member of a terrorist organization? What are the personal motivations and psychological makeup that leads the individual to terrorism to begin with? Some answers are hinted at in examining the motivation and characteristics of organizational dynamics but do not explain individual decision making to join the organization. This section of the chapter will address the motivations and psychological characteristics of the terrorist as an individual.

Concerning individual motivations, Kidder (1990) suggested motivations for resorting to terrorism included political repression, economic inequality, social upheaval, and ethnic and military conflict. In addition, she suggested people were motivated to become terrorists because of resistance to colonial rule, ethnic separation, ideological belief, political and external factors, humiliation because of personal inadequacies, and a need for others to know the person exists. Kidder also suggested religious minorities are more prone to become terrorists because of perceived threats against them, and these religious-based terrorists were more likely to convince others to join their movement because they are able to raise other people's consciousness. The person motivated by religious reasons translates this religious justification into political, ethnic, and economic justifications.

While Kidder (1990) raises some interesting issues, she does not really explain what motivates people to become terrorists. For example, many people resist colonial rule, but colonial rule in and of itself is not a motivation. Colonial rule may provide an external justification, but it does not explain what motivates. Likewise, ethnic separation may be a rational, but it is not a motivation. Neither are external factors nor ideological beliefs a motivation. They may provide a reason people engage in terrorism, but they do not tell us why a person is motivated to join a terrorist movement. Neither of these reasons indicates that some internal need state of the individual is satisfied by becoming a terrorist.

Bremer (1990) said individuals were motivated to engage in terrorism because of a need for belonging and because of unjust treatment. Terrorists commit violence because of unjust treatment and are seeking justice. Violence is the avenue they have selected to seek justice. Belonging to the organization is the motivation, while the cause of the organization is the individual's rationale. To support his position, Bremer indicates that terrorist suicide attacks are very infrequent and that few operations are intended to kill the terrorist. Most operations are designed so the terrorist can escape to commit further atrocities in the future.

Bremer (1990) provides two motivations for individuals to turn to terrorism: belonging and need for justice. According to Bremer's theory, individuals who are "loners" and outcasts of society enter the world of terrorism because terrorists will accept them. These individuals turn to the organization not for political reasons but because the organization will let them. Their motivation is not to change a political system but simply to be accepted. Second, people become terrorists because of a need to see justice prevail. They perceive the world as full of inequity and injustice, and terrorism provides an avenue to right the wrongs of the world.

George and Wilcox (1992) provided several other motivations. They suggest that terrorists are motivated by a sense of "moral superiority" over others, want power over others, to relieve a personal sense of worthlessness and insecurity in an organized movement trying to achieve "noble aspirations," are addicted to propaganda, are jealous and envious of the success of others, and the terrorist organization provides a substitute for one-to-one relations.

Sederberg (1993) explained individual motivation in terms of Erich Fromm's theory of aggression. Fromm said people engage in two types of aggression: defensive aggression, which is a violent response to an individual threat of personal interest, and malignant aggression, or aggression simply for the sake of violence. Sederberg argued terrorists engage in malignant violence and have selected coercive violence from among the repertoire of available responses. People turn to terrorism as a response to discontent and that the terrorist believes in the use of violence because of their alienation from the political system. Terrorists validate their use of violence through exposure to other terrorists and their commitment to ideology. That is, terrorists are initially motivated to commit senseless violence, and that exposure to the organization within a culture of violence reinforces the need to commit violence and leads to contagion (success in the use of violence is learned from watching other terrorists commit violence).

These theories of individual motivation assume that at the heart of the person's motivation is some need to engage in violence. The need for justice, moral superiority, power over others, relieve worthlessness and insecurity, and jealousy suggest that violence is a part of the terrorist's motivation. Sederberg's (1993) concepts of malignant violence, discontent, violence validation, and contagion deal more with the behavior of violence than of violence to fulfill a need state. Likewise, George and Wilcox's (1992) theory of the terrorist organization as a substitute for interpersonal relationships hints at the motivator of violence more so than the psychological need for affiliation.

The exception is the motivational theory of addiction to propaganda. It is not believed these are significant motivational factors concerning terrorism. The satisfying of addiction fulfills a physiological and/or psychological need, but not as a motivator for behavior. It is even doubtful that the fulfilling of an addiction will lead one to engage in terrorism. Addictions lead individuals to engage in crime, but these addictions often revolve around some deep-seated physiological and psychological addiction, such as drugs or alcohol abuse. An addiction to propaganda is certainly not strong enough to lead one to engage in senseless violence to change a political system. Even the violence committed by serious drug addicts is not political violence, it is violence to obtain drugs. If the person could obtain drugs in another manner, they would not engage in crime. If a person were addicted to propaganda, they would satisfy this addiction in other ways.

The above motivational theories assume that engaging in violence is part of the motivation for becoming a terrorist. Most psychologists argue that violence is a behavior rather than a need state, emotion, or motivation (see, for example, Baron & Byrne, 1977). Violence is a by-product of other motivations and does not fulfill some internal drive condition. Assumptions that terrorists are motivated by violence indicates a lack of understanding of what terrorists are about. As stated previously, violence is a by-product of terrorism, not a causal factor in terrorism.

The above factors of individual motivation are shared among terrorists and many people who do not engage in terrorism. For example, hundreds of thousands of people have a deep need for belonging and of moral superiority over others, yet they do not turn to terrorism to satisfy these needs. They instead join clubs, become business leaders, politicians, or enter other professions that will satisfy these cravings. The need to belong, to hold power over others, relieve worthlessness and insecurity, etc., does not identify those who may become terrorists.

In sum, the motivations described above describe images of an individual's self-image of themselves. A need to belong, moral superiority, power over others, worthlessness and insecurity, and jealousy of others are all part of a broader self-image individuals have of themselves. All of the above are somewhat related and a component of an even larger perception of the self. Self-image is also on a continuum of high to low. It is likely that terrorists are at the lower end of the self-image continuum, but their position there does not fully explain terrorist motivations.

It is likely that part of the motivations discussed above must be combined with a willingness (not a motivation) to use violence to satisfy those needs. Toch (1969), in a study of prison inmates, categorized people according to reasons they used violence. One category of inmate were self-image compensators, or people who used violence to elevate their self-esteem and self-worth. A second category of person were bullies and sadists. These individuals had learned to use violence because of the pleasure it gave them from seeing others suffer. Toch's third category of persons were the self-defenders, or those who used violence because of their fear of others. Terrorists could fit any one of the three categories identified by Toch.

The use of aggression, like self-image, is arranged on a continuum from likely to not likely. Many people with a low self-image, or bullies, or self-defenders, do not rely upon violence to satisfy inner needs. An individual's position upon this continuum, however, would not be a function of motivation but would instead be a function of the individual's past learning history. People who have somehow learned that the use of violence is internally (or externally) rewarding would be the individuals who engage in violence. Terrorists and criminals would be at one end of the continuum.

Finally, it may be that the needs described above are only one part of the continuum of more broader motivations for engaging in any type of behavior. Maslow (1970) proposed a theory of motivation that is widely accepted today. To Maslow, motivation was the satisfying of need states on a hierarchical level, with the lowest needs states satisfied first and the highest need states satisfied last. In Maslow's hierarchy, needs are arranged in ascending order from biological/physiological needs, safety needs, social needs, ego needs, and, at the highest rung, self-actualization. Figure 3.2 illustrates Maslow's hierarchy.

Physiological needs are those of shelter, food, water, etc. Once the person has satisfied those needs, he can then satisfy needs pertaining to safety and security. After the person is secure, they will then satisfy social needs by forming friendships, getting involved in relationships, getting married, etc. Next, the person will satisfy ego, or internal psychological

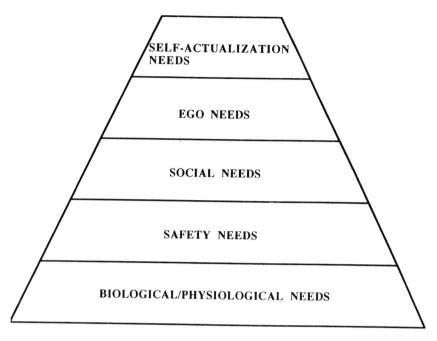

Figure 3.2. Maslow's need hierarchy.

needs, such as happiness, contentment, etc. Finally, after all other need states have been satisfied, needs of self-actualization will be addressed. Self-actualization needs are those of career contentment, feelings of self-worth, self-content, contributing to the collective welfare, etc.

Like political ideologies, Maslow's (1970) hierarchy can be represented on a continuum, with the least number of people trying to satisfy (on an ongoing basis) biological and self-actualization needs, and most people satisfying social needs. Time spent fulfilling needs can likewise be represented on a bell curve, with most time spent (by people who have moved through the hierarchy) satisfying social needs and the least time spent satisfying physiological and self-actualization needs. Figure 3.3 represents number of people and time spent at the various need states.

Putting the concepts of self-image, use of violence, and Maslow's (1970) theory of motivation together, a model of individual motivation for terrorism can be presented. This model is presented in Figure 3.4. The axes are concept of self-image, disposition toward violence, and position within Maslow's need hierarchy. Terrorists would have low self-image and have learned to solve problems by using violence. In some instances, the terrorist may even use violence to elevate their self-image. As the use of violence increases, so does the individual's

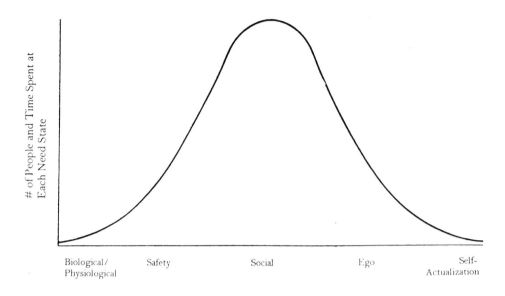

Maslow's Need States

Figure 3.3. Maslow's need hierarchy and population proportions and time spent by individuals at each need state of the hierarchy.

self-perception of themselves. Terrorists would have low self-image and high disposition to violence as a solution.

The terrorist would also be within the safety and social levels of Maslow's (1970) hierarchy. This would be consistent with their low self-image and disposition toward violent solutions. Persons below or above these need states would not need to engage in terrorism to satisfy their needs, nor would persons not disposed to violence or those with high self-images. Persons at the ego or self-actualization level of Maslow's hierarchy would be more likely to become involved in other forms of organized criminal behavior, such as the Mafia or drug cartels. Regardless of the hierarchical level or concept of self-image, people with a low disposition to violence would not engage in criminal activities, with the exception of possible drug addiction. To become a terrorist, the individual would have to meet all three requirements. Only then would the person be motivated to engage in terrorism.

PSYCHOLOGY OF THE TERRORIST

The Hollywood depiction of the terrorist is a criminal psychotic or psychotic schizophrenic individual who kills for the enjoyment of killing.

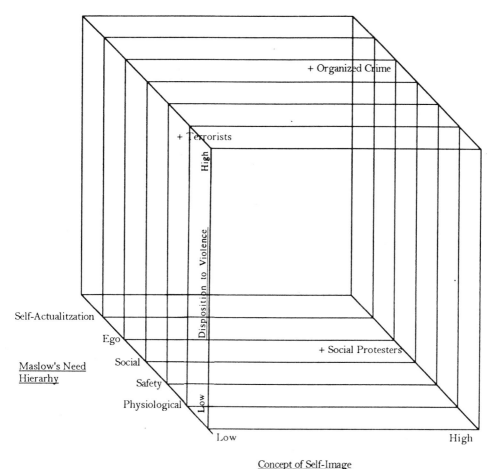

Figure 3.4. A model for individual motivation for terrorism.

Hundreds of movies have depicted terrorists with this personality, each movie introducing more terrorist violence than the last. Terrorists kill indiscriminately and without remorse. They are driven by some internal demons that can never be satisfied. Killing only serves to worsen the demons. Neither are the killings usually associated with a political agenda. The terrorists of Tinseltown kill for the simple sake of killing. The public has adopted this characterization of the terrorist, believing the terrorist is some wild-eyed Charles Manson-type creature with serious personality disturbances. Even law enforcement officials have fallen prey to the silver screen depiction of terrorists. Law enforcement officers routinely speak of the "insane maniacs" that populate the terrorist world and view terrorists as "homicidal serial murderers."

The stereotype of terrorists hardly fits the reality of the terrorist. Most terrorists have no serious personality disorders, are not psychotic or neurotic, and are not wild-eyed raving lunatics (Simon, 1994). Terrorists do kill, but not for the sake of killing. Terrorists kill to achieve a political goal and then kill only when necessary. Killing is not always necessary to produce fear. Only when a last resort do terrorists kill. It is doubtful anyone could have looked at suspect Timothy McVeigh prior to his arrest for the Oklahoma City bombing and predicted he would become one of the most notorious terrorists of the twentieth century.

Like the general population, terrorists come in all sizes, shapes, and psychological makeup. There are certain psychological characteristics terrorists share. The psychological makeup of followers is different than that of leaders and each will be discussed separately. These general psychological traits are ones shared generally by terrorists and do not apply to every single terrorist. The psychological traits presented below will, however, apply to the vast majority of terrorists and provide a good profile of the terrorist mentality.

Terrorist Followers

Most terrorists have a history of being an outsider. They have a lengthy background of being shunned and humiliated by their peers and, in many cases, by their families. They also have a background history of personal failure (Strentz, 1987). One thing they are seeking, and the terrorist organization provides, is being liked and accepted. Their past history of failed social interactions leads to lowered self-esteem, social isolation, and a negative self-image (Freedman, 1974). For example, the actions of Donald DeFreeze of the Symbionese Liberation Army have been attributed to exposure to family pathology and social maladjustment as a child (Kifner, 1974).

The terrorist organization ends the social isolation, and the person finally perceives a sense of belonging and that their life has meaning and purpose (Mullins, 1988). The person is with fellow losers in the game of life and has finally found a group which provides the social interaction and peer acceptance which has been lacking. The person may not even believe in the revolutionary or political ideas of the organization. Instead, they are members only for the social camaraderie the organization provides. To remain in the organization and with people who accept them as a person, they will do whatever is required, even to the point of catering to the organizational/social pressure of engaging in homicidal or suicidal missions. With time, the person usually does come to accept and personalize the ideology of the organization. Many college students of the 1960s joined the SDS and Weather Underground because it was socially acceptable. A few later became key members of the organization.

To the terrorist, the organization is the first true family most have ever known (Kidder, 1993). By engaging in terrorist activities with the organization, their sense of belonging and self-esteem is elevated (Hacker, 1983). The notion of the organization as a family unit is further intensified, and the individual develops a love of their comrades. Additionally, by defeating or humiliating others, the terrorist improves his worth as a human being, both as an individual and as a contributing member of his family. At the same time, reliance on other members of the organization is increased.

Part of the psychology of the terrorist and his activity is the desire to get non-terrorists to recognize him as a person (Simon, 1994). Engaging in terrorist activities, to many terrorists, is a way to let the world know he exists and has meaning in the world. The lower a person's self-esteem and less he belongs, the more important this need may become. To many terrorists, terrorist acts may be the only way to gain attention. Some want to be known for their notoriety, and terrorism provides the perfect vehicle to establish a national or international reputation.

The terrorist has learned and carefully nurtured a misperception of reality (Crenshaw, 1985). They feel inferior, helpless, have a low self-esteem, and are personally insecure (Freedman, 1983; Kaplan, 1978). Terrorists are hostile and suspicious by nature because they have learned to not trust others. They perceive everyone else as conspiring against them (Wilkinson, 1983). Left-wing terrorists tend to perceive themselves as the oppressed of society, or as the victims of an unfair political system or regime. Right-wing terrorists perceive themselves as elite, having a superior morality, and as heroes with their destiny as that of saving others. To both left- and right-wing terrorists, the world is easily divided into black and white, good versus evil. There are no areas for compromise or negotiation. This can lead to a lack of sophistication on the part of the terrorist. Thinking in simplistic terms, they tend to plan operations simplistically (Strentz, 1987). A simplistic operation does not necessarily mean a small operation. The Oklahoma City bomb was one of the simplest types a person could make and the operation was extremely simple. The outcome, however, was devastating.

Many terrorists believe themselves to be morally, intellectually, and rationally superior to other people (Wilkinson, 1983). They see their cause as the only true cause, and it is their inherent duty to bring that cause to the masses and to cleanse humanity and purify society. The far right, for instance, perceives their duty to purify and cleanse humanity of all persons who are inferior to themselves. Race has a different connotation to the right-wing terrorist than it does to other people. Race is not restricted to skin color, it also implies similarity of political and ideological beliefs. The right-wing terrorist rejects intellectualism as a rational and has a deep hatred of intellectuals. Arguments of rationality are perceived as a direct attack on their superiority.

The right-wing terrorist tends to be more authoritarian, dogmatic, and militaristic than their left-wing counterpart. The right-wing organization, as a result, tends to be more rigid and structured (Mullins, 1993). Operations are conceived and conducted using military phraseology and tactics. Writings, propaganda, dress, and organization conform to military standards. The common uniform of the far right is camouflage fatigues. Training is conducted along military standards and is highly regimented. They see all-out war as a necessity for achieving their racial destiny.

The terrorist belief system is maintained by selective listening and carefully screening out any discrepant information. Conversely, the terrorists may reinterpret any discrepant information to fit their belief system. Snow and Machalak (1982) have pointed out that the unconventional belief systems of the terrorist are very rigid, persistent, and resistant to change. The right-wing terrorist in the United States believes the only law is God's law and that law enforcement officials are the agents of Satan. No amount of argument or debate will alter that perception. They will make convoluted arguments to support this position, misquoting or altering Scripture to fit this belief system. The arguments they make are merely a reiteration of the leader's statements, arguments, and beliefs. Once they have found a cause to believe in, they blindly follow and accept whatever contorted belief system that is forced upon them. There is no original thought on their part, which is one of the reasons it is impossible to reason with them or to change their belief system. As mentioned previously, the organization discourages independent thought. Even when the terrorist thinks independently he has difficulty processing and integrating that information. If cognitive information does not fit his perception of the world, it is irrelevant and is discarded. To put it another way, if the information does not agree with his outlook on the world, it "goes in one ear and out the other."

One other type of terrorist organization member is the ideologist. These persons, like other members, need a cause and are looking for guidance in finding this cause. They are naive, immature, and innocent in the ways of the world. They are often malcontent individuals and will join the organization simply because the organization offers a different way of doing things. Although dated, Hoffer (1951) summed up the ideologist when he stated, "He's a fanatic, needing a Stalin (or Christ) to worship and die for. He's a mortal enemy of things-as-they-are."

The ideologist is often from an upper- or middle-class family whose parents were politically and/or religiously liberal. They were taught at an early age that an injustice against them represented an injustice against humanity. To most, their parents failed to achieve their goals and were frustrated by their station in life (Decter, 1975). Some individuals become terrorists because of injustices suffered by their parents at the hands of a government or religion (Post, 1984). Many Black Panthers joined the movement because of the humiliations and degradations experienced by their parents under Jim Crow laws.

The ideologist turns to terrorism primarily out of frustration. Their mission in life is to construct an utopia, and anything which frustrates them is an injustice to humanity (Kidder, 1993; Stenhoff, 1976). If the ideologist is frustrated by some injustice, then everyone must be frustrated by the same injustice. Compounding the problem is the impatience of immaturity. The ideologist wants immediate change and is not willing to work within the system, for the system takes time to change. The terrorist organization is able to take full advantage of this sense of injustice, naiveté, and immaturity by offering widespread and immediate change. The ideologist sees this revolutionary promise of movement as the only salvation for society.

The ideologist is the most dangerous member of the terrorist organization. Besides being fanatical to the cause, he is willing to sacrifice himself for the rest of humanity. The organization often uses this dedication and fanaticism to its advantage and survival. The ideologist is the individual exposed to, and/or given, the most dangerous assignments. The ideologist is the member designated to gather intelligence, perform criminal acts such as bank robberies, and assigned to suicidal or other high-risk missions. The ideologist is only too happy and willing to comply, as their actions, no matter how insignificant, are perceived as being the cornerstone of the ultimate revolution.

The ideologist has an extreme sense of moral righteousness and are highly self-oriented (Simon, 1994). Their way is the only right way and it is their destiny to direct the future of others. For the ideologist, some innocents may have to be sacrificed in the pursuit of utopia and perfection. Individuals lose their identity to the more overpowering need to serve the most of the masses. The moral righteousness of the ideologist makes them a self-centered individual. While acts of terrorism are for the good of the masses, it is the ideologist who wants ultimate control should the revolution succeed. All the talk of Marxism-Leninism, nationalism, etc.

are ruses to get the power. Once the revolution succeeds, the ideologist will take complete control.

The ideologist is similar to the sacrificial victims of traditional religion (Juergensmeyer, 1993). Socially marginal individuals, the ideologist perceives himself to be physically and spiritually pure. He has been chosen by society for self-sacrifice and is a victim of social pressure and a government conspiracy. The concept of self-sacrifice is a dominant part of the ideologist's psychology and can be overpowering. Juergensmeyer has indicated that some terrorists get so involved in the idea of self-sacrifice that they begin competing with other terrorist organizations to see who can sacrifice the most (i.e., Hezbollah and Amal). Juergensmeyer calls this competition "mimetic rivalry."

Waterman (1990), in discussing the religious ideologist, points out they are possibly the most difficult of all terrorists to deal with because of five factors. One, the religious ideologist is more of a threat to kill innocents because they have been ordained by God to commit the act and it is not murder. Two, their threats of self-sacrifice are part of a holy crusade and their death is a religious event. Three, their absolutist religious convictions are harder for intelligence-gathering operatives to penetrate and their ideology is a barrier to infiltration by law enforcement agents. Four, when cornered by authorities, they usually "hole up" in holy places and shrines, making military-type assaults unacceptable. Five, in general, there is more community support for the terrorists as persons. There is more public sympathy for their cause which hinders law enforcement efforts to end their activities.

The psychological characteristics of followers, whether they be outsiders or ideologists, usually result in organizational groupthink, where the psychological characteristics of the individual become enmeshed in the group collective. Individuals lose their unique identity and all members become one in thought, cognitions, speech, dress, demeanor, etc. Living in the underground of society, internal stressors of this life-style, and each member striving to be accepted are all conducive to the development of groupthink (Simon, 1994). This phenomenon also results in a general deterioration of mental functioning and reality testing that turns terrorists into robots who will blindly follow the leader.

Contrary to the popular perceptions, terrorists do not necessarily enjoy killing (Bell, 1972). Violence is used to achieve another goal, it is not an end unto itself. Most terrorists experience some level of guilt over having to kill and will employ several strategies to reduce this guilt. One, the terrorist depersonalizes and stereotypes their enemies and victims (Holsti, 1972). Depersonalizing the enemy and referring to them as capitalists, communists or, more severely, by using racist names removes the human identity. The enemy or victim becomes an object of terrorism, not a human sufferer of terrorism. It is worth noting that law enforcement and military personnel do the same thing when referring to criminals or an enemy. Criminals are "slimebags," "a—holes," and "scrotes." Military foes are "krauts," "gooks," or "ragheads."

Two, this depersonalization helps the terrorist not have to face the reality of their actions. The more depersonalized the terrorist can make the victim, the more likely the terrorist is to do violence to the victim (Duvall & Stohl, 1983). When the Moluccan terrorists took Dutch hostages in 1975, one of the hostages selected to be killed was Gerard Vaders. The terrorists allowed Mr. Vaders to compose and deliver a farewell message to his wife. In this message, he summarized their marriage, family, and life together. As a result of this, Gerard Vaders came to be seen as a human being by the terrorists and they were unable to depersonalize him. Consequently, Mr. Vaders was returned to the hostage group and not executed. Unfortunately, another hostage was selected and shot by the Moluccans (McMains & Mullins, 1995; Ochberg, 1982).

Three, in order to further remove guilt or responsibility for their actions, the terrorist blames others (and sometimes fate) for the victim's suffering (Knutson, 1981). This may even serve to further strengthen their ideological beliefs (Crenshaw, 1985). American victims of foreign hijackings and hostage-taking episodes are referred to in terms of suffering for the sins of the government. They are victims because of the U.S. government's repression and mistreatment of citizens of the world. Most right-wing terrorists feel little remorse for the victims of the Oklahoma City bombing, because those victims were not killed by a far-right fanatic, they were killed by a corrupt government.

Four, to even further distance himself from a victim's suffering, the terrorist may couch their actions in legalistic terminology (Margolin, 1977). Victims are not assassinated, they are "executed after a people's trial." Victims are not kidnapped, they are "held in a people's prison." Using legalistic jargon also serves to strengthen and reinforce the belief that true justice and right is on the side of the terrorist.

Simon (1994) has shown that the newest generation of terrorists are much more brutal than their past counterparts. This new generation is well-versed in killing, has a higher threshold for violence and death, sees violence as one of the only redresses for grievances, and is more radical and factionalized than their predecessors. They feel hopeless and betrayed by the government, and their belief systems are more rigid and structured than those of past terrorists. Although poor, uneducated, and alienated by society, they are much more dangerous because of their knowledge of technology, information systems, computer systems and data bases, and financial networks. Simon sees this new generation of terrorists as being more involved in technology as a tool of terrorism than their predecessors.

Both Kidder (1993) and Sederberg (1994) have attempted to summarize the psychology of the terrorist. Kidder's summary addresses seven psychological characteristics. One, terrorists oversimplify issues. The terrorist perceives the world as black or white, is inward-looking, and politically naive. The terrorist lives in a world of self-created fantasy, believing his cause has widespread public support. Two, the terrorist is highly frustrated by the world around him and he has no patience. Three, the terrorist is self-righteous, intolerant, dogmatic, authoritarian, and ruthless. Four, the terrorist believes in utopia. The destruction of the present political structure will lead to the creation of the perfect political system. Five, the terrorist is socially isolated and lonely. Six, terrorists engage in acts of symbolic overtones designed to show the world they exist as a person. Seven, the terrorist is willing to kill to achieve their goals and his victims are perceived as objects, not people.

Sederberg's (1994) summary of the terrorist mentality is somewhat similar to Kidder's (1993). According to Sederberg, terrorists have three substantive and three stylistic traits. Substantive traits are: (1) a polarized world view. To the terrorist, the world is divided into good and evil. Everything the terrorist stands for is good, all else is evil. Three subtraits of the polarized world view are: (a) a single force for evil is the cause of all problems and the solution resides in a single force for good. Evil usually translates into the government and good translates into the terrorist organization. (b) Behavior is moral if it contributes to the victory of good. Behavior is immoral if it delays or endangers victory. (c) Beliefs and values are highly structured and simplistic. The world is clearly polarized into right and wrong, good and evil, and black and white. There are no gray areas or middle ground for compromise. (2) The terrorist is a populist. The masses will rally behind the terrorist cause and help lead the terrorist to victory. Once victory is achieved, the terrorist will be adored, glorified, and a hero to the people. The people will display absolute loyalty to the terrorist once the struggle is over because the terrorist has freed them from their chains of oppression. (3) Terrorists have a strong power orientation. Cynicism and elitism are produced by the struggle for power and power is the dominating force behind terrorist actions.

Stylistic traits of the terrorist are: (1) extreme dogmatism. The terrorist is intolerant of others who dare to disagree or be different. He is extremely resistant to different belief systems, regardless of the circumstances. The terrorist ideology is a simplistic ideology and he is discouraged from thinking about that ideology. (2) The terrorist is committed to a path of activism and rapid change. The normal process of political change is not sufficient nor fast enough for the terrorist. He wants change and wants it now. (3) The terrorist is willing to destroy to accomplish his goals. Innocents are victims of circumstance and their individual suffering is necessary for the collective good.

Terrorist Leaders

In contrast to the follower, the terrorist leader has a high self-esteem and extraordinary self-confidence. They have a past learning history of being leaders; not leaders of the masses, but leaders of the lost and misguided (Mullins, 1986). They sought out and cultivated those who needed and were seeking guidance and direction. The terrorist leader is very charismatic (Crayton, 1983) and is able to use this charisma to get people to follow them. The leader is able to use their charisma and abilities to lead and direct followers in the direction the leader wants. They use followers to serve their purpose. In essence, followers are commodities to be used and discarded when they are no longer useful.

The terrorist leader tends to be paranoid and often borders on a psychotic paranoia. He is overly suspicious of others and perceives others as being responsible for his faults and inadequacies (McNeil, 1970). His perception of the world is that others are out to get him, in part because he is intellectually and morally superior to others. Everyone is an enemy, but an inferior enemy which can be defeated through his cunning and strategy. Since this delusional system is not built on logic, rational arguments against the delusion are not effective. Anyone who does make an argument against the delusional system is seen as a traitor and enemy (Coleman, 1976). The delusional system is constructed around a small truth, but rapidly becomes convoluted by the leader's paranoid tendencies.

The belief system of the leader is based on the political and social past (Crenshaw, 1985). The past history is important in that it shapes present ideology (Wilkinson, 1977), and this past history can be social, cultural, political, or religious. Most terrorist leaders believe these past ideologies were flawed and it is their mission to improve upon them. The leaders of the far left are constantly revising the tenants developed by Karl Marx, believing him to be almost perfect, but still with room for improvement.

Most leaders are millenalists, believing the time is ripe for widespread and sweeping political change. The recent collapse of communism in Europe has reinforced this millenialism for both the left and right wing. To the left, it is imperative for the United States to turn to communism to rebuild from the ashes of Europe, and America is the last hope for securing communism as the dominant political system of the world. To the far right, the collapse of communism signifies the edge of a new world order they are responsible for producing. The communist collapse is a message from God signifying the beginning of a new world order they are destined to be a part of.

Crenshaw (1985) has indicated there are five components to millenialism. One, it assists the cause. People are more inclined to follow when sweeping changes are on the horizon rather than small, inconsequential change. Pronouncing the overthrow of a government will get more recruits than will promises to change a division of the government. Two, concrete gains are not necessary. Morale is kept strong merely by the promise of change. The leader often justifies no action because "the time is not right," or that the organization could go out and cause small change, but that is not sufficient. Three, there is a promise of complete separation from the old ways. When change comes, all social order will be turned upside down, as well as the government being completely overthrown and a different form of government instituted. Five, the leader is able to assure the personal salvation of the members (Wilson, 1973), thus strengthening their loyalty to the organization. Members are promised positions of power and authority in the new regime.

The terrorist leader is a messianic figure (Mullins, 1987, 1988, 1991). This religious reverence is reinforced and increased by the leader sending the organization on two or three quick operations designed to be fail-safe. For example, the leader may send people out to conduct a brief series of seemingly well-planned bombings. These bombings are, in reality, quick strikes randomly selected, are events which law enforcement could not possibly prevent or arrest for, and they serve to make the leader the perfect godperson to the members of the organization. These brief forays increase group cohesiveness (Janus, 1968), as danger naturally increases group cohesiveness by making each member responsible for the safety of the other members.

The terrorist leader is unethical and amoral, having no conscience for anybody or anything. They are almost totally machiavellian, rejecting any morality and being totally ruthless to reach their goals. People are merely objects to help the leader in achieving his goals. Followers are used and rejected. The leader has no loyalties except to himself. Suffering and death, of followers or the victims of his terrorism, serve to make the leader believe even more in his own omnipotence. The leader believes he has the absolute power of life and death. He feeds off suffering, becoming stronger and stronger as more and more people suffer. He is God.

Because members of the organization are almost totally dependent upon the organization, the leader uses this dependence to further strengthen the organization and further isolate the members from reality. The leader can deepen the emotional support network members have established by having the members share their beliefs and feelings with each other. One of the reasons members initially joined the organization was because of the member's weak psychological makeup. By further weakening the person and making them see strength through the organization, the person becomes more deeply attached to the organization. The member initially joined the organization because of its attractiveness, not necessarily because of the ideology of the organization. By improving the emotional interactions and emotional appeal of the organization, the leader can increase both loyalty and increase membership.

As much as followers, the leader is a loner. The leader, however, is not a loner because others reject him, he rejects others. He is a loner by choice. He lives in an emotionally isolated world. His emotions are directed toward work, self-sacrifice, and dedication to his ideology, not to other people. His world is one of self-denial, self-interest, self-service, and narcissism. He is fanatically devoted to ideology and goal-oriented. Nothing will sway him from his destined path.

Terrorist leaders have rigid, inelastic personalities. Everything the leader does is correct and anything that deviates from the beliefs, ideology, or teaching of the leader is wrong. As with members, the leader lives in a black-and-white world with no room for gray areas. Any operations that fail or do not work as planned are not the fault of the leader's preparation but are the fault of someone else. For example, if a law enforcement agency were to infiltrate and compromise the terrorist organization, it would not be the leader's fault for allowing the infiltrator to join the organization but rather a member of the organization having misplaced priorities, having talked to outsiders, etc. If questioned concerning this faulty logic, the leader would blame other organizational members for not being attentive enough to the "alleged" defector's disloyalty. The leader is thus able to dissolve and separate themself from all blame.

Sederberg (1994) has identified several contributions the terrorist leader makes to the organization. Divided into instrumental and expressive contributions, the leader provides instrumental contributions of goal-setting, communication, and mobilization. Expressive contributions include ego support, inspiration, and the development of a collective identity. He further divides leaders into three types: (1) ideologists, (2) agitators, and (3) administrators. Leaders are usually good at only one or two of these functions at the neglect of the others. A few state leaders, such as Castro, Lenin, Mao Tse-tung, and Adolph Hitler, were good at all three. Leaders that excel at all three are usually the most effective and most dangerous leaders.

Because of the nature of terrorist organizations, the motivation and psychology of members, and the psychological attributes of leaders, there are certain organizational problems associated with leadership (Sederberg, 1994). One, the most serious problem facing the terrorist organization is that of leader succession. If the leader is killed or imprisoned, the organization will probably die. Most organizations do not have an adequate pool of leader material so if the leader is deposed, the followers are left without someone qualified to take over and run the organization. Additionally, most leaders believe they are invincible and that nothing can happen to them. When something does happen to them, there is no mechanism for transmitting authority. Two, the leader is the only decision maker within the organization. When the leader is removed, there is no one left within the organization that can pick up the reins and make the necessary decisions. Three, if the organization fails in a terrorist operation, members are likely to become disenchanted with the leader's abilities. The strong will of the leader assures success. Failure destroys expectations of members. Four, most followers are sycophants and "yes men." Shortcomings and failures of the leader are ignored and problems ignored. Organizational inbreeding leads to internal destruction of the organization over time and there are no outside forces to reduce this organizational apathy.

Fanaticism to an ideology, supreme self-confidence, unshakable belief in ideology, a messianic complex, persuasive communication ability, and inelasticity of personality all combine to make the terrorist leader a dangerous opponent for law enforcement. Throughout history, these traits and abilities have made the terrorist leader an opponent of fear and trepidation. Robespierre, Lenin, Stalin, Mao, Hitler, Guevera, Castro, and Charles Manson all shared these personality characteristics. All have led the masses with a dementia based upon a paranoid concept of deity. All believed themselves operating on some higher level of morality and consciousness than the rest of civilization and saw it as their duty to save civilization from corruption, self-destruction, and death. They all saw themselves as the only person who could do that, as no other person had their insights, knowledges, and abilities.

DEMOGRAPHICS OF THE TERRORIST

Terrorists come in all races, nationalities, ages, from various occupations, and are both male and female. It is difficult to categorize terrorists according to demographic characteristics. It cannot be said that terrorists come from underprivileged backgrounds or that all terrorists are college educated. Some generalizations by demographic data can be made. Much of the demographic information is provided by two excellent studies, one conducted by Russell and Miller (1978), and the other from Smith (1994). Russell and Miller examined the demographic composition of 18 terrorist organizations located in Germany (Movement Two June and the Baader-Meinhof Gang), Ireland (Provisional Wing of the Irish Republican Army), Italy (Red Brigades and Armed Proletarian Nuclei), Japan (Japanese Red Army), Latin America (Argentine Montoneros, Trotskyite Revolutionary People's Army, Uruguayan Tupamaros and followers of Carlos Marighella), Palestine (Popular Front for the Liberation of Palestine and the Black September Organization), Spain (Basque Fatherland and Liberty Movement, Patriotic Revolutionary Front and ETA–V), and Turkey (People's Liberation Army).

Smith's data on terrorist demographics is concerned with terrorists who have operated in the United States. Foreign terrorists operating in the United States represented the Provisional Irish Republican Army, Japanese Red Army, Omega 7, Amal, Libyans, and the Syrian Social Nationalist Party. Domestic terrorists included members of the El Rukns, Macheteros, FALN, May 19 Communist Organization, United Freedom Front, New Afrikan Freedom Front, Provisional Party of Communists (all left wing), Aryan Nations, Arizona Patriots, CSA, KKK, the Order, the Order II, Sheriff's Posse Comitatus, and the White Patriot Party (all right wing).

In addition, observational data is used to supplement these studies. This observational data was obtained from various published media reports, government reports, and electronic media sources. As with the data from Russell and Miller (1978) and Smith (1994), this data is limited in terms of its generalizability, but it does add to our knowledge of the terrorist operating in the United States.

In terms of age, Russell and Miller (1978) found that the terrorist was usually between 22–25 years old. Terrorists in Germany and Japan were somewhat older (31 and 28, respectively) but not significantly so. They also found that the age of the terrorist appeared to be falling, especially in Ireland, Latin America, Spain, and Turkey, where many of the terrorists were teenagers in secondary schools. Some Ireland terrorists were as young as 12 years old.

In the United States, international terrorists averaged 36 years of age (Smith, 1994) and domestic terrorists averaged 35 (left wing) and 39 (right wing). Deviations from the mean for the far left tended to be younger and for the far right tended to be older. Some of the leaders of the far right were over 60 years of age. Leaders of the far left tended to be younger, many in their twenties.

All data indicate that the vast majority of terrorists are male. Well over 90 percent of all terrorist followers are males, except for United States left-wing terrorists, where the male-to-female ratio is 73%–27% (Smith, 1994). Almost all terrorist organizations were led by males. Most females are in support areas with less than 16 percent involved directly in operations (Russell & Miller, 1978). The one exception was Germany, where 33 percent of terrorists were female. Although not numerous, there are notable exceptions to the leadership data and almost all those exceptions are in left-wing organizations. Examples include Ulrike Meinhof of the Baader-Meinhof Gang, Fusako Shigenobu of the Japanese Red Army, Nancy Ling Perry of the Symbionese Liberation Army, and Bernadine Dohrn of the Weather Underground. In general, when females lead the terrorist organization, a male is appointed as a "front," appearing to the outside world to be the true leader of the organization, such as Donald DeFreeze of the Symbionese Liberation Army.

Although there are not many women terrorists, some have played a significant role in terrorism. In addition to the females mentioned above, women held several key roles in most Russian revolutionary organizations, where almost one-quarter of revolutionaries were women (Gaucher, 1968). Some more notable females in the revolutionary movement were Tatiana Leontieve of the Social Revolutionaries, daughter of vice governor of Yakustsk and conspirator to assassinate the tsar; Marie Spiridonova, who assassinated counselor Luzhanovsky in 1907 and participated in the 1917 revolution; Lydia Sture, who shot several police officers in St. Petersburg and was executed by hanging with Anna Rasputin; Vera Zasulich, who attempted to assassinate Governor-General Trepov in St. Petersburg; and Vera Figne who attempted to kill the tsars by planting mines along their travel route (Gaucher; Laqueur, 1987; Vetter & Perlstein, 1991).

The vast majority of women, however, have been used in support roles, such as nursing, maintaining safe houses, and intelligence collection. The exception has been in Italy, where women have been involved in the full range of terrorist activities (Weinburg & Eubank, 1987). Reif (1986) has suggested that the reasons for less women's involvement in operational issues has been due to societal constraints and roles women have historically been assigned to and lack of revolutionary concern with women's issues. Women have historically been "protected" by male members of society and these same attitudes permeate the terrorist world. Neither are terrorist agendas directed toward gender issues. Terrorists have not been concerned with improving the women's role within society.

Russell and Miller (1978) have suggested that in left-wing organizations women have served in support roles primarily because of security reasons and not so much for chauvinistic male attitudes. Law enforcement is not likely to consider three single females living together as terrorists operating a safe house. Women, because they are perceived as less threatening, might be able to enter areas males could not enter and gather intelligence and perform surveillance activities.

Burton (1975) and Laqueur (1977) have said that even though women are a minority in terrorism, their presence and role is changing. According to them, women are moving out of the traditional roles they have long held in society. Women consigned to the role of wife, mother, and roles of passivity and gentleness are becoming frustrated by their lack of opportunity for advancement, and some of these women see terrorism as the opportunity for advancement. Two, women have acquired new skills they can use as terrorists. As women have moved into the work world, they have learned the same skills as men and can transfer those skills to terrorism. Three, the increase in feminist and socialist organizations have provided women the opportunity to move into terrorism. Four, women are demanding immediate change and are becoming more forceful in those demands.

Female terrorists tend to be more free lance than their male counterparts, offering their services to a variety of organizations which share the female's ideals and philosophy. She is more overtly hostile than her male counterpart, is ruthless, aggressive, tough, and displays little moral constraints for violence and killing. Many female terrorists exhibit male personality traits, physical traits, and other masculine qualities (Georges-Abeyie, 1983).

In the United States, right-wing terrorists are almost exclusively male, with the few involved females serving as supporters for the males. According to Richard Butler (Butler, undated), leader of the Aryan Nations, the purpose of the female is to provide a "well-run home to refresh and inspire her man." John Harrell, another leader of the right-wing extremist movement, says there are different worlds for males and females (Harrell, undated). According to Harrell, males are the guardians and females are to provide a family life for the male. In the U.S., the right-wing extremist tends to be highly religious, following rigidly the teachings of the Bible. As part of this belief system, the female is seen as being subservient to the male.

Most terrorists are unmarried. In Russell and Miller's (1978) study, 75%–80% of all terrorists were single. The same figure probably holds true for the left-wing terrorist in the United States. The figure for single right-wing terrorist is probably much lower. Being older and religiously oriented, many right-wing extremists are not only married but also have children. This is consistent with their religious and/or extremist beliefs which dictate a family life run by the male. It is the obligation, therefore, of the male to have a family. Based on personal knowledge and an assessment of published reports from various sources, probably about 60 percent of right-wing extremists are married (Mullins, 1989).

Russell and Miller (1978) found that most terrorists (66%) had a university degree. The high was in Germany (80%) and the low in Ireland (20%). Surprisingly, about 75 percent of Latin American terrorists had university degrees. The degrees included economics, education, engineering (most among Mideast terrorists), history, the humanities, law, medicine, philosophy, and the social sciences. The terrorist with an engineering degree is at a decided advantage over law enforcement personnel, as terrorists have the knowledge of technology which can be used to construct sophisticated explosive devices. In the United States, the majority of left-wing terrorists have degrees or some university education (Demaitre, 1973). Smith (1994) found 54 percent had college degrees and only 12 percent had only high school educations. Right-wing terrorist typically do not have any university education (Blumberg, 1986). Smith reported only 12 percent had college degrees and 33 percent had a GED equivalent or less. This lack of formal education is offset by the fact that many have specialized special forces military training. Many were in the military, while the majority received training from ex-special forces mercenaries hired to conduct paramilitary training (Mullins, 1990). Finally, according to Smith, most foreign terrorists in the United States had no college (56%) and only 8 percent had a university degree.

In terms of socioeconomic background, most terrorists (66%) came from middle- or upper-class backgrounds (Horowitz, 1973). Their parents were from professional disciplines, government service, police and military officers, diplomats, and the clergy. The one exception was the IRA, where the terrorist came from the lower classes. In the United States, most left-wing terrorists also come from middle- or upper-class urban backgrounds (Deakin, 1974), while most right-wing terrorists come from lower-class backgrounds.

Smith (1994) reported that foreign terrorists operating in the U.S. had varied occupations and worked at a variety of part-time jobs. Many posed as students and very few (only Omega 7 members) held regular full-time jobs. Left-wing terrorists worked in a variety of occupations and many were professional workers such as physicians, attorneys, teachers, and social workers. On the far right, most terrorists were unemployed, impoverished, or self-employed in service industries or agriculture.

Table 3.2 summarizes the demographic profile of international terrorists.

Table 3.2.
Demographic characteristics for international terrorists.

Variable	Demographic Characteristic	
	Russell & Miller, 1978	*Smith, 1994**
Age	22–25	23–48, Average — 36
College Degree	66%	8%
Ethnicity	None reported	13% Hispanic
		50% Irish
		34% Mideastern
		3% Oriental
Sex	Males — 80% of leaders	100% male
	74% of followers	
Socioeconomic Status	Left — middle/upper class	Left — middle/upper class
		Right — lower class

*Smith examined only those international terrorists arrested in the U.S.

SUMMARY

The terrorist is highly motivated, dedicated, and committed to a political cause. They are psychologically prepared to do whatever is necessary to accomplish their goals and bring about political change. They are fanatical to a cause but not psychotic. Major psychological pathology among terrorists is relatively low, although many leaders are paranoid to some degree. There is nothing to distinguish the terrorist from any other citizen. They do not stand out in a crowd, glow in the dark, have signs around their neck proclaiming them to be terrorists, nor advertise in newspapers. Except for their political beliefs and the manner in which they attempt to enforce those beliefs on everyone else, the terrorist is not distinguishable from anyone else.

Terrorist followers are basically insecure and looking for acceptance from someone. The terrorist organization provides that acceptance and provides a sense of belonging. Because the follower has finally found someone who will accept them, he is willing to do anything for the organization to keep that acceptance. Ideologists likewise are willing to do anything the organization asks. Ideologists are dedicated to their ideology and prepared to make any sacrifices necessary to bring about political change.

Leaders tend to be very charismatic, forceful, and seen by the organization as messianic figureheads. To many followers, they are the "father one never had." Their personal power over the individual is enormous and omnipotent. Anything they want, followers are willing to do. The leader's strength is also his weakness. If the leader is deposed, the organization usually dies because there is no other person capable of assuming leadership, either organizationally or psychologically. Most followers are not leader material and are not able to assume control of the organization.

From a motivational and psychological perspective, it is to the terrorist's advantage that law enforcement underestimates their dedication and willingness to operate in the shadow netherworld of terrorism. Misperceptions and misconceptions about the psychological characteristics of the terrorist works to the terrorist's advantage. Inability to "know and understand thy enemy" is to the terrorist's benefit. Until we understand the motivation and psychology of the terrorist, we will not be effective in preventing terrorism. It is imperative that law enforcement and citizens learn what drives the terrorist and what motivates the terrorist to engage in violence. When we understand the internal states and emotional makeup of terrorists, we can begin to understand the terrorist and predict future behavior on the part of the terrorist. Being able to effectively predict what the terrorist is going to do will enable us to stop the threat posed by terrorists.

Chapter 4

AN ORGANIZATIONAL PERSPECTIVE

The vast majority of any law enforcement agency's time is devoted to intelligence gathering. From the newest patrol person to the most experienced administrator, the key to the success of the law enforcement agency revolves around their ability to collect and operate on intelligence information. For serious criminal activity, such as organized crime, the agency may spend close to 100 percent of its time on intelligence gathering. Organized criminal activity is that activity in which two or more persons, with continuity of purpose, engage in (1) supplying illegal goods and services and/or (2) engage in predatory crime (State of California; Task Force on Organized Crime, 1976). Organized criminal activity may involve such activities as burglary rings, drug cartels, fencing operations, gang activity, loansharking operations, racketeering organizations, subversive groups, and terrorist organizations.

For most organized criminal activities, law enforcement intelligence-gathering operations have proved to be quite successful. Relying on informants, undercover operations, person and electronic surveillance, interagency file sharing, business records, and tax records, law enforcement agencies have been able to successfully compete against organized crime interests (see, for example, Stewert, 1980).

In the 1990s, intelligence-gathering activities by law enforcement agencies have been greatly enhanced by science and technology. Ion-argon lasers for fingerprint detection, DNA analysis of body fluids, and other advances in science have been applied to law enforcement uses for the purpose of gathering information on crime suspects. Computer technology has been heartily applied by law enforcement agencies in intelligence-gathering efforts. The ability to scan records, search for information (all with a court order), and the ability to rapidly communicate and interact with other law enforcement agencies have proved to be a major benefit in the collection of intelligence. The smallest of municipal agencies can instantly communicate with a variety of federal and international law enforcement agencies and obtain information concerning an ongoing case and then utilize this information in the arrest and prosecution of the case.

It may be argued that advances in science and technology have been the most important development in law enforcement in the history of policing. The improvements in intelligence gathering due to science and technology are immeasurable in terms of their impact on the ability of law enforcement to affect organized criminal activity. Almost all forms of organized criminal activity have suffered significantly because of improvements in intelligence gathering.

The only form of organized criminal activity which has remained impervious to law enforcement intelligence-gathering activities has been terrorism. With very few notable exceptions, improvements in intelligence gathering have not resulted in improvements on the part of law enforcement to catch terrorists, and the exceptions are not usually the result of intelligence-gathering activities. Catching terrorists has remained primarily a function of luck or terrorist stupidity. For example, members of the Order of the Rising Sun were arrested in Chicago, Illinois in 1972, en route to poison the Chicago water system with typhoid bacillus. A patrol officer stopped them on a "routine traffic stop" and subsequently discovered the biological agent (Clark, 1980). The fundamentalist Islamic terrorists responsible for the World Trade Center bombing were caught when the lead terrorist returned to the rental car agency to retrieve his deposit on the van used to hold the explosives.

Other terrorists are caught for complicity in ordinary crime. Robert Mathews, leader of the Order, was killed on Whidby Island, Oregon, in 1984, by federal agents because of his involvement in the robbery of a Brinks Armored truck. Other terrorists, such as members of the Puerto Rican FALN and left-wing UFF, have been arrested and convicted for crimes ranging from murder, to bank robbery, to robbery of armored trucks. Attempts to arrest and prosecute terrorists for their involvement in terrorist activities by law enforcement authorities have been largely unsuccessful. In one of the more famous and well publicized of such failures in 1987, 14 leading members of the far right were arrested and tried for seditious activity (one of the few statutes applicable to terrorist activity). All defendants were tried in federal court in Fort Smith, Arkansas in 1988. All were acquitted (Haddigan, 1987). A jury found that the government case was not sufficient to prove an attempt to overthrow the federal government (Mullins, 1989). In other words, the defendants were freed because of a failure of adequate intelligence gathering.

Why is intelligence gathering so difficult against terrorists? There are several reasons law enforcement has such a difficult time collecting intelligence. First, too few authorities understand the scope and extent of terrorist activities within the United States. Few realize, for example, that between 1980–1986, there were 190 terrorist incidents within the United

States, accounting for 18 deaths and 82 injuries (Mullins, 1988). In numerous seminars and training sessions the author has conducted for police on terrorism in the U.S., it is remarkable that most police officers do not recognize that terrorists operate in the U.S. or the scope and breath of the problem.

Many law enforcement officers, for example, believe members of the Ku Klux Klan are disenfranchised racists that want to resurrect the South. Very few authorities realize the Klan is several unified organizations, having a membership of several thousand and chapters in almost every state of the nation. It literally amazes these officers to discover that some of states with the largest Klan membership are not located in the South but in the North and West. Few officers are aware that many Irish organizations in the northeast are merely "fronts" for the Irish Republican Army (IRA) and that even police unions have been suspected of providing funds to the IRA. Even fewer still realize foreign terrorists operate in this country (although that perception has been changed somewhat in the wake of the World Trade Center bombing).

A second reason for the failure of law enforcement intelligence-gathering efforts is the lack of understanding of law enforcement personnel of the motivation and desire of the terrorist. Most law enforcement officers believe terrorist incidents are completed by "crazies," "nut cases," and otherwise mentally unstable or disenfranchised "lone wolves." Few authorities understand terrorists are not crazy and are highly committed and dedicated to bringing about political change through violence. The lack of understanding of the motivation of the terrorist leads to an underestimation of the capabilities of the enemy—a dangerous state of preparedness.

Even in the wake of the Oklahoma City Federal Building bombing, most law enforcement authorities believe the individual responsible is one of the fringe "crazies," and are unaware of the cohesiveness, unity of purpose, and dedication to a political goal of the far-right militias in the U.S. Most, in fact, were simply amazed to discover that an American citizen had committed that atrocity. Most officers the author spoke with immediately following the blast believed that "Mideast crazies" were responsible. When it was revealed that a member of the far right was responsible, many of these same people refused to believe it, arguing instead that federal officials had made a mistake.

A third reason intelligence-gathering efforts are largely unsuccessful against terrorists is that terrorists do not operate the same as do other organized crime figures. For example, terrorists do not usually operate illegal or illegitimate businesses as do drug cartels or organized crime families. Terrorists generally are not involved in money laundering, loansharking, or other illegal business ventures that provide records that can be used to prosecute. When terrorists do operate a business, it is often a legitimate business outside the scope of their illegal activities. Records reflect the operation of the business, taxes are paid, and activities of the terrorist are kept separate from business concerns.

Intelligence-gathering efforts rely heavily upon the use of informants. Most informants are either individuals who have become disenchanted with the criminal organization and want to harm that organization, or are members of the criminal organization who have criminal charges pending and have been assured that by working as an informant the charges will not be filed. Both types are readily found in crime families, drug cartels, and gangs. Terrorist informants, however, are few and far between. Terrorists are dedicated to a political cause and are unlikely to provide information concerning their activities or comrades. The few who become angered by the organization will usually not turn to the authorities to seek revenge. Members charged with criminal activity will not become informants, preferring instead to suffer in jail or prison for "the cause." Many hope prison will make them martyrs and rally the masses around their political agenda.

The most significant hindrance to law enforcement intelligence-gathering efforts, though, is the organizational structure of the terrorist organization. Unlike most other organized criminal activity, the terrorist organization is highly mobile, utilitarian, close-knit, autocratic, and functional (Mullins & Mijares, 1995). The dynamics of the terrorist organization make it virtually impossible for law enforcement authorities to infiltrate, but more importantly, the organizational dynamics are vastly different than other organizations. Many personnel in law enforcement do not understand the dynamics of the terrorist organization and thereby do not understand how these dynamics work to hinder intelligence-gathering activities. Only by understanding the organizational structure of terrorist organizations can law enforcement make significant inroads and then begin to collect adequate intelligence gathering against terrorists.

THE CIRCULAR ORGANIZATION

Organizations, whether private businesses, law enforcement agencies, organized crime units (or families), or terrorist organizations, all have goals and objectives, engage in planning and decision making, have leadership and chains of command, and engage in problem solving. Because of these similarities, most people assume terrorist organizations are similar to other organizations, both legitimate and illegitimate. The above-listed items are, however, about the only organizational similarities between terrorist organizations and any other organization.

The Bureaucracy of Business and Law Enforcement

Businesses and law enforcement agencies are bureaucracies and are structured as hierarchies as illustrated in Figure 4.1. Leaders are at the top and workers at the bottom. In this organization, management is separated from the workers. Communications are vertical, following a well-defined chain of command and religiously adhered to.

When communications are successfully accomplished and a course of action established, it becomes virtually impossible to change that course of action.

Program implementation is a lengthy process, often taking weeks or months. Various departments and administrators have to approve the program, decide upon necessary resources and prepare logistical flowcharts. Personnel have to be reassigned (or hired) for the program, necessitating changes in other personnel.

Rules, regulations, and policies are a way of life in the bureaucracy. Every aspect of employee behavior and conduct becomes regulated and controlled. As policies keep being added, the organization becomes static and grows laterally, not vertically. Support personnel are added exponentially while operations personnel are added linearly. In Vietnam, for example, the U.S. military required over 100 support personnel to support one combat soldier: clerks, typists, cooks, mechanics, supply specialists, and other administrative personnel.

Organizational change becomes almost impossible to achieve, and maintaining the status quo of the organization becomes almost as important as the organizational mission. Personnel are reluctant to change, will resist change, and may covertly and overtly rebel against change.

Eventually, the organization becomes overburdened with support personnel to the exclusion of operational personnel (as evidenced by the American organizational experience in Vietnam). The organization may have, for instance, well over 50%–60% of personnel in support functions. Figure 4.2 shows the flowchart of a bureaucracy suffering from this problem. Furthermore, regardless of intentions, all bureaucracies will, without drastic interventions, eventually balloon with support personnel and become more inefficient; in a sense, the business equivalent of the physical Second Law of Thermodynamics (order will become chaos).

Even most organized crime operations are similar to classic bureaucracies. Abadinsky (1987), for example, discussed the bureaucratic structure and format of Italian-American crime families. He described them as

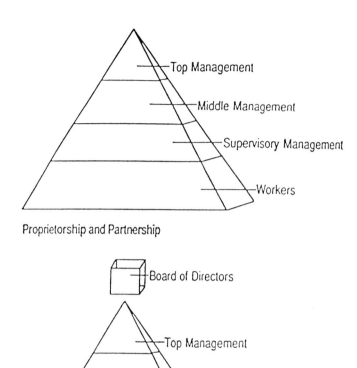

Figure 4.1. The hierarchy of the pyramidal organization.

having the classic pyramidal bureaucratic structure. Salerno and Tompkins (1969), in discussing the flowcharts of organized crime syndicates, stated: "The major difference between the diagram of an organized crime family and the chart of a major corporation is that the head of the enterprise—the boss—does not have a box over him labeled 'stockbroker.' Many of the other boxes are paralleled in the underworld."

But this organizational structure is the only one most police officers have ever experienced and the only organizational structure they are familiar with. Those officers attempting to understand and deal with the terrorist work from this organizational perspective and believe the terror-

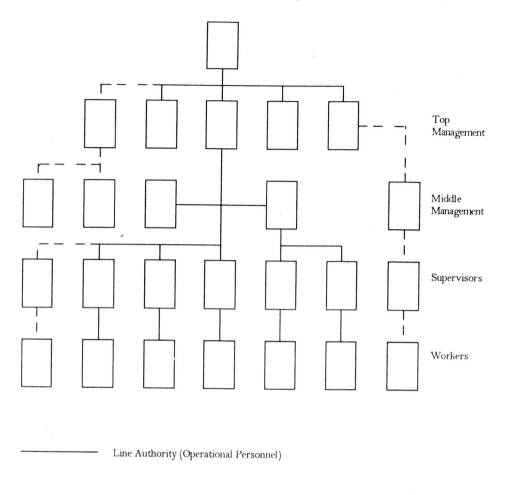

Figure 4.2. Flowchart of a typical hierarchical organization.

ist operates under the same organizational deficiencies. The officer does not realize how organizational efficiency translates into operational success, nor how this same efficiency leads to prevention of law enforcement to prosecute terrorists. The failure to understand the organizational structure of terrorism is as fatal a flaw as failure to understand the motivation and sincerity of the terrorist.

White (1991) has argued that terrorist organizations are based on the classical bureaucratic model. According to White, terrorist organizations are pyramidal in structure with four organizational levels. At the top of the pyramid are the leaders of the organizations. At the second level are the active cadre. These personnel conduct operations and are the true terrorists of the organization. At the third level are active supporters. These people are not terrorists but instead provide various forms of support for the organization: publishing and disseminating propaganda, handling administrative details, managing finances, etc. At the bottom of the pyramid are passive supporters, persons who are in the background or not members of the organization. Like the supporters described below, passive supporters are outsiders who may not even be aware of the true activities and philosophy of the organization. Supporters assist the organization based upon their limited knowledge of the organization, or may succumb to misleading information published and disseminated by the terrorist organization.

The Centrifugal Organization of Terrorism

While White (1991) provides a simplistic overview of the terrorist organization, it is inaccurate in its description of not only the terrorist organization but bureaucracies in general. Even in classical legitimate bureaucracies, workers are at the bottom level of the hierarchy and supporters (active and passive) are outside the normal lines of authority and chains of command. Additionally, organizational supporters rarely outnumber workers as White suggests. His depiction of the terrorist organization conforms to the perception of terrorism held by many law enforcement authorities who work within a bureaucratic structure, and that is one of the advantages for the terrorist. Not understanding the organizational dynamics of terrorism works for the terrorist and against the authorities.

The terrorist organization attempting to duplicate the bureaucratic organization would be doomed to failure. It is critical to terrorist success that the organization support rapid communications, speedy decision making, constant organizational change, and ability to adapt to changing circumstances (Mullins & Mijares, 1993). All personnel are involved in operational activities. As a result, terrorists have abandoned the classic pyramid bureaucracy for a circular, or solar system organizational arrangement (Zawodny, 1983), as illustrated in Figure 4.3. The leader is at the center of this arrangement and the members surrounding him. In the solar system analogy, the leader would be the sun and members the planets.

Bureaucracies tend to be open-ended organizations, with outsiders able to enter at almost any node of the flowchart. The circular organization, however, is a closed system, making it impossible for outsiders to penetrate the organization without the leader's knowledge. The leader being in direct contact with members prevents any covert intrusion into the organization. Thus, the leader has a direct influence on and direct control of all members and actions of his organization (leaders will be referred to in the masculine, as almost all terrorist leaders are male). In addition to being a closed organization, the circular organizational structure provides other benefits for the organization (as indicated by Zawodny, 1983).

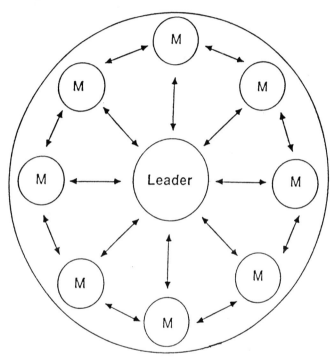

Figure 4.3. The circular, or solar system, organizational structure of the terrorist organization.

1. Leaders are participants. Leaders not only decide the course of action, they participate in operations. In other organized crime operations, leaders are far removed from the operation. If members are caught, there are numerous buffer layers between the participant and leader, and the insulation of rank keeps the leader from being implicated by the authorities. Arrest of one of these leaders usually takes years or decades of intelligence work and even then is very seldom tied to a specific criminal activity of the organization. Additionally, when caught, members are often willing to talk about the organization in exchange for a reduction of charges.

The terrorist leader, on the other hand, is visible on a daily basis to provide a role model for his followers, to share in the physical and psychological stresses which affect the organization, and share in the consequences of operations. This daily contact with the leader and his involvement in high-risk activities helps build intense loyalties among the followers and makes those loyalties personalized on an individual basis. Thus, each member of the organization feels personally allied with the leader and has a perception of being special and unique. Because of this, members are more likely to engage in actions which could result in capture, injury, or death.

For law enforcement authorities, this means that if the terrorist organization is compromised or caught committing an act, the leader is usually caught as well. Che Guevera was caught with his terrorist followers in Bolivia. In the terrorist world he became such a cult hero that the Bolivian government has refused to divulge the location of his burial site. Fidel Castro gained a fanatical following among Cuban old guard communists because he led the revolutionary action and suffered along with them in overthrowing the Batista regime. In 1985, the FBI raided the compound of the Covenant, the Sword and the Arm of the Lord (CSA). Arrested and sentenced with the members was Jim Ellison, leader of the CSA.

The vast majority of terrorist organizations are small, numbering less than 15–20 people. When the leader is killed or captured, the organization usually dies. Countless terrorist organizations have disbanded or died because the leader died or was arrested. Some notable examples in the United States include the Weather Underground, the United Freedom Front, and the Order.

2. **The power of the leader is directly reinforced.** Most terrorists are "followers." They are persons with low self-esteem, have a history of personal failure, and are looking for a direction in life. In contrast, most leaders are very strong-willed, charismatic, and able to prey on the psychological weaknesses of others. Daily contact between leader and followers tightens the bond between the leader and followers. Eventually, the leader becomes godlike and a mystical persona (Wilson, 1973).

Most terrorists do not initially join the terrorist organization as fanatical believers in the organization's political philosophy. Most are looking for a purpose in life, have a distorted sense of reality, perceive themselves as inferior, helpless, and outsiders. For the most part, they are insecure, hostile, and believe the world is conspiring against them (see, for example, Crenshaw, 1985; Freedman, 1974 & 1983; Kaplan, 1978; Strentz, 1987; Wilkinson, 1983). Once within the organization, the leader can shape these followers' behavior and belief structures and make them idealists.

Once the follower has adopted the ideology of the organization, then the leader can begin reinforcing the notion that the old world order needs destroyed and the ideal world can be built from the ashes (Steinhoff, 1976). Law enforcement personnel are often attacked as exemplifying the old, established order and being a mortal enemy to the new order (Coleman, 1976). As idealism becomes more predominant, the leader can then turn the followers into true fanatics of "the cause." One clear example of this process is the Charles Manson family. Most of Manson's followers were little more than 1960s "hippies" looking for acceptance of their radical dress, drug usage, and unconventional sexual mores. Within a short period of time, Manson had led them to believe he was the messiah and had convinced them to commit multiple murders in his behalf.

This strong personal devotion is not seen in other organizations. In most organizations, including other organized crime families, most members never even meet the leader, much less have any type of ongoing contact with him. This lack of contact between the leader and members does not lead to personalized loyalty and obedience as in the terrorist organization. As a result, most people cannot understand the devotion of members to a particular person.

3. The leader controls membership. Through his close control of the members and daily alliance with the terrorist organization, the leader directly controls, selects, and supervises the introduction of new members to the organization. The leader may use members to recruit, but it is he who ultimately allows new members into the "inner circle" of the organization. With new members, the leader can directly assess their sincerity, dedication, motivation, and fanaticism to the organization's cause.

Some terrorist organizations have relied on sophisticated techniques to screen potential members and keep informants from penetrating the organization. Robert Mathews of the Order, for example, gave potential members a polygraph using the Voice Stress Analyzer. Members were also periodically tested with this instrument to insure they remained sincere to the organization's goals and had not become informants for law enforcement. Although few organizations go to this extreme, most leaders have the same level of paranoia concerning penetration by the "enemy."

No other organized crime syndicates resort to these measures, nor is the leader involved in recruitment and selection to the extent that terrorist leaders are. In non-crime bureaucracies, recruitment and selection is conducted by support personnel and little regard is given to political motivation. One of the reasons intelligence networks of nations are able to infiltrate and penetrate the intelligence networks of other countries (i.e., double agents in the CIA or KGB) is lack of participation in this process by the key cadre of leaders.

4. Direct control of the leader over the behavior of members. The leader can administer punishment rapidly and directly over the members of the organization. The leader is able to keep his followers under constant surveillance and supervision. Any mistakes or deviations from group norms can be quickly remedied. Deviations from organizational philosophy can be directly corrected, and possible defectors can be dealt with before they can compromise the organization.

Other organized crime syndicates also exercise close control over members and administer swift and severe punishment, but this punishment is usually administered by a peer in the organization and not the leader. In the terrorist organization, the leader's involvement in the punishment serves a second function missing in other crime syndicates, that of serving to reinforce the behavior of other members and increasing their esteem for the leader. That is, the leader's total domination over the organization and involvement in all aspects of organizational life only serves to enhance his mysticism and supernormal characteristics to the group.

5. Internal stressors are recognized and can be eliminated. Daily contact with the organization allows the leader to recognize when internal pressures and stressors are building up in the organization. These internal stressors can be greater for the terrorist organization than most other organizations (legitimate or illegitimate) because of the close and almost constant proximity of members to one another. Being a closed organization, members have more constant contact with other members than seen in other types of organizations. They not only work together, they often travel and live together. This constant contact often leads to personality disputes and organizational stress. Being in close contact with the organization, the leader is able to recognize and diffuse these stressors. The leader may give the organization some external target on which to focus their frustrations (Zawodny, 1978). They may, for example, conduct an attack on an enemy target, engage in a quick and simple act of sabotage, or engage in some other activity directed against external sources. A side benefit of an action such as this is that it helps increase group cohesiveness (Hacker, 1983).

6. Improved organizational communications. The communications network in the terrorist organization does not involve paperwork or telecommunications. Lines of communication are horizontal, not vertical.

Instead of going through lengthy chains of command, communications go directly from the leader to the receiver. Miscommunications, misunderstandings, and mistakes in communications are avoided. Any garbling of communications can be immediately rectified and clarified.

The flexibility of the organization is increased during operations, greatly enhancing their chances of success. Rather than conducting an operation with rigid operational plans, the organization can change as the situation dictates, improvising as necessary. The leader is available for the communications that allow for this strategic and tactical flexibility. The American military experience in Vietnam serves to illustrate the advance of flexible communications. Regular military units, when conducting an operation, were constrained by a formalized communications chain of command. If a unit saw a target of opportunity, the unit radioed their command, command radioed headquarters, who, in turn, had to get approval from MACV (overall command of American military forces in Vietnam). MACV had to get approval from the government of South Vietnam. Once up the chain, communications then had to be reversed and go down the same command chain. By the time the field unit was given approval, the target of opportunity had vanished. Special forces units (Green Berets, Seals, Marine Recon teams, etc.) did not operate under such communication restraints. When they saw a target of opportunity, their commander was on the scene and was able to give immediate approval for tactical action. As a result, special operations teams were more successful in the conduct of the war than other military units.

Other crime organizations rely on typical bureaucratic chain-of-command communications. These communications often leave a paper trail for law enforcement to use in investigation and prosecution. Phone calls, letters, computer mail, etc. are used by these organizations to communicate. By using these trails and/or using electronic surveillance/eavesdropping equipment, authorities can gather intelligence against the organization. This cannot be done with the terrorist organization.

7. Enhanced tactical flexibility. Related to communications flexibility is the ability of the terrorist organization to operation against targets of opportunity. Terrorist organizations generally do carefully select targets and make extensive plans of action against that target. Occasionally, a target will unexpectedly present itself. When this happens, the terrorists are able to take advantage of the situation and exploit the target in the furtherance of their goals. Should a primary target become unavailable, the organization can readily adapt and attack another target.

Security experts advise their clients to make themselves secure targets not only for their safety but also because target-hardening will lead to the terrorist selecting an easier target. In Italy, for example, Aldo Moro was not the primary target of the Red Brigades (Scotti, 1986). He was kidnapped because the primary target had secured himself. The decision to kidnap Moro was made on the scene when he presented himself as available.

If law enforcement authorities do manage to obtain intelligence concerning a terroristic tactical operation, the ability of the terrorist organization to make last-second changes in the operational plan makes the intelligence worthless. One of the major difficulties in capturing terrorists resides with this tactical flexibility. Avoiding the trap of being locked in to a plan makes the terrorist much more effective than law enforcement attempting to capture the terrorist.

8. Freedom from support networks. All members share in all tasks and the group as a whole does whatever work needs to be done. All members perform support functions, secondary to their primary function of conducting operations. Members are involved in medical functions, operating a clandestine press, making and repairing weapons, mending clothes, cooking, etc. Whatever needs arise, members see to those needs.

Other organized crime syndicates rely on outside persons and businesses for certain tasks and operations. For example, many activities of the "Mafia" (i.e., drugs, prostitution, loansharking, etc.) require non-members as growers, suppliers, for transportation, etc. Without these non-members, the syndicate cannot do business. For example, syndicates do not grow drugs. They buy drugs from an outside source and resell. If the terrorist organization, on the other hand, needs something, their members get it. If the organization needs weapons, members perform the necessary activities to obtain those weapons.

9. Enhanced organizational efficiency. The terrorist organization is extremely efficient at the organizational level. There is no bureaucratic paperwork, no complex chain of command to retard decision making, no lengthy communication sequences, no complicated hierarchy, and no support personnel to detract from the primary mission. The primary function of every member remains focused on the primary objectives of the organization. The details and minutia which bog down most bureaucracies are not present in the terrorist organization. For law enforcement authorities attempting to investigate the terrorist organization, there are no paper trails to follow and no bureaucratic administrative details by which to build an intelligence case. No terrorist organization in the United States has ever been shut down because of a bureaucratic intelligence trail.

10. Organization can remain anonymous to outsiders. Because the terrorist organization is self-contained, very few people outside of the organization are aware of who the members are in the organization. Many terrorist organizations do not even come to the attention of law enforcement agencies until they commit an act. There have, in fact, been numerous instances where law enforcement authorities believed they had put a terrorist organization out of business only to see it resurrected in the future, often with some of the same key personnel involved in the new organization.

In larger terrorist organizations, where the organization is divided into cells, the same principle applies internally. The members of one cell do not know of the existence or identities of the other cells. Thus, if one cell is compromised, the members of that cell cannot compromise other members in different cells. One of the primary reasons the French Underground was so successful in World War II was the devotion to secrecy concerning the identities of cell members. When members of the French Underground were captured by the Nazis, they could not "give up" their comrades because they did not know who their comrades were. Even when different cells worked together in operations, the people involved did not know the names of those they were working with.

11. The organization seeks support from other terrorist organizations or weak third-world nations. Most terrorist organizations do not receive direct support from the superpower nations such as the USSR or China. Instead, they rely on nations such as Chad, Cuba, Iran, Iraq, Libya, Syria, North Korea, etc. to provide arms, finances, safe havens, supplies, training, and manpower. The superpower nations do support terrorism, but for the most part, their support is indirect by feeding through third-world nations or by using various fronts (such as "legitimate" businesses sympathetic to the terrorist's cause).

Third-world nations see terrorism as a path to political prominence and power. A nation such as Libya knows it cannot compete economically or militarily with the United States (as amply evidenced by Desert Storm against Iraq). Instead, they use terrorists to compete for them. By directly supporting terrorists, these nations can enhance their own standing among other third-world nations and help bring about the collapse of the superpowers in the free world. With the collapse of communism in Europe, many of these nations stand ready to fill the void by directly supporting terrorist activity.

Terrorists also rely on other terrorist organizations for support, supplies, manpower, and financing (Anable, 1978). In the United States, the far right has developed extensive networks for sharing information, manpower, equipment, and finances. Computer bulletin boards, telephone hot lines, radio shows, and television programs broadcast over satellite have all been utilized to form a nationwide support network for the far right. It is common, for example, to find members of the far right holding joint membership in several different terrorist organizations. All of this interaction is done within a closed and tightly controlled society that is off limits to outsiders.

The advantages listed above also overcome most of the management problems facing the terrorist leader. Some of these management problems include: (1) the need for secrecy and communications within the organization, (2) the ability to coordinate activities, (3) maintaining internal discipline, (4) preventing fragmented ideologies, (5) maintaining logistics, (6) training, and (7) financing (White, 1991). The leader as the organizational center and his direct and almost constant contact with members helps reduce or eliminate all of these management problems. Communications are enhanced and secrecy is maintained because communications are direct from leader to member, coordination of the organization is improved, discipline conforms to the behavioral precepts of punishment, ideological uniformity can be maintained, and logistics, training, and financing can be immediately remedied as they become an issue.

These organizational advantages provide the terrorist a significant advantage in conducting operations, maintaining organizational security, and preventing interception by law enforcement. Being fluid, highly mobile, compartmentalized, and dynamic enables the terrorist to remain outside of the reach of law enforcement intelligence-gathering activities until "after the fact." Because of these organizational advantages, law enforcement is reduced, for the most part, to being reactive instead of proactive. The terrorist has almost free reign to conduct a war of fear and dread against the American public.

CELLULAR STRUCTURE OF
THE TERRORIST ORGANIZATION

As terrorist organizations grow in size, they become more complex and more compartmentalized. With increased size, the terrorist organization becomes less efficient (as does any organization), but this loss in efficiency is negligible in comparison to the formal bureaucratic organization. Any terrorist organization with more than ten to twelve members will become compartmentalized to some degree and have an internal structure, or division of labor. Several of these internal structures are common across different terrorist organizations.

As the terrorist organization grows in size, the structural makeup of the organization will become specialized (Mullins, 1987). Although individuals will be required to have a variety of skills and be able to perform highly diverse functions, the organizational units will become highly specialized. The members assigned to an organizational unit can then be expected to concentrate on a specialty function. Some members will concentrate on and perform sabotage acts, some in bombing operations, some in ambushes, etc. Although all will be cross-trained in other operations, they will be assigned to a unit that specializes in one particular type of operation.

The Red Army Faction in Germany had a three-tier circular arrangement (Horchem, 1993). Basic cells consisted of 15–20 persons and were the operations units of the organization. Cells were surrounded by the Illegal Militants and provided plans and instructions to the cells. The third ring was composed of organization members who called themselves the Political Fighters and formed the Legal Arm of the Red Army Faction. They established philosophy, ideology, and strategy for the Red Army Faction. There were approximately 400 members of the organization in the early 1980s and about 200 of these were Illegal Militants or Political Fighters. All members participated in terror operations.

One unusual dynamic of the Red Army Faction was the communications structure. In the late 1970s, the leaders were arrested and imprisoned. The organization continued to receive instructions from these leaders using sophisticated communications links between the prisons and outside world. To reinforce earlier statements concerning the need for leaders to maintain almost daily contact with the organization and illustrate the individual power of the leader, by the early 1990s, the Red Army Faction had almost ceased to exist as a terroristic organization because the imprisoned leaders could not provide the ongoing fervor in organization members. Members of the organization began to tire of the fight, got disenchanted and quit, retired and returned to mainstream society, and lost the passion for political terrorism. New members were not recruited and the leaders had no influence on bringing in a continuing stream of future terrorists.

This again is a difference between the terrorist organization and other bureaucracies. In a crime syndicate, for example, a member may be assigned to one unit but may be required to perform, on an ongoing basis, many other functions. A person involved in loansharking may be required to collect "numbers," distribute drugs, operate a prostitution ring, etc. In contrast, the terrorist assigned to a specialized unit can concentrate on the one specific task assigned to that unit.

The terrorist organization typically has two distinct types of organizational units, operational units and non-operational units. Operational units are those entrusted with tactical responsibilities (conducting terrorist operations), while non-operational units are responsible for performing non-tactical functions. Non-operational units engage in tasks and assignments necessary to keep the organization operating. Members in this second type of unit have typically been employed in operational units and transfer to a less hostile environment as a reward for past performance. Realize, however, that even non-operational units may be tactically deployed if and when the need arises. Terrorists are, first and foremost, fighters. Everything else the organization is involved in is secondary to the primary function of the organization, the conduct of terrorism.

Operational Units

The most basic operational unit within the terrorist organization is the cell. The cell is responsible for conducting tactical operations against enemy targets (Sterling, 1982, 1986). Cells are limited in membership to 3–10 persons and are purposely kept this small to reduce the chance of organizational compromise. By keeping cells small and close-knit, the organization can help avoid penetration by law enforcement agents or informers (Michel, 1972). Furthermore, each cell is completely autonomous, no one cell knowing of the existence of any other cell. Thus, if one cell is caught or compromised, organizational integrity can be maintained. A cell may even be allowed to conduct operations under a different name than the parent organization, thus further distancing and concealing the parent organization.

In the largest of terrorist organizations, members of a cell may not know of the full extent of the overall plans and goals of the organization. Instead, they will be told only what they need to know to complete an assignment. Each cell will have its own internal leader, an individual who has earned the position by virtue of loyalty and bravery to the organization. The cell leader is also a charismatic individual like the organization leader. The cell leader must be able to motivate the members just like the organizational leader would. The cell leader will typically be the only cell member to have direct contact with the organizational leader.

As the organization increases in size and membership, cells will likely become more specialized, becoming proficient in one or more operations

(Dalager, 1984; Wolf, 1978, 1981). The terrorist organization may have cells that specialize in assassination, communication, escape and evasion, intelligence, passive resistance, propaganda, sabotage, supply and finance, surveillance and security, and operations of bombing, hijacking, etc. An assassination cell, for example, would do nothing but conduct tactical assassination operations. This cell would most likely not even be involved in the planning of the assassination nor the escape and evasion planning of the operation. Instead, other cells may be called upon for those portions of the assassination operation. The assassination cell would enter, "hit" the target, and disappear.

A communications cell would be responsible for planning and establishing the terrorist organization's communication system, including mail drops, phone drops, code systems, and emergency signals. An escape and evasion cell would establish and maintain safe houses and hideouts, develop escape networks, make counterfeit money, make and provide false identification papers, and forge documents. An intelligence collection and target selection cell would engage in intelligence-gathering activities and select operational targets. A passive resistance cell would organize boycotts, demonstrations, marches, riots, sit-ins, strikes, and work slowdowns. In addition, this cell would have the responsibility for decoy operations, such as disturbances and other disruptive activities, while the organization was performing the primary operation. A propaganda cell would print and distribute leaflets, posters, the underground newspaper, prepare radio and television broadcasts, pass rumors, and conduct word-of-mouth campaigns. A sabotage cell would carry out sabotage operations. A supply and finance cell would use methods of coercion, purchase, and theft to obtain supplies and money, as well as distribute the supplies and moneys to the rest of the organization. A surveillance and security cell would be responsible for organizational security and conduct surveillance activities against potential targets, enemies, and suspected infiltrators and/or traitors. The terrorist cell would be the pure operations cell in the organization, conducting operations such as ambushes, bank robbery, bombing, execution, hijacking, kidnapping, and the torture and murder of hostages and/or prisoners. Members of the terrorist cell would have to work up to that position, having to excel in their work and loyalty in other cells.

Burton (1976) suggested groups of similar cells formed columns within the organization. According to his organizational typology, cells (with 4–6 persons each) had specialties and groups of similar cells formed a column. Thus, the organization was arranged like stacks of coins, with leaders as individual coins linking two or more columns. Each column was a semiautonomous unit, each cell having a different but related specialty and a single command structure governing the organization.

Burton (1976) argued this organizational arrangement was too cumbersome for operational utility and such an arrangement was to the benefit of law enforcement authorities because secrecy is too difficult to maintain. Further, he suggested this arrangement would lead to intercolumn friction and competition and this arrangement would only work for operational support. Many terrorist organizations have been and are aligned according to this conceptualization of organizational structure, and most have been highly successful. Some examples would include the various resistance movements in World War II, the North Vietnamese Army, Shining Path in Peru, Castro's revolutionary Cuban freedom fighters, and the Abu Nidal Organization. Figure 4.4 illustrates the columnar arrangement as employed by the Iranian Overseas Network in 1982. Notice that the organizational structure is more boxlike than pyramidal in form and how units are "stacked" rather than laterally disbursed.

From an organizational perspective, the cell-column arrangement actually works to the advantage of the terrorist organization. One, similar units are clustered together within the organization. This simplifies command and control, communications and responsibilities. Two, having similar units functionally aligned enhances command and control responsibilities and improves operational efficiency. Three, from an operational perspective, tactical flexibility and probability of success is increased. Additional units can be readily called in to an operation and add their skills to completing the mission. Four, a columnar arrangement of cells would have little or no effect on organizational security as cells are only informed of organizational information on a "need-to-know" basis, regardless of their position within the organization. Five, cooperation among cells is not dependent upon their positioning within the organization, it is dependent upon the ethos of the organization. Functional placement is irrelevant.

The Red Brigades (Brigate Rosse) had two divisions composed of numerous cells each (Horchem, 1993). Each cell was responsible for a particular type of operation, but each branch was dedicated to a particular ideology of the organization. One branch, the Red Brigades for the Construction of the Fighting Communist Party (BR–PCC), based operations on the notion of anti-imperialism and its operations were international in scope. The other branch, the Union of Fighting Communists (UCC), was dedicated to the concept of proletarianism and was geared to class struggle issues.

The Islamic Hezbollah has three distinct branches (Brooks, 1993). One

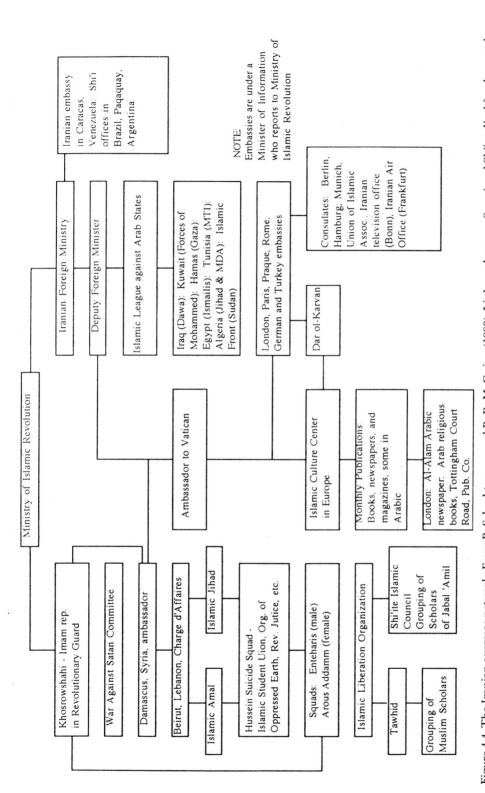

Figure 4.4. The Iranian overseas network. From B. Schechterman and B. R. McGuinn (1990). Linkages between Sunni and Shi'i radical fundamentalist organizations: A new variable in recent middle eastern politics? In B. Schechterman and M. Slann (Eds.), *Violence and terrorism*. Guilford, CT: Dushkin Publishing Group, Inc. Reprint from *The Political Chronicle*, 1989, *1*.

branch engages in technical work and cells construct booby traps, bombs, land mines, placing explosive charges, and camouflage operations. Different cells are responsible for different tasks. The second branch of Hezbollah is responsible for intelligence work. Operatives usually are natives of the Lebanese towns they are assigned to. An additional responsibility of this branch is to penetrate enemy organizations, governments, and other terrorist organizations. The third branch of Hezbollah is the operational arm of the organization and is responsible for performing military and terrorist operations. Each branch operates according to a cellular structure, with different cells responsible for different tasks.

The Abu Nidal Organization (ANO) is a more formal organization than Hezbollah, having two distinct structures (one political and one military) with six functional departments (Wege, 1993). The departments of the ANO are: (1) Organizational Departments charged with developing and maintaining relations with foreign governments and private non-governmental organizations such as student unions. The department also coordinates operational units in the field with the assistance of six regional committees. (2) The Information Department is responsible for security for ANO personnel and functions and for gathering intelligence, counter-intelligence operations, and planning operations. (3) The Political Department has responsibility for organizational propaganda. The ANO, through this department, publishes a news weekly, *Filastin al-Thawra,* and an international monograph, *Al-Tarig,* explaining ANO philosophy, ideology, policy, and personnel issues. (4) The Finance and Economic Department maintains financial records, payroll, other accounting functions, and operates ANO commercial activities. (5) The Lebanon Affairs Department of the ANO is responsible for organizational activity in Lebanon and to establish and maintain relations with other Lebanese terrorist organizations. (6) The Administration Department is responsible for all routine administrative tasks. In addition, the ANO is organized along geographical lines to allow strength and resilience through operational cross-checks. Realize, however, the ANO and PLO are more similar to formal bureaucracies than any other terrorist organizations due to their size, goals, and objectives. Both are larger than many third-world militaries and it is difficult to consider them representative of terrorist organizations in general.

Non-Operational Units

As the terrorist organization gets larger and larger, it becomes necessary for them to add non-operational personnel functions and to form non-operational units. These units and personnel are in non-critical or non-tactical operations within the unit. But to reemphasize a point made earlier, these non-operational personnel are drawn from operational units and are still terrorists first and foremost. Assignment to one of these units may be a reward for gallant service to the unit, reassignment because of age or injury, or assignment for some related reason. If the need arises, these personnel will be placed back into operational units and used to participate in terrorist operations.

Figures 4.5 and 4.6 contrast the two types of larger terrorist organizations. Figure 4.5 illustrates the general terrorist organization, where each cell may perform a myriad of types of operations and other functions. Figure 4.6 illustrates the more specialized organization. In the specialized organization, each cell would be responsible for particular types of operations, such as ambush, or bombing, or sabotage, etc. Additionally, in non-operational areas, each cell would have a different area of expertise, such as propaganda, finance, etc.

This is different from most bureaucratic organizations. In other organizations, support personnel are usually hired and trained to perform only those support operations. They will not participate in organizational operations. In a police department, for example, secretaries and administrative support personnel will not be given a firearm and other hardware and sent out into the streets during an emergency or crisis situation. They may be called in during an emergency, but to perform support functions. In the terrorist organization, the terrorist is a terrorist first, foremost, and always.

One non-operational unit may be the clandestine press. This unit would be responsible for the preparation and dissemination of propaganda efforts, newspapers, leaflets, and distribute general information about the organization. In some terrorist organizations, the clandestine press may utilize sophisticated satellite telecommunications equipment to spread propaganda. The Aryan Nations has a radio show they use as a forum to spread their philosophy and recruit new members (Staff, 1987). Thomas Metzger, former Grand Dragon of the Ku Klux Klan and self-proclaimed leader of the skinhead movement, produced and hosted a satellite television program called *Race and Reason.* Also, the clandestine press is responsible for claiming responsibility for activities of the organization and making news releases.

Terrorist organizations are the only criminal organizations to employ a clandestine press unit. Most other criminal syndicates do not want the public to know of their criminal activities. The last thing drug cartels want to do, for example, is to broadcast the location, amount, and sale

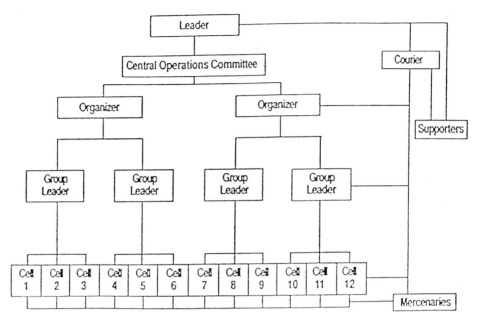

Figure 4.5. Flowchart of the generalist terrorism organization.

price of drugs they produce. To these organizations, a press unit would be a "red flag" for law enforcement authorities to home-in on and destroy the operation. To the terrorist, a press is merely part of doing business and the associated risks are merely part of the terrorist's world.

A second non-operational unit within the terrorist organization are couriers. Couriers are individuals selected to establish and maintain communication networks within the organization. Couriers are highly trusted individuals who relay communications between cells and/or leaders within the organization. Couriers may not personally know any members of the organization, or if they do, they will know very few individuals and not be able to compromise the organization if caught. Neither is it usually necessary for couriers to come into direct contact with any members of the organization. They can receive communications via telephone, newspaper, radio, satellite, etc.

In delivering messages, couriers utilize drop points or cutouts, locations where messages and communications are traded by members of the organization. These help insure that members never have to come into contact with one another. Not only are the drop points and cutouts constantly changed, couriers may utilize "dead" drops to lead authorities astray. Additionally, couriers constantly monitor communication points for any hint of surveillance or compromise.

Couriers may also have the responsibility of purchasing arms, equipment, and supplies for the terrorist organization. It is suspected that the individuals responsible for PanAm Flight 103 over Lockerbee, Scotland utilized couriers to obtain the Toshiba radios and plastic explosives used

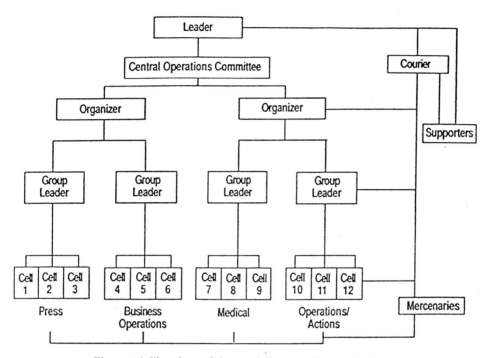

Figure 4.6. Flowchart of the specialist terrorist organization.

to make the bombs that brought down that airplane. The trust in couriers must be absolute. A courier who becomes an informant or who is captured and compromised can bring about the downfall of the entire terrorist organization. Carlos Marighella, in the later stages of his career as a terrorist, was employed as a courier. Not a good fighter, Marighella was nevertheless loyal and dedicated to the cause of the overthrow of the Bolivian government and served the terrorist movement superbly as a courier.

Supporters are another non-operational unit employed by terrorist organizations. Supports are individuals who voluntarily or unknowingly assist the terrorist organization. Supporters are primarily used for monetary contributions. In many instances, supporters may not be aware of the true nature and purpose of the terrorist organization. For example, the author recently received a letter asking for donations to support a congressional lobby concerned with pressuring Congress to demand a search for Vietnam MIAs. Any money donated would have actually gone to a far-right organization and used for conducting a terrorist campaign against the government, minorities, and Jews. Gordon Kahl, member of the Sheriff's Posse Comitatus, was provided shelter by several supporters during his flight from federal authorities. These people were not members of the Posse Comitatus but were sympathetic to the cause of that organization.

Supporters may also be fringe members of the organization, or persons of the same nationality as the terrorists and sympathetic to their cause. In the United States, for example, many former citizens of Cuba have been utilized to assist in Cuban drug dealing, assisting representatives of Castro's government while in the U.S., and for providing arms caches, safe houses, money-laundering activities, and providing other resources and support to Castro.

Terrorists may utilize umbrella businesses as part of their nonoperational structure. The purpose of having these businesses is to provide financial support for the terrorist organization. Most organized crime syndicates operate umbrella businesses. The major difference between organized crime and terrorist organizations are who operates these businesses. In the case of organized crime, umbrella businesses are usually operated by non-members. For example, the "Mafia" often makes loans to non-member citizens to open legitimate businesses (Anderson, 1979) and are then used by the "Mafia" to make a profit, launder money, provide a meeting place, provide a tax shelter, dispose of stolen merchandise, hire syndicate members who are on probation or parole, etc. Eventually, the business owner may tire of the illegal activities or constant interference and turn informant against the organization. Thus, law enforcement authorities can build an intelligence case and prosecute the syndicate through the activities of this business.

The terrorist organization, on the other hand, uses organizational members in operating the business and avoids using the business in direct operational support of the organization. Primarily, the business remains legitimate and is for the purpose of generating income for the organization. On occasion, the business may be used to launder money, provide employment for members, serve as a drop point or cutout for communications, be a meeting place, repository, or delivery point for arms, receive supplies, and serve as a storage place for organizational equipment. The PLO, for example, operates duty-free shops at airports, raises chickens and eggs in Guana, and invests on Wall Street. Jim Ellison of the Covenant, Sword and Arm of the Lord operated a religious

bookstore in Harrison, Arkansas. Other right-wing organizations operate paramilitary/survivalist stores.

Finally, terrorists may employ mercenaries to assist the organization
in accomplishing its goals. Mercenaries are soldiers for hire employed
by the organization on a per-job basis. Mercenaries are not members of
the organization, may not be aware of the organization's philosophy or
goals, and may not even know who actually hired them. Mercenaries are
typically employed by couriers or supporters and are nothing more than
"hired guns." They may be brought in to the organization as consultants, trainers, to conduct a specialized operation, or participate with
members in a large-scale operation. In addition, mercenaries, because of
their military expertise, may be brought in to help plan a specific
operation.

The use of mercenaries is risky for the terrorist organization because
they work strictly for the money. The mercenary has no loyalty to the
organization, to a political purpose, or to some higher morality. They
work for the highest bidder and if the going gets too tough, they may
pull out of the operation or become an informant for law enforcement
authorities. Terrorist organizations operating in the United States have
little history of employing mercenaries to conduct operations, although
some U.S. citizens have served as mercenaries for foreign-based terrorist
organizations. In the U.S., domestic terrorist organizations typically have
employed mercenaries for training purposes. This has also been true for
foreign terrorists located in the U.S. For example, the assassins of Anwar
Sadat were trained at a paramilitary/survivalist training center in Alabama run by a member of the Ku Klux Klan. The persons who operated
this training camp were mercenaries, offering to train anyone who had
the money.

LEADERSHIP IN THE TERRORIST ORGANIZATION

In the very smallest of terrorist organizations, the leader of the organization is in direct and daily contact with the rank-and-file membership.
The leader is a member of the cell and works side by side with members.
As the organization grows, the leader will become more removed from
everyday operations and become more of a manager. His role will still be
to guide daily and long-term operations of the organization, but his role
becomes less of a terrorist operative and more of a terrorist manager. He
will still remain in contact with the organization, exert his absolute
control over the organization, and retain the mystical aura of leadership,
but his time will become more consumed with management functions. At

one point, if the organization continues to grow, he will need a cadre of leaders to assist him in managing the organization.

As cells are added, the organization will employ group leaders whose responsibility will be to control several cells. Group leaders rise from the rank and are promoted based upon their courage and loyalty to the organization. The number of cells any one group leader has responsibility for will be limited. More than a span-of-control issue, the limit on the number of cells commanded is due primarily to issues of organizational penetration or compromise. As the span of control increases, the more possible it becomes for infiltration into the organization. If captured, the group leader could do significant damage to the organization by having too large a span of control.

A second responsibility group leaders have is to make detailed plans for tactical operations. Group leaders are not involved in target selection or strategic decision making. They merely work out the tactical arrangements once targets have been selected and strategic priorities established. Group leaders may not know of the overall objectives of a particular tactical operation, or the long-range goal the operation is to accomplish. Their role is purely tactical command and their position is analogous to the mid-level commander in the military or police agency.

Above the group leaders are the organizers, who have responsibility for both strategic and tactical operation planning. Organizers are comparable to the executive vice-presidents in legitimate bureaucracies and underbosses and caporegime in organized crime syndicates (Cressey, 1967). Organizers select targets which fit into the overall goals of the terrorist organization and which will arouse the most sympathy for the organization. Organizers have a heavy responsibility in the terrorist organization, as their decisions on targets will result in fear and advance the organization's goals, or result in anger and be detrimental to the organization. Organizers may be in command of several group leaders and report directly to the organization's leader.

At the very top of the terrorist organization is the central operations committee, composed of organizers and leader. This "board of directors" is responsible for establishing the short- and long-term goals for the organization, maintaining discipline and order within the organization, strategic planning, and insuring the goals of the organization are being achieved or moved toward. In short, the central operations committee has the task of keeping the organization on course to its goals.

In the Abu Nidal Organization, the Central Committee served as decision makers answerable to the organization's Politburo (top leaders). The Politburo, led by Al-banna, was formed by organizational constitution in 1985 and had ten members. The Central Committee consisted of 40 members, some elected and some appointed by the Politburo of Abu Nidal. In addition to responsibility for daily operations, the Central Committee was entrusted to establish organizational ideology (Wege, 1993). In a 1989 purge designed to streamline the Abu Nidal Organization, some powers were removed from the Politburo and Central Committee and the units became largely functionary.

When applicable, the central operations committee will work with governments sympathetic to the terrorist's cause and establish relationships beneficial to both parties. The central operations committee may even establish embassy-like offices in foreign countries. If there is more than one government interested in helping the organization, the central operations committee has the added responsibility of serving as mediator between those governments so harmonious, working relationships can be developed, with neither government feeling slighted. If the organization has to negotiate with a government, as in the case of a hostage situation, the central operations committee will conduct those negotiations. They will establish demands, modify demands, and either ultimately accept or reject demand packages.

On occasion, the central operations committee of several terrorist organizations may work together to reach mutual accords, common strategies for common goals, and divide operations. Joint operations between terrorist organizations are not uncommon events. In 1982 in Hayden Lake, Idaho, leading members from several right-wing terrorist organizations met to draft a new American "Constitution." At this meeting were leaders from the Aryan Nations, Ku Klux Klan, Mountain Church of Michigan, and Texas Emergency Reserves (Sapp, 1986). This meeting was one of the biggest single factors leading to the unification of the far right in the United States. Similar meetings have occurred between leaders of foreign-based terrorist organizations as well. Examples include the PLO–Baader-Meinhof Gang, Red Brigades-Red Army Faction, and Hezbollah-PLO, to name just a few.

The fully integrated terrorist organization is a dynamic, organized, and efficient force to contend with. American law enforcement officials are at a decided disadvantage when dealing with terrorists, in large part because they do not understand the organizational dynamics of the terrorist. Successful counter-terrorist units such as Delta Force, the Navy Seals teams, Israeli Mossad, English SAS and SBS, and German GS–G9 are effective because they do understand the organizational dynamics at play in terrorist organizations. Most of these counter-terrorist units, in fact, are organized along the same lines and operate in the same manner as the terrorist organization. This organizational structure often presents difficulty for the counter-terrorist unit, because it is a structure at odds with the larger military bureaucracy they work within.

FINANCING TERRORISM

Just as with the legitimate organization, it costs money to be a terrorist. Organizational operations, the production and distribution of propaganda, terrorist operations, supplies, weapons, logistics, materials, the operation of safe houses, transportation, and routine feeding and caring for terrorists requires financial expenditures. A political idea without the capital funds necessary to achieve the political goal will not make for a very successful or long-lived terrorist. Even if terrorists were to steal enough arms and ammunition (or explosives) to conduct a terrorist operation, it would still require money to actually conduct that operation. One of the major objectives of the organization, even if unstated in the organization's goals, is to obtain financing to maintain the organization and engage in terroristic activities.

There are several avenues open to the terrorist to obtain money, some legitimate, others not legitimate. One method of obtaining money is through the use of supporters. The terrorist can solicit funds directly from those sympathetic to their cause. Conversely, terrorists can solicit funds through a seemingly legitimate front organization and divert the funds to their organization. Libya has provided millions of dollars to Palestinian, Latin American and European terrorist organizations (Kidder, 1990). Saudi Arabia donates $30–$40 million annually to the PLO. North Korea, Iran, Iraq, Syria, Chad, Cuba, the USSR, and China are just a few of the countries which financially support terrorist organizations.

The terrorist organization can also raise funds by operating a legitimate business. Net profits from this business would be funneled to support the terrorist organization and its activities. Jim Ellison of the CSA operated a religious bookstore, other right-wing organizations operate paramilitary/survivalist stores, and other organizations have been involved in a range of businesses (Mullins, 1986). Most Mideast and European terrorist organizations have been owners and operators of legitimate business concerns used to finance their terrorism. The Abu Nidal Organization operated the SAS Trade and Investment Company in Warsaw, Poland. This business was a sales brokerage house for black market arms and other goods and was primarily for government trading, including East Germany, Poland, Iran, and Iraq (Wege, 1993). In addition Abu Nidal received government subsidies from these and other governments to support their organization.

One of the most popular methods to raise money for United States terrorist organizations has been robbery and theft. Members of the Order conducted a series of bank robberies and armored truck robberies in the western part of the United States in the 1980s. The most infamous occurred in Ukiah, California, when over $3 million was stolen in the robbery of a Brinks armored truck. The United Freedom Front conducted a series of bank robberies on the East Coast to finance their campaign of bombings. Several Puerto Rican separatists organizations, including the FALN, were involved in numerous robberies of banks, stores, shops, and armored trucks to finance their terrorist campaign. Most of the leaders of the FALN were arrested and convicted in Connecticut for their role in the robbery of a Wells Fargo depot.

Theft of weapons, arms, ammunition, and explosives are common in the terrorist world. Most weapons used by terrorists, particularly in the United States, have come from thefts of police and military armories. Most U.S. bombings, incidentally, have involved homemade explosive devices. Both the World Trade Center bombing and Oklahoma Federal Building bombing involved homemade explosives using ammonium nitrate as the explosive. Even using homemade components, explosives are still expensive. Members of the Weather Underground made the FBI's "top ten" fugitive list for the theft of arms from a Texas National Guard armory. Many of the weapons found in possession of Order members, at the CSA compound, and in various Klan seizures were traced to weapons thefts from various sources.

Weapons are also supplied by sympathetic governments. U.S.-based and foreign terrorist organizations have all received arms from governments. Iran, for example, has received over $1 billion worth of arms from North Korea (Pollack, 1990). Libya has supplied weapons to the Sandinista's in Nicaragua and terrorists in Grenada. Cuba, Syria, Iran, Iraq, Chad, Russia, China, Bulgaria, East Germany, Poland, Tunisia, and Turkey have all supplied arms to terrorist organizations.

Terrorists also make money from the growth, distribution, and sale of drugs. Shining Path in Peru makes millions of dollars annually from drug sources. The South American Tupameros are involved in the drug trade, M19CO in Colombia, the ANO, PLO, Red Army Faction, and both the far left and far right in the United States have made money from the drug business (Mullins, 1990c). To the terrorist, drugs are not only a way to secure funds, they also help achieve political goals and objectives.

Many organizations use multiple sources to obtain funds. The world's largest and most organized terrorist organization, the PLO, exemplifies the diversity of fund raising terrorists engage in. The PLO has numerous business ventures, including an airline company in the Maldive Islands, operating duty-free shops in African airports, exporting pineapples to France and Russia, farms and ranches throughout the Mideast, Asia, and Africa, and investment companies in several nations (Rosewicz & Seib, 1990). They own and operate news agencies, produce children's clothes in factories in Thailand and shoes in Lebanon. In fact, the PLO is the largest egg producer in Guinea. They receive donations from foreign governments sympathetic to their cause, donations from individuals, and are involved in various illegal operations. Palestinians living in Arab countries pay a PLO tax of 5%–7% of gross pay per year. Total, the annual operating budget of the PLO exceeds $220 million.

The PLO has a branch to manage their financial affairs, the Palestine National Fund. Approximately $87 million annually is dedicated to the Palestine Liberation Army, $10 million to health care for Palestinians, and $10 million to support their diplomatic missions. Money made by the PLO is spent in a variety of ways. The PLO distributes over $52 million per year in social security payments. Payments are made to approximately 60,000 Palestinian families per month. If a PLO soldier gets killed, for example, his family receives a lifetime pension and free medical care for life. They support a standing force of approximately 14,000 persons and operate a military air force. The PLO owns and operates hospitals, universities, and other social welfare agencies for Palestinians. They provide loans to foreign governments. In the 1980s, the PLO loaned Egypt several million dollars. In addition, the PLO operates diplomatic missions in over 90 countries (Rosewicz & Seib, 1990).

TRAINING OF TERRORISTS

The public and many law enforcement personnel have a mental conception of the terrorist being a wild-eyed, fanatical, raving maniac or psychotic. This is the image terrorists want the public to have. Terrorists are none of those things. They are motivated, dedicated individuals who are calculating and cunning. Terrorist operations are conducted by individuals who not only have the necessary political agenda for brutality, they are also well-trained to be successful in conducting operations. In point of fact, most terrorists receive more training than the majority of law enforcement personnel.

Most police officers receive 400–800 hours of initial training and then may average 40 hours of training per year for the rest of their career. This 40 hours of additional training usually revolves around some basic, state-mandated requirement, such as firearms requalification, driving techniques, baton or nightstick training, and handcuffing procedures. If the officer is promoted or progresses through the career ladder, she may receive specialized training for her new position. Investigators, for example, will go to a criminal investigation course. These specialized courses typically range in length from 40–80 hours of instruction, with possibly an additional 8–20 hours at a later date.

In contrast, the terrorist's initial training period may be six months or more, which translates to roughly 1,000 hours of initial training (Mullins, 1987, 1988). Following this training, many terrorists continue the training regime for the rest of their careers. Terrorist training is comparable to training received by specialized military units, and much of this training follows the guidelines for terrorist training outlined by Carlos Marighella in his *Minimanual of the Urban Guerrilla* (Deakin, 1974).

Individual Training

Even though the potential terrorist already espouses the tenets and doctrines of the terrorist organization, the early part of their training will consist almost entirely of political indoctrination. This political indoctrination will permeate all of their training and be an underlying part of everything they are taught. In terrorist training camps in North Korea, Lebanon, Iran, Iraq, and the United States, all recruit terrorists receive massive doses of political indoctrination that lasts from the start of training through their entire career as terrorists. This political indoctrination blends political philosophy with organizational doctrine to insure the recruit fits into the organizational framework. For an example, to the Ku Klux Klan, it is not sufficient that the recruit believes in racial superiority and separatism. The recruit needs to practice the particular "brand" of racism of the KKK and to understand Klan tactics in order to practice this form of racism.

The recruit will receive physical training consisting of regular physical endurance training (such as running, calisthenics, weight lifting, etc.) and specialized training in physical fighting techniques. The recruit will be taught boxing, offensive combat fighting, defensive fighting, martial arts, hand-to-knife, and knife-to-knife techniques. The recruit will be taught a variety of techniques for killing, including killing by hand, using materials available on the scene, garrotes (wires used for strangling), and blade and impact weapons. In most terrorist training sites, this physical training is modeled after military training and, in most cases, taught by military or ex-military personnel. Many paramilitary/survivalist training sites in the U.S. use ex-special forces mercenaries to conduct this training.

The recruit will be well-schooled in the operation and maintenance of various firearms. He will be taught to competently use a wide range of firearms, including various handguns, rifles, shotguns, automatic weapons, heavy weapons such as surface-to-air missiles (SAMs), light anti-tank weapons (LAWs), and rocket-propelled grenades (RPGs). The recruit will become proficient in the use of all of these weapons because he may, without notice, have to use any one of these weapons during an operation. Weapons caches of the IRA and extremist organizations in the United States have been found to contain a wide variety of handguns, several different calibers of rifles, a range of automatic weapons, and the heavy weapons like SAMS, LAWs, and RPGs. The recruit will be required to learn how to maintain and care for these weapons, repair the weapon in field conditions and "kit-bash" parts and how to make or reload ammunition for these weapons.

In addition to use of weapons, the recruit will be taught how to make various weapons, ranging from single-use pistols and shotguns to heavy weapons. The making of "zip" guns, single-use weapons made from scrap parts and firing a variety of cartridges ranging from .22 calibers to 12-gauge shotgun shells will be taught. Homemade RPGs will be covered. While easy to make, the skills necessary to make these weapons are important skills and valuable to the terrorist.

The recruit will be taught how to make and use explosive devices. The recruit will be taught the difference between high and low explosives, explosive charges, detonators, fuses, and constructing shape charges. The recruit will learn how to use purchased or factory-made devices such as hand grenades, dynamite, nitroglycerin, and various forms of plastique (C-4, RDX, PETN, etc.). Additionally, the recruit will receive instructions in the construction of homemade explosive devices utilizing readily bought compounds. Because so many terrorists are killed in the construction of explosive devices, safety issues will be emphasized.

At many training sites, advanced weapons of mass destruction are covered and taught. Nuclear, biological, and chemical weapons construction and usage are taught to the recruit. This training will include instruction on the construction of clandestine biological and chemical laboratories and the making of biological and chemical weapons. Materials used, obtaining materials, producing materials, delivery system construction, and safety issues are part of the training regimen (Mullins, 1991, 1992).

The full range of paramilitary skills will be taught to the recruit. Paramilitary tactics, police tactics, and techniques for countering rescue forces will be taught. Techniques to slow or defeat police and rescue forces will be taught. The strengths and weaknesses of specific counterterrorist organizations will be discussed and the recruit taught how to exploit these organizations for their own purposes.

The use, collection, analysis, and dissemination of intelligence and intelligence gathering will be taught. Types of intelligence, handling intelligence information, and the proper use of intelligence will be covered and the recruit taught to operate with intelligence data. The need to carefully maintain and disseminate intelligence information will be emphasized.

Outdoor skills will be taught to the recruit. Hiking, camping, swimming, mountain climbing, map-reading and mapmaking, and orientation skills (using a compass and/or sextant to find one's way) will be part of the training curriculum. The recruit will be taught outdoor survival skills such as foraging for food, obtaining shelter, and making clothing. Urban survival skills will also be covered in this part of training. Blending into a particular society or segment of society, blending into a crowd, site surveillance, mapping skills, and site selection are part of the urban survival curriculum.

The recruit will learn to drive and repair many different types of vehicles. In addition to land vehicles, training may include learning to sail, operate motor boats and ships, flying planes, and piloting helicopters. The recruit will be taught how to use evasion techniques when using these vehicles. Part of this training will focus on the theft of vehicles, for the terrorist organization will rarely use purchased vehicles during operations.

Training in surveillance techniques will be taught, along with how to detect and evade surveillance. The recruit will be taught how to use disguises and how to blend in with the environment. The establishment, operation and maintenance of safe houses will be covered, including how to remain unobtrusive to neighbors. The Red Brigade manual, *Security Rules and Methods,* cautions the recruit:

> [You] should appear respectable, proud of your homes and regularly employed. Apartments should be proletarian, modest, clean, neat and completely furnished. Use curtains, entrance light, and nameplate in place. Window boxes are recommended to help provide an air of respectability. Don't make noise at night and do everything possible to reassure the neighbors. Make sure hideout is on a street where the police would find it difficult to watch. Dirty cars attract attention. . . .

An important part of this training involves escape and evasion techniques and how to endure interrogation and torture. Along similar lines, a training manual for the Order advises members:

> Cars being used for anti-ZOG activities should be registered to a completely fictitious third party. . . . Every time you are stopped for a ticket it becomes necessary to sell your car and purchase another (because your driver's license and car tag are tied together by authorities). . . . (Kansas City Star, 1985; Wiggins, 1986)

The final portion of combat operations training focuses on conducting specific types of terrorist operations. The recruit will learn to booby-trap buildings and vehicles, conduct operations of sabotage, set up ambushes, carry out assassinations, and perform kidnappings (including victim selection, ransom demands, victim release, checking for surveillance, etc.). Hostage-taking operations will be taught, including the selection of hostages, care of hostages, and demand issues. Along with this training in hostage taking, skills used by hostage negotiators are taught so the terrorist is familiar with the strategies negotiators will use in trying to resolve the situation. Knowing what negotiators do enables the terrorist to counter those strategies.

After the recruit has been taught the basic skills of terrorism, the recruit will learn other related skills to increase their proficiency. Basic and advanced first-aid and medical care will be taught. Many terrorists have as much knowledge and skill in treating injuries as many emergency room personnel. The recruit will learn stamping and forgery techniques for the construction of false documents and identity. Electronics will be taught so the recruit is proficient in using, maintaining, and repairing (or ruining) radios, telephones, televisions, computers, satellite receivers, and other machines of electronic communications.

Terrorist training emphasizes computer skills. Basic computer operations and programming, linking via computer, and breaching computer systems will be taught. Planting and detecting viruses and computer security will be part of the curriculum.

Depending upon the goals and objectives of the terrorist organization, specialty topics will be part of the training program. An eco-terrorist organization might, for example, be taught how to "spike" trees, cut power poles, or sabotage road machinery. Methods for interfering with whaling operations may be part of the training. If a terrorist is planning a specific type of operation, they may receive more specialized training in that specific operation, including full-scale mock-ups of the target and actual practice on taking out that target. The Abu Nidal Organization, for example, isolates a cell once it is selected for an operation (Pollack, 1990) and brings in specialists such as the Japanese, Germans, or Cubans to provide training specific to operational objectives (Wege, 1993).

To more fully understand the training terrorists receive, Table 4.1 lists the training programs conducted by three right-wing extremist organizations in the United States. Many of these training concepts have been outlined in the novel, *The Turner Diaries* (Holden, 1986).

Upon completion of the training program, the recruit may be tested before being allowed to join the organization or participate in operations. This test will most likely be some form of practical examination, where the recruit is required to perform some type of terrorist action. The Montoneros in Argentina, for example, use both written and practical examinations before allowing the recruit to join the organization. For the operational part of the examination, the recruit is required to kill a police officer.

Training Centers

Most foreign terrorist training camps are sponsored by communist regimes or third-world dictators and are located in these countries (Dobson & Payne, 1982). The Soviet GRU sponsors many training facilities (Ledeen, 1986) and have trained European, Asian, Mideast, Central and South American terrorists (Goren, 1984; Vaksburg, 1991). Soviets have trained the Motoneros in Argentina, the Bandera Roja in Venezuela, the FMLN in El Salvador, and FSLN in Nicaragua (Kirkpatrick, 1986). Soviet in-country terrorist training centers are located at Simferpol and Lumumba University in Moscow, and Soviet personnel have been involved in training activities at the old East German training center at Pankow and the Czechoslovakian training center at Ostrova. In addition, Soviet trainers and military members have provided terrorist training to organizations all over the world. The Soviet military and KGB conduct training worldwide for various terrorist organizations (Douglas, 1990; Ehrenfield, 1990).

The Soviet Union and other Eastern bloc countries not only provide training for terrorists, they also support terrorists politically, legally, morally, and with equipment and supplies (Netanyahu, 1986; U.S. Department of State, 1985). Additionally, the Soviets have provided legal assistance to captured terrorists and worked to prevent passage of international treaties and agreements providing for the extradition of terrorists. Evidence suggests the Soviets also played a role in he attempted assassination of Pope John Paul II (1986). The Soviets perceived the Pope as a

Table 4.1.
Training curricula for three United States right-wing terrorist organizations.

The Covenant, Sword, and Arm of the Lord	*Christian Patriots Defense League Citizen's Emergency Defense System*
Attack formations	Archery
Basic rifle and pistol	Brainwashing techniques
Christian martial arts	City escape
Christian military truths	Combat medicine
First aid	Crossbow
Hand signals	Unarmed defense
Military dress	Government control by the Jews
Military equipment	Guns and reloading
Military fieldcraft	Intelligence gathering
Personal home defense	Knife making and use
Searching landscapes	Legal use of lethal force
Special weapons	Marksmanship and handgun use
Urban warfare	Military fieldcraft
Weapons proficiency	Organizing CEDS units
Wilderness survival	Personal and home defense
	Protection dog training
	Recruitment of new members
	Safe houses (patriots in flight)
	Security control
	Security weapons
	Self-defense
	Stick fighting
	Weapons selection

Armed Resistance Movement	
Actions against tanks/armored vehicles	Intelligence gathering
Ambushes	Interrogation techniques
Assassinations	Personal combat
Base camps	Physical & photographic security
Booby traps	Physical & psychological training
Camping and woodcraft	Posting of sentries
Code and cipher systems	Principles of organization
Combat & reconnaissance patrols	Psychological defense against communism
Combat tactics	Raids
Communications & security	Recruiting new members
Counter-intelligence techniques	Rifles
Escape & evasion techniques	Sabotage
Espionage	Scouting & patrolling
Explosives	Scouts & snipers
First aid	Security
Guerrilla warfare	Small arms
Hunt & kill groups (techniques)	Small unit combat
Improvised weapons & techniques	Subversion
Infiltration & espionage	Theory of resistant movements
	Unconventional weapons & warfare
	Underground warfare

political threat and helped in the hiring and training of a member of the Turkish Mafia to assassinate him. The belief of the Soviets was the assassination would not bring down world condemnation upon them for eliminating a political threat.

Since the dissolution of the old Soviet republic, other communist regimes have replaced Soviet training of terrorism (which does not imply that the Soviets no longer train terrorists). South Yemen, Vietnam, and North Korea have stepped forward to fill the void left by the Soviets (Levy, 1978; Johnson, 1986). Predominant among these have been the North Koreans. According to Pollack (1990), North Koreans have been involved in terrorist training and support in Africa, Central America, South America, Grenada, Puerto Rico, Mexico, and Costa Rica. Zambia uses North Koreans for the training of defense and security personnel. In 1982, in Zimbabwe, the Zimbabwe Fifth Brigade, with assistance from North Korean forces, killed thousands of people in the Matabeleland massacre. The North Koreans have trained over 5,000 terrorists since 1969 in more than 30 training camps. Terrorists organizations the North Koreans have provided training for include the Sandinista National Liberation Front, Angolan People's Movement for the Liberation of Angola, the PLO, the Mozambique Liberation Front, Red Brigades, Baader-Meinhof Gang, and Abu Nidal Organization.

South Yemen operates terrorist training camps and uses the Popular Front for the Liberation of Palestine to train other terrorists. Terrorist organizations that have trained in Yemen include the Basque ETA, Red Army Faction, IRA, Italian Red Brigades, PLO, and other Palestinian organizations (Kidder, 1990).

Bulgaria has been involved in training and aiding terrorist organizations. Most notably, the Bulgarians assisted the Red Brigades in 1981 to kidnap General Dozier and were implicated for intelligence assistance in the attempt upon the life of Pope John Paul II (Mullins & Mijares, 1992). Bulgaria has also housed terrorist embassies, provided safe havens, and supplied money, arms, equipment, and manpower to terrorist organizations.

On the other side of the world, the Cubans have been a mainstay in the training of terrorists since the early 1960s. They provide terrorist training in Cuba as well as traveling around the globe to train terrorists. The Cuban presence has been observed in terrorist acts throughout Central and South America, Africa, the Mideast, Europe, and Asia.

The Mideast continues to be the major center for terrorist training activities (Segal, 1986). In Libya, which operates over 20 terrorist training camps, training centers are located at Tocra, Tarhuna, Misurato, Sirte, Rabta, Sebha Oasis, and Mahad near Tripoli (Nordland & Wilkinson,

1990). Even the spring 1986 bombing by President Reagan of the Tocra, Tarhuna, Misurato, and Sirta camps did not slow Libyan involvement in terrorist training. At these camps, terrorists from Barbados, Chile, Colombia, Costa Rica, Dominica, El Salvador, Honduras, St. Lucia, Surinam, Oceana, Asia, western Europe, the Mideast, and Africa have received training (Pollack, 1990). Libyans have supplied arms and training to the Sandinista's in Nicaragua, El Salvador, and Grenada.

Training sites are located near Sabra, Shatila, Burj al-Barajneh, Beirut, Hammara, and the Bekaa Valley in Lebanon (Hammara is the Abu Nidal rear base camp). European terrorists from Italy, Germany, Spain, and Turkey regularly train at these camps (Becker, 1986). Syria, Tunisia, Iraq, and Iran all have numerous training facilities. The Abu Nidal Organization, for example, regularly trains at Habbaniyah (near Ramadi) and Hit, Iraq. Terrorists from around the world have trained at these and similar camps throughout the Mideast. At Qom, Iran, over 2,000 terrorists from over 20 countries have received training, including the terrorists involved in the 1985 Rome and Vienna airport massacres, the terrorists who attacked the U.S. embassy in Kuwait in 1985, and the Shiite terrorists who bombed the Marine barracks in Beirut that same year (Kidder, 1990).

In Central and South America, terrorists are routinely trained and welcomed with open arms. In Nicaraguan camps, staffed by Nicaraguans, Cubans, Libyans and PLO terrorists, Latin American terrorists have received extensive training. Organizations who have received training at the camps include the Montoneros, Tupameros, Shining Path, and others. Additionally, European terrorists such as the Baader-Meinhof Gang, IRA, and Italian Red Brigades have trained in Nicaragua.

Some foreign terrorists have received training in the United States. One of the Sikh terrorists accused of planning the murder of Rajiv Gandhi and suspected of having sabotaged the Air India jet which crashed into the North Atlantic, killing 329 people, was trained at Frank Camper's Reconnaissance Commando School near Birmingham, Alabama (Stinson, 1993; World Press Review, 1985).

In the 1970s and 1980s, numerous terrorist training facilities have sprung up in the United States. These training sites attempt to disguise themselves as survivalist/paramilitary training centers to avoid close examination by law enforcement authorities. The Aryan Nations has training facilities in Idaho and Oregon. The CSA conducted training in the Ozark Mountains near Harrison, Arkansas, in the northwest part of the state. The Jewish Defense League trains in the California desert. The Ku Klux Klan operates several different training facilities throughout the southern and eastern United States (Mullins, 1990a, 1990b). At many of these facilities, the indoctrination and training of children receives as much attention as does the training of adults, as the extreme far right sees the early training of children crucial to their long-range goals (Sapp, 1985). Some law enforcement authorities believe the Sheriff's Posse Comitatus is developing a training site in south Texas (personal communication). Many far-right organizations are relocating their training compounds from the mid-American Ozark mountain region into the desert country of the Southwest, west Texas, Arizona, New Mexico, Utah, and Colorado because of the population growth in the Ozarks (Mullins, 1993).

Regardless of where they are trained, terrorists receive much more extensive training than do their adversaries in law enforcement. At the international level, counterterrorist units receive comparable training (i.e., Navy Seals, Delta Force, GS–G9, British SAS, etc.). For domestic terrorist organizations, however, the Constitution prevents using military units to respond to domestic issues. The law enforcement personnel assigned to combat the problem of terrorism are at a distinct disadvantage due to training differences. Combine this with the perception law enforcement has of a "bunch of nuts running around" and the terrorist is a formidable foe.

SUMMARY

The terrorist organization is highly efficient, fluid, and able to dynamically change as circumstances or situations dictate. The terrorist organization is much more efficient and operationally effective than the bureaucracies law enforcement works within. The leader as a catalyst for action applies not only to operational programs and actions but also to maintaining the integrity of the organization. His personal intervention within daily organizational life keeps the terrorist one step ahead of law enforcement and keeps the terrorist constantly in a ready-alert state.

The inability to understand the dynamics and workings of the terrorist organization assists the terrorist in accomplishing his goals and has proven to be a hindrance to stopping terrorism. Few people understand, and fewer still recognize, just how important the functional organization is to the terrorist and achieving his objectives. By understanding the terrorist organization and knowing how to intercede into the organizational life of the terrorist, inroads can be achieved in putting the terrorist out of business.

Understanding and knowing the skills and abilities of terrorists are just as crucial in stopping terrorism. Most people were surprised that a lone terrorist could produce an explosive device capable of destroying a building the size of the Oklahoma City Federal Building. Had they understood the regime of training the terrorist is exposed to, it should not have been a surprise. The device used in Oklahoma City was one of the simplest devices terrorists are taught how to use. The ability to reconnoiter, surveil, and place the bomb were all basic skills taught the terrorist.

Failure to recognize the training received by terrorists and the extent of their skills will prevent us from ever stopping terrorism. It is vital that law enforcement personnel fully understand and know their adversary. The belief that terrorists are untrained, unskilled, and have deep-seated psychological problems will continue to hamper our efforts of arrest and continue to serve the terrorist's goals by increasing public fear of terrorism.

Knowing the organizational structure and training programs of terrorists will allow us to be much more proactive in our efforts to stop terrorism. It will also help us to predict future terrorist activity, where that activity may occur, and who may be involved in that activity. A dedicated proactive approach based upon a full understanding of terrorist society is necessary before we can become proactive, however. Continuing our approach of reactive response will continue to cost lives, keep the citizens fearful, and lead to even more terrorist atrocities.

Chapter 5

UNITED STATES TERRORIST ORGANIZATIONS*

Although no accurate estimates exist, there are probably somewhere around 2,500–3,000 terrorist organizations throughout the world (although Aho, 1990, suggested at least 3,500 in the United States in 1986). Some of these, such as the PLO, have hundreds or thousands of members, massive budgets, and the necessary resources to conduct world-wide campaigns of terrorism. The vast majority, however, consist of only a few politically dissatisfied individuals who form a loose-knit coalition, engage in one or two terrorist activities, and are either arrested or disband.

The large majority of these organizations present no threat to the United States or to U.S. citizens overseas. Most employ terrorism directed at a local or regional political system and have no interest in the United States or its government. As history has shown, however, there are many that do. The downing of PanAm flight 103 over Lockerbee, Scotland, and the bombing of the World Trade Center are examples of foreign-based terrorists directing attacks against U.S. citizens and interests. The 1980s and 1990s, particularly, have shown an increase in foreign-based terrorism directed against U.S. interests, both in number and magnitude (Kelly & Rieber, 1992; Ross & Gurr, 1989).

To reinforce an earlier point, most citizens have the perception that the only threat of terrorism comes from these foreign-based terrorists (Mullins, 1988). As will be shown in this chapter, the greatest fear comes from internal sources. Domestic terrorism affects more Americans per year than does foreign-based terrorism. Terrorism does exist in the U.S. and is caused by American citizens. More citizens are terrorized, wounded or killed, and more property destroyed per year within the U.S. by domestic terrorists than by all foreign-based terrorism directed against U.S. targets combined.

Not including foreign terrorists operating in the United States, domestic terrorism can be classified as one of three types: left wing, right wing, or special interest. Each type will be explored and the major organiza-

---

*The author was assisted in the preparation of this chapter by Lisa K. Zottarelli.

tions of each type examined. The distinctions between the three types, especially left and right wing, are based as much on convention as on theoretical pedagogy. Some terrorist organizations easily fit within a left-right typology. Others are more difficult. For example, right-wing terrorism is more nationalist oriented than left wing, although the Puerto Rican nationalists are considered left wing. The IRA is also treated the same way historically. Other organizations, such as the Jewish Defense League (JDL), seem to fit within any category. In some respects, the ideology and methodology of the JDL conforms to left-wing typology, but in other respects, the philosophy of the JDL fits within the far right.

Another caveat emptor is in order. Some of the organizations to be discussed are not active as this was written. That does not mean they will be inactive six months or a year from now. There have been numerous instances of law enforcement proclaiming a terrorist organization no longer active because its members and leaders were in prison, only to see a rebirth of that organization before the announcement was finished. On at least four occasions, for example, M19CO was announced to have been deactivated by the arrest of key personnel, only to have it reappear in one form or another more active and more violent than ever before (Stinson, 1987). Another example is the Order and Order II.

Finally, the reader should be wary of any numbers presented in this chapter. Because of the way terrorism is defined, by both scholars and law enforcement agencies, numbers differ. Counting beans is easy if agreement can be reached as to what is a bean. Unfortunately, terrorism is a more elusive concept than beans, and very few incidents lend themselves to everyone calling the incident terrorism. Federal law enforcement agencies define terrorism differently than do organizations that track terrorists. The FBI and ATF disagree on the annual number of domestic terrorist incidents because they define terrorism differently. One watchdog agency may claim terrorism from a particular organization is decreasing, while another watchdog agency claims activity from that organization is on the rise. Without agreeing upon a common definition and methodology, figures presented are "best-guess" estimates at best. Realize, however, that regardless of who is counting or how they count, terrorism is undergoing a general increase, will continue to increase, and will become more deadly. Any lull in terrorist activity is only temporarily at best and upswings in the curve of activity almost always rises higher than the previous upswing. The organizations discussed in this chapter have not gone away (if so claimed), will not go away, and, despite all efforts, will reemerge more active and deadly than previously. Names and faces may change, but political ideology and hatred will always be with us.

LEFT-WING TERRORISM

The far left is fairly easy to classify and describe. Regardless of the organization, the basic political ideology of the far left centers around some form of Marxist-Leninist doctrine and abolishing capitalist systems. To the left, capitalism and democracies oppress the working masses and deliberately establish power structures in favor of the select few. For the masses to be free of this oppression, socially and economically, a socialist system of government must be established. Although terrorist organizations of the far left do not often cooperate and assist each other, they all share several common traits, including ideology and belief, beliefs of economic system and distribution of wealth, tactics, and targets (Smith, 1994).

In general, there are three types of socialists. One are the Stalinists. These left-wing terrorists believe the USSR provided the ideal model of government while under the direction of Lenin, Stalin, and Kruschev. They believe the Soviet system was the perfect system until Gorbachev ruined it through poor leadership and misguided loyalty to the principles of socialism. To the Stalinites, the dissolution of the Soviet Union and reunification process of East Germany was due to the socialist system becoming perverted through individual greed and mismanagement, not because communism does not work. They see events in Europe as temporary setbacks and as a cleansing process. To them, the Soviet Union will rebuild in the years ahead and be stronger than ever (Mullins & Mijares, 1992). In the meantime, it is their responsibility to stop those (meaning the U.S.) that would hinder this rebirth process. Additionally, the capitalist system is collapsing under its own weight of the power elite's greed. Their manifest destiny is to assist the collapse of democracy and prepare the way for the Soviets to rule as an international government.

The second faction of the far left are the Trotskyites. They also believe in a pure form of Marxism-Leninism, but not under Moscow-dominated control. To the Trotskyites, revolution must occur worldwide and each nation has the right to establish a socialist government. Where the Stalinites see one globally dominated form of government, the Trotskyites see many different nations controlling their own sphere, but all following the principles of socialism. Further, they believe the only way to bring about this change is through violent revolution.

The third faction on the far left are the Maoists. This faction are considered neo-Stalinists and are true believers in Mao Tse-tung, the late Albanian dictator Enver Hoxha, or Kim Il Sung of North Korea. To them, the Soviet Union collapsed because its leaders, beginning with Stalin after World War II, strayed from the principles of socialism established by Marx and Engels. China and North Korea have remained true socialist states because leaders of those countries have remained uncorrupted by power and Western influences. They believe violent revolution is required to bring about world socialism and that, as nations adopt socialism, these nations should allow themselves to be guided by China and North Korea in establishing new governments.

There are some elements of turn-of-the-century anarchism present in the far left, although it is not a pure form of anarchism. The modern anarchist believes if the government is destroyed and the people allowed to select a system of government, the people will choose socialism (Mullins & Mijares, 1995). Part of the primary motivation of the far left, more so than seen in the far right, is the desire of terrorists themselves to control. The far left preaches socialism, equality, and eliminating the power elite. What they really want, however, is the power for themselves. Throughout the twentieth century, when the far left has taken control, terrorist leaders of the movement have seized power and refused to relinquish that power. Closest to the U.S. is Castro. He may deceive some onlookers by appearing in public dressed in the green fatigues of the revolution, but he has never relinquished the power gained during the overthrow of the Batista government. Nor has he allowed the people to decide who should lead. Like almost all left-wing terrorists, he hid his true motivation behind the rhetoric of revolution and became his own power elite when he seized control. His revolution was not for the Cuban people but for himself.

Communist Party USA

Next to the Ku Klux Klan, the Communist Party USA (CPUSA) is the oldest terrorist organization in the United States. First founded in 1919 as the Worker's Party, it changed its name to CPUSA in the 1920s. By 1939, CPUSA claimed membership of over 100,000. Membership stabilized in the 1940s, and for a year in 1944, the CPUSA disbanded. In the 1950s, membership in the CPUSA fell to an all-time low, primarily because of the Red Scare witchhunts of Senator Joseph McCarthy and the House Unamerican Activities Committee. In the 1960s and 1970s, membership again increased, stabilizing in the 1980s and falling insignificantly in the 1990s. At present, membership is somewhere between 3,000–20,000 people (George & Wilcox, 1992).

Membership in the CPUSA represents all three factions of the far left (Levy, 1978). These subdivisions represent Stalinites, Trotskyites, and Maoists. The Stalinites believe Moscow is the heart of communism and all governments should come under the control of Moscow. The Trotskyites believe communism is an international form of government and each country is responsible for running their own government. The Maoists are the most violent, believing that pure revolution is necessary and that any who oppose revolution must be killed. A brief history of CPUSA is given in Table 5.1.

Table 5.1.
Brief history of the Communist Party, USA.

Date	Activity
1918	Communist Propaganda League formed
1919	National Left Wing Manifesto adopted in New York Congress
1919	Communist Labor Party of America formed in Chicago on 31 August
1920	United Communist Party of America formed in Michigan on 1 May
1921	Communist Party of USA formed as part of Communist International
1922	Young Communist League formed
1923	Communist Party and Worker's Party of USA combined to form Communist Party USA
1929	Trotskyites thrown out of Communist Party USA
1943	American Youth for Democracy named to replace Young Communist League
1944	Communist Party USA disbanded
1945	Communist Party USA reestablished
1947	Young Progressives for America named to replace American Youth for Democracy
1948	Leaders of Communist Party USA arrested and deported
1949	Labor Youth League named to replace Young Progressives (disbanded in 1957)
1950	Communist Party USA began present-day activities, strengthened their position, and became sponsoring organization for left-wing organizations, activities which continue today
1956	FBI begins counter-intelligence program (COINTELPRO) against CPUSA (lasts until late 1960s)
1956	Hungarian uprising and Khrushchev revelations about Stalin cause membership to significantly decline
Late 1950s–1960s	McCarthy era and House UnAmerican Activities Committee actions severely weakens CPUSA and causes significant loss of membership
1961	DuBois Clubs for youth began (disbanded in 1971)
1983	Young Communist League formed

CPUSA also serves as an umbrella organization for other left-wing organizations. Some of these include the Abraham Lincoln Battalion of the 15th International Brigade, the Labor Research Association, the U.S. Peace Council, the National Lawyer's Guild, the National Emergency Civil Liberties Committee, the Center for Constitutional Rights, and the Revolutionary Youth Movement.

In the late 1920s and early 1930s, the Trotskyites were barred from CPUSA as the Stalinists had taken control of the party. In Russia, Stalin had risen to power upon Lenin's death and Leon Trotsky had fled the country and was in exile and hiding. Within CPUSA, members perceived the cowardice of Trotsky to be the ultimate sin and followers of Trotsky not worthy of membership. In 1940, Trotsky was killed in Mexico by Ramon Mercado, a Spanish Communist. Following his death, Trotskyites were again allowed membership in CPUSA.

In the late 1940s and 1950s, hundreds of members of CPUSA were arrested and imprisoned and others deported because of their socialist beliefs. Russia had developed the atomic bomb and the Cold War was becoming a national concern. America was developing a deep fear and paranoia of anything communist and perceived members of CPUSA to be Russian agents, either sent by Moscow to overthrow the government or under the direct control of Moscow. Because they were most visible, this national hysteria was taken out on members of the CPUSA.

In the wake of 1950s McCarthyism, the CPUSA began to rebuild itself in the 1960s. Many members of the organization were older and had lost the passion for revolution, so CPUSA targeted the college audience. In 1966, CPUSA had become strong enough once again to hold a national convention. Participants at this convention included the Student Non-Violent Coordinating Committee, Students for a Democratic Society, DuBois Clubs, Youth Against War and Fascism, Young Socialist Alliance, and the Progressive Labor Party.

In 1965, CPUSA began an organization especially for teens called the DuBois Club. Many of the new members CPUSA were recruiting, however, did not have children and there were not enough youth to support the DuBois Clubs in the 1960s so they were disbanded. In 1971, CPUSA tried again and formed the Young Workers Liberation League. In 1983, the name was changed to the Young Communist League.

The CPUSA published two periodicals, a weekly called *People's Weekly World* and a quarterly newspaper, *Political Affairs.* Unlike most extremist publications both have survived the decades and both can be purchased at newsstands that choose to carry them. The publications report on CPUSA activities, atrocities of the U.S. government, developments concerning communism at the international level, and provide tips on how to begin and conduct the revolution.

In 1991, *Rossiya,* a Soviet paper, revealed KGB documents that showed the Soviet Union paid CPUSA approximately $2 million per year, with periodic supplements of $1 million or more. This money was to support CPUSA activities in overthrowing the U.S. government, recruitment of new members, and to purchase materials necessary for beginning a revolution.

Although CPUSA has a long and illustrious history of fighting capitalism, one of the most notorious incidents involving CPUSA members occurred in August 1970. Jonathan Jackson, a Black Panther and suspected CPUSA member, entered a Marin County courtroom where three confederates from San Quentin were on trial. Jackson pulled a pistol and took five people hostage. In a gun battle with law enforcement officers, Jackson, two of the inmates, and the judge were killed. The guns were believed to have been purchased by Angela Davis, member and active spokesperson for CPUSA. Angela Davis had taught at UCLA, but had been fired for her membership in CPUSA. She filed a civil suit and won her job back, only to be later dismissed for other reasons. Following the Marin County shoot-out, Davis fled California and was listed on the FBI's Ten Most Wanted list. In October of the same year, she was captured in New York, returned to California, and tried as an accomplice to Jackson. It was alleged she purchased the pistols for Jackson to use in freeing the inmates. A jury acquitted Davis and she returned to teaching and lecturing. Her flight and trial became a rallying point for the far left and did more for recruitment than did all the stacks of printed material being produced and public demonstrations combined.

Socialist Worker's Party

In terms of the far left, second only in size and age to the CPUSA, the Socialist Worker's Party is the official arm of Trotskyite belief in the U.S. Initially they called themselves the International Socialist and in 1934 joined with the American Worker's Party to form the Workers Party U.S.

In 1937, over an ideological split, the Trotskyites were dismissed from the Workers Party U.S. In 1938, the exiled members formed the Socialist Workers Party and grew to over 1,200 members. Another division and factioning over ideology occurred in 1940. In 1953, the Socialist Workers Party factioned again, with a new organization called the Spartacist League being formed. Finally, in 1963 a last division occurred and the Workers League was formed. All of the splinter organizations have long since disappeared, their members returning to either the Socialist Workers Party or CPUSA.

In 1928, the Socialist Workers Party began publishing the weekly newspaper *The Militant* and the quarterly *International Socialist Review* (George & Wilcox, 1992). Surprisingly, both are still published today.

Like CPUSA, the Socialist Workers Party has been involved in numerous criminal and terrorist activities through the years. In the 1960s, FBI agents working in the COINTELPRO program infiltrated various radical organizations throughout the U.S., including the Socialist Workers Party, gathering intelligence, recording names, building personnel files on members and contacts, and establishing surveillance of members. In 1970, the Socialist Workers Party filed suit against the FBI because of the COINTELPRO program. The Socialist Workers Party suit requested $40 million for violation of civil rights of members. A federal court ruled the FBI had been involved in unconstitutional activity in the COINTELPRO program and awarded the organization $246,000.

Other Left-Wing Communists

The CPU and Socialist Workers Party are the two largest communist left-wing organizations in the U.S., but they are not the only ones. The Progressive Labor Party was formed in 1962 and was Maoist until 1971. Their philosophy now is a combination of Leninism, Stalinism, Trotskyism, and Maoism. Most of the early members of the Progressive Labor Party were dissatisfied members of CPUSA. Membership today is primarily on university and college campuses, with chapters in most large cities on the East Coast, Midwest, West, and South. Larger chapters include New York, Boston, San Francisco, Chicago, and Los Angeles. In 1973, they formed the International Committee Against Racism (InCAR), dedicated to eliminating racism in the U.S. Whenever a racist organization demonstrates, InCAR will appear and counter-demonstrate. One of their favored tactics is to throw rocks, bottles, and other debris at the racist protesters, attack radio and television stations, and demonstrate at movie theaters showing "racist" movies. In August 1978, they forced their way into Kansas City radio station KCKN and physically assaulted several neo-Nazis being interviewed on a talk show. George and Wilcox (1992) estimate their national membership at about 500.

The Communist Workers Party, an organization founded by Jerry Tung in 1973, had their most infamous activity occur in November 1979. In Greensboro, North Carolina, at a Klan and neo-Nazi rally, members of the Communist Workers Party engaged in a violent confrontation with the right wingers. Five people were killed in a gunbattle between the two factions. In August 1980, members wearing gas masks and riot gear attempted to storm the Democratic National Convention at Madison Square Garden but were repelled by police. Membership reached its high in the mid-1980s at about 500 people. Today, there are only about 100 members nationally.

The New Afrikan Freedom Fighters are based in New York City.

Founded by members of the Black Panthers and Black Liberation Army, one of the political agendas of the New Afrikan Freedom Fighters was the creation of a separate black nation in the Deep South, including Alabama, Georgia, Louisiana, Mississippi, and South Carolina (Smith, 1994). Another goal was the establishment of a socialist republic in South Africa. In 1985, eight members were convicted for the attempted bombing of New York City Police Officers Benevolent Association building. The bombing was designed to be a diversion while other terrorists freed member Nathaniel Burns from prison, who had been convicted and sentenced for his role in a 1981 Brinks armored truck robbery. A police search of their safe house found an extensive weapons cache, ammunition stores, and explosives (Harris, 1987). In 1985, members of the New Afrikan Freedom Fighters attempted to rescue Donald Weems from prison. Weems was a member who was also involved with the United Freedom Front. He was in prison for his role in the 1981 robbery of a Brinks armored truck in Nyack, New York, that left two police officers and one guard dead. Ten members of the New Afrikan Freedom Fighters were arrested and convicted for their role in the rescue attempt. Most were acquitted for the attempted escape, but were convicted for carrying illegal weapons. On this charge, the terrorists were given a suspended sentence and probation. Following these arrests, the organization became much less active and violent. Most of the activities in the late 1980s and early 1990s were directed toward apartheid policies in South Africa. Since Nelson Mandela became president of South Africa, the New Afrikan Freedom Fighters have become less active and membership has declined.

Other left-wing socialist organizations with a violent history and little recent terrorist activity include the All African People Revolutionary Party, the Coordination of United Revolutionary Organisations (CURO), M19CO, New Afrikan People's Organization, Prairie Fire Organizing Committee, Revolutionary Action Movement, Revolutionary Communist Party, Spartacist League, Workers League, and Workers World Party. For those wanting to keep track of what the far left is involved in, *The Guardian,* a weekly newspaper devoted to far-left activities, can be purchased at many newsstands.

El Rukns

The El Rukns were also known as the Blackstone Rangers and Black P. Stone Nation during their heyday during the late 1960s and early 1970s in Chicago. Led by Jeff Fort, the El Rukns were a conglomeration of 21 Chicago street gangs named after the cornerstone of the Kaaba, an Islamic shrine in Mecca, Saudi Arabia. At its height, the El Rukns numbered about 250 members. In 1983, Jeff Fort was sent to federal prison for distribution of drugs but continued to lead the organization from the Bastrop, Texas Federal Correctional Institute.

In March 1984, the top lieutenants of the El Rukns went to Libya to attend Kaddafi's Second General Mathaba Conference for combating American imperialism (Smith, 1994). At that conference, Kaddafi promised the organization $2.5 million if they would assist in overthrowing the American government. The El Rukns developed a five-stage plan to get the money. One, they planned to make threatening calls from throughout the U.S. to the Capitol Building. It was hoped these calls would show the American public was dissatisfied with U.S. diplomatic policy toward Libya. Two, they would produce a videotape, with the El Rukn lieutenants posing with Kaddafi to show he was not the evil enemy most U.S. citizens perceived him to be. Three, they planned to assassinate an anti-Kadaffi government official. Four, they would attack business interests unsympathetic to Kadaffi. Five, they would then escalate their attacks to bombing attacks or missile attacks on federal buildings.

To carry out their progressive terrorist plan, they planned to purchase a LAWs rocket. The FBI intercepted the telephone call and arranged for an undercover operative to meet with the El Rukns and sell them a rocket. When the Rukns attempted to purchase the rocket, they were arrested and the organization disbanded. The case of the El Rukns is the first time a domestic terrorist organization has actively worked with a foreign government to conduct terrorist activity.

Irish Republican Army and Provisional Irish Republican Army

Units of the Irish Republican Army (IRA) operate in the U.S. The U.S. units are known as the Provisional Irish Republican Army (PIRA). Primarily, PIRA has concentrated on obtaining weapons and explosives for the IRA (Pomerantz, 1987). Many members of PIRA have joint residences in the U.S. and Ireland, and many have been arrested in the U.S. for their involvement in illegal activities. In May 1983, IRA members Joseph Cahill and James Drumm were arrested for illegal entry into the U.S. In June 1983, Joseph P.T. Doherty was arrested in New York City as a British fugitive for the murder of a British army officer and as a member of the notorious M60 Gang.

In April 1984, Joseph Murray Jr., Patrick Nee, and five other PIRA members purchased large quantities of weapons, ammunition, rockets, weapons manuals, bulletproof vests, and other military equipment. These items were purchased in small lots from gun stores and paramilitary shops across the U.S. At a U.S. Marshall's auction, they purchased the cargo ship *Valhalla* and transported the goods to Ireland. Before unloading, they were arrested by the Irish navy and extradited to the U.S. In May

1986, Noel Murphy and Cairan Hughes were arrested for attempting to purchase M-16 rifles and a Redeye surface-to-air missile for shipment to the IRA. In 1987, Joseph Murray and Robert Anderson were convicted under RICO statutes for drug smuggling when they were caught bringing over 1,000 pounds of marijuana into the country to finance their PIRA activities.

A sub-organization of PIRA is the Irish Northern Aid Committee/Northern Irish Aid (NORAID), the primary fund raiser in the United States for the IRA.

One anti-IRA organization in the United States is the Ulster Volunteer Force (UVF). In 1966, the UVF began on the East Coast for the purpose of violently opposing the IRA. The UVF believes the IRA and Catholicism are a threat to Protestantism in Ireland and that if the British leave Ireland, the IRA and Catholic church will take control and begin a campaign of Protestant persecution. No UVF members have yet been arrested for terrorist activity in the U.S., although several have been suspected of purchasing and shipping weapons to the Irish UVF.

Omega 7

Omega 7, founded in 1974 by Eduardo Arocena, is an organization of exiled Cubans living in the United States who are anti-Castro. Their primary targets have been businesses considered favorable toward the Castro government and individuals who are pro-Castro. They have been responsible for over 50 bombings and assassinations against pro-Cuban interests (Smith, 1994). More notable attacks have included: (1) the bombing of the Venezuelan Consulate in New York City on 1 Feb 1975, (2) bombing the Cuban delegation to the UN in June 1976 and December 1979, (3) bombing the Soviet cargo ship *Ivan Shepetkov* at Port Elizabeth, New Jersey, in August 1976, (4) bombing a TWA flight in March 1979, (5) attempted bombing of Cuban UN ambassador Raul Roa in March 1980, (6) the assassination of Felix Garcia-Rodriguez, attaché to the Cuban UN mission, and (7) involvement in drug trafficking to finance their terrorism (Boyce, 1987).

In September 1985, Eduardo Arocena was arrested and convicted for his participation in several Miami, Florida bombings. After his arrest, activities of Omega 7 fell to very insignificant levels and it is believed the organization is not active at this time.

The 1960s Revisited

Many of the radical terrorist organizations formed in the 1960s still have an influence on terrorism in the 1990s. Most persons involved with these 1960s movements have tired of the practice of terrorism and fighting the system externally and have established middle-American lifestyles (or are in prison, exile, or dead). A new generation of activists are beginning to pick up the reins and some of the described organizations are poised to make a comeback.

Black Panther Party

Founded in 1966 at Merritt College in Oakland, California, by black radicals such as Anthony Bryant, Huey Newton, Bobby Seale, Eldridge Cleaver, David Hilliard, H. Rap Brown, and Stokely Carmichael, the Panthers proclaimed an agenda for the liberation of blacks. Their political objectives included: (1) all black "political" prisoners released from prison, (2) military service exemption for blacks, (3) federal payments to blacks, and (4) the establishment of a black homeland on the West Coast.

The Black Panthers believed black America should arm itself for protection against fascist federal and state governments. In one nationally reported incident, 30 Panthers entered the California State Assembly carrying a variety of unloaded weapons to protest a state bill providing criminal sanctions for carrying weapons in urban areas. Their claim was this law was merely another attempt by white America to keep blacks oppressed.

Members of the Panthers ambushed and killed several police officers in the U.S. In 1967, Huey Newton was tried for this offense and sentenced to prison. His conviction was overturned on appeal. In 1974, he was tried for the murder of a prostitute, but both of the trials ended in a hung jury. Newton voluntarily went into exile in Cuba, returning to the U.S. in the mid-1980s. He was killed in a drug deal in Oakland in 1989.

In 1968, wanted for a parole violation, Eldridge Cleaver fled to Cuba and later Algiers. He returned to the U.S. in the mid-1980s and has lived a quiet life since. Anthony Bryant was convicted in 1968 of skyjacking a plane to Cuba and served 12 years in prison. Bobby Seale was tried for the murder of Alex Rackey, a suspected federal informant, in 1969. Acquitted, Seale ran a losing campaign for mayor of Oakland in 1975.

By the late 1980s, law enforcement authorities believed the Panthers had finally disbanded, but in 1991, the newspaper *The Black Panther* appeared on the streets in Oakland. The newspaper preaches the 1960s Panther philosophy and argues for blacks to arm themselves against fascist America. According to editorials in the paper, the only way blacks can rid themselves of oppression is to overthrow the white, racist government. No estimates exist on the number of members in this newest resurrection of the Black Panther party.

SDS

In 1905, Jack London, Upton Sinclair, and other literati formed the League for Industrial Democracy as an intercollegiate socialist society. In 1930, it was renamed the Student League for Industrial Democracy, and in the late 1930s, it merged with the National Student Union to form the American Student Union.

At a national convention in Port Huron, Michigan, in 1962, it was renamed the Students for a Democratic Society (SDS). The SDS became a loose national coalition of socialists on college and university campuses. The SDS was organized so each university campus could form its own chapter with no national ideology to guide the local chapter. This lack of unifying political ideology was apparent during the 1960s demonstrations. SDS chapters at one campus would protest America's involvement in Vietnam, others would protest for civil rights, and still others would advocate the overthrow of the federal government.

In 1968, a national convention of the SDS was held in Michigan in an attempt to unify the SDS movement. Bernardine Dohr, Mike Klonsky, and Fred Gordon were elected to head the SDS and give it a national direction. The first act of the new SDS was a coordinated takeover of Columbia University on 27 March 1968. Five campus buildings were seized in a takeover that lasted five days. In the accompanying riots, the police arrested 712 demonstrators and 148 were injured. When the incident was resolved, Colombia closed the campus for the remainder of the school year.

A more violent faction of the SDS, including Bernardine Dohr, separated from the SDS and formed the Weathermen (later changed to Weather Underground because of the sexist connotations of the original name). In October 1969, in response to mistreatment and abuse in Chicago during the 1986 Democratic National Convention, the Weather Underground staged "Four days of rage" in Chicago, when members stormed downtown Chicago, destroying shops, attacking police and citizens, and creating general mayhem. During the riot, 72 police officers were injured and over 300 members of the Weather Underground were arrested, with bail totaling over $2.6 million (George & Wilcox, 1992).

In December of that same year, a war council meeting of over 400 Weather Underground members determined that armed struggle, assassinations, and a bombing campaign were necessary to cause a revolution that would topple the government. On 6 March 1970, preparing a bomb destined for Fort Dix, New Jersey to begin the revolution, three Weather Underground members were killed in New York City when their home-made bomb exploded. The deaths of Ted Gold, Diana Oughton, and

Terry Robbins in Greenwich Village sent the Weather Underground into deep underground. Most of the members dropped out and only the hard-core remained to carry on the revolution.

Their first bombing occurred in June 1970 at the New York City Police Department headquarters building and injured eight people. Later that same year, the Weather Underground bombed buildings in Berkeley, California, Chicago, Detroit, and New York. In March 1971, a Weather Underground bomb was detonated at the U.S. Capitol and another at the Pentagon in May 1972. Altogether, in 1969–1970, the Weather Underground was suspected in about 800 bomb explosions nationwide and approximately 20,000 bomb threats. During those two years, George and Wilcox (1992) present data that show there were a total of 975 explosions, 3,333 incendiary incidents (of both, 1,175 failed to detonate) and 35,000 bomb threats. Twenty percent of the incidents occurred during campus demonstrations. Seven percent were caused by black extremists, 5 percent by white extremists, and 64 percent of unknown origin. Most of those unknown origin bombs have been attributed to the Weather Underground and related movements.

M19CO

In the mid-1970s, remnants of the Black Panther Party, Black Liberation Army, SDS, and Weather Underground formed the M19CO, or May 19th Communist Organization, one of the most violent left-wing organizations in recent history. The organization was named for the birthdays of Ho Chi Minh and Malcolm X. Some leading members included Kathy Boudin, Sam Brown, Marilyn Buck, Nathaniel Burns, Judith Clark, JoAnne Chesimard, Dave Gilbert, Samuel Smith, Donald Weems, Jeral Wayne Williams, and Laura Whitehorn. M19CO first established associations and ties with foreign terrorist organizations. In 1986, for example, 20 M19CO members went to West Germany to meet with members of the Red Army Faction (Stinson, 1987). The organization also expressed solidarity and relationships with the Popular Front for the Liberation of Palestine. In a ten-year career of terrorism, the M19CO was involved in numerous bank robberies, bombing incidents, the murder of a state trooper in New Jersey, and the attempted murder of two Massachusetts state police officers. On 21 October 1981, the UFF robbed a Brinks armored truck in Nyack, New York that resulted in the death of one Brinks' guard, two police officers, and the wounding of two others. Cathy Boudin, Judith Clark, and David Gilbert were arrested (along with several other M19CO members) and charged with murder, robbery, and planning the armored truck robbery.

The M19CO was also responsible for bombing the U.S. Capitol, National

War College, Washington Navy Yard computer office, the FBI office on Staten Island, the South African Consulate in New York, and the New York Patrolman's Benevolent Association building. In claiming responsibility, the M19CO often referred to themselves as the Armed Resistance Unit, Revolutionary Fighting Group, or the Red Guerrilla Resistance, names designed to deceive investigating authorities (Smith, 1994).

Another offshoot organization from the SDS and Weather Underground was the United Freedom Front (UFF). Led by Raymond Luc Levasseur, Patricia Gros, Thomas Manning, and Carole Manning, the UFF was small but violent. Between 1974–1985, the UFF was involved in at least nine bank robberies and numerous bombings. By 1984, almost all members of the UFF had been arrested for their illegal activities.

Puerto Rican Left-Wing Terrorist Organizations

In the last half of the 1980s, over 60 percent of left-wing terrorist acts in the United States were attributable to Puerto Rican organizations. According to Smith (1994), the six primary Puerto Rican terrorist organizations have been the Armed Forces of National Liberation, the Organization of Volunteers for the Puerto Rican Revolution (Ejercito Popular Boricua), Macheteros, Armed Forces of Popular Resistance, Guerrilla Forces of Liberation, and the Pedro Albizu Campos Revolutionary Forces.

The Puerto Rican nationalist movement actually began in 1936 when Pedro Albiza Campos formed the National Party in Puerto Rico and attacked a police station, killing a police commander. He was extradited to the U.S. and tried for plotting to overthrow the government and spent seven years in prison. The Puerto Rican separatist movement continued in the 1950s, when two leftists attempted to assassinate President Truman in Blair House in Washington D.C. in 1950, and in 1954, when four nationalists fired onto the floor of the House of Representatives, wounding five congressmen (Simon, 1994).

Since 1975, the Armed Forces of National Liberation (FALN) has been responsible for over 100 bombing incidents in the United States and Puerto Rico (Conley, 1987). In 1975, in New York, four people were killed and 54 wounded when a FALN bomb exploded in the Fraunces Tavern. In December 1979, with assistance from the Organization of Volunteers for the Puerto Rican Revolution (OVRP), they bombed a naval bus in Sabana Seca, Puerto Rico, killing two U.S. servicemen and wounding nine others. To end the decade, FALN member William Morales escaped from Bellvue Hospital in New York City with assistance from Dr. Alan Berkman of M19CO. He was tended to in a M19CO safe house in New Jersey by Marilyn Buck. He later escaped to Mexico and was arrested for killing a police officer. Released from a Mexican prison in 1988, he fled to Cuba, where he remains to this day.

In March 1980, members of FALN seized the Carter-Mondale and Bush campaign headquarters in Chicago and New York, respectively, destroying property and spray-painting pro-Puerto Rican slogans on the walls (Poland, 1988). In January 1981, the Macheteros bombed nine airplanes at a National Guard base at Muniz Airport in Isla Verde, Puerto Rico. That same month, members of the organization ambushed and killed one navy seaman who was ashore on liberty. In 1985, OVRP conducted five separate attacks against U.S. Army recruiting offices in Puerto Rico. Also in 1985, the OVRP and Macheteros combined for a rocket attack against a federal courthouse in Old San Juan, and the OVRP assassinated an U.S. Army major at his home in Puerto Rico. In 1986, the OVRP and Macheteros were responsible for planting six bombs and the assassination of Alejandro Malave, a former police officer. That same year, one of the organizations (unknown which one) planted ten bombs, two of which exploded at the naval recruiting station and at Fort Buchanan in Puerto Rico. In 1987, the Guerrilla Forces of Liberation planted a series of seven bombs at four banks, two government buildings (Customs and Postal Service), and a department store. No deaths resulted from those bombings. In 1988, the Pedro Albizu Campos Revolutionary Forces bombed Citibank, a travel agency in Rio Piedras, Puerto Rico, Motorola headquarters, and International General Electric, both in Puerto Rico. Again, no deaths were recorded.

To finance their activities, the Macheteros turned to robbery. In September 1982, members attempted to rob a Wells Fargo armored truck in Puerto Rico but were unsuccessful. In November 1982, they robbed a supermarket and Wells Fargo armored truck. In that robbery, one person was killed and the Macheteros got over $312,000. In July 1983, they again robbed a Wells Fargo truck, killed the driver and stole $600,000. In September 1983, in West Hartford, Connecticut, a Macheteros member, Victor Gerena Ortiz, secured a job at the Wells Fargo depot. On 12 September, he pulled a gun on the depot manager and, along with other Macheteros, stole $7.1 million. This act led to the arrest of 18 leading members of the Macheteros. Most have been convicted and sentenced to prison. It is worth noting that less than $100,000 from that robbery has ever been recovered. Many authorities believed it ended up in Cuban hands to be used by Castro in his continuing efforts to destroy the United States.

As of this writing, most leaders of the Puerto Rican leftist movement have been arrested or killed in confrontations with law enforcement. The FBI has conducted a concerted effort to arrest leading members of the

FALN (Webster, 1986), most Macheteros were arrested or fled the country following the Wells Fargo depot robbery, and leaders of the other four Puerto Rican organizations have been arrested by federal authorities for a range of offenses. Stinson (1987), however, suggested that in 1987, after all members had supposedly been arrested, the FALN still had over 120 dedicated members and a support base of over 2,000 people in New York, Chicago, El Paso, Denver, Milwaukee, Los Angeles, and Washington D.C. He also claims the FALN is a front organization for the Movement for National Liberation, Crusade for Justice, California Committee Against Repression, Colorado Committee Against Repression, and La Raza Unida. Also, in 1995, the citizens of Puerto Rico voted to remain a territory of the U.S. This vote to remain a U.S. territory will undoubtedly increase Puerto Rican terrorism in the coming years. Those wanting independence from U.S. control may perceive that this vote removed the last legitimate avenue of recourse for independence and that the only redress available is terrorism.

RIGHT-WING TERRORISM

The basic belief structure of the far right is based on notions of racial superiority. The far right is intensely nationalistic and racist, despises Jews, and believes in Holocaust revisionism (Merkl & Weinberg, 1993). To the far right, the people have been deceived by an illegitimate government and it is their duty to enlighten and protect the citizens. The basis of this belief varies depending upon the organization being examined. The rise in the 1980s of the far right is likely due to several factors, including social and racial emancipation, the rise of the women's movement and as a response to the new far left of the 1960s and 1970s, legalization of abortions, mandatory busing for school desegregation, relaxed immigration laws, a polarization of rich and poor, rise of special-interest groups, and a liberal Congress (Aho, 1990; Merkl, 1993). As Kelly and Cook (1995) stated, "the capacity to absorb newcomers of different cultural backgrounds seems to be exhausted." The collapse of world communism also played a role in the growth of the far right. They offer an alternative to the disenfranchised and alienated, and the idea of a classless society as proposed by Marxism has disappeared.

Most of the far right is from rural America, are older than their left-wing counterparts (with the exception of the skinheads), over 80 percent are Protestant (Aho, 1990), are married (and not divorced; Aho, 1990), and have some college education (Weinberg, 1993). Most work in agriculture or blue-collar occupations (Mullins, 1986). According to Aho (1994), the far right has its largest membership in the Northwest states of

Montana, Idaho, Oregon, Wyoming, Colorado, Arizona, Washington, and Alaska. In part, this is due to the isolation of the Far West, vast regions of uninhabited areas, and freedom to live undisturbed.

Unlike the far left, the far right is more difficult to classify. Coates (1987) suggested there were six categories of right-wing organizations: (1) True terrorists, such as the Order, whose reason for existence was to conduct terrorist attacks against minorities; (2) Identity Churches, whose beliefs of racial superiority are founded upon Protestant religious principles and their interpretation of the Bible; (3) Protest organizations, who were more specific-agenda oriented, such as the Posse Comitatus, a tax protest organization; (4) Lone wolves fighting the system, who are organizations that are not part of the right-wing movement; (5) Survivalists, who believe Armaggedon is at hand or nuclear devastation between the U.S. and a foreign enemy; and (6) Compound dwellers, who want to escape society (for a variety of reasons) and isolate themselves in the wilderness away from any other population.

In the Coates (1987) schema, many organizations could be multiply classed. The Ku Klux Klan could be a terrorist organization, a protest organization, lone wolves, and survivalists. Many survivalists are also compound dwellers. The inclusion of a category as terrorist organizations is somewhat misleading, since most of the organizations of the far right engage in terrorism.

Suall and Lowe (1987) classified the far right into four categories: (1) Racist by membership in a majority group. These organizations are racists to be racist; (2) Christian Identity organizations, whose racism is based upon Scripture; (3) Nazis, who are followers of Adolph Hitler and want to bring about the rise of the Fourth Reich; and (4) Hybrid organizations, who are not true terrorists but instead limit their activities to political expression and freedom of speech and politics (White, 1991).

Suall and Lowe's (1987) is imprecise and overlapping. Neo-Nazi organizations are racist. Survivalists are not considered in this classification. Their hybrid category includes those on the right who are not terrorists nor, in some instances, even extremists. Further, organizations such as Posse Comitatus and the Arizona Patriots fit no category.

Sapp (1985, 1986c) suggested the far right could be classified as: (1) White supremacist; (2) Patriotic and survivalist; or (3) Christian Conservative Identity. There are some minor problems with Sapp's categories. Almost all far-right organizations are white supremacist. Their reasons, however, for being white supremacists differ based upon some internalized belief structure. With some minor refinements, Sapp's classification best describes the far right. It is suggested an appropriate classification of the far right would include: (1) the Christian Identity movement—

those organizations who base, their supremacist beliefs upon Scripture; (2) Secular based—organizations in this category would be supremacist organizations that believe in racial superiority without any religious justification; (3) Paramilitary/survivalist organizations would be those who foresee Armaggedon in the not-so-distant future and are anti-government and isolationists; (4) Neo-Nazis—those organizations who want to see the rise of the Fourth Reich.

Even this schema has difficulties. One, organizations among the far right often practice a combination of ideology. Members of the Posse Comitatus, for example, would primarily be paramilitary/survivalist, but they also have a component of secular-based supremacy. Many members of the Klan are also members of Identity churches. Two, organizational philosophy often overlaps. Many Christian Identity movements, as an organization, preach survivalism in the face of government stricture. Three, organizations change their political focus. The Klan, again, has undergone somewhat of a philosophical change from purely racism to the more general issue of the federal government being an enemy which must be destroyed. Although not a great help in classifying the far right, possibly the best classification is that proposed by Mullins (1993): (1) secular or (2) Christian Identity. Even at that, however, some organizations fit both categories.

Many of the far-right organizations in the United States have in recent years adopted the Christian Identity philosophy. There are several reasons for this shift from secular to Scripture-based ideology. One, many of the leaders of the far right began in secular-based organizations, were converted and now preach Christian Identity theology. Many have not changed organizations. Instead, the members of their organization adopt their theology. Two, the leaders of the Christian Identity movement tend to be more charismatic and persuasive than other organization leaders. Thus, the Christian Identity organizations are able to grow and expand faster than others. Three, Christian Identity provides a moral and ethical justification and rationale for supremacist belief structures. Four, Christian Identity ties in with the conservative Protestantism many far-right followers grew up with, so it fits more generalized cognitive belief structures. Five, Christian Identity offers the ultimate goals of Aryan dominance, Aryan government, and eternal life for Aryans.

Regardless of classification, most far-right organizations believe n the concept of postmillenialism, or the belief that Jesus cannot return to earth until God's law has been reestablished. The white race must reestablish dominance and control before the Second Coming of Christ can occur. To the white race, this means defeating the agents of Satan (Holden, 1986a). According to the postmillenialist belief, Satan's agents on earth are the Jews, who control the world's governments. They must be overthrown so Christ can return to earth. To these persons, Christ will establish His Second Kingdom in the United States, so there is some religious urgency to depose the federal government (Holden, 1987). The far right, in fact, refers to the federal government as the Zionist Occupational Government (ZOG).

The Satan-Jewish link is the fundamental cornerstone of the Christian Identity movement. Begun in the 1800s by Richard Brothers, the anti-Jewish doctrine was part of a broader philosophy of Anglo-Israelism (Benware, 1984), which preached that true Israelites as described in the Old Testament are really the Aryans. Accordingly, Adam was created in the image of God which was white (Finch, 1983). Not only did Adam and Eve begin the white race, God gave Adam power over other inferior races. Adam was given the power, not Eve. The Mannasah tribe was given the United Kingdom by God and was responsible for spreading the gospel. American settlers in the 1600s were the descendants of the Mannasah tribe, and America is the land God promised Moses.

In the late 1940s and early 1950s, the Reverend Wesley Swift introduced racism and Aryan supremacy into Anglo-Israelism. Thomas Robb most appropriately described this addition when he stated: "... it is a lie. The Jews are not the Chosen people of God. The Bible is an Israel book. It does not give the history of the negroes, or any other people or any other race. It gives the history of only one race" (WMAQ, 1985).

The historical beginnings of the black and Jewish races are given different explanations, depending upon which Christian Identity movement is queried. Many believe Jews came about as the result of Satan's seduction of Eve. Others, such as William Gale, said minorities are agents of Satan descended from an alien race called the Enosh. The Enosh then mated with primates, and the offspring of this mating resulted in the Jewish race (Holden, 1986b). Additionally, God is at war with the Jews because they crucified His son Jesus.

Violence against Jews and minorities is justified for several reasons. One, Jews and minorities are not human according to the Bible and so there is no moral sanctions against killing them. The death of a minority or government agent of ZOG is not a violation of God's commandments. Two, because Jews are agents of Satan, they cannot be peaceably stopped. Violence is the only way to overthrow ZOG. Other minorities have also been condemned by God for abetting Satan and they must also be destroyed. Three, the far right practices eschatology. They literally interpret the New Testament book of Revelation and believe Armageddon is at hand. During Armageddon, Christians will rise to battle the agents of Satan and help speed the Second Coming. Four, without other justification, the Christian Identity movement reinterprets the Bible to suit their purposes (White, 1986). To most, Jews are responsible for most of the problems in the world, including the economic recession, race mixing, drugs, crime, immorality within society, and other problems that plague modern America. To save society, the white race, and Christianity, the Jews must be destroyed, along with their assistants, the minorities of the world (Mullins, 1989, 1991).

Originally, according to Anglo-Israelism, the U.S. Constitution and Declaration of Independence were holy covenants between God and man. Through the years, largely because of the ZOG influence, both have lost their true meaning and are no longer holy pacts. In 1982, in Hayden Lake, Idaho, Richard Butler of the Aryan Nations convened a meeting of leaders of the far-right movement and drafted a new U.S. Constitution which came to be called the Nehemiah Township Charter and Common Law Contract (Sapp, 1986b). Representatives which helped draft this document included representatives from the Aryan Nations, British Colombia Ku Klux Klan, Ku Klux Klan of the United States, Mountain Church of Michigan, and Texas Emergency Reserves (Mullins & Mijares, 1993).

The Nehemiah Township Charter reestablished and reaffirmed the holy contract between God and man and will be the new constitution once ZOG is overthrown. Jesus is chief executive officer of the new government and the purpose of the government is to "safeguard and protect the Christian faith.... Thus, we declare that our nation must choose HIS LAW as its ONLY way of LIFE" (Mullins, 1988). There will be no legislative body, no taxation, no governmental laws other than those already specified in the Bible and only freemen (Aryans) will have personal freedoms. Additionally, freemen can possess any type of weapon they wish, including automatic weapons and heavy weapons such as rocket launchers and missiles. Courts will base decisions on the Bible and word of God. A posse comitatus will be formed to fight wars and protect freemen. War with the unholy (all non-whites) is required to be waged and fought in accordance with Deuteronomy, Chapter 20. In part, Deuteronomy 20 reads:

When you advance on a city to attack it, make an offer of peace. If the city accepts the offer and opens its gates to you, then all the people in it shall be put to forced labour and shall serve you. If it does not make peace with you but offers battle, you shall besiege it, and the Lord your God will deliver it into your hands. You shall put all its males to the sword, but may take the women, the dependents, and the cattle for yourselves, and plunder everything else in the city. You may enjoy the use of the spoil of your enemies which the Lord your God gives you. That is what you shall do to cities at a great distance, as opposed to those which belong to nations near at hand. In the cities of these nations whose land the Lord your God is giving you as a patrimony, you shall not leave any creature alive. You shall annihilate them ... as the Lord your God commanded you, so that they may not teach you to imitate all the abominable things that they have done for their gods and so cause you to sin against the Lord your God. (New English Bible)

Under the Nehemiah Township Charter, only Aryans could live in the United States, to wit: "We declare and announce and intend that this government and all territory subject to its control is dedicated to the preservation, protection, and sustenance of our Aryan Race and civilization indigenous to that Race."

Law enforcement officers are agents of ZOG and are subject to attack and murder (Sullivan, 1990). Law enforcement are worse agents of Satan than even other minorities because law enforcement is working with Satan to end Christianity (Mullins, 1990b). The far right, even more than with minorities, have a moral obligation to exterminate law enforcement agents. Members of the far right may attempt to provoke law enforcement officers by refusing to carry licenses and automobile registrations, have no vehicle insurance, refuse to produce identification, and/or refuse to sign citations (Melnichak, 1986b). Several police officers and federal agents have been killed by far-right terrorists, including two federal marshals and an Arkansas sheriff by Gordon Kahl of the Posse Comitatus (Bowers, 1987).

Secular believers of the far-right movement see the civil rights movement, racial equality, affirmative action, Equal Employment Opportunity and American's with Disabilities Act laws, and other governmental control as an attempt to erode the superiority of the Aryan race. To them, there is a moral obligation to restore the white race to its place of prominence. Actions directed against other races are attempts to both destroy the minority race and to overthrow a liberal and permissive government that wants to destroy Aryans. To them, like the Christian Identity movement, Jews control the government and are engaged in a conspiracy to control world economics and destroy Aryans. Hate crimes are political crimes, designed as the first step in the ultimate wrestling governmental power away from the Jews (Mullins, 1993).

They also believe the Jews fabricated the Holocaust in order to gain world sympathy for the Jewish plight and to foster discord against the Aryan race. An offshoot organization of the Liberty Lobby, the Institute for Historical Review (IHR), was created in 1979 to provide "evidence" that the Nazi holocaust never occurred an is a hoax of the Jews. Using non-credentialed scholars, IHR publishes the *Journal of Historical Review* and holds public meetings seeking to prove the holocaust a Jewish conspiracy. In 1991, the IHR bought a series of revisionist advertisements in university newspapers calling for open debate on the holocaust issue. Today, IHR is based in Newport Beach, California and operated by Willis Carto (ADL, 1994).

IHR argues several points regarding the holocaust and claims that it never occurred. One, the holocaust did not occur because there was no single "master plan" for Jewish annihilation. That is, no one Nazi document details plans to exterminate the Jews. Two, there were no gas chambers at Auschwitz and other camps. Three, holocaust scholars rely on the testimony of survivors because there are no objective documents proving the Nazis practiced genocide. Four, no Jews were killed between 1941–1945 by the Nazis. Five, the Nuremberg trials were a "farce of justice" staged for the benefit of the Jews. Mark Weber, one of the leading holocaust revisionists, stated in the IHR Newsletter, "Don't for a minute think that indoctrinating wide-eyed school children with the lies and slanders against Germans, Slavs, Catholics, Christians, Europeans, and whites in general isn't a primary purpose of the Holocaust-managers.... The Holocaust is a religion. Its underpinnings in the realm of historical fact are non-existent—no Hitler order, no plan, no budget, no gas chambers, no autopsies of gassed victims, no bones, no ashes, no skulls, no nothing.... Secondly, it's a religion for losers.... Suffice it to say that the rise of religions such as this generally coincides with the decline and fall of nations which tolerate them" (ADL, undated).

The neo-Nazi movement is similar in many respects to secular ideology, the major difference being they wish to see a Nationalist/Fascist government modeled after the Third Reich. To them, the Jews have also gained control of the government, control the world economy, and have corrupted society with the express purpose of subjugating the white race. They want government controlled by whites and the elimination of the Jewish race. To most, minorities are Jews with different color skin. In addition to the neo-Nazis discussed in this chapter, other neo-Nazi organizations include the Bruder Schweigen Task Force 3, Central New York White Pride, Christian Guard, Cuban Nationalist Association, Euro-American Alliance, National Alliance, National Socialist German Workers Party, New Aryan Empire, New National Socialist, Robert Mathews Brigade, Seymour Supremacist Group, Southern Liberation Front, SS of America, USA Nationalist Party, White Alliance, White Citizens Council, and the White House Network.

The paramilitary/survivalists, while also racist and anti-Semitic, believe the corruption of society has gone beyond the point of no return. To them, the only hope is to dig in and wait for Armageddon. The "war to end all wars" will not necessarily be God's revenge against man but will be caused by communists, minorities, drugs, loosening of moral values, advent of the nuclear family, etc. Whatever their rationale, to all the government is responsible. Government interference has intruded into the lives of citizens, the constitution has been bastardized, and rights of citizens have slowly been eroded to the point where total destruction of society is inevitable. The only hope people have to prevent the final destruction of the world or American society is to overthrow the government. They believe the future of the country can only be secured by getting rid of the bureaucracy, which to them means the entire government structure. Some even want to form their own army and secede part of the country from the United States.

Regardless of ideology, almost to a person, the far right believes Armageddon is at hand (and, to many, will occur before the turn of the century). The final destruction of America could come from one of five sources. One, nuclear war could cause Armageddon (Wiggins, 1987). Nuclear war will devastate the world and it will become the responsibility of Aryans to rebuild a new world from the ashes of the old. The collapse of Eastern Europe has not dimmed the perception that nuclear war is on the horizon. Many believe that if China, North Korea, or another country does not begin the nuclear holocaust, then the U.S. government will in its attempt to control the behavior of citizens. Many of the militias believe the United Nations, being communist-controlled, will bring about nuclear destruction upon the United States.

Two, natural disasters could bring about the end of the present world order. Massive earthquakes, volcanic explosions, floods or droughts, tidal waves, or other natural disasters will be God's revenge for race-mixing, Jewish domination, or to defeat Satan. God will use these natural disasters to destroy mankind, who have been unfaithful to the word of God because of their race-mixing, and to establish a new world under the government of the Second Coming.

Three, communism is still a possibility for the destruction of the world. Many nations still practice communism, and some of these nations have the potential to launch a strike against the U.S. As proof, the far right will point to the proliferation of nuclear weapons in North Korea and other third-world nations. Additionally, the communist threat will come from within the U.S. The Jewish controlled, or Zionist Occupational Government (ZOG), depending upon which faction of the far right is discussing the topic, has eroded democracy to the point where the U.S. is virtually communistic already. Every minute, hour, day, and week, the Zionist-controlled government brings the country a little closer to the brink of total domination and the complete loss of the rights of free man. To the far right, the communists in government already control the world banking system, media, law enforcement, and are intent on destroying Aryan society (Blumberg, 1986). In the mid-1990s, far-right members point to federal law enforcement actions at the Randy Weaver siege in Idaho, and the Branch Davidian compound in Waco, Texas, as proof of the communist control of the government.

Four, Armageddon will be brought about by changing economics, societies, and technology (Besser, 1982). The Jews, who already control the world economy, will collapse the economic and agricultural markets of the world (Gurr, 1988; Mitchell, 1983). When farms, ranches, and agriculture collapse, the Jews will have it all and society will collapse. Only those who are self-sufficient will be able to survive (Marty, 1983).

Five, race wars will bring about Armageddon (Stimson, 1986). It is the duty of Aryans to promote these race wars. One of the reasons the far right has become involved in drug trafficking is to hasten the race war (Mullins, 1990c). According to the far right, Aryans would never use drugs (other than alcohol, nicotine, caffeine, amphetamines, tranquilizers and a multitude of prescription drugs, of course). Only Jews and minorities use drugs. By trafficking, Aryans are fulfilling their destiny by promoting the coming race war. Also, the race war will be shorter and easier to win because thousands of minorities and Jews are killing themselves by using drugs, as evidenced by inner-city gang violence. Those not dead will be in no condition to fight when the time comes. Instead, they will be easy to kill because of being drugged up.

One of the primary reasons, overthrow of the government aside, the far right is heavily involved in paramilitary/survivalist training is because of their belief in Armageddon. John B. Harrell, late leader of the Christian Patriots Defense League, identified a mid-America survival zone, stretching from west Texas, north to southern Nebraska, east to southern Pennsylvania, and south to northern Alabama. According to Harrell and many members of the far right, this survival zone will be the only safe place for Aryans when the end comes. This area of the country is relatively free from minorities, isolated, and mountainous. Other far-right patriots have expanded the survival zone to include west Texas, New Mexico, and Arizona. Still others see the northwest forests of Washington, Idaho, and Montana as the survival zone.

Having identified and described right-wing philosophy and ideology, the remainder of this section will examine some of the more prominent organizations of the far-right movement. A few of these organizations are not presently active, but those are the ones with the potential to reappear. Only the enduring organizations will be covered and discussed. New organizations, churches, and coalitions appear almost monthly. Many of these disappear as fast as they appear, others become part of another organization. To discuss all right-wing organizations might make this volume timely in 1996, but it would be out of date by 1997. Even between the writing and publication, this book would be out of date if all organizations were described. Klanwatch (1993) provides data suggesting the magnitude of the far-right problem in the United States. Figure 5.1 shows Klanwatch reporting of white supremacist organizations in the United States for 1992. Table 5.2 lists other far-right organizations active in the U.S. As can be seen, claims the far right is in disarray and falling apart appear unfounded.

Realize also that unlike the far left, members of far-right organizations hold multiple memberships. It is not unusual to find a person in the far-right movement having membership in Christian Identity, paramilitary/survivalist, and neo-Nazi organizations. One of the reasons law enforcement has had such difficulty in reducing far-right terrorism is the unity of the movement. The far right is extremely cooperative and helpful, each organization helping all others when needed. Unlike any movement at any time or any place, the far right can truly be considered one national organization. It is similar to a large corporation with international offices. Each branch has specific responsibilities, tasks and localized goals, but the overall mission of the organization is the same (Mullins, 1988, 1990a).

Members of the far right, unlike their left-wing counterparts, are primarily rural (Smith, 1994). More than the far left, the far right relies on modern technology to help spread their message of hate. The right employees bulletin boards, E-mail, and addresses on the Internet, relies on satellite television such as Thomas Metzger's show *Race and Reason,* and has numerous radio shows throughout the nation, like Sheldon Emory's (pastor of Lord's Covenant Church) program in Phoenix, Arizona, *America's Promise.*

Ku Klux Klan

The KKK is the oldest terrorist organization in the United States. The original KKK was formed in Pulaski, Tennessee in 1868 by Civil War general Nathan Bedford Forrest (Wiggins, 1985). Forrest formed this organization to terrorize blacks and drive the Northern carpetbaggers from the reconstructive South. Forrest structured this Klan into state realms, country provinces, and individual dens. The state realm was led by the Grand Wizard, county province by the Grand Dragon, and individual dens by Grand Titans and Grand Cyclopses. Lesser functionaries were titled Giants, Genii, Hydra, Furies, Goblins, and Nighthawks (Poland,

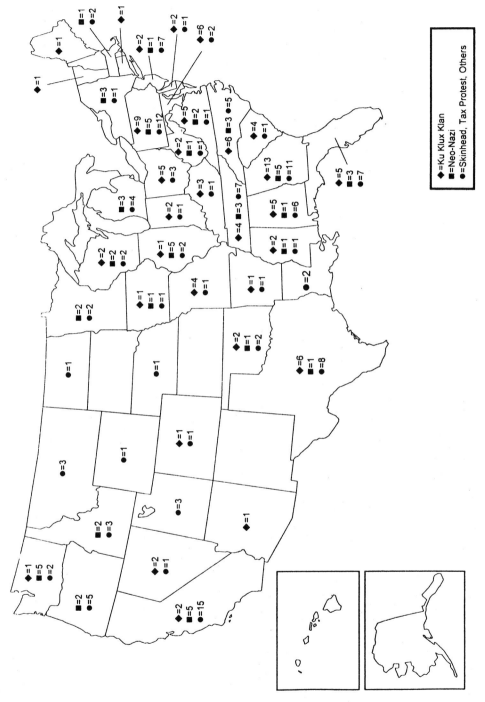

Figure 5.1. White supremacist organizations in the United States in 1992. From Klanwatch (1993). *Intelligence Report*, 65, 13.

Table 5.2.
Far-right extremist organizations in the United States in 1996.

Organization	Organization
Albanian Boys	Mountain Church of Jesus Christ
American Covenant Church	National Agriculture Press Association
America First Committee	National Association for the Advancement of White People
American Resistance Movement	National Democratic Front
American Spring	National Socialist League/World Front
American White Nationalist Party	National Socialist Liberation Front
American Workers Party	National Socialist Movement
Arizona Patriots	National Socialist Vanguard
Arizona Rangers	National Socialist White Worker's Party
Aryan Militant	National Sozialistiche Deutsche Arbeiter Partei/Auslands Organisation (NADAP/AO)
Barristers Inn	
Catholic Defense League	National States Rights Party
California Rangers	Nationalist Movement
CAUSE Foundation	Nationalist Socialist White American Party
Church of the Creator	New Dawn
Church of Israel	New Order Legion
Church of the Living Word	North American Front
Citizen Emergency Defense System	Oklahoma White Man's Society
Citizen's Emergency Network	Oregon Militia
Civilian Military Assistance	Phineas Priesthood
Committee of the States	Present Truth
Crusade Against Corruption	Pure American Freedom Party
Elohim City	Resistance
Emergency Committee to Suspend Immigration	Romantic Violence
Euro-American Alliance, Inc.	Security Services Action Group
Farmers Liberation Army	Social Nationalist Aryan People's Party
Final Solution	SS Action Group
Florida National Socialist Party	Texas Emergency Reserves
Georgia Patriots	United Citizens for Justice
Guardian Nights of Justice	United White People's Party
Heritage Library	Universal Order
Heritage Society	Western Front
Institute for Applied Marine Research	White American Resistance
Institute for Historical Review	White Cause
Iowa Society for Educated Citizens	White Knights of Liberty
Knoxville White Action	White Patriots Party
LaPorte Church of Christ	White Student Patriot Union
League 88	White Student Union
Legion for the Survival of Freedom, Inc.	White Supremist Party
Liberty Lobby	World Service
Lord's Covenant Church	Wyoming Rangers
Ministry of Christ Church	Yahwah Church (Black Hebrews)
Minutemen	Young and Wasted
Minute Men Association	

1988). The hood and robe were adopted as the official uniform and the night cross burning selected as the Klan symbol.

In 1867, Congress passed the Reconstruction Act of 1867, which allowed for military governments instead of locally created governments (i.e., no carpetbaggers). Later that same year, at a national convention in Nashville, Tennessee, Forrest proclaimed the Klan to be for the "maintenance of supremacy of the White Race in this Republic" as the primary mission of the Klan (ADL, 1988). Additionally, the Klan would oppose the "harsh Reconstruction measures" adopted by the federal government. Between 1867–1871, thousands of blacks were killed by Klansmen. In Florida, it was estimated that at least one black per day was killed, and the commander of federal troops in Texas reported, "The murder of Negroes is so common as to render it impossible to keep accurate accounts of them" (ADL, 1988).

By 1872, local, state, and federal pressure led to a Congressional investigation and federal legislation that led to the Klan's dissolution. Forrest himself claimed the Klan had disbanded in 1869, stating publicly it was no longer needed to protect the South.

In 1915, William Simmons resurrected the Klan in Atlanta, Georgia as an organization for white Christian patriots. As much as toward blacks, the second Klan was anti-Semitic, anti-Catholic, and anti-foreigner. In 1920, Simmons hired Edward Clarke and Elizabeth Tyler to conduct a publicity campaign for the Klan and increase membership. In 1923, with membership somewhere around 1–1.5 million, Simmons was ousted by Texas dentist Hiram Welsey Evans, who continued Klan growth and national influence.

Under Evans, Klan membership had grown to 4–5 million members by the mid-1920s and had a chapter in every state. A 1925 Klan rally in Washington D.C. drew over 25,000 robed Klansmen, and members were sheriffs, judges, state legislatures, and governors of three states. Members served in the U.S. Senate and House of Representatives. While it was growing, however, members continued to murder and torture blacks, Jews, Catholics, and foreigners. The ADL (1988) reported that many punished by the Klan were guilty of violating moral law: gambling, liquor dealing, dope peddling, and marital infidelity.

The downfall of the second Klan began in the late 1920s. Clarke, who was married, and Tyler were discovered to be having an affair. D.C. Stephenson, Grand Dragon of Indiana, was charged with the murder of an underaged female with whom he had been having sexual relations. Third, various state legislatures and federal government were passing laws banning certain types of Klan violence and controlling Klan activity. Fourth, various Klan leaders were beginning to infight over the distribution of funds designated as campaign contributions. These events, by

1926, had begun to cost membership. By the end of that year, membership had fallen below 2 million and by the end of 1927 had fallen to around 321,000 (ADL, 1988).

In 1939, James A. Colescott, a Klansman from Indiana, took over the Klan from Hiram Evans as Imperial Wizard and began an association with the Nazis. In 1940, the Klan held its national rally at the German-American Bund Camp Norland in New Jersey. The association with Nazis further hurt Klan membership, and by 1941, membership had fallen to less than 10,000 nationwide. On 23 April 1944, the Ku Klux Klan, Inc., at its annual meeting, the Imperial Klonvocation, dissolved itself, but not before the IRS had filed a $685,305 lien for back taxes.

In a response to school desegregation (*Brown* vs. *Board of Education*), the Klan resurfaced in the 1950s with an ideology based on racial purity and white supremacy (Randell, 1965). The ideology of the first Klan was resurrected, as many in the "old" South saw this legislation as a direct threat to the South's way of life and standard of living. Shortly after, many Klan chapters opened in the North and Midwest, as racists all over the country were threatened by new legislation giving minorities equal rights. These racists saw in the Klan white salvation. In its most recent history, the KKK has been the most active and violent of all far-right organizations. Members have been involved in thousands of acts of murder, assassination, execution, lynching, bombing, and harassment.

The Klan is often identified as a single movement, when in reality the Klan is organized into numerous subdivisions. One faction of the Klan is the Invisible Empire, Knights of the Ku Klux Klan. The Invisible Empire was headquartered in Denham Springs, Louisiana and led by Bill Wilkenson (ADL, 1988). In 1986, James Farrand was chosen its Grand Dragon (ADL, 1991). Presently headquartered in North Carolina, the Invisible Empire has its largest chapters in Louisiana, Alabama, Connecticut, and Pennsylvania.

The Invisible Empire runs several paramilitary/survivalist training camps in the South. One, called My Lai, after the Vietnam War massacre of Vietnamese by American soldiers, is a youth training camp. At this camp, children are indoctrinated in Klan philosophy and ideology, given weapons training, and taught guerrilla warfare tactics. As an example of the thoroughness of Klan training, Louis Ray Beam, former Klan Grand Dragon, once remarked, "The Klan training in Texas is more rigorous than that which is given to members of the United States Army at Fort Hood." Beam was charged in April 1987 by a federal grand jury with sedition. He fled the country and was found in November 1987, in Guadalajara, Mexico, and returned to the United States after a confrontation with Mexican authorities (Byrd, 1987).

A second major Klan faction is the Knights of the Ku Klux Klan (KKKK). Founded by David Duke in 1974, Duke stepped down as Grand Dragon to enter Louisiana politics (ADL, 1995b). Don Black became the Grand Dragon, and, in 1981, Black and nine other KKKK members were arrested by federal agents for conspiracy to take over the island of Dominica for the purpose of establishing a white nation. Upon Black's arrest, the KKKK fragmented into two separate organizations: one in Tuscumbia, Alabama, and led by Stanley McCollum, the other in Metairie, Louisiana with various leaders (including David Duke).

In the late 1980s, Arkansas minister Thomas Robb reunified the KKKK under his leadership. Living in Harrison, Arkansas, Robb heads the Church of Jesus Christ, an Identity church. Robb has directed his ministry toward the elimination of Jews. Robb once stated, "I hate Jews. I hate race-mixing Jews. We've let anti-Christ Jews into our country and we've been cursed with abortion, inflation, homosexuality and the threat of war" (ADL, 1991).

A third national Klan faction is the United Klans of America (UKA), historically the most violent, secretive, and conservative of the three major Klan subdivisions (Wiggins, 1985). In 1959, the largest Klan membership in the United States belonged to the U.S. Klans, headed by Eldon Lee Edwards. In 1960, Edwards was replaced as Grand Dragon by Robert Davidson. In 1961, the U.S. Klans merged with the Alabama Knights and became the UKA. Robert Shelton became Grand Dragon. Headquartered in Tuscaloosa, Alabama, and led by Robert Shelton, the UKA is most active in Alabama, Florida, Kentucky, North and South Carolina, and Virginia.

In 1987, UKA member Henry Hays was convicted in the murder of Michael Donald, a black youth killed in Mobile, Alabama. In one of the very few cases of its kind, Donald's mother and the Southern Poverty Law Center sued the UKA for civil rights violations and was awarded $7 million in a judgment against the UKA (Kornbluth, 1987). The civil judgment against the UKA seriously hurt UKA activities in the late 1980s, although they have reorganized and are rebuilding.

Klan leaders have been encouraged by the successes of David Duke in the legitimate political arena and are moving toward a revisionist policy to begin working inside the system. The Klan is attempting to seat its members in legitimate political positions so they can bring about change from inside the government. Their legitimate political agendas focus on affirmative action, EEO laws, immigration policy, crime, drugs, welfare, and AIDS.

In addition to these three major Klan factions, there are numerous other localized Klans scattered throughout the U.S. Table 5.3 lists some of the more active sub-factions of the Klan. A favored recruiting tactic of the Klan was to recruit outside of military bases. Military personnel were young, conservative, trained, and motivated to become engaged in Klan activity. On 5 September 1986, however, Defense Secretary Casper Weinberger issued a new directive prohibiting the recruitment at military installations and forbidding participation or membership in the Klan of military members (ADL, 1988).

Aryan Nations

One of the largest and most enduring of all Christian Identity organizations has been the Aryan Nations. Founded by ex-aerospace engineer Richard Butler in the late 1970s, the Aryan Nations is headquartered in Hayden Lake, Idaho. Sometimes called the Church of Jesus Christ Christian, the Aryan Nations is the masthead of the entire far-right movement. In 1995, Butler retired as leader of the Aryan Nations and turned control over to Harold Wheeler Hunt. Another assistant to Butler was William Fowler, former Grand Dragon of the California Ku Klux Klan.

Richard Butler was an engineer at Lockheed in California when he met William Gale, founder of one of the first far-right organizations, the California Rangers. Gale introduced Butler to Wesley Swift at the Church of Jesus Christ Christian in Hollywood. Butler soon converted to Christian Identity and refined the philosophy of the Church to include two categories of man: one was the true man, the Aryan descendants of Israel; the other satanic man, or homo bestialis, sons of Lucifer, Jews, and blacks—Satan's foot soldiers. In 1970, when Swift died, Butler took over the Church and moved it to Idaho. Richard Gale formed the Ministry of Christ Church and moved to Mariposa, California. Shortly thereafter, two of Gale's parishioners were arrested for the torture/murder of two people, including a five-year-old boy.

Richard Butler has repeatedly stated that neither him nor the Aryan Nations believe in violence. His actions and those of the organization say otherwise. The Aryan Nations has developed a formula whereby members can become an Aryan Warrior, an exalted position based on Norse mythology. By killing certain members of ZOG, members can work toward becoming an Aryan Warrior (Stinson, 1987). One-tenth of a point is earned for killing FBI agents and federal marshals, one-twelfth of a point for journalists and local politicians, one-sixteenth of a point for judges and the FBI director, one-fifth of a point for congressmen, and one point for killing the president of the U.S. If a member gets one point, they are considered an Aryan Warrior.

Table 5.3.
Ku Klux Klan organizations in the United States in 1996.

State	Organizations
Alabama	Alabama Empire Knights of the Ku Klux Klan
	Alabama Invisible Knights of the Ku Klux Klan
	Elmore County Key Club
	Knights of the Ku Klux Klan
	United Klans of America
California	American Knights
	California Knights of the Ku Klux Klan
	Invincible Empire, Knights of the White Rose
	White Knights of the Ku Klux Klan
Connecticut	Invisible Empire Knights of the Ku Klux Klan
Delaware	Territorial Klans of America
Florida	Church of the Christian Knights, KKK
	Dixie Knights of the Ku Klux Klan
	Florida Biker Knights
	Fraternal White Knights
	Militant Knights of the Ku Klux Klan
	Templar Knights
	White Knights
Georgia	Aryan White Knights
	Association of Georgia Klans
	Christian Knights of the Ku Klux Klan
	Confederate Forces
	Confederate White Knights
	Federated Knights of the Ku Klux Klan
	Forsyth County Defense League
	Fraternal White Knights of the Ku Klux Klan
	Improved Order of U.S. Klans
	Lookout Mountain Knights
	Loyal Order of White Knights
	National Knights of the Ku Klux Klan
	New Order Knights of the Ku Klux Klan
	Rebel Knights of the Ku Klux Klan
	Royal Confederate Knights
	Southern White Knights
	True Knights of the Aryan Nations
	Winder Knights
Indiana	Blood Klan
	Northwest Territory Knights of the Ku Klux Klan
Iowa	White Knights of the Ku Klux Klan
Kentucky	Christian Knights of the Ku Klux Klan
Louisiana	Original Knights of the Ku Klux Klan

Table 5.3. Continued

State	Organizations
Maryland	Confederate Independent Order Knights
	Independent Order Knights
	Invincible Empire Knights of the Ku Klux Klan
	Mason Dixon Knight Riders
	Territorial Klans of America
	United White Brotherhood of America
Michigan	White Ku Klux Klan
Mississippi	Cavalier Club
	Mississippi Knights of the Ku Klux Klan
	New Order Knights
	White Knights of the Ku Klux Klan
Missouri	Christian Knights of the Ku Klux Klan
	Confederation of Independent Orders
	Knights of the Ku Klux Klan
	National Knights of the Ku Klux Klan
	New Order Knights
	New Order Ku Klux Klan
	White Knights of the Ku Klux Klan
Nevada	Nevada Ku Klux Klan
	Southern National Klan Church
New Jersey	Confederate Knights of the Ku Klux Klan
	Flaming Sword Ku Klux Klan of the Confederate Knights of America
	Invisible Empire Knights
New York	White Knights of the Ku Klux Klan
North Carolina	Aryan Riders Motorcycle Club
	Aryan Christian Knights
	Carolina Ku Klux Klan
	Christian Knights of the Ku Klux Klan
	Confederate Knights of America
	Federated Knights of the Ku Klux Klan
	New Empire Ku Klux Klan
	White Knights of the Ku Klux Klan
	White Knights of Liberty
Oklahoma	White Knights of the Heartland
	White Knights of the Ku Klux Klan
Ohio	Belpre Dixie Knights
	Independent Invisible Knights
	National Knights of the Ku Klux Klan
	Ohio Knights of the Ku Klux Klan
	U.S. Knights of the Ku Klux Klan
Pennsylvania	Confederate Knights of America
	Kauker Knights
	Ku Klux Klan White Unity Party
	Mountaineer Knights of the Ku Klux Klan
	United Empire Knights of the Ku Klux Klan
	White Christian Knights
	White Knights of Pennsylvania
	White Unity Party

Table 5.3. Continued.

State	Organizations
South Carolina	Associated of South Carolina Klans
	Christian Knights of the Ku Klux Klan
	Confederate White Knights
Tennessee	Confederate Knights of America
	Dixie Klans
	Dixie Knights
	Justice Knights of the Ku Klux Klan
	Soddy Knights of the Ku Klux Klan
	Tennessee Knights
	United Empire Knights of the Ku Klux Klan
	White Rights Association
Texas	Confederate Knights of the Ku Klux Klan
	Knights of the White Camelia
	White Knights of Texas
	White Worker's Union
Virginia	Christian Knights of the Ku Klux Klan
	Confederate Knights of America
	Robert E. Lee Society Invisible Empire
Washington	Northwest Knights of the Ku Klux Klan
West Virginia	Christian Knights of the Ku Klux Klans
	Independent White Knights of the Ku Klux Klan
Wisconsin	National Knights of the Ku Klux Klan

The Aryan Nations also has developed plans for the establishment of an Aryan country in the northwestern United States, encompassing Washington, Oregon, Idaho, Montana, and Wyoming. The Aryan Nations has stockpiled weapons, harassed and killed minorities, defaced currency, participated in and led tax protests, trained in guerrilla warfare, and advocated the violent overthrow of the federal government (Broadbent, 1987). In the 1980s, the Aryan Nations contacted the government of Syria to discuss purchasing weapons and secure finances (Melnichak, 1986a).

One major activity of the Aryan Nations is hosting a yearly convention of the far right (Hoffman, 1986). The Aryan National Congress is open to all members and organizations of the far right. Topics discussed focus on white rights, and seminars are given in effective techniques for overthrowing the government (Barker, 1985; Sapp, 1987; White, 1991). Guest speakers have included Robert Miles of the Michigan Mountain Church of Jesus Christ, Louis Ray Beam of the Ku Klux Klan, author of *The Turner Diaries* William Pierce, and Manfred Roeder, a leading German neo-Nazi. Additionally, the Aryan Nations operated the Aryan

Nations Liberty Net computer bulletin board to spread its message to white America (ADL, 1985).

In 1979, Butler began a prison outreach program (ADL, 1995c). White inmates were invited to join the Aryan Brotherhood, a protective association for white inmates. Butler stated the purpose was to bring Christianity to prison inmates. The unstated purpose was to provide a manpower pool for the Aryan Nations, and a pool well-versed in violence. Prisoners who join the Aryan Brotherhood are required to sign a contract. Two clauses are particularly relevant to terrorism: (1) Upon release, the member will kill the police officer responsible for sending them to prison; and (2) upon release, the member will stay in the Aryan Nation organization. The Aryan Brotherhood has chapters in almost all prisons, federal and state, within the U.S., with the largest chapters in the penal system of California and Texas (ADL, 1986; Mullins, 1993).

The Order

The Order was formed in 1984 by Robert Mathews and, in its brief life, was one of the more violent of all far-right organizations (Harris, 1987). Members of the Order were from the Aryan Nations who believed a violent and widespread campaign to overthrow the federal government was needed. The Order went by several names, including the Bruder Schweigen (Silent Brotherhood), the White American Bastion, the Aryan Resistance Movement, and the White American Army of National Liberation for the Aryan Nations (Sapp, 1986a; Wiggins, 1986a; White, 1991).

During their short-lived career, members of the Order were involved in numerous criminal and terrorist activities, including the robbery of City Bank in Seattle, Washington (1983), robbery of a Continental Armed Transport in Seattle (1983), murder of Walter Earl West (an Order member suspected of being an FBI informant, 1984), murder of a Missouri state trooper (1984), murder of Denver radio talk-show host Alan Berg in Denver (1984), robbery of a Brinks armored truck in Ukiah, California (1984), planned assassination of presidential candidate Jesse Jackson (1988), and other confrontations with law enforcement authorities.

Relying on intelligence provided by a federal informant, the FBI closed in on Robert Mathews in 1984 (Dubin, 1988). Attempting to serve an arrest warrant at his hideout on Whidby Island, Oregon, Mathews confronted the agents and was killed in the ensuing firefight. Searching the wreckage of his house, authorities discovered an extensive hit list of federal judges, prosecutors, FBI agents, civil rights leaders, and other law enforcement authorities (Wiggins, 1986c), plans for blowing up Boundary Bridge in Seattle, disrupting shipping lanes in Puget Sound by destroying a liquid natural gas ship (LNG) with LAWs rockets, and poisoning various municipal water supplies.

In 1985, the remaining members of the Order were indicted by a federal grand jury for numerous crimes, including murder, counterfeiting, robbery, and various weapons violations (Wiggins, 1986b). In 1987, a federal grand jury in Fort Smith, Arkansas charged leaders of the Order, along with other leaders of the far-right movement, with sedition (Haddigan, 1987; Mullins, 1989). Those charged included: (1) Richard Joseph Scutori, chief security officer of the Order, (2) Bruce Carroll Pierce, suspected assassin of Alan Berg, (3) Jean Margaret Craig, female "warrior" in the Order, (4) David E. Lane, accomplice in the Alan Berg assassination, (5) Richard Butler, (6) Robert Miles, founder of Mountain Church of Jesus Christ the Savior in Cohoctah, Michigan, (7) Louis Ray Beam, Jr., former Grand Dragon of the KKK, (8) Ardie McBrearty, intelligence chief and legal advisor to the Order, (9) Robert N. Smalley, member of the CSA, (10) Richard Wayne Snell, member of the CSA, (11) Andrew V. Barnhill, member of CSA, (12) William Wade, member of CSA, Posse Comitatus and KKK, (13) David M. McGuire, son-in-law of Jim Ellison, and (14) Lambert Miller, member of CSA. Wade, McGuire and Miller were also indicted for attempting to murder Chief U.S. District Judge Franklin Waters and FBI agent Jack Knox. All 14 defendants were acquitted of all charges (Mullins, 1989; 1993). Other federal prosecutions of Order members are shown in Table 5.4 along with the outcome of those trials. One long-term outcome of the sedition trial and other prosecution efforts are that they have unified the far right and further demonstrated the illegitimacy of the federal government (Mullins, 1990a).

The Order II

In 1987, shortly after the death of Robert Mathews, Bruder Schweigen Strike Force II, or the Order II, was organized by other members of the Aryan Nations. Leaders of the Order II included Robert Pires, Elden "Bud" Cutler, and David and Deborah Dorr (David and his wife were leaders). Their first activity was to begin counterfeiting $20 bills to supply finances to the Order II. On 6 May 1987, the Order II sent a bomb to Gary Solomon, Jewish owner of a Hayden Lake trucking company. On 7 August 1987, members planted explosives in Fred Bower's Classic Auto Restoration business in Kootenai County, Idaho and two weeks later assassinated Kenneth Shray for being a suspected federal informant. In that same year, members bombed the residence of Father William Wassmuth of the St. Pious X Catholic Church on 16 September, and on

Table 5.4.
Federal prosecutions of members of the Order.

Name	Plea or Trial	Sentence	Age
Andrew Virgil Barnhill	Trial	40 years	29
Thomas Bentley	Plea	7½ years	57
Jean Margaret Craig	Trial	40 years	51
Randolph George Duey	Trial	100 years	34
James Sherman Dye	Unknown	Unknown	Unknown
Randall Paul Evans	Trial	40 years	29
Mark Franklin Jones	Plea	Suspended	Unknown
Richard Harold Kemp	Trial	60 years	39
Ronald Allen King	Plea	5 years	46
David Eden Lane	Trial	190 years	46
Kenneth Joseph Loff	Plea	5 years	34
Robert Jay Mathews	Deceased	None	31
Ardie McBrearty	Trial	40 years	57
Robert E. Merki	Plea	20 years	50
Sharon K. Merki	Plea	20 years	47
William Anthony Nash	Plea	Credit for time served	Unknown
Michael Stanley Norris	Trial	5 years	26
Jackie Lee Norton	Plea	Suspended	Unknown
Charles Ostrout	Plea	5 years	51
Denver Daw Parmenter	Plea	20 years	Unknown
Bruce Carroll Pierce	Trial	250 years	30
Randall Eugene Rader	Plea	6 years, suspended	34
Frank Scutari	Plea	3 years	Unknown
Richard Joseph Scutari	Plea	60 years	39
Frank Lee Silva	Trial	40 years	27
Ian Royal Stewart	Plea	5 years, 4½ suspended	21
David Tate*	Not tried	None	22
Gary Lee Yarbrough	Trial	60 years	29
George Franklin Zaengle	Plea	Suspended	Unknown

Source: Reprinted from *Terrorism in America: Pipe bombs and pipe dreams* by B.L. Smith by permission of the State University of New York Press. Copyright 1994, State University of New York.
*Tate is serving a life sentence in Missouri for killing a Missouri state trooper.

29 September placed four bombs in various locations around Coeur d'Alene, Idaho (telephone company, restaurant, finance company, and federal building). These bombings were meant as a diversionary attack while the Order II robbed the First National Bank in Rathdrum, Idaho and the Idaho Army National Guard Armory at Post Falls, Idaho. As a result of this last activity, all five members were arrested. Pires pled guilty to the murder of Shray and the others were convicted under RICO statutes (Smith, 1994).

Christian Defense League

Founded in Baton Rouge, Louisiana in 1977 by James K. Warner, the Christian Defense League operates a mail-order book service called the Sons of Liberty and publishes the *Christian Vanguard*, a periodical that is a forum for attacking Jews and minorities. Articles have included "Inequalities of the Negro Race," "New Research Into Jewish Ritual Murder," and "Sex Practices of the Jew" (ADL, 1983). *The Christian Vanguard* is nothing more than a forum for the far right to spread their messages of hate.

Christian Patriots Defense League

Founded in 1977 by John R. Harrell, the Christian Patriots Defense League (CPDL) is not active at present. They are presented because they were one of the early far-right identity movement organizations, and many of the precepts of the CPDL are cornerstones for the far-right movement. The CPDL held an annual Freedom Festival in Missouri for the far right. At these conventions, members of the far right were taught survivalist tactics, ideological indoctrination, paramilitary tactics to use against law enforcement and the government, and combat tactics to use against Jews and minorities. One role performed by the CPDL was that of an umbrella for the Christian Conservative Churches of America, the forerunner to today's Identity churches. The CPLD also established the Citizens Emergency Defense System, a private militia for the "new" government. Many active members of the far right received their initial training and philosophical indoctrination at CPDL Freedom Festivals. David Tate, killer of a Missouri state trooper, trained at a Freedom Festival just prior to killing the trooper.

The Covenant, The Sword and The Arm of the Lord

Jim Ellison founded the Covenant, the Sword and the Arm of the Lord (CSA) on a 224-acre compound in Marion County, Arkansas he called Zaraphath-Horeb. Ellison operated the Endtime Overcomer Survival Training School, where the Christian soldiers of the far right were taught survival and paramilitary skills, training in weapons proficiency, and received instructions in terrorist tactics. The rifle range at Zaraphath-Horeb, called Silhouette City, had Stars of David painted on the chests of targets (Weinberg, 1993). Ellison published the *CSA Journal and Basic Training Manual*, a paramilitary manual that discussed urban warfare, personal home defense, Christian martial arts, and Christian military truths.

Ellison was one of the more public and vitriolic leaders of the far right. He was willing to express his views on race, Jews, and the government to anyone who would listen. In one CSA tract, Ellison wrote

> Jesus gives us (Revelation 13:10) the authority to use the weapons of the Beast against those in rebellion to God. Our age not only suffers the travesties of drug addiction, prostitution and abortion, but also witches sexually mutilating people, sodomite homosexuals waiting in their lusts to rape, negro beasts who eat the flesh of men, Seed of Satan Jews sacrificing people in darkness, city-living white Christians, and "do-gooders" who've fought for the 'rights' of these groups. As we of the Adamic race are made "in the image of God," to then our anger at the world's sin is His, our wrath His, our vengeance the Lord's. (In Aho, 1990)

During the 1980s, Ellison was arrested numerous times. In 1980, in an arson-for-hire crime, Ellison was indicted for burning his sister's house. In 1983, he was indicted for burning a homosexual church, a Jewish community center, and bombing a natural gas pipeline. In 1985, Zarephath-Horeb was raided by federal agents, who found stockpiles of semiautomatic and automatic weapons, LAWs rockets, land mines, hand grenades, explosive devices, dynamite, kinetic explosives, military C-4 explosives, detonation cord, smoke grenades, military trip flares, South African Kruggerands, and thousands of rounds of ammunition. His compound was also heavily booby-trapped, with claymore mines around the perimeter and other booby-trap explosive devices in compound buildings. In September 1985, Ellison and two other CSA members were charged and sentenced to prison under RICO statutes. In 1988, Ellison turned government witness at the Fort Smith sedition trial.

In 1984, CSA member Richard Wayne Snell killed a Texarkana, Arkansas pawn shop owner and Arkansas state trooper Louis Bryant. Just prior to the killing of Bryant, Snell had attended a CPDL Freedom Festival. In 1995, Snell was put to death for the murder of Trooper Bryant. His execution was conducted on the same day as the Oklahoma City Federal Building was bombed.

National Alliance

Located in Arlington, Virginia, the National Alliance was founded in 1974 as a reorganization of the National Youth Alliance, an organization of George Wallace supporters. The National Alliance believes in white supremacism and espouses a platform of anti-Zionism. Membership is ultraconservative and spends a great deal of effort on controlling leftists and liberals on university and college campuses. The organization has published numerous books and pamphlets on how to construct and use homemade explosives and incendiaries.

In 1978, a member of the National Alliance, William Pierce (pen name Andrew MacDonald) wrote *The Turner Diaries,* a novel which has become the blueprint for survival for the far right (ADL, 1995a). Timothy McVeigh, suspected bomber of the Oklahoma City Federal Building, was a reader and avid believer of the book. Many suspect his bombing attack was planned directly from suggestions offered in the book (see Table 5.5). Following the bombing, Pierce, now director of National Alliance, said on 29 April in his weekly radio broadcast, "...we'll see some real terrorism, planned, organized terrorism—before too long. I suspect that a growing number of exasperated, fed-up Americans will begin engaging in terrorism on a scale the world has never seen before" (Klanwatch, 1995).

Table 5.5.

A comparison of a terrorist bombing attack described in *The Turner Diaries* and the actual bombing of the Oklahoma City Federal Building.

The Turner Diaries	*Oklahoma City Federal Building*
Target was federal law enforcement building	Target housed federal law enforcement
Truck bomb	Truck bomb
Bomb was about 5,000 pounds	Bomb was 4,400 pounds
Bomb was fuel oil and ammonium nitrate	Bomb was fuel oil and ammonium nitrate
Bomb detonated at 9:15 A.M.	Bomb detonated at 9:05 A.M.
Bomb designed to blow off front of building causing upper floors to collapse	Bomb blew off front of building and collapsed upper floors
Bombing caused passage of federal gun control act	Suspects violently opposed to federal gun control
Main character, Turner, considered himself a "patriot"	Suspects considered themselves "patriots"
Turner was member of anti-government underground cell	FBI believes suspects were members of underground anti-government cell
Terrorists robbed banks to fund war	Despite having no jobs, suspects had thousands of dollars, ski masks and pipes similar to those used in 13 bank robberies
Turner was openly racist	Prime suspect is openly racist

FROM: Klanwatch (1995). Over 200 militias and support groups operate nationwide. *Intelligence Report, 78,* 4. Klanwatch Intelligence Report is produced by the Southern Poverty Law Center, Montgomery, Alabama

National Socialist Liberation Front

The National Socialist Liberation Front (NSLF) was formed in 1969 by Karl Hard, Jr. in Metairie, Louisiana. Of all neo-Nazi parties, the NSLF has been the most outspoken and one of the most violent. The NSLF has held demonstrations and marches throughout the South, attempting crowds to incite to violence to regain the country for the white race. Hand has directed recruiting efforts at prisons, looking for ex-convicts to fill NSLF ranks. Felons have the necessary skills to conduct campaigns of violence against Jews and minorities, as well as a deep-seated racial hatred developed by their prison experience.

National Socialist Party of America/American Nazi Party

The American Nazi Party (ANP) arrived on the scene in 1970 in Chicago, Illinois. Its founder, Frank Collins, was convicted of child sexual abuse in 1980 and sent to prison. In 1980, Harold Covington took control of the party. He was suspected by members of being a federal informant, so in March 1981, Michael Allen of St. Louis was named as party leader. Unfortunately, Allen was an ATF informant and provided federal agents with enough information to lead to the arrests and convictions of many ANP members. In 1982, Jim Burford took command and the organization began to wither under his direction. As membership decreased, two factions of the ANP appeared: one was the American Nazi Party under control of Dennis Milam, and the other the America First Committee lead by Art Jones (George & Wilcox, 1992). Both are still active and have rebuilt the party. A favored tactic of the ANP is to hold a demonstration, provoke the audience into reacting to their inflammatory message, and then attack the crowd in the guise of "self-defense."

In the late 1970s, the ANP petitioned to demonstrate in Skokie, Illinois, a community with a large WWII European Polish population. The city refused the request and a court action was threatened. The city relented and issued a permit. At the demonstrations (one held in 1977, the other in 1978), the ANP stressed the legitimacy of Hitler's extermination program, provoking a violent confrontation between citizens of Skokie and the ANP.

The ANP perceives itself as international in scope and actively recruits neo-Nazis from other countries, including Canada and Germany. John Hinkley, who attempted to assassinate President Reagan, claimed membership in the ANP. The ANP, in response, claimed Hinkley had been thrown out of the organization because he was too violent.

New Order/National Socialist White People's Party

The National Socialist White People's Party is the oldest neo-Nazi organization in the United States. It was founded on the coattails of the great Red Scare of the 1950s by George Lincoln Rockwell (Holden 1985). By 1960, the name of the party had been changed to the New Order. In August 1967, Rockwell was assassinated by ex-member John Patler in a Chicago laundromat and Matthias Koell took control of the New Order. He moved the headquarters to Arlington, Virginia and immediately made it national, forming chapters in Chicago, Cleveland, Milwaukee, Minneapolis, Los Angeles, San Francisco, and Orange County, California (ADL, 1983). In 1983, its headquarters was again moved, this time to New Berlin, Wisconsin (George & Wilcox, 1992). The New Order (still sometimes referred to as the NSWPP) has an 800 telephone number, the White Power Message, which provides daily hate messages against minorities and Jews.

In the 1990s, the New Order has recruited actively on university and college campuses. They preach a message of National Socialism which is based upon three principles: (1) Natural order, the belief that the universe is governed by natural laws that humankind must follow. Today's society is in violation of those natural laws and must be changed or the white race will die out. (2) Racial idealism. Race is the most important component of the natural order and the race must be protected at all costs. Races are not created equal, and it is the right and duty of Aryans to maintain the biological, cultural, and political independence of the race. (3) Upward development of the white race. Whites must selectively procreate, allowing only the strongest, most intelligent, and healthiest to live and further procreate. Hereditary weaknesses, illnesses, and defects must be eliminated.

The New Order has in the past formed subdivisions for special interests. These include the National Socialist Youth Movement, the National Socialist Women's Organization, and the Storm Troopers. The last are trained guards responsible for protection at public demonstrations and protests.

Posse Comitatus

In 1973 in Portland, Oregon, Gordon Kahl, Henry Beach, and William P. Gale founded the Posse Comitatus as a tax protest movement. Their name was derived from the Posse Comitatus Act of 1878, which prohibited military involvement in local law enforcement and enabled the sheriff to deputize any citizen of the county to assist in keeping the peace. Also referred to as the Sheriff's Posse Comitatus and Citizen's Law Enforcement Research Committee, the ideology of Posse Comitatus includes the elimination of all taxes, the overthrow of the Jewish federal government and a return to Anglo-Saxon origins, elimination of all federal, state, and municipal law enforcement, establishment of county government as the primary form of government in the U.S., and hate campaigns directed against minorities and Jews.

In 1984, Gordon Kahl killed two federal marshals who were attempting to arrest him for tax evasion, fled to Smithville, Arkansas, and killed a county sheriff before himself being killed by federal marshals (Bowers, 1987). After his death, Pastor James P. Wickstrom of the Wisconsin Life Science Church, and Wilhelm Ernst Schmitt, formerly of Lockeed Missile and Space Company (where he worked on the Polaris missile) declared themselves new leaders of the Posse Comitatus.

Schmitt had been convicted in 1969 of threatening an IRS agent, and moved to Bemidji, Minnesota. There he linked up with Harry Mott, Roger Luther, and Ernest Foust, and the four were soon arrested again for threatening to kill an IRS agent. When federal authorities searched their homes, they found weapons, explosives, hand grenades, machine guns, military trip flares, a grenade launcher, and various ammunition and supplies, most secreted in underground and interconnected bunkers (Smith, 1994).

In 1985, Wickstrom and Donald Minniecheske attempted to create the new township of Tigerton Dells, Wisconsin, and establish a paramilitary camp. This new township would be its own "country" and not have to abide by the laws of the nation or state of Wisconsin. In response, the state arrested Wickstrom and he was convicted of impersonating a public official. That was the end of Tigerton Dells.

The Posse Comitatus has been involved in paramilitary/survivalist training, stockpiling of weapons, and creation of armed compounds around the nation. In addition, the Posse Comitatus has engaged in drug trafficking to finance their activities. In July 1979, a member of Posse Comitatus wounded three AFT agents in a drug-buy attempt. The Posse Comitatus has no national leadership. Each county chapter is responsible for its own maintenance and organization. As a result, many chapters of the Posse Comitatus have different names. In Dallas, Texas, the chapter is named Citizens for Constitutional Compliance; in San Diego, California, the Know Your Rights Group; in Canton, Ohio, the Citizens for Constitutional Rights; and in Racine, Wisconsin, the Christian Posse. Many members claim to be "preachers" in the Life Science Church and call their homes chapels and their guns church property. Any income received is considered "donations" to the church ministry.

Arizona Patriots

In 1982, Hollywood actor Ty Hardin founded the Arizona Patriots in Prescott, Arizona. Like the Posse Comitatus, the Arizona Patriots believed county government was the only legitimate form of government. Many of their members came from other far-right organizations. In preparation for the communist invasion from Mexico, the Arizona Patriots began building an armed encampment in the Arizona desert. In June 1984, the organization threatened all public officials in Arizona. If elected officials did not resign within 30 days, the Arizona Patriots would "force" them to resign.

Plans were made to conduct a series of terrorist activities in late 1984. The Arizona Patriots selected a Jewish synagogue, the IRS regional center at Ogden, Utah, and various hydroelectric plants on the Colorado River for a campaign of bombing. Needing money, members devised a plan to rob Las Vegas casino armored trucks. The robbery conspiracy members included Steve Christensen, David Gumaer, J. R. Hagan, Foster Thomas Hoover, Jack Oliphant, Tom Palmer, Monte Ross, and Patrick and Rita Schlect. All were sent to prison except Gumaer, who escaped and became a federal fugitive.

Skinhead Movement

In the late 1980s, a new youth movement was brought from Europe, the skinhead movement. In Europe, skinheads were originally counter-culture youths who dressed weird, danced "slam dances" to punk rock music, and got identifiable tattoos. In the U.S., the skinhead movement adopted the ideologies of neo-fascism and Christian Identity, today two philosophies which are the trademarks of skinheads.

The first U.S. skinhead organization was Romantic Violence in Michigan. In 1988, there were only an estimated 300 skinheads nationwide. In 1991, the movement had over 5,000 members, with chapters in most major cities. The ADL (1993) indicated that in 1993, membership was approximately 3,300–3,500, up from 3,000 in 1990, 3,000 in 1989, 2,000 in 1988 and 1,000–1,500 in 1988. Skinhead organizations do not come under a national organization, nor are they unified into a national coalition. Instead, each local chapter governs ideology and action (ADL, 1990a). Table 5.6 provides an overview of the more active and larger skinhead organizations in the U.S.

Although there is no national organization, Californian Thomas Metzger and his son John proclaim themselves leaders and have attempted to unify the skinheads into a national organization.

Table 5.6.
Skinhead organizations in the United States in 1996.

State	City	Organization
Alabama	Birmingham	Aryan National Front, Birmingham Area Skinheads, Confederate Hammer Skins
	Fultondale	Family Assistance Project
	Helena	White Reick
	Homewood	NO NAME
	Huntsville	Alabama Confederate Hammer Skinheads, Aryan National Front
Arizona	Phoenix	Arizona Hammer Skinheads
	Tucson	NO NAME
	Yuma	NO NAME
Arkansas	Harrison	Aryan Women's League
California	Bakersfield	War Skins
	Bonsall	Aryan Women's League
	Fontana	Aryan Identity
	Garden Grove	American White Separatists
	Lomita	Lomita White Boys
	Los Angeles	Western Hammer Skins
	Modesto	American Front Vikings
	Orange County	18 organizations
	Sacramento	Sacto Skins
	San Diego	American Front and War Skins
	San Francisco	American Front, San Francisco White Aryan Resistance
	San Luis Obispo	Peni Skins
	Santa Barbara	Santa Barbara Boot Boys
	Santa Rosa	WAR Skins
	Simi Valley	SVH Skins
	Turlock	American Front Vikings
	Upland	White Flesh
	Ventura	Ventura Boot Boys and Skinhead Dogs
	Yucaipa	Nationalist Skinhead Knights
Colorado	Castle Rock	Rocky Mountain Confederate Hammer Skins
	Denver	Aryan Alliance, Boot Boys/Boot Girls, Rocky Mountain Confederate Hammer Skinheads
Connecticut	Various Cities	NO NAMES
Delaware	Newark	Eastern Hammer Skins
Florida	Anthony	Frydung
	Jacksonville	New White Working Youth
	Kathleen	Aryan Southern League
	Longwood	Florida Corps Skinheads
	Nokomis	National Socialist White Workers Party

Table 5.6. Continued.

State	City	Organization
	Orlando	Florida Corps Skins, Old Glory Skins, Young Southern Nationals, Youth Corp 87
	Tampa	Bros
	Temple Terrace	NO NAME
	Treasure Coast	American Front
	West Palm Beach	American Front, Aryan National Front
Georgia	Albany	American Front
	Armuchee	Aryan Resistance League, Northwest Georgia Skinheads
	Atlanta	American Front, Aryan National Front, SS Strike Team
	Duluth	National Socialist Political Action League
	Marietta	Christian Guard, Georgia White Unity Association
	Roswell	Frydung
Illinois	Chicago	Blue Island Skinheads, Chicago Area Skinheads, Chicago White Viking
Indiana	Indianapolis	Pure American Freedom Party, Northern Hammer Skins
Kentucky	Louisville	Louisville Aryan Skinheads
Louisiana	New Orleans	National White Resistance
	Shreveport	Shreveport Metropolitan Area Skinheads
Maryland	Baltimore	American Resistance, Baltimore Area Skinheads, Maryland Knights, Nationalist Skinheads of Baltimore
	Prince Georges County	NO NAME
	Southern Maryland	Southern Maryland Area Skinheads (SMASH)
Massachusetts	Quincy	North Quincy Skinheads, South Boston Skinheads
	Stoughton	Confederate Vanguard
Michigan	Clio	United White Youth of Clio
	Detroit	Northern Hammer Skins
	Grand Rapids	Pit Bull Boys, Northern Hammer Skins
Minnesota	Minneapolis/St. Paul	Northern Hammer Skins, Nordic Fist
Missouri	St. Louis	American Patriotic Army
Montana	Billings	Northwest United Skinheads
Nevada	Las Vegas	Aryan Long Hairs, Las Vegas Skinheads, Operation White Nurse
New Jersey	Atlantic County	Atlantic City Skinheads
	Berlin	Aggravated Assault
	Burlington	White Combat Skinheads, White Power Skinheads
	East St. Paul	Bound for Glory
	Elizabeth	Aryan Women's League

Table 5.6. Continued.

State	City	Organization
	Hudson County	Bayonne Bulldog Bootboys
	Mercer County	Trenton Guards, Trenton Posse, White Justice
	Middlesex County	Brunswick Skins
	Monmouth County	Aryan Resistance, Third World, New Way, Throckmorton Boys
	Newark	Eastern Hammer Skins, White Rights Union
	Ocean County	Brick Town Guards
New Mexico	Albuquerque	NO NAME
New York	Long Island	NO NAME
	Rochester	Buffalo Rochester Area Skinheads (BRASH)
North Carolina	Asheville	Southern Aryan Warriors
	Fayetteville	Nationalist Socialist Front
	Waxhaw	Skinhead Power
Ohio	Cincinnati	Northern Hammer Skins
	Enon	Voltairian Philosophers
Oklahoma	Tulsa	Boot Boys, Tulsa Skinhead Alliance
Oregon	Medford	Southern Oregon Skinheads
	Portland	American Front, American White Aryan Resistance (AWAR), United White Front, National White Separatists, Nationalist Front, Southern Justice Skinheads
Pennsylvania	Allentown	Allentown Skinheads
	Clifton Heights	Clifton Heights Skins
	Philadelphia	Eastern Hammer Skins, White Combat, White Justice
	Pitcairn	Aryan Women's League, Pennsylvania Aryan Independence Network
	Pittsburgh	NO NAME
	Swarthmore	White Power Skinheads
Tennessee	Butler	Confederate Hammer Skins, ANP
	Chattanooga	Chattanooga Area Confederate Hammer Skins
	Knoxville	Knoxville Area Skinheads, Southern Aryan Women's Assoc.
	Memphis	Memphis Area Skins
	Nashville	Aryan Women's League, Nashville Area Skinheads (NASH), Confederate Hammer Skins
	Ooltewah	Christian Guard
Texas	Austin	Creativity Skins, Teutonic Order of Skinhead Aryan Youth Movement, United Skins of America
	Dallas	Confederate Hammer Skins, Confederate White Vikings
	Ft. Worth	Aryan Legion

Table 5.6. Continued.

State	City	Organization
	Houston	Kingwood Skins, National Socialist Skinheads of Houston
	San Antonio	San Antonio Metropolitan Area Skinheads (SMASH)
Utah	Hurricane	Army of Israel
Washington	Kingston	Aryan Women's League
	Seattle	American Front, League of American Workers (LAW)
	Vancouver	Southern Justice
Wisconsin	Milwaukee	Northern Hammer Skins
Wyoming	Casper	Casper Area Skinheads (CASH)
	Evanston	Christian Patriot Women

The far-right movement sees the skinheads as the future warriors of the far right. The Klan, Aryan Nations, CSA, and other far-right organizations have provided political indoctrination, training, weapons, and other supplies and materials to skinheads. Richard Butler and various Klan factions have used the skinheads as security guards at conventions, meetings, and public demonstrations. The KKKK in Tuscumbia, Alabama has established links with skinheads from Oklahoma, Illinois, and Texas. Joe Grego, head of the Oklahoma White Man's Association and Klan member, has hosted several Skinhead Aryan Fests in Oklahoma (ADL, 1990b). Skinheads have been involved in Klan functions in Arkansas, Florida, Georgia, Illinois, Pennsylvania, Tennessee, and Texas.

In 1987, 13 Palo Alto, California skinheads went to Modesto to provide security for a Klan cross-burning rally. Four of those were inducted into the Klan. In the 1988 sedition trial in Fort Smith, Arkansas, skinheads performed security functions for far-right demonstrators. In 1988, the KKK and skinheads rioted at the Democratic National convention and were led in this activity by Richard Barrett, who runs the Nationalist Movement. In March 1988, a Tulsa skinhead was named Racist of the Month for his "professionalism" while a security guard at a Klan rally in Mansfield, Arkansas (ADL, 1990c). *The Oklahoma Separist,* a publication of the Oklahoma Knights, classifies skinheads under the heading, "The Fourth Reich." The Texas Knights Klan has assisted the Confederate Hammer Skinheads of Dallas. In 1990, skinhead and KKK members demonstrated at the Economic Summit meeting in Houston, Texas (they were joined by Richard Butler, Charles Lee, Kirk Lyons, and Thomas Robb).

As the far right ages, the skinheads are the salvation for white America and the ones who will lead the white race to victory. Richard Butler, speaking of the skinheads, said, "... natural biological reaction of white teenagers banding together after they have been taught that non-white kids are great and that white kids are scum. Skinheads will clean up the streets after receiving proper guidance" (Mullins, 1991).

In the 1990s, skinheads nationwide have been charged and convicted of vandalism against Jewish property, assaults against blacks and Jews, and murder of minorities. Skinheads in Texas, California, Colorado, Florida, Nevada, Oregon, and Pennsylvania have been sentenced. The most notable case against skinheads occurred in Portland, Oregon in 1989. Kenneth Mieske (aka Ken Death) and Kyle Brewster, members of the East Side White Pride Skinheads, were charged with killing Mulugeta Seraw. The Southern Poverty Law Center and ADL filed a wrongful-death suit against the two defendants, Thomas and John Metzger, and the White Aryan Resistance (ADL, 1990b). In 1990, a Portland jury returned a $12.5 million verdict against the five defendants: $3 million against Thomas Metzger, $4 million against John Metzger, $5 million against the White Aryan Resistance and $500,000 each against the two skinheads.

In addition, the U.S. skinhead movement has had a significant influence and impact on the European skinhead movement. Most European skinheads have adopted the racist philosophies and ideologies of their American counterparts. In England, in 1991, there were over 70,000 skinhead incidents and over one skinhead concert per month on the European mainland (Waxman, 1993). Of the European skinheads, the fastest-growing organizations are in Germany and Eastern Europe. There are an estimated 2,000 skinheads in Dresden, Germany alone. In Hungary, a skinhead magazine is regularly published called the *Panon Bulldog*. Skinheads have adopted the racist-matched names to coincide with their political beliefs. Organizations have names such as German National Front, German Alliance, Wiking Jugend (Viking Youth), and British Extremist National Front.

In the past couple of years, the skinhead movement has been undergoing some transformations. One, younger members are joining the skinheads. Reports of 12- and 13-year-old members are being received. In part, this movement is likely a response to inner-city gang growth. Two, skinheads are becoming more mobile, moving around the country to avoid law enforcement. Three, the skinheads are changing their physical appearance back to more mainstream dress, again in an attempt to thwart law enforcement and confuse the public. Four, the far right is assisting even more in recruitment and indoctrination of skinheads and involving them more in far-right activities.

The Militia Movement

The militia movement of the 1990s had its beginnings almost 30 years ago when William Potter Gale formed the California Rangers (Klanwatch, 1995). In 1968, several right wingers claiming themselves to be Minutemen bombed the Redmond, Washington police department and attempted to rob three Seattle banks. Three of those arrested and other leaders of the Minutemen, including Dennis Mower (an Identity preacher), Walter Peyson, and Keith Gilbert, were shown to be members of Swift's California church. Gilbert was also indicted for stealing 1,400 pounds of TNT to kill Reverend Martin Luther King, Jr. at the Hollywood Palladium. From those beginnings, the present far right grew throughout the 1970s, exploded in the 1980s, and has led in the 1990s to the militia movement. The militia movement has attracted many of the far-right members from the 1980s, who have changed organizations but not stripes. In the militia movement of 1995 are people such as Glen Miller, Harold Covington, James Wichstrom, Joe Grego, and many others from the various Klans, Aryan Nations, CSA, and other movements of the 1980s.

Two incidents in the early 1990s gave impetus and focus to the militia movement: the Branch Davidian siege in Waco, Texas in 1993 and the Randy Weaver siege at Ruby Ridge, Idaho. In 1992, at Estes Park, Colorado, over 160 leading members of the far right, including Louis Beam, Richard Butler, and Pete Peters, members of the Aryan Nations, Posse Comitatus, various Klan factions, and other Identity organizations, planned a strategy for the coming revolution (Klanwatch, 1995). Calling the tactic "Leaderless Resistance," the strategy called for the development of underground militia units and small leaderless terrorist cells to conduct campaigns of terrorism against the government.

The Randy Weaver saga in Idaho is highly significant to militias, so it is worth describing at this point. In 1986, Randy Weaver moved his wife, son, and three daughters to Ruby Ridge, on the Selkirk Mountains in northern Idaho, after attending the Aryan World Congress at Hayden Lake, Idaho (Aho, 1994). His intent in moving there was to protect his family values. He called his family Yahweh believers, practiced a doctrine of white separatism, referred to Jews as "Christ killers," would not permit any toys, paintings, or furniture with pictures of flowers, and made his wife Vicky move into an outbuilding during menstruation (to wait for the Last Days)

In January 1991, Weaver was arrested in Kootenai County for selling two sawed-off shotguns to a federal informant. He fled, returned to Ruby Ridge, and vowed never to surrender. For 18 months, government surveillance watched Weaver, using video cameras and flyovers by military

F-4s. Weaver found one of the cameras and destroyed it, an action the government used to charge him with destruction of federal property. U.S. Marshall Jack Cluff attempted to talk Weaver into surrendering. Weaver was close to surrendering, but his wife, Vicki, convinced him to continue to resist.

In May 1992, Cluff surveilled the property posing as a real estate agent and was confronted by Weaver, Vicki, and a friend of Weaver's, Kevin Harris. He retreated from the property. U.S. Marshall William Degan, member of the national SWAT team and Special Operation's Group, entered the Weaver property without a search warrant. Degan said he was going to recover one of the surveillance cameras. Dressed in jungle camouflage fatigues and armed with automatic rifles, Degan and Cluff went up the mountain. Weaver's dog caught their scent and began barking. Sammy (Weaver's son), Kevin Harris, and Randy Weaver went to investigate. As Degan was killing the dog, Sammy and Harris stumbled upon him. In an ensuing gun battle, Sammy was fatally struck in the back by a round from Degan's rifle, and Degan was killed by a bullet which hit him in the thorax.

The FBI assumed command of operations, and supposedly, snipers were given an order to shoot when they got a target, an order outside normal FBI policy and procedure. About 38 hours later, Weaver appeared in the cabin doorway and an FBI sniper fired a round. The sniper's bullet hit Randall in the shoulder and killed Vicki. Harris was hit in the chest by bone fragments and suffered several broken ribs and a collapsed lung. Weaver put Vicki's corpse under the dining room table for the remaining ten days of the siege.

After ten days, including four in which Bo Gritz, a Christian patriot, negotiated for a surrender, Weaver came out and ended the siege. Weaver and Harris were charged with "provoking and sustaining a violent confrontation with federal, state and/or local law enforcement officers" (according to the federal indictment, in Aho, 1994). Weaver, Harris, Vicki, Sammy, and all three daughters, including a 10-month-old, were charged with "unlawfully, willfully, deliberately . . . kill(ing) and murder(ing) one William F. Degan."

In April 1993, in the Boise Federal District Court, 56 government witnesses were called to testify for the prosecution. Weaver's attorney called no witnesses. After 20 days of deliberation, a jury acquitted Harris on all counts. Weaver was acquitted of murder and provoking a violent confrontation but was convicted of the two lesser charges of failure to appear for the original trial and committing an offense while on release from a federal magistrate.

The Attorney General of Idaho wanted to charge the FBI sniper with murder, and a federal Senate hearing concerning the Ruby Ridge incident was convened in 1995. In 1996, Weaver was awarded over $3 million in damages. To the far right, the entire incident illustrated the danger of the federal government and gave rise to a movement to overthrow the government before it hurt more citizens.

Between the meeting in Estes Park and late 1995, the militia movement grew to include over 224 militias in 39 states. Table 5.7 and Figure 5.2 list and show the location of some of these militias. As reported by Klanwatch (1995), at least 45 have direct links with neo-Nazi and other white supremacist organizations. Michigan alone has 30 militias, California has 22, Alabama and Colorado have 20 each, Missouri and Texas have 14, and Florida has 13. Militias with racist ties are in at least 22 states. The Militia of Montana, one of the most visible and vociferous, was founded by John Trochmann, speaker at the Aryan Nations conventions. One issue of their monthly newsletter, *Taking Aim,* printed shortly before the Oklahoma City Federal Building bombing, stated that 19 April was that day "Lexington burned . . . Warsaw burned . . . The feds attempted to raid Randy Weaver . . . The Branch Davidians burned" (ADL, 1995d). The implications and comparisons of the federal government to the Nazi genocide are obvious.

Unlike their predecessor organizations, the militias are small and fluid. Most believe an apocalyptic showdown with a tyrannical federal government is on the horizon. They are permeated by a deep-rooted paranoia that the government is intent on enslaving white Americans and is conducting continual surveillance on white America. Theories of black helicopters surveiling citizens, concentration camps being constructed for resisters, foreign troops encamped on U.S. soil, laser weapons trained on "patriots," and secret markings on road signs to guide invading forces abound. Militia members believe the government has already trained over one million agents to regain control of America and take it away from the people. Additionally, some of these militias believe there are massive crematoriums with gas chambers and guillotines throughout the country, over 100 established concentration camps are awaiting "patriot" inmates, that the United Nations has control of the U.S. Air Force, over 2,000 Russian tanks and other military vehicles have landed in Gulfport, Mississippi, that Fort Polk, Louisiana is a Russian military installation under the United Nations flag, that the National Security Agency records every single telephone conversation and fax transmission on Cray computers in Virginia and England, and new money is being printed with the United Nations New Order symbol on the back. Militias also believe Christianity is about to be banned by the government. Behind most of this paranoia is the great Jewish Satan, the United Nations. President

Table 5.7.
Militia and support organizations in the United States in 1996.

State	Militia	
Alabama	American Rangers	Central Alabama Militia
	Committee of Seventy Six	Committee to Defend the
	Crispus Attucks Detachment	Constitution
	Dogtown Rangers	Free People's Militia
	Gadsden Minutemen	Jefferson County Militia
	Mobile Regulators	Montgomery Militia
	Shelby County Group 19	Sons of Liberty
	Sons of Liberty Southern Command	
Arkansas	Citizen Militia	Marion County Militia
	Washington County Militia	
Arizona	American Citizens and Lawmen	
	Assoc.	Arizona Constitutional Rangers
	Arizona Patriots	Chino Valley Militia
	Citizens for America	Constitutional Militia
	Guardians of American Liberties	Sovereign Citizens Movement
California	Citizens Armed for Responsible	
	Educ.	Cool Company
	Critical Issues Advocate	El Dorado County Militia
	Garden Valley Company	Georgetown Company
	Georgetown Divide Battalion	Guardians of American Liberties
	Kelsey Company	Morongo Basin Militia and Yacht
	Morongo Militia	Club
	Pilot Connection Society	Placer County Militia
	RP Installation	Second Amendment Committee
	Shingletown Militia	Tehama County Militia
	Unorganized Militia of California,	We The People
	Ft. Bragg Unit	
Colorado	American Agricultural Movement	American Citizens Militia
	Boulder County Militia	Colorado Free Militia
	Financial and Monetary Consultants	Colorado Patriots
	Guardians of American Liberties	Longmont Citizens of the Republic
	National Commodity and Barter	
	Assoc.	Paladin Arms
	Patriots	Remnant Resolves Committee
	Save America Militia	Stewards of the Constitution
	Tenth Amendment Committee	USA Patriot Network
	White Knights of the KKK	
Delaware	Delaware Minutemen	Delaware Regional Citizen's Militia
Florida	American Citizens Alliance	Central Florida Militia Assoc.
	Constitutional Common Law Militia	Florida State Militia 2nd Regiment
	Florida State Militia 7th Regiment	Gold Coast Patriots Club
	Guardians of American Liberties	Highlander Militia 7th Regiment
	Liberty Group	North Central Regional Militia,
		Florida

Table 5.7. Continued.

State	Militia	
	Operation Freedom	Outpost of Freedom
Georgia	Citizens for a Constitutional Georgia	Citizens for a Safe Government
	11th North Georgia Militia	
Hawaii	Honolulu Unorganized Militia, Unit Alpha	Militia of Hawaii
	The Phoenix Project/Committee of 50 States	
Idaho	Idaho Citizens Awareness Network	Northwest Liberty Network
	Stewards of the Range	SPIKE
	United States Militia Association	Unorganized Militia of Idaho
Illinois	Southern Illinois Patriots League	
Indiana	Black Panther Militia	Brown County Militia
	Delaware County Patriots	Marion County Militia of Indiana
	North American Freedom Council	Ripley County Militia
	Switzerland County Militia	
Iowa	North American Freedom Council	
Kentucky	Defenders of Liberty	Kentucky Citizens Militia
	Voice of Liberty	
Louisiana	Citizens Against the Waco Atrocities	
Michigan	American Freedom Network	Central Michigan Regional Militia
	Citizens for Justice	Committee to Restore the Constitution
	Fully Informed Jury Assoc.	
	Gun Owners of (16 different counties)	Justice Pro Se
	Michigan Militia	Michigan Militia-at-Large
	Michigan Militia of Isabella County	Michigan Militia Southern Region, 5th Brigade
	Muskegon County Citizens Militia	Northern Michigan Regional Militia
	Oakland County Militia	
Minnesota	People's Reform Movement	
Mississippi	Mississippi Militia, Jones County Unit	
Missouri	1st Missouri Volunteers	24th Militia
	Continental Militia	First Missouri Volunteers
	Missouri 51st Militia HQ	Missouri Patriots
	Missouri White Militia	South Central Regional Militia
Montana	Citizens Against Military Enforcement of the Law	Militia of Montana
		United States for Justice
Nebraska	Department of Council Patriarchs	
	Militants of Nebraska	
New Hampshire	Constitution Defense Militia	White Mountain Militia
New Mexico	Christian Crusade for Truth	
New York	Broome County Militia	Chemung County Citizens Militia
	Orange County Militia	Unorganized Militia Affiliate

Table 5.7. Continued.

Nevada	Information Down Link America	Guardians of American Liberties
	National Refounders Empowerment Center	Nevada Volunteers
	United States Constitutional Rangers	
North Carolina	Citizens for the Reinstatement of Constitutional Government	
Ohio	Guardians of American Liberties	Ohio Unorganized Militia
Oklahoma	Cleveland County Militia	Oklahoma Citizens Militia, NW
	Oklahoma Militia	
Oregon	Central Oregon Regional Militia	Northwest Oregon Regional Militia
Pennsylvania	Bradford County Citizens Militia	Keystone Militia
	Perry County Militia	Posse Comitatus—Penn.
	Unit Alpha of Penn. State Militia	
South Carolina	American Patriots Private Intelligence Network	South Carolina Militia
South Dakota	Tri-State Militia	
Tennessee	Christian Civil Liberties Association	
Texas	Concerned Americans	Freedom Fighters
	Guardians of American Liberty	Texas Constitutional Militia, Bexar Cty
	Texas Constitutional Militia, North Gulf Region	Texas Constitutional Militia, Northern Region
	Texas Constitutional Militia, Southern Region	Texas Light Infantry
		Texas Militia Correspondence Comm.
	U.S. Civil Militia Organization	U.S. Special Forces National Militia
	War and Emergency Powers	
Utah	Rocky Mountain Resistance	
Virginia	Blue Ridge Hunt Club	Gun Owners of America
	Waco Remembrance	
Washington	Clark County Militia	Guardians of American Liberties
	Lake Chelan Citizens Militia	We The People
Wisconsin	Black Panther Militia	Family Farm Preservation
	Free Militia	

FROM: Klanwatch (1995). Over 200 militias and support groups operate nationwide. *Intelligence Report, 78,* 1–16.

NOTES: 1. There are at least 28 other militias whose names are not known at this time.

2. At least 44 militias have ties with other right-wing, racist organizations.

Bush, in a 1991 speech praising the international coalition that helped win Desert Storm, referred to the "New World Order." This innocuous statement became a rallying point for the militia, who fear a U.N.-dominated global government and end to American sovereignty. The Weaver and Waco sieges and anti-assault weapon laws are proof of the government conspiracy.

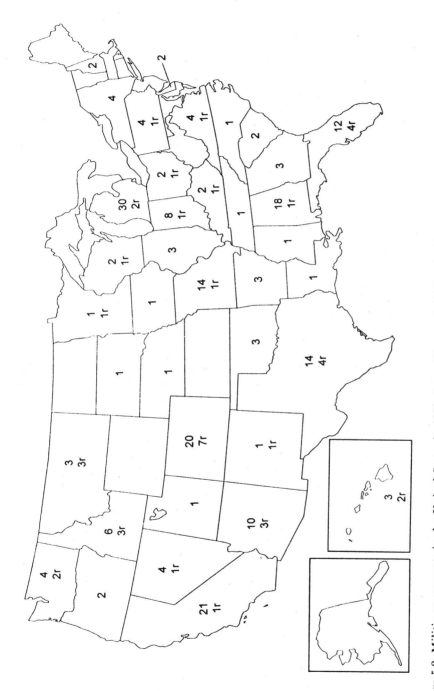

Figure 5.2. Militia movements in the United States in 1996. From Klanwatch (1995). *Intelligence Report, 78,* 8–9. Note: Number with r indicates militias with racist ties.

In Michigan in September 1994, three militia members were arrested when military assault rifles, semiautomatic pistols, a revolver, 700 rounds of armor-piercing ammunition, 21 magazines, six knives and bayonets, night-vision binoculars, and other military equipment were discovered in their vehicle. They were conducting surveillance on police departments. Also in Michigan the next month, two militia members were arrested when in their van was found body armor, assault weapons, 100-round magazines, a shotgun and a handgun, all with armor-piercing rounds. A search of their residence turned up assault weapons magazines and ammunition, a gas grenade, gas masks, and other military gear. In September of the same year in Missouri, a Missouri state trooper was shot in his home following a raid on the paramilitary compound of the organization Citizens for Christ. At the compound, authorities found dynamite, blasting caps, machine guns, and ammunition. The trooper was the police officer who arrested the organization's leader, Bob Joos, in Virginia. The same month, also in Virginia, members of the Blue Ridge Hunt were arrested for carrying automatic weapons. Members were planning a robbery of the National Guard armory in Pulaski, Virginia.

In March 1995, in Minnesota, two members of the Minnesota Patriots Council were convicted of conspiracy of planning to use a biological toxin to kill federal employees and law enforcement agents. They had produced enough Ricin to kill 1,400 people. Additionally, those arrested were planning to blow up a federal building, assassinate a sheriff's deputy, and steal assault weapons. In March, in Nye County, Nevada, two U.S. Forest Service Officers were bombed after receiving threats from "patriots." In May 1995, in Montana, three militia members and leader of the North American Volunteer Militia from Indiana were arrested for threatening to kill judges, law enforcement officers, and public officials. At the home of one suspect, the police found a stockpile of automatic weapons (including a .50 caliber machine gun) and ammunition.

The above compendium is in no regard a complete listing of the far right in the U.S. There are dozens of organizations and movements that are not discussed. Some of the more prominent organizations not discussed are listed in Table 5.8.

Other Right-Wing Organizations

There are several organizations that do not fit within the classification schema of the far right. The most visible of these has been the Jewish Defense League. Founded in 1968 by Rabbi Meir Kahane, the organizational goals of the JDL were to prevent attacks against Jewish interests and people by the Soviets, Arabs, and other anti-Jews. The JDL began

Table 5.8.

Far-right extremist organizations in the United States in 1996.

Organization	Organization
Albanian Boys	Mountain Church of Jesus Christ
American Covenant Church	National Agriculture Press Association
America First Committee	National Association for the Advancement of
American Resistance Movement	White People
American Spring	National Democratic Front
American White Nationalist Party	National Socialist League/World Front
American Workers Party	National Socialist Liberation Front
Arizona Patriots	National Socialist Movement
Arizona Rangers	National Socialist Vanguard
Aryan Militant	National Socialist White Worker's Party
Barristers Inn	National Sozialistiche Deutsche Arbeiter
Catholic Defense League	Partei/Auslands Organisation (NADAP/AO)
California Rangers	National States Rights Party
CAUSE Foundation	Nationalist Movement
Church of the Creator	Nationalist Socialist White American
Church of Israel	Party
Church of the Living Word	New Dawn
Citizen Emergency Defense System	New Order Legion
Citizen's Emergency Network	North American Front
Civilian Military Assistance	Oklahoma White Man's Society
Committee of the States	Oregon Militia
Crusade Against Corruption	Phineas Priesthood
Elohim City	Present Truth
Emergency Committee to Suspend	Pure American Freedom Party
Immigration	Resistance
Euro-American Alliance, Inc.	Romantic Violence
Farmers Liberation Army	Security Services Action Group
Final Solution	Social Nationalist Aryan People's Party
Florida National Socialist Party	SS Action Group
Georgia Patriots	Texas Emergency Reserves
Guardian Nights of Justice	United Citizens for Justice
Heritage Library	United White People's Party
Heritage Society	Universal Order
Institute for Applied Marine Research	Western Front
Institute for Historical Review	White American Resistance
Iowa Society for Educated Citizens	White Cause
Knoxville White Action	White Knights of Liberty
LaPorte Church of Christ	White Patriots Party
League 88	White Student Patriot Union
Legion for the Survival of Freedom, Inc.	White Student Union

Table 5.8. Continued.

Organization	Organization
Liberty Lobby	White Supremist Party
Lord's Covenant Church	World Service
Ministry of Christ Church	Wyoming Rangers
Minutemen	Yahway Church (Black Hebrews)
Minute Men Association	Young and Wasted

peacefully, but rapidly escalated into physical violence and bombing attacks. In 1971, Meir Kahane moved to Israel and became a member of Knesset, the Israeli parliament.

Reins of the JDL were taken by Steven Rombom, who renamed the JDL the Jewish Armed Resistance (JAR). A bounty was placed on any "Nazi attacking a Jew." The bounty ranged between $500–$1,000. The JAR patrolled Jewish neighborhoods with guns and weapons and even attacked moderate Jewish institutions. In October 1977, for example, JAR bombed the Beth Star Shalom Religious Center in North Hollywood because of the temple's call for peaceful solutions of acts of anti-Semitism.

Members of JAR also engaged in anti-Semitic acts themselves to raise the consciousness of the Jewish community. In February 1979, in Philadelphia, James Guttman (aka Mordechai Levy) applied for a neo-Nazi parade permit for a rally to be held in Independence National Historic Park (George & Wilcox, 1992). The intent was to inflame the city's Jewish community into supporting the Jewish Armed Resistance. The plot was uncovered and he was denied a permit.

In Los Angeles in 1981, Mordechai Levy formed the Jewish Defense Organization. Just outside of Los Angeles by the Los Angeles National Forest, he operated a guerrilla training camp called JUDO (Jews United to Defend Ourselves; Menuez, 1986). On weekends, members of the Jewish community could go to this survivalist camp and receive instructions on the usage of pistols, rifles, shotguns, and automatic weapons. Targets often contained pictures of anti-Jewish enemies, such as Kaddafi, Arafat, Hussein, and Gorbachev.

In 1985, Meir Kahane officially resigned from the JDL and command was given to Irv Rubin and the organization became even more violent. In 1985, the JDL was suspected of bombing the American-Arab Anti-Discrimination Committee headquarters in Boston. In the next several years, they attacked the Russian embassy in New York, the Russian Embassy housing complex on Long Island, were suspected of planting an explosive device in New York's Kennedy Center of the Performing

Arts to protest a performance by the Soviet ballet, and attacked suspected Nazi war criminals.

In 1990, Meir Kahane returned to New York to give a speech at a Jewish function. Shortly after the speech he was assassinated by El Sayid al-Nosair, one of the terrorists convicted for the World Trade Center bombing. After Kahane's death, the JDL became less active and membership began falling. With the death of Israel's Prime Minister Rabin and the uncertainty his death will bring back to the Mideast, activities of the JDL can be expected to increase in the later part of the 1990s.

SPECIAL-INTEREST TERRORISM

The 1980s and 1990s have seen a unique form of terrorism strike America: special-interest terrorism. This form of terrorism is that conducted by organizations that are interested not in changing the entire government but only a specific set of laws. The three primary types of special interest terrorism are eco-terrorists, animal rights terrorists, and anti-abortion terrorists.

Eco-Terrorism

The eco-terrorists attempt to preserve the environment by confronting issues head-on through direct action, engage in actions designed to protect biological and ecological diversity, and perform individual action with no organizational support (Scarce, 1990). The tenets of ecological terrorism are rooted in the philosophies of ecological consciousness and ecocide. Ecological consciousness is the belief that humans have to change themselves to repair human destruction of nature. Ecocide is the philosophy that humans have constructed an eco-wall and keep adding bricks to that wall. That is, there is a fundamental schism between humans and nature. Humans use nature for human needs and do not mind destroying, while nature attempts to peacefully coexist among species. By taking an alternate path from coexistence, humans are destroying nature, themselves, and the planet.

Eco-terrorists typically select one aspect of nature on which to focus their activities. Greenpeace concentrates on the marine environment, Sea Shepards have historically worked to save the seals, and Earth First! operates on land issues. It is worth emphasizing that only a very small minority of environmental activists, like their animal rights and anti-abortion counterparts, engage in terrorist activity. Most environmentalists, such as the Sierra Club, Wilderness Society, Audubon Society, Natural

Resources Defense Council, National Wildlife Federation, etc., work within the system to improve and save the environment.

The environmental philosophy of eco-terrorists takes one of two forms. The belief in deep ecology is rooted in the premise that humans are only part of all of nature and must realize that they are part of a much larger environment. Deep ecology accepts the tenet of ecocentrism, that everything in nature has intrinsic value and humans do not have the right to destroy any part of nature. According to deep ecology, humans are no different than trees, animals, or grass. The goal of deep ecology is to reduce the population and live as tribal cultures in an ordered anarchy. Only by disbanding society and adopting small tribal cultures can humans embark upon a spiritual quest with nature. Deep ecology blends Western and Eastern religion, mysticism and Indian spirituality.

The philosophy of eco-feminism (coined in 1974 from the French *ecofeminisme*) believes that humanity has roots in male values and social constructs and practices androcentrism, or male-centeredness. According to the eco-feminist philosophy, the causes of ecological problems is this androcentrism. Males are rational, dominate, competitive, stress individualism, and need to control things, including nature. Females are egalitarian, connected with the world around them and non-aggressive. Females are more in touch with nature because of their historical gender role and the birthing process. To save the environment, humans need to live a "cruelty-free" life-style, which means learning to promote women's Earth-nurturing values.

The two most prominent eco-terrorists have been Greenpeace and Earth First!. Greenpeace began in 1969 in Vancouver, British Columbia as the Don't Make A Wave Committee. The purpose of forming was to go to Amchitka Island in the Aleutians (Alaska) and prevent a nuclear test. Sailing aboard their boat *Greenpeace,* they sailed into the nuclear detonation zone and dropped anchor. They also developed a tactic eco-terrorists have used ever since: they notified the media of what they were doing. After successfully preventing the nuclear test, they renamed the organization the Greenpeace Foundation.

In 1972, Greenpeace members sailed to Mururoa Atoll near Tahiti to prevent a French nuclear test. French navy commandos rammed Greenpeace's boat and severely beat two protesters. In 1973, Greenpeace began their anti-whaling activities, attempting to halt Japanese whalers by blocking the whaling vessel harpoons with a Zodiac boat (small rubber, two-man boat). In 1975, Greenpeace began efforts to halt Russian whaling.

In the early 1980s, Greenpeace went international and increased their activities. In addition to whaling and nuclear tests, members began patrolling the beaches in French Guiana to protect sea turtle eggs, destroying Japanese drift nets, opened a research station in Antarctica, and hung radiation signs on U.S. and USSR warships. In 1985, Greenpeace returned to Mururoa Atoll in their new ship, *Rainbow Warrior,* to prevent another nuclear test. On 10 July, the ship was bombed by French commandos and one member of Greenpeace was killed. The seven commandos who planted the bomb (on orders of the French government) were taken to New Zealand and tried. Two were convicted and jailed. Under diplomatic pressure and the threat of economic sanctions, New Zealand was forced to release the commandos.

In the United States, Greenpeace has protested, demonstrated, and sabotaged nuclear testing, fought against toxic waste dumping, worked actively on ocean ecology issues, and protested for atmosphere and energy issues. For example, at the DuPont factory, members of Greenpeace often lay on the railroad tracks to prevent trains from delivering chlorofluorocarbons.

At present, Greenpeace headquarters are in Amsterdam, Netherlands. They employ over 400 full-time people in 35 field offices. Their annual budget is over $100 million and membership is slightly more than two million.

The more terroristically active environmental organization is Earth First! Founded by David Foreman, Mike Roselle, Bart Koehler, Howie Wolk, and Ron Kezar, Earth First! is organized into local cells with no overall bureaucracy. Organizational philosophy is "No compromise in defense of Mother Earth!" Earth First! came to the attention of the public in 1981, when the founders put a large, black plastic "gash" on the Glen Canyon Dam on the Colorado River. Many of their activities involve "monkey-wrench" sabotage terrorism. Monkey-wrench terrorism was described by eco-cult writer Edward Abbey as a form of low-technology sabotage of equipment (or "ecotage" as Earth First! calls it).

In 1983, Earth First! proposed the Wilderness Preserve System, a plan whereby the government would establish 50 reserves of 716 million acres that would be off limits to human visitors. In 1987 and 1988, members cut nuclear power lines to the Palo Verde nuclear power plant, cut power poles at Fairfield Snow Bowl, and toppled power poles leading to an uranium mine near the north rim of the Grand Canyon. In 1987, a faction of Earth First!, called Circle-A, splintered off because Earth First! was not violent enough. Circle-A believes chronic anarchy must be achieved before society will change, and their avowed goal is to bring down industrial society.

In 1989, David Foreman and other radical Earth First! members, who were by then calling themselves the Evan Meacham Eco-Terrorist International Conspiracy, were arrested for cutting through a tower support that delivered electricity to a power company substation. All members plead guilty but got light sentences. Foreman's sentencing was delayed until 1996, when his felony conviction will become a misdemeanor if he stays out of trouble and fulfills his probation.

Animal Rights Terrorism

Animal rights activists focus their terrorism around one of three issues. One, the animal welfare organizations want better treatment of animals. Two, the animal rightists believe in non-passive activism to protect animals used by humans. Three, the animal liberators use legal and illegal protests against any use of animals for human goals. Most terrorism has been performed by the animal liberators. Primary concerns of the animal liberators center around vivisection, animals used in agriculture, hunting and trapping of animals, and animals used in the entertainment industry. Organizations that have engaged in terrorist activities to protect animals include the Animal Liberation Front (ALF), Band of Mercy, True Friends, Last Chance for Animals, the Animal Rights Militia, and People for the Ethical Treatment of Animals (PETA). Of those, PETA is the largest and has been the most active and radical. PETA, founded in 1980 by Alex Pacheco and Ingrid Newkirk, has 240,000 members nationally, recruiting about 40–50,000 new members per year, and a budget of over $7 million. ALF has approximately two million members in 10,000 local ALF organizations (Scarce, 1990). Altogether, the animal liberation movement has over 7,000 organizations with 10 million members and receives over $50 million annually in contributions and donations (Vetter & Perlstein, 1991).

In April 1987, ALF members burned the University of California at Davis research laboratory and vandalized eight university vehicles. In November 1988, Fran Stephanie Trutt attempted to kill Leo Hirsch, founder and director of the U.S. Surgical Corporation in Norwalk, Connecticut, because of his company's use of animals in research. In 1989, ALF members destroyed two research laboratories and burned a research center at the University of Arizona (Hueston, 1990). In 1993, ALF members engaged in a series of bombings around the country, including one at Texas Tech University which caused over $1 million in damage to a research laboratory.

Anti-Abortion Terrorism

The most violent of all special-interest terrorists have been the anti-abortionists. Between 1982–1986, over 40 abortion and birth control clinics were bombed, including 25 in 1984 and 11 in 1985. Two people were injured in the 1986 bombing of a New York City abortion clinic (Hoffman, 1987). Clinics have been bombed, invaded, vandalized, burned, patients harassed as they attempt to enter or leave, and fake clinics established so pregnant women can receive anti-abortion lectures and see graphic examples of abortions in progress and aborted fetuses. One Illinois doctor and his spouse were taken hostage for eight days. Others have received hate mail, death threats, and have had their property vandalized (Kort, 1987). On 10 March 1993, Michael Griffin, founder of Defensive Action, shot and killed Doctor David Gunn at the Women's Medical Services Clinic. On 29 July 1994, Paul Hill killed three people, including an abortion doctor at a Pensacola, Florida abortion clinic. Hill was a militant anti-abortion protester who preached the legitimacy of murdering abortion doctors.

Many right-to-life advocates, such as Joseph Scheidler, believe violence against abortion clinics and abortion personnel is legitimate violence if it is designed to stop abortions. Scheidler said, "When the law is so twisted, it is obvious that one has to fight it, and when the law sanctions the killing of innocent people, maybe you have to break the law to save lives" (Ginsburg, 1989). The Reagan administration strengthened the anti-abortion movement when he stated that their attacks were not terrorism because they were not conducted by organized groups claiming responsibility. In January 1989, Representative Poirer of Massachusetts introduced legislation to provide for the death penalty for anyone having or performing an abortion (Cook, 1993).

Hardly any issue faced by the American public in the last 50 years has inflamed public passions as has the abortion issue. Abortion beliefs, much more than ecology or animal rights, is usually based on emotion more than reason. The response to abortion, likewise, is emotional. One seldom hears, even in controlled debate situations, rational arguments put forth for or against abortion. In uncontrolled situations, such as at an abortion clinic, it is not surprising that the response of both sides to the other is violence.

FOREIGN TERRORIST OPERATING IN THE UNITED STATES

Foreign terrorist incidents within the U.S. are rare. Between 1982–1987, for example, there were no incidents of terrorism committed by foreigners within the U.S. (Revell, 1987). When foreign-generated incidents occur on U.S. soil, they tend to be grandiose events. The World Trade

Center bombing in 1993 is one example. In that incident, Siddig Ibrahim Siddig Ala, along with eight other Sudanese Muslims, planted 1,200 pounds of ammonium nitrate in the parking garage at the World Trade Center and detonated it. Six persons were killed and hundreds of others wounded. Members claimed to be associated with the Liberation Army Fifth Battalion.

Armenian terrorists in the U.S. have targeted Canadian, Swiss, and Turkish interests in the U.S. In 1982, members of the Justice Commandos of Armenian Genocide (JCAG—aka, Armenian Revolutionary Army) assassinated the Turkish Consul General in Los Angeles (January) and the Honorary Turkish Consul General in Boston (May). Four members of the Armenian Secret Army for the Liberation of Armenia have also been arrested by the FBI in the 1980s for their illegal and terroristic activities (Smith, 1994).

Indian Sikh terrorists have operated in the U.S., or attempted to. In 1985, the FBI successfully prevented two planned assassinations by Sikhs, one against Indira Ghandi when she visited the U.S., and the second the Chief Minister of the Indian State of Harya during his visit to New Orleans. Other Sikh terrorists are suspected to be in the U.S., although they have not committed any terrorist acts.

Mideastern terrorists, including Iranians, Iraqis, Libyans, Syrians, and Palestinians, have been in the U.S. Four Palestinian/Syrian terrorists were arrested for planning terrorist operations (Smith, 1994). Libyans pose one of the most serious threats, as Kaddafi has ordered Libyans to form suicide squads and hurl "human bombs" at Americans whenever they can (Watson, Walcott, Barry, Clifton, & Marshall, 1986). Representatives of Al Fatah, the PLO, the Democratic Front for the Liberation of Palestine, and the Popular Front for the Liberation of Palestine are suspected to have agents in the U.S. Some PLO members even trade actively on the New York Stock Exchange (Adams, 1986).

The FBI has arrested various other foreign terrorists in the U.S., or suspect foreign terrorists of being in the U.S. to conduct future operations. A member of the Japanese Red Army was arrested in New Jersey with homemade explosives in his van. He was driving to New York to plant the devices in federal buildings. Many European neo-Nazis are in the U.S. In the 1990s, the American far right and European neo-Nazi movement have worked closely together to unify the far-right movement on the international level (Mullins & Mijares, 1995). Representatives of the Freedom Party of Austria, the Republican Party in Germany, German People's Union, and National Party of Germany have visited the U.S. on several occasions (Breslau & Sullivan, 1993).

SUMMARY

Terrorism is more of a threat to citizens on the domestic level than on the international level. International events usually make for bigger and bolder headlines. A 747 airplane being blown out of the sky is more newsworthy than the murder of a black individual in rural America. In any one year, however, more people will die from domestic terrorist incidents than all the international incidents combined.

Many scholars and law enforcement authorities claim that domestic terrorism is on the decline. These individuals usually produce death and injury statistics to support their claims. As in any statistical endeavor, though, "there are lies, damn lies and statistics." Terrorism, in frequency, severity, or any other psychometric measurement, is not decreasing. A temporary lull in the figures that lasts for one or two years will be followed by an even larger upswing during the next cycle of activity. Just as with international incidents, the magnitude of individual incidents are also increasing. In 1993 it was the World Trade Center bombing, in 1995 the Oklahoma City Federal Building. In 1996 it is liable to be a sports stadium with 80,000 in attendance.

Many also claim the far right to be in disarray, dishevel, and dismissed. An examination of the figures showing locations of far-right organizations will disavow those claims. There may have been some decrease in Christian Identity churches, or the Klan may not be as strong as it once was, but the increase in militia activity more than makes up for those losses. War is coming, and law enforcement had better be prepared to receive the threat.

Many states have enacted hate crime laws and other special legislation in an attempt to reduce far-right activity (ADL, 1994). Every state in the union has some type of law dealing with bias-motivated violence, civil action provisions, criminal penalties, and/or institutional vandalism laws. Many of these laws, while well-intentioned, have made the job of law enforcement more difficult, as they increase the burden of proof required for an arrest and conviction. Most hate crime statutes require as proof a person's intent to do harm to a minority or Jewish interest. Assault is rather easy to prove; one merely has to examine the bruises, cuts, or broken bones. Why the assault occurred is an entirely different matter. Is a black-white fight in a bar on Friday night a hate crime? Or what about an interracial couple who gets into a domestic dispute? Is that hate crime? Hate crime laws are not necessarily the solution to domestic terrorism.

The first half of the 1990s saw significant increases in special-interest terrorism. Throughout the history of the United States, special-interest organizations have always used terrorism as a tool to promote a special concern. In the 1970s and 1980s, the most common were the tax protest organizations. These organizations are still active and dangerous. Some include the Christian Sons of Liberty in Whidbey Island, Washington, Freedom Law Center in Tampa, Florida, Golden Mean Team in Missoula, Montana, John Doe School of Law in Nebraska, Liberty Township in Utah, Sane Citizens Revolt Against Politicians in North Dakota, and Taxpayers for a Responsible Government, in Roseville, Minnesota (Klanwatch, 1992). Recently, ecologists, animal rights activists, and the anti-abortion movement have turned to terrorism to bring about political change. Some have argued that inner-city gangs are a form of special-interest terrorism at the local level (Mullins & Mijares, 1994). Gangs want political concessions just like other special-interest organizations. The difference is that gangs want change and concession from the local or municipal level of government rather than from the federal level.

The best defense against domestic terrorism is a good offense. Offense begins with knowing who the enemy is, why they are an enemy, how they operate, and what their tactics are. By knowing who the enemy is, then we can begin to defeat the enemy, and on our terms, not theirs. The militias arose, in large part, because of the siege at Ruby Ridge. We are now confronted with having to battle the militias on their terms, by their rules, and on their "turf." By understanding the causes of Ruby Ridge, how to avoid such confrontations and using other legal means to resolve similar incidents, then we can fight on our terms, by our rules and on our "turf."

Chapter 6

TERRORIST TARGETS

Terrorists employ an endless variety of methodologies and have unlimited targets from which to select. Office buildings, homes, restaurants, airplanes, ships, buses, playgrounds, etc. have all been targeted by terrorists. A person can be victimized by terrorists anywhere and without warning. No place on earth is safe from terrorist attack. In 1994, even the White House was subject to two attacks. These were not terrorist operations but do show how vulnerable anyone and anyplace is to terrorism. Target-hardening can reduce the probability of a terrorist attack, but it cannot completely prevent attacks.

The terrorist is not an undisciplined raving lunatic. Neither are most operations random events. Whether a cross-burning in a person's front yard or the bombing of a federal building, terrorist targets are carefully chosen. The planning and precision of most operations rivals that of any military or police operation. Military operation planning considers several factors: determining the target of the operation, the value of conducting an operation against the target, selecting secondary targets, collecting intelligence on the target, developing an operational battle plan, developing a contingency plan of action, determining manpower requirements, assessing logistical and material support, developing casualty assessments, and determining egress routes. The terrorist tactical operation considers the same factors and is planned just as carefully.

Some operations are conducted without extensive planning, but these operations usually involve targets of opportunity. They are also the exception to the rule. One mistake law enforcement is often guilty of is making the assumption that terrorist operations are unplanned and spur-of-the-moment events. This type of thinking works for the terrorist as much as violent operations. Following the Oklahoma City Federal Building bombing, many media pundits and law enforcement officials they interviewed kept saying the bomber selected the building because it was available and an easy target to strike. The unstated assumption was the bomber was driving around looking for a target and happened to find the federal building in Oklahoma City. The terrorist, of course, wants law enforcement to believe terrorist operations are random and unplanned. This type of thinking advances the terrorist cause, produces more fear in the public, and helps assist in achieving their political goals.

Terrorist operations can be expressive or instrumental. Expressive operations are those intended to directly achieve the goals of the organization. The Iranian embassy siege was an expressive operation. The terrorists intended the operation to obtain specific concessions from the United States government. Instrumental operations are designed to express frustration with a government or body of laws. Instrumental operations are designed to publicize the existence of the organization, demonstrate the organization's capability for resisting established order, demonstrate the consequences of resisting the organization, and to make geographical territory ungovernable or for provoking an ill-conceived and thought-out governmental response to terrorism (Sederberg, 1994). Instrumental operations have less to do with achieving goals than they do with demonstrating the power of the organization.

Terrorist operations are most frequent under one of four conditions: one, the society has been disrupted by economic crisis or war; two, they will be supported by fellow citizens of the same ethnic, national, racial, or religious group; three, operations are limited to those which will destablize the government in power and strengthen opposition groups; and four, when opponents lack the finances, manpower, equipment, psychological skill, and political strength to conduct any extended counter-terrorist campaigns.

In recent years, terrorists have expanded their operations from more traditional or classical terrorist operations and criminal activity and have become involved in the international drug trade. Terrorists have become active in all facets of drugs, including growing, distributing, selling, and protection. The terrorist drug link will be explored in this chapter, including reasons for this involvement.

The terrorist has become more sophisticated in operational methodology over the years. Advances in telecommunications and technology have largely been responsible for this increased sophistication. Terrorists have also become more sophisticated at public relations and have become masters at using and manipulating the media to serve their purposes. Largely due to reasons related to media coverage, terrorists have turned to larger and larger operations to gain attention. Terrorists and the media use each other for self-serving interests, and the media has become almost as much of a problem as terrorists. The terrorist-media relationship will be discussed and methods that can be employed to reduce the media influence on terrorism will be presented. As much as any anti-terrorism or counter-terrorism measures the government or law enforcement could use, the media can do as much, if not more, to reduce terrorism. The media is discussed in this chapter because, at present, the media is a tool of terrorism, not counter-terrorism.

TERRORIST INCIDENTS

Terrorism is here to stay. Nothing the government, law enforcement, nor the public does is going to stop terrorism. Terrorists have not been defeated, nor even dealt a serious blow. The 1960s was the decade of the airplane hijacking. Governments, law enforcement, the Federal Aviation Administration and others developed procedures, tactics, laws, treaties, international treaties, and increased airport security in an attempt to reduce airplane hijackings. Tables 6.1 and 6.2 show the result of these measures. Table 6.1 shows aircraft hijackings between 1969–1985. The data for the United States fluctuates but is overall fairly stable. International airline hijackings are less variable and just as stable. Table 6.2 lists explosions aboard aircraft from 1949–1984. Incidents peaked in the 1970s, after measures were taken to reduce airplane terrorist incidents. The numbers fell in the 1980s, not due to measures to protect airlines, but because terrorists turned to other methodologies.

Table 6.1.
Attempted hijacking of aircraft, United States and foreign, 1969–1985.

Year	United States	Foreign	Total
1969	40	47	87
1970	27	56	83
1971	27	31	58
1972	31	31	62
1973	2	20	22
1974	7	19	26
1975	12	13	25
1976	4	14	18
1977	6	26	32
1978	13	18	31
1979	13	14	27
1980	22	19	41
1981	8	24	32
1982	10	22	32
1983	19	15	34
1984	7	21	28
1985	5	31	36

Table 6.2.
Aircraft incidents involving explosions and death, 1949–1985.

Year	Incidents	Number Killed	Year	Incidents	Number Killed
1949	2	36	1970	9	84
1950	1	0	1971	3	25
1952	1	0	1972	7	114
1955	2	60	1973	5	92
1956	1	0	1974	5	161
1957	2	1	1975	4	1
1959	1	1	1976	5	168
1960	2	47	1977	1	0
1962	1	45	1978	3	5
1964	1	15	1979	2	0
1965	1	52	1980	1	0
1966	1	28	1981	3	2
1967	4	66	1982	2	1
1968	1	0	1983	2	112
1969	4	33	1984	3	0

FROM: U.S. Department of Transportation, Federal Aviation Administration, Office of Civil Aviation Security (1985). *Explosions aboard aircraft.* Washington, D.C.: U.S. Government Printing Office. In Poland, J.M. (1988). *Understanding terrorism: Groups, strategies, and responses.* © 1988, pp. 179. Adapted by permission of Prentice-Hall, Upper Saddle River, New Jersey.

Table 6.3 lists bomb and incendiary incidents in the United States for 1984. The data for any year between 1960–1995 would appear similar. Of interest in Table 6.3 is the last column, indicating bomb incidents where the site was notified of the threat before the bomb detonated. As shown, very few incidents had an associated threat warning, strongly suggesting the terrorist wanted people to die in the blast, not necessarily to kill people, but to gain media attention and produce fear in the public. Bomb threats may produce fear in the people in the building, but they do not garner media attention. Also, because of the high number of bomb threats in recent years, people in the building are usually no longer afraid. The number of terrorist bombing incidents is so great the media becomes uninterested and the public apathetic. Between 1983–1986, bombing incidents accounted for 47 percent of all terrorist attacks in the U.S., followed closely by arsons at 32 percent (Hoffman, 1993). On the international terrorist front, bombings accounted for 50 percent of all terrorist incidents. In response, terrorists turn to larger-scale bombing operations to regain media attention and produce public fear, evidenced by PanAm 103, the World Trade Center, and the Oklahoma City Federal Building.

Some would argue that terrorism is on the decline. Terrorism is not on the decline, either on the international or domestic front. Wardlaw

Table 6.3.
**Bomb and incendiary event history in the United States for 1984
showing percentage of devices with a threat report preceding detonation.**

Month	Explosive Devices	Incendiary Devices	Total	Percent with Threat Report Before Detonation
Jan*	—	—	—	—
Feb	98	27	125	4.0
Mar	109	46	155	5.8
April	56	40	96	8.6
May	69	192	261	12.2
June	106	100	206	11.5
July	154	71	225	6.5
Aug	95	84	179	12.7
Sep	105	86	191	9.4
Oct	94	53	147	10.1
Nov	301	62	363	5.7
Dec	92	29	121	9.8
TOTAL	1279	790	2069	6.2

FROM: National Bomb Data Center (1984). Incident summaries. U.S. Department of Justice (FBI–LEAA). Dover, NJ: Picatinny Arsenal.
*A total of 156 incidents were reported for January, but no other data was provided.

(1985) showed that in 1982 there were 117 terrorist organizations representing 71 different nationalities involved in terrorist operations. In 1995, there were over 3,000 terrorist organizations in the world. Smith (1994) argued that by 1990, the far right in the United States was virtually nonexistent. If that were true, there would not be over 440 militia organizations in the U.S. in 1996 and there would be no threat from the far right. The 1990s have not supported Smith's claim. In fact, many terrorist organizations thought long defunct have made a comeback (see, for example, Bolton, 1984; Hoffman, 1984; and Horchem, 1985). Terrorists do not disappear because of arrests, changes in political administration, or changes in society values and mores. Terrorists change organizations, operational strategy or tactics, and geographical locations.

Terrorism throughout the 1980s and 1990s has become more violent than ever before (Cordes, Hoffman, Jenkins, Kellen, Moran, & Slater, 1984). Terrorists are killing more people each year than the year before. There may be yearly lulls or downturns in deaths, but considered on a continuous time line, the death rates continue to rise. One reason for this increase is that terrorists are concentrating more on individuals as targets than on federal structures and buildings (Oakley, 1985). Over 50 percent of terrorist operations are directed against people. Terrorists are selecting the citizens rather than the institutions and symbols of political systems (Rodriquez, 1986). The 1960s and 1970s taught the terrorist that attacking the institutions of government did not produce political change nor terrorize citizens. The change of targeting began in the 1970s. Between 1970–1980, there were 2,072 international terrorist attacks on U.S. citizens, and 32% were aimed at corporate facilities and executives (Davis, 1988). Russell (1985) pointed out that between 1970–1982, 48% of terrorist abductions were directed against wealthy business leaders. In the 1980s and 1990s, terrorists have changed their tactics to target the individual citizen. Two, these attacks on citizens have become much more violent, with the terrorist more willing to kill to achieve his objective. Bombing attacks of the 1970s were designed to damage structures during periods of low human activity. In the 1990s, the attacks are designed during peak periods. Both the World Trade Center and Oklahoma City Federal Building bombings occurred during peak building usage.

There are many reasons terrorists have become more violent and more prone to cause deaths. One, the media has become indifferent to terrorist attacks that do not kill. Deaths are news; the destruction or sabotage of an empty building is not. Two, the public has become inured to violence. In our violent society, one or two deaths has become commonplace. Multiple deaths are necessary to gain public attention. Three, violence in society has inoculated people to death and destruction. One or two deaths does not produce fear and terror. It merely produces a shrug of indifference. Personally, I was amazed in the wake of the Oklahoma City Federal Building bombing how students, coworkers, friends, and law enforcement personnel discussed the tragedy in impersonal and non-emotional terms. The degree of desensitization to this massive tragedy was literally amazing. Four, terrorists have learned it takes death to produce change. If people do not die, governments do not make concessions. Five, terrorists are merely keeping up with the violence in society. The overall insensitivity to pain and suffering of the citizen population applies equally as well to the terrorist. Six, the technology terrorists use has improved. The terrorist has become more sophisticated in operational methodology, weapons, and skilled at conducting operations. Better weapons mean more deaths.

For the foreseeable future, there is no possibility of these trends being reversed. Terrorists will become more active, more violent, their operations more grandiose, their numbers larger, and the death toll will continue to rise. Terrorist techniques and operations will become more technologically sophisticated and even more insulated from attempts to stop them. The extreme fringes of society will continue to become more and more disenfranchised and disenchanted. Their frustration will be manifest in violence, and the book of the dead will need additional volumes.

TERRORIST TARGETS

There are no limits nor constraints on what can be a target of terrorism. Targets can be as diverse as the terrorist wishes and as varied as his imagination. Unsuspecting citizens to the president, Forbes 500 companies to mom-and-pop storefront businesses, PanAm 747s to a dilapidated automobile are all equally as likely to become terrorist victims. The diversity of targets available to the terrorist is one of the primary factors in making their behavior unpredictable and so difficult to stop.

Schmid (1985) argued that terrorists have four primary types of targets. First and foremost is the actual target of the violence itself. These are the people who suffer directly at the hands of the terrorist. Passengers on a hijacked airliner, people visiting a building to be bombed, or persons targeted for assassination are primary targets. The second target of the terrorist is the target of terror. Targets of terror are secondary victims of the terrorist operation, such as persons who suffer because of their relationship to a primary target. The families of hostages or an assassination victim would be the targets of terror. The third target of the terrorist is the target of demand. This target would be the group or interest the terrorist act was designed to warn or force to change. A government, business, supporters of either, or a group of citizens would be demand targets. The fourth target of the terrorist is the audience whose attention the terrorist is hoping to gain. This target would include the civilians the terrorist is hoping to terrorize, by producing fear, changing their behavior, or turning them against the government.

The terrorist targets delineated by Schmid (1985) are comprehensive but overly complex and mis-prioritized. Under Schmid's classification, primary targets are the direct victims of the terrorist operation: hostages, citizens who are injured, or those killed. The last, and presumably least important, category of targets is the audience watching. As explained in the chapter on definitions, the audience watching is the *most important target* of the terrorist atrocity. He further identifies as a target the relatives of the primary victims. These are not terrorist targets. The terrorist has no concern or regard for relatives of his victims. Like the primary victims, relatives are innocent bystanders to the terrorist activity.

A better target categorization would include three targets, prioritized as targets of fear, institutes, and violence. Targets of fear would be the citizens who watch the terrorist atrocity, become fearful and change their behavior because of that fear. This is the primary audience the terrorist is hoping to reach. The second target is that of the institutions the terrorist is hoping to coerce or change. Governments and industry are the primary institutions terrorist activities attempt to influence. Through the years, terrorists have learned direct change is not possible, so their activities are planned to make these institutions secondary targets. Governments, for example, will not change policy or function if terrorist attacks are directed specifically against those institutions (in most instances), so the terrorists direct activities against the citizens in hopes of using them as institutional change agents. The third target of terrorism, and the least important, are the targets of violence. These targets are selected as only a tool to affect the first two targets. With the exception of assassination and certain hostage situations, the victims are not selected because of who they are but for what they can do to influence the first two targets. In the Iranian Embassy takeover, the hostages were important only in the sense that they were American. In Oklahoma City, the victims were immaterial to the goals of the bomber. They were victims because they were in the building.

Collectively, there are certain groups of people that terrorists target. The primary and historically most popular target of terrorism is national government. The terrorist can target persons within the government, government buildings and facilities, government-regulated industry such as a power plant or transportation network, and military installations. Any person within the government or any type of facility, no matter how remotely associated with government, is subject to attack. Very often, for example, when an airplane is attacked or sabotaged, even though the airplane is owned and operated by a civilian carrier, the terrorist is attacking the government.

The second category of targets are private corporations. At the international level, the terrorist may attack the American corporation to obtain money, force the corporation to leave the country, obtain concessions from the host country, or turn the population of the host country against the corporation. Domestically, the terrorist attacks the private corporation to force some political change. Animal rights terrorists attack corporation and university animal research facilities in an effort to force the government to change laws regarding animal research. Anti-abortion protesters' attacks against abortion clinics are designed as much to change a set of laws as they are to force the clinic to close. Occasionally, the terrorist may attack the corporation to gain financial concessions to support further terrorism. Threatening to sabotage a corporate building or taking corporate hostages may be an act designed as much to obtain money as to force political change.

A third category of targets are innocent citizens. The citizen may be attacked to force political change, gain support for the terrorist cause, or obtain finances. In the 1970s, executives of an American corporation with major offices in South America repeatedly had its South American executives captured and held for ransom. The motive of these attacks were merely to gain money for the terrorists. Most often, citizens are victims of terrorist attacks to force political change. Hostage taking, whether international or domestic, is usually done to force political concessions.

A fourth category of terrorist attack is the political organization. Left-wing attacks on Carter and Bush campaign headquarters in the late 1980s were an example of this type of terrorism. Almost every presidential political convention is subject to some type of terrorist activity, ranging from non-peaceful protest to physical attack.

A fifth category of terrorist attack is labor unions. The terrorist may either incite a labor group against a corporation or government, sabotage the work place, or directly attack the labor group to cause unrest, work stoppages, or panic. Labor unions were frequently targeted by terrorists in the 1920s–1960s, but since then have significantly declined, in large part due to the decrease in economic power of the labor unions and decline of the far-left movement.

The sixth category of terrorist attack are specific minority, ethnic, or religious groups. Domestically, throughout the 1980s and 1990s, the far right has been the most active of the terrorists within the U.S. and they have targeted these groups more than any other category of people. As federal legislation and society values have moved minorities, religious organizations, and women more into mainstream society, terrorist attacks against these groups have significantly increased. White males have lost their power base within society, and many perceive a threat to their status, social standing, economic security, and career goals from these groups. The problem of terrorist attacks have become so severe and widespread against these groups, special laws have been created to address this form of terrorism: hate crime laws. Hate crime will be discussed more fully later in this chapter.

DISCRIMINANT AND INDISCRIMINANT TERRORIST OPERATIONS

Discriminant Operations

Terrorist operations can be discriminant or indiscriminant (Dalager, 1984). Discriminant terrorist operations are directed against specific governments, agencies, or corporations and are designed to result in specific outcomes. Against a government, discriminant operations are designed to first produce confusion and fear within the government. Government officials will have to spend their time and energy trying to protect themselves to the neglect of their official responsibilities. Government leaders become secluded and inaccessible, officials do not show for work, and meetings and activities of the government focus on the problem of terrorism to the exclusion of solving more pressing social and legal problems. The government becomes focused on dealing with the attacks against itself rather than working for the common good. The success of this strategy was evidenced by the Carter administration during the Iranian embassy siege. The government virtually ignored all other issues and concentrated solely on attempting to resolve the embassy situation.

Two, the reputation of the government can be made to suffer in the eyes of the international community. Other nations will question the attacked government's ability to govern and manage its own affairs. In the 1980s, the United States government lost considerable stature in the world community because of its inability to control terrorist attacks against it. The inability to protect citizens from terrorist attack gave other nations the perception the U.S. government was weak and ineffective. This perception soon generalized to include perceptions that if the government cannot deal with the terrorist problem, it must also be ineffective in dealing with other problems confronting the international community. Soon, the U.S. was perceived as being incompetent in the whole realm of foreign policy affairs.

Three, the government will lose the respect and trust of its own population. By not being able to counteract or control the terrorists, citizens soon begin to question the government's ability to handle other governmental responsibilities. A side benefit to the terrorist is that citizens come to believe the government cannot protect them and so the citizens take it upon themselves to provide personal protection. This can lead to the destruction of government and social institutions, lead to further terrorism against the government, and ultimately result in anarchy. Many of the present problems in the old Soviet Union are a result of this perception. Increased crime, vigilantism, and terrorism have all been experienced by the Soviets as a result of the citizens believing they need to protect themselves since the government cannot.

Four, in an attempt to deal with and control terrorist operations, the government will enact legislation which impinges upon and suppresses the freedoms of the common citizen. This may range from increased security at buildings and airports to roadblocks, stringent curfews, and a declaration of martial law. These governmental actions only serve to lead an already disenchanted populace to begin reactive or even revolutionary actions against the government. The rise in the 1990s of the militia movement is largely attributable to the perception of excessive government control over the citizens and a continued decrease of individual rights guaranteed by the Constitution.

Governments which use terrorism to control their population are using a discriminant form of terrorism. State terrorism can range from the mild, such as intimidation used to discourage dissent and opposition, to coerced conversion designed to alter or change a national life-style, to severe, where the government engages in selective genocide designed to eliminate a class, ethnic group, minority group, or religious group for political reasons (Slann, 1993). Genocide is most likely to be effective when the target group of people are a weak minority of the total population, the minority population is perceived by the majority group with fear and/or contempt, and the world community is indifferent to the victim's fate (Sederberg, 1994).

Discriminant operations against a corporation (whether international, national, or foreign) serve a similar purpose. By having to deal with the terrorist threat, the corporation has to expend other valuable resources of manpower, equipment, finances, etc. Productivity declines, workers become afraid, untrusting, frustrated, and leave the corporation, the reputation of the corporation suffers and expenses increase, until ultimately the corporation's local operation becomes too expensive and the corporation may close its doors at that location or go out of business altogether. The local workers are out of a job and they turn their frustrations against the government for not doing a better job in stopping the terrorist. By conducting operations against a corporation, the terrorist is ultimately attacking the government. The corporate attack strategy is most effective during periods of recession, when workers are already uncertain and fearful of the future, dissatisfied with downsizing efforts, and disenchanted with the corporation's inability to deal with the recession. Through the end of the 1990s, American business will undergo major transformations and massively downsize operations in an effort to become more efficient. Combined with an economic recession, corporations have become particularly vulnerable to terrorist attack.

Through the use of discriminant operations, the terrorist has a forum for communication, propaganda, and bargaining. The terrorist organization makes its goals and philosophies known to the target audience. As the terrorist saying goes, "Kill one, scare ten million." The discriminant terrorist operation also provides the opportunity for coercive bargaining. Operations of hijacking, kidnapping, sabotage, bombing, etc., enable the terrorist to obtain finances, free colleagues from prison, change government policy, and/or rally the public to adopt the cause of the terrorist. Instances of bombings of abortion clinics in the United States opened the way for other pro-life supporters to begin actions against abortion clinics. Additionally, many reactionaries who were afraid to conduct illegal operations see the terrorists get away with conducting illegal operations, and this lowers their inhibitions against conducting illegal operations. Thus, these extremists turn from oratory to terrorism.

Successful discriminant operations lead to increased status and prestige for the terrorist organization. Membership increases, finances improve, supporters increase in number and willingness to support the organization, the population begins supporting the organization, and the international community lends moral and/or physical support to the terrorist organization. Government and law enforcement agencies become frustrated in trying to stop the terrorists, and this frustration makes them even more ineffective. Agencies stop cooperating and sharing information, become distrustful of each other, and even become competitive in nature, each trying to outdo the other in stopping the terrorists. In the failed attempt to rescue the American embassy hostages from Iran in 1981, each branch of the military wanted to assume the lead role in the rescue attempt. Although never publicly stated or admitted to by the government, this infighting probably contributed significantly to a delay in making a rescue attempt and led to the ultimate failure of the mission. Following the Branch Davidian siege in Waco, Texas, the FBI and ATF kept blaming each other for the mistakes and failures during the siege. During the siege, in fact, tensions between the two agencies often reached the breaking point and had to be mediated on a regular basis.

Indiscriminant Operations

Indiscriminant terrorist operations are seemingly random attacks on a populace. Bombings of nightclubs, restaurants, and shopping malls would likely be indiscriminant operations. The far right in America uses indiscriminant operations much more than do left-wing or foreign terrorists. Where discriminant operations are carefully planned and conducted, indiscriminant operations require little planning and are more "targets of opportunity." The terrorist still has a target audience, such as a government, as its goal but is using a more indirect method to reach that audience. European terrorists commonly bomb places where Americans congregate, such as restaurants, nightclubs, military bases, and airport terminals. Attacks against minorities, hate crimes and similar types of crimes are primarily indiscriminant operations.

There are several purposes to indiscriminant operations. One, the terrorist hopes to create fear and uncertainty in the population. This fear will translate into a societal fugue, whereby people will avoid public places, stop traveling, and remain in their own homes. This fear could also lead to an exodus from an area of the country. People may be so afraid that, en masse, they leave a geographical area. In the summer of 1986, fears of increased operations by Mideast terrorists reduced American tourism to Europe by almost 40 percent. Two, continued indiscriminant operations will frustrate the government and law enforcement agencies. This frustration will soon affect the citizens, for the public will not know where to turn for assistance and protection or assurances of safety. The public will soon quit believing in the government and quit listening to the government. Three, this frustration will lead to acts of civil disobedience against the government. The people will take their frustrations out on the government and law enforcement agencies. Protests, demonstrations, and riots will increase and become a norm of behavior. Four, indiscriminant operations may actually lead to major concessions on the part of a government or, ultimately, lead to the overthrow of the government. Many of the activities of the Cuban revolutionaries fighting against the Batista regime were indiscriminant.

Indiscriminant operations can be risky for the terrorist, for if the targets are not carefully or properly chosen, the operations will work against the terrorist. Instead of producing fear, they may produce anger and frustration. Moreso than discriminant operations, indiscriminant operations have the potential to cross the invisible line between fear and anger. Governments sympathetic to the terrorist's cause may condemn the organization and discontinue their support. The bombing in West Germany of a nightclub popular among American servicemen was an indiscriminant operation that ultimately resulted in President Reagan's bombing of Libya. Libya finally stepped over that fine line separating fear from anger when they bombed the nightclub.

TYPES OF TERRORIST OPERATIONS

Terrorists have a variety of methodologies from which to choose. Like the military, terrorists have a variety of options available for attacking a target. Some may be large-scale operations and require extensive planning and numerous operatives, others may be small-scale and only require one or two terrorists. Some of these operations may take hours, days, or weeks to accomplish, others may take only seconds or minutes. The most typical terrorist operations will be presented and discussed.

Ambushes

Ambushes can be either discriminant or indiscriminant operations. Basically defined, an ambush is an event where one or more terrorists hide in a concealed location and wait for the victim to pass the location. At the location, the victim is killed by either clubbing, knifing, shooting, or bombing. Most ambushes occur when the victim is on foot or traveling in a vehicle. Ambushes are one of the oldest type of all terrorist operations, being used by the Jewish Sicarri against the Romans and later methodologically refined by Hassan ben Sabbah. Historically, German and Italian terrorists prefer shooting the victim, while the IRA and Basque ETA have preferred bombing. American terrorists have employed all ambush techniques but have preferred bombing.

Assassination

Assassinations are usually a discriminant operation and are the primary purpose of ambushes, although not all assassinations are ambushes. Assassinations are historically planned operations, although many far-right ambushes, especially the hate crime assassinations, may be unplanned. Victims of ambushes are usually killed outside a building, entering or exiting from a vehicle, while in a moving vehicle when the vehicle can be intercepted, or when the victim is at a public speaking engagement (Siljander, 1980). The most commonly used weapons in assassinations are handguns, explosives, rifles, blade and impact weapons, shotguns, machine guns, and poison. Most assassination victims are political figures, law enforcement officials, or racial, ethnic, or religious minorities.

There are many definitions of assassination. One rather simplistic definition is "the truncidation of a political figure without due process of law" (Padover, 1943). A second definition defines assassination as "the killing of a person in private life from a political motive and without legal process" (Encyclopedia of the Social Sciences, 1937). Bell (1978) defined ambushes as a violent crime with political implications. The most comprehensive definition, provided by Jaszi and Lewis (1957), defines assassinations as "the premeditated killing of an individual in order to get, maintain, or extend the power of the state in the interest of an individual or organization." They further add that if the killing is directed toward a well-known individual, the purpose is political.

Assassination is a special category of murder (Schmid & DeGraaf, 1982) as identified by the elements of assassination. One, the target for assassination is a public figure of political importance. Two, the motive for the assassination is political. Three, the assassination occurs outside the context of war, revolution, insurrection, or is controlled by the potential victim. Four, legal procedures for establishing guilt are either nonexistent or are controlled by the potential victim. Five, the target is specifically selected by the terrorist organization. Six, the assassination is committed in a public place and the assassin is at risk. Seven, the political impact of the assassination is significant.

Crotty (1971) has identified five types of assassins. The first is the Anomic assassin, or the murderer of a political leader for private motives. This would include mentally disturbed assassins who are not necessarily terrorists (Gross, 1978). Second is the Elite Substitution assassin, or where the murderer intends to replace a political leader with a leader of an opposing political faction. Third are Tyrannicide assassins, or those who kill a dictator or despot to replace him with a more compassionate leader. Fourth are Terroristic assassins, those assassins of a government who attempt to control insurgents, rebels, revolutionaries, and the opposition to neutralize the allegiance of a population. Fifth are assassins who engage in Propaganda by Deed, those assassins who are attempting to bring the public's attention to larger political or nationalistic problems.

The National Commission on the Causes and Prevention of Violence (1970) has identified five types of purposes for assassinations. One purpose of assassination is to eliminate a political elite to be replaced with another political elite with no change in the political structure or ideology of a government. A second purpose is to create fear and demoralize the legitimacy of the ruling power structure to effect political change. The third purpose of assassination is that conducted by governments to suppress political challenges from rival political organizations. A fourth purpose of assassination is to engage in propaganda by deed. The fifth purpose of assassination is that conducted by the mentally disturbed against highly visible political figures.

Bank Robbery

Bank robberies are discriminant operations designed to raise money for the terrorist. The bank robbery may occur in conjunction with some other operation, such as a bombing, where the bombing would serve as a diversionary tactic. In the United States, more so than any other terrorist operation, bank robberies lead to arrests of the terrorist. The armored car robbery by the Order in Ukiah, California, the bank robberies of the United Freedom Front, and the Wells Fargo robbery by the FALN are recent and well-known examples of arrests of terrorists for their involvement in bank robberies.

Bombings

Bombing operations can be discriminant or indiscriminant. A terrorist bombing is defined by Rummel (1966) as, "Any use of explosives to damage or destroy private or public property or wound or kill individuals including those used against the property of persons of foreign governments or their subjects, excepting what occurs in the conduct of open warfare between two countries." For many terrorist organizations, bombings are the favored tool of the terrorist. In Latin America, bombings account for well over 50 percent of all terrorist attacks. Risks International (1979) provided data indicating that between 1970 and 1978, over 62 percent of all Latin American terrorist incidents against U.S. targets were bombings.

Bombings are one of the terrorist's most effective tools. The terrorist may bomb to scare or frighten, to kill several innocent victims, to kill a particular victim, to destroy a particular facility, or to illegally enter a bank, business, or military establishment to obtain money, equipment, weapons, or other supplies. Bombs may be packaged and placed long before the explosion, mailed, or shot from weapons such as a grenade launcher or shoulder-operated rocket. The British SAS regularly conducts exercises at London's Heathrow Airport to practice for terrorist missile attacks against aircraft. Bombings are one of the safest of all terrorist operations. Bombing operations draw attention to the terrorist cause and are virtually risk free (Hoffman, 1993).

Contrary to popular belief, it is rare the terrorist will alert anyone prior to detonation. As shown in Table 7.3, most bombs detonate with no forewarning, thus increasing the probability of injury and/or death. Bomb threats are also used by terrorists to disrupt normal activities and produce fear and disorganization. Bomb operations are preferred by many terrorists for a variety of reasons. One, bombing operations offer limited risk to terrorists because of the variety of delivery methods, small sizes, and use of delayed detonators. Many modern explosive substances such as PETN and RDX can be molded into a variety of shapes and are completely unrecognizable, even by trained EOD personnel. Two, because of the delivery methods, the terrorist can avoid any type of confrontation with law enforcement authorities. Three, because of delay detonation devices, bombing operations offer an excellent opportunity for escape. By the time the bomb detonates, the terrorist can be half a world away. Four, by notifying persons of the bomb, the terrorist can eliminate unnecessary or unwanted casualties (Mickolus, 1980). In fact, in bomb threat situations, only one of one hundred bomb threats actually involve an explosive device (Kendall & Moll, 1974). Most bombing operations in the U.S. are directed against government offices, businesses, structures, military installations, and airlines. Person targets, at least in the U.S., are not often bombed.

Execution

Executions are discriminant operations. In an execution, the terrorist organization acts as both judge and jury, deciding the victim has to die for any one of a variety of reasons: disloyalty, repression of a population, sins against the people, crimes against the government, law enforcement officials investigating the organization, etc. After an execution, the organization will make a public statement taking credit for the execution and explaining why the execution had to occur. The key element in the execution is the public explanation, which is designed to deter future similar behavior.

Executions differ from assassinations in that executions are less well planned, the reasons for the execution are publicly announced by the terrorists, and usually involve the victim being taken hostage. Executions may also be conducted as part of another terrorist operation, such as a hijacking. In these cases the victim may be executed to demonstrate the sincerity of the terrorists, control the behavior of other hostages, force a ransom, or prevent law enforcement authorities from tactically assaulting the hostage site.

Extortion

Extortion is a discriminant operation and is used in conjunction with one of the other types of terrorist operations. Extortion is an operation where terrorists use human lives or the threat of taking human lives as leverage to get a target population to agree to terrorist demands. An extortion operation is modeled along the lines of, "if you (a government) do not do A, then we (terrorist organization) will do B." A terrorist organization may threaten to bomb nightclubs or other public gathering places unless a government agrees to make concessions to terrorist demands and move the terrorist organization in the direction of their goals. The major difference between extortion and hijacking operations is that in extortion, the only terrorist behavior occurring is a threat, where in hijacking, other criminal behavior occurs.

Hijacking/Hostage Taking

Hijacking/hostage-taking operations can be discriminant or indiscriminant and are operations where terrorists take control of some public conveyance (i.e., airplane, bus, train, etc.), or other public building or gathering place containing innocent persons, with the intent of using the lives of those persons as bargaining chips in forcing the target audience or a government to grant the terrorist's demands. In a hijacking, the target audience may also assist to bring pressure upon a government to grant the terrorist's demands for the security of the hostages. Hijackings can also generate publicity for the terrorist's cause (Gallimore, 1991). The major disadvantage of hijacking/hostage-taking operations is the high risk of failure, capture, and death.

Hijackings of aircraft are the most common, although buses, trains, and ocean liners have been hijacked by terrorists as well. Hijackings do involve the taking of hostages, innocent victims caught by circumstances beyond their control. Netanyahu (1986) has called hostage taking as the classic terrorist attack. Hostage taking is deliberate and an assault on civilians because they are non-combatants. Hostage taking transforms a criminal act into a political act, with the purpose to legitimize the terrorists as a political force to be dealt with. The U.S. government was forced to concede to terrorist's demands in the Iranian embassy siege, making the hostage-takers heroes to most of the Mideast nations.

Law enforcement agencies are more likely to be involved with hostage situations than they are in any other type of terrorist operation. Hostage situations require time. Time has to pass for the incident to develop, time for the terrorists to make it known they have hostages, time to make their demands known, and time for their demands to be satisfied. On the law enforcement side, time is required to respond to the incident, time to allow emotions to decrease, time to negotiate, and time to resolve the incident (McMains & Mullins, 1995). Because hostage taking is a popular terrorist operation and is an incident that law enforcement can successfully deal with, a later chapter will discuss the hostage situation in detail.

As an historical footnote, the first airline hijacking occurred on 21 February 1931, when a group of Peruvian revolutionaries hijacked a Peruvian mail plane for the purpose of dropping propaganda leaflets to the Peruvian public (O'Ballance, 1979; Mickolus, 1980).

Kidnapping

Kidnappings are discriminant operations and are conducted for the purpose of obtaining money, political concessions, reparations, or the release of prisoners. Kidnappings may also be conducted to obtain publicity for the terrorist's cause (Evans, 1977), harassment and demoralization of political leaders (Madruga, 1974), polarization of a society, or aggravation of state-to-state relations. Kidnappings are not random but usually are well-planned, well-thought-out events (USAF OP Plan 208-85, 1985). Law enforcement agencies are mostly involved with kidnapping events on an intelligence-gathering level or, if the kidnappers are located, for tactical operations.

Kidnappings differ from hostage situations in that in hostage situations, the terrorists and hostages are confined in a known location and the situation is open to negotiations. Kidnapping operations are not contained and are not negotiable operations. The location of the kidnappers and victims are not known, nor is there any way to contain the terrorists or victim in any one location. The terrorists will not negotiate in a kidnapping. Demands are not presented in a two-party conversation but are presented in such a way that the authorities and government cannot negotiate. If the kidnappers are located and contained, then the kidnapping becomes a hostage situation.

Kneecapping

Kneecapping operations are a discriminant and non-fatal form of execution first popularized by the IRA. Kneecapping involves the shooting of the victim in a knee with a small caliber (.22, .38, 9 mm) pistol. The purpose of the operation is to serve notice to others who may be contemplating actions similar to the victim. A terrorist who attempts to quit the organization may be kneecapped to serve as an example to other members. A hostage may be kneecapped to control the behavior of other hostages. A citizen may be kneecapped to produce fear in other citizens.

Rescue of Prisoners

A discriminant operation, rescue of prisoners is an operation that may be accomplished indirectly through one of the other types of operations discussed, such as extortion, hijackings/hostage takings, sabotage, etc. France is experiencing a series of terrorist bombings in an attempt to force them to release the terrorist Carlos. Rescue operations may also be conducted directly, where the organization physically attacks a prison. The terrorist may seek to free political prisoners, members of the organization (including a leader), a needed specialist such as a chemist, a person to use for ransom, or the general prison population.

Sabotage

Sabotage operations can be discriminant or indiscriminant, direct or indirect. Direct sabotage involves the use of explosives, incendiaries, weapons, etc., to disable facilities and/or equipment. Indirect sabotage involves the use of harmful additives such as abrasives, acids, alkalis, halogens, salts, or other contaminants in equipment, machinery, fuels and lubricants, foodstuffs, tampering with equipment and machinery, and using incendiary devices. The terrorist may seek to disrupt the functioning of a government or corporation by destroying buildings, equipment, tools, etc., or may want to strike fear into the general population by disabling aircraft, destroying bridges, railroads, etc. In 1995, an Amtrak passenger train was derailed in Arizona, killing one passenger and injuring several dozen others. The person(s) responsible, who called themselves the Sons of the Gestapo, removed the bolts securing adjacent sections of rail.

Acts of sabotage may be designed to disrupt a political or religious movement as well. Sabotaging the Republican National Headquarters, convention sites, hotels, and vehicles could disrupt the Republican Party to such an extent the party would not be able to nominate a presidential candidate. Several years ago, poisoned Tylenol killed several innocent people. In October 1984, Japan experienced a wave of copycat type of poisonings, where over 100 packets of cyanide-laced candy was placed on store shelves. This was followed in March 1986, in the U.S., of poisonings of Tylenol, Contac, Diatec, and Teldrin (Poland, 1988). Additionally (and suspected to be copycat), this was about the same time the widespread poisoning and malicious tampering with children's Halloween candy became popular. The fear induced by the poisoner changed people's consumer habits and changed an entire set of government laws concerning packaged food and drug products. American business lost over $1 billion in changing packaging to meet the new government standards. Tampering with Halloween candy changed the way Americans celebrated the holiday. Children were discouraged from "trick or treating," parents would not let children eat unwrapped candy and fruit, and hospital emergency rooms offered to x-ray candy. Many parents simply would not let their children celebrate the holiday because of fear over tampering with candy.

Table 6.4 summarizes the terrorist operations listed above. Of those operations, armed assault, assassination, bombing, hijacking, hostage taking, and kidnapping account for 95 percent of all terrorist operations (Jenkins, 1985). As Jenkins stated, "Terrorists blow up things, kill people, or seize hostages. Every terrorist operation is merely a variation on these three activities." These six operations are also ones where it is easy for the terrorist to use force multipliers, or increase the attack power of the organization without increasing manpower requirements (White, 1991). Three commonly used force multipliers are media manipulation to increase the perception of the power of the organization, utilization of transnational support networks for logistical support and mobility, and use of technology to increase the potency of their weapons.

Table 6.4.
Summary of types of terrorist operations.

Operation	Discriminant	Indiscriminant	Causes Death	Law Enforcement Interventions*
Ambushes	Yes	Yes	Yes	No
Assassination	Yes	No	Yes	No
Bank Robbery	Yes	No	Doubtful**	No
Bombing	Yes	Yes	Likely***	No
Execution	Yes	No	Yes	No
Extortion	Yes	No	No	No
Hijacking/hostage taking	Yes	Yes	Possible	Yes
Kidnapping	Yes	No	Doubtful	No
Kneecapping	Yes	No	No	No
Rescue of prisoners	Yes	No	Doubtful	Possibly
Sabotage	Yes	Yes	Possible	No

*Assumes the law enforcement agency has not received prior specific intelligence from infiltrators, traitors, etc.

**Purpose of act does not involve killing, although persons may die from interference.

***If the bomb detonates, probability is high persons will be killed. Some bombs are specifically intended to kill victims.

PLANNING THE TERRORIST OPERATION

The majority of terrorist operations are planned events, including indiscriminant operations. Operations are planned to ensure that the operations accomplish the terrorist's goal for the operation, lead to the overall goals of the organization, guarantee the safety and escape of the terrorist, and deliver a specific message to a target audience and government. The only way to produce fear in the public and guarantee political change is through successful operations. If operations are not successful, fear is not produced, the terrorists are themselves perceived as incompetent and ineffective, and the organization will lose support. Operations have to succeed, so the planning function is crucial to the terrorist.

Planning of an operation typically involves three phases: target analysis, intelligence gathering, and development of an operational plan.

Target analysis is the first phase of operational planning and involves narrowing the list of possible targets in an area down to two or three potential targets for detailed analysis. After two or three potential targets have been identified, each target will be analyzed in terms of five variables: criticality, vulnerability, accessibility, recovery ability, and impact on the government and/or citizens.

Criticality of a target refers to how important the target is to citizens and/or the government. Criticality can be assessed on the services it provides and how important those services are to the public, how necessary the target is for the government to continue functioning, what the psychological effects would be on the public if the target was destroyed, and the meaningfulness of the target to the society or government. Assuming criticality was the only variable in the target analysis, a power plant would likely be selected over a government building, a government building over a public library, a public library over a public monument, and a public monument over a convenience store.

Vulnerability refers to the ease or difficulty a target would be to attack. Vulnerability assessment would first include target-hardening measures, such as fences, barricades, gates, doors, windows, locks, alarms, video surveillance, etc. The presence or absence of security forces would be considered. A target would be more vulnerable if guarded by a private security force than by armed military security police. Personal security would be a factor in vulnerability assessment. Buildings are being discussed, but bear in mind the vulnerability of a human target would be assessed in the same manner.

Accessibility of the target would be considered. Ease of entry and movement within the potential target would be assessed. The ease or difficulty of reaching the target would be evaluated, along with egress. Human targets are particularly vulnerable but can be made unaccessible by developing and implementing an executive protection program. Accessibility can also be evaluated in terms of how difficult destruction of the target would be for criminal investigators to collect evidence. Pan Am 103, for instance, was intended to be destroyed over the ocean so the wreckage could not be recovered and subject to investigation.

Recovery ability refers to the ease with which the target could be rebuilt or the victim replaced without loss of continuity. Targets which have a difficult recovery are the preferred target because their loss is usually more devastating to the public. The assassination of Prime Minister Rabin in Israel in November 1995 may well destroy any peace initiate in the Mideast, as Rabin was the driving force behind bringing a lasting peace to the Mideast. Recovery from his assassination may take years or decades. To destroy peace in the Mideast, terrorists would have been hard-pressed to select a better target.

Impact on the government and/or citizens refers to the target's importance to functioning of the government or need of the citizens. The target will be assessed for its likelihood of producing fear, panic, unrest, and disruption in the government and society. Ideally, the destruction of the target should turn the civilian population against the government and affect the operation of the government. Destruction of the target will be geared toward forcing the government to change its methods of operation, cede to the terrorist's demands, or lead to the collapse of the government. Terrorists would be more effective in accomplishing these goals by destroying an in-session Congress than by assassinating the president. Losing Congress would impact the government much more severely than killing the president.

The selection for destruction of the Oklahoma City Federal Building was a wise choice for the terrorists involved because of the number of federal agencies housed in the building. Almost 50 federal agencies had regional or district offices in the building, including the IRS, Social Security, DEA, military recruiting, and the Attorney General. Bombing the building affected a variety of federal functions and affected those functions not only for Oklahoma City but for a large portion of the Midwest. In addition to government functions being severely affected, many of those functions were ones citizens used on a daily basis. The terrorists were able to disrupt both the government and citizens.

The second phase of planning is that of intelligence gathering. Once a final target has been selected the terrorist will attempt to learn all they can about the target. If the target is a person, this might involve travel times and routes, bodyguards, information about their home and workplace, work schedule, family life issues, friends, social engagements, workplace and home information, and times the target is most vulnerable. For important dignitaries, the terrorist may have to plan for the presence of an executive protection team (Wurth, 1985). Executive protection teams will provide a much higher level of target security than will bodyguards. Lee Harvey Oswald, assassin of President Kennedy, carefully mapped out and considered his shooting location before the day of the parade. Unsuccessful presidential assassins such as Squeeky Fromme and John Hinkley failed in intelligence gathering and failed to accomplish their mission.

If the target is a building or facility, intelligence gathering will help determine the most effective attack method to use on the target, what type of explosives may be needed, where they should be placed, etc.

Security equipment and physical barriers will be examined for weaknesses, routines of security guards will be learned, shift changes in security determined, routines of workers established, occupancy periods mapped, etc. Drawings of the target or blueprints may be obtained and photographs of key locations made. A surveillance team may be assigned to the target to provide detailed information on production, schedules, equipment inventories, shipping and receiving schedules, locations and patrol routes of security personnel, and passive security devices such as alarms, video equipment, etc. The surveillance team may also be responsible for obtaining items necessary for the operation, such as keys, entry cards, computer-access codes, uniforms, and other specialized equipment.

One of the primary reasons the World Trade Center bombing did so little damage is because the terrorists did an inadequate job in intelligence gathering. The location of the van containing the explosives in the underground parking garage was inappropriate for the type of bomb used. When the bomb detonated, the location of the van allowed the parking garage structure to work as a giant shape charge, forcing the majority of the force of the blast out the garage opening rather than forcing it inward where it would damage the building's support structure. Placing the van in another location in the garage would have significantly worsened the blast and done much more damage to the structure.

The third phase of planning is developing the operational plan. The operation plan consists of identifying manpower and supply requirements, materials to use to attack the target, entrance and egress avenues, timing of activities, preparation of explosives or incendiaries or obtaining other weapons necessary to complete the operation, transportation requirements, routes, and contingency plans, secondary targets, and targets of opportunity. After the operation plan is complete, the terrorist organization may have a "dry run" to ensure the plan is workable and that everyone is familiar with their role. Finally, before the operation plan is put into practice, diversions may be planned and organized. In Coeur d'Alene, Idaho, members of the Order II placed a series of explosives around the town designed to detonate at the same time to cover their robbery of a bank and National Guard armory in a neighboring town.

Targets of opportunity are often identified in the operational plan. These targets are ones the terrorists could attack if the opportunity presented itself. For example, in a direct sabotage attack on a power plant, the terrorist plan may be to attack the primary transformers. During the operation, the terrorists discover the main generators are unguarded and open to attack, so the terrorist may seize advantage of the situation and sabotage the generators as well. Targets of opportunity may be identified along the egress route and those attacked while exiting the scene. Other members of the organization may be assigned to secondary targets during the primary operation. The terrorist may bomb a building, while at the same time other members walk down a public street and throw small explosive devices into storefronts.

Terrorist operations are very similar to military operations but more flexible. Terrorist operations center around specialized tactics that emphasis logistics, application of force, and intelligence (Sederberg, 1994). Logistical concerns of terrorists include the self-reliance on supply networks and trails, use of enemy supplies, decentralized logistics, and efficiency and austerity. Factors pertaining to the application of force include non-attachment to territory, dispersion and concentration, and flexibility and surprise. Intelligence concerns center around knowledge or organizational capabilities, knowledge of enemy capabilities, knowledge of geography, and knowledge of the target population. Excellence in each of these areas is crucial to success of the terrorist operation. When operations are unsuccessful or terrorists are caught, there is usually a weakness or deficiency in one or more of these areas.

HATE CRIME ACTIVITY IN THE UNITED STATES

One type of terrorism the United States has been particularly vulnerable to, and a form of terrorism only recently recognized as terroristic, is hate crime terrorism. Hate crime is an insidious form of low-level terrorism practiced·almost exclusively by the far right. It is indiscriminant terrorism that can assume any of the types of terrorist operations described above. Many people, including a large faction of law enforcement, do not consider hate crime a terrorist activity. It is argued here that hate crime is terrorism. It conforms to the basic definition of terrorism used in this book, has a political purpose and outcome, and is intended to produce fear. Hate crime is a more personalized form of terrorism and may produce greater fear than more large-scale terrorist operations. Random attacks on black citizens as individuals would likely produce more fear than the bombing of a black church, club, or business. Hate crime not being "officially" classified as terrorism is one of the political goals the far right is attempting to maintain.

Hate crime is that terrorism directed toward an individual because of that individual's race, national origin, or religion. It is terrorism directed at an individual but designed to produce fear in the affected group and designed to change the behavior and/or social structure of the affected group, and to change political legislation designed to protect and assure constitutional rights of the affected group. This section will explore the prevalence of hate crime in the United States.

There are a multiplicity of problems in attempting to list hate crimes during any one period of time. One, not all hate crimes are reported. Hate crimes are often not reported for fear of retaliation, fear of further violence, or because of peer pressure from other members of the affected group. Two, many hate crimes are not classified as hate crime. Motives for the act may be unclear. Three, crimes may be falsely reported as a hate crime when the motive is not hate related. A dispute between different-race neighbors may be classified as a hate crime when the motives are a dispute between the location of a fence. Both reasons two and three are almost entirely contingent upon the discretion of the reporting officer. Four, hate crimes have not historically been assessed, by law enforcement, the government, the media, or the public, in terms of their political intent. Hate crime is not a "crime against persons" or "crime against property." Hate crime is crime against a political system and the political intent of these crimes, until recently, has never been recognized.

The data in this section was from Newton and Newton (1991), who provided a comprehensive chronology of hate crime incidents from 1501–1989. Although the most comprehensive listing of hate crime available, their listing of hate crime incidents, and the following data analyses, suffers from several limitations. One, the Newton and Newton listing is a biased sample. They relied on archival data to produce their chronological listing. Two, the data of Newton and Newton was content analyzed and any incident not clearly identified as a hate crime was omitted. Three, police brutality was not included unless the officer(s) involved specifically indicated the incident of brutality was a hate crime. Four, prison and jail incidents were omitted from the following analysis. Five, minority-instigated sniper attacks on law enforcement officers and fire fighters were omitted. The Black Panther party intentionally sniped law enforcement and fire fighters because they represented authority, not because of race. In these incidents, there was no way to discern race from authority-motivated attacks. Six, some multiple hate crimes were classified as single incidents. If one person or organization detonated a bomb in multiple locations on one day, or if a riot lasted multiple days, that event was treated as a single incident. Seven, in cases where several activities occurred at one location or to one person, the incident was classified according to the worst activity. If a person was assaulted and murdered, that incident was classified as a murder. If a building was vandalized and bombed, the incident was classified as a bombing. Eight, not all incidents reported by Newton and Newton (1991) or reported were committed by the far right. Only about 10 percent of all incidents reported or used in the data analysis can be directly attributable to the far right, although probably about 80–90 percent are due to far-right activities. This is understandable, since one of the goals of the far right is to avoid responsibility for their activities, instead attributing their terrorism to other citizens or for providing the impetus for action by others. As indicated here, the far right has been achieving their goals.

Figure 6.1 lists the number of hate crimes for 1951–1989. The significant rise in hate crimes in 1956 corresponded with school desegregation. In 1964, court-ordered school desegregation reached Mississippi. In 1964, of 169 hate crime incidents, 137 occurred in Mississippi. In 1968, Martin Luther King was assassinated, leading to a three-year reversal in hate crimes by race. In 1968, 1969, and 1970, almost 40 percent of hate crimes were committed by blacks, as compared to other years, when whites committed over 90 percent of all hate crimes. The rise in hate crime activity in 1980, 1985, and 1986 can be explained by several factors (Mullins, 1993). Membership in the far right increased during the 1980s. The country entered a recession, when it is common for whites to blame minorities for economic woes. During the 1980s recession, the white blue-collar worker was the population segment most affected, the very population that comprises the majority membership in the far right (Flynn & Gerhardt, 1989; Strentz, 1990). The Republican administration of the mid-1980s virtually ignored the social, economic, and racial woes of America. The Reagan administration gave the implied signal that minorities were second-class citizens by the actions of the administration. Jobs, housing, education, and equal rights activities were ignored by the administration. During the mid-1980s, the far right got younger. Young adults began entering the far-right movement and many became skinheads. Taken together, these factors gave impetus to the far-right movement and all contributed to increases in hate crimes.

Table 6.5 gives the frequency of hate crimes by state. States of the Deep South, long considered the most racist of all states, are generally no worse than many other states. In Mississippi, when the school desegregation incidents of the 1960s are factored out, the number of incidents falls from 288 to 24. Non-southern states with significant numbers of hate crimes include New York (181), California (117), and Illinois (110).

Table 6.6 indicates hate crime incidents by geographical region. Most hate crime occurred in the Southeast (44%), the least in the Northwest (2%). In the past two decades, these geographical divisions have somewhat disappeared, and hate crime has been fairly evenly distributed throughout the country. Incidents of hate crime have been decreasing in the Southeast and increasing in the Northeast. This trend is supported by the ADL (1991), who reported that in 1990, 55% of all reported instances of vandalism-related hate crime occurred in the Northeast, 9%

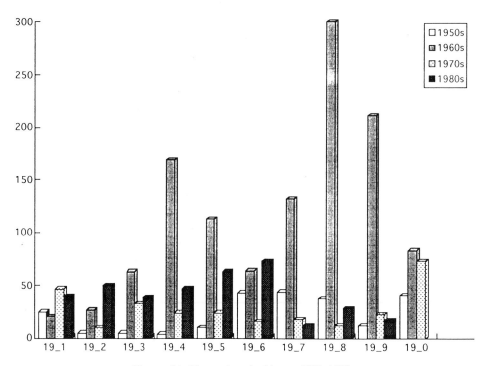

Figure 6.1. Hate crime incidents, 1951–1989.

in the Southeast, 13% in the Midwest, 1% in the Midsouth, 5% in the Northwest, and 17% in the Southwest.

Table 6.7 lists types of hate crime incidents by decade. Five issues concerning the data in Table 6.7 need explanation. One, for a multiple-crime incident, only the most serious is included. If a building were vandalized and burned, the incident was classified as an arson. Two, if an individual was killed with no further explanation, that incident was classified as an assault. Three, all categories include attempted crimes. Four, assaults include beatings, knifings, use of other weapons (i.e., clubs, chains, bottles, etc.), abduction, and threats of violence. Five, mobs or riots had to involve four or more people and had to involve multiple acts such as beatings and vandalism. Otherwise, the incident was classified as an assault. The 1950s was the decade of bombing, the 1960s the decade of riots, the 1970s the decade of shootings and assaults (discounting mobs/riots as most occurred in the early part of the decade and were a trace element of that previous decade), and the 1980s the decade of assaults. This data indicates that as law enforcement became proficient at solving or preventing one type of hate crime, terrorists changed methodology. It is believed total incidents of vandalism may be underrepresented

Table 6.5.
Hate crimes by state, 1951–1989.

State	1951–1960	1961–1970	1971–1980	1981–1990	Total
Alabama	50	85	23	8	166
Arizona	0	3	1	2	6
Arkansas	10	15	5	2	32
California	1	50	37	29	117
Colorado	0	2	1	3	6
Connecticut	0	22	3	6	31
Delaware	3	5	0	2	20
Washington D.C.	0	10	1	0	11
Florida	19	62	14	12	107
Georgia	23	59	13	54	149
Hawaii	0	1	0	0	1
Idaho	0	0	0	10	10
Illinois	5	74	10	21	110
Indiana	0	11	8	9	28
Iowa	0	6	0	1	7
Kansas	0	8	1	1	10
Kentucky	4	10	1	6	21
Louisiana	7	46	5	6	64
Maryland	1	16	1	17	35
Massachusetts	0	11	18	14	43
Michigan	0	39	7	8	54
Minnesota	0	4	2	1	7
Mississippi	12	266	3	7	288
Missouri	2	11	2	5	20
Nebraska	0	4	3	1	8
Nevada	0	3	1	0	4
New Hampshire	0	0	0	2	2
New Jersey	0	58	16	4	78
New Mexico	0	1	1	1	3
New York	1	101	39	40	181
North Carolina	18	40	10	29	97
Ohio	2	34	7	6	49
Oklahoma	1	0	2	0	3
Oregon	0	4	0	4	8
Pennsylvania	0	43	3	13	59
Rhode Island	0	8	0	2	10
South Carolina	14	11	1	4	30
South Dakota	0	0	24	0	24
Tennessee	30	19	5	6	60
Texas	12	11	7	20	50
Utah	0	0	1	1	2
Vermont	0	0	1	1	2
Virginia	9	10	1	2	22

Table 6.5. Continued.

State	1951–1960	1961–1970	1971–1980	1981–1990	Total
Washington	0	7	0	3	10
West Virginia	3	1	0	1	5
Wisconsin	0	12	2	4	18
Wyoming	0	0	0	1	1

FROM: Mullins, W.C. (1993). Hate crime and the far right: Unconventional terrorism. In K.D. Tunnell (Ed.), *Political crime in contemporary America: A critical approach.* New York: Garland Publishing Co.
NOTE: Maine, Montana, and North Dakota reported no hate crime incidents.

Table 6.6.
Hate crime incidents by geographical area for the decades since 1951.

Area	Number of Incidents Percentage of Incidents				Total & % of Total
	1951–1960	1961–1970	1971–1980	1981–1990	
Northeast	71	285	83	104	489
CT, DE, DC, ME, MD, MA, NH, NJ, NY, PA, RI, VT, VA, WV	.07	.24	.30	.28	.24
Southeast	166	542	69	120	897
AL, FL, GA, MS, NC, SC, TN	.73	.46	.25	.33	.44
Midwest	13	213	67	63	356
IL, IN, AI, KS, KY MI, MN, MO, NE, OH, SD, WI	.06	.18	.24	.17	.17
Midsouth	30	72	19	28	149
AR, LA, OK, TX	.13	.06	.07	.08	.07
Northwest	0	13	2	22	37
CO, ID, OR, UT, WA, WY		.01	.00	.06	.02
Southwest	1	58	40	32	131
AZ, CA, HI, NV, NM	.00	.05	.14	.09	.06
TOTAL	227	1183	280	369	2059
	.11	.57	.14	.18	

FROM: Mullins, W.C. (1993). Hate crime and the far right: Unconventional terrorism. In K.D. Tunnell (Ed.), *Political crime in contemporary America: A critical approach.* New York: Garland Publishing Co.

by as much as 50–70 percent, as most incidents of vandalism are either not reported or not classified by law enforcement as hate crimes.

Table 6.8 lists deaths from hate crimes. Race riots of the 1960s significantly elevated hate crime deaths. Although it may appear that

Table 6.7.
Types of hate crime incidents by decade.

Incident type	1951–1960	1961–1970	1971–1980	1981–1990	Total
Bombing	97	139	22	62	320
Burning/Arson	13	135	16	49	213
Mob/Riot	39	613	86	29	767
Assault	52	152	63	140	407
Shooting	21	129	89	58	297
Vandalism	5	15	4	31	55
TOTALS	227	1183	280	369	2059

FROM: Mullins, W.C. (1993). Hate crime and the far right: Unconventional terrorism. In K.D. Tunnell (Ed.), *Political crime in contemporary America: A critical approach.* New York: Garland Publishing Co.

deaths due to hate crime have been decreasing throughout the 1980s, the proportion of deaths to total number of yearly incidents has been increasing. In the 1980s, hate crimes decreased slightly while deaths increased.

To illustrate the severity of the problem of collecting information on hate crime in the U.S., Table 6.9 lists acts of hate crime vandalism and assaults, threats, and harassments for 1980–1989 as collated by the ADL (1991). The ADL listing is significantly greater than that reported by Newton and Newton (1991). One disturbing trend reported by the ADL was the increase of hate crimes on college and university campuses. As reported by the ADL, 69 hate crime incidents occurred on 54 separate campuses in 1989 and 95 hate crimes on 57 campuses in 1990. Some of the very people who should be most resistant to the hate of the far right are those becoming involved in spreading the message of hate.

Hate crime terrorism has been a part of this nation since its founding. It has only been within the past decade that hate crime has been recognized for what it really is: a form of right-wing terrorist tactics. Hate crime is not usually represented nor understood as terrorism because it does not fit preconceived notions of what terrorism should be. Hate crime is directed at individuals as persons rather than individuals as representatives of government structure. Terrorism is directed against the individual because of what the individual represents. This tactic hides terrorism behind a facade of normal criminal activity. Thus, members of the far right can move toward their goals while not becoming labeled as terrorists. It is not likely that the immediate future will see the far right abandon this insidious tactic.

Table 6.8.
Deaths from hate crime incidents by year.

Year	Number	Year	Number
1951	3	1971	11–3
1952	0	1972	6
1953	0	1973	25[b]
1954	0	1974	10[b]
1955	6	1975	10
1956	12	1976	10
1957	2	1977	10[c]
1958	1	1978	10[c]
1959	1	1979	10[c]
1960	2	1980	50–16
1961	1	1981	1
1962	4	1982	18
1963	11	1983	4
1964	9	1984	4
1965	9	1985	14
1966	7	1986	9
1967	84–81[a]	1987	4
1968	75–61	1988	3
1969	15–9	1989	5
1970	23–9		

FROM: Mullins, W.C. (1993). Hate crime and the far right: Unconventional terrorism. In K.D. Tunnell (Ed.), *Political crime in contemporary America: A critical approach.* New York: Garland Publishing Co.

[a]Whenever a second number appears, that number indicates the number of deaths which occurred during mob/riot incidents for that year.

[b]Black Muslim splinter group Death Angels were responsible for a series of Zebra killings in California. In 1973, there were 10 Zebra killings, in 1974 there were 6.

[c]Racist serial killer Joseph Paul Franklin killed 3 people in 1977, 3 people in 1979, and 9 people in 1980.

TECHNOLOGICAL TERRORISM IN THE UNITED STATES

Americans like to believe the United States is immune from terrorism. This belief is often reinforced by federal, state, and local law enforcement officials who reassure the citizens of the safety and invulnerability of the country against terrorist activities. Nothing could be further from the truth. The United States is one of the most vulnerable countries on earth to terrorist attack. Robert Kupperman, staff member at the Georgetown University Center for Strategic and International Studies, stated, "The United States is probably more vulnerable and less prepared to deal with major acts of terrorism than are most other countries" (in Yeager, 1986).

The United States has been and remains particularly vulnerable to

Table 6.9.

ADL summary of vandalism and other hate crime incidents, 1980–1989.

Year	Number of Vandalisms	Number of Assaults, Threats, Harassment
1980	377	112
1981	974	350
1982	829	593
1983	670	350
1984	715	363
1985	638	306
1986	594	312
1987	694	324
1988	823	458
1989	845	587
TOTALS	7159	3755

FROM: Mullins, W.C. (1993). Hate crime and the far right: Unconventional terrorism. In K.D. Tunnell (Ed.), *Political crime in contemporary America: A critical approach.* New York: Garland Publishing Co.

technological terrorism. Technological terrorism refers to terrorist operations that target the technological heart of American society. Power networks, nuclear facilities, transportation networks, and computer systems are major components of this technological network and are especially vulnerable to terrorist activity. The United States has become dependent upon these technological networks to provide services we take for granted, foodstuffs, and other comforts of modern life. Unlike in other nations, Americans have come to accept these networks as a fact of life, that these services are guaranteed and an inalienable right of the freedom of America. In reality, these networks are fragile webs that can easily be disrupted or destroyed by well-timed attacks by terrorists.

Technological targets provide attractive targets for the terrorist. The terrorist has a virtual plethora of technological targets to select from. These targets are seldom guarded heavily, if at all; attacks can produce higher damage, destruction, and death; and terrorists can impact a significant portion of the population. Technological terrorism also refers to the ability of terrorists to conduct larger-scale operations against non-technological targets, as technology has impacted weapons and other tools of the terrorist trade (Simon, 1994). Firearms, plastic explosives, and the more exotic weapons of nuclear, chemical, and biological warfare are all available to the terrorist. The United States is continually in competition to stop terrorists on the technological front, while terrorists continue to outwit technological efforts to prevent operations. The best example of this is airline security. Terrorists have a vast array of weapons that can defeat air travel security measures. Plastic guns, plastic explosives, and chemical weapons are all used by terrorists to defeat security measures. The government and airlines are continually attempting to develop detectors, bomb-resistant glass, fortified cargo containers, and x-ray devices that will detect these technologically sophisticated weapons. Whenever the airlines successfully compromise a weapon, the terrorist turns to a different weapon.

Rather than be well-protected from technological terrorism, the United States has been lucky. As one example, in 1985, the FALN bombed the Senate chamber in Washington D.C. By fortune, the Senate had adjourned early on that particular day, so there were no injuries. As the IRA has repeatedly told British Prime Minister Margaret Thatcher, "You have to be lucky every time. We have to be lucky only once" (McGee, 1987).

The United States is a vast playing board of networks. Power supplies, communications, railways, highways, shipping lanes, natural resource pipelines, and computer services are each national interconnected webs that provide services to vast geographical areas and millions of people. Both citizens and the government have become totally dependent upon these networks to function legislatively, financially, organizationally, and socially. These networks have become the lifeblood of American society in all respects, and as Yeager (1986) has indicated, a terrorist operation conducted by a small organization of terrorists against any one of these networks would produce a great deal of fear in the public and virtually paralyze and isolate large segments of the country.

The destruction of the electric power grids in New Mexico would shut down most of the western and West Coast of the United States, including Los Angeles. Figure 6.2 illustrates the varieties of ways this power grid could be sabotaged and the ease with which it could be accomplished. Disabling a power network would do much more than simply cause a power blackout. Computer networks would be closed or destroyed, West Coast ports would be forced to close, vehicular traffic would be brought to a standstill, rail lines would have to cease operations, airports would be forced to close, businesses would be unable to operate, water purification plants would be unable to produce potable water, and sewage treatment plants would cease operations. Crime would become rampant and the police would be powerless to do anything about it, as police communication networks would be affected and patrol operations would be immobilized. In essence, the entire West Coast would be isolated and alone.

Any part of the United States transportation network is just as vulnerable as power networks. Airplanes are kept flying by a series of isolated radar stations, computer and communications antennae, and a series of 20 Air Traffic Control centers. Any act of sabotage or destruction at any

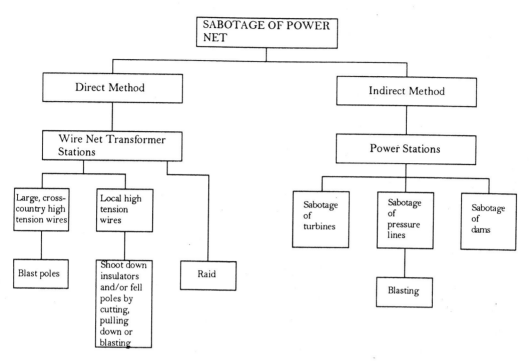

Figure 6.2. Techniques which could be used to sabotage a power network.

part of this chain would likely close all civilian and most military aircraft operations. Passenger and cargo air services would cease to operate. In spite of the increased security measures, airports in the United States are just as vulnerable to terrorist operations as ever. Table 6.10 shows the results of screening procedures at airports for the years 1980–1985. As can be seen, thousands of persons attempt to board aircraft with all manners of weapons. Airports are secured by minimum-wage security guards who have inadequate training, are unmotivated to thoroughly check every passenger, and are ill-equipped to search for more sophisticated weapons. One senior official of the Federal Aviation Administration (who wished to remain anonymous) confided that only about 20–30 percent of all weapons smuggled aboard aircraft are detected by airport security services.

Airlines are particularly attractive targets for the terrorist and provide an international forum for political statements. Palestinian terrorists first demonstrated the usefulness of terrorist acts against airplanes and passengers, including both hostage taking and bombing (Media Analysis Center, 1990). Airlines are symbols of nations and governments and are overt representations of the success of a nation (Jenkins, 1993). From an

Table 6.10.
Airline passenger screening results, 1980–1985.

	1980	1981	1982	1983	1984	1985
Persons Screened (millions)	585.0	598.5	630.2	709.1	775.6	992.7
Weapons Detected						
Firearms	2022	2255	2676	2784	2957	2987
Handguns	1878	2124	2559	2634	2766	2823
Long Guns	36	44	57	67	100	90
Other*	108	87	60	83	91	74
Explosive/Incendiary Devices	8	11	1	4	6	12
Persons Arrested						
Carrying Firearms/Explosives	1031	1187	1314	1282	1285	1310
Giving False Information	32	49	27	34	27	42

FROM: Federal Aviation Administration (1986). *Reports of passenger screening activities at U.S. airports.* Washington D.C.: U.S. Department of Transportation.
*Includes knives, mace, CO_2, ammunition, etc.

operational perspective, airplanes are convenient sealed containers for hostages. A small number of terrorists can completely control a large number of hostages and counter-terrorist response teams. Airplanes also can be used to accomplish more than one goal. Airplane incidents can be used for publicity purposes, escape attempts, achieve political goals, demonstrate the terrorist organization's strength and power, and make a government appear weak and ineffectual.

The nation's rail network, the major carrier of freight within the United States, would be even easier to disable. Two or three well-coordinated attacks on the rail system would effectively immobilize rail traffic for most of the country. Sabotage of rail networks would be the most effective and simplest of all networks for the terrorist to attack. Bombing the Potomac River rail bridge in Washington D.C. and the main track-line in Cincinnati, Ohio would halt all rail traffic in the Northeast corridor and entire eastern seaboard. The supply of foods, consumable goods, and other material supplies would come to a complete stop for several weeks.

Not as critical as the air or rail systems, but just as unprotected and vulnerable, is the inland water system. Destroying a ship in the St. Lawrence Seaway would stop all traffic between the Great Lakes and the Atlantic Ocean. Strategically sinking a ship in the Intercoastal Waterway would bring a halt to the shipping of 40 percent of the nation's bulk cargo. River traffic to middle America could be completely disrupted by sabotaging a lock-and-dam system or bombing a bridge across the Mississippi River.

Possibly the most vulnerable of all systems is the United States oil and natural gas pipeline system. Most of these pipelines are in isolated areas and are totally unprotected. The most exposed of all pipelines is the Trans-Alaska oil pipeline, the largest of all pipeline supplies to the U.S. This pipeline is a four-foot pipe running for 800 miles between Prudhoe Bay to Port Valdez, Alaska. It carries over 1.2 million barrels of oil per day. One control center in Valdez is responsible for monitoring the entire pipeline. A terrorist bombing along the pipeline would not only disrupt the flow of oil, but it would turn the 140-degree oil into a semisolid which would require over one year to clean up. Three other pipelines equally as vulnerable are the Capline pipeline between St. James, Louisiana and Patoka, Illinois (632 miles), the Colonial pipeline on the East Coast, and the Plantation pipeline in the South. Even more vulnerable (and destructive) are the natural gas pipelines. A small charge which would let air into one of these pipelines would destroy several miles of pipeline and millions of dollars of property and countless lives (Stephan, 1973). By gaining control of a control center and increasing the pressure of natural gas, the terrorist could cause a major explosion.

It should be evident that the United States is extremely vulnerable and open to large-scale acts of terrorism. A large-scale operation does not imply that the terrorist strike force has to be large in number. One or two persons could conduct operations such as those described above. In the United States, the government, business, nor the individual take the most basic precautions against terrorist operations, nor take the "conscientious and disciplined protection" which will deter terrorists (Clutterback, 1975). The central issue remains not if but when.

TERRORISM AND DRUGS

Many people, civilian and government, uniformed and expert, uneducated and educated, low skilled and law enforcement, see many of the present problems in society as resulting from the exponential increase of drug use. This drug epidemic is seen as responsible for the increases in crime, teenage and young adult violence, the murder rate, teen pregnancy, birth defects, divorce, and homelessness. Drugs have filled the prisons and turned our society into an armed compound where citizens are not safe in their own homes. In the 1990s, the demand for drugs is so great that terrorists have entered into the drug business and found new opportunities for advancing their cause and achieving their goals. Terrorists organizations ranging the entire gamut from left to right wing, completely autonomous to state-sponsored or supported terrorism, have become involved in the drug business, including anti-U.S. governments who use terrorists to wage war on the U.S. (Mullins, 1990b).

The United States is the single largest user of illicit drugs in the world. Because of this, most of the narco-terrorist activity concerns, either directly or indirectly, the United States. Drugs are shipped to the United States from all corners of the world. Most of the marijuana imported into the U.S. comes from Latin America, most of the cocaine from South America, and most of the heroin from Asia (Balsiger, 1990). The profits to be gained and low risk of being caught has made narco-terrorism an ideal form of terrorist activity.

At the lowest level of involvement in the drug business, terrorist organizations use drugs to obtain finances. Peru's Shining Path was one of the most heavily involved terrorist organizations in the financial proceeds end of the drug trade. In the "cocaine capital of the world," Uchiza, Peru, in the Upper Huallaga valley, Shining Path controls and operates the largest cocaine processing network in the world. In Uchiza, Shining Path has gained political control of the area from the Peruvian army. Shining Path regulates the drug commerce for the Colombian drug cartels. In July 1987, in the town of Tochache, Shining Path took the Huallaga Valley from another terrorist organization, the Tupac Amaru Revolutionary Movement, by armed force. Once they gained control of the drug fields, Shining Path realized profits of $15–$34 million per year, with good growing years reaping the organization almost $100 million (Trujillo, 1993).

Between 1988–1992, some estimated Shining Path earned over $250 million from growing and processing cocaine (Brooke, 1993). As part of their narco-terrorist activities, Shining Path forced businessmen to contribute to a "war tax" and either extorted businesses or kidnapped business executives who refused to pay this tax. Using sophisticated computer files to organize and maintain intelligence information, Shining Path kept complete dossiers on hundreds of Peruvian businesses and CEOs, including finances, net worth statements, information on executive's private lives, and travel plans. Shining Path terrorists have even attacked U.S. interests, shooting down a DEA helicopter in 1992. In a country where the average monthly income is only $56, many local citizens support and work for Shining Path in the lucrative drug business (Dillon, 1993). In a country where millions of people survive by eating trash, community service programs operated by Shining Path are seen as salvation. They operate soup kitchens, support charities and hospitals, and sponsor education and life-survival programs. Many Peruvians ignore the fact that in the decade of the 1980s, over 24,900 people were killed by

Shining Path violence and over 6,000 Peruvian prisoners are Shining Path members.

Operating in a manner similar to Shining Path, the Tupac Amaru extorted, kidnapped, and murdered business executives who refused to pay a monetary tribute to the organization. In 1992, Victor Polay Campos, leader of Tupac Amaru, was arrested and over 50 computer disks seized at Optimisa S.R.L., a front business for the terrorist organization. From the computer files of the chief financial officer for Optimisa S.R.L., Maria Luisa Benza Pflucker, law enforcement authorities found complete intelligence files on members of pharmaceutical manufacturers, soft drink bottling companies, and printers. This information cataloged economic and financial movements, company directories, addresses, telephone numbers, and other private and personnel information. When companies paid extortion money, Optimisa S.R.L. even provided receipts (Brooke, 1993).

Some drug cartels use terrorist organizations to provide security and protection, harass the government, or to conduct terrorist campaigns to force a government to not investigate and prosecute the cartel. The most famous example of this is the M-19 attack on the Colombian supreme court. Over 200 people, including 12 Supreme Court justices, were killed by a series of explosions and assassinations. The purpose of this attack was to discourage the Colombian government from investigating cartel activities and to not permit U.S. drug enforcement agents into Colombia to investigate the cartels. In all, the Colombian drug cartels employ several different terrorist organizations to provide security and engage in drug cartel-sponsored terrorism (Unnamed, 1993). Drug cartels have not only employed local terrorists to assist in narco-terrorist activities, they have also engaged terrorist organizations such as the IRA, PLO, FARC, Red Brigades in Italy, Gray Wolves in Turkey, and the Shan United Army and Burmese Communist Party in Burma (Mullins, 1990c).

The drug trade can also spawn insurgent organizations that threaten existing governments. In Latin America, hundreds of terrorist organizations have sprung up around drug-producing areas, each hoping to realize the financial windfalls of the drug business to support political overthrow. In Burma, both the Burmese Communist Party and Shan United Army use drugs to support their movements to overthrow the Shan state (Vetter & Perlstein, 1991). The Burmese Communist Party wants Burma to become a communist state, and the Shan United Army wants to return Burma to its pre-1948 democracy. Both organizations are active in the Golden Triangle, the most fertile poppy growing area in the entire world, and both gain finances from taxing poppy growers, producing heroin, smuggling drugs, and the sale of heroin in the United States. In the Bekaa Valley, Lebanon, terrorists from different organizations work hand in hand in the growing, production, and sale of hashish. Opium and heroin are refined and processed in Beirut by numerous terrorist organizations (Williams, 1990). This uneasy symbiotic relationship between philosophical enemies is maintained by the enormous profits to be made by all by working in the drug business.

States that support and sponsor terrorism use the drug trade to wage their war of terrorism against the United States. In a sentiment echoed by Fidel Castro, Carlos Lehder of the Medellin Cartel once said, "Coca has been transformed into a revolutionary weapon against American imperialism" (Mullins, 1990c). Castro sees cocaine as the white path of destruction for the U.S. Charging $800,000 per boat load for safe passage through Cuba, Castro said, "We are going to make the people up there white, white with cocaine" (Balsiger, 1990). In 1983, Jaime Guillot, Colombian drug dealer and member of M-19, was tried for smuggling over 25 million tablets of methaqualone and 80 pounds of cocaine into the U.S. through Cuba. He paid the Cubans for his use of their ports, and they paid him to transport weapons to M-19 in Colombia (Williams, 1990). He was arrested in 1981, when his ship, the *M/V Karina,* was sunk by the Colombia navy, along with 100 tons of weapons. M-19 and FARC are also believed to be responsible for the murder of Colombian presidential candidate Luis Carlos Galan in 1989 and the bombing of an Avianca flight in New York in 1989.

In Latin America, other major state-sponsored narco-terrorist governments have included Nicaragua, Panama, El Salvador, and Colombia, who all have used narco-terrorism. Manuel Noriega provided a safe haven for drug cartel leaders, a conduit for drugs headed for the U.S., and assistance and protection for terrorists. Drug boats, stolen in the U.S., were taken to Cuba, loaded with fuel and arms shipments, and then the arms delivered to Nicaragua. In Nicaragua, the boats would be loaded with drugs, sent to Colombia to be loaded with more drugs, sent on to Cuba for fueling and provided a Cuban escort, and then returned to the U.S. to off-load their drug shipment. U.S. Customs Commissioner William Vonn Raab called this route a "nifty twentieth century version of the old triangle trade" (Balsiger, 1990).

In the Mideast, Syrian drug profits are channeled into anti-West terrorist activity, as are those of Iran, Iraq, Libya, and Chad. In the Iranian embassy siege, Hezbollah terrorists financed the operation through profits realized in narcotic trafficking. In Europe, Bulgaria and the USSR have both used narcotics profits to support terrorism. Bulgaria is a primary funnel for Mideast drugs to enter Europe, and the Bulgarian secret police funded their failed attempt to assassinate Pope John Paul II with drug proceeds.

In the United States, foreign and domestic terrorists have been involved in the drug trade. Foreign organizations such as the Provisional IRA, Palestinian Fawaz Younis (Smith, 1994), and M-19CO have used drugs to support their terrorist activities. Other left-wing terrorist organizations have been involved in drug trafficking to both finance their operations and as a means to an end. The far left believes drugs can be used as a revolutionary tool. The far right has also become involved in the drug trade. To the far right, only minorities are weak enough to dare use drugs. Thus, drugs become a means for the far right to eliminate minorities and establish dominance of the Aryan race. By promoting drug use among minorities, the coming race war can be prompted to occur and give the advantage to Aryans, since the minorities will be "stoned" and unable to fight (Mullins, 1990a). A side benefit to the far right are the profits to be made from drugs which will allow these organizations to increase their activities against the government. Many far-right organizations preach that the federal government is deliberately encouraging drug usage (and secretly supplying drugs) as a method of social control as the government becomes a dictator, allows the communists to take control, or takes freedom from white Americans (Mullins, 1989, 1991; Mullins & Mijares, 1993).

At all levels of the drug business, from growing, to distribution, to sales, terrorists have found uses for the drug business and have become involved to support their organizational goals and provide funds for terrorist operations. Drugs have become an integral part of the world of terrorism. At heart, terrorists see drugs as just another way to spread fear and panic throughout the public and overthrow the government. Drugs are one additional tool in the terrorist arsenal.

TERRORISM AND THE MEDIA

On 9 March 1977, Hamaas Abdul Khaalis and 12 members of the Hanafi Muslims took 134 people hostage in three locations in Washington D.C. Khaalis' two primary demands were that the murderers of his family be given to him so he could punish them according to Muslim law and that the sacrilegious movie, *Mohammed, Messenger of God*, be banned from American movie screens (McMains & Mullins, 1995). During the initial stages of what proved to be a three-day siege, one news reporter was killed and several other hostages injured. Television broadcast the events live and kept telephoning Khaalis to ask him questions and update him on police activities. At one point during the siege, the media told Khaalis the police were preparing to assault his location. At another point during the siege, a reporter called and asked why the police were attempting to trick Khaalis into surrendering. Police negotiators were also able to diffuse these threats and eventually persuaded Khaalis and the other hostage takers to surrender. During the incident, ABC devoted 40 percent of their national news coverage to the hostage story, CBS devoted 31 percent to the story, and NBC 53 percent (Schmid & De Graaf, 1982).

In 1985, Shiite terrorists hijacked TWA flight 847. Their demands included the release of 700 Lebanese prisoners in Israel, the release of 17 Lebanese prisoners in Kuwait, Lebanese prisoners in Greece, two Lebanese in Spain, the overthrow of King Hussein in Jordan and President Mubarak in Egypt, an end to U.S. aid to Israel, and a change in U.S. policy in the Mideast. During the 17 days this incident lasted, it became a major media story, dominating the airwaves for the duration of the incident. The media became allies and partners with the terrorists, arguing that the prisoners of Israel were no better off than the hostages on the airplane.

These two incidents forced people to begin examining the relationship between terrorism and the media. In Washington, the way the media treated the incident, continually talked to the terrorists, prompted the terrorists on police actions, and delayed the resolution of the incident clearly showed that the media did indeed influence terrorist activity. The media glorification of the terrorists at the hostage takeover of TWA flight 847 made many people question the value of media reporting of terrorist incidents. People believed the media to be undermining U.S. interests and weakening the government's ability to deal with terrorists, that the media were being manipulated by the terrorists for self-serving purposes, that the media crossed the line from reporting to being participants in the drama, and that network competition lengthened the incident and delayed resolution.

Television is the obviously preferred medium for terrorists. Television can cover the incident live and broadcast the story in real time to a worldwide audience. Television cameras can provide close-up views of the actions and provide a visual forum for the terrorists. Even if the terrorists cannot be heard by television microphones, the visual images can be translated into clearly discernible actions of "street theater." Cameras are also on the responders, political, law enforcement, and military. The eye of the camera can influence policy, response strategy, and tactics. In Somalia, most are familiar with the CNN camera crews on the beach awaiting the Navy Seal teams who were responsible for securing the landing beaches. Unit effectiveness was completely compromised by the presence of the cameras.

Television has become more than a simple reporter of the story, it has become part of the story. Jeffrey Cohen, Fairness and Accuracy of Reporting, once stated, "The media covers terrorism like a sporting event with easy emphasis on scoring wins. It trivializes. How can someone deal seriously with a medium whose motto is, 'if it bleeds, it leads'" (in Elkin, 1990)? Unfortunately, his comments apply equally as well to other forms of the media, including radio, newspapers, and even magazines. Miller (1993) agreed, arguing that live cover of a terrorist incident precludes being able to censor the events. Miller suggested most media representatives covering terrorist incidents completely disregarded ethical issues in their coverage and that the media would do whatever necessary to get ratings, the public safety be damned. He referred to media coverage of terrorist incidents as a "cult of objectivity," in that merely by observing and transmitting the story altered the story and that terrorist operations are essentially terrorist hijackings of the news media. Koppel, Podhoretz, Krauthammer, Besacon, O'Sullivan, Schorr, Will, and Woodward (1986), however, indicated it is important to separate popular press coverage and quality press coverage of terrorist incidents. They suggest that the popular press assumes terrorists are important for what they do, while the quality press assumes that terrorists are important for what they say. Either way, the issue of media influences on terrorism remains.

Several authors have addressed the role of the media and how their actions can affect terrorism. Most agree that media coverage of terrorist incidents leads to a contagion effect, where coverage of one act leads to a series of similar acts (Crenshaw, 1983). Schmid and De Graaf (1982) examined 26 parachute hijacking attempts and concluded the media played a significant role in copycat acts. Similarly, Oots (1986) suggested the media could influence less violent organizations to emulate the high-publicity violence of terrorists. Wardlaw (1982) suggested the media can prolong a terrorist incident by increasing the perception of power held by the terrorists and can increase the severity of the consequences of the incident. Finn (1993) argued the media could affect the form terrorism takes. Kidnapping incidents were common in the 1960s and 1970s, hijackings and car bombings in the 1970s, and hostage taking in the 1980s. Through the media, terrorists learned response strategy and tactics and altered their operations accordingly. Finn also suggested the media can influence how participants, terrorists, victims, and response units react.

Schmid and De Graaf (1982) also suggested media influence could affect public reactions by instilling fear in a mass audience, polarize public opinion, terrorists could gain publicity by agreeing to interviews, demand publication of their political agenda, provoke government overreaction, spread false and misleading information, force the release of prisoners, attract persons to their cause, achieve political goals from the free advertising, discredit public officials, send messages to comrades in other areas or countries, incite the public to rebel against established authority, improve organizational morale, achieve a "Robin Hood" status by appearing to fight injustice, obtain counter-terrorist information and intelligence, identify future victims, and appear to be more powerful than they really are by manipulating the media. Terrorists could also use the media to create celebrities among terrorists, incite other organizations to violence, and divert public attention by conducting an operation intended to reach the headlines. Most damaging, possibly, is that the media provides a "built-in escalation imperative," where it requires larger and more violent activities to obtain media coverage.

Simon (1994) has addressed some of these concerns, attempting to separate the myths of the media-terrorism link from the facts about terrorism. A journalist, Simon offers the following as myths and facts concerning the media and terrorism:

1. *Myth:* Most terrorists attempt to use the media to the terrorist's advantage.

   Fact: Most terrorists do not use the media. Some do utilize the media for political purposes, but most terrorists, including state-sponsored and state-supported, attempt to avoid the media. Media coverage of the terrorist organization can make them less effective, bring pressure from the government, lead to identification or capture, and disrupt and interfere with future operations. Media coverage can also turn public opinion away from the terrorists.

2. *Myth:* The media fosters an image of "crisis" over terrorism.

   Fact: Media coverage masks the role presidents and government play in creating a crisis atmosphere during a terrorist incident. The media is used by the government as much as the terrorist may attempt to use the media. This can lead to pressure on the government and lead to them making mistakes.

3. *Myth:* The media can limit a government's options in responding to terrorism.

   Fact: The media could negatively affect a government's response plans by disclosing sensitive information or intelligence, but the media usually focuses on the human and personal element during . terrorist incidents than on government responses.

4. *Myth:* The media can help prolong terrorists incidents by giving widespread and continuing publicity to the terrorists.
   Fact: The attention given an incident has little effect on its duration.
5. *Myth:* The media are not interested in providing context and causal explanations for terrorist incidents. Simon cites the NBC news interview in 1986 of Tom Brokaw's interview with Abu Abbas, mastermind of the *Achille Lauro* incident. NBC news received widespread criticism for this interview, because NBC did not reveal the location of the interview or Abbas and simplified the complexity of the situation.
   Fact: The media does provide context to terrorist incidents, but since terrorism raises strong emotions in people, any discussions about terrorist motives may appear too sympathetic and forgiving to the terrorists. The public wants easily grasped symbols and terrorism does not lend itself to those symbols.

Whether one accepts the influences of the media on terrorism, or the explanations offered by Simon (1994), and although no empirical data exists, it must be agreed that at some level the media does influence terrorist behavior. Whether this influence is in a contagion effect, motivating other organizations to turn to violence, increase the duration of an incident, increase the danger to victims, or affect response options is unknown. What is known is that neither terrorism nor the media coverage it receives occurs in a vacuum and that the two are linked in unexplained ways. It must then be asked, what has the media done to limit possible influences on terrorism?

In April 1977, immediately following the Hanaafi Muslim incident in Washington D.C., CBS became the first major network to develop guidelines for the reporting of terrorist incidents (Simon, 1994). Their guidelines included: (1) not providing an excessive platform for terrorists; (2) paraphrasing terrorist demands; (3) a prohibition against live coverage except with permission of the president of CBS news; (4) no interference with telephone links between law enforcement authorities and terrorists; (5) utilizing a hostage negotiation expert to advise on issues to determine if questions or phraseology may influence the situation; and (6) balancing the length of coverage with other news events. It is worth noting that most of these guidelines were violated during the 1979 Iranian embassy siege.

Following CBS's lead, NBC developed guidelines for covering terrorist incidents. Their guidelines specified that: (1) terrorist incidents were newsworthy and would be covered; (2) reporters should use professionalism and common sense in reporting on these incidents; and (3) the news should be balanced with keeping the public informed, avoidance of being used by either side, and avoid exacerbating or sensationalizing the situation. NBC's guidelines, unlike CBS's, recognized that terrorist events were diverse and different, that third parties could be introduced into the incident, and that speed of coverage was essential as terrorist events unfolded with rapidity.

Following the 1985 hijacking of TWA 847, CBS news, the *Chicago Sun Times,* and UPI developed revised or new guidelines for dealing with terrorist incidents (Rosen, 1993). These guidelines said: (1) avoid providing an excessive platform for the terrorist; (2) do not sensationalize the story beyond it already being sensational; and (3) that no specific rule can exist for every terrorist incident and that reporters and news directors should use common sense and the circumstances and facts of the story in deciding how to report the story. Guideline (3), in essence, removes all guidelines.

In 1991, Gallimore examined the guidelines of almost all major news organizations in the United States and identified ten common guidelines. These were: one, do not rely on either the terrorists or responding agency as the sole source of information. Two, balance the volume of news between the terrorist incident and other news of importance. Three, provide a context and background to the terrorist event. Four, do not disclose counter-terrorist operations or plans. Five, avoid using inflammatory words or rumors. Six, do not disclose the identification of hostages if the disclosure would or could result in harm. Seven, do not provide a platform for the terrorists. Eight, involve the news' organizations top management in major decisions concerning coverage. Nine, do not participate in incidents nor become a negotiator in the incident. Ten, respect the privacy of victims and their families.

These are good guidelines for the media to follow, but there are other guidelines that should be included. The National News Council (in Miller, 1982) suggested: (1) do not give the names of terrorists and avoid providing additional credit and strength to the terrorist; (2) do not prevent the methodology employed in the operation; (3) limit coverage as much as possible; (4) show the incident as a despicable act committed by disenfranchised and losers; (5) report that no hostage incident has ever been successful; (6) make no direct calls to terrorists; (7) do not use continuing on-site coverage. It is recommended that item (5) not be used, as it is not true. Many terrorist hostage incidents have been successful. The National Advisory Committee on Criminal Justice Standards and Goals (1977) also added: (1) avoid creating any media presence at the scene than is necessary to provide full, accurate, and balanced reporting; (2) omit no important detail and place all details in context; and (3) follow the principle of minimal intrusiveness that could include the use of pool reporters, limitations on use of high-intensity lighting, obtrusive camera equipment and special equipment, limitations on interviews with any incident participant, use of official spokespersons for information, and avoid making inquiries into tactical operations. Other measures that could be taken to adhere to minimal intrusiveness might include: avoiding coverage of the spectacular qualities of the incident or that which would bring spectators to the scene; verifying information concerning injury, death, or property damage; balancing reports of participant statements with contrasting information from official sources; reporting on risks to non-involved persons; delaying disclosure of any tactical information; delaying reporting on location if location is not known and when not likely to become public until potential for growth of incident is no longer present; and delaying reporting of details that have the potential for inflammation or aggravation.

Bremer (1990) has suggested guidelines for the individual journalist covering a terrorist incident. Several of these cannot be written into an organizational policy and must be ethically adhered to by the newsperson. One, obey the Hippocratic Oath and first and foremost, do no harm. Two, keep your competitive instincts in control and do not let competition drive reporting of the incident. Three, assess the benefit or harm in releasing professional and personal history of victims. Four, weight all statements given based upon the stress and duress of the persons making those statements. Five, carefully consider all statements released by the terrorists and assess why they released those statements. Six, consider editing live coverage before broadcast by evaluating information before release. Seven, use the same criteria for assessing information sources as you would in a non-crisis situation. Eight, consider the harm that could be done by releasing any tactical information on resolving the incident. Nine, consider the family members of victims before releasing information on them. Families and victims are as guiltless as any other non-participant. Why harm them if not essential to reporting the story?

While these general guidelines make sense and provide a context for the reporting of a terrorist incident, either during or after the incident, no set of guidelines or statements of professional ethics will guide the news media in reporting a terrorist incident. Many have suggested that the news media should be censored when a terrorist incident occurs. Finn (1993), in fact, argues that civil liberties and the Constitution should, on occasion, be sacrificed for national security. Some countries, in fact, have laws that restrict press coverage of terrorist incidents. Belgium, Canada, Denmark, England, France, and the Netherlands have all enacted legislation restricting the news media. In Ireland, the 1960 Broadcasting Authority Act, Section 31, prohibits any broadcast containing IRA, Sean

Fein members, or any other organization member as proscribed under the Northern Ireland Emergency Provisions Act of 1973. Section 3 of the Canada War Measures Act, which covers terrorist activity, specifies that the governor in council can regulate censor, control, and suppression any written publication, map, plan, photograph, communication, or means of communication concerning terrorist activity.

Regulating by legislating the activities of the media beyond reasonable control is a dangerous precedent. Media censorship or undue regulation is in itself a form of state-sponsored terrorism and would rapidly lead to an erosion of many other constitutional guarantees. The 1976 Prevention of Terrorism Act, Sections 10 and 11 (Miller, 1993), comes close to censorship by prohibiting any person from giving aid resulting in contributing to terrorism and requiring any person with knowledge of the whereabouts of terrorists or potential terrorists to report that knowledge to rightful authorities. In numerous cases, the courts have ruled that the media has no more right to the scene of a crime than any other citizen (Miller, 1982). That is all the censorship the government needs to impose. Any greater degree of censorship and the constitution is in danger.

Schmid and De Graaf (1982) addressed the censorship issue and offered various pros and cons of censorship. Eleven pros included: (1) terrorists use the media for political purposes and to recruit new members; (2) terrorists conduct some operations for the media coverage; (3) the media provides a model to increase terrorist success rates; (4), the information released during an incident can be useful to the terrorists; (5), news reporting can endanger victims; (6) media coverage will produce copycat terrorists; (7) in a hostage or kidnap incident, news reports could endanger hostages; (8) terrorists use violence to gain public attention; (9) terrorist incidents lead to public sadism; (10) reporting of terrorist incidents could result in vigilantism and public revenge against terrorists or the terrorist organization; and (11) the negative news could demoralize the public.

Corresponding to the eleven arguments for censorship presented above, the arguments against censorship are: (1) Terrorist violence will be judged in a negative light by the public; (2) publicity can substitute for violence and media coverage reduces violence by allowing terrorists to use threats; (3) terrorists would increase their level of violence until the media was forced to use even more violence; (4) during an incident, if not reported, rumors about what was occurring would spread and the rumors would be worse than the facts; (5) law enforcement would be prevented from using tactical solutions and the public would be endangered; (6), government responses to terrorism would be uncontrolled if there was no reporting and the government could call any act terrorist; (7) censorship of terrorism could lead to other censorship (or the suspicion of censorship) and media credibility would suffer; (8) the public would develop a false sense of security by coming to believe no terrorism was occurring; (9) the public would not understand the political situation; (10) the public would come to distrust the government because of the lack of information; and (11) terrorist claims that democratic states are not democracies would gain credibility because of government-imposed censorship.

SUMMARY

The terrorist has many options to choose from when conducting an operation against a target. The operation may be indiscriminant or discriminant, may involve a single individual or multiple individuals, and may involve destruction or sabotage of a building, equipment, or network of some society support system. The wide range of target options open to the terrorist almost insure that law enforcement will be prevented from being able to prevent the activity. Knowing the motivation and goals of the terrorist organization, along with an understanding of their strategy and tactics, can increase the ability to predict, but not enough to completely prevent terrorist operations.

Further, terrorists depend upon the misperceptions of the government, law enforcement, and public concerning terrorist operations. If perceived as a lunatic, the terrorist increases the probability of conducting a successful operation. This perception prevents the authorities from understanding the full scope of terrorist planning and leads to an attitude on the part of the authorities that terrorists are not strategists or tacticians. Time and again, terrorists have proven this mislabeling to be costly. Even with the evidence of successful terrorist operations and the rising toll of dead, this attitude persists. Until the terrorist is recognized as a trained and capable master operational planner, the public will suffer, law enforcement will be unable to prevent terrorism, and society will increasingly become embittered with the government.

Drugs and technological terrorism have presented new terrorist threats to the public in the 1990s. Drugs are seen as another avenue for changing political systems and achieving political goals. Many terrorist organizations, both international and domestic, realize enormous profits from the drug business. These profits fuel their organization, provide funds for weapons and equipment, and finance operations. Some terrorist organizations use drugs to advance their political agenda. The far right sees drugs as helping prompt and speed the coming race wars that will return America to a white power state.

Technological terrorism refers to the weapons of terrorism and the targets for terrorists. Weapons are covered separately in other chapters. Technological targets permit the terrorist to reach a much larger population with less effort. Air, rail, and vehicle transport networks, utility grids, communication networks, and power plants and nuclear facilities are all especially vulnerable to terrorist operations. Water supply reservoirs, fuel pipelines and repositories, and storage facilities are virtually unguarded and open invitations to terrorists. Terrorist operations could wreck havoc with computer systems and networks. Financial data bases, citizen records, and military computer systems are available for tampering, theft, and destruction to the person familiar with computer systems. Many of these systems could be compromised and cause massive damage long before anyone would be aware of the compromise.

Technological terrorism will become one of the preferred forms of terrorism in the future because of the numbers of people that can be harmed and the relative ease with which these targets can be attacked. Most technological systems are open, unguarded, and not secured. The terrorist has a virtual guarantee of being able to destroy that target without being detected or captured. The terrorist can operate in an isolated area to damage a system at his own pace and vanish long before any response unit could get to the location.

In many instances unwittingly, the media becomes part of the terrorist operation and provides the stage for the context and dissemination of terrorist philosophy. The media does influence terrorism, usually negatively, and leads to increases in terrorist activity and the severity of terrorist activity. As the media moves evermore toward tabloid journalism, the terrorists will increase their reliance on the media as part of their operational strategy. Every terrorist act leads to a public outcry of anger against terrorists. While people call for increased action against terrorists; few outpour the same emotions for media responsibility. The media-terrorist link is the ideal symbiotic relationship for the terrorist. The terrorist actively uses the media for his own purposes; the media unwittingly uses the terrorist.

The balance between the freedom of the press and responsibility of the press is an extremely fine line. Straying either direction from this line has severe consequences for a free society. Governmental controls on the press removes freedoms guaranteed by the Constitution. Requesting that the media self-regulate their activities and reporting would be like asking a pig to fly. With the first is the danger of it occurring; with the second the shame that it does not occur.

Chapter 7

TERRORIST WEAPONS

Terrorists use a wide variety of weapons. Terrorists have used their hands, knives, bows and arrows, pistols, shotguns, rifles, automatic weapons, hand-held rocket launchers, conventional and homemade explosives, and chemical and biological weapons. In the twentieth century the most popular weapons have been firearms and explosives. These two types of weapons have the advantages of producing the maximum damage with minimal risk to the terrorist. In a hostage situation, a pistol will produce enough fear to keep hostages obeying orders. A knife may not produce fear, and hostages may feel they could overpower the terrorist. If the terrorist used explosives, the hostages may not take threats seriously because they would not believe the terrorist would kill himself by detonating the explosives. In large part, the type of operation chosen dictates the weapon the terrorist will use.

Firearms and explosives have been weapons of choice because they produce fear. They are easy to obtain or make, relatively simple and straightforward to operate and require no special expertise, and are easy to conceal and travel with. This chapter will discuss the conventional weapons of terrorism: firearms and explosives.

FIREARMS

The terrorist can choose from several types of firearms: pistol versus rifle, shotgun versus grenade launcher, semiautomatic versus automatic, small versus large caliber, etc. In making this selection, there are several criteria the terrorist needs to consider (Dobson & Payne, 1982). The first criteria is firepower. The weapon should appear intimidating to the terrorist's victim. A .22 caliber firearm is actually more deadly than a .38 caliber or 9 mm caliber weapon, as the small projectile of a .22 tends to "bounce" around inside a victim, while the larger calibers travel through the victim. The perception of the victim, however, is that the larger caliber weapon will do more damage because it looks bigger. Victims tend to equate size with killing ability. Shotguns are much more intimidating than most rifles because shotguns have a large bore (size of the

287

barrel opening), although if used at distances much farther than 10–15 feet the shotgun has a low kill probability.

The rate of fire of the weapon is an important consideration for the terrorist, especially if the weapon is an automatic. Militaries and the police have unlimited stocks of ammunition. The terrorist, on the other hand, has limited supplies of ammunition. If the weapon's rate of fire (number of rounds per time unit, usually per minute) is too great, ammunition may be totally expended before the operation is complete. One example of this from the U.S. military experience in Vietnam is the M-16 rifle. The M-16 rifle had an extremely high rate of fire and servicemen were running out of ammunition before the enemy was killed. To solve the problem, makers of the M-16 put a burst suppresser on the weapon, which limited the rate of fire to three rounds of ammunition expended per trigger pull.

Three, the terrorist wants a weapon with stopping power. Stopping power refers to the ability of a weapon to stop a person instantly. Unlike the movies, where people who are shot "fly" through the air, weapon projectiles and humans obey the basic rule of the physical world that dictates that for every action, there is an equal and opposite reaction. Bullets are small and lightweight and travel at high velocities. The smaller the bullet and the faster it travels, the smaller the reaction when it hits a person. Many persons hit by a bullet, even fatally, will continue with whatever action they were engaged in for a short period of time. In the 1980s, the FBI engaged in a shootout with two bank robbers in Miami, Florida. One of the bank robbers was struck with a fatal round in the first few seconds of the shootout. He continued on for approximately four more minutes, even managing to walk over 10 yards and kill two FBI agents. The terrorist prefers a large, slow-moving projectile, such as a .45 caliber, as these have greater stopping power than smaller calibers, including many rifles.

Four, the terrorist wants a weapon that is concealable. Weapons should be small enough to be able to be carried under a coat, in a purse, in a briefcase or package, or under the seat of an automobile. Not many terrorists use an M-60 heavy machine gun because of its large size. Pistols, shotguns with the barrels sawed off, and short barrel/short stock rifles are preferred. Many manufacturers produce rifles and automatic weapons that have folding stocks, short barrel lengths, and compact magazines that can fit under a short coat or in a briefcase.

Five, terrorists prefer weapons that are easy to obtain. Weapons that are unusual, rare, or not readily available on the open market are not preferred by terrorists. One of the favorite automatic weapons in the terrorist arsenal is the AK-47 or its various variants. Millions of these weapons have been made by the Soviet Union and China and are in the hands of militaries and terrorist organizations all over the world. Additionally, ammunition for the weapon should be readily available. European terrorists prefer 9 mm firearms because most police and military in Europe carry those calibers and ammunition is plentiful.

Finally, the sixth criteria in a terrorist weapon is simplicity. Terrorists prefer weapons that are easy to operate, disassemble, and repair. In many instances, terrorists do not get extensive training in using a weapon. They do not have the resources or ammunition to spend countless hours on a firing range practicing with a weapon. Unlike the police, military, and other gun owners, the terrorist cannot take their weapon to a gunsmith to be repaired. Neither do they have the luxury of swapping guns during an operation, nor stopping to unjam or repair a firearm. If a weapon needs repair, they must be able to repair it. Many of the Chinese-made AK-47s are constructed of stamped metal parts. With many parts on the weapon that may wear or break, a soda can, pocket knife, and hammer are the only tools needed to make a replacement part.

There are various sources terrorists can use to obtain weapons (Gander, 1990). One, they can purchase weapons from black market arms dealers. There is a vast worldwide network of arms dealers who sell to the underground market. These weapons have been originally obtained from a variety of sources, including thefts and secondhand sales. When a piece of military hardware becomes obsolete, rather than destroying the weapon, the country may auction it off. Black market arms dealers buy these weapons and then resell them to the highest bidder. Any weapon from a small revolver to exotic military hardware such as tanks and airplanes can be purchased from these dealers. The weapons, however, tend to be expensive. To obtain weapons in this manner, terrorists will often turn to other criminal activity, such as bank robbery, kidnapping, or dealing drugs to raise the needed money.

Second, terrorists can steal the weapons. Weapons dealers, gun shops, police storehouses, and military armories are all sources of weapons for the terrorist. Most repositories where guns are stored, including many military armories, are secured to the extent that the armory can be protected from criminal behavior. They are not target-hardened enough to prevent the trained terrorist from breaking in. As Gander (1990) said, "If you have a knife, you can obtain a sword. If you have a sword, you can obtain a rifle. . . . "

Sympathetic nations can provide the terrorist with weapons. Nations like Libya, Syria, Iraq, Russia, North Korea, Cuba, and China have a long history of providing weapons to terrorist organizations. Sympathetic nations usually provide any weapon the terrorist requests. Many terrorists who use heavy weapons such as portable rockets and anti-aircraft missiles obtain them from nations.

Fourth, the terrorist can make their own weapons. Small-caliber fire-arms can be produced with some pipe and a nail ("zip gun"). Shotguns can be similarly made. Heavier weapons such as rocket-propelled gre-nade launchers, including the projectile, can be produced with material purchased from a hardware and plumbing supply house.

Pistols and Submachine Guns

Pistols, although sometimes used, have limited utility to the terrorist. Pistols meet most of the criteria of terrorist weapons, but their drawbacks outweigh their advantages. They have a short lethality range, are unsafe, and have limited usages. The effective range of pistols is only around 15–20 meters, and even at that range, most users cannot consistently hit a target. The pistol is used primarily as a weapon of assassination, in hostage situations, and in conducting criminal activities. For large-scale operations, the pistol is more of a liability than an asset. Displaying a pistol will usually not produce enough fear to assure compliance. British SAS instructors, in teaching how to use the Smith and Wesson revolver, stress one point that applies to all pistols: the best way to bring down an opponent with a pistol is to throw it at them.

Popular fiction (film, television, and novels) has glamorized the terror-ist using the "silenced" pistol as a tool of terrorism. Primarily, this is myth. First, silencers do not silence. The correct name for silencers are sound moderators or suppressers. They do not "silence" the pistol, they only reduce the volume of noise. With a silencer, the sound of a fired pistol will be about the same as a loud hand clap. Second, sound modera-tors significantly reduce the lethal range and accuracy of a pistol. Third, sound moderators are only good for 2–4 shots before they lose their effectiveness. Fourth, there are only certain types of pistols that sound moderators can be used on. They cannot be used on revolvers, and on many semiautomatic pistols, they will disperse gas blow-back so much that the receiver mechanism will not work and fail to eject the spent shell and chamber the next shell. Fifth (and a problem no sound moderator can overcome) is that the majority of noise from a fired shell comes from the projectile breaking the sound barrier. Sound suppressers do not slow the speed of the projectile. To be truly quiet, a pistol would have to employ sub-sound barrier ammunition, and that ammunition can only be used in .22 caliber pistols, which is not used by anybody on a regular basis except target shooters.

A few pistols that have been employed by terrorists include the Soviet

TT-33 or Tokarev, produced from 1933–1954 by the Soviet Union. This pistol fires a 7.62 × 25 cartridge and is still manufactured in China as the Type 54 and in Yugoslavia as the Model M57. The Tokarev was the most widely produced pistol in the world, and the Soviets freely gave them to third-world nations and terrorist forces. Another pistol widely used by terrorists is the M-52. Made in Czechoslovakia, the M-52 has one of the highest muzzle velocities of any pistol on the market, approximately twice that of the U.S. Army Colt .45. The M-52 was used to kill Michel Moukharbel, the friend that betrayed Carlos. The projectile passed through Michel, the floorboards, the ceiling of the apartment below, a molded plastic table, and then buried itself so deeply into the floorboards it could not be extracted. The American Colt .45 M 1911 has been used by terrorists worldwide. A heavy pistol, the Colt .45 delivers super stopping power.

The submachine gun is actually an oversized pistol-style of weapon that fires a pistol cartridge on full automatic. Introduced shortly after World War I, the submachine gun did not become popular until the introduction of the British Sten in World War II. Several million Stens were produced during WWII and were widely distributed to Allied troops and guerrilla forces. After the war, many of these weapons found their way into terrorist hands, where some still are today. Another submachine gun used by terrorists is the Israeli Uzi and Ingram Model 10 (Mac-10). Both are small, can fire either a .45 or 9 mm shell, and take little or no training to use. Except for their high rate of fire, both meet the weapon's criteria of the terrorist. The Skorpion VZ-62 was the standard submachine gun of Czechoslovakian security forces. It fires either a .32 ACP or 9 mm cartridge, with a fire rate of 700 rounds/minute. With the butt folded, it will fit into a holster and not take up more space than a large pistol. An earlier version of the VZ-62, the VZ-61, was the weapon used to kill Aldo Moro in Italy.

Shotguns

Shotguns have been used throughout the century by terrorists all over the world. Shotguns are numerous and easy to obtain, ammunition is plentiful and, at close ranges, they are extremely lethal. Shotguns are sized by gauges and, unlike pistols and rifles, come in limited, universal sizes: 12-gauge (approximately 20 mm in diameter), 16-gauge, 20-gauge, and 410-gauge, with the 12-gauge being the most popular. The 12-gauge is extremely popular, plus, regardless of geographical location, 12-gauge ammunition is easy to obtain.

Many shotguns used by terrorists are modified. The barrels are shortened (i.e., the sawed-off shotgun) and the stock is shortened and reconfigured. These modifications serve two purposes. One, it makes the shotgun easier to conceal (some can be carried in a shoulder holster under a jacket) and two, it increases the lethality of the weapon. Shortening the barrel increased the fan of the cone and hence the killing radius. That is, as the shot exits the barrel, it has wider lateral dispersion than in a full-barrel gun. The disadvantage is that the lethality range is reduced. Shotguns have the disadvantage to begin with of being a "close-in" weapon. With shot (numerous small pellets per cartridge), the effective range of the shotgun is under approximately 15 feet. With slugs (one large pellet per cartridge), the effective range is only marginally higher, at about 20–25 feet. With the barrel shortened, the effective range can be reduced to one-half of that.

Shotguns require very little training, experience, or aiming. One simply points and pulls the trigger. Maintenance is low, as they have very few moving parts. Also, the projectiles can penetrate wood, steel, or other hard surfaces, can be used to shatter some locks, and otherwise used to penetrate locked areas. Finally, shotguns can be produced in a home workshop. A length of pipe and some type of striker mechanism are all necessary to produce a homemade shotgun.

Recent advances in technology have made the shotgun more suitable to the terrorist. In the past, shotguns were available as barrel-loaders or pump. With the barrel-loader, one opened the weapon at the rear of the barrel, loaded it, fired, opened the weapon, loaded, fired, etc. With the pump shotgun, several shells were inserted into the breech, and a mechanical pump mechanism fed shells into the firing position. The operator fired a shell, pumped the mechanism, and the spent shell was ejected and a new shell slipped into place for the next shot. Semiautomatic and automatic shotguns are now on the market. The Italian Franchi SPAS 15 holds six rounds and can be used as a semiautomatic or pump shotgun. The Italian Franchi SPAS 12 is an automatic shotgun that can fire armor-piercing projectiles or grenades from a muzzle launcher (Gander, 1990).

Rifles

Rifles, unlike shotguns, come in an infinite variety of sizes, shapes, calibers, and styles. Rifles can be single-shot, semiautomatic, or automatic. They can be breech-operated, bolt-operated, or magazine-fed. Calibers can range from .22 to .50 (calibers are the diameter of the shell, either in hundreths of an inch or millimeters). Length can vary from about one foot to five feet. The effective killing range can be as great as 500–600 yards, and some specially made rifles can be effective at 1,500–2,000 yards.

Rifles can be equipped with specialized equipment such as sound suppressors to reduce the noise, telescopic sights for aiming accuracy at long distances, laser-guided sights, tripods to steady the weapon, and larger magazines. They can be equipped with interchangeable barrels, folding stocks, and other special hardware to adapt them to special circumstances.

Although any rifle is apt to be found in the hands of terrorists, the two most popular are the Kalishnikov AK-47 and the Armalites, general category of the U.S. M-16A1. The AK-47 is the most widely produced weapon in the world, with well over 12 million having been produced by the Soviets, Chinese, and other manufacturers (Gander, 1990). Hogg (1978) estimates that over 35 million have been produced since the weapon's introduction in 1953. Following World War II, Germany researched the development of a weapon that would be effective at around 400 meters and used low-power ammunition (better stopping power). Using this data, they designed the Sturmgewehr 43, which fired a 7.92 mm kurz patrone round.

Using the German research data, the Soviets designed the AK-47 which fired a 7.62 × 39 mm round. The designer of the weapon was Mikhail Timofeyevich Kalashnikov. The AK-47 assault rifle is low-powered and can fire single shot or fully automatic, with a maximum effective range of around 400 meters. The AK-47 is a very stable weapon that is typically used on single shot at long distances and full automatic in close combat situations. The AK-47 is gas-operated. When a round is fired, the gas blow-back activates an internal piston which ejects the spent shell, feeds the next shell, and sets the cocking mechanism. Ammunition is fed to the weapon from a 30-round magazine inserted into the bottom of the receiver.

The basic AK-47 weights 4.3 kg, is 869 mm in length with a barrel length of 414 mm, holds a 30-round magazine, can fire 600 rounds per minute on automatic, and has a muzzle velocity of 710 meters/second.

Early AK-47s used machined parts, making the weapon extremely durable. The stock was constructed from a single piece of wood, along with the pistol grip on the weapon. Some AK-47s were produced with a metal folding stock for use by airborne troops. In the late 1950s, due to production costs, the machined parts were replaced by stamped and riveted parts. These later models are known as AKMs. By the late 1980s, the Soviets were producing an improved version of the weapon called the AK-74, which fires a smaller 5.45 × 39 mm cartridge. A variant is the AKS-74, which has a folding-butt stock.

Because of Soviet economic pressure, almost all Eastern bloc and Asian socialist nations used the AK-47. Most of these countries produced their own version of the AK-47. Romania produced an AKM, East Germany produced the MPiKM, Yugoslavia the M70, Hungary the AMD-65, and the Chinese the Type 56 and Type 56-I. Even non-communist nations have produced weapons similar to the AK-47, such as Israel (Galil), Finland (Valmet M60), and South Africa (R-4).

Later AKMs have a muzzle compensator, which reduces muzzle jump when fired, and a folding bayonet and scabbard, which can also be used as wire cutters. A cleaning kit can be carried under the butt plate. Ammunition is easy to obtain and even Western nations produce 7.62×39 mm ammunition for the weapon. The most common types of ammunition for the AK-47 are ball, tracer, incendiary, and armor-piercing.

Armalite refers to a series of weapons that have been mass produced and have found their way into the terrorist arsenal. Primary Armalite weapons include the AR-10, AR-15, AR-16, and AR-18. Armalite first produced the AR-10 in the 1960s for military use. The military had just replaced their M1 Garands with M-14s and were not interested in mass purchasing another new weapon. The AR-10 was a revolution in military weaponry. It fired the standardized 7.62×51 mm NATO round, employed an all-in-line layout with the barrel in line with the butt, sights raised over the barrel and built into a carrying handle, had a muzzle brake and flash suppresser, used a 20-round straight box magazine, and had a rotary bolt-into-barrel lock with locking lugs and a two-part bolt (Gander, 1990). The weapon was gas-operated and used light-alloy metals. Since the U.S. military did not purchase the AR-10, Armalite sold them to third-world countries such as Sudan and Guatemala.

In the late 1950s, the U.S. military wanted to adopt a light automatic weapon for the military and Armalite developed the AR-15 to meet these needs. The AR-15 was virtually a smaller-sized AR-10. It used light-alloy castings and nylon-plastics for the butt, fore stock, and pistol grip. The cocking piece was moved from the side to the back, and it fired the new 5.56×45 mm high-velocity cartridge (1,000 meters/second). Military interest in the AR-15 increased in the early 1960s as the U.S. got involved in Vietnam and the M-16A1, a variant of the AR-15, began being produced.

The M-16A1 fired the 5.56×45 mm cartridge, weighted 3.18 kg, was 990 mm in total length with a barrel length of 508 mm, could use either a 20- or 30-round magazine, had a muzzle velocity of 1,000 meters/second, and could fire between 750–900 rounds per minute. Production switched to Colt Patent Firearms Manufacturing Company and it became the standard-issue weapon for the U.S. military. In addition to Colt, M-16A1s were produced in Singapore, South Korea, and the Philippines. Taiwan produced the Type 65 and the Chinese produced the Type 311, or Type CQ copies.

During American involvement in Vietnam millions of M-16s were distributed to different nations. Throughout Southeast Asia, Africa, Latin America, and Europe, nations were given M-16s merely for the asking. It has, of course, found its way into the terrorist world. For the terrorist, the weapon satisfies all criteria except rate of fire, and even there, the newer M-16s with the burst suppressor overcome that handicap.

Following Vietnam and into the 1980s, ArmaLite developed the AR-18. Similar to the AR-15, the AR-18 is smaller, lighter, uses metal stampings, and is cheaper to manufacture and purchase. It fires the standard NATO 5.56 round, is slightly smaller than the M-16, weights 3.17 kg, has magazines that hold 20, 30 or 40 rounds, has a muzzle velocity of 1,000 meters/second, and will fire 850 rounds per minute on automatic.

The AR-15, M-16, and AR-18 have been used by terrorists worldwide. The AR-18 is one of the preferred weapons of the IRA. Over 8 million M-16s have been produced by Colt and they are readily available. As reported by Gander (1990), the IRA has adopted the slogan, "Politics of the ballot box and the Armalite." In the Philippines, the New People's Army uses the M-16. Tamil in Sri-Lanka, and terrorists in Lebanon, throughout Central and South America, Africa, and Europe have used the Armalite series of weapons.

Other rifles that have found their usage in the world of terrorism will be briefly mentioned. The American Springfield M1903 series rifles are used by many organizations in the Far East, along with thousands of M-14s left over from Vietnam. M-14s have also been used by African and Latin American terrorists. The Lee-Enfield series of rifles, used in World War I, was produced in England and Australia until the end of the 1950s and many are still available. Many have been rebored to fire the 7.62 × 51 NATO round. Many Mideastern and South American terrorists use the World War II German Mausers, rebored for the NATO cartridge. Many German Mausers (Model 98k) were used by Israel in the late 1940s and 1950s in gaining their independence from England and are now used by various Mideast terrorists. Many Central and South African terrorists use the Soviet Mosin Nagant Model 1944 and SKS, World War II-era rifles the Soviets freely distributed to "freedom fighters" around the world. The Belgian 7.62 mm FAL (Fusil Automatique Legere) was produced by the hundreds of thousands in the 1950s, 1960s, and 1970s, and some countries still produce it. Terrorists worldwide have been found in possession of the FAL. The Heckler & Koch G-3 (West Germany) is produced by seven countries, including Iran, and has been used by the

IRA and Kurds in Iraq. Many of the terrorists at the American embassy situation in 1979 used the Heckler & Koch G-3.

Machine Guns

With a few exceptions, not many terrorists employ machine guns. Some terrorists in the U.S. have been discovered with machine guns, the IRA has used machine guns in rural areas, and terrorists in Central and South America have used machine guns. Machine guns are heavy, the lightest weighing approximately 9 kg, most require a tripod, they are large and not concealable, they waste a lot of ammunition, take practice to be used effectively, and require considerable maintenance.

Machine guns are classified as either light machine guns (LMG) or general-purpose machine guns (GPMG). Most employ an air-cooled barrel and are belt- or magazine-fed. Heavy machine guns require the use of a heavy tripod, while light machine guns are usually equipped with a bipod. Both were designed for squad and company level military actions and are not suited to use by small, mobile bands of terrorists. Some, however, have been used by terrorists. One such weapon is the LMG Soviet RPK, an upsized AK-47. It has a larger barrel, bipod, and larger magazine. It can hold a box magazine of 40 rounds or a 75-round drum magazine. One deficiency of this weapon is that the barrel will overheat and warp during sustained bursts of fire. Similar models are the Yugoslavian-produced M-72BA and M-72AB1. Another machine gun used by terrorists is the Soviet PK, a newer and heavier version of the RPK that uses a belt feed and fires at a cyclic rate of 720 rounds/minute. A third popular terrorist machine gun is the American M-60. The M-60 is a belt-fed GPMG and too heavy to use as a LMG (Rambo movies notwithstanding). Thousands were used in Vietnam and from there have made their way into the terrorist arsenal. Many were stolen from U.S. arsenals in the 1970s and 1980s. The M-60 has been popular with the IRA and right-wing terrorists in the U.S.

In the Mideast, Europe, Africa, and Latin America, the Czechoslovakian ZB-26 has been popular among terrorists. An LMG, the ZB-26 began production in the mid-1920s and is still produced in some Asian countries today. It fires a 7.92×57 mm cartridge with a cyclic fire rate of 500 rounds/minute. The ZB-26 was the weapon of choice for the Chinese Koumintang, and once they were overthrown, the ZB-26 began making its way into the terrorist arsenal.

Heavy Weapons

One thing that has helped terrorists conduct operations on a large scale has been the introduction of heavy weapons into the terrorist arsenal. Even as recent as nine or ten years ago, it was unheard of for terrorists to use unguided or guided missiles. Today, however, it is rare that the well-armored terrorist organization does not have at least one or two of these heavy weapons in their stockpile. The British SAS, for example, regularly practices anti-missile attacks at London's Heathrow Airport so great is the proliferation of these weapons among terrorists.

Unguided rockets are the oldest form of missile, appearing during WWII with the Soviet Katyuscha, a multiple rail system carried on a truck. Most modern unguided rockets are 122 and 140 mm. The 140 mm rocket weighs approximately 40 kg, carries a 15–20 kg warhead, and has a range up to 9,800 meters. Although heavy, they can be carried to the launch site by one person. The PLO made extensive use of unguided rockets against Israeli border towns throughout the 1970s and 1980s. The Afghan Mujahadeen obtained Chinese 107 mm Type 63 12-tube rockets (along with the PLO) for use against the Russians during their war.

The most popular unguided rockets have included the Soviet RPG-2, RPG-7, and American M-72. These are smaller with a lighter warhead and fired by one person using a shoulder launch position. Most will fit into the trunk of a vehicle and many can be homemade. The RPG-7 uses an 85 mm shell, a 2.25 kg rocket, and, overall, weighs only 10.15 kg. The effective range of this weapon is approximately 500 meters. Newer versions are even more compact, having a barrel that breaks into two parts. Similar models are produced in China and Yugoslavia.

The American M-72 uses a 66 mm projectile, weights 2.37 kg and has an effective range of 300 meters. It is often referred to as a LAWs, or light-anti-tank weapon, although the projectile is too small to penetrate heavy steel. The M-72 employs a collapsible tube and a flip-up sight. It is designed as a single-use weapon, meaning it is fired and discarded. Many terrorists in the U.S. have been found with M-72s in their possession.

Guided missiles used by terrorists have included the Soviet SA-7 (surface-to-air), American Stinger, British Blowpipe, and the heavier projectile Strela or Grail missiles. Most of these weapons are small and will easily fit into the back seat of a vehicle, can be operated by one person, and have ranges from 4,000–10,000 meters. Most employ an infrared seeker that locks onto a heat source, such as jet engine exhaust. The major disadvantage of these weapons are that they require a considerable amount of training to properly use. The operator has to insure the missile is "locked on" to the target before firing, and this usually involves a complex sequence of switching on a thermal battery, warming up the electronics, tracking the target until the missile locks the target, and, after firing, remaining still until the missile ignites and exits the tube. The entire sequence can take several minutes.

Even when everything is done correctly, the odds of hitting a target are low. The missiles can be thrown off course by wind shifts, release of flares, or even the heat of the sun. Most guided missiles have to be fired at the rear exhaust of an aircraft, and the aircraft in forward motion relative to the missile can allow the plane to pass out of fuel range of the missile. These weapons have proven themselves to be most effective against helicopters, not airplanes. Irregardless, terrorists from the Mideast, North Korea, Peru, Iraq, Cuba, Cyprus, Iran, Syria, Uganda, Asia, Africa, and Latin America have employed guided missiles in terrorist acts. The PLO has attacked El-Al airplanes with RPG-7s and SA-7 missiles (Poland, 1988). The PLO, in addition to guided missiles, has also been discovered to be in possession of even heavier weaponry, such as Russian B-21 rocket launchers and T-34 and T-54 Russian tanks (Arens, 1986).

EXPLOSIVE DEVICES

Explosive devices are by far the most favorite weapon in the terrorist arsenal. Explosives are so popular among terrorists that nothing else comes in second place. Between 1970–1984, there were 10,107 terrorist bombings in the world that accounted for 3,407 deaths, 15,111 injuries, and $473 million in property damage (Risks International, 1985). Between 1977–1983, 63.5 percent of all terrorist activity involved explosive devices (U.S. Department of State, 1983). In 1984, over half of all terrorist incidents, both within the United States and on the international front, involved explosives (U.S. Department of State, 1985). According to U.S. Department of Transportation (1985) figures, between 1949–1984, 80 aircraft were damaged by explosives, 17 were destroyed, and 1,184 people were killed. Internationally, 38 countries and 43 different airlines were affected by terrorist airplane bombings, and in the United States, 15 aircraft were downed and 126 lives were lost.

Every year, a greater percentage of terrorist atrocities are committed with explosives than the year prior. In the United States, in 1989, there were over 2,000 explosive incidents. In 1990, the number had risen to 3,541, a 20% increase (Popkin, 1993). During that same year, 185 pounds of C-4 were recovered by law enforcement, 623 detonators were recovered, and 143 hand grenades confiscated, which were being sold on the street for $150 each. Between 1985 and 1989, over three-fourths of all explosive incidents in the U.S. were caused by pipe bombs or other homemade devices. During the same time period, over 90,000 pounds of explosives were stolen from construction sites, quarries, and explosive manufacturers. Included in the figures was over 80,000 pounds of dynamite. Between January 1989 and June 1990, military bomb squads assisted law enforcement agencies respond to over 1,127 explosive incidents. Recovered in those incidents were 85 rockets, 400 grenades, 200 pounds of military C-4, 45 tons of TNT, and over one dozen military land mines. During the same period, firearm seizures by law enforcement more than doubled (Gugliotta & Isikoff, 1993).

In June 1991, Sergeant Michael Tubbs was arrested and sentenced to eight years in a federal penitentiary for stealing over 90 pounds of military C-4, military TNT, claymore anti-personnel mines, hand grenades, and anti-aircraft and anti-tank machine guns from Fort Bragg, North Carolina, and Fort Campbell, Kentucky. An ATF agent said, "There were enough explosives to blow up the Gator Bowl." Sergeant Tubbs was linked to a white supremacist organization that had utilized Tubbs to "dedicate (their) blood to this great nation and the white race."

There are several reasons terrorists like explosives. One, they are easy to obtain or produce. In many states, a person can buy explosives simply by showing a driver's license. Explosives, as indicated above, are relatively simple to steal. The terrorist could make homemade explosives. There are thousands of chemicals that can be purchased at a grocery store, pharmacy, or chemical supply company that can be used to produce explosive devices. Two, explosives are a low-cost alternative for the terrorist. Even when purchased legitimately, explosives are not very expensive. Three, one person can make and place the explosives. Thus, the organization is somewhat protected should the person placing them get caught. Four, explosions attract media attention. Five, a great deal of public fear can be produced through one explosion.

Explosives for the terrorist are a low technology, low expense, and low training operational technique. The production and use of explosives requires little technical knowledge. For the novice, several books and pamphlets completely describe the making of homemade explosives. *The Anarchist's Cookbook* (Powell, 1971), *The Poor Man's James Bond* (Saxton, 1986), *150 Questions for a Guerrilla* (Bayo, 1975), *Explosives and Homemade Bombs* (Stoffel, 1972), and a variety of military manuals, such as *Boobytraps* (Department of the Army, FM 5-31, 1965), *Unconventional Warfare Devices and Techniques: Incendiaries* (TM 31-201-1, 1966) and *Improvised Munitions Handbook* (TM 31-210, 1969), are books available at many bookstores and military supply stores. These books show the step-by-step construction of simple, yet lethal, homemade explosive devices. Before running out to purchase one or more, a word of warning is in order. Several of the formulas in these books are not entirely correct and could lead to the user's death. Even the formulas that are correct are highly unstable and could detonate just sitting in a room. One of the above authors, for example, blew both his hands off making one of the formulas in his book. The terrorist can now learn bomb-making over the Internet. There are at least two home pages which list the formulas and instructions for constructing homemade explosive devices. Table 7.1 lists some of the more common substances used in the construction of homemade explosives.

Table 7.1.
Common substances used to construct homemade explosives.

Substance	Generic Name	Purchase Site
Acetic Acid	Vinegar	Grocery Store
Ammonium Hydroxide	Ammonia	Grocery Store
Ammonium Nitrate	Fertilizer	Garden Store
Calcium Sulphate	Plaster of Paris	Hobby Store
Carbon Carbonate	Chalk	Drug Store
Carbon Tetrachloride	Cleaning Fluid	Hardware Store
Ferric Oxide	Rust	Paint Store
Graphite	Pencil Lead	Numerous Sources
Glycerin	Candle Wax	Numerous Sources
Hydrogen Peroxide	Peroxide	Drug Store
Magnesium Silicate	Talc	Grocery Store
Magnesium Sulfate	Epson Salts	Grocery Store
Naphthalene	Moth Balls	Grocery Store
Potassium Chlorate	—	Drug Store
Powdered Aluminum	—	Automotive Store
Potassium Nitrate	Fertilizer	Garden Store
Sodium Bicarbonate	Baking Soda	Grocery Store
Sodium Chloride	Salt	Grocery Store
Sodium Hydroxide	Lye	Grocery Store
Sodium Nitrate	Fertilizer	Garden Store
Sucrose	Cane Sugar	Grocery Store
Sulfuric Acid	Battery Acid	Homemade

In the fourth century, the Chinese, Romans, Hindus, Greeks, Arabs, Germans and English were all using black powder, the earliest explosive. This powder was used to create hot fires and for fireworks. It was several centuries later before black powder came to be used as a projectile. In fact, the Englishman Roger Bacon is often credited with inventing black powder in the thirteenth century. It was not, however, until the fourteenth century that a German inventor, Berthold Schwarz, used black powder as a propellant in firearms. In Europe, black powder was called Schwarzpulver, after its inventor (Poland, 1988). In the seventeenth century, the English figures out how to use black powder as an explosive. In the first recorded terrorist bombing operation in history, the Fenians bombed Clerkenwell Prison, killing 12 people and injuring 120 (Laqueur, 1977).

At the University of Turin, Italy, in 1847, nitroglycerine was invented (Van Gelder & Schlatter, 1973). In a liquid form, nitroglycerine was not of much use to anyone because it was so unstable. Temperature changes in the atmosphere were enough to detonate a vial of nitroglycerine. In 1867, Alfred Nobel mixed nitroglycerine with an absorbent material and produced the first dynamite, which immediately became popular with the military and terrorists.

Prior to World War I, dynamite remained an unstable weapon. It often "sweated," where the nitroglycerine leached out of the absorbent material. This leaching made dynamite almost as unstable as liquid nitroglycerine. Military uses dictated improvements in dynamite, and much more stable compounds were eventually produced. During WWI, TNT (trinitrotoluene) was invented. TNT was much more powerful and more stable than dynamite. TNT had greater shattering effects, was insensitive to impact, heat, temperature gradients, and shock. After WWI, research into explosive devices increased, and shortly before WWII, C-4 (Composition 4) was invented. C-4 has a consistency much like children's clay and can be shaped and formed for specific uses. C-4 is a much stronger explosive than TNT. Another more powerful explosive was developed about the same time, PETN (pentaerythritol-tetranitrate). Looking like a dirty cotton rope, PETN is also referred to as detcord, primex, and primacord. After WWII, hundreds of powerful explosives were developed and employed by the military. Today, the terrorist has a virtual cookbook of explosives to select from.

High Explosives

High explosives are characterized by a fast rate of detonation, require no confinement container, and are the explosives preferred by terrorists. No confinement refers to the fact that the explosive does not have to be within a secondary container such as a bottle or pipe for the explosive effects to be produced. When detonated, the high explosive changes in milliseconds from a solid or liquid to a gas. The change in physical state produces a shock wave much like a sonic boom, except thousands of times faster and stronger. The gas requires more physical volume than the solid or liquid and this increased pressure causes the destructive forces produced by the high explosive. This is called "shattering shock" and is like a hammer blow.

High explosives can produce air pressures of 700 tons per square inch, and the pressure wave can travel at speeds up to 7,000 miles per hour (Poland, 1988). The pressure wave of the explosive is divided into two parts. First is the positive pressure wave. When the explosive detonates, the first effects are caused by the shattering shock expanding radially from the point of detonation. The positive pressure wave then pushes the structure, adding to the damage. As the pressure wave expands, behind it is a negative pressure area, much like a vacuum. Air rushes the reverse direction into this negative pressure area, pulling at the structure. The rising mushroom cloud in a nuclear detonation is an example of air rushing to fill the vacuum. The positive pressure wave lasts only a fraction of a second; the negative pressure phase lasts three to five times longer. Figure 7.1 illustrates the effects of high explosives.

Secondary effects are produced by a thermal effect. As the explosive changes from a solid or liquid to a gas, incredible amounts of heat are generated by this change, sometimes as hot as 10,000–15,000 degrees Fahrenheit. This is the associated fireball seen with high explosives. This heat will combust materials near the point of detonation.

Tertiary effects can be produced by wrapping the high explosive with some type of fragmentation device. The military claymore mine uses high explosives surrounded by steel ball bearings. The pressure wave pushes the ball bearings before it, ripping into whatever objects they touch. The fragmentation devices have a farther lethal radius than the pressure wave. The pressure wave dissipates as a function of the square of the distance from the explosion, or for every two feet traveled, the pressure waves loses four amounts of force. The fragmentation devices lose only two units of velocity for every two units of distance traveled (a linear relationship).

High explosives were used at the Marine barracks in Beirut (collapsing a four-story building, leaving a 20 × 40 foot crater and killing 241), the World Trade Center, and the Oklahoma City Federal Building.

There are literally hundreds of high explosives terrorists can employ. Dynamite is one of the most common. Dynamite typically comes in stick form and weighs approximately one kilogram. Dynamite, except for military dynamite, contains nitroglycerine mixed with oxidizers and some type of absorbent material. The strength of dynamite depends upon the amount of nitroglycerine in the unit of dynamite. The most powerful dynamite contains over 90% nitroglycerine, sodium nitrate to supply oxygen, and some solid binder such as wood pulp or ground meal. This high-grade dynamite will explode at a rate of 23,000 feet per

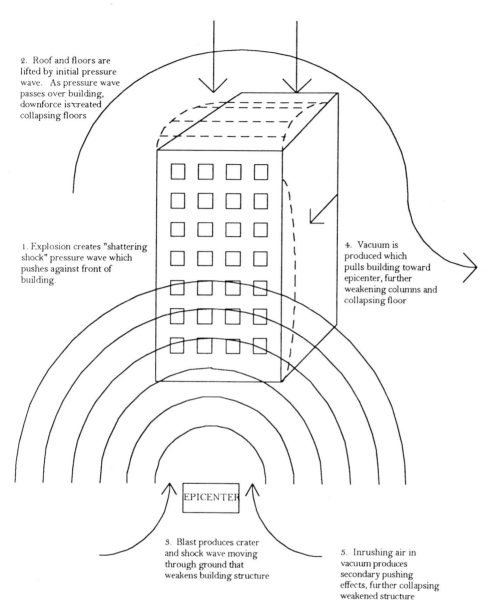

2. Roof and floors are lifted by initial pressure wave. As pressure wave passes over building, downforce is created collapsing floors

1. Explosion creates "shattering shock" pressure wave which pushes against front of building.

4. Vacuum is produced which pulls building toward epicenter, further weakening columns and collapsing floor

EPICENTER

3. Blast produces crater and shock wave moving through ground that weakens building structure

5. Inrushing air in vacuum produces secondary pushing effects, further collapsing weakened structure

Figure 7.1. Effects of high explosives on a structure.

second (speed of the positive pressure wave). Other dynamite might be 75%, 60%, or 50%, numbers which refer to the percentage of nitroglycerine in the mixture. Dynamite comes in stick form in a wide variety of shapes, sizes, strengths, and packaging material. Dynamite is somewhat unstable and can be detonated by a variety of methods.

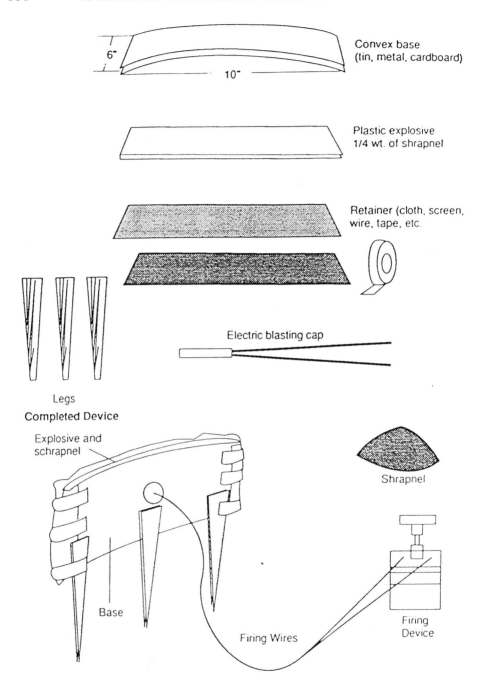

Convex base
(tin, metal, cardboard)

Plastic explosive
1/4 wt. of shrapnel

Retainer (cloth, screen,
wire, tape, etc.

Electric blasting cap

Legs

Completed Device

Explosive and
schrapnel

Shrapnel

Base

Firing Wires

Firing
Device

Figure 7.2. The claymore mine.

Some terrorists use nitroglycerine in its liquid form. In liquid form, nitroglycerine is yellow-brown and extremely unstable and highly dangerous. Minor shocks, such as simply moving the liquid, can detonate nitroglycerine. To stabilize it somewhat, it can be mixed with nitric and/or sulfuric acid. It can be left in a drinking glass on a table, in a bottle on a countertop, and even as a puddle on the ground. Moving the container or stepping in the puddle will usually be enough to detonate the nitroglycerine. If found, nitroglycerine should never attempted to be moved.

TNT (trinitrotoluene) is made of nitric acid, sulfuric acid, and toluene. It is commonly produced in sticks weighting one-half to one kilogram. TNT is usually used to damage or destroy heavy structures of brick, concrete, and/or steel. Unlike dynamite, TNT is insensitive to shock and is relatively stable under the most adverse handling conditions. One of the drawbacks of TNT is its toxicity. Handlers should avoid breathing dust and having skin contact with TNT.

C-4 is an off-white plastic explosive composed of cyclotrimethylene trinitramine, isomethylene, motor oil, and plastic binder (Yost, 1985) and has a detonation velocity of approximately 26,400 feet/second. It comes in "brick" form and is stable under a wide range of environmental and handling conditions. Being pliable, C-4 is easily molded into a variety of shapes and is most effectively used as a shape charge (see below). Because of the motor oil binder, C-4 is fairly readily detectable by its greasy feel or grease on the container of the explosive. The most common legitimate (and illegitimate) use of C-4 is against heavy structures.

RDX (cyclotrimethylenetrinitramine) is one of the most powerful of all high explosives, having a detonation velocity of approximately 42,000 feet/second. RDX is more pliable than C-4 and is not greasy. It can be molded into virtually any shape imaginable, such as shoelaces, pressed flat in a briefcase, molded to the corner bead of a suitcase, or worn like a belt. In the 1980s, many terrorists used mercury fulminate to detonate RDX, but because of the instability of mercury fulminate, RDX is now usually detonated with azides, such as lead, mercury, or silver azide. RDX was the explosive used to bomb the Marine barracks in Beirut in 1983 (Biddle, 1986).

PETN (pentaerythrite tetranitrate) comes in brick or pellet form and has a detonation velocity of 21,000 feet/second. PETN is the primary component in detonating cord. It is odorless, stable, lightweight, virtually undetectable, and easily concealable. PETN may be detonated in a variety of manners, but the most common is flame or other non-electric detonator.

Ammonium nitrate can be purchased at most garden, agricultural supply centers, and feed stores. Ammonium nitrate is the primary ingredient in fertilizer, although mixtures vary widely. In recent years, the government has required that the amount of ammonium nitrate in fertilizers be reduced so the fertilizer is inert. The World Trade Center and Oklahoma City Federal Building bombings are ample proof that some fertilizers still have too high an ammonium nitrate concentrate. Ammonium nitrate is a white crystalline powder and has one of the lowest detonation rates of all high explosives, approximately 3,600 feet/second. Most terrorists mix ammonium nitrate with motor oil or diesel fuel as a binder and to serve as a secondary initiator or sensitizing agent. One drawback to ammonium nitrate is that the initiator must be extremely powerful to begin detonation.

Low Explosives

Low explosives are slow burning and require a containment vessel. The explosive burns in the tenth of seconds and changes from a gas to liquid much slower so no shattering shock or massive pressure wave forms. Most low explosives burn at rates below 3,000 feet per second, compared to dynamite, for example, which burns at 7,000–18,000 feet/second. If detonated in the open air, low explosives will merely burn and not produce an explosion. The pressure from the change from a solid to liquid has enough time to disburse in the surrounding air.

Low explosives require a containment vessel for them to be used as an explosive. Black powder in a bullet is an example. Inside the containment vessel (shell casing), the powder burns and pressure builds up because the expanding gas cannot dissipate. When the pressure builds high enough, the bullet is pushed away from the cartridge at a high velocity. If the black powder were placed inside a solid container and burned, the pressure buildup of gas would eventually shatter the container, spraying fragments. This is exactly what occurs with a hand grenade.

Some low explosives can be made into high explosives by packing them into a brick or cake. Nitrocellulose (gun cotton/modern smokeless powder) is an example. A low explosive in normal form, if compressed, can be used as a high explosive. Low explosives are usually detonated by heat, flame, or spark and are often used as secondary initiators for high explosives. French Ammonal is an easily produced, homemade low explosive composed of ammonium nitrate, stearic acid, and aluminum powder which can be used as a secondary initiator.

The most common of the low explosives is black powder. Black powder is a mixture of potassium nitrate (saltpeter), charcoal or carbon, and sulfur. The amount of potassium nitrate in the mixture determines the strength of black powder. The most common mixtures are 75%, 15%, and 10% potassium nitrate. Black powder is not actually black but comes in a variety of colors, including dark gray, brown, and yellow. The quality of black powder is also a function of grain size. The smaller the grain, the more powerful the powder and the quicker the change in form from a solid to a gas. Black powder is somewhat unstable, easily ignited, and can explode even when not confined. It can be prematurely detonated by heat, friction, and static electricity (Poland, 1988). According to the ATF (1983), for instance, in 1982, 35 percent of all recorded bomb injuries in the United States were done to the bombmakers while using black powder.

It should be mentioned at this point that many terrorists are killed in the construction of explosive devices. Approximately 30 percent of those people killed by homemade explosives are the explosive makers. Almost always, the constructor is killed by introducing a detonator to the explosive device. Several members of the Weather Underground were killed in Greenwich Village, New York while constructing explosive devices. Authorities believe one of the constructors was smoking a cigarette and accidentally detonated the devices. The British are fond of referring to the bomb maker self-destructing as "scoring one's own goal."

Detonators and Initiators

To ignite the explosive, two additional components are required: a detonator and an initiator. The detonator is some type of substance which provides the necessary heat to begin changing the explosive from a solid or gas to a liquid. The initiator is some type of heat system which ignites the detonator. The simplest example to illustrate these three components is the "classic Hollywood" stick of dynamite with a fuse sticking out of one end. A match lighting the fuse is the initiator, the fuse burns (detonator), and ignites the dynamite. Another example would be the same stick of dynamite with a blasting cap inserted into one end and hooked via wires to an electric current source. Turning on the electric current (initiator) heats the blasting cap (detonator) which begins the burn process in the explosive.

The Molotov cocktail is a common terrorist explosive. The Molotov cocktail is a jar filled with gasoline with a rag stuck into the neck of the bottle. A match (initiator) lights the rag (detonator) which in turn begins the gasoline burning. The preceding examples describe flame fuse systems. Flame fuse systems are the most dangerous and unstable of all detonator and initiator systems. Flame fuses may burn at a faster or slower rate than advertised, may "bridge" or jumps across the fuse system, or fail to completely burn to the explosive.

Some flame fuse systems can be quite exotic. In World War II, the Germans were known for placing a small amount of explosives in the stem of a pipe and then leaving the pipe laying in a place where the British would find it. The British would fill the pipe with tobacco, light the pipe, and, drawing the flame and heat of the burning tobacco through the stem, would ignite the explosive.

Next to flame, mechanical initiators are the most common and simplest systems used. The hammer on a firearm is an example of a mechanical initiator. The hammer in the firearm falls forward and strikes a flame primer in the base of the bullet (detonator), which starts the powder burning. A mechanical type initiator is often used in booby-trap devices.

A third common initiator system is electric. Electric initiators produce heat, which in turn begins the detonator burning. Electric devices using clocks or watches are the most commonly found type of this initiator. A very fine bare wire is placed in the explosive. One end of the wire is connected to the body of the clock and the other end of the circuit is connected to a screw set in the crystal of the clock. A battery is placed in the circuit to provide the electric current. When the hand of the clock hits the screw, the electric circuit is completed, the wire heats up, and the heat sets off the detonator. Many electric initiators are nothing more than two metal plates connected to a wire. Bringing the metal plates into contact with each other completes a circuit. Probably more than any other type of detonation system, electric detonators present the greatest threat to law enforcement personnel because of their small size and ease in being concealed.

Chemical initiators and detonators are becoming more common among terrorists. Chemical initiators are simple and efficient. A chemical which will interact with a detonator is introduced to the detonator system. Potassium chlorate (weed killer) in a balloon and dropped into an automobile's gasoline tank is an example of a chemical detonator/initiator system. The gasoline eats through the rubber balloon, the potassium chlorate reacts with the gasoline and an explosion occurs. In this case, the initiator is the chemical reaction of the gasoline eating the rubber balloon. The detonator is the chemical reaction between the gasoline and potassium chlorate which produces enough heat to ignite the gasoline.

Recently, drug dealers and terrorists have begun using an ingenious chemical system. Red phosphorus and potassium chlorate are soaked in alcohol and then mixed together and placed in aluminum foil. When the alcohol evaporates, the dried chemicals become highly unstable and explosive. When the foil package is moved and opened, exposure to the air produces an explosion. To the victim, the foil container appears to be nothing more than a wadded-up leftover scrap of foil or foil bag containing drugs.

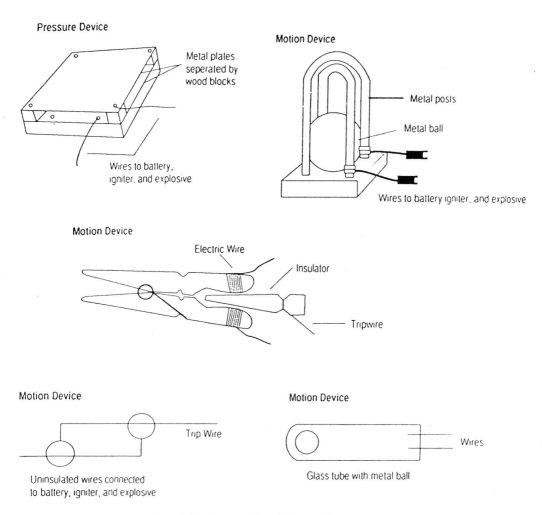

Figure 7.3. Common electric detonation systems.

A fourth type of initiator system is the pressure initiator. These initiators are sometimes used with explosive compounds sensitive to pressure and are primarily used in incidents involving aircraft. The explosive is placed in a container with a plunger arrangement on one end. Barometric pressure changes cause the plunger to move (initiator), igniting a detonator which ignites the explosive. A more complicated device involves the use of a double-switch arrangement. When the aircraft passes a certain altitude, the first switch arms the initiator. When the aircraft then descends, the second switch begins the initiation process.

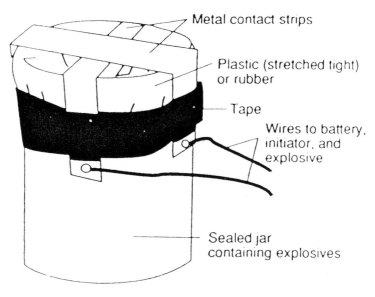

Figure 7.4. Simple altimeter switch.

Triggering Mechanisms

After the explosive has been constructed and placed, it still requires a triggering mechanism. Explosive devices are detonated through the use of three types of triggering mechanisms. One type is the time delay. The triggering mechanism is set so the explosive device detonates after a specific amount of time has elapsed. A clock or watch can serve as the triggering mechanism, or they can be such items which melt (i.e., ice blocks), evaporate, leak, or expand or contract.

A second type of triggering mechanism are remote control devices. With a remote control, the explosive device is placed and the terrorist uses some type of radio signal to active an electric detonator.

The third, and most common type of triggering device, is the target-activated mechanism (booby trap). The explosive device is attached to a wire, door, window, telephone, vehicle starter mechanism, etc., so that when the victim moves the trigger, the explosive device is detonated. Most target-activated trigger mechanisms are some type of motion-activated device. Motion-sensitive devices are of particular concern to law enforcement because terrorists not only use motion-sensitive devices against targets they also use these devices to protect themselves. For instance, the terrorist may use motion-sensitive devices to booby trap their headquarters, safe houses, business fronts, vehicles, and specific rooms inside different buildings. A pull switch, for example, may be attached between a door jamb and the door, so that when the door is opened, an electrical circuit is completed, detonating the device.

Additionally, the terrorist may guard themselves with primary, secondary, and tertiary devices. A primary device would be claymore mines planted in the yard surrounding their safe house. Secondary devices would be explosive charges attached to all entry points, such as doors and windows. Tertiary devices would consist of booby-trap devices within the building. Lights, books, desk drawers, sofa cushions, etc., may all contain explosive devices.

TERRORIST USE OF EXPLOSIVES

The use of explosive devices by terrorists is limited only by their imagination. In order of preference, terrorists prefer military explosives, construction explosives, and, as a last resort, homemade explosives. Military explosives are by far the most potent explosives, producing large amounts of chemical energy from a small volume of substance. Some even contain an integral booster to assist detonation. The most common commercial explosive used by terrorists is dynamite. It is easy to obtain and use, and many of the newer dynamites on the market do not contain nitroglycerine, making them extremely stable and safe to use.

Fragmentation devices are commonly used by terrorists. The most common fragmentation device is the hand grenade, nothing more than a steel case containing PETN in stabilized powder form. The steel is serrated or etched, so that when the PETN is detonated, the steel casing breaks along the serrations, sending metal shards flying in all directions. Damage is produced primarily by these pieces of steel, not the explosion. Older grenades were called "pineapples" and were serrated on the outer surface. It was discovered, however, that the exterior serrations made no difference to fragment production. Effective lethal radius was about 10 meters. Newer grenades are serrated or etched on the inside and produce thousands of pieces of shrapnel, with effective lethal radii of up to 25 meters.

Some terrorists have increased the effectiveness of the grenade by using a launcher device, such as a rifle grenade or grenade cartridge. Rifle grenades are rifles fitted with special barrels that propel the grenade for up to 100 meters before the grenade explodes. The grenade cartridge is a special weapon designed to do nothing but propel grenades. Grenade cartridges can propel the grenade for up to 150 meters before it detonates. Additionally, the grenade cartridge can fire special grenades that are high explosive, armor-piercing, filled with CS (tear) gas, flares, and smoke. Most grenade cartridges, like the American M-79 and Soviet AGS-17, fire either 30 or 40 mm grenades.

The vast majority of fragmentation devices employed by terrorists are homemade devices. Fragmentation devices can be as simple as a glass container filled with gasoline, wrapped with nails or scraps of metal, and a rag for a fuse. Additionally, blocks of explosives can be wrapped with metal shards, combining fragmentation effects with blast effects. The IRA, for example, commonly uses tin cans packed with explosives in a shape-charge configuration and capped with nails. Strips of cloth are attached to the rear end of the can to keep it oriented through flight. Used against an armored vehicle, the shape charge will blow a hole in the exterior skin of the vehicle and the fragmentation shards will penetrate and injure or kill persons in the vehicle (Gander, 1990).

In many instances, the terrorist will prefer an incendiary device over an explosive device. Incendiaries are designed to burn but may have an associated explosive effect. The Molotov cocktail is an incendiary device. If the container has an extremely small neck or is plugged, the Molotov cocktail will explode first and then produce incendiary effects. Incendiaries are almost always homemade devices and can be made from thousands of ordinary chemicals and substances. Napalm, for example, widely used in Vietnam, was nothing more than motor oil or diesel fuel mixed with a gel soap (which caused the burning fuel oil to stick to surfaces). Other commonly used gelling agents include soap, candle wax, egg whites, lye (alcohol and/or balsam), latex, and animal blood. Other liquid incendiaries include kerosene, alcohol (benzene), fuel oil, naphtha, turpentine, diesel fuel, and toluene. Thermite, a commercial incendiary, can burn through metal, such as transformers, automobile engines, storage tanks and pipelines, or weld metal together. Thermite is made from ferric oxide (iron rust) and aluminum powder.

Like explosive devices, incendiaries require an initiator, although many do not require a separate detonator. The initiator produces the first fire in the incendiary system. The only time detonators are used in incendiary devices is when the initiator may not produce enough heat to ignite the incendiary material. Most incendiary devices also employ a time-delay mechanism to allow the terrorist to flee before the device ignites.

One common incendiary initiator is fuse cord. Fuse cord can be purchased at most hardware stores and consists of a fast-burning material encased in a waterproof sheath. Most fuse cord is marked in one- or five-foot intervals so the user can time the burn. String fuse can be improvised by soaking cotton string or twine in a mixture of potassium chlorate and granulated sugar, or in potassium nitrate and granulated sugar.

Sulfuric acid is another common initiator for incendiaries and is easily made from battery acid. Sulfuric acid can be used to initiate incendiaries such as match heads, sugar and chlorate, and fire fudge. Most often, sulfuric acid is used with a delay mechanism. For example, sulfuric acid can be placed inside a balloon and thrown inside a sugar-chlorate mixture. When the acid eats through the balloon, a fire is produced.

Water is an effective initiator and can be used to ignite aluminum powder and sodium peroxide, silver nitrate and magnesium powder, and sugar and sodium peroxide. Almost always, water is used with a delay mechanism. Water is placed in a container and either dissolves the container or is spilled from the container onto the igniter, starting the initial fire.

Incendiary igniters have to burn at an extremely high temperature to set off the incendiary, so are often made from combining two or more chemicals. Some commonly used igniters include a mixture of sugar and chlorate (potassium or sodium), granulated sugar and sodium peroxide, barium peroxide and magnesium powder, silver nitrate and magnesium powder, and aluminum powder and sodium peroxide. Fire fudge is a moldable igniter made of a mixture of hot water, granulated sugar, and potassium chlorate. If the fire source is flammable, such as paper, hay, wood shavings, or a combustible liquid, the igniter may serve as the incendiary.

Incendiary delay mechanisms may be as simple as a lighted cigarette placed in a matchbook or as complex as a string tied between a clock-winding mechanism and a bottle containing the initiator. As the string winds around the clock mechanism, the initiator bottle is pulled over and the initiator spilled on the igniter.

Actions such as airplane hijackings and hostage situations may involve the placement of hidden explosive devices. Most military explosives such as C-4, PETN, and RDX cannot be detected by airport metal detection devices. More dangerously, these explosives can be molded, shaped, and painted to resemble articles of clothing, shoelaces, belts, or worn next to the skin. They can be placed in the lining of suitcases or briefcases, inside candy wrappers, flattened and put inside folders, or placed inside cosmetic bottles. If used as carryon luggage, the terrorist can, using a portable radio or similar device, complete the mechanism after boarding the airplane. Two common airplane explosive devices are shown in Figures 7.6 and 7.7. Figure 7.8 shows the explosive device used to bring down Pan Am flight 103.

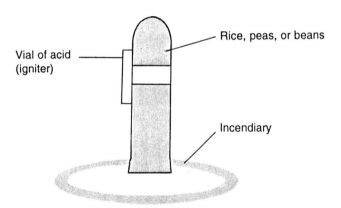

As beans expand, vial tips, spilling initiator onto ignitor, which lights incendiary.

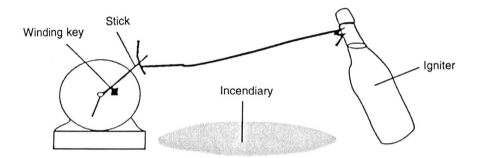

As clock hand turns, initiator is pulled over onto incendiary.

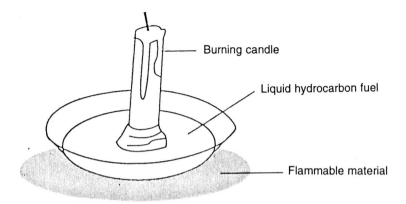

Figure 7.5. Commonly used delay mechanisms for incendiary mechanisms.

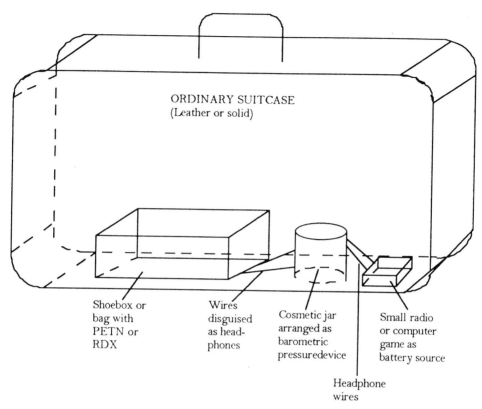

ORDINARY SUITCASE
(Leather or solid)

Shoebox or bag with PETN or RDX

Wires disguised as head-phones

Cosmetic jar arranged as barometric pressuredevice

Small radio or computer game as battery source

Headphone wires

Figure 7.6. Airplane suitcase bomb.

One use of hidden explosives is to place the law enforcement officer in a position of jeopardy or prevent an assault on the location. Every year, law enforcement personnel are killed by booby-trap devices. The law enforcement officer is at a distinct disadvantage when it comes to dealing with booby traps, as they receive no training concerning the recognition of these types of devices.

Terrorists may employ booby traps in any type of operation, although the use of booby traps would most likely be employed in sabotage, ambush, assassination, hostage-taking operations, and in the protection of their properties. Law enforcement raids on United States terrorist compounds have almost always uncovered booby-trap devices. When the FBI raided the CSA compound in Harrison, Arkansas they discovered an elaborate system of claymore mines and trip wires throughout the property.

Motor vehicles have been a favorite booby-trap target of terrorists. Vehicles are easy to booby trap and the explosive device is almost impossible to detect. The most common method of booby trapping the

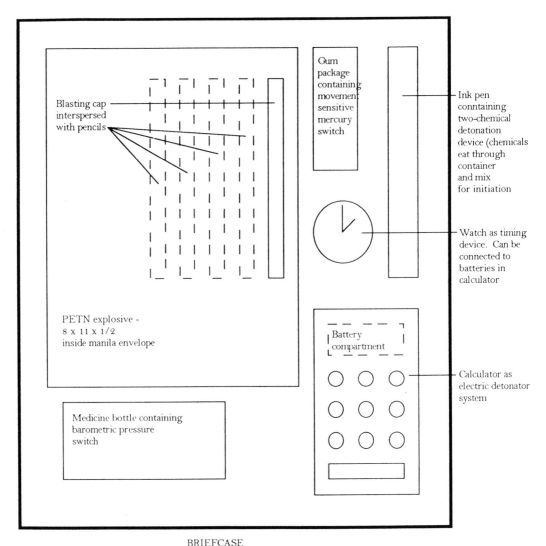

BRIEFCASE

Figure 7.7. Under-seat hand-carried airplane bomb.

vehicle involves placing two–five pounds of dynamite under the engine or the driver's side, under the front seat, under the dashboard or attached to the gas tank (Brodie, 1972). Most use an electric initiator, with the wire leads connected to the alternator. If the explosive is placed under the driver's seat, pressure-sensitive switches are usually employed.

In addition to booby trapping the vehicle, terrorists also use vehicles as fragmentation devices, as the bomb itself in suicide attacks, as an anti-personnel device in ambushes, and multiple vehicle bombs in coordinated attacks. On 23 October 1983, the Marine barracks in Beirut was

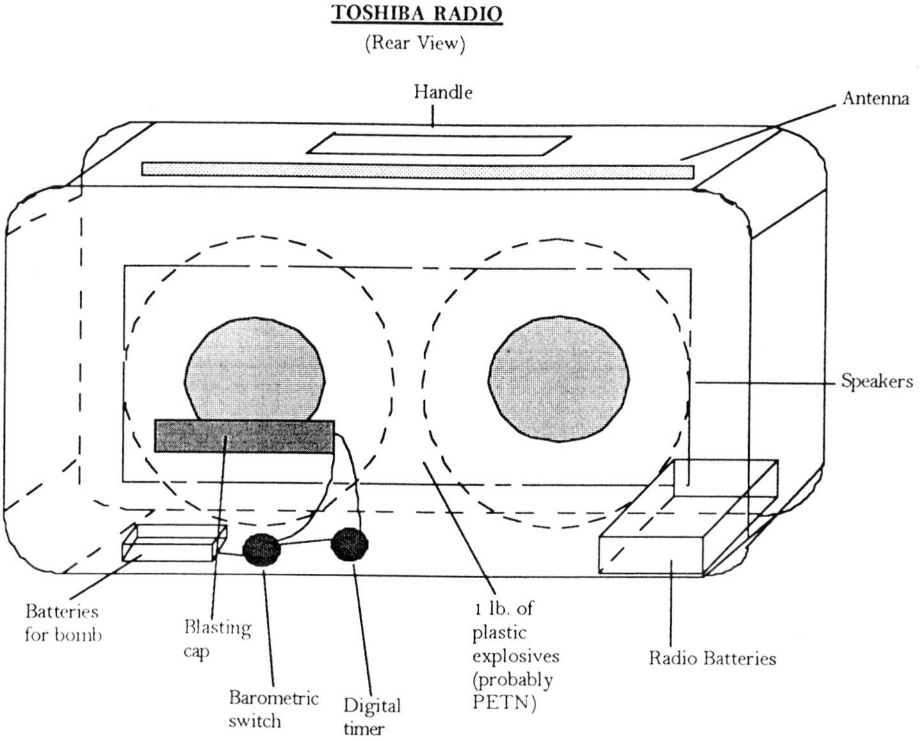

TOSHIBA RADIO

(Rear View)

Handle   Antenna

Speakers

Batteries for bomb

Blasting cap

Barometric switch   Digital timer

1 lb. of plastic explosives (probably PETN)

Radio Batteries

Figure 7.8. Toshiba radio bomb used on Pan Am Flight 103.

destroyed by a car bomb (Department of Defense, 1983). On the same day, 58 French paratroopers were killed in Beirut by a second car bomb. On 5 November 1983, the same terrorist organization killed 60 Israeli soldiers in Tyre, Lebanon. In just under two weeks, over 359 U.N. troops were killed by three car bombings. The PIRA conducts many assassination and ambush attacks using two vehicles. The first vehicle is used for the initial kill and the second to kill the rescuers. On 27 August 1979, 18 British paratroopers were killed on the North Ireland and Republic of Ireland border by this tactic (Poland, 1988). Ten paratroopers were killed in the initial blast and eight when they went to rescue their comrades.

The fear of car bombs is so great that governments go to extraordinary lengths to protect themselves. In front of embassies and government buildings worldwide, one can find steel and concrete barricades, sloped revetments, trucks filled with dirt, armed guards, and extensive vehicle search procedures.

Another favorite booby-trap device employed by terrorists is the letter bomb. In the United States over the past decade, numerous people have been killed and injured by a person or organization dubbed the Unabomber. The Unabomber mails packages to the victim, who is killed when he opens the package. Letter bombs first appeared in Germany in 1895, when one was sent to a local police headquarters office. Between 1977 and 1983, 84 letter bombs exploded in 23 countries, 19 in the United States. Forty-seven letter bombs were used in Europe, 40 sent to diplomats, and these letter bombs killed seven people.

The letter bomb is designed to kill a target, to injure or maim, or to harass and intimidate the public (Poland, 1988). Injuries or death from a letter bomb is due to shattering shock and blast pressure. High-risk targets for letter bombs are embassy personnel, corporate managers, defense-related industries, police officers, and government offices. The typical letter bomb weighs 2–3 ounces and fits within a $5\frac{3}{4} \times 4\frac{1}{4}$ inch envelope (Knowles, 1976). C-4 is the most common explosive used in letter bombs, and the most common fuse is the percussion fuse, which operates like the firing pin in a gun. When the package is opened, a spring releases a striker that impacts a detonator, igniting the explosive.

Characteristics that help identify a package as a letter bomb include: (1) the envelope is usually bulky and unbalanced, being heavier on one side than the other; (2) the package may have wires or spring holes in the outer wrapping; (3) if C-4 is used, a part of the envelope may be greasy; (4) it may have an unusual smell (may smell like almonds if C-4 is used); (5) will be stiff and unyielding; and (6) may be taped on all sides, indicating a spring-loaded mechanism.

In hostage situations, the terrorists are apt to booby trap entry points and the hostages. In an aircraft, this may include doors, hatches, windows and other surface openings. In a structure, doors, windows, and basement and roof accesses may be booby trapped. The purpose of these booby traps is not necessarily to kill but to prevent law enforcement personnel from forcibly and rapidly entering the confinement area. Terrorists have been known to booby trap themselves, so that killing the terrorist will detonate the explosive device. A pressure-release detonator would be used by the human booby trap (i.e., a deadman switch).

The booby traps listed above represent only several of the hundreds of types of booby-trap devices terrorists have been known to employ. A complete listing of booby traps would comprise a book in itself. Rather than try to explain all booby-trap devices and cover all situations in which booby traps may be employed, a brief synopsis will be given as to how the terrorist organization might booby trap their headquarters or safe house with primary, secondary, and tertiary devices. The booby traps discussed will be limited to the most common devices which have been employed by terrorists.

Primary booby traps would consist of two main types: claymore mines and trip-wire activated devices. Claymore mines can be readily made.

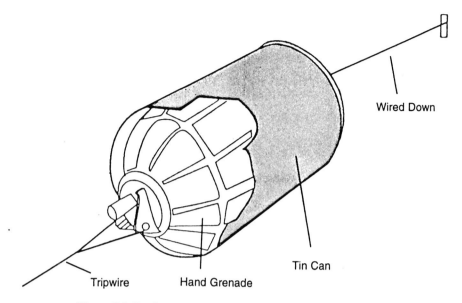

Wired Down

Tin Can

Tripwire　　Hand Grenade

Figure 7.9. Booby-trap grenade employing a simple trip wire.

The only materials required are tin, plastic or castable explosives, shrapnel (nails, barbed wire, bolts and/or nuts), window screen, tape, a detonator, wire, and electric source. The claymore could be detonated by a trip wire or by the terrorists. Pressure-sensitive devices could also be used to activate the booby trap.

Secondary booby traps would be placed at all entry points. These secondary booby traps will often be built into the walls around the entry points of the structure. Newly patched or repaired walls around entry points may indicate the presence of this type of booby trap. These booby traps would employ mechanical or electrically-initiated explosive devices. The most common of these devices employ pull-switch initiators, although trip-wire devices are not uncommon. Some devices may employ reverse polarity contacts, so that a separation or breaking of a contact causes the explosive device to detonate. Many of these secondary booby traps are placed at the top of doors or windows. Most personnel searching the area will concentrate on the lower levels of the area and pay little attention to what is overhead. Thus, the chance for successful detonation is improved.

Tertiary booby traps are the most difficult of all to uncover and avoid, as these can be placed in a multitude of locations and in a variety of objects. Books, drawers, countertops, desks, light bulbs, and sofa cushions have already been mentioned. Telephones, cabinets, refrigerators, closets, inside clothes, light switches, and under moveable objects, such as chairs, hollowed-out floor spaces, and in electric appliances, are other

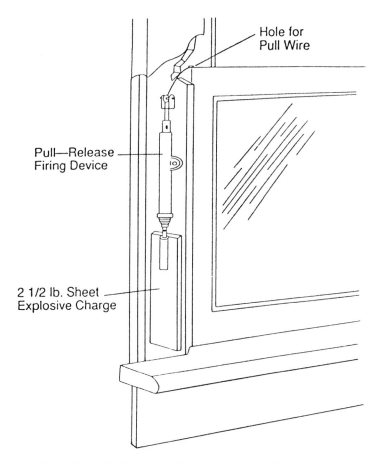

Figure 7.10. Window unit with a secondary booby-trap device.

likely places for booby traps. Items which are "out of place" can alert law enforcement personnel to potential booby traps. A neatly stacked book-shelf in an otherwise messy room could indicate a booby trap in the books. Other indicators might include a different hue of carpet, a "fluffed up" pillow or couch cushion, a tightly closed drawer when other drawers are ajar, a "conveniently" placed cigarette lighter, a shade-darkened room (where the light switch must be turned on), a piece of furniture "out of place," and a closed interior door.

Whatever the location or situation, the law enforcement officer must be extremely cautious when entering any area of terrorist, or suspected terrorist, activity. The terrorist is an expert in explosives and booby-trap devices, and the law enforcement officer is treading unknown waters. Terrorists often employ state-of-the-art military technology in the construction and use of explosives, incendiaries, and booby traps. The IRA,

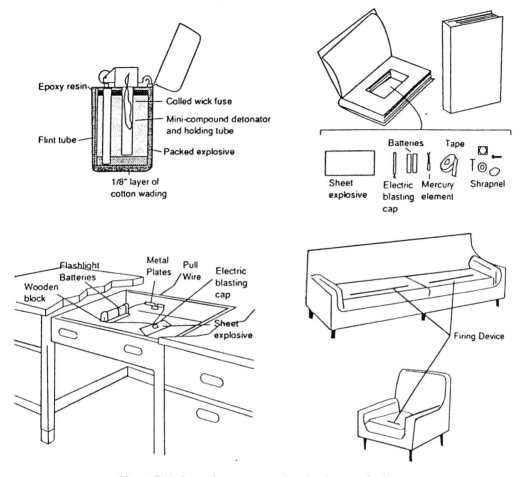

Figure 7.11. Several common tertiary booby-trap devices.

for example, stays one step ahead of British EOD (Explosive Ordinance Demolition) personnel and are responsible for taking many lives per decade because of their skill with explosive ordinance.

SUMMARY

The weapons terrorists employ in operations have only two constraints. One, weapons are selected on an operation-specific basis. The type of operation the terrorist is planning will dictate the selection of weapons to be used. Conversely, the type of weapons the terrorist has may dictate the operation. If a terrorist wished to destroy an airplane and did not have explosives, they may instead resort to taking hostages aboard an airplane, an operation that would only require firearms. Two, weapons are only limited by the imagination, creativity, training, and intelligence of the terrorist. It is not necessary for the terrorist to purchase weapons or even to steal weapons. Any weapon in the terrorist arsenal can be produced in the kitchen, a workshop, or machine shop.

In terms of firearms, pistols, shotguns, rifles, submachine guns, and automatic weapons have all been owned and used by terrorists. There is not a correlation between the sophistication of the organization and the firearm used. One or two terrorists could, and have, make effective use of a surface-to-air missile and crash an airliner. The PLO and IRA still rely on more conventional small arms, such as pistols and shotguns. One favored weapon among the IRA faithful is the old U.S. Thompson machine gun.

Since their invention, explosives have been the favored weapon of terrorists. No other weapon has produced more destruction, caused more deaths or resulted in more paralyzing fear than explosives. There are literally no constraints on the types of explosives terrorists can use. Everything from sophisticated military explosives to homemade bombs cooked up in a kitchen have proven deadly to the public. Those responsible for the World Trade Center and Oklahoma City Federal Building bombing used one of the oldest and simplest explosive devices known. The terrorists who brought down Pan Am 103 over Lockerbee, Scotland used sophisticated military explosives and a sophisticated arming and detonation device.

As long as there are terrorists, there will be explosive incidents for the public to contend with. As long as chemistry advances, terrorists will make use of this science to produce and employ even larger and more deadlier explosive devices. As the public becomes inured to acts of mass destruction, the terrorist will be forced to employ larger and larger explosives, killing ever greater numbers of people to gain media attention. The bombing of the Oklahoma City Federal Building held the nation's attention for several weeks on a daily basis. The next similar blast will hold the nation's attention for a few days at most, the next for a few hours, the next for a few minutes, the next not at all. To gain the notoriety they seek, terrorists will be forced to resort to more grandiose acts that cost even more lives.

Chapter 8

NUCLEAR, BIOLOGICAL, AND
CHEMICAL TERRORISM

In June 1994, eight people died and over 200 were injured in Matsumoto, Japan when sarin gas, a deadly nerve agent, was released in a courthouse. On 20 March 1995, five Tokyo subway stations and trains were the sites of a chemical attack. At these sites, small amounts of sarin were free-released. Twelve people died and over 5,000 required hospitalization. A Japanese terrorist cult, the Amu Shinri Kyo (Supreme Truth), was linked to both attacks. At a cult complex named the Seventh Satian in Kamikuishiki, Japan, investigating authorities discovered a complex chemical processing plant containing tons of chemicals needed to make sarin, processing machinery and equipment for making chemical containers and release mechanisms. Also found in a cult laboratory was the biological agent clostridium botulinum, one of the deadliest bacteriological agents on earth.

Further investigation revealed the Amu Shinri Kyo had planned to take over the Japanese government by the year 2000 and rebuild the Japanese military machine into one of the most powerful in the world. Members of the cult included former members of the Japanese military and of Japan's Home Guard among its 5,000 plus members. Plans to wage global war once Amu Shinri Kyo gained power were also uncovered by police investigators.

One of the most fearsome forms of terrorism is NBC, or nuclear, biological, and chemical terrorism. Just the mention of these weapons can produce an almost paralyzing fear when linked to terrorists. The fear of the unknown, of unseen "bugs" and viruses, the misunderstanding these weapons are associated with, and the awesome potential for destruction can scare even the most hardened anti-terrorist's hearts. While the lack of knowledge, misperceptions, and misunderstandings concerning these weapons produce inordinate fear, the truth is far worse. The NBC weapons are the terrorist's "Pandora's box" of fear, death, and political change.

With the exception of nuclear weapons, developed first in the 1940s, biological and chemical weapons have been around (and used) for decades and centuries. Biological weapons have been available and employed by governments since ancient biblical times. Various strains of anthrax, plague, and typhus have been used for centuries by warring factions. In the early part of the twentieth century, the scientific investigation into and development of these weapons became a priority of military strategists and planners. The development of biological weapons began in earnest in World War I as scientists and researchers developed new theories on immunology, microbiology, and carrier agents. Research efforts were increased during World War II, as both the Allies and Axis powers developed biological weapons. Gruinard, a small island off the Scottish coast, for example, has been rendered uninhabitable (and unvisitable) for centuries because of the anthrax experiments conducted there during WWII. During the Cold War, efforts into the creation of biological weapons increased exponentially as both the U.S. and Russia attempted to develop weapons that were alternatives to nuclear strikes.

Chemical weapons research also began during WWI and these weapons were widely used during that war. Mustard gas, phosgene, and chlorine gas were widely used. In WWII, Germany developed Zyklon-B, an early nerve agent for the gas chambers of the extermination camps. Japan's Unit 731 attempted to create chemical weapons for use in the war, as did the U.S. at Fort Detrick, Maryland (Harris, 1994; Mullins, 1995). Again, during the Cold War, research and development of chemical weapons reached a fevered pitch as both the U.S. and Russia attempted to outmaneuver and out-duel each other for strategic advantage. In the 1980s and 1990s, these weapons proliferated into the hands of third-world nations intent upon recreating the world order. Part of Reagan's intent in the 1984 raids on Libya was to destroy two chemical warfare production plants. Hussein used chemical and biological agents in the war against Iraq, the Persian Gulf War, and his war against the Kurds.

In the later part of the 1980s and 1990s, chemical and biological weapons found their way into the hands of terrorists. The CSA compound of Jim Ellison was found to contain large quantities of potassium cyanide, along with plans to poison the water supplies of several major U.S. cities. As will be shown in this chapter, that is only one example of the proliferation of NBC terrorism.

NBC terrorism is discussed by many authors as part of the broader category of technological terrorism. Including NBC terrorism within techno-terrorism is not entirely accurate. Techno-terrorism refers to acts of terrorism directed against technological targets such as computer systems, electric grid networks, power plants, refineries, etc. (Kupperman & Trent, 1979). NBC terrorism, while employing technologically sophisticated weapons in some forms, is not directed against the targets of a technological society. The NBC weapons are directed against the simplest and most basic of all terrorist targets: citizens. Nor are all the NBC weapons technologically sophisticated. Virtually all of the biological weapons are the simplest life forms on the planet, as are the delivery systems for these weapons. Most of the NBC weapons do not require any technological sophistication to produce or release, do not require large expenditures of money, do not require large and complex laboratory facilities, nor require a large international organization. One terrorist working in a kitchen can produce many of these weapons and then release these weapons on an unsuspecting public.

This chapter will discuss the NBC weapons, what they are, what they do, and how they may be employed by terrorists. The issues surrounding NBC terrorism will be explored, including the ethical and moral sanctions for or against the use of these weapons. Understanding what these weapons are and how they may be used by the terrorist helps provide an estimate of the probability of their use and general strategies which may be employed to prevent their use.

NUCLEAR TERRORISM

One of the primary images of the second half of the twentieth century imprinted upon the world's consciousness is the mushroom cloud. Introduced to the world in August 1945 over the skies of Hiroshima and Nagasaki, the world has lived under the nuclear threat for the past 50 years. In the 1950s and 1960s, the U.S. and USSR were the agonists of the world's paranoia of nuclear destruction. In the 1980s and 1990s, the fear worsened as nuclear weapons proliferated among the world's nations. At present, even small third-world countries possess nuclear weapons or the technological capacity to make nuclear weapons. Countries with a nuclear capability or working on producing a nuclear weapon, in addition to the U.S. and USSR, include Argentina, Brazil, China, France, India, Iraq, Israel, North Korea, Pakistan, South Africa, Taiwan, and the United Kingdom. As early as 1986, Iraq had over 200 tons of raw uranium, over 14 kilograms of enriched uranium, and the host cells necessary for reprocessing uranium (Cranston, 1986). By the early 1990s, Pakistan had an uranium enrichment facility at Kahuta, an uranium reprocessing facility at Pinstech, a plutonium diversion plant at their Kanupp reactor, and a nuclear weapon design team in place at Wah. Most of Pakistan's nuclear capability was purchased from the West, including materials from Emerson Electric in England, Saint Gobain Techniques Nouvelles in France, Vat and Cora in Switzerland, and Keybold Heraeus in West

Germany (Cranston). By the end of the twentieth century, over 40 nations will have nuclear capability (Vetter & Perlstein, 1991).

In 1991, in his popular fiction novel, *The Sum of all Fears,* Tom Clancy presented a scenario involving a terrorist organization producing and detonating a nuclear device during a Denver, Colorado football game. This novel played out a theme long debated in the government, military circles, the academic community, and law enforcement confines—that of the possibility of terrorists obtaining and using a nuclear weapon. This issue consists of two components: one, the issue of whether terrorists could obtain a nuclear device, and two, whether terrorists would actually use the device if they obtained it.

In regards to the first issue, the possibility of terrorists obtaining a nuclear weapon, there are several components that must be addressed (Clark, 1980). The first concerns the technical knowledge necessary to construct a nuclear device. Is the technical knowledge known or is it available to terrorists? The second involves more actual production concerns. If the knowledge is available, would the terrorists have access to the technical knowledge necessary to actually construct a nuclear device? The third is a material issue. If the knowledge and technical capabilities are available, could terrorists obtain weapons-grade nuclear material to use in a bomb?

Is the technical knowledge that is necessary for constructing a nuclear device available to terrorists? In 1970, the city of Orlando, Florida was the victim of a nuclear blackmail scheme (Mickolus, 1980). The city was sent a package containing plans for a nuclear device, along with a letter explaining the device would be detonated unless a ransom was paid. Experts examining the plan claimed the device was workable. The investigation revealed the material came from a 14-year-old junior high school student. In 1974, Boston was victimized by the threat of a potential homemade nuclear device within the city (Gates, 1987), and nuclear threats were received in Des Moines, Iowa, Lincoln, Nebraska, and San Francisco (Dobson & Payne, 1982). In 1976, an undergraduate physics student at Princeton University, as part of a class project, designed a workable nuclear device that would fit into an automobile trunk. All of his information came from journals and technical manuals available to the general public.

Any person intent on constructing a nuclear device could easily obtain the technical knowledge necessary to construct a nuclear device. Any technical information they would need is contained within a well-stocked library. All the technical information necessary is available within the public domain and not too difficult to find (Mullen, 1979; Spector, 1985).

Terrorists could easily acquire the necessary technical knowledge needed to build a nuclear device from "scratch." Some background in physics and engineering would be required to translate the scientific jargon into useful designs. Terrorists with some physics and/or engineering in college would not have much difficulty understanding and then in using the technical jargon of scientific writing.

If the terrorists obtained the technical knowledge to construct a device, could they create the technical laboratory needed to physically construct a nuclear bomb? This question ignores the actual nuclear mass for the bomb, but instead focuses on the technical aspects of the casing and detonating a nuclear mass. Mullen (1979) argued that the development and production of a nuclear device would require an extremely high technological laboratory, a massive security program to keep the project secret, millions of dollars in capital and equipment, a group of scientists with degrees in physics and engineering, and years of dedicated effort.

The laboratory required to construct a nuclear device would be beyond the capabilities of almost all terrorist organizations. There are probably no more than three to five terrorist organizations in the entire world which could construct such a facility. Even if the entire far right in the United States were to unite and work together, they as a cohesive unit probably could not develop the necessary laboratory. Advances in technology is helping overcome the laboratory difficulties for the terrorist. Computer-aided design, computer-aided drafting, and robotics all make the job of actually constructing a device easier and easier. The legions of highly trained and skilled technicians required in the U.S. government's nuclear program are no longer required. Much of their expertise and many of their skills in machining parts to infinitesimal tolerances can now be done more swiftly and accurately by computers and robots. The programs that drive these computers and devices are available to the general public.

The security required at a terrorist nuclear production facility would be the project's Achilles' heel. The abilities of intelligence-gathering organizations such as the CIA, NSA, Mossad, etc., are phenomenal. It is doubtful the terrorist organization could maintain the level of security required to keep the laboratory secret. Even with sophisticated computers, it would still require hundreds of personnel to construct a nuclear device. As the size of the team grew linearly, the inability to keep the laboratory secret would increase exponentially. That is, if ten people were involved in the project, it would be 10,000 times more likely a leak would occur than if only one person were involved in the laboratory.

The money necessary to fund such an operation would easily reach into the hundreds of millions of dollars. Again, few terrorist organizations have the money available to finance such an operation. They could, however, obtain funding from a sympathetic government or coalition of governments, but the trail of money would likely compromise the operation.

Mullen (1979) argued that a person or team of persons with an advanced knowledge of physics would be required to direct a nuclear production laboratory. There are millions of physicists and engineers who would agree to assist and work for the terrorists in a nuclear project. Additionally, hundreds of machinists, computer programmers and operators, chemists, metallurgists, and other technicians would be just as crucial to the project. Some of these specialty persons would be more difficult to find.

The nuclear project would require several years from the start of the project to final product. Time from site location to initial production would take between five and seven years, from initial production to finished project about one to two years. As with personnel, the longer the project is in the works, the greater the probability the project would be compromised by intelligence efforts. A terrorist operation that took seven to nine years would, almost without question, be uncovered and closed.

The next concern centers around finding and obtaining the actual nuclear material to put into a bomb. Related to this concern is the question of the amount of material necessary for a bomb. To construct a bomb, the terrorist would need special nuclear material (SNM; Poland, 1988). SNM is fissionable nuclear material consisting of enriched uranium isotopes U-233 and U-235, or weapons-grade plutonium P-239 containing approximately 7% P-240. The terrorist would need only 11–15.42 kilograms of U-238, 25 kilograms of metallic uranium (U-235), 35 kilograms of highly enriched uranium oxide (UO-2), 200 kilograms of intermediately enriched UO-2, 4–7 kilograms of enriched plutonium or 10 kilograms of plutonium oxide (Clark, 1980; Rosenblum, 1978; Willrich & Taylor, 1979). This amount of either uranium or plutonium would be equivalent to approximately 100 tons of TNT, while keeping the device small enough to be able to fit in the trunk of a small automobile.

Terrorists could obtain SNM in one of four ways (Mullins, 1992). One, terrorists could steal the material from a processing site, storage site, or weapons facility. This would be the most dangerous and difficult for the terrorist, but it is not beyond the capabilities of many terrorist organizations. There are only a few facilities in the world that have the capability of producing weapons-grade nuclear material and they tend to be heavily guarded. It would take a large, well-coordinated effort by the organization to steal the material from one of these facilities, but it is conceivable.

Two, terrorists could hijack or divert materials during the transport of weapons-grade material. The production facilities that produce SNM are not the facilities where weapons are constructed. The SNM has to be shipped from one facility to the other. A coordinated attack on a transport system would require less effort than attacking the production facility. It would still be a highly risky operation for the terrorist organization, but it is not outside the realm of possibility.

Three, terrorists could obtain the material from an employee who worked at the production facility. Several types of employees could assist the terrorist. An employee who is dissatisfied with the facility could steal the material. Millions of workers are dissatisfied with their employers and wish to retaliate in some manner. An employee dissatisfied with the government may assist the terrorist organization simply to retaliate against the government. Many workers in the U.S., for example, do not necessarily agree with the tactics or philosophy of the far right but are angered at the government for a variety of reasons. Assisting the terrorist organization obtain SNM may displace this anger. An employee could be sympathetic to the terrorist's cause and want to assist the organization. Employees working with SNM are carefully screened, but this screening cannot determine their political ideology. An employee could be compromised by the terrorist organization. Monetary payments, threatening to make public harmful personal details of the employee's private life, or threatening the family of an employee could be leverage used by the terrorist organization to coerce an employee to steal SNM. A worker could steal enough SNM in a four-month period to construct a weapon with the same power as the one dropped on Nagasaki in World War II (Dobson & Payne, 1979).

Four, using any combination of the above techniques, terrorists could obtain SNM through "MUF." MUF stands for Material Unaccounted For and is an accounting system to track SNM. Developed by the Nuclear Regulatory Commission, MUF recognizes losses of SNM somewhere in the production, transportation or usage areas of SNM. MUF is nothing more than a bureaucratic system used to explain why the output side of the SNM equation is lower than the input side of the equation. How the material disappeared, how much disappeared, and where it disappeared to is unknown. In the U.S., some estimates suggest the yearly MUF of nuclear material to be between 1,500 and 6,000 pounds (Rosenblum, 1978). No figures are available for other nations, but it is likely that the MUF figures in other countries are even higher than the U.S. as their accounting procedures are not as stringent (Mullins, 1991b).

Iraq's Development of Nuclear Weapons

To illustrate the difficulties in developing an atomic weapon for terrorist purposes, it is instructive to examine Hussein's attempts to develop a nuclear arsenal in Iraq. Following the successful invasion of Kuwait in 1990, Hussein ordered his nuclear research team to have a nuclear weapon ready for use by April 1991. The Persian Gulf War and the threat of massive retaliation by President Bush closed Iraq's nuclear development program. After the war ended, however, Iraq returned to the development of an atomic warhead. Repeated inspections by U.N. inspections teams following the Gulf War have revealed that Hussein's development of an atomic weapon continues virtually unabated.

Inspection teams first discovered small amounts of enriched plutonium at a reactor site in Tuwaitha, Iraq. This reactor was also the site of the chemical enrichment plant for plutonium. U-238 was being irradiated and then the plutonium created was separated out by chemical methods. Weapons-grade U-235 was discovered at an uranium extraction plant in Akashat. Iraq was producing weapons-grade U-235 by three methods. At Tarmia and Al-Sharqat, inspectors found 23 calutrons. A calutron separates ionized uranium gas into U-235 and U-238 using electromagnets. The calutron was the device used in the Manhattan project. Calutron component and assembly plants were discovered at Al-Dijjla, Al-Dura, Al-Rabesh, and Augba bin Nafi (Milhollin, Dolley, & Spector, 1991). Two, centrifuge extractors were discovered at Al-Furat. Inspectors discovered Iraq planned to build 600 centrifuge separators. The centrifuge separator splits the uranium isotope by passing it through a rotating cylinder, pulling the lighter U-235 to the top of the cylinder. Three, Iraq experimented with chemical enrichment techniques that use catalysts to separate U-235 and U-238.

Inspectors found explosives and electronic equipment that Iraq had imported from foreign governments to use for an implosion bomb. In an implosion bomb, a spherical core of uranium or plutonium is surrounded by a high explosive (conventional), which when detonated drives the nuclear sphere together with great force, causing an initiator to release free neutrons. The combination of the critical mass and chain reaction produced by the free neutrons bombarding the mass lead to a nuclear detonation.

Finally, U.S. inspectors discovered peripheral equipment required for the production of a nuclear weapon. High-grade metals required for the bomb casing had been imported by Iraq from Europe. The high explosive HMX, required to collapse the spherical nuclear mass, was discovered at a weapons plant. Capacitors and krytrons bound for Iraq were seized in Europe by a U.S.-British team. Capacitors are used to control the detonation of the conventional explosive, and krytrons are switches that set off implosions.

Iraq was a nation attempting to develop a nuclear weapon. Approximately 20 different laboratory, processing, and enrichment facilities were being employed to construct the device. Thousands of scientists, engineers, technicians, and machinists were employed in the process, millions of dollars expended, and most parts purchased from other nations. Iraq has been working at full capacity on producing a nuclear weapon for almost eight years and is still not close to producing a weapon that would be ready for detonation before the year 2000.

The foregoing discussion assumes terrorists would need to construct a nuclear device to obtain a nuclear device. Terrorists constructing a nuclear device is a low probability event and the least likely avenue to be used by terrorists in obtaining a nuclear weapon. There are many other ways the terrorist organization could obtain a nuclear weapon. Terrorists could obtain a nuclear weapon from a sympathetic government (Cranston, 1986; Crenshaw, 1977). Iraq, North Korea, and Pakistan, all of whom have nuclear weapons capabilities, are only three of the many governments who have nuclear capabilities and who are unsympathetic to the United States. Donating a nuclear weapon to a terrorist organization would accomplish their political goal and remove them from any retaliation by the U.S. The terrorist organization could do their dirty work and absolve the nation from condemnation among the world community, unless it was discovered which nation gave the weapon to terrorists.

Two, terrorists could steal a nuclear weapon. Several years ago, such a theft would have been unthinkable. Nuclear weapons were massive in size and stored in strongly fortified bunkers. Today, however, the idea of theft is not farfetched. The U.S. and USSR both have developed "backpack" nuclear weapons, used primarily by NATO forces. These low-yield weapons are carried and detonated by a two-man crew. The backpack, weighing approximately 60 pounds, is carried by one person. The carrier and one other person have to enter a secret code into the Permissive Action Link (PAL) system to arm the nuclear device. Once armed, the device is placed in a secure spot, such as a locker, and then at a predetermined time it detonates. The small size, light weight, and portability of the backpack make them an ideal weapon for the terrorist.

Although secured, the security surrounding backpacks is not as stringent as with other nuclear weapons, especially considering they are assigned to NATO forces in Europe. For the terrorist, the major difficulty to overcome in using a backpack nuclear device would be in defeating the PAL arming system (Norman, 1978). Although a serious difficulty for the terrorist organization, defeating the PAL system is not an insurmountable obstacle.

Three, the terrorist could purchase a nuclear weapon. The dissolution of the Soviet Union left thousands of nuclear weapons and nuclear material in various locations within the confines of the new regional governments. Deep in a depression, the Russians are living hand to mouth and these newly formed governments are unable to raise capital to establish programs for the people. A quick way to raise millions in capital is to sell these weapons. Over 38,000 nuclear warheads are in the Georgian states alone (Mullins & Mijares, 1992, 1993, 1995). Holding a Wild West attitude towards capitalism, newly formed Russian organized crime syndicates could obtain and offer these weapons on the open market. In 1992 and 1993, an organized crime syndicate in Vilnius, Lithuania attempted to sell 4.4 tons of SNM uranium-contaminated beryllium to an unknown syndicate in Zurich, Austria for $2.7 million. This syndicate, in turn, had arranged for another unknown buyer to pay $24 million. Authorities suspected the end buyer was North Korea (Zimmermann & Cooperman, 1995). Beryllium is used in nuclear weapons as a neutron deflector, allowing for less nuclear material to be used in a device. In the Vilnius shipment of beryllium, the SNM uranium could be extracted, bypassing the need to enrich regular uranium. Other countries such as Iraq, Pakistan, and North Korea could sell a nuclear device for a lower price to terrorists who intended to use the weapon against the U.S.

Most of the Soviet weapons unaccounted for from the dissolution of the USSR are the "dirtier" nuclear weapons, meaning the radioactive fallout is significantly greater than from the ICBMs and other large weapons. These dirty nuclear weapons include land mines, artillery shells, short-range missiles, surface-to-air missiles, torpedoes, and small bombs. Because of their small size, the smuggling of these weapons is a very viable threat. Some are small enough to fit within a small suitcase, and their military configuration makes them indistinguishable from conventional shells (Steinberg, 1993). Additionally, compared to other nuclear weapons, these are much cheaper to purchase.

The actual detonation of a nuclear weapon by a terrorist organization is the most unlikely use of nuclear terrorism but not the only form nuclear terrorism could take (White, 1991). There are numerous other ways terrorists could conduct a campaign of nuclear terrorism (Jenkins, 1986). Terrorists could merely fabricate a nuclear threat, make the threat public, and demand a ransom. A threat alone would produce the fear the terrorist wishes to accomplish and, if successful, could produce the desired political change. Accompanied by the appropriate supporting documents, such as sources of obtaining SNM, detailed blueprints of the device, etc., the government would have no option but to take the threat seriously. Even if the government's intelligence services investigated and determined the threat to be a hoax it is unlikely the general public would believe the government. In the wake of Pan Am 103, the World Trade Center bombing, the Tokyo subway gassing, and the bombing of the Oklahoma City Federal Building, government statements would mean very little to the public.

Second, terrorists could actually steal nuclear material and demand a ransom. Because of public ignorance concerning the physics involved in a nuclear weapon, the terrorists would not even have to steal SNM; any nuclear material would be sufficient. Merely knowing that terrorists had stolen some nuclear material and were threatening to detonate a nuclear weapon would produce the fear the terrorist is wishing to produce. Once again, government disclaimers would do little to allay the public's fear. In 1986, Hoffman suggested the greatest threat to nuclear facilities were from Islamic fanatics and right-wing extremists. There is no evidence in the mid-1990s to suggest the threat from these two groups is any less than it was a decade ago.

Associated with the theft of nuclear material, the terrorists would not have to claim possession of a nuclear weapon. The terrorist organization could threaten to free release nuclear material into the atmosphere. The general public has not forgotten the near disaster at Three Mile Island nor the devastation produced by the Chernobyl reactor meltdown. Threatening to release nuclear material could produce as much or more panic than the threat of a nuclear weapon. To legitimize the threat, the terrorists could actually release a small amount of nuclear material. Using some type of radioactive dispersal device, terrorists releasing only three-and-one-half ounces of plutonium into a closed space, such as an office building, could cause the death of several thousand people from primary and secondary radiation effects (Alexander, 1983). Three ounces of plutonium is over 20,000 times as toxic as curare (cobra venom) or potassium cyanide. Hundreds to thousands would die in a free-release incident, and the psychological ramifications would be politically and economically disastrous (Schelling, 1976; Krieger, 1977).

Free release may be the most fearsome form of nuclear terrorism. While the possession of a nuclear device by terrorists would produce paralyzing fear, most of the public would see this threat as a one-time use by the terrorist organization. Free release would be an ongoing threat to the public.

Fourth, terrorists could attack a nuclear facility and use the facility for ransom or as a weapon. Out of all the above terrorist options, this would be one of the more unlikely. The planning, manpower, and logistics required to actually conduct an operation to capture a nuclear facility would be overwhelming for many terrorist organizations. The chances for failure are great and holding a nuclear facility would require time to negotiate demands. In this type of operation, time would work against the terrorists and turn fear into anger. The takeover of a nuclear facility is not outside the bounds of reasonable probability, however. Between 1969 and 1977, for example, the U.S. experienced 194 threats against nuclear facilities, four pipe bombs were discovered at nuclear facilities, and 15 people penetrated the intrusion alarm systems of nuclear facilities (Norton & Greenberg, 1979).

Related to the above is the terrorist operation directed at sabotaging a nuclear facility, such as a power generation plant, a reprocessing plant, a nuclear storage site, or a fuel fabrication center. A meltdown of a core reactor would cause thousands of deaths, result in environmental damage lasting thousands of years, and close an area to human habitation for centuries. The fear and panic caused by the sabotage of a reactor core would lead to social and economic chaos that could topple a government. With the rapid proliferation of nuclear facilities in the world, many experts believe it is just a matter of time before a sabotage incident occurs (Flowers, 1976).

Poland (1988) has indicated there are several realistic scenarios for terrorists taking a nuclear facility. He suggests the most likely incidents might include religious fanatics with suicidal tendencies (which would include the majority of the U.S. far right), anti-nuclear activists attempting to end nuclear energy and research, organized criminal gangs attempting to extort a government (money, release of prisoners, change in drug laws, etc.), emerging third-world nations attempting to influence international policy, terrorists wanting to escalate their strategy by producing a nuclear threat, and highly trained terrorists destroying a facility.

Finally, the morality of terrorists actually engaging in nuclear terrorism must be explored. Would terrorists engage in an operation of massive death such as that produced by nuclear terrorism? Given the history of terrorism, the motivation of terrorists, and the need to continue escalating terrorist atrocities to gain the needed media attention, the 1990s has witnessed a philosophical shift in the answer to this question. Even five years ago, the answer would probably have been no. A terrorist atrocity on the magnitude of nuclear destruction would have been beyond the lack of morality of even the most hardened terrorist.

Today, in light of the recent history of terrorist activity and the reaction of the public to those events, the answer is yes. Perceptions and expectations of the terrorist, the government and, most importantly, the public have been elevated by recent events in the world of terrorist operations. To achieve the same goals of 1990, the terrorist has to resort to larger and larger acts of mass destruction. There is an upper limit to these acts when using conventional weapons. The terrorist will have to employ unconventional weapons to achieve the same reaction. One of these unconventional weapons is nuclear weapons. In a sense, the terrorist has been forced to consider nuclear weapons, regardless of the motivation, morality, or ethics of the terrorist.

At present, the only sanction against third-world nations or terrorists in employing nuclear terrorism is the threat of the U.S. and U.N. military response (Berard, 1985; Forrest, 1976; Livingstone & Arnold, 1986; White, 1991). Nuclear terrorism would bring about a full-scale military response. Even the threat of usage would bring about this response (aka, Saddam Hussein in Iraq). Because of the proliferation of nuclear weapons and threat of this form of terrorism, the U.S. has attempted to reduce the threat, primarily by calling for stringent controls on exports of nuclear technology (Cranston, 1986). The U.S. and Soviets entered into numerous agreements attempting to limit the spread of nuclear technology and prevent nuclear terrorism, a point on which both nations agreed (Nunn & Warner, 1987). As has been shown, however, the breakup of the Soviet Union has resulted in less than an ideal situation. Today, the Soviets and U.S. are working closely together to rein back in the "nuclear genie."

In the U.S., nuclear emergency search teams (NEST) were developed to handle not only emergencies involving nuclear materials (i.e., reactor malfunctions, discovered nuclear materials, etc.) but to respond to the terrorist threat. The Atomic Energy Commission, in 1975, created the NEST concept in the wake of the Boston bomb scare of 1974 (Gates, 1987). If the FBI receives intelligence suggesting a nuclear threat, NEST personnel are brought into the investigation to assist. NEST personnel are specifically trained to respond to nuclear terrorism, including bombs, free-release agents, or incidents at a nuclear facility.

Of the different forms of NBC terrorism, nuclear terrorism has the lowest probability of occurring. The problems inherent in the use of nuclear materials are simply too great for the terrorist to contemplate and the response too massive to suggest this as a viable terrorist alternative. As will be shown, there are other methods the terrorist can employ to achieve the same ends and there are alternatives that produce much less risk to the terrorist than nuclear terrorism.

BIOLOGICAL TERRORISM

The use of biological agents for war and terrorist activities has a long history. Biological agents are by far the oldest and most used of all NBC weapons (Day, 1989). One of the first recorded episodes of biological warfare occurred in 1343, when the Black Sea fort of Caffa, Genoese was attacked by the Tartars, who catapulted plague victims inside the fortress (Vetter & Perlstein, 1991). The Genoese then inadvertently spread the plague aboard their trading vessels, introducing the disease to Europe. Within three years, the Black Death had claimed over 30 million victims. In 1710, the Russians launched plague corpses against the Swedes at Reval. Francisco Pizarro conquered the Incas by introducing a smallpox epidemic, killing over 50 percent of the Incan race. Cortez introduced smallpox to the Aztecs, claiming over 10 million Indians during the course of the disease. As America expanded westward, the settler's took smallpox, influenza, cholera, tuberculosis, plaque, malaria, typhus, measles, and chickenpox with them. Many of these diseases were deliberately introduced to Indian populations (Connell, 1984).

In WWII, the U.S., England, Germany, Russia, and Japan experimented with biological agents, as did Belgium, Canada, Holland, France, Italy, and Poland. At Fort Detrick, Maryland, Biloxi, Mississippi, and Utah, the U.S. Army opened their Chemical Warfare Service, researching such exotic diseases as botulism, brucellosis, glanders, tularemia, psittacosis, coccidioidal granuloma, neurotopic encephalitides, shellfish poison, potato blight, southern blight, and plaque (Harris, 1994). Japan used flea-borne plaques to infect the citizens of Chuhsien, Ningpo, Chanhteh, and Kingwa, China. In 1944, the Allied forces infected the German potato crop with the Colorado Beetle, devastating the primary food crop of the Germans. After the war, the CIA had agents searching South American and African jungles looking for new biological agents that could be used if the Cold War heated up (Thomas, 1989).

In the 1990 Gulf War, Saddam Hussein was planning to release biological agents. Anthrax, botulin toxin, and other biological agents were prepared and loaded into over 200 warheads for use against the Allied coalition forces. Only the threats by President Bush of massive and total retaliatory action and the threats of a nuclear reaction by Israel prevented those weapons from being used.

In the U.S. in the 1940s, the search for biological warfare agents was given second priority behind the Manhattan Project. Presidents Roosevelt and Truman had no reservations about using biological agents if they would have shortened the war. In 1963, responding to the U.S. use of biological agents in WWII, Theodor Rosebury said, "We were fighting a fire, and it seemed necessary to risk getting dirty as well as burnt.... We resolved the ethical question just as other equally good men resolved the same question at Oak Ridge and Hanford and Chicago and Los Alamos." Within the entire government and military complex of the time, only the chief of staff to President Roosevelt, Admiral William Leahy, opposed the use of biological agents, saying that their use "would violate every Christian ethic I have ever heard of and all of the known laws of war" (Harris, 1994).

In 1970, the leftist terrorist organization, the Weather Underground, was planning to steal biological agents from Fort Detrick, Maryland to contaminate the water supplies of various cities around the country (Griffith, 1975). In 1972, the right-wing organization Order of the Rising Sun was planning to infect the Chicago water supply with typhoid bacteria. In 1975, the Symbionese Liberation Army was found with military technical manuals on the production of biological agents for germ warfare. In the late 1970s, the Italian Red Brigades were caught with large amounts of botullinum toxin in their possession.

Biological agents are a more insidious form of terrorism than nuclear terrorism, and the probability of terrorists turning to biological agents is greater than them using nuclear weapons (Mengel, 1979). As with nuclear terrorism, there are several questions which must be addressed concerning the possible use of biological agents. Like nuclear terrorism, these questions focus on availability of technical knowledge, necessary expertise, availability of materials, and willingness to use the biological agents in terrorist atrocities. Before examining these issues, however, it is necessary to describe the biological agents available for use.

Biological agents can be classified as anti-animal agents, anti-plant agents, or anti-personnel agents. The anti-animal agents are designed to attack livestock and animals necessary for a society to function. These agents are designed to either destroy the animals or to allow the target personnel to become infected by eating the contaminated meat. Anti-plant agents are designed to destroy foliage and/or crops or poison the crops so they cannot be used as a food source. Anti-personnel agents are designed to work directly on the human targets by introducing illness or death. Whether anti-animal, anti-plant, or anti-personnel, biological agents are classified by their size as either viruses (smallest; 100 times smaller than bacteria), protozoa, bacteria, rickettsia (gram-negative microorganisms), or fungi (largest in size).

Unlike nuclear devices, there is almost no technical knowledge necessary for cultivating or using biological agents. The only knowledge necessary could be obtained in any high school biology textbook. There is no special knowledge required, no technical obstacles to overcome, no high-technology laboratories to contend with, costs are minimal, and security would be easy to maintain. Most biological agents could be produced in simple dishes containing a small amount of a saline solution in the kitchen. Many biological agents could be allowed to free-grow on an old piece of food and then introduced to the target audience by introducing that food to the audience.

In terms of obtaining, biological agents are the anti-thesis of nuclear material. Many biological agents which would be of interest to the terrorist can be obtained through the mail. As stated by Douglas (1984), biological agents are the "Saturday night specials" of terrorism. In the 1980s, police discovered a clandestine laboratory in the kitchen of a Paris, France apartment. The Red Army Faction was producing clostridium botulinum (Livingstone, 1986; Douglas & Livingstone, 1987). This biological agent produces botulinal toxin (BTX), the most lethal toxin on the planet, only eight ounces of which would be ample to kill every living creature on earth (Hersh, 1968). Exposure to 1/100,000 of one gram would be a lethal dose (Investigative Reports, 1995).

The terrorist wanting to use a biological agent would have the same concerns as the U.S. military has had in their search for a biological warfare agent. First, the agent would have to be one for which there is no natural occurring immunity. Persons affected by the agent would have to become ill or die by the agent for it to be effective as a weapon of terrorism. Second, the biological agent would have to be highly infectious. The biological agent would have to be one in which the spread occurred rapidly and consistently. Third, the ideal terrorist agent would have no readily available vaccine. Once people were infected, the agent would have to be able to run its course without medical intervention or medical prevention from further infection. Fourth, the biological agent would have to be able to reproduce rapidly and be hardy enough to survive until ample contamination occurred.

The list of biological agents available to the terrorist is almost endless. Some of the available agents would have to be artificially synthesized in a culture facility (which could be a kitchen or bathroom), others could be used in their naturally occurring state. Some of the biological agents which would be attractive to terrorists might include anthrax, cryptococcosis, escherichia coli, haemophilus influenzae, brucellosis (undulant fever), coccidioidomycosis (desert fever), psittacosis (parrot fever), yersina pestis (the Black Death of the fourteenth century), tularemia (rabbit fever), malaria, cholera, typhoid, bubonic plague, cobra venom, and shellfish toxin. Of these agents, anthrax is the most toxic and would infect the most people. In an enclosed environment, for example, the release of anthrax in an aerosol spray could infect approximately 70,000 people within the first hour of its release (Mengel, 1979). The drawback with anthrax, as with many of the biological agents, is that the area infected by anthrax would remain infected for years or centuries (Harris & Paxman, 1982). This would defeat the terrorist purpose. Table 8.1 lists some of the biological agents conducive to terrorist usage.

Naturally occurring biological agents, like anthrax and botulinum toxin, are extremely lethal agents. Science, however, has produced even more deadly strains of biological agents. Recent advances in bioengineering and recombinant DNA technologies have provided the knowledge necessary to take naturally occurring agents and make them even deadlier. The eshcerischia coli, a harmless bacteria which resides in the human intestinal tract, can, by using recombinant DNA procedures, be turned into diphtheria toxin (Murphy, Hay, & Rose, 1984). Using bioengineering, a biological agent could be made more resistant to antidotes and vaccinations, made more virulent, made to last longer and produce worse effects, and made to disperse faster and affect more human biological systems. Some (see, for example, Day, 1989) have even suggested that "ethnic bombs" could be created, where the biological agent would only attack certain races of people, one sex or age group, or certain areas of a country. These radical biological weapons could introduce "ethnic cleansing by test tube" (Investigative Reports, 1995). With more technical sophistication, novel "treatment specific" agents could be developed. These agents would be ones which required medical treatment, and the medical treatment would cause a second, more severe agent to form in the person's system.

The research into biotechnology has produced several new categories of biological agents which could be used by the terrorist. One category has already been alluded to: the agents that are genetically altered that would make any vaccine worthless. These agents would resemble the original organism when viewed through a microscope, but their genetic structure would be altered just enough that existing vaccines would be useless in killing the organism.

A second category would be those agents that were previously dismissed as a weapon system because they were so difficult to collect. Many spider venoms and naturally occurring toxins could be produced artificially and in such quantities that they would become a viable weapon system. One example would be brown recluse spider venom.

A third category would be the unique combination of agents into new, more potent, and more lethal agents. These combination biologics would consist of multiple toxins combined into one bacteria, fungia, rickettsia, or virus, essentially a new and unique strain of a disease for which there would be no anti-toxin or vaccine.

Table 8.1.
Selected biological agents and their dissemination methods.

Disease, Target, and Type	Causative Agent	Dissemination
Anti-Animal Agents		
Fungi		
Aspergillosis	Aspergillus Funigatus	Food or dust
Lumpy-Jaw	Actinomyces Bovis	Food or dust
Viruses		
Foot and Mouth	FMD Virus	Food, water, aerosol
Newcastle Disease		Food, water, aerosol
Vesicular Stomatitis		Food, water, aerosol
Cattle Plague		Food, water, aerosol
Anti-Personnel Agents		
Bacteria		
Anthrax	Bacillus Anthracis	Aerosol
Brucellosis	Brucella	Aerosol
Cholera	Vibrio Comma	Water
Dysentery	Shigella	Food, water
Glanders	Actinobacillus Mallei	Aerosol
Plague	Pasteurella Pestis	Aerosol, fleas
Tularaemia	Francisella Tularensis	Aerosol
Typhoid	Salmonella Typhosa	Food, water, aerosol
Fungi		
Coccidioidomycosis	Coccidioides Immitis	Aerosol
Rickettsia		
Epidemic Typhus		Aerosol
Q Fever	Coxiella Burnetti	Aerosol
Rocky Mountain Fever		Aerosol, tick
Tsutsugamushi	Rickettsia Tsutsugamushi	Mites
Viruses		
Chikungunya		Aerosol, mosquito
Dengue Fever		Aerosol, mosquito
Haemorrhagic Dengue		Aerosol, mosquito
Influenza		Aerosol
Psittacosis	Chlamydia Psittaci	Aerosol
Rift Valley Fever	RVF Virus	Aerosol, mosquito
Yellow Fever		Aerosol, mosquito
Anti-Plant Agents		
Bacteria		
Corn Blight	Pseudomonas Alboprecipitans	Aerosol, dust
Rice Blight	Xanthomonas Oryzae	Aerosol, dust
Fungi		
Potato Blight	Phytophthora Infestans	Aerosol, dust
Rice Blast	Pyricularia Oryzae	Aerosol, dust
Rice Brown-Spot	Helminthosporium Oryzae	Aerosol, dust

Table 8.1. Continued.

Disease, Target, and Type	Causative Agent	Dissemination
Viruses		
Corn Stunt		Aerosol, windblown
Hoja Blance		Aerosol, windblown
Potato Yellow Dwarf		Aerosol, windblown
Sugar Beet Curly-Top		Aerosol, windblown

Fourth, biological regulators and hormones that occur naturally in the human body could be deregulated by certain biological agents. Unregulated, these hormones could produce lethal results.

Fifth, nanotechnology has made it possible to manufacture organisms at the molecular level. Biological agents could be produced one gene at a time in nanomachines, including programmable genes (replicating or non-replicating—Simon, 1994). These nanomachines would enable a scientist to create radically unique biological agents, not merely clones off known organisms. Botulis, for example, could be combined with anthrax to produce an organism which could infect a human with both biologics.

Sixth, as the world population expands and moves into rain forests and other remote locations, new biological agents are appearing with regularity. Most of these agents are extremely lethal and resist any attempts to develop vaccines and treatments. These "emerging infections" can be devastating to human populations and some are ideal for terrorist purposes. The AIDS virus, familiar to all, is an example of one of these viruses. The virus first appeared in Mossegah, Uganda and is 100 percent fatal. By the year 2010, over 100 million people will be infected with AIDS.

Another of the emerging viruses is the Ebola with three different strains: Marburg, Sudan, and Zaire. The Ebola strain of filoviruses (similar to measles, mumps, and rabies) is the perfect terrorist biological weapon. These virus strains have lethality rates between 50 percent and 100 percent, have no anti-serum or vaccine and are prone to extreme amplification, meaning they multiply so rapidly they turn the host into the virus (Preston, 1994). More ideally for the terrorist, and unlike AIDS, these viruses are hypermutant. Hypermutation is the case where the virus mutates within the course of one infection, making them totally resistant to any treatment. Fast acting, these viruses kill within two to seven days and can spread throughout a host population before the biological agent can even be identified, a condition Preston refers to as an explosive chain of lethal transmission.

The Ebola strains are so virulent that even corpses are infectious. The viruses liquefy the human body (Learning Channel, 1995). As explained by Preston (1994), the Ebola strain stuffs victims "with clots, and yet you bleed like a hemophiliac who has been in a fist fight. Your skin develops bruises and goes pulpy, and tears easily. Your intestines may fill up completely with blood. Your eyelids bleed. Ebola kills so much tissue that after death the cadaver rapidly deteriorates. In monkeys, and perhaps in people, a sort of melting occurs, and the corpse's connective tissue, skin, and organs begin to liquefy."

The extreme danger of the Ebola (and other emerging biological agents) was illustrated in an outbreak among monkeys in Reston, Virginia in the early 1990s. Monkeys from the Philippines were being quarantined in the Hazleton Research Products building, a division of Corning, Inc., when an Ebola outbreak occurred. Early in the 30-day quarantine period, one of the Crab Monkeys caught (or brought with him) the Ebola virus. Within one week, almost all of the monkeys had either died or become infected with the Ebola strain, later named Ebola Reston, after the quarantine facility. To stop the outbreak and ensure it did not spread beyond the monkey facility, USAMRIID (U.S. Army Medical Research Institute for Infectious Disease) teams completely sealed the building, killed all remaining monkeys, sprayed with bleach, and spread formaldehyde throughout the facility. To insure the building was sterile, USAMRIID introduced Bacillus Subtilis Niger, a harmless but extremely tough virus, into the facility. When the building was clear of traces of niger, the building was opened. The primates had initially been infected with Ebola Zaire, but somehow had mutated it into a harmless pathogen for humans. Disturbingly, the Reston infection was the first time Ebola had transmitted itself through the air (all previously known transmissions had occurred through contact with an infected host). Livingstone (1995) suggested that had this form of Ebola not mutated and infected humans, over 10,000 people in the Washington D.C. area would have been infected and the government would have had to close down. Relocating the government would have spread the virus to any location the government moved to.

Along similar lines, viruses have been inexplicably mutating as they move to different geographical areas. Dengue hemorraghic fever, for example, common to Asia, Latin America, Cuba, and other tropical locations, has been discovered in the United States. In Texas, Asian dengue cases first appeared in the early 1990s and has spread to over 17 states. It has mutated into unknown strains and has mutated to attack the human immune system. At present, scientists do not know how or why the virus mutated, nor do they know how to prevent mutations.

Other recently emerging viruses include lassa, rift valley fever, oropouche, ricio, Q guanarito, vee, monkeypox, chikungunya, hantaviruses, machupo, junin, mokola, devenhage, la dante, kyasanur forest brain virus, semliki forest agent, crimean-congo, sindbis, o'nyongnyong, and sao paulo. Most of these are amplification viruses and hypermutate. Their source is unknown, host organism has not been identified, transmission routes have been undiscovered, and antibodies not able to be developed. Most of these viruses have been replicated in research labs. If science can replicate these strains, so too can terrorists.

Finally, new agents could be produced which are smaller than bacteria which could freely pass through filters designed to keep out biological agents. These low-weight molecular agents could render obsolete gas masks, protective suits, clean rooms, etc.

As the Weather Underground was planning to do, a terrorist organization could steal a biological agent from a governmental research facility. Additionally, governments unsympathetic to the U.S. could sell or give biological agents to a terrorist organization. Virtually every government on the planet is engaged in biological research. Some of the leading governmental research programs, excepting the U.S. and Soviet Union, include Iran, Iraq, Libya, North Korea, and Syria, all anti-United States (Livingston, 1986). Moreso than with nuclear weapons, biological information and data are shared and readily available. Most nations have stockpiles of basic biological agents, and many would be willing to share with terrorist organizations.

Terrorists could steal biological agents from millions of university and private industry research laboratories. Most of these facilities have virtually no security systems in place. The penetration of most of these facilities would be easier than attempting to steal weapons from a private arms dealer. The terrorist would not necessarily need to steal the agent. They could enter, free release the organism, and leave. Table 8.2 lists some of the primary governmental and military biological research facilities in the U.S. and Soviet Union. To list the university and private biological research facilities would run the list into the thousands. Additionally, these university and private facilities have less security than government facilities. Many university laboratories have no security and are open 24 hours per day. Additionally, researchers at these university facilities undergo no security clearances.

If obtaining biological agents would be easy, the release of those agents would be easier. Biological agents could be placed into foodstuffs and liquids as a contaminant, spread as a vapor in an enclosed area, dispersed into an enclosed area via aerosol spray, or dispersed into an open area via vapor or aerosol (Hersh, 1968). The CIA has coined a term

Table 8.2.
United States and Soviet Union biological warfare research sites.

United States	Soviet Union
Center for Infectious Diseases at the Center for Disease Control	Aksu, Malta (rumored)
	All Union Research Institute for Molecular
Department of Commerce	Biology (Novosibirsk Oblast)
Department of Energy	Berdsk (rumored)
Department of the Interior	Byelorussian Research Institute for
	Epidemiology and Microbiology,
Government Services Division, the Salk Institute, Swiftwater, PA	Minsk
	D.I. Ivanovsky Institute for Virology,
Lawrence Livermore Laboratory	Moscow
Los Alamos National Laboratory, New Mexico	Irkutsk Anti-Plague Scientific Research Institute of Siberia and the Far
National Academy of Sciences	East, Irkutsk
National Cancer Institute, Frederick Research Facility, Frederick, Maryland	Kurgan (rumored)
	Moscow Research Institute for Viral
National Institutes of Public Health Service, Bethesda, Maryland	Preparations, Moscow
	N.F. Gamaleya Institute for Epidemiology
NASA	and Microbiology, Moscow
Naval Research Laboratory	Omutinisk (rumored)
Plum Island Animal Disease Center, Plum Island, NY	Penza (rumored)
U.S. Army Chemical Research, Development and Engineering Center	Pokrov (rumored)
	Scientific Research Institute for Poliomyelitis
U.S. Army Dugway Proving Ground	and Viral Encephalitis, Moscow Oblast
U.S. Army Human Engineering Laboratory	The Microbiology and Virology Institute, Sverdlovsk
U.S. Army Nataick Research, Development and Engineering Center	
	The Scientific Research Institute of Sanitation, Zagorsk
U.S. Army Research Office	
	Vozrozhdeniya Island (Aral Sea)
U.S. Atmospheric Sciences Laboratory	
Uniformed Services University of Health Sciences	
U.S. Army Medical Research Institute of Infectious Diseases, Ft. Detrick, Maryland	
Walter Reed Army Institute of Research	

for a biological agent release mechanism: *nondiscernible microbioinuculator* (Day, 1989). None of these dispersal methods would require any specialized knowledge or equipment. A pump spray bottle and a little water would be all that is required.

The most logical, and simplest, release mechanism for the terrorist would be nature. Fleas, flies, rats, and other small animals could be used for a natural spread of the biological agent by infecting a host population and then releasing the population into an area. The common housefly is capable of carrying and spreading over 30 diseases which would infect a human population, including cholera, typhoid, dysentery, bubonic plague, leprosy, cerebrospinal meningitis, diphtheria, scarlet fever, smallpox, and infantile paralysis. Anopheles, or malarial mosquito, could be free released. Mosquitoes can carry over 100 biological agents, and only two to five host mosquitoes would be needed to introduce a biological agent. In sum, the use of biological agents would be a low-risk option for the terrorist.

The one major drawback to the use of biological weapons in a terrorist operation is the ability to control the spread of the agent. With biological weapons, the terrorist would be just as much at risk as the target population. Almost any dispersal technique would expose the terrorist to as much risk as the target population. Once released, the organism is released. There is no ability to control the organism and prevent non-targets from becoming infected. The exception, obviously, would be the "ethnic bomb." Once again, however, science has assisted in overcoming this problem. Many biological agents can now be microencapsulated (Simon, 1994). Microencapsulation with biological agents is similar to the time-released medicine many people take to control colds and flu symptoms; the biological agent is released over a period of time as the containment vessel deteriorates. Using microencapsulation, the terrorist could release the organism at some point after departing the area and release would continue for a specified period of time, depending upon the capsule release rate.

Although the probability of terrorists employing biological agents is significantly higher than their use of nuclear weapons, biological terrorism has only a moderate likelihood. Unlike with nuclear weapons, it would be virtually impossible to gather intelligence on who released the agent. The probability of the terrorist being able to avoid detection is high. This advantage would be offset by the high probability of the terrorists themselves becoming infected with the agent. Self-infection would be the primary factor in causing the terrorist to avoid biological terrorism.

CHEMICAL TERRORISM

On 22 April 1915, at Ypres, France, the first recorded chemical attack of the twentieth century occurred when the German army released a large quantity of liquid chlorine over Allied lines. Over 10,000 French, Canadian, and Algerian soldiers were killed. This attack opened the way for large-scale chemical attacks by both sides, including the release of mustard gas (dichlorethyl sulphide). In these gas attacks, over 90,000 soldiers on both sides died from exposure to mustard gas. In the last 18 months of WWI, one of every six deaths was as a result of exposure to chemical agents (Harris & Paxman, 1982). During WWI, over 124,000 tons of chemical agents were used, killing over 91,000 people and injuring another 1.3 million.

During WWII, Hitler used Zyklon B as the death agent in the concentration camps, killing approximately 8–12 million Jews and Europeans. The Japanese used chemical agents against the Chinese, killing untold numbers. Development also began on a unique class of nerve agents that today have become the mainstay of the chemical arsenal. Zyklon-B was one of the first nerve agents used.

During the Vietnam War, the United States dropped over 11 million gallons of DDT in Vietnam and hundreds of thousands of gallons of napalm. Between 1983 and 1988, in the Iraq-Iran War, Saddam Hussein released large amounts of chemical agents on his enemies. In over 60 separate gas attacks, Hussein killed thousands of Iraqis and Kurds. One of the worst attacks occurred at the village of Halabja, where over 5,000 Kurds were killed and the entire village exterminated. Analysis has indicated Hussein used mustard gas, tabun, and cyanide in these attacks (Nova, 1990).

Governments have long attempted to regulate chemical weapon production and usage. The first chemical weapon treaty was the Hague Convention of 1899, which outlawed the use of any chemical weapons in warfare. In 1921, the Washington Treaty outlawed the use of any poison gases, but, because of France's refusal to sign the treaty (no doubt the result of that country's experience in WWI), the treaty never went into effect. In 1925, the Geneva Convention, signed by 28 major world powers, outlawed the use of chemical weapons. For the past 17 years, the Geneva Convention has been attempting to ban chemical weapons, without success. The banning of many chemical weapons would halt production of useful chemicals, and that is why the convention has not been able to pass a majority resolution against chemical weapon production. In September 1989, President Bush was able to get the Non-Chemical Treaty passed by the U.N., but it is doubtful any nation will abide by the terms of the treaty for the same reason they do not want to ratify any ban by the Geneva Convention.

Terrorists have used chemical agents (Alexander, 1983). In 1975, in Stuttgart, Germany, terrorists threatened to release mustard gas if all political prisoners in German prisons were not released. In 1976, U.S. postal authorities discovered a sealed envelope filled with a nerve agent. In 1978, the Israeli citrus fruit crop was contaminated by the Arab Revolutionary Army with liquid mercury, requiring the entire harvest to be destroyed. In 1985, the CSA compound was found to house over 200 liquid pounds of potassium cyanide (Bowers, 1988; Mullins, 1993). Force 17 of Fatah and Hezbollah have both trained in the use of chemical weapons (Alexander, 1993). In 1995, the Tokyo subway system was attacked with sarin, a derivative of parathion and one of the more powerful nerve agents. The mixture of sarin used was relatively weak. If they wished, the terrorists could have killed thousands of people. The delivery system chosen also suggests the terrorists did not want to kill numerous people. The chemical agent was allowed to slowly leak out of sealed plastic containers. By using an aerosol delivery system, the terrorists could have killed everyone in the subway system.

Chemical weapons may be the perfect NBC weapon for terrorists. Chemical agents have none of the problems associated with nuclear weapons, all of the advantages of the biological weapons, and are controllable in their dispersal (Douglas & Livingstone, 1987; Mullins & Becker, 1992). There are practically no disadvantages to the terrorist with chemical weapons.

Chemical agents can affect people in one of four ways (Vetter & Perlstein, 1991). One, chemicals can be blood agents, such as hydrogen cyanide and cyanogen chloride. Blood agents block the oxygen carrying capacity of blood cells and work by causing choking, tearing, and death. Two, there are the choking agents, such as chlorine, phosgene, and chloropicrin. These chemicals sear the lining of the respiratory passages. In essence, the person drowns in their own body fluids. Three, the blistering agents, such as sulfur mustard, nitrogen mustard, and lewisite, produce eye and skin irritations, temporary blindness, and respiratory problems. Victims usually die from respiratory complications. Four, and most deadly, are the nerve agents, such as tabun, sarin, soman, and VX. Nerve agents block the neural activity in the central nervous system. The fastest acting of the four types of chemicals, the nerve agents, can be absorbed through the skin.

Murphy, Hay, and Rose (1984) classified the chemical agents as lethal anti-personnel agents, harassing non-lethal personnel agents, incapacitating agents, anti-plant agents, and incendiaries. Lethal anti-personnel agents would consist of the nerve agents such as tabun and sarin. Non-lethal harassing agents would include chemical agents such as tear gas. Incapacitating agents would include chemicals such as BZ, similar to LSD. The anti-plant agents would include chemicals such as agent orange, a defoliant. Incendiaries are burning agents such as napalm and are designed to burn whatever they come into contact with.

The classification schemes of Vetter and Perlstein (1991) and Murphy, Hay, and Rose (1984) are somewhat incomplete and too general. A more comprehensive schema is proposed below and outlined in Table 9.3. One group of chemicals can be considered anti-plant agents, chemicals designed to affect plant life. Categories of anti-plant agents would include anti-crop agents, such as cacodylic acid, which are agents designed to attack and destroy one particular type of food crop. A second category would be the defoliants, such as 2,4-D and 2,4,5-T, those chemicals designed to kill any plant they come into contact with. A third category of anti-plant agents are the soil sterilants, such as bromacil, which are designed to prevent any plants from growing in the soil.

A second group of chemical agents are the casualty agents, designed to kill or seriously impair humans and animals. Categories of casualty agents are: (1) incapacitants, such as BZ, which are designed to tempo-rary impair and incapacitate; (2) incendiaries, such as napalm, which burn on contact; (3) nerve gases, such as sarin, which affect the nervous system and cause death; and (4) poison gases, such as chlorine, which can either kill or seriously injure. The mechanism in the poison gases category can involve blood, respiration, or other human systems.

The third group of chemical agents are the harassing agents. These irritants are designed to temporarily interfere with a human's ability to operate normally (i.e., fighting back, producing resistance, preventing a person from being able to work, etc.). The tear gases, pepper sprays, and similar chemicals are example of harassing agents.

The development and use of chemical agents would require the terror-ist to have some technological sophistication. Very few of the chemical agents attractive to terrorists are naturally occurring, although a hybrid category of chemical/biological agents, animal venoms, could easily be extracted from its host organism. Animals venoms, depending upon route of effect, could fit either the biological or chemical weapons category. Most chemical agents would have to be produced in a laboratory, and the laboratory would have to be more complex than a petrie tray in a refrigerator. With a basic working knowledge of chemistry, however, a chemical processing laboratory would not be difficult to build in an apartment or garage. One of the deadliest chemicals in the chemical arsenal, VX nerve gas, can be produced from information supplied in

Table 8.3.
Selected chemical agents and their dissemination methods.

Types of Agents	Common Name	Dissemination	Lethal Dose Mgs/ min meter
Anti-Plant Agents			
Anti-Crop	Cacodylic Acid	Diesel, Kerosene	100,000
Defoliants	2,4-D	Diesel, Kerosene	3,500–35,000
	2,4,5-T	Diesel, Kerosene	35,000–350,000
	Picloram	Diesel, Kerosene	
Soil Sterilants	Bromacil	Diesel, Kerosene	
	Monuron	Diesel, Kerosene	
Casualty Agents			
Incapacitants	BZ	Aerosol	None
Incendiaries	Napalm	Petrol Fuel	
	Magnesium	Solid	
Nerve Gas	Sarin (GB)	Vapor, liquid	100
	Soman (GD)	Vapor, liquid	50
	Tabun (GA)	Vapor, liquid	400
	VX	Vapor, liquid	10
Poison Gas	Chlorine	Vapor	19,000
	Hydrogen Cyanide	Vapor	2–5,000
	Lewisite	Vapor	1,300
	Mustard Gas	Vapor	1,500
	Phosgene	Vapor	3,200
Harassing Agents			
Irritants	CN	Aerosol	11,000
	CS	Powder	25,000
	CR	Liquid, Aerosol	25,000

books at the local library and requires no special materials or knowledges. Ball-point pen ink is only one chemical step removed from sarin.

Other chemicals can be purchased from chemical supply houses in ready-made form. Cobalt 60 and TEPP insecticides, for example, can be purchased at chemical supply houses, greenhouses, agricultural supply stores, and hardware stores (Alexander, 1983). Terrorists could also obtain chemicals from governments sympathetic to their cause. Kaddafi in Libya has stockpiled large quantities of tabun. Iran, Iraq, Russia, China, North Korea, Cuba, and a number of other countries could make chemicals available to terrorists. Libya and Syria have added their names to the chemical agent list (Corddry, 1988). The Libyan chemical manufacturing plant at Rabta was destroyed by fire in March 1990 but has since been rebuilt. Kaddafi is also building a chemical weapons plant at Sebha. Additionally, most of these countries have the full range of lethal chemicals in vast quantities.

Iraq has been one of the leading abusers of the production and use of chemical weapons. In the Iran-Iraq War, Hussein used mustard gas, cyanide, and nerve gasses against the Iranians and Kurds. These chemicals were produced at the Samarra plant in north Iraq in the early 1980s. More disturbingly, most of the manufacturing facilities and chemicals used to produce Hussein's chemical arsenal were provided by European and even U.S. companies, as has many other Mideastern chemical weapons plants. A chemical plant in Tessenderlo, Belgium, owned by Phillips Petroleum Company in Bartlesville, Oklahoma, filled three Iraqi orders for thiodiglycol (TDG), used to produce mustard gas. Over 500 metric tons of TDG were shipped to Iraq before the Belgiums refused to ship any more. SEPP, used in the production of mustard gas, cyanide, and nerve gas, was sold to the Iraqi Samarra plant by a West German company. In the late 1980s, U.S. authorities seized a shipment of potassium fluoride on its way to Iraq. Potassium fluoride is one of the primary ingredients in sarin. The German company Hippenstiel-Imhuasen was sentenced by the West German government for helping build the Rabta, Libya chemical weapons plant (Tuohy, 1989). Although the U.S. has banned export of many chemicals used in chemical warfare agent production, many of these chemicals are sold to hostile nations by other countries. Some of the restricted chemicals include potassium fluoride, dumethyl methylphosphonate, methylphospohonyl, phosphorous oxychloride, and thioglycol, all chemicals used in nerve gas production (Verrengia, 1995). Banning chemicals, however, will not slow the production of chemical weapons. Any factory that produces agricultural pesticides can produce a plethora of chemical warfare agents.

With the huge military storehouses of chemical weapons, terrorists could steal chemical agents. Compared to nuclear facilities and biological research laboratories, chemical agent storage sites would be the easiest to penetrate. Chemical storage sites are the least "target hardened" and have the laxest security. In the past two decades, governments have disposed of millions of tons of chemical agents in underground burial sites, pumped them into vast underground chambers, and sunk them in the ocean. All that would be necessary to recover the chemical is to locate the disposal site and go retrieve the chemical agent. Some U.S. disposal sites of nerve gases are the Umatilla Army Depot in Oregon, Bluegrass Army Depot in Kentucky, Anniston Army Depot in Alabama, Tooele and Pueblo Army Depots in Colorado, Johnson Island in the Pacific Ocean, and the Pine Bluff Arsenal in Arkansas (Greve, 1995). The Soviets have over 50,000 tons of similar chemical weapons stored at various sites throughout Eastern Europe (Nova, 1990). To illustrate the enormity of the readily available chemical agent problem, Tables 8.4 and

8.5 list some of the stockpiled chemical agents in the United States and USSR. For every pound of chemical agent listed, it is reasonable to assume that 100 pounds of that chemical has been disposed of by burial, underground internment, or dumped at sea.

Table 8.4.
Chemical warfare agents stockpiled in the United States.

Chemical	Common Name	Estimated Quantity
Anti-Plant Agents		
Anti-Crop	Cacodylic Acid	Millions of tons
Defoliants	2,4-D	Millions of tons
	2,4,5-T	Millions of tons
	Picloram	Unknown
Soil Sterilants	Bromacil	Millions of tons
	Monuron	Millions of tons
Casualty Agents		
Incapacitants	BZ (3-Quinuclidinyl Benzilate)	Few tons
	DM (Adamsite)	Few tens of tons
Incendiaries	Napalm	Few tens of tons
	Magnesium	Few tens of tons
Nerve Gas	Sarin (GB)	30 million pounds
	VX	10 million pounds
Poison Gas	Cyanogen Chloride	Few hundred pounds
	Hydrogen Cyanide	Few hundred pounds
	Mustard Gas (H, HD, HT)	35–40 million pounds
	Nitrogen Mustard (HN1)	Obsolete
	Phosgene (CG)	Residual stocks
Harassing Agents		
Irritants	CN (Chloroacetophenone)	Tens of tons
	CS (2-Chlorobenzal-malononitrile)	Few tens of tons

As with biological agents, the ability of the terrorist to synthesize, store, and use chemical agents would be virtually undetectable by intelligence and law enforcement agencies until after the fact. Few people would have to be involved in production and no sophisticated facilities would be required. An adequate laboratory could be built using locally obtained materials in any apartment or garage (Douglas, 1984). The terrorist would be caught only if unlucky (Livingstone & Arnold, 1986).

There are numerous methods by which chemical agents could be dispersed. Contamination of foodstuffs and liquids, vapor or aerosol in an enclosed or opened area, and individual administration are all techniques readily usable for chemical agent dispersal. Chemical agents

Table 8.5.
Chemical warfare agents stockpiled in the USSR.

Chemical	Common Name
Anti-Plant Agents	
UNKNOWN	
Casualty Agents	
Incapacitants	Psychochemicals
	DM (Adamsite)
	DA (Diphenylchloroarsine)
Incendiaries (UNKNOWN)	
Nerve Gas	Sarin (GB)
	Soman (GD)
	Soman, Thickened (GD)
	VR-55 (GD)
	Tabun (GA)
Poison Gas	Chloropicrin (PS)
	Cyanogen Chloride (CK)
	Diphosgene (DP)
	Hydrogen Cyanide (AC)
	Mustard Gas (H)
	Mustard/Lewisite (HL)
	Nitrogen Mustard (HN3)
Harassing Agents	
Irritants	CN (Chloroacetophenone)

could be released via unitary or binary delivery system. Unitary refers to a delivery system where the chemical agent is produced prior to use and delivered intact and fully operational. A binary delivery system keeps the chemical compounds separated and inert until delivered, whereupon the casement breaks and mixes the two chemicals to produce the lethal combination. For example, most delivery systems for nerve gasses are binary systems as a safety measure. With sarin, isopropanol is stored in one chamber and methyl phosphonyl diflouride in another chamber. When the weapon is released, an internal membrane bursts, mixing the two chemicals. The U.S. military rocket, the Bigeye, operates on the binary principle. Bullets, flechettes, and shrapnel could be impregnated with a chemical and used as contaminants (Robinson, 1977). In addition to wounds from the projectile, victims would be infected with the chemical agent. Tables 8.6 and 8.7 show some of the military delivery systems developed by the U.S. and Soviet Union for delivery of chemical weapons.

One major advantage of chemical agents over nuclear or biological weapons is that by using the right chemicals, any effects could be delayed for a period of time. The agent could be dispersed and it could be hours

Table 8.6.
United States chemical warfare munitions delivery systems.

Weapon System	Munition	Agent
Air Force Weapons	CBU-16 Dispenser	BZ
	TMU-28 Spraytank	VX
	Aero-14B Spraytank	GB, VX
	CBU-15 Dispenser	GB
	BLU-52 750 pound bomb	CS
	All 500 and 750 pound bombs	GB
	M-10 Spraytank	HD
	M-10 Spraytank	HD
	XM80/XM99	CS
	E158/XM15 Cluster Bomb	CS
	M44/M43/CBU-5	BZ
Naval Weapons	All Naval Delivery Weapons	GB
Ground Forces	Land Mines	HD, VX
	M79 40 mm Grenade Launcher	CS
	M30 107 mm Mortar	H, HD, HT, CS
	Howitzers (all sizes)	HD, GB, VX, CS
	M2 155 mm Gun	HD, GB
	M107 175 mm SP Gun	GB, VX
	M91 115 mm 45-tube MRL	GB, VX
	M51 Little John	GB
	M50 Honest John	GB, VX
	SRBM	GB, VX

or months before any effects appeared in the target population. In 1971, Iraq purchased 100,000 tons of grain contaminated with methylmercury dicyanidamite. It was several weeks before any signs and symptoms of mercury poison appeared in those who had ingested the grain, and by then it was too late. Over 6,000 people died and another 100,000 were blinded or paralyzed. In Michigan in 1983, Firemaster (a PBB flame retardant) was inadvertently introduced into cattle feed. It was estimated that over 9 million people were affected, and in those affected, symptoms may not appear for years. Although neither case is terrorist related, they do illustrate the delayed effects of chemical poisoning.

Another advantage of chemical agents over biological agents is the storage life of chemical agents. Chemical agents have an active life significantly longer than that of biological agents. With biological agents, the terrorists have to use the agents virtually immediately or the biological agent will die. Chemical agents can remain stored for years and decades without losing any potency. VX nerve gas, when dispersed, can remain active anywhere from 3–16 weeks, depending upon climatic

Table 8.7.
USSR chemical warfare munitions delivery systems.

Weapon System	Munition	Agent
Air Force Weapons	Rotational Scattering Bombs	AC, GD
	Incendiary Bombs	AC, GD
	Fragmentation Bombs	Mustard, or BZ
	AK-2	Phosgene
	BATT	AC
Ground Forces	Land Mines	Mustard, Lewisite
	Mortars	Mustard, Lewisite
	Tube Artillery	Mustard, Lewisite
	BM 21/40 122 mm 40-tube rocket	AC, GD
	BM 14/16 140 mm 16-tube rocket	AC, GD
	BMD 25, 250 6-rail rocket	AC, GD
	All FROGs	AC, GD
	SCUD–A SS-1b & SCUD–B SS-1c	AC, GD
	Shaddock SSC-1	AC, GD
	Scaleboard SS-12	AC, GD

conditions. Thus, it is not necessary that the target audience come into immediate contact with the chemical agent. Nerve agents can also be stored for generations and still retain their full potency.

Another way terrorists could use chemical agents would be by making the agent itself the weapon. A well-coordinated attack on a liquid natural gas (LNG) ship would produce an explosion comparable to that of a small nuclear weapon. LNG is made by reducing natural gas to less than one six-hundredth of its vapor volume by liquefying the gas at -260 degrees Fahrenheit. When the liquid contacts normal air, it expands. This expansion would produce the initial explosion. Being heavier than air, the gas would settle toward the ground, and if contacted by a spark (such as static electricity or a friction spark from the metal shrapnel), the gas would then detonate. All of this, of course, would occur in milliseconds. The total explosive energy of LNG in one large tank would be greater than the total energy released by all of the bombs dropped on Tokyo during WWII (Clark, 1980).

The use of chemical agents could be controlled to a much greater extent than could nuclear or biological agents. The delivery of chemical agents could be accomplished with exact precision, thus insuring that only the target audience was affected. Additionally, most chemicals disperse rapidly and the target would be clear for the terrorists to enter. There would be no trace elements as there would be with nuclear or biological agents. The target area would be safe for habitation. Massive amounts of chemical agents could be delivered in one terrorist operation. Thatcher and Aeppel (1989), for example, have stated that 15 tons of nerve agents could be delivered by one strategic bomber over a 24-square-mile area, kill 50 percent of the exposed population and contaminate the entire area for several months.

With chemical agents, the only detection mechanisms are reactive. The agent cannot be detected until after it has been released. The U.S. military is working on several systems to detect chemical agents, including specialized ground vehicles and helicopter laser systems that reflect energized ions that are spectral analyzed. Although these systems are effective in detecting chemical agents and can help protect military forces from exposure, they are virtually worthless should a terrorist decide to employ chemical terrorism. If they detected a terrorist release of a chemical agent, the sensor systems could do nothing to stop the attack or deter the immediate population from becoming infected by the agent.

In sum, millions of casualties could result in a single chemical episode; there would be no insurmountable technological problems in obtaining, producing, or using chemicals; dispersal would be simple and widespread, controllable by the user of the agent; and there would be minimal risk of detection (Mullins & Mijares, 1995; Stephens & Mackenna, 1988). Chemicals are as close to the perfect terrorist weapon as is possible. Of the three NBC alternatives, chemical weapons are the most suited to and those with the highest probability of terrorist usage (David, 1985). It is extremely possible that terrorists will rely on chemical agents extensively in the future, producing massive casualty rates and the greatest fear terrorism has ever produced.

SUMMARY

The IRA has oft repeated to the English government, "You have to be lucky every time. We have to be lucky only once." These words become even more chilling and infinitely horrendous when applied to the terrorist use of NBC weapons. One unlucky stroke for the U.S. government or law enforcement could prove devastating. NBC weapons, long a staple of military control and supervision, have been released and made available to the terrorist. The question of interest concerning the terrorist use of these weapons is not if but when. When will terrorists be forced to escalate to using these weapons to gain the attention they desire and produce the fear they require? When will terrorists obtain a sufficient quantity of these weapons to make their use a viable tool for terrorism? When will we be unlucky in catching the terrorists before they can unleash these weapons? When will the face of terrorism be changed by one or more political fanatics? When will the public suffer at the hands of an unseen and unrecognizable weapon?

NBC weapons are terrorism of the future (Mullins, 1990a, 1990b, 1991a). Nuclear weapons have a low probability of terrorist usage, chemical weapons a high probability. Like throwing dice, probabilities are just that—probabilities. Probability theory calculates not if an event will occur but when that event will occur. As the NBC weapons become more available, as the technology of science improves, and as information becomes more readily available, the when becomes more assured of occurring on the time line. "When" will happen. Of that there is no question.

Nuclear terrorism, if nuclear detonation is considered the only form of nuclear terrorism, is still several years away. The major threat of nuclear terrorism is the release of radioactive material into the atmosphere, either via releasing a radioactive material or destroying a power plant or other nuclear facility. Operations of those types are now within the ability of the terrorist. Obtaining a nuclear weapon is still several years away, although there are several governments more than willing to assist the terrorist cause. Even with this assistance, there are too many factors working against the terrorist to make this a viable option.

Biological terrorism is more of a threat than nuclear terrorism. The biological agents attractive to terrorists are readily available. There are few restrictions to prevent terrorists from employing biological terrorism other than self-inflicted infection. To the suicidal terrorist, however, this is not a restriction. Biological agents may produce the most fear of all the NBC agents. Perceptually, disease scares people more than any other event. Diseases work from the inside out, they cannot be seen, and the unknown cannot be treated proactively. Only after the unexpected disease has been acquired can preventive measures be undertaken, and by then it is too late.

Chemical agents are the most likely NBC agents to be employed by terrorists. The terrorist has a wide range of weapons to select from; most are easy to produce, store, and use. The terrorist can release the agent in delayed action form and avoid any intelligence efforts to determine who was responsible. In all, chemical agents are the perfect terrorist weapon. Assume that instead of being bombed, the Oklahoma City Federal Building had been subjected to a delayed chemical attack. The attacker could have placed the chemical weapon in an unobtrusive place and delayed release for several months. Many more could have been killed with no property damage. No incriminating evidence would have been left at the scene. Media coverage would have been greater. Fear in the public would have exponentially increased, especially if the terrorist threatened to repeat the attack at another location. An attack of this nature would make the bombing pale by comparison.

Morally, there are little sanctions against using any of the NBC weapons. Terrorists have learned that political change can only be produced by mass casualty actions or actions they can "win" (i.e., Iranian embassy takeover). An NBC threat or attack is a winnable action. If an operation requires massive casualties, then the terrorist is willing to conduct that operation.

What can prevent NBC terrorism? Very little. Education can reduce the threat by providing answers to what options are available to the terrorist. Education cannot prevent the terrorist from obtaining, developing, constructing, or using the NBC weapons. Education can help law enforcement understand what is occurring, which in turn can help in allaying the public fear of these weapons. Education and understanding, in turn, can assist in minimizing the damage once these weapons are released. Education can also reduce the probability of these weapons from being used. Knowing what and where to look will delay the use of these weapons and minimize damage when released.

Chapter 9

COUNTER-TERRORISM AND LEGAL ISSUES

Whenever a terrorist atrocity occurs, the immediate question asked by the public is why the government or law enforcement did not do more to prevent the event. When people become victimized by terrorism and afraid for their safety, they also become angry with the government for not doing more to prevent terrorism. The perception of the public is that terrorism can be treated like more ordinary criminal behavior. That is, the public perceives that once the government has identified terrorists, or organizations with the potential to engage in terrorist activity, the government should immediately arrest those individuals.

What people do not recognize nor understand is that the very complexity of the political agenda of the terrorist is the very factor that makes it so difficult to deal with terrorists. Barring a physical criminal act, terrorism is a political ideology. Terrorists want political change, and under the current Constitution of the United States, calling for political change, in and of itself, is not illegal. People can hold any belief they wish, can argue for that belief in public forums, and can demonstrate and protest for change. The documents which assure the freedom to live in the U.S. provides the same freedoms to disagree.

With few exceptions, what this means is that the government is almost forced into the position of dealing with terrorists on a reactive basis. That is, terrorists have to commit a physical criminal act before they can be arrested. The system could be changed so it is more proactive in terms of responding to terrorism. Basic rights and freedoms could be taken away from the public and the government made to be more proactive. But what would be the cost of taking this approach? This approach would realistically mean taking away the rights guaranteed by the Constitution to disagree. Under this approach, extremists on both the left and right of the continuum could be arrested for believing and arguing for political change. That would significantly reduce terrorism in the United States.

That approach would also cost the public many other freedoms, however. It would mean that any dissent, argument, or protest would be banned.

Any deviation from the party line would place the citizen in jeopardy of harassment and arrest by the government. It would also mean the end of the right to peacefully assemble, the freedom to move around unimpeded by the government, the end to select where and how to live one's life, and the end to the ability to choose. Tightening the legal strictures on terrorists would bring about an end to the U.S. way of life and place the nation within the same system as the Soviets operated under Lenin and Stalin.

It would also mean government intrusion into the private lives of citizens. Unannounced searches, loss of protection from unreasonable search and seizure, unwarranted intrusion into private affairs by the government, loss of autonomy and right to live one's life as one wished, and constant surveillance and interference in all other aspects of the individual's life would become the standard in the United States. No area of life would be free from government interference. In 1995, people complained about heightened airport security and the inconveniences the increased security made in their ability to travel. Image the same or worse level of intrusion into everyday life. Imagine roadblocks at every other intersection to inspect for proper documentation (i.e., ID cards, driver's license, not drinking and driving, no contraband, etc.). Imagine agents conducting random and unannounced searches of private residences at all hours of the day and night. Imagine not having the ability to move about freely, nor being able to live as you wish. Imagine both the press and individual thoughts being subject to censorship.

The ability to completely counter terrorism and reduce terrorism to zero occurrence would require the creation of a totalitarian state. Further, who would be responsible for labeling an organization terroristic? What organizations would be considered terroristic? It is conceivable the Boy Scouts of America could be considered terroristic. They do, after all, wear uniforms, march around, learn survival skills, and have a code of honor. Other youth organizations, church societies, labor unions, and even professional associations could be targeted as terrorist organizations. Once begun, the restrictions placed upon the public would never end.

This solution does not take into consideration the problem presented by foreign-based terrorists. Halting immigration and completely sealing the borders could prevent foreign terrorists from conducting operations within the U.S. What measures would be necessary to prevent Americans from being attacked while overseas? The only effective measure would be to prevent citizens from traveling overseas.

Terrorist attacks overseas often produce a hue and cry for rapid and massive military retaliation. The ramifications of such actions often carry political concerns over and above the necessity of preventing terrorism. France, for example, threatened to withdraw from NATO following Reagan's 1984 bombing of Libya. England filed formal protests, and other nations publicly condemned the U.S. strikes. To eliminate terrorism would result in the U.S. becoming a world dictator of foreign policy and economics.

This chapter will explore the alternatives open to the U.S. in stopping terrorism, the response options open to the government and law enforcement, and the legal attempts undertaken to control terrorist behavior. As will be shown, these attempts have ranged from the passive to active. Passive measures might include doing nothing more than being politically reactive when terrorists commit a criminal act. Active measures could range to conducting full military retaliatory strikes.

RESPONSE OPTIONS TO TERRORISM

There are only two general options available in responding to terrorism. One option involves proactive measures. Proactive measures are things which can be done prior to terrorist activities to stop those activities from occurring. The severity of measures employed can range from collecting and analyzing data to conducting preemptive military strikes against potential terrorists. The other available response option is reactive, or attempting to catch terrorists after they engage in a terrorist operation. Reactive measures can range from investigative and identification strategies to full-scale military reactive strikes.

Sandler, Enders, and Lapan (1993) define response options as being either active or passive. Their range of response option categories redefines somewhat the concept of proactive and reactive. Active responses are measures designed to pursue terrorists, both on a proactive and reactive basis. Active responses could range from organization infiltration (more proactive) to retaliatory raids (reactive). Passive responses could include measures such as making international treaties (proactive) to instituting stricter laws (more reactive). The typology of responses elucidated by Sandler, Enders, and Lapan assumes both proactive and reactive terrorist responses can range from passive to active.

Whether reactive or proactive, responses to terrorism can include both anti-terrorist and counter-terrorist measures. Anti-terrorist measures are more defensive in nature and designed to protect, while counter-terrorism measures are more offensive oriented and designed to respond to terrorist incidents (Vetter & Perlstein, 1991). Anti-terrorist measures might include barricades, intelligence collection, and education. Counter-terrorism would involve more active measures such as specially trained units to use intelligence and arrest terrorists, specially trained military teams designed to attack terrorist strongholds, or special legislation enacted following a terrorist atrocity.

Sloan (1987) added a third category to the response options: preemption. Terrorist preemption is offensive reactions initiated against terrorists, sponsoring states, or terrorist supporters. Preemption is designed to prevent or deter terrorist operations or campaigns directed against U.S. citizens. Preemption is primary proactive and more military-response oriented than anti- or counter-terrorism usually is. The Gulf War was preemptive in nature concerning Iraq activities against the U.S. Preemptive terrorism could also include economic or legal sanctions designed to prevent terrorism.

Responses to terrorism can range from the political to military. Political responses to terrorism might include the establishment of treaties, legal arrangements with other nations, or international laws designed to prevent or respond to terrorism. Military responses would involve military actions undertaken to respond to terrorism. Somewhere along the continuum between these two responses would be law enforcement. In many respects, the law enforcement response to terrorism usually involves some combination of political and military-type responses.

Finally, responses to terrorism, proactive versus reactive, anti-terrorism and counter-terrorism, preemptive operations and political versus military responses, can be designed to respond to terrorism within the U.S. or to foreign-based terrorism. The responses, obviously, available within the U.S. are different than ones that might be employed overseas. Very few military options, for example, can be employed within the U.S. Many legal options available within the U.S. cannot be employed overseas. The ability to respond to terrorism is greater with domestic terrorists than for foreign terrorists operating externally to the U.S. Dealing with foreign terrorists involves political ramifications of the U.S. operating within foreign countries. Responses are limited to the rules established by that government. A government may, for example, not permit U.S. law enforcement agencies to collect intelligence data, nor arrest terrorists, nor extradite terrorists. Also, the range of options available in responding to domestic terrorism or foreign terrorists operating within the U.S. are greater than those available for responding to foreign terrorism.

The responses to terrorism are on an overlapping continuum, meaning that the responses available interact and are somewhat limited by other variables. A decision to be completely proactive in preventing terrorism would be limited if the government decided to employ military counter-terrorist measures. Focusing on only domestic terrorism, likewise, would limit completely reactive military responses. A purely political, anti-terrorist approach would limit reactive measures to stop terrorism. Examining proactive-reactive, anti-counter-terrorism, preemptive responses, government-military responses, and responses designed for the U.S. versus abroad would require a spatial model that represented these response options (or factors) on a four-dimensional model. The ability to visualize and understand the complex interplay between the various response factors would serve to confuse the issue of responses more than clarify.

Introducing one response option may reduce one type of terrorism but may increase another type of terrorist activity. The installation of metal detectors at airports will decrease terrorist incidents of hijacking but lead to increases in hostage taking, bombings, and assassinations. Fortifying buildings reduces bombings and hostage taking but increases assassinations. More drastic responses such as military raids and military strikes tend to increase threats, assassinations and bombings but has no long-term effect on terrorist activity (Sandler, Enders, & Lapan, 1993). Terrorists are well-schooled in adapting their operations to exploit the weaknesses of response options. Terrorists use unexpected operations and tactics to create situations the government and law enforcement are not able to deal with (Wardlaw, 1982).

Responding to terrorism must involve a multidimensional approach. Using only limited responses to terrorism will be ineffective and unconstructive. Placing barricades in front of buildings without taking other measures to prevent terrorism will only serve to change the form of terrorist operations without significantly reducing those operations. To be effective, the government must rely on multiple response options to counter terrorism. The full range of responses must be employed if terrorism is to be effectively reduced and the citizens protected. A drastic military response to one organization may prevent that organization from continuing operations, but will do little to prevent other organizations from conducting terrorist operations. Increasing airport security will not prevent terrorists from bombing buildings. Strengthening immigration laws will not prevent domestic terrorism.

Also, concentrating on foreign terrorism reduces resources to combat domestic terrorism and vice versa. Resources available to counter terrorism are very limited. Expending those resources in one area reduces available resources in another. The only way to truly be effective at preventing terrorism is to increase and diversify the available resources.

Policy Issues

Any responses made to terrorism must be made based upon a standardized and firm policy regarding terrorism. At the international level, the government has attempted to establish a policy line in dealing with terrorists. According to Gist (1990) and Bremer (1990), the U.S. government policy on countering terrorism consists of three elements. One, the government has a no concession and no ransom policy in dealing with terrorists. Two, the U.S. government works with other countries to put pressure on terrorists. The countries that usually support terrorism, such as Cuba, Iran, Libya, North Korea, etc., have been subjected to international economic, political, diplomatic, and military pressures. Three, the government works with ally nations to develop counter-terrorist measures, such as sharing of intelligence to identify terrorists, their goals, ideologies, area of operation, tracking their movements, confiscating weapons and dangerous materials that could be used in weapon systems, apprehending terrorists, and prosecuting and punishing the terrorists.

The weakest of these political response options concerns the U.S. non-negotiation policy (Simon, 1994). Since the early 1960s (and even to a degree under the Eisenhower administration), the U.S. has publicly announced the government will not negotiate with terrorists nor provide any ransom. The reality is, however, that the U.S. does negotiate and does pay ransom. In countless hostage incidents, including the Iranian embassy, TWA flight 847, and a variety of Beirut hostage situations, the government has negotiated and acceded to terrorist demands. For a policy strategy to be effective, it must be adhered to without exception. The non-negotiation policy has not been adhered to; thus, terrorists see a basic weakness on the part of the U.S. and will continue to take hostages.

On the domestic front, the government has no unified policy concerning treatment of terrorists. Instead, law enforcement agencies are left to their own resources concerning the handling of terrorists. Almost every agency has their own policies in handling terrorism, and most of these policies are reactive (some proactive measures will be discussed later in this chapter). Some incidents are negotiated, some are met with force. Two recent examples of the latter include the Randy Weaver standoff in Idaho and the Branch Davidian incident in Waco, Texas. State and municipal agencies have their own policies concerning terrorists. Some agencies negotiate, some rely on tactical solutions, and others rely on federal agencies.

The lack of consistency in responses to terrorism is one of the single greatest deterrents in the government's ability to stop domestic terrorism. The fragmentation and infighting of agencies responding to terrorist activity leads to a loss of ability to be proactive in fighting terrorism. The lack of response consistency actually reinforces the terrorist to commit activities. The terrorist knows that disunity actually assists their cause and makes people more sympathetic to the terrorist cause. Growth of the militia movement literally exploded following the Randy Weaver siege and Branch Davidian standoff. People perceived an inappropriate government response to terrorism and supported these types of movements to show their displeasure with the government response.

Another political option available to the government is the erection of physical barriers. The placement of physical barriers is a political reaction to terrorism and is often a measure taken instead of more drastic legal changes. Physical barriers are generally seen as less intrusive on individual rights than are legal remedies. For example, physical barriers around the White House are not as psychologically imposing as are laws which restrict all access and visitations to the White House. Physical barriers can range from the totally unintrusive (fences around a building that do not limit access) to totally intrusive (draconian airport security measures). U.S. foreign embassies typically have a high degree of physical security and multiple barriers, including concrete fences, concrete barricades to prevent vehicle bombs, armed guards that personally check every visitor, badges for visitors to wear, and U.S. Marine Corps guards for the property and embassy personnel. Many have bulletproof glass and are target-hardened to prevent heavy weapons attacks.

In the U.S., many federal buildings have fences, metal detectors, visitor passes, armed guards, vehicle barriers, and camera surveillance systems. For fear of terrorism, parts of Pennsylvania Avenue near the White House were closed to vehicle and foot traffic. In the wake of the Oklahoma City Federal Building bombing, physical security measures have been increased at all federal buildings. Most state and municipal buildings have followed suit and increased their security. Airport security has always been present, but has increased in recent years.

The development of physical security measures is a multi-million dollar industry. All efforts are directed toward further target-hardening buildings and airplanes. In the airline industry, for example, new physical security measures include bombproof cargo containers and new x-ray technology which can detect certain types of plastic explosives in stored luggage. The search for more perfect barriers has extended to the consideration of plants to provide security. Trifoliate Orange is a plant marketed as a security system for buildings (Stone, 1990). Trifoliate Orange, a member of the citrus family, can grow up to 25 feet in one year and has four-inch thorns. The bush is so dense it can stop a slow-moving jeep.

Most physical security measures serve merely to produce the perception in the public that they are secure from terrorist attack when visiting these buildings or flying. History and experience have shown that these physical security measures do little to deter terrorists. Very few security devices are going to prevent the dedicated terrorist. Airplanes and military installations are the most target-hardened of all structures. Terrorists still attack these structures on a frequent and regular basis. Every measure taken to target-harden these structures has been defeated by the terrorist. Even when these physical measures do deter, the terrorist selects another type of operation.

If physical security measures become too severe, the public will not tolerate the security and perceive the terrorists to have "won." The public will demand security be relaxed to the point that inconvenience is reduced or eliminated. Reducing security to lesser levels, in essence, means no security. In many cases, such as air flight, the public wants to be secure but not inconvenienced. Inconvenience means security from terrorism, but it also means distress in one's personal life. The public does not want distress, even though it means more personal threat.

Additionally, target-hardening physical structures does not protect the terrorist's victims when away from the building. If the terrorist is intent upon killing or kidnapping certain individuals, target-hardening the physical workplace only provides a temporary respite from the terrorist. The terrorist could attack the victim while traveling, at home, at other businesses, etc. In all respects, physical security measures mean little to the terrorist. They are only minimally effective in deterring terrorists and do nothing to prevent terrorism.

Other political solutions to terrorism have been proffered. Lopez (1993) suggested effective counter-terrorism measures would include the establishment of international criminal courts to try terrorists, the establishment of an international grievance agency under the control of the United Nations, the development of international mediation agencies, creation of a U.N. commission to examine human rights violations and abuses, developing international arms sale treaties, and the development of new international economic orders. Lopez also suggested governments could significantly reduce terrorism by including non-governmental political actors in policy decisions. Ethnic minorities, stateless peoples and refugees could be provided forums to air grievances and explore their political agenda. Further, forums could be established within the international community for dissatisfied actors and organizations. For example, the PLO could be provided representation within the U.N. An open political forum in which the PLO could express its grievances would likely reduce PLO terrorism.

This last course of action is unwise, because it legitimizes not only the terrorist organization but the legitimacy of terrorism as a tool for political change. Making international concessions to terrorists would not reduce terrorism, it would increase terrorism. Legitimizing terrorism by allowing terrorists legitimate forums to express their political ideology would significantly increase the number of terrorists in the world, as anybody with any type of grievance would lead people to use terrorism to gain political recognition.

Lopez (1993) also suggested that the development and enforcement of a behavioral code for multinational corporations and governments could reduce terrorism. These codes could standardize government actions in attempting to lure businesses. South Africa, for example, provides favorable climates for international businesses by deliberately suppressing the population (i.e., extremely low minimum wage laws). By creating these conditions, governments foster the growth and use of terrorism. Additionally, the international code of behavior would prohibit businesses from paying ransoms to terrorists. This business code of conduct is not reasonable or realistic. The establishment of such a code would remove the sovereign right of government to rule as they wished and would not reduce terrorism. If economic conditions were improved, for instance, political extremists would find another outlet for their terrorism.

To the above suggestions, Kidder (1990) proposed improved international cooperation and more careful attention to U.S. foreign policy decisions. According to Kidder, many terrorist attacks on U.S. citizens are not the fault of inadequate security but the result of mistaken U.S. foreign policy decisions. Lack of security at the Marine barracks in Beirut provided a simple explanation that covered a more serious flaw in government foreign policy. According to Kidder, a reexamination of government policy would significantly reduce terrorism.

Intelligence Issues

Almost all would agree that the single most significant drawback to effectively countering terrorism is the lack of adequate intelligence efforts. On all intelligence fronts, political, economic, scientific, technical, political, and ideological, there is a lack of the collection, dissemination, and use of intelligence information. Producing useful intelligence requires three steps (Poland, 1988). Step one involves the collection of intelligence data on terrorists. Intelligence can be collected from open records sources, criminal information sources, clandestine agents and informants, and intelligence services such as the military, CIA, NSA, FBI, and Interpol. Step two involves the usefulness of the intelligence information. Intelligence data should be analyzed as it meets the Three R criteria: relevancy, reliability, and rationality. Step three in the intelligence response involves the complete dissemination and disposition of intelligence data. The information needs to be collated, evaluated, trends analyzed, a threat analysis conducted, relevant intelligence stored for easy retrieval and relayed to the political decision makers and law enforcement agencies who need the intelligence.

At present, each of the three intelligence response steps are inadequate. First, there is no concerted effort to collect appropriate intelligence, nor are there any common criteria nor priorities for collectors and evaluators (Amit, 1993). Most intelligence is descriptive in nature, not analytical, and comes from secondary source materials (Ross, 1993). Much of the intelligence American law enforcement officials rely upon is provided by the *FBI Bomb Summary, Uniform Crime Reports,* or *FBI Analysis of Terrorist Incidents and Terrorist Related Activities in the U.S.* This data is biased by the FBI's definition of terrorism and has no statistical analyses to summarize the data and make it useful. All federal, state, and most municipal agencies collect their own data and there is very little effort to share that data among agencies that may benefit from the intelligence. At the Randy Weaver and Branch Davidian incidents, one federal agency began the situation without working with other agencies in collecting intelligence. Neither did the federal agencies work with state or munici-pal agencies in collecting intelligence information. Had there been a unified intelligence collection apparatus, neither situation would likely have occurred. The very concept of multijurisdictional law enforcement is a benefit to the terrorist because of the problems in law enforcement intelligence cooperation and sharing (Stinson, 1993).

Finally, and most serious of intelligence problems within the law enforcement community, intelligence on terrorist organizations is not disseminated nor shared among different agencies. There is a degree of provincialism in the law enforcement community centered around "protecting one's own turf." Thus, when intelligence is collected, there is a reluctance to share with other agencies. Furthermore, the more serious the criminal activity, the less the sharing between agencies. Because terrorists move around quite a bit, the intelligence collected by one agency, if not disseminated, becomes useless. Efforts to capture members of almost every terrorist organization in recent history has been thwarted by lack of willingness to share intelligence.

Amit (1993) suggests that for intelligence to become useful as a tool in the war against terrorists, several things must occur. One, a static network for the collection of intelligence must be established. This unit, agency, or group must be the repository for all intelligence, regardless of what agency collects the intelligence. Two, criteria must be established for evaluating and analyzing this data. The criteria must be prioritized using threat assessment procedures so the most dangerous terrorist organizations are given the highest priority, or those organizations who have the highest probability of becoming violent are given the highest priority. Three, a communications network must be established between the intelligence collectors and law enforcement agencies at all levels. Federal, state, and affected local law enforcement agencies must have equal access to the intelligence data and must work together to bring their full, collective weight against the organization. One agency cannot be omitted from the loop. Four, priorities and criteria for decision making and resource allocation must be developed. Five, the intelligence collectors and operational personnel must work together. The combined resources of the law enforcement community must be brought to bear on terrorists for any measures to be effective in stopping terrorism.

Stinson (1993) argues the greatest detriment to counter-terrorist efforts is the lack of centralized intelligence and data analysis. As did Amit (1993), Stinson argues there must be a centralized intelligence collection unit, and threat assessment methodologies are necessary to prioritize the intelligence. Stinson suggests that at both the international and national levels, the intelligence-gathering efforts could be better served by having regional intelligence networks that funnel intelligence data to the primary collection agency. For such a system to be viable, mechanisms would have to be established to reverse the intelligence flow to ensure the analyzed data got back to the agencies that need the intelligence data. These regional networks would also have to realize that law enforcement agencies have different capabilities and specialties in the areas of use of informants, interception techniques, surveillance and counter-surveillance capabilities, intelligence collection ability, agent handling, and investigative capability. Agencies would have to be utilized according to their strengths and weaknesses.

Systematic threat assessment procedures must be utilized by all agencies attempting to collect and collate intelligence data on terrorist organizations. These procedures must conform to the fundamental principles of threat assessment methodology. First, the context of potential violence must be identified. As Fein, Vossekuil, and Holden (1995) indicate, violence does not occur in a vacuum but is the result of the violent perpetrators, stimulus or triggering conditions, and a setting that facilitates or permits the violence. Second, attack-related behaviors must be identified. Terrorists will perform behaviors that precede and are related to operational behavior. Terrorists develop strategy, plan, and prepare for an operation. In industrial/organizational psychology, an old axiom states: "The best predictor of future behavior is past behavior." Terrorists are predictable in their operations. By examining attack-related behaviors, it becomes possible to predict future behavior.

Third, multi-agency resources must be used to investigate pre-operational contexts and behaviors. The threat assessment must be focused toward identifying terrorists with a potential for violence, assessment of violence as a function of time, and management of the threat, both of terrorists and the targets.

Once terrorists capable of violence have been identified, the threat assessment must concentrate on evaluating the threat the terrorists pose. This process involves a comprehensive investigation of the terrorist and an evaluation of the risk. The investigation should focus on interviews with the terrorists (when possible): materials the terrorists possess, such as books, magazines, articles, personal writings, etc.; persons familiar with the terrorists, such as family, coworkers, friends, neighbors, etc.; and historical and archival information such as law enforcement records, propaganda, and other data material. Data must also be collected on potential targets. This data should concentrate on identifying and rating potential targets based upon information gained concerning the terrorists, potential weaknesses and vulnerabilities of the target, resources available to the target, target-hardening capabilities, etc. Evaluation should focus on behaviors and actions consistent with an attack and whether these indices suggest the terrorist is moving toward or away from an attack.

Next to centralizing intelligence collection and analysis, the next most crucial need in counter-terrorism efforts at the proactive level is the establishment of criteria for the use of this intelligence. Terrorists are dependent upon law enforcement not being able to react on a proactive basis. Terrorist tactics are predicated upon this lack of ability. Law enforcement could become proactive if intelligence use criteria were established and clearly defined. Having cogent guidelines regarding proactive law enforcement response procedures would take the advantage away from terrorists. This criteria should include past history, tactics and operational strategy, location, size, organizational structure, and political philosophy.

REACTIVE RESPONSES TO TERRORISM

Proactive responses to terrorism are limited. The right to privacy, public safety and security, and government intrusion into the affairs of citizens must all be balanced in attempting to stop terrorists. In terms of reactive responses to terrorism, there is a much wider range of response options available to the government and law enforcement. Reactive responses can run the gamut from purely political sanctions against supporting governments to full-scale military responses. Factors that could influence a response to terrorism would include the political ideology of the terrorist organization, the size and influence of the organization, the purposes of the terrorist operation, external support for the organization, the type of terrorism committed (i.e., international, transnational, state, or domestic), and political climate (Sederberg, 1993).

Political Responses

The most difficult form of terrorism to respond to is state terrorism. The U.S. has a long-established policy regarding state-sponsored terrorism, but opposing state terrorism in a practical manner presents a difficult challenge. Factors to include in any response to state terrorism must take into account the reasons why terrorism is employed by a government, the support for the regime, degree of institutionalization of governmental terrorism, and susceptibility of the government to external pressure (Sederberg, 1993). A complete discussion of state-sponsored terrorism is beyond the scope of this text, but it is mentioned because it affects the U.S. A recent example is the U.S. response to Hussein in Iraq. American servicemen (and their dependents) were affected directly by his actions in the Mideast. The U.S. military was sent to the Mideast to oppose Hussein, travelers were at risk of reprisal, and citizens within the U.S. were subjected to tightened government controls for fear of Iraqi-backed terrorism. Any discussion of reactive responses to terrorism must consider state-sponsored terrorism.

Political measures can range from public condemnation to economic sanctions. Between are responses of breaking diplomatic relations, diplomatic expulsion, trade restrictions, and arms embargoes. At times, all of these diplomatic measures have been employed, more often than not unsuccessful. Repeatedly, the U.S. has diplomatically condemned nation states that sponsor or support terrorism, such as South Africa, the European Eastern bloc countries, Mideast sponsors of terrorism, China, and North Korea. This political posturing has never been successful. It is unreasonable to suspect nations that condone terrorism will respond to political rhetoric against their strategies. U.S. citizens may feel better by the government condemning nations that use terrorism, but it does nothing to strengthen the safety or security of citizens.

Similarly, the U.S. has repeatedly severed diplomatic ties with nations that engage in terrorism. Nicaragua, Cuba, El Salvador, South Africa, North Korea, Yemen, Iraq, Iran, Libya, etc., have all, at one time or another, been diplomatically banished by the U.S. Like political condemnation, terrorist sponsors do not respond to diplomatic breaches by the U.S. More often than not, severing diplomatic ties worsens terrorism directed against the U.S. and increases the support for those anti-U.S. nations.

Trade restrictions have been little more successful. Trade restrictions can range from limiting the amount of trade with a nation, prohibiting certain items from being exported to that country, to totally isolating the nation from foreign trade. Trade-restricted items can range from military hardware such as weapons, weapons systems or components of systems, to basic foodstuffs. In the 1960s, 1970s, and 1980s, certain computer parts were prohibited from trade with the Eastern bloc countries. In the 1980s, grain exports were restricted to several Mideast nation sponsors of terrorism. The most famous example of trade restriction was during the 1963 Cuban missile crisis, when President Kennedy completely isolated Cuba from any foreign commerce. Cuba was finally forced to have the Russians remove their nuclear missiles, but this commerce tactic did not reduce Cuban terrorism. Trade embargoes are still being used by the U.S. in the 1990s, with no greater success than in the 1960s, 1970s, or 1980s.

Arms embargoes are a more specialized form of trade restriction strategies. The U.S. and U.N. have prohibited the sale or export of hundreds of types of weapons systems to terrorist nations. Like its more general relative, arms restrictions have not prevented nor slowed terrorists from obtaining weapons. All efforts to prevent the proliferation of nuclear weapons have failed. Isolating North Korea from the technology necessary to make nuclear weapons has not prevented that nation from developing the capability to produce nuclear weapons. Extensive restrictions placed on Iraq has not prevented Hussein from developing biological and chemical weapons (Mullins & Becker, 1992).

The most severe political responses to terrorism are economic sanctions. Many of the nations that support terrorism are third- or fourth-world nations. Isolating those nations economically can have the greatest impact of all political sanctions, although even economic sanctions are not particularly effective, even if applied long term (Turner, 1993). Typically, economic sanctions change the form of terrorist operations. In the late 1970s, the U.S. economically isolated Iran because of Iran's involvement in terrorism. These economic sanctions led to the Iranian takeover of the U.S. embassy in Tehran. Ultimately, the U.S. was forced to unfreeze Iranian assets and pay Iran millions of dollars in recompense. Economically preventing one type of terrorism leads to another type of terrorism.

Domestically, reactive political responses to terrorism are extremely dangerous. In the U.S., political responses mean either tightening security at buildings and airports, restricting immigration, or enacting laws that impinge upon personal freedoms and liberties. Any of these responses reduce personal liberties and involve further government intrusion into the lives of citizens. By using reactive political responses, the terrorist is winning, not the government. The rise of the militia movement in the 1990s, in fact, is largely due to government responses to terrorism. Increased security responses, banning of certain types of weapons, investigative efforts, the actions of the federal government at Ruby Ridge and Waco, and similar responses to terrorist activity have led to an increased militancy and sense of paranoia in thousands of American citizens who perceive the government as a greater threat than the terrorists. Governmental responses to terrorism have led many to terrorism—a vicious circle where no one wins.

Related to reactive political responses to terrorism are increased offensive security measures designed to reduce terrorism. Barriers on buildings, security checkpoint stations for visitors, and increased airport security have all been used as offensive security measures in the wake of terrorist attacks. Many federal buildings resemble bank vaults more than places to conduct routine business. Again, the effectiveness of such measures must be questioned from two perspectives. One, are these measures effective in stopping terrorism and two, are these measures a reduction in personal freedoms and liberties? The answer to the first question is no, offensive security measures do little to reduce terrorist activity. The terrorists merely select another target or another type of operation. If a structure is target-hardened to prevent terrorist attacks, the terrorists will choose another building or another type of activity, such as assassination, hostage taking, etc. To the second question, the answer is probably. The perception of the public outweighs the actual threat to the public. Offensive security measures suggest the perception of a government under siege and advance the terrorist's cause.

Covert Operations

The next level of reactive counter-terrorism would be covert operations, either law enforcement or military. As with political responses, there is a range of possible covert operations against terrorists the government can employ. Civilian covert operations conducted overseas would be done by the CIA, Department of State, or Customs Department; covert operations in the U.S. could be handled by the FBI, ATF, Secret Service, or Customs Department. Figure 9.1 illustrates the counter-terrorist organizational flowchart in the U.S. Efforts to combat terrorism are multi-jurisdictional, although the lead agency overseas is the CIA and within the U.S. the FBI. The organizations listed in Figure 9.1 are responsible for developing proactive responses to terrorism and developing and implementing reactive responses to terrorism.

Most covert operations have been and are conducted by the Central Intelligence Agency. The CIA has the primary responsibility for maintaining the security interests of the United States overseas, including terrorism. The range of options for the CIA include providing political advice, infiltrating terrorist organizations, providing economic subsidies to individuals and governments, offering financial support to political democratic organizations, operating disinformation and propaganda campaigns, provide training to insurgent forces, assisting in paramilitary operations designed to overthrow governments, and conducting assassinations (Marchetti & Marks, 1983; Poland, 1988).

Covert operations have had many more successes than failures, although the public typically only hears about the failures. Any civilian-operated covert strategy is fraught with peril, however. Many of these operations would be condemned by the world as another attempt for the U.S. to exert its influence on neutral governments and likely lead to increased terrorism. Other governments resent the intrusion into their affairs by the United States, leading to further political schisms and disharmony. Providing assistance to a pro-U.S. foreign government can backfire as political winds shift direction. Many governments covertly supported by the U.S. have become political enemies in time. The U.S. supported Iraq during the Iraq-Iranian War, only to have many of the weapons and resources provided by the U.S. turned against U.S. soldiers during Desert Storm. Training of insurgent forces is seen as the U.S. attempting to dictate world affairs and often leads to political problems more severe than the terrorist problem (i.e., Nicaragua). Actually engaging in a paramilitary operation designed to overthrow a government or end a campaign of terrorism by a non-governmental organization usually leads to recriminations far beyond the political arena. Terrorists may increase their activity, other terrorists may begin conducting operations against U.S. targets, and neutral nations may side with and support the terrorists.

Following the Munich Olympic attack in 1972, Israeli Mossad agents systematically assassinated the masterminds and participants in that terrorist attack. In October 1995, the assassination of the leader of the Islamic Jihad made front-page headlines. Israeli Mossad is suspected in that assassination. People often wonder why the U.S. does not take similar action against terrorists who attack U.S. citizens and property. Simply stated, assassination is not an effective tool in combating terrorism, nor does political assassination fit within the framework and operations of a democratic society. Political leaders who order, encourage, or condone assassination are condemned by their citizens and other world

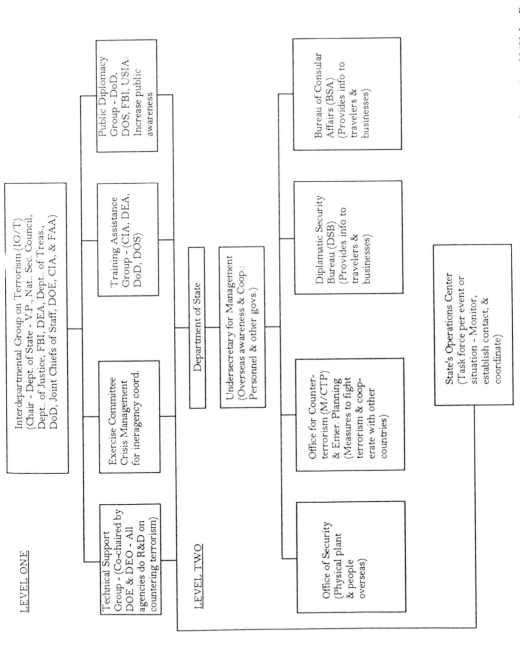

Figure 9.1. Counter-terrorist flowchart of the United States government. From ANNUAL EDITIONS: *Violence and terrorism 90/91* by Bernard Schechterman and Martin Slann. Copyright 1990, The Dushkin Publishing Group/Brown & Benchmark Publishers, a Times Mirror Higher Education Group, Inc., Company, Guilford, CT. All rights reserved. Reprinted by permission.

leaders. In addition, political assassinations usually result in increased terrorism against those who ordered the assassination. Countering terrorism with terrorism is not, by any measure, an effective strategy (Turner, 1993).

In essence, covert operations against terrorism is itself terrorism. During the Vietnam War, the CIA operated a program named Operation Phoenix. The purpose of the operation, as stated publicly and on paper, was to remove North Vietnamese cadre from South Vietnamese villages. Suspected North Vietnamese were to be removed from the villages under arrest, thus removing pressure on the villagers to support North Vietnam. In reality, Operation Phoenix was an assassination program, where any person even remotely suspected of being North Vietnamese or a sympathizer was assassinated. The entire program was a purposeful terrorist campaign controlled by the U.S. government and directed against the Vietnamese. Further, the operation was not a military component of winning the war. It was a political program designed to achieve political objectives and had no military value.

Covert military operations are more forceful than civilian covert operations. These usually involve limited military strikes designed to neutralize or eliminate the terrorist threat. The aborted attempt to rescue the Americans held in the Tehran embassy is an example of a covert military operation. The Iranian embassy siege in London in 1980 was resolved by specially trained Special Air Service anti-terrorist units (Almond, 1990). Several military units have been developed and tasked with providing covert operations, including the Army's Delta units, Navy Seals, and Marine Force Recon units. Covert military operations can be directed at the terrorists who committed the activity, organizations or government who support the terrorists, or governments who sponsor the terrorists.

Covert military operations can lead to the terrorists losing prestige by discrediting the terrorists' ability to conduct successful operations. Limited military strikes have the advantage over full-scale military operations in that they are less costly and time consuming, the strikes are selective and casualties can be reduced, civilian casualties and collateral damage is reduced, and the forces are already trained and prepared for specialized missions (Poland, 1988). In the political arena, covert strikes are less objectionable than full-scale military operations. Targeting only those responsible for a terrorist atrocity has less moral and ethical repercussions within the world community than more general military actions. In the U.S. populace, covert military strikes are more acceptable than committing thousands of troops to an action.

Covert military options have a greater potential of failure than almost any other reactive counter-terrorist measure. If the mission does not succeed, U.S. foreign policy can be severely damaged or discredited. The intelligence information necessary for covert operations is often lacking and either inadequate or inaccurate. There is always the danger the wrong organization or government could be targeted for the strike. If the operation is not successfully completed, the terrorist problem is worsened instead of lessened, such as was the case with the Iranian embassy incident. Often, the cooperation of other nations is needed. Many times these nations will not provide assistance because of fear they will be targeted by the terrorists. There is always the danger of small wars becoming large wars. A limited covert operation could rapidly escalate into a full-scale war, requiring massive commitments of U.S. troops. Korea and Vietnam both began as limited actions that later escalated beyond control (Poland, 1988).

Poland (1988) argues that the history of U.S. covert military operations indicates this response strategy is not effective in dealing with terrorists. I disagree with this assessment. It is believed the history of military covert operations shows the exact opposite: that a well-planned limited strike can be an effective weapon in the war on terrorists and covert military operations are possibly the best counter-terrorist tactic employed by the government. The mistakes in Korea and Vietnam were not military mistakes, they were political mistakes. When conducted properly, covert military operations are a powerful and effective tool. For illustration, successful military operations include the invasion of Grenada, the arrest and capture of Noriega in Panama, air operations in Libya in 1984, the arrest of the hijackers of the *Achille Lauro,* and numerous others that have not been generally publicized. By definition, covert military operations are not detailed to the public. Successful missions often go unrecognized and unrewarded. Only the mistakes become public. For every Desert Eagle (Iranian embassy rescue mission), there are dozens of successful operations that never reach the public newspapers.

Military Responses

At the far end of the continuum of reactive responses to terrorism are full-scale military operations, such as Desert Storm in Saudi Arabia and Iraq. These operations bring the full resources of the U.S. government to bear on terrorists and are a limited option for only the worst cases. Part of the reason President Bush authorized Desert Storm was not only because of Hussein's invasion of Kuwait, but because of Hussein's potential to allow Iraqi terrorism to spread much farther than Kuwait. Hussein was making preparations to spread his terrorism throughout the Mideast and Europe. A military response was the only possible way to stop him.

The military response can also be used to prevent terrorism. The invasion of Somalia was intended to limit the reign of terror of the gang lords within that country and prevent them from expanding into neighboring African countries. A show of force can be effective in preventing terrorism, but only if the government is prepared to back up the show with force. Whether reactive or proactive, military responses must be used sparingly and only as a last recourse. A military response to every single terrorist incident would be self-defeating and cause other governments to censor the U.S.

For domestic terrorism, military intervention, either covert or overt, is not an option. The U.S. Constitution prevents the use of military force within national borders except in cases of national emergency (when the National Guard and military reserves can be used) or in the event of invasion by a foreign power. Terrorist activity does not qualify on either count. The military can, when requested and if in the best interests of national security, provide assistance to law enforcement agencies. This assistance can include providing intelligence data and services, providing military equipment and material, and providing training and guidance.

LEGAL RECOURSES

The most often used and most successful strategies to stop terrorism have been legal remedies, both at the international and national level. Legal actions are most consistent with our system of government and societal values and provide a measure of moral satisfaction. Although not entirely effective, legal actions hold more promise for reducing terrorism than any other strategy employed. Internationally, laws and other legal remedies have attempted to define what terrorists are and when terrorists violate international principles. Domestically, legal remedies revolve around criminal violations, not political ideologies.

International Legal Remedies

Internationally, each individual country defines crime. What may be a crime in the U.S. is not necessarily a crime in England. Most nations agree on common law crimes, or crimes against persons or property. Murder, theft, robbery, assault, etc., are common-law crimes. Few nations can agree on what constitutes political crime, or crime where a person expresses freedom of thought, expression or belief by words, acts, or writings which do not incite to violence, or freedom of association and religious practice (Vetter & Perlstein, 1991). Many nations have statutes preventing such conduct (Bassiouni, 1975). In many nations, it is illegal to speak or write against the political regime. Many Islamic nations prohibit the practice of other religions.

In some of the nations which have political crime statutes, common law crimes are legal if the crime is conducted against an enemy of the state. An Iraqi that murders an American, Kurd, or other "infidel" would not be in violation of Iraqi law. Schreiber (1978) refers to these types of activities as complex crimes, or common crimes with political overtones. Complex crimes are considered international crimes regardless of the stance of any particular government and should not free a person from liability of punishment. For example, the downing of Pan Am 103 occurred in international airspace. Was this crime an act of murder or was it a political crime? Another example is the killing of Leon Klinghoffer aboard the *Achille Lauro*. Was this murder or a political crime? What about the hijacking of the ship itself? Was it piracy or a political crime? Some nations would regard it as a political crime while others a common crime.

This discussion illustrates the fundamental problem in bringing international terrorists to justice. There are no definitions that are commonly agreed upon between nations, no common international laws to use against terrorists, nor are there any international courts to bring to justice those accused (Vetter & Perlstein, 1991). There are some criminal acts in international law (Lynch, 1987), such as aircraft hijacking, murder of diplomats, theft of nuclear material, etc. Even where international law specifies a criminal act, the nation who arrests the violator tries and punishes the violator. The punishment for a crime may depend upon the political climate of that country. Libya, Syria, Iraq, Iran, and Chad have never tried and punished a person who has committed international common law acts of terrorism against Americans. The only exception to complex laws are the Hague Hijacking Convention and the Montreal Sabotage Convention which define acts against airplane hijacking and sabotage as international crimes. Even with these international statutes, however, nations are authorized to refuse extradition of terrorists who commit such acts on political grounds.

Under international law, terrorists are *hostes humani generis,* or common enemies of mankind, and are subject, theoretically, to international jurisdiction (Beres, 1990). As early as 1758, poisoners, assassins, or incendiaries were defined by Article 38 of the Statute of International Court of Justice as international criminals. The article further granted nations the authority to impose the death penalty on such criminals because their crimes were directed against all nations.

Following World War II, at the Nuremberg Military trials in 1945, the tribunal decreed the concept of *nullum crimen sine poena*, or no crime without a punishment. Directed toward the international terrorism conducted by the Nazi Party, the Nuremberg court said that in certain circumstances, exceptional crimes against humanity should surpass the established bounds of due process and that, for these crimes, strict adherence to due process could be the greatest of all injustices. The court said, "so far from it being unjust to punish him, it would be unjust if his wrongs were allowed to go unpunished" (Beres, 1990).

At the conclusion of WWII, the United Nations was formed to help insure international peace. One of the first tasks undertaken by the U.N. was to establish the International Law Commission to prepare draft codes dealing with international crimes affecting the peace and security of mankind (Finger, 1990). Formed by U.N. General Assembly Resolution 177 (II), on 21 November 1947, the commission presented its first draft to the General Assembly in 1954. Article 2, Paragraph 6, of this draft stated, "The undertaking or encouragement by the authorities of a State of terrorist activities in another State, or the toleration by the authorities of a State of organized activities calculated to carry out terrorist acts in another State," was an international offense against all mankind. This document did not, however, define what terrorism constituted, and that was its greatest weakness. Each nation was allowed to determine what acts and crimes were terrorist.

Further weakening the draft was Article 51 of the U.N. Charter, which stated, "Nothing in the present Charter shall impair the inherent right of individual or collective self-defense if an armed attack occurs against the Member of the United Nations, until the Security Council has taken measures necessary to maintain international peace and security" (Bremer, 1990). Article 51 prohibits the training of terrorists or supporting terrorism, but gives individual nations the right to engage in those activities if national security is threatened. Many nations use Article 51 to justify their use of terrorism. The PLO has defended its actions against Israel citing this article.

In October 1970, U.N. General Assembly Resolution 2625 (XXV) endorsed the Declaration on Principles of International Law Concerning Friendly Relations and Cooperation Among States in Accordance With the Charter of the United Nations. "Every State has the duty to refrain from organizing, instigating, assisting or participating in acts of civil strife or terrorist acts in another State or acquiescing in organized activities within its territory directed towards the commission of such acts, when the acts referred to in the present paragraph involve a threat or use of force." Article 3, Paragraph 3, of the same declaration condemned, "Sending by or on behalf of a State of armed bands, groups, irregulars or mercenaries, which carry out acts of armed force against another State of such gravity to amount to the acts listed above, or its substantial involvement in therein." Article 7 stated, "Nothing in this definition, and in particular Article 3, could in any way prejudice the right to self-determination, freedom and independence, as derived from the Charter, of peoples forcibly deprived of that right and referred to in the Declaration on Principles of International Law Concerning Friendly Relations and Co-operation" (Finger, 1990).

This Declaration significantly strengthened the U.N.'s position on terrorism and explicitly specified the illegality of employing terrorism to achieve political goals. It condemned nations that train, support or employ terrorists, and outlawed any use of terrorism against other nations. Article 7, however, took almost all the bite out of the Declaration, affirming the right of states to do whatever necessary to protect their sovereignty. The 1970 Declaration is still the primary statement of the U.N. addressing international and state-sponsored terrorism.

In general, the U.N. and U.N. resolutions have been ineffective in combating terrorism. One of the difficulties experienced by the U.N. has been their inability to arrive at a common definition of terrorism (Wilkinson, 1986). Some U.N. nations even argue that certain forms of terrorism are legitimate and should not be regulated. Nations have argued that political terrorism is a legitimate form of conduct and revolutionary activities should be allowed (Green, 1979; Sofaer, 1986). The only agreement among nations concerning the problem of terrorism is that individual nations should pursue treaties and multilateral agreements independently and that the issue of terrorism should not be a United Nations concern.

The Geneva Convention, designed to regulate conduct by nations during wartime, has addressed terrorism. As relevant to this discussion, the Geneva Convention has established rules of warfare, which include the protection of civilians against deliberate attack, prohibits the taking of civilian hostages, provides for the humane treatment of those captured by an enemy, and specifies that combatants must wear uniforms or insignia identifying their status (Bremer, 1990). In a special 1974–1977 convention, the Geneva Convention added the Geneva Diplomatic Conference on the Reaffirmation of International Law Applicable in Armed Conflict. Protocol I, Article 1(4), of the convention declared it is an act of war if armed conflicts are directed against colonial domination, alien occupation or racist regimes, and the combatants are fighting for independence or self-determination. Protocol I, Article 44(3), legalized non-uniformed combatants when the combatant is among a civilian population and does not have time or resources to become uniformed as long as the combatant carries arms openly when engaged in a military action and when visible to an adversary (Vetter & Perlstein, 1991).

The addendums to the Geneva Convention clearly prohibit certain forms of terrorism and legalize others as acts of war. Transnational and international terrorism are prohibited and not classified as acts of war, while certain forms of domestic terrorism are allowable as acts of war. Mostly, terrorist operations directed against the citizens or interests of another nation are not acts of war and do not fall under the protection of the Geneva Convention. Domestic terrorism intent upon ending a fascist or dictatorial rule can, in certain circumstances, be considered as acts of war. Recent activities in Rwanda are terroristic; recent activities in South Africa are not. Any act targeted against civilian populations are not acts of war.

In the recent past, many terrorist organizations, both international and domestic, have made the argument that they are at war with the United States and should be treated accordingly. Based upon the Geneva Convention, terrorists clearly are not soldiers and do not have the rights and protections afforded military personnel. Attacking U.S. citizens is not a defense under Article 1(4), Protocol I. The U.S. government is not a racist regime, nor does it engage in colonial domination or occupation. Terrorists attacking U.S. military targets often claim rights under the Geneva Convention. As shown, however, they have no legitimate grounds for making such claims.

In 1972, the Third International Symposium of the International Institute for Advanced Criminal Sciences established guidelines for the punishment or extradition of terrorists. Referred to as the *Aut Dedire Aut Punire* (either extradite or punish) and as published by and herein quoted by Schreiber (1978), these guidelines specified:

1. An alleged terrorist offender in custody should be effectively prosecuted and punished or else extradited to a state which requested him and intends to prosecute him.

2. Extradition to a requesting state should be granted if the state with custody chooses not to prosecute, unless an international court is created with jurisdiction over such matters, in which case the accused should be surrendered to the court's jurisdiction.

3. All states should be vested with universal jurisdiction with respect to crimes of terrorism.

4. Whenever a state other than the state in which the act of terrorism was

committed seeks to prosecute a terrorist, a reasonable number of observers should be allowed to see the evidence and attend all proceedings.

5. Whenever extradition is contemplated, the ideological motives of the accused should not be the sole basis for the granting of asylum or for denying the extradition request.

6. If the act at issue involves grave crimes, extradition should be granted regardless of the ideological motives of the actor.

7. In all other cases, when a grave common crime has not been committed and the defendant alleges he is being charged with a political crime and thus should be immune to extradition, the court making the decision must weigh the harm committed against the values the defendant was seeking to preserve and the means he employed in relation to the goal he sought.

8. In the event of multiple extradition requests for the same offender, priority should be given to the state relying on territorial jurisdiction in its request.

9. The rights of the individual in extradition proceedings must always be upheld and he or she should not be precluded from raising any defenses available under extradition law and other relevant aspects of national and international law.

10. Extradition should not be granted when the individual sought is to be tried by an exceptional tribunal or under a procedure in patent violation of fundamental human rights. In such cases, however, the state with custody must prosecute the accused.

11. To prevent circumstances from arising in which states seeking an alleged terrorist will resort to extralegal measures to secure him, extradition procedures should be expedited but without sacrificing the protection afforded to the individuals, and states that do not choose to extradite should prosecute their prisoners without delay.

12. Finally, judges, public officials, lawyers, and others who may become involved with terrorists in the course of their duties should become familiar with international criminal law, in particular those provisions relating to the extradition of those charged with terrorism.

As stated previously, many nations will not abide by these recommendations because they support the terrorists, believe in the terrorists' cause, or do not agree diplomatically with U.S. policy. Thus, terrorists can seek safe refuge in these nations without fear or extradition to the U.S. or fear of punishment by the host country.

Legal avenues to stopping terrorism on the international level are beset not only by problems with defining terrorism and lack of cooperation and agreement among nations concerning the terrorist problem. Once terrorists are arrested, prosecution of the terrorists is extremely difficult. The investigation, arrest, and prosecution of terrorists is an emotional event. They are high-profile criminal justice cases that have a high degree of audience interest and government involvement. As such, many law enforcement authorities, attorneys, prosecutors and judges may take shortcuts in the investigation and prosecution of the case. Illegal methods for collecting evidence may be employed, evidence may be fabricated or tampered with, the civil rights of the accused may be violated, rules of evidence may be relaxed, biased testimony may be allowed, prosecutors and defense attorneys may engage in collusion, and judges may purposely prejudice the case (Crelinsten, Laberge-Altmejd, & Szabo, 1978).

Witnesses for the prosecution may be reluctant to testify against the terrorists for several reasons. One, they may have been victims of the terrorist operation. They may be emotionally scared or experiencing post-traumatic stress disorder, may be biased beyond normal bounds, may be afraid to testify for fear of retribution or retaliation by the terrorists or supporters, may not want to publicly address their conduct while a victim, may not want to be identified by the media, or may want to put the entire incident behind them (McMains & Mullins, 1995). Two, the witness may not want to return overseas for reasons of safety and security. The witness may be afraid of retribution, loss of income, cannot afford the expenses involved (even though the prosecution will reimburse or pay them for travel, lodging and meals), or may feel insecure away from their home and country. Three, the witness may be a collaborator or ex-member of the terrorist organization and may retain some loyalty to the terrorists. This witness may also fear from retribution. Four, the witness may have been only an observer of the event and may be terrified to become involved in such a case. This witness was in the wrong place at the wrong time and wants nothing to do with the case.

Sentencing options available to the court in normal criminal cases include a fine, probation, suspended sentence, imprisonment, and capital punishment (Vetter & Perlstein, 1991). Fines, probation, and suspended sentences are not options in cases involving terrorists by the very nature of their crime. Thus, the courts are left with a very restricted range of options for sentencing terrorists. The evidence of proof has to be overwhelming for the courts to find terrorists guilty, a level of proof extremely difficult to achieve in such cases. Also, the purpose of sending terrorists to prison, at the psychological level, is different than for common law criminal behavior. Common law criminals are sent to prison for either rehabilitation or punishment. Terrorists are sent to prison to keep them from committing further acts of terrorism. The issue of rehabilitation and punishment is not a determining factor.

Some nations may be hesitant to prosecute terrorists because of their fear of retribution or an increase in terrorist incidents against their nation. France, for example, has imprisoned the infamous terrorist Carlos. Although the French government has taken great care to keep Carlos's whereabouts secret, moving him periodically to maintain security, the nation has been subjected to increased terrorist activity because they have Carlos. Colombia, Bolivia, Brazil, and Peru have been victims of terrorist campaigns because of their efforts against terrorists and the drug cartels. The attack by M-19 that resulted in the death of 12 Supreme Court judges was a political message sent to the government. Every nation who has arrested, tried, or sentenced a terrorist has been subjected to increased terrorism directed against that nation.

Some countries have resorted to extraordinary measures to protect law enforcement and the judiciary from terrorist reprisal. France, for instance, tries terrorists in special courts, using panels of seven judges chosen on a case-by-case basis rather than juries. This practice began in the late 1970s, when the leader of Direct Action, Regis Schleicher, threatened citizen jurors at his trial (Lief, 1990). West Germany has passed the State Witness laws, which reduces punishment if the terrorist will turn state's witness and testify against other terrorists (Clough, 1990). England has established special tribunals and special laws of procedure and evidence in terrorist cases. The English system bans certain media coverage of terrorist trials and uses special precautionary and security systems at trials and in prisons.

Nations may refuse to extradite terrorists to the United States. They may not agree with U.S. foreign policy, may wish to protest certain actions by the U.S. government, may want to avoid the appearance of giving in to U.S. demands, or may not agree with or trust the U.S. judicial system. Canada refused to extradite the person responsible for 13 murders in the Seattle Wah Mee massacre until the federal government promised the death penalty would not be invoked. Likewise, West Germany refused to extradite Mohammed Ali Samadhi for murdering Robert Stetham in 1985 while aboard hijacked TWA flight 847 due to the U.S. having the death penalty. Israel will not extradite terrorists for the opposite reasons. Israel considers the U.S. criminal justice system weak and ineffective. They perceive the constitutional rights of the accused as being too great and would prefer to try terrorists themselves.

Within the United States, two major laws have been passed to allow the U.S. to bring international terrorists to trial. One law, the Anti-Crime Bill of 1984, authorizes U.S. federal courts to prosecute terrorists who take hostages and sabotage aircraft irregardless of where the act was committed. The 1984 Anti-Crime Bill was passed specifically to deal with overseas terrorism committed against U.S. interests. The second law, the Omnibus Diplomatic Security and Anti-Terrorism Act of 1986, establishes U.S. jurisdiction over any terrorist crimes committed anywhere in the world against U.S. citizens. The Omnibus Diplomatic Security Act also has provisions for assisting other governments fund witness protection programs for persons who testify against terrorists, authorizes funding for diplomatic and embassy protection, and increased the funding for the State Department's terrorist reward program. This last activity provides rewards to anyone, anywhere in the world, for providing information leading to the arrest and conviction of any terrorist who has committed a terrorist act against any U.S. interest or citizen.

Legal Recourse Within the United States

Within the United States, the government has been somewhat successful in prosecuting terrorists, especially domestic terrorists. According to Smith (1994), over 210 terrorists (domestic and international) were indicted by the FBI. Federal court conviction rates for these terrorists were: 54.2% for left-wing terrorists, 26.8% for right-wing, and 25.7% for international. Guilty pleas were 22.9%, 43.3%, and 62.9%, respectively. The remaining percentages were dismissed cases, acquittal, or mistrial. It is likely that terrorists are using the guilty plea to make a political statement as much as for admitting guilt. Many of the guilty pleas are likely an attempt to gain public support or to illustrate "government oppression."

In federal courts, terrorists are more likely to receive prison terms than probation and are likely to receive more severe sentences than are common criminals tried for the same offense. Comparing terrorist sentences to criminals, Smith (1994) reported 63.9 percent of terrorists sentenced received lower than average rates of probation, and that when sentenced to prison, 66.3 percent of terrorists received sentences higher than other criminals. It is likely that the lack of use of probation and the heavier sentences received by terrorists are an attempt by the courts to send a message to other terrorists. The higher rates of probation for domestic right-wing terrorists was explained by Smith as being used in plea-bargain situations where the defendant was given probation (and time served while awaiting trial) in return for testifying against other right-wing terrorists, particularly among members of the Order and CSA (Mullins, 1989). For terrorists convicted of federal crimes, ones receiving probation were most likely to have been convicted of conspiracy to commit robbery, embezzlement, firearms violations (conspiracy or possession), sedition, and contempt of court.

As mentioned previously, the only federal law dealing with terrorism per se is U.S. Code 18, Chapter 115, Treason, Sedition and Subversive Activities. Most terrorists are tried in federal court for violations of criminal law. Between 1982–1989, 1,363 terrorists were charged with federal crimes. Only 22 were charged with sedition (Smith, 1994). The rest were charged under federal criminal statutes. Criminal charges included racketeering, firearms and explosive violations, conspiracy, RICO, stolen property, robbery and burglary, international emergency economic powers, and mail fraud. Just over 40 percent of the charges were for organized crime activities, either racketeering (30.2%) or RICO (9.3%). Over one-fourth were for weapons violations of some type, including illegal weapons, firearm violations, and possessing or using explosive materials (27.7%).

At the state level, 25 states have criminal violations for engaging in or threatening terrorism. Table 9.1 lists states with terrorism statutes and whether it is a felony or misdemeanor. Most terroristic threat laws apply to acts that are not necessarily terrorism. They apply to situations where one individual threatens to do harm to a government official, group of people, or public facility. Many of the persons charged under these laws are not terrorists, nor is the purpose that of terrorism. Usually the person is irritated at the target for personal reasons, such as having a utility shut off for non-payment, having been fired or laid off from work, or having a personal grudge against a group of people.

Hate Crime Laws

In a further attempt to legally combat terrorism, and primarily in response to a significant increase in right-wing activity, many states have undertaken a different legal strategy to fight the terrorists: the enactment of hate crime statutes. At the time of this writing, the federal government was considering a federal hate crime statute. With terrorists, hate crime laws are like any other criminal violation but provide two additional weapons to fight terrorists. One, they provide another layer of legal recourse state governments can use to combat terrorism, and two, they recognize terrorist-motivated interference with the civil rights of citizens. Most criminal code crimes require that criminal activity has to actually occur before a violation is committed. Most hate crime laws, on the other hand, specify a violation when intimidation or threats occur. Table 9.2 lists hate crime laws by state.

Hate crime laws are of three major types. The first type of hate crime laws prohibit intimidation or interference with civil rights. This category of hate crime laws address civil rights violations based on force, the threat of force, interference with, or intimidation of persons because of the person's characteristics. The second category of hate crime laws are those statutes which create separate bias-motivated crimes. One group of

Table 9.1.
Terrorist laws by state.

State	Crime	Punishment
Alaska	Terroristic threatening	Felony
Arkansas	Terroristic threatening	Felony
California	Terroristic threat	Felony
Colorado	Terrorism	Felony
Connecticut	Terrorizing	Misdemeanor
Florida	Terrorism	Felony
Georgia	Terroristic threatening or acts	Felony
Hawaii	Terroristic threatening	Felony/Misdemeanor
Idaho	Terrorism	Felony
Iowa	Terrorism	Felony
Kansas	Terroristic threat	Felony
Kentucky	Terroristic threatening	Misdemeanor
Louisiana	Terrorizing	Misdemeanor
Maine	Terrorizing	Felony/Misdemeanor
Michigan	Terror	Felony
Minnesota	Terroristic threat	Felony
Mississippi	Terrorism	Misdemeanor
Montana	Terrorism	Misdemeanor
New Jersey	Terroristic threat	Misdemeanor
Pennsylvania	Terroristic threat	Misdemeanor
Rhode Island	Threat by terror	Felony
Texas	Terroristic threat	Misdemeanor
Utah	Terroristic threat	Felony/Misdemeanor
West Virginia	Terrorism	Felony
Wyoming	Terroristic threat	Felony

SOURCE: Reprinted from *Terrorism in America: Pipe bombs and pipe dreams* by B.L. Smith by permission of the State University of New York Press. Copyright 1994, State University of New York.

these crimes is where the terrorist engages in criminal activity and commits the activity by reason of the victim's characteristics. A second group is where the terrorist engages in criminal activity and commits the act because of the victim's characteristics. The third group of bias-motivated crimes is where the terrorist acts to intimidate or harass the victim because of the victim's characteristics and the defendant commits a criminal act. The third category of hate crime laws provides for penalty enhancements when a crime is committed and the crime is a bias crime. Some statutes require the victim of the activity to be intentionally selected, others require that the victim be knowingly selected, while others require the victim be selected because of a victim characteristic. The federal hate crime statute under consideration, the Hate Crimes Sentencing Enhancement Act, as the name implies, would increase penalties for federal

Table 9.2.
Hate crime laws by state.

State	Laws
Alaska	Alaska Statute 12.44.155(c)(22)
California	California Penal Code 422.6
	California Penal Code 422.7
	California Penal Code 190.2
	California Penal Code 422.75
	California Penal Code 1170.75
	California Penal Code 1170.8
	California Penal Code 11410
	California Civil Code 51.7
Colorado	Colorado Revised Statute 18-9-121
Connecticut	Connecticut General Statute 46a-58
	Connecticut General Statute 53a-40a
	Connecticut General Statute 53a-181b
District of Columbia	D.C. Code Annotated 22-4001
	D.C. Code Annotated 22-4003
Florida	Florida Statute Chapter 775.085
Idaho	Idaho Code 18.7901
	Idaho Code 18-7902
	Idaho Code 18-7903
	Idaho Code 18-7904
Illinois	720 Illinois Comp. Statute 5/12-7.1
	730 Illinois Comp. Statute 5/5-5-3.2
Iowa	Iowa Code 729A..1
	Iowa Code 729A.2
	Iowa Code 729.5
Maryland	Maryland Code Annotated article 27,470A
Massachusetts	Massachusetts General Laws Annotated chapter 265,37
	Massachusetts General Laws Annotated chapter 265,39
	Massachusetts General Laws Annotated chapter 12, 11(h)
	Massachusetts General Laws Annotated chapter 12, 11(i)
Michigan	Michigan Comp. Laws Annotated 750.147b
Minnesota	Minnesota Statute Annotated 609.2231
Mississippi	H.B. No. 768
Missouri	Missouri Annotated Statute 574.090
	Missouri Annotated Statute 574.093
Montana	Montana Code Annotated 45-5-221
	Montana Code Annotated 45-5-222
Nevada	Nevada Revised Statute Annotated 207.185
New Hampshire	New Hampshire Revised Statute Annotated 651:6
New Jersey	New Jersey Revised Statute 2C:12-1
	New Jersey Revised Statute 2C:33-4
	New Jersey Revised Statute 2C:43-7
	New Jersey Revised Statute 2C:44-3

Table 9.2. Continued.

State	Laws
New York	New York Civil Rights Law 40-c
	New York Civil Rights Law 40-d
	New York Civil Penal Law 240-30
	New York Civil Penal LAW 240.31
North Carolina	North Carolina General Statute 14-401.14
North Dakota	North Dakota Cent. Code 12.1-14-05
Ohio	Ohio Revised Code Annotated 2927.12
Oklahoma	Oklahoma Statute Annotated title 21,850
Oregon	Oregon Revised Statute 166.155
	Oregon Revised Statute 166.165
Pennsylvania	Pennsylvania Constitutional Statute title 18, 2710
Rhode Island	Rhode Island General Laws 11-42-3
	Rhode Island General Laws 11-53-1
South Dakota	South Dakota Codified laws 22-19B-1
Tennessee	Tennessee Code Annotated 29-17-309
Texas	Texas Penal Code 12.47
	Texas Code of Criminal Procedure article 42-12, 13A
	Texas Code of Criminal Procedure article 42.12, 16(e)
	Texas Code of Criminal Procedure article 42.014
Vermont	Vermont Statute Annotated title 13, 1454
	Vermont Statute Annotated title, 13, 1455
Virginia	Virginia Code Annotated 18.2-57
Washington	Washington Revised Code 9A.36
	Washington Revised Code 9A.36.080
West Virginia	West Virginia Code 61-6-21
Wisconsin	Wisconsin Statute 939.645

FROM: Anti-Defamation League (1994). *Hate crime laws: A comprehensive guide.* New York: Anti-Defamation League of B'nai B'rith.

crimes if victims were selected because of their actual or perceived race, color, religion, national origin, ethnicity, gender, disability, or sexual orientation. Table 9.3 summarizes hate crime statutes by state and hate crime provisions in those statutes.

In using the hate crime laws to prosecute terrorists, states have to demonstrate three elements. One, it must be shown the defendant had specific intent to commit a crime and that it was motivated by bias. To remain within the guarantees of the First Amendment, it is not sufficient to demonstrate that the terrorist was prejudiced. The prosecution must demonstrate the victim was selected specifically because of their characteristics. Two, the state must demonstrate that the terrorist's biased motivation was a motivation for the crime. As stated by the ADL (1994), "the defendant's biased motivation must be a *substantial,* rather than an

Table 9.3.
Hate crime statute provisions by state.

State	Bias Motiv. Viol.	Civil Action	Crim. Pen.	Race Rel., Ethnic	Sexual Orient.	Gend.	Other	Inst. Vand.	Dat Coll.	Training of LE
Alabama								X		
Alaska	X		X	X		X	X			
Arizona								X	X	
Arkansas								X	X	
California	X	X	X	X	X	X	X	X	X	
Colorado	X	X	X	X				X		
Connecticut	X	X	X	X	X	X	X	X	X	
D.C.	X	X	X	X	X	X	X	X	X	
Delaware								X		
Florida	X	X	X	X	X			X	X	
Georgia								X		
Hawaii								X		
Idaho	X	X	X	X				X		
Illinois	X	X	X	X	X	X	X	X	X	X
Indiana								X		
Iowa	X	X	X	X				X		
Kansas								X		
Kentucky								X		
Louisiana			X					X		
Maine								X		
Massachusetts		X	X	X	X			X	X	X
Michigan		X	X	X	X		X			
Minnesota		X		X	X	X	X	X	X	X
Mississippi	X		X	X		X		X		
Missouri		X	X	X	X				X	
Montana		X		X	X				X	
Nevada		X		X	X	X			X	
New Hampshire		X		X	X	X	X			
New Jersey		X	X	X	X	X			X	X
New Mexico									X	X
New York	X		X	X		X	X			
North Carolina	X		X	X				X		
North Dakota	X		X	X		X				
Ohio	X	X	X	X				X		
Oklahoma	X	X	X	X			X	X	X	
Oregon	X	X	X	X	X			X	X	X
Pennsylvania	X	X	X	X				X	X	X
Rhode Island	X	X	X	X				X	X	
South Dakota	X		X	X						
Tennessee	X		X	X				X		

Table 9.3. Continued.

State	Bias Motiv. Viol.	Civil Action	Crim. Pen.	Race Rel., Ethnic	Sexual Orient.	Gend.	Other	Inst. Vand.	Dat Coll.	Training of LE
Texas	X		X					X	X	
Utah										
Vermont	X	X	X	X	X	X	X			
Virginia	X	X	X	X				X	X	
Washington	X	X	X	X	X	X	X	X		
West Virginia	X		X	X		X	X	X		
Wisconsin	X	X	X	X	X		X	X		

FROM: Anti-Defamation League (1994). *Hate crime laws: A comprehensive guide.* New York: Anti-Defamation League of B'nai B'rith.

NOTES: Nebraska, South Carolina, and Wyoming have no statutory provisions.

incidental, motivation for the crime. But, while the prosecution must show that the selection on the basis of the defendant's characteristic was more than an incidental motivation for the crime (a 'de minimis cause'), the prosecution need not show that in the absence of the bias motivation the crime would *not* have occurred (a 'but-for cause')." Three, the state must establish bias motivation beyond a reasonable doubt. In cases of penalty enhancement, a preponderance of the evidence is the standard of proof. Also, penalty enhancement statutes have been held to be constitutional "because a bias-motivated crime is simply a more harmful manifestation of the underlying criminal activity" (ADL).

The major drawback to hate crime statutes is they require an additional level of proof for conviction. Kevin abducts and hangs Fred, a 14-year-old black youth, from a tree. Agent Jones, the lead investigator, with probable cause, searches Kevin's apartment. Inside the apartment, Jones finds neo-Nazi and KKK literature, the white robe and hood of a klansman, and a personal diary describing how blacks are evil and must be eliminated. Agent Jones also discovers a piece of rope, which, under laboratory scrutiny, is determined to be of the same type as that used to hang Fred. Based upon this evidence, Agent Jones files murder-hate crime charges against Kevin. At the trial, the jury determines that Kevin did hang Fred but is not convinced the crime was committed because Fred was black and acquits Kevin because the burden of proof was not met regarding the element "by reason of" Fred being black.

In this example, the prosecution proved that Kevin engaged in a criminal act but could not prove Fred was selected for murder "by reason of" his race. Because both elements of the crime were not satisfied, the jury had no choice but to acquit, even though jury members believed Kevin committed the crime. Kevin was a racist, member of the KKK, and had written of the danger to the United States of allowing blacks to be citizens. The state failed to prove, however, that Kevin selected his victim because of race.

Hate crime statutes can overcome this deficiency by separating the two elements of the crime into two separate crimes—one for the criminal behavior, the second for the element of hate. That way, if the evidence is not enough to convict for both, the evidence can convict for the other element. In states with penalty enhancement, this is how the law is written. Convicting on the offense is one crime, penalty enhancement for the element of bias is separate. Thus, the state proves two separate crimes. All hate crime statutes should consist of two distinct components: the criminal activity and bias motivation. Even those states with statutes prohibiting intimidation or interference with civil rights could follow this model. Force or threat of force could constitute one crime, bias motivation the other crime.

Working to strengthen the impact of hate crime statutes, the FBI has been actively working to train and educate law enforcement personnel in hate crime laws and investigative techniques. The FBI maintains a data file on hate crimes and conducts training for state and municipal law enforcement personnel. Training focuses on identifying, responding, reporting, investigating, and prosecuting hate crimes. In addition to the FBI and ADL, the International Association of Chiefs of Police, U.S. Conference of Mayors, National Association of Attorney Generals, National Sheriffs' Association, Fraternal Order of Police, Association of State Uniform Crime Reporting Programs, and International Association of Directors of Law Enforcement Standards and Training have given their support to adopting uniform hate crime laws and training of law enforcement personnel (ADL, 1994).

Civil Recourse

Another legal recourse in the fight against terrorism is civil action. A relatively recent tactic, civil action has proved to be an effective tool in the fight against terrorism. In the late 1980s, Henry Hays and other members of the United Klans of America killed Michael Donald in Mobile, Alabama. The participating UKA members were tried and convicted in criminal court of murder. In a civil action, the Southern Poverty Law Center and Mrs. Donald (mother of Michael) sued the UKA in civil court under federal law for violations of civil rights. Mrs. Donald was awarded $7 million. In 1991, the Del Dotto family won a $1.8 million civil judgment against Lucielle and Neil Olsen, a mother and son team who were harassing and terrorizing their neighbors, the Jewish Del Dotto's.

In 1989, the Chicago Lawyers' Committee for Civil Rights Under Law, Inc., formed the Project to Combat Bias Violence in Chicago to prosecute terrorists under civil law statutes. Supported by the ADL, the Chicago Lawyers' Committee works *pro bono* to combat terrorism. In their four cases to date, they have won judgments for Mack Green, an African American truck driver assaulted by a white racist ($475,000), Dorothy Stirgus, an African American living in a white neighborhood who was attacked by four white racists ($300,000), Mary Lampkin, an African American bus driver attacked by three neo-Nazi skinheads ($1.75 million), and Alexis Dodds, an African American beaten with baseball bats by members of an all-white gang ($1.2 million) (data from ADL, 1994).

Civil action may become the most effective *modus operandi* of combating terrorism in the future. As discussed in previous chapters, it costs money to be a terrorist. Taking the financial resources from the terrorist through civil action may prove to be the Achilles' heel of terrorism. Since the Donald civil suit, the UKA has virtually ceased operations. The skinheads and Thomas Metzger have suffered severe setbacks in their operations due to civil action. Several militia members are facing long and expensive civil action and do not have the resources, physical or financial, to continue terrorist activities until these suits are resolved. Civil lawsuits, although the data is limited and far from conclusive, shows the highest success rates of any counter-terrorist measure yet employed within the United States.

SUMMARY

There are many deficiencies in our war on terrorism. Most of the weaknesses are attributable to the lack of any unified policy or program to address terrorism. These problems are apparent at both the international level and domestic level. The lack of any cohesive, encompassing policy regarding counter-terrorism efforts has given the advantage to the terrorists.

Every political change, whether presidential or top-level federal administrator, produces a change in counter-terrorist philosophy. Eisenhower and Bush were hard-liners, the Kennedy and Clinton administrations were more passive, and the Carter administration allowed terrorism to bring about the downfall of that administration (Simon, 1994). Nixon vacillated. With some terrorists, he took a hard-line approach, others he virtually ignored. Reagan preferred to negotiate but was willing to use limited military responses to the terrorist problem, as evidenced by the 1984 attack on Libya. President Johnson endorsed political pressures on supporting nations, although he was willing himself to allow terrorism to be used to help end the Vietnam War.

All presidents since Eisenhower strongly endorsed and publicized a non-negotiation policy with terrorists. All had to renege on that philosophy when confronted with terrorist atrocities. Throughout the world, terrorists turned the non-negotiation philosophy into a white albatross, making the current administration appear weak, ineffectual, and unable to protect the people. Every time the government announces a counter-terrorist position, terrorists violently attack that position in such a manner that the government is forced to retreat from the position.

Much of the reason the government is forced to retreat from policy is that most policies are unidimensional. The government adopts a singular approach in counter-terrorist efforts rather than developing a more comprehensive policy that attacks terrorism at many different levels. In the Iranian embassy takeover, Carter placed all his hopes on a diplomatic solution. When diplomacy did not work, the U.S. had no fallback position and put together a hastily conceived rescue operation that failed. A multidimensional effort that combined diplomacy, sanctions against other governments, a full-scale intelligence effort, and a military response together may have been more effective.

This is not to imply that law enforcement has taken the same approach. Working under their own initiatives, law enforcement personnel throughout the U.S. have approached counter-terrorism proactively and worked diligently to protect the citizens. Law enforcement agencies have been hampered by the current political philosophy, however. It is difficult to mount a multidimensional, proactive counter-terrorism program without the support or resources necessary to operate a program.

What is called for is a complete, unified and multifaceted approach to terrorism that includes the full range of response options available within the framework of our societal values. The first step must be the agreement on a standardized definition of what terrorism is and who the terrorists are. Coordinated intelligence efforts must then be established using these criteria to identify, locate, and isolate terrorists. We cannot continue to fight different enemies at different levels of the system.

Once an intelligence network has been established, the government must be willing to act upon the intelligence. We must be prepared to risk international wrath and foreign policy disagreement and do what is necessary to protect U.S. citizens and interests from terrorism. Government counter-terrorism policy must concentrate on a combination of response options employed together. The non-negotiation, non-ransom policy must be abandoned in favor of a more reasonable approach. Reasonable might include using negotiations to set up a limited military strike.

Additionally, the U.S. must establish counter-terrorism treaties and pacts that have some meaning in the world community. Formulating international agreements in principle do more harm to counter-terrorist efforts than good. Agreements, treaties, and pacts should not be developed unless they can be abided by and enforced. If enacted, governments should be forced to abide by the conditions of the agreement.

Domestically, the government has to employ the same multidimensional approach to terrorism. This approach must concentrate on proactive interventions. The challenge within the U.S. is to balance the rights and guarantees of the public with safety and security. Law enforcement must be given the tools to combat terrorism while retaining the basic freedoms of a democratic society. Proactive efforts must be concerned with preventing violent activity. Threat assessment programs must be developed to guarantee that only those planning violence are targeted for investigation, not those protesting for political change. Anything more and the terrorists have won the war.

The most daunting task in the fight against terrorism is balancing the responsibility of government to prevent terrorism with the right of a free people to live free. In the 1980s, the government was too far to the freedom side of the equation; in the 1990s, the government moved too far to the terrorist side of the equation. Hopefully, the latter half of the 1990s will find the government finding that delicate balance point that will allow them to stop terrorism while still recognizing the right of the citizens to protest and disagree. If we are fortunate, this will occur before another World Trade Center or Oklahoma City Federal Building disaster, or before the militia movement gains significantly more strength from mainstream America.

Chapter 10

VICTIMS OF TERRORISM

Victims of a terrorist attack include many more persons than just those killed or injured in the attack. Surviving victims, relatives, witnesses, bystanders, and other members of the general public may all be victimized behaviorally and psychologically by a terrorist attack. Following the Oklahoma City Federal Building bombing, hundreds of victim services workers, counselors, psychologists, ministers, trauma debriefers, and other mental health professions were called to the city. Their primary responsibility was to provide emotional debriefings for survivors, families and relatives of victims, workers, witnesses and observers outside the building; citizens of the city who did not see the explosion but were traumatized by the event; hospital workers who received the dead and injured; and rescue workers. The explosion lasted for seconds, the psychological aftermath will last for decades.

As the preceding paragraph indicated, people are victimized by terrorism at two times. One, people are victimized during the actual incident. Being victimized by a terrorist incident can occur physically, as when persons are injured or killed by the terrorist. People are also victimized emotionally and psychologically. The incident produces fear, terror, dread, emotional numbing, and various other psychological responses. In incidents that continue for more than a few seconds, the emotional reactions continue to build and change as the physical dynamics of the incident play themselves out. For the duration of the incident, people continue to respond emotionally to the incident. Two, people remain victimized following the terrorist incident. The physical resolution to an incident does not remove the emotional components and psychological reactions to that incident. The incident produces trauma which can last for days, years, decades, or even the remainder of the victim's life.

This chapter will focus on the victims of terrorism and examine what occurs to victims both during an incident and following the incident. Because it is a preferred terrorist operation and lasts for a significant length of time, hostage incidents will be explored. The reactions and responses to being a hostage will be described and the psychological and emotional consequences of being captive explained. Keep in mind that

396

hostage incidents are being used to explain the effect on victims, but victims of any type of terrorist incident experience the same effects. Also, while the discussion focuses on hostages, other peripheral victims experience the same psychological trauma—relatives and friends of hostages, the public watching the event, and law enforcement or military response units. Similar types of psychological reactions are being experienced by all of these individuals as the incident develops and continues.

The aftereffects of being victimized by terrorists will be discussed and explained. Many victims of terrorism never fully recover and return to pre-incident levels of functioning, behaviorally, emotionally, or psychologically. The aftereffects of being a terrorist victim can be completely debilitating and can last for the rest of a person's life. The vast majority of World War II POWs, released from captivity over 50 years ago, still suffer debilitating emotional trauma from their captivity. Far too often, we concentrate on the immediate victims of the terrorist attack and ignore secondary victims. Even more often, once the terrorist incident is over or resolved, the victims of the incident are completely forgotten and passed into the annals of history. There is a tendency to believe that when the incident ends, the incident is over for everyone and it becomes time to prepare for the next situation. The victims are left to suffer in quiet silence and desperation. In many instances, the burden of grief becomes too much to bear for the victim and they commit suicide. Years after an incident, the terrorist claims yet another victim.

The long-term psychological ramifications of being victimized do not have to be debilitating, life-threatening, or lifelong. There are some relatively easy treatments for victims that can be used by law enforcement authorities, mental health professionals, or even friends of the victim. For the most part, these short-term interventions are extremely effective in moving the victim past the trauma of the incident and return them to pre-incident levels of functioning. Almost all of these interventions are just as effective if used by a trained law enforcement officer or someone close to the victim. Psychologists and mental health professionals are effective and can be used, but are not entirely necessary if others are trained in using these interventions. This chapter will discuss the interventions used to move victims past the trauma of the incident and return them to what they once were: normal, functioning, productive members of society.

PSYCHOLOGICAL ASPECTS OF
THE TERRORIST INCIDENT

A terrorist incident can be broken into four stages: pre-crisis, crisis, accommodation, and resolution. The pre-crisis stage is the planning stage. Emotions are normal, reasoning ability is high, and terrorists and victims are going about their everyday lives. The terrorists are beginning to become aroused because the operation is eminent, but the arousal is primarily physiological. The adrenal gland begins releasing adrenaline and the body is becoming prepared for activity. Victims are operating at normal levels because nothing has occurred to them. Passengers, for example, are boarding the airplane, finding their seats, and settling in for the flight.

The actual start of the incident signals the beginning of the crisis stage. The terrorists aboard the airplane pull guns or explosives and announce the hijacking of the aircraft. The crisis stage is the most dangerous part of the entire incident and the time at which most hostages are likely to be killed (Defense Intelligence Agency, 1982). The terrorists are most aggressive during the crisis stage. They are pumped on adrenaline, stress levels are high, emotions are high, and reasoning ability is low. They are attempting to gain control of a situation that is not under control and are attempting to establish order from the chaos.

The terrorists are wary of everybody since they do not know who may be among the hostages (i.e., police, military, etc.). Any hostage who does anything of an aggressive nature is immediately suspect and may be killed. A hostage may be killed to serve as a warning to other hostages. To the terrorist, the hostages are not people. They are merely objects to be used to achieve an end. Any hostage who displays human qualities, positive or negative, may be perceived as a threat and be killed (Eitenger, 1982). The terrorists expect certain emotional reactions. Any hostage who does not display those reactions is dangerous and a threat. Even the hostage who remains quiet, calm, and explicitly obeys instructions is just as much a threat as the hostage who may become violent and attempt to overpower the terrorists.

During the crisis stage, hostages become immediately stressed and their emotions are at higher levels than the hostage takers. Many may attempt to resist and some may be killed (Derrer, 1985). The hostages will be fearful, tense, panicky, and may deny the reality of the situation (Ochberg, 1979; Strentz, 1987). The fear may be so overwhelming the hostage denies the reality of the situation (i.e., "this is not really happening to me"). Symonds (1975) refers to this paralyzing fear as "frozen fright." The hostage is experiencing fear so intense, profound, and overwhelming the hostage feels totally hopeless about surviving the incident. The hostage experiencing this frozen fright may even go into shock.

Hostages are experiencing four fear-producing threats (Fields, 1982). First is the threat to life. Hostages, rightfully so, expect to be killed. Second is the threat of bodily injury. Just as frightening as death may be the fear of injury, disfigurement, or disability. To some, the fear of bodily injury may be a greater fear than that of death. Third, hostages experience a threat to security. People expect the world to be an ordered place, using established routines to deal with the stresses of life. Suddenly, the world of the hostages has lost all security and orderliness. The routine has been disrupted and the world is no longer a predictable place. Fourth is the threat to self-image (Lanza, 1986). People expect to be in control of their environment. Being taken hostage removes that control. People may believe something is wrong with them, that they are not worthy to live because they have been taken hostages, and they are somehow less than full persons to lose personal control. The hostage may perceive that people watching the incident will attribute a sense of personal fault on the hostage's part because they were taken hostage.

Hostages may experience sensory overload, delusions, and hallucinations (Hillman, 1981; Hillman, 1983; Siegel, 1984). This overwhelming sense of unreality may last well into the incident and may behaviorally manifest itself in symptoms of dryness of the mouth, insomnia, lack of hunger and thirst, numbness, shock, distortion of time, and a lack of spatial or social orientation. The hostage may lose all touch with reality and enter into a world of delusional systems and even hallucinations. As the hostage comes to accept the reality of the situation, he may experience confusion and defenselessness (Rahe & Geneder, 1983).

The third stage of the incident is the accommodation stage. During this stage, emotions decrease to near normal levels and rationality increases. It is during the accommodation stage that the hostage will employ adaptation, defense mechanisms, and coping skills to deal with the situation. During this stage, the Stockholm syndrome appears and becomes part of the dynamics of the situation. The danger of death or injury during this stage is significantly reduced. Not all adaptive and defense mechanisms are positive strategies and adaptive to survival. Some are maladaptive responses that increase the hostage's chance of getting harmed.

During the accommodation stage, the terrorists also become less emotional and more rational. They have gained control of the situation. The terrorists have control of the hostages, have the perception of control over the responding units, and are in command of the internal and external dynamics at work during the incident. They are engaging in problem-solving behavior, attempting to develop strategies and solutions to resolve the incident and then to get away without being captured or killed. The terrorists also come to experience the Stockholm syndrome during the accommodation stage.

The fourth and final stage of the incident is the resolution stage. The terrorists are surrendering, escaping, or the tactical assault is prepared. The resolution stage, for all participants, is almost as dangerous as the crisis stage. Emotions rise and rationality decreases. The resolution stage, like the crisis stage, brings change to the environment, which produces stress and anxiety. If surrendering, the terrorists are fearful of what may await them when exiting the scene and need assurances that they will not be harmed. One strategy law enforcement uses with criminal or mentally disturbed hostage takers to is carefully develop a surrender plan and go over all the details with the hostage takers so there are no surprises during the surrender. The hostages become tense and emotional and may be more fearful of law enforcement than the terrorists. Because emotions are high and the ability to reason is reduced, hostages may not obey instructions from either terrorists or law enforcement authorities. They may instead rely on instinct to get out of the situation, and these instincts may be contrary to other survival skills. The authorities are also more emotional and nervous. Tactical units are operating under tremendous amounts of adrenaline and stress, negotiators are stressed, and commanders are on edge. Many incidents have ended in disaster because of the high emotional content of the resolution stage.

All terrorist incidents go through these four stages. The duration of each stage varies according to the type of incident. Bombings, for the terrorist, have a very short crisis, accommodation, and resolution stage. Placing the bomb and waiting for the explosion are the crisis and accommodation stages. In an assassination, waiting on the target comprises the crisis and accommodation stage, actually killing the target and escaping the resolution stage. With some terrorist incidents, the crisis, accommodation, and resolution stage can last only seconds. Victims of a terrorist bombing, if not killed outright, experience the crisis stage when the bomb detonates, the accommodation stage following the blast and awaiting help, and the resolution stage while being transported to a hospital and while being cared for in the emergency room.

STRESS AND TERRORIST VICTIMS

The victim of a terrorist incident, especially in a prolonged incident, is subjected to extraordinary stressors. Hans Selye (1956) defined stress as "the nonspecific response of the body to any demand made on it."

Selye's definition focuses on the physiological responses to stress. Within this definition are three important components. One, responses do not depend upon the nature of the demand. Physiological responses, such as increased heart rate, increased blood pressure elevation, etc., occur in any stressful situation. Physiological responses are automatic and are designed to protect the organism. Two, the physiological defense reaction has three sequential stages: alarm, where the body shows arousal to the threat; resistance, where the body's reaction stabilizes and the person copes with the higher arousal levels through learned skills; and exhaustion, where the person has expended all energy available for adaptation and then shuts down. Three, when the stress is prolonged, diseases appear as a result of the overextension of expending energy (Cox, 1979). Additionally, chronic stress leads to both psychological and physical problems (Everly, 1989).

Seyle's (1956) definition does not account for the fact that the physiological responses produced when under stress depend upon both the nature of the stressor and the person's interpretation of the situational meaning of the event (McMains & Mullins, 1995). A person's response to stress depends upon a person's environment, assessment of their abilities, plans for dealing with the demands, and feedback received about those plans (Cox & Mackay, 1976).

The effects of stress are experienced behaviorally, cognitively, emotionally, and physically (Cox, 1979). Behaviorally, acute stress can lead to an increase or decrease in appetite, increased smoking and drinking, increased impulsivity and excitability, and increased proneness to accidents. Cognitively, ability to concentrate and make decisions is impaired, forgetfulness and mental blocks are common, and people function from habit rather than reason. Acute stress may lead to psychological problems, including adjustment disorders, affective disorders, anxiety disorders, post-traumatic stress disorder, and reactive psychosis. Emotionally, persons experiencing acute stress experienced increased anxiety, aggressiveness, boredom, fatigue, irritability, moodiness, tension, and loneliness. Physically, stress increases blood sugar, catecholamine release (neurotransmitter which plays a role in controlling emotional behavior), heart rate, blood pressure, pupil dilation, and respiration rates. Cortisteroids, produced by the adrenal glands, are released. Increased cortisteroids are associated with a rise in aggression, depression, helplessness, and object loss.

In the terrorist operation, terrorists and victims are both affected by stress. To the terrorist, stress is produced by the newness of the situation. The terrorist is in a new environment that is unique. This in itself produces stress. The terrorist faces an unknown future, especially in a hostage incident. Most future options are perceived to be negative (i.e., capture, failure, death). The stress of what the future holds may overwhelm the terrorist and he becomes unpredictable. The terrorist is also stressed by having hostages. He is now responsible for a group of people and must use them for his safety and security. The terrorist must protect himself and provide for this group of strangers. He must deal with their emotions, their needs, and their behaviors. If a hostage is injured or killed, stress is further elevated for the terrorist. The terrorist is stressed by the presence of the authorities. He does not know their plans or actions. As time passes, increases in basic need states elevates stress. Needs of safety and security are at risk. The most basic need of survival is threatened by the potential for violence and the authority's response. Decision-making skills are affected by stress. Emotions are elevated, physiological processes are speeded up, and cognitive processing ability is reduced. With time, the number of decisions that need to be made increases, producing a corresponding increase of the demands on the system.

Hostages are under even more stress than the terrorist. Hostages are faced with loss of life and freedom, serious injury, and a loss of self-respect. They are anxious, fearful, panicky, and uncertain of the future (Oots & Wiegele, 1985). The helplessness, fear, and sensory input overload may completely overwhelm the hostages (Hillmann, 1981). The hostages are victims of circumstance and their orderly world has suddenly become chaotic and unpredictable. Their every action, thought, and emotion is controlled by someone else.

The hostages will experience an increase in heart rate and blood pressure, neural interference, and may experience loss of muscular control (Gilmartin & Gibson, 1985). They may hyperventilate, experience an asthma-like attack, lose bladder control, vomit, faint, or even experience severe debilitation such as a heart attack or stroke. If they have a medical condition, the hostage situation may exacerbate that condition (Nudell & Antokol, 1990). Some hostages may hallucinate (Lanza, 1986; Siegel, 1984).

Hostages are experiencing a loss of self-respect and this will increase stress levels. The hostages perceive themselves as somehow being bad people because they have been taken hostage. Families and friends might think less of them and this perception elevates stress, often more so than being taken hostage. The hostages may experience stress because of guilt feelings for having been taken hostage and not taking action to prevent or resolve the situation. Many ex-POWs, for example, express sentiments that they let down their country by being captured (Mullins, 1994).

As time passes, the hostages begin to calm down and the initial stress response dissipates. With time, however, stress increases as basic needs are not fulfilled. Hunger, thirst, sleep deprivation, lack of bathroom facilities, etc., lead to increased levels of stress. The presence of response units increases stress, as the hostages do not know what these response units are doing or how they are going to resolve the incident. The response units are seen as great a threat to hostage lives as the terrorists.

Finally, as the incident is resolved, stress increases. Over time, the hostages have adapted to and become familiar with the situation and have learned to cope. Resolution of the incident produces uncertainty, anxiety, and emotional turmoil. The hostages realize the hostage takers may become even more irrational and unpredictable. Also, with release, the hostages are treated as if they were terrorists by the response units, and this unexpected and unnecessary treatment increases stress.

ADAPTATION, COPING, AND DEFENSE MECHANISMS

As the crisis stage moves into the accommodation stage, emotions begin to decrease and the situation begins to stabilize. The hostages begin to settle down, the adrenaline rush is over, stress reduces, and they begin to develop cognitive strategies for surviving the incident. All hostages will begin to cope with the incident, some better than others. Some hostages will employ positive strategies for survival, others negative strategies for survival. Inappropriate adaptive mechanisms decrease the probability of remaining unharmed during the incident (Goldaber, Pizer, Remsberg, Reber, Shaw, & Tilton, 1979). Each hostage will rely on the emotional, cognitive, and behavioral strategies he or she brought to the situation for life experiences, and ones each believes will lead to survival (Welch, 1984). Hostages will also have to change their survival strategies as the dynamics of the situation change. Terrorist incidents such as hostage situations are not static events. They are fluid and change with time. The hostage has to be able to adapt with the situation and change their coping strategies to match the changing nature of the incident.

Hostages will have to rely on adaptation mechanisms to successfully survive the incident. Adaptation is the use of different behaviors, responses, and strategies to reduce stress and maximize chances for survival (Tinklenberg, 1982). Adaptation uses defense mechanisms and coping strategies to meet the various demands of the situation. Defense mechanisms are unconscious psychological responses made to reduce the danger and anxiety inherent in the situation and are largely a function of one's personality and prior learning history. Coping is the use of innovation by hostages to adjust to the situation as it evolves and responds to the various demands of the incident (Green, 1985). The hostage must use both defense mechanisms and coping during the incident.

Characteristics of the incident will influence the ways in which hostages adapt and cope. One, the duration of the incident will affect how hostages adapt. If hostages do not adjust their coping strategies to respond to the temporal demands of the incident, the stress and anxiety will overwhelm them and the hostages will suffer from deteriorating judgment and engage in erratic, self-destructive behavior. The hostages will become panicked, lose the ability to give their attention to survival, and fail to stay alert to situational changes. Two, the number of terrorists and hostages will affect adaptive mechanisms. Several terrorists may require different adaptive and coping strategies than being held by just one captor. Similarly, the number of other hostages will affect individual adaptation and coping. One thing a hostage will do, since this is a unique and never before experienced event, is examine how other hostages are coping and model their behavior. Three, the notoriety and attention given the incident will affect adaptation and coping. Having an international audience may reduce a person's ability to handle the situation. The hostage may not use adaptive and coping mechanisms in his personal repertoire of behavior, but may instead use ones he believes will not embarrass him in the public eye. Four, the response to the incident will affect adaptation and coping. Diplomatic and negotiated responses will produce different responses in hostages than will tactical and military responses.

Ladewig, Jessee, and Strickland (1992) identified individual variables that can affect adaptation and coping. One, a person's age is important. Persons who are older adapt and cope better than do younger persons. Age brings more life experiences and a greater diversity of experiences from which to draw upon when determining how to cope. Two, and related to age, prior life experiences influence adaptation and coping. The more life experiences, the better one is able to cope and adapt. Persons who are culturally, socially, and environmentally diverse will be able to deal with the situation much better than the person who has lived a sheltered life. Certain hostages do not cope well because of their prior life experiences. Military personnel, for example, do not adapt and cope as well as non-military persons. Military personnel have learned to obey, not question, and work within a group structure. As hostages, they are not as flexible as non-military personnel in reacting to the incident.

Three, education is a variable that is important in adapting and coping as a terrorist victim. Those with higher educational levels are better at adaptation and coping. Persons with higher educational levels are better able to generalize from other situations and apply responses from those situations to the victim scenario. Four, training in hostage situations makes a person better able to adapt and cope as a hostage. Knowing the dynamics involved in hostage situations and preparing for being a hostage will enable a person to better adapt and cope than a person who knows nothing about hostage situations. Executive protection training given by the U.S. Department of State, and numerous private consultants teach hostage situation dynamics just for this reason.

Five, the length of captivity affects adaptation and coping ability. The longer the incident lasts, the worse the adaptive and coping ability of the victim. With the passage of time, stress increases, fatigue becomes greater, and a sense of hopelessness and helplessness build. The victims will become tired and inattentive and unable to keep up with the changing dynamics of the situation. Hostages will become more cognitively rigid, less emotionally flexible, and more focused on what they have been doing rather than what they should do in the future.

Six, hostages who have had many social relationships will adapt and cope better than hostages who are "loners" or who have not affiliated socially. Social relationships teach persons how to interact with and deal with people in a variety of situations. Social relationships also prepare a person for unique and uncharacteristic situations they may be faced with. Seven, hostages who affiliate with other hostages will adapt and cope better than hostages who do not affiliate.

Eight, persons who have a spiritual outlook or spiritual anchor in their lives adapt and cope better than other hostages. Spirituality provides an inner resource for the hostage to draw upon and they perceive themselves to not be alone in trying to survive the situation. Nine, persons prone to depression or depressive episodes are not as effective as others in adapting and coping. This applies also to persons with a negative and fatalistic outlook concerning the world around them.

Defense Mechanisms

Part of the adaptive response employed by victims of terrorists include the use of defense mechanisms, unconscious psychological responses used to reduce the situational danger, and emotional anxiety of being victimized or being held hostage. The specific defense mechanisms a hostage will employ is both a function of the person's personality and prior learning history. Hostages may employ either beneficial or detrimental defense mechanisms or a combination of both during the duration of the incident. Most people will employ more than one defense

Table 10.1.
Factors that may influence adaptation and coping during a terrorist incident.

Incident Characteristics
    Duration of incident
    Number of terrorists and/or other victims
    Attention given incident
    Response to the incident
Individual Variables
    Prior life experiences
    Education level
    Prior training
    Length of captivity
    Prior social relationships
    Affiliating with other victims
    Spiritual outlook or anchor
    Proneness to depression.

mechanism if the terrorist incident lasts for any period of time or changes rapidly over time.

Beneficial defense mechanisms include intellectualization, creative elaboration, and humor. Intellectualization is the defense mechanism whereby the hostage removes the emotional components of the incident and views the incident in terms of its logical and rational components. The hostage cognitively assesses the actions of the terrorists and determines how to respond to these actions, while ignoring fear, stress, anxiety, and other emotional components. When the *USS Pueblo* was seized by the North Koreans, many crew members knew they would be released because the physical beatings of the North Koreans were designed to not leave any physical marks or scars. These hostages determined that if the North Koreans were not going to release them, it would not matter if the beatings left visible marks (Ford & Spaulding, 1973).

Creative elaboration, or fantasy, is the case where the hostage engages in fantasy to cope with the situation. Fantasy allows the hostage to briefly escape the emotional reality of the situation and remember and concentrate on more hopeful times or more positive activities. Many POWs engage in creative elaboration to maintain sanity and remain positive concerning their predicament. POWs may mentally prepare elaborate meals, repair automobiles, play complex card games (including shuffling the deck so the cards are randomly dealt), write novels, and engage in other mental activities (Mullins, 1995).

Humor is another beneficial defense mechanism employed by successfully adapting hostages. Humor, usually bizarre, allows the hostage to examine a situation in an unconventional manner and reduces stress and anxiety. Captors may be seen in caricature form, slight physical defects may be exaggerated, or life-threatening events may be turned into morbid jokes. It provides an escape mechanism that allows the person to emotionally escape the seriousness and life-threatening nature of the situation.

Detrimental defense mechanisms include counter-phobic reactions, denial, and reaction formation. A counter-phobic reaction is where a hostage engages in responses opposite to basic survival. The hostage may argue with the terrorists, may dare the terrorists to shoot him, or refuse to obey instructions or orders. If told to sit, the hostage may stand. If told to not talk, the hostage may talk. Hostages engaging in counter-phobic reactions may engage their captors in political, philosophical, or religious arguments, or may threaten them with later retaliation. The counter-phobic hostage may survive the ordeal with the terrorists, only to be injured or killed by a rescue team. If the rescue team storms the hostage location and orders everyone to lay on the floor, the hostage may jump to his feet.

Denial is where the hostage refuses to believe she is in fact a hostage and denies the incident is occurring (Jacobson, 1979). This hostage may get up and attempt to walk out the door, or may continue doing whatever she was doing prior to the crisis stage. If ordered to do something by the terrorists, the hostage may ignore them altogether or refuse to obey them. Either way, the hostage in denial is in great danger of injury or death.

The defense mechanism of reaction formation is where the hostage adopts attitudes opposite to his true beliefs and/or behaviors. Fear becomes admiration for the terrorists, anger becomes respect, and anxiety becomes compliance. Often, the hostage engaging in reaction formation becomes overly compliant and attempts to continually provide assistance to the terrorists. The hostage may even attempt to convince other hostages to admire, respect, and comply with the terrorists. The greatest danger in reaction formation is that the hostage stands out from the other hostages. The person using reaction formation is behaving different than other hostages and becomes noticed for this difference. Because he is distinguished and identified, the hostage may be killed to serve as an example.

A final defense mechanism is identification, and this defense mechanism can be either beneficial or detrimental. The hostage becomes psychologically allied with the terrorists and perceives himself to be in the same predicament as his captors. He may even assist his captors in making demands, attempting to defeat response teams, or physically assisting the terrorists. Identification is a component of the Stockholm syndrome and will be more fully discussed in that section.

Coping Mechanisms

Coping mechanisms are strategies employed by a hostage to adapt to the changing dynamics of the situation. Some coping mechanisms are similar to defense mechanisms in form, but they are less pervasive behaviors. Defense mechanisms are difficult to alter as the situation changes, being more permanently etched within one's personality. Coping mechanisms are more cognitively related and are more fluid and changeable. Most coping mechanisms are beneficial to the hostage but can become detrimental if overused.

One coping strategy is relinquishing control. From the very inception of the incident in the crisis stage, the hostage cannot show anger, hatred, fear, anxiety or other similar emotions, but must accept the fact they have been taken hostage and cede control to their captors. Relinquishing control helps the hostage realize the reality of the situation and reduces the probability of the hostage getting injured or killed.

A second coping strategy is controlling emotions. Screaming, shouting, crying, and wailing are behavioral manifestations of the emotions experienced in the hostage situation. The only thing these behavioral displays gain for the hostage is recognition by the captors. Displaying these behaviors may also elevate the emotions of the terrorists, and, in an attempt to reduce those emotions, they may kill the hostage. Controlling emotions will also reduce stress and anxiety, increase the ability to think clearly, and help cognitive processing of information. The two major advantages of controlling emotions are not standing apart from the rest of the hostages and forcing one's self to explore other, more positive techniques to adapt and cope.

A third coping mechanism is role rehearsal. The hostage will, at every opportunity, rehearse her role and attempt to foresee and predict upcoming situations and terrorist actions and will then mentally rehearse how she will behave and react in those situations. The hostage who engages in role rehearsal will have some internal control over the situation and will not feel so hopeless and overwhelmed.

Gathering information is a fourth coping strategy. The hostage will pay attention to the surrounding environment and analyze and assess events as they occur. Information will be collected on the location, other hostages, the terrorists, treatment of hostages, and the response units. As mentioned previously, *Pueblo* crewmen determined the North Koreans would ultimately release them because the beatings were designed to not leave visible marks. Gathering information combined with role rehearsal provides a complete picture of the predicament so the hostage can cognitively prepare for the future.

A fifth coping strategy is establishing positive bonds with the terrorists (National Advisory Committee on Criminal Justice Standards and Goals, 1976). When South Moluccan terrorists took a passenger train hostage in a siege that ultimately lasted 30 days, this coping mechanism kept one hostage, Gerard Vaders, alive. The South Moluccans decided to execute Vaders as a demonstration to authorities of their sincerity. Prior to his execution, the terrorists allowed Vaders to speak to his wife on the telephone. Vaders spent approximately 15 minutes reviewing his life and saying good-bye to his spouse. Following the conversation they monitored, the South Moluccans took Vaders back to his seat and selected another hostage. After the incident ended, the terrorists explained that they could not kill Vaders because he had become human, with similar problems, troubles, cares, desires, and wants as the terrorists (Ochberg, 1982). As an historical footnote, the other hostage did not die from his wounds.

Forming relationships with other hostages is a sixth coping mechanism. The coping hostage will bond with other hostages and come to perceive the situation as a group problem, not an individual situation. The hostage group will support and assist each other, serving in essence as a psychological support group and reducing the stress and anxiety for all hostages. Gerard Vaders and several other hostages on the Dutch train formed such a group. Every day of their captivity they sat and worked together. One activity the group used to psychologically survive was to "write" a book. One hostage would write a sentence, pass the book to the next hostage who would add a sentence, pass it on to the next hostage who would add the next sentence, etc. When any one of the group became depressed or emotional, the others were there to help.

A seventh coping strategy is finding a purpose for survival. The will to live under any circumstances can carry the hostage through the worst of times. Surviving prisoners of war, for example, have been found to make the decision to live early in captivity (Segal, Hunter, & Segal, 1976). POWs developed the will to live to see their captors punished, to ensure the world knew of their hardships, to see a spouse or family member again, or just to not give the enemy the satisfaction of them dying. This will to live may be the factor around which the hostage can develop and utilize other coping skills. The hostage who cannot cope and does not develop the overpowering desire to live may allow himself to succumb to the stress, anxiety, and fear to such a degree that he will die of non-deliberate causes. Dimsdale (1974) found that the failure to develop the will to live was the primary reasons prisoners of the Nazi concentration camps suffered non-deliberate death.

Coping hostages may utilize and rely upon either emotion-focused or problem-focused coping strategies (Strentz & Auerbach, 1988). Emotion-focused strategies are intended to reduce the emotions of the situation and may involve attendance redirection, avoidance, denial, relaxation, wishful thinking, and attention-like activities such as seeking social support, engaging in group activities, or forming relationships with other hostages. Problem-focused strategies are an attempt to reduce the emotional impact of the situation, are centered around the environment, and may involve using information, intelligence, and instructions concerning the surrounding to reduce negative emotions. Strentz and Auerback found that hostages who use emotion-focused strategies were better able to cope with the situation than were hostages who relied upon problem-focused strategies.

Table 10.2.
Coping mechanisms employed by victims of terrorism.

Coping Strategies
Relinquish control
Control emotions
Role rehearsal
Gather information
Establish positive bonds
Form relationships with other hostages
Develop purpose for survival
Emotion-versus problem-focused strategies

Survivors and Succumbers

Some persons are better able to cope with being a hostage than are other persons. Strentz (1987) divided hostages into two groups: survivors and succumbers (see also Ford & Spaulding, 1973; Richardson, 1985; and Wesselius & DeSarno, 1983). Survivors remain relatively stable and non-emotional during the hostage situation and have very few long-term psychological problems following the incident. Succumbers are very emotional and distraught during the incident and tend to have serious physical and psychological problems following the incident.

During the hostage situation, survivors are able to blend in with the rest of the hostage group. They do not attempt to be leaders, do not attempt to organize the hostages into a formal group, do not argue with the terrorists, or do things on their own without being ordered. Survivors do exactly as told, do it promptly, and do it carefully. Succumbers, on the other hand, attempt to assume leadership roles, may be argumentative, and draw attention to themselves in other ways. Succumbers may also draw attention to themselves by being too subservient and too compliant. Strentz (1987) illustrates this by telling of the bank clerk who "cried, held her hands high over her head while her peers walked with their arms at their sides, and said, 'yes sir!' while the others said 'okay.'" Later, when the terrorists selected a hostage for execution, they chose this hostage. Although being compliant, she stood out and was remembered by the terrorists.

Survivors are able to contain and hide their hatred and disdain for the hostage takers. Survivors do not make inflammatory remarks, make demands, nor engage in hostile expressions or body language. Neither do survivors engage in religious, philosophical, or political discussions with the hostage takers. Nardini (1952) provided an excellent example of how survivors suppressed their emotions in describing how American troops survived the Bataan Death March in World War II. The surviving POWs did nothing at all to antagonize their Japanese captors. They walked when told to walk, kept their eyes straight ahead, did not talk, did not lag behind, and showed no outward emotions. They contained their fears, anxieties and anger behind a mask of neutral indifference. Succumbers do just the opposite and engage in the London syndrome. They let their anger and hostility show. These hostages argue, make demands, and may even threaten the hostage takers (i.e., "Just wait until I get out of this and I'll teach you a lesson"). Rather than concentrate on survival, succumbers concentrate on retaliation.

Survivors are able to control their outward appearance and project a persona of confidence, high self-esteem, professionalism, and decisiveness. Their outward appearance is often able to calm the hostage takers and reduce tensions. Succumbers, on the other hand, will be the proverbial "bowl of Jell-O" and succeed only in raising the tensions of the other hostages and of the hostage takers. Survivors have faith in themselves and in their government. These hostages maintain a positive mental attitude and believe that the authorities are doing everything possible to secure their release. Survivors do not believe they have been abandoned, deserted, and left to die. Succumbers believe that the world has forgotten about them and that they are isolated from outside assistance.

One of the major problems faced by hostages is boredom. Hostages are often confined to small spaces such as airplane seats, sitting in corners, locked in closets, etc., with nothing to do. Hostages are deprived of radios, television, cassette players, reading material, paper and pencils, playing cards, and other items which could be used to relieve boredom. Survivors successfully engage in fantasy and daydreaming to relieve the boredom (Ascencio & Ascencio, 1983; Neihouse, 1980). Many American prisoners of war in Vietnam constructed elaborate code systems for communicating with other POWs, designed complicated buildings, wrote mental novels, plays, poetry, songs, and mentally played games of monopoly, bridge, solitaire, and other games. Crew members of the *Pueblo,* after taken hostage by the North Koreans, fantasized about preparing elaborate meals, building a computer, and planning a full-scale retaliatory raid against the North Koreans (Spaulding & Ford, 1972). Succumbers fill the empty hours by dwelling on the hopelessness and despair of the situation and in imagining how the terrorists are going to harm, torture, and kill them.

Survivors keep to routines. They write (if allowed), engage in physical exercises, assist other hostages, and set short- and long-term goals for themselves. Survivors affiliate with the other hostages and hostage takers (Hauben, 1983). With other hostages, survivors provide encouragement, mutual support, and reassurances. Survivors assist other hostages in coping with the situation. Survivors use the hostage takers to provide information and try to determine and deal with the attitudes, intentions, and ideologies of the hostage takers. Succumbers do not set goals or daily routines. These hostages spend their time commiserating over their plight and potential fate and will avoid engaging in activities which would be beneficial and help to pass the time. Succumbers will also isolate themselves from the other hostages.

Survivors do not engage in self-pity. They maintain a positive mental attitude and assist others in maintaining a positive mental attitude. Survivors realize they were a victim of circumstances and realize the authorities are working to secure the hostage's freedom. Succumbers, on the other hand, let their depression control their situation and constantly question why they were taken hostage. In a sense, succumbers somehow attribute blame to themselves for being caught up in the flow of events.

Survivors accept their fate and adjust to the situation. These hostages keep looking at the bright side of the situation (i.e., "I'm still alive") and do not try and over-rationalize their fate. Survivors accept the situation and changes in the situation and try to turn the negatives into positives. Succumbers attempt to convince themselves they should have done things differently (i.e., "I knew I should have stayed home today") and cannot accept their fate and cannot adjust to the changing circumstances of the situation.

Survivors are able to find humor in the situation or attempt to interject humor into their predicament. They use imagery and may assign humorous names or descriptions to their captors. Succumbers dwell on the seriousness and morbidity of the situation.

In sum, survivors dwell on whatever positive aspects can be found in the situation, and succumbers dwell on all of the negative aspects of the situation. Survivors do whatever is necessary to survive the situation intact, both psychologically and physically. Moreover, survivors fight to survive and make preparations for survival. Strentz (1987) has shown that the trauma of the hostage situation can be significantly reduced by being prepared. Being prepared means expecting certain reactions in oneself and assuming roles which will minimize stress, anxiety, and fear. Strentz has shown that persons can be trained to psychologically survive a hostage situation. This training can teach people how to react in the situation by utilizing certain personality characteristics and providing them with skills and strategies that would be beneficial if they were ever to be taken hostage.

THE STOCKHOLM SYNDROME

In 1973, Jan-Erik Olsson and Clark Olofsson entered the Sveriges Kreditbank in Stockholm, Sweden with intent to relieve the bank of some of its extra cash. During the robbery, the police arrived and a 131-hour standoff began. During the incident, Kristen Enmark, an employee of the bank and a hostage, called a local television station and reported she was more afraid of the police than of the robbers. She felt the police were playing with the lives of the hostages (Cooper, 1978). The police were stunned at this public statement, but not nearly as much as they were following the incident when several ex-hostages refused to testify against their captors and when one ex-hostage became engaged to one of the robbers. These hostages were responding normally to the hostage situation, as we now know. Named after this incident, the Stockholm syndrome is a fairly typical response of hostages to the stress of captivity.

The Stockholm syndrome is an emotional survival reaction to being held hostage. As has been previously mentioned, the defense mechanisms of counter-phobic reactions, denial, reaction formation, and identification with the aggressors all contribute to the formation of the Stockholm syndrome but do not fully explain the phenomenon. Defense-oriented reactions are most prevalent during the early phases of the hostage incident. As the hostage situation begins to drag out, defense-oriented reactions are replaced with more positive coping behaviors. The defense mechanisms mentioned previously may help predispose the hostages to the later formation of the Stockholm syndrome.

There are three components to the Stockholm syndrome (Ochberg, 1980b; Olin & Born, 1983; Strentz, 1982). The first component is positive feelings on the part of the hostages toward the hostage takers, the second

Table 10.3.
Survivor and succumber differences.

Survivors	Succumbers
Blend in with other hostages	Stand out from other hostages
Do not try to lead	Try to lead
Do not formally organize	Organize hostages
Do not act without being ordered	Argumentative
	Too subservient/compliant
Contain and hide disdain and hatred	Show hatred and disdain
Do not make inflammatory remarks	Make inflammatory remarks
Do not make demands	Make demands of hostage takers
Show no hostile expressions	Make hostile expressions
Concentrate on survival	Concentrate on retaliation
Control outward appearance	Let emotions show
Confident	No self-confidence
High self-esteem	Low self-esteem
Professional	Non-professional
Decisive	Cannot make decisions
Reduce tensions and anxiety of all	Raise tensions of everyone
Believe in themselves and rescuers	Feel forgotten by world
Relieve boredom with fantasy and daydreaming	Dwell on hopelessness and despair
Keep routines	No routines
Set goals	Do not set goals
Affiliate and provide support	Isolate themselves from other hostages
Gather information	Do not gather information
Maintain a positive mental attitude	Do not maintain a positive mental attitude
Realize they were a victim of circumstances	Attribute blame to themselves
Accept fate and adjust to situation	Do not adjust to situation
Do not over-rationalize	Over-rationalizes
Accept situation	Do not accept situation
Adjust to dynamics of situation	Do not adjust to situation
Use humor and imagery	Dwell on seriousness and morbidity

is negative feelings on the part of the hostages toward the police, and the third is, after the resolution of the incident, compassion and sympathy of the ex-hostages toward the hostage takers. As part of the development of the Stockholm syndrome, the hostages are in a cognitive bind (Simon & Blum, 1987). On the one hand, hostages are dependent upon the hostage takers for survival, so there is a desire not to make them irritated. On the other, the hostages are dependent upon the police for their rescue. These two competing interests leave the hostage in a quandary that is difficult to resolve. In large part, the Stockholm syndrome helps resolve this cognitive bind.

    The Stockholm syndrome begins forming shortly after the crisis stage passes and hostages begin developing a positive affect for the captors. Hostages develop positive affect toward their captors for several reasons. Once the hostage accepts being a hostage, they come to believe they will be freed (U.S. Congress, 1975). At least initially, the hostage believes that outside authorities will successfully resolve the incident. With this belief, the hostage does not want to do or say anything that will upset, anger, or antagonize the hostage takers for fear they will do something to the hostage or something to preclude the resolution of the incident. At the very least, the hostage will be obedient and react civilly to the hostage takers. This civility allows the hostage to view the hostage taker as a person. Even if the hostage takers wear masks or hoods, by responding socially, the hostage realizes he is interacting with another human being.

Two, positive bonding begins to occur because of gratitude on the part of the hostage toward the hostage taker (Eitinger, 1982). The hostage taker allowed the hostages to live. The crisis stage is highly emotional and dangerous. Combining the emotions of fear and anxiety with the threats to life and bodily injury, the sense of relief following the crisis stage is enormous. This sense of relief is greatly magnified because of the strength of the emotions present during the crisis stage. In a sense, the hostage "owes" a debt to the hostage taker. Being allowed to live is one of the most crucial components in the development of the Stockholm syndrome. The hostage takers had the power of life and death and exercised the right to life. The hostage believes he is alive through the benevolence of the hostage taker. The more the positive contacts between hostage and hostage taker, the stronger the Stockholm syndrome becomes. That is, the lack of beatings, physical abuse, or verbal degradation lead to more positive affiliations and positive feelings on the part of the hostages toward their captors. The strength of the Stockholm syndrome is greatly enhanced by the frequency of these positive contacts.

Conversely, if the crisis stage was violent and hostages were injured or died during the initial takeover, the Stockholm syndrome will be stronger than if violence were just threatened (Soskis & Van Zandt, 1986). When violence is committed, the surviving hostages experience consuming relief that they were not injured and see the hostage takers as saviors. To these hostages, the strength of the Stockholm syndrome may be greater than in the above case, where no violence was committed.

Some have likened this identification as a regression to childhood on the part of the hostages (Ochberg, 1980a; Strentz, 1979). As a child turns to a parent for physical and emotional support, the hostages turn to the hostage takers for this support. The hostage taker becomes a surrogate parent for the hostage and provides basic safety and security needs. Symonds (1983) refers to this parent-child relationship in the hostage situation as "pathological transference." The hostages have been severely traumatized, or as Symonds refers to it, "traumatic psychological trauma," and regress emotionally to a simpler and less complex time. As they were with their real parents when they were children, the hostages become dependent, compliant, and agreeable toward the hostage takers (Quarles, 1988).

Three, hostages develop positive feelings toward the hostage takers as the hostages come to recognize the human qualities of the hostage takers (Turco, 1987). The hostages come to realize that the hostage takers have the same human attributes as any other persons. Hostage takers have desires, wants, families in some cases, emotions, concerns, etc. More importantly, the hostages come to the realization that the hostage takers are just as much victims as are the hostages. Gerard Vaders, speaking of the South Moluccan terrorists, summed up this belief when he said:

> You had to fight a certain feeling of compassion for the Moluccans. I know this is not natural, but in some ways they came over as human. They gave us cigarettes, they gave us blankets. But we also realized that they were killers. I also knew that they were victims, too. In the long run they would be as much victims as we. Even more. You saw their morale crumbling. You experienced the disintegration of their personalities. The growing of despair. You couldn't help but feel a certain pity. For people at the beginning with egos like gods — impregnable, invincible — they ended up small, desperate, feeling that all was in vain. (In Soskis & Ochberg, 1982)

Five, the hostages may develop positive feelings toward the hostage takers because of the stress and closeness of the group. People who share and experience an intense group experience develop close-knit relationships, affiliations, and bonds. The hostage takers as well as the hostages will participate in this group bonding. The stress and closeness of the situation may result in a reverse Stockholm syndrome, whereby the hostage takers affiliate with the hostages and come to view the hostages as humans trapped in circumstances beyond their control. When negotiators negotiate with hostage takers, one area always worked on is developing the humanness of the hostages for this reason.

In 1976, Israeli citizens on an El Al flight were taken captive by Arab terrorists and flown to the Entebbe Airport in Uganda. The hostages were placed in one room and a terrorist was assigned the task of killing the hostages should a tactical assault be attempted. Israeli commandos mounted a rescue operation to free the hostages. When the commandos stormed the airport, the terrorist shot at the commandos instead of executing the hostages (Stevenson, 1976). The terrorist was killed, so his motivation for not killing the hostages will never be known. It is known that during the incident, the hostages and terrorists became friendly with each other and would sit and talk for hours about the Mideast, families, friends, interests, hobbies, etc. It is likely the terrorist had developed a personal relationship with the hostages and could not bring himself to kill them when the assault came.

The second component of the Stockholm syndrome is fear, disdain, or even hatred towards the authorities and/or police who are attempting to resolve the incident. The hostage is identifying with the hostage takers and identifying with the hostage takers' perceptions of the external dangers caused by the authorities. The hostages perceive the weapons of the police pointed at them as well as the hostage takers. The hostages, not familiar with police and military assault procedures, believe that when the police assault, the police will kill indiscriminately, regardless of whether a person is a hostage taker or a hostage. It is worth noting at this point that in terrorist hostage incidents, most hostages do die during a tactical assault, but not necessarily by the weapons of the police (Jenkins, Johnson, & Ronfeldt, 1977).

At one airplane hijacking incident in the early 1980s, the tactical response team stormed the airplane and employed "flash bang" grenades during the assault. Flash bang grenades are relatively harmless devices that detonate with a loud noise ("bang") and a blinding white light. They are designed to disorient persons in the area so the tactical unit can obtain an advantage during the assault. At this particular incident, the flash bang grenades worked as they were supposed to and the terrorist incident was resolved with no injury to any hostage. The hostages refused to believe the tactical team used "harmless" grenades, arguing instead the grenades malfunctioned. Several days later, the tactical unit took the hostages to a field and demonstrated the grenades. The hostages still refused to believe the tactical unit, arguing that the demonstration was staged to cover the fact that during the assault the real grenades failed to operate properly.

A second component of the resentment of the police is that the police response may force the hostages to take rash and unpredictable actions which could result in the death of hostages. The police have contained and sealed the area, are not granting the demands of the hostage takers, and are provoking the terrorists into taking unplanned action, including killing hostages to gain respect and control of the police. The police are responsible for the elevation of emotions, stress, and tension within the hostage arena.

Third, the hostage may believe the authorities are responsible for dragging the incident out. If the authorities were not present, the hostage takers would resolve the incident and leave, and the hostages could then leave. The longer the incident continues, the stronger this resentment becomes. The perception is the police presence is endangering the hostages; the reality is the police response is reducing the danger to hostages.

In the past several years, there have been several well-publicized hostage-taking incidents where the hostage takers traded clothes and identities with the hostages. Should this occur in a hostage situation, the resentment and fear of the hostage toward the authorities would become more severe. In this case, the hostages have lost their identities as individuals and will now believe the authorities believe them to be part of the hostage takers. This change in identity serves to cause a reappearance of the fears, anxieties, stressors, and defense-oriented reactions present in the crisis stage. The hostages may well lose the ability to cope with the incident and adapt to the dynamics present. A survivor may well become a succumber.

Upon resolution of the incident, the authorities treat everyone released as if they were a terrorist. Until the authorities can establish the identity of the participants, people released from the incident are searched, handcuffed, and guarded. If a hostage is released prior to the resolution of the incident, the hostage is usually kept at the scene and under guard lest they attempt to help the hostage takers from the outside. Released hostages have been known to grab weapons, ammunition, food, etc., and return to the confinement area in an attempt to assist the hostage takers. Some have passed on information and intelligence to the hostage takers concerning police activities, tipped off the hostage takers as to an impending assault, and used media sources to keep hostage takers informed of what is occurring outside the scene. Others have notified the press, held moratoriums and demonstrations at the scene, and publicly berated the authorities attempting to resolve the incident. Hostages do not understand the actions of the authorities and become indignant that they are being treated as a criminal, which strengthens anti-police sentiments.

The third component of the Stockholm syndrome begins when the incident is over. Hostages maintain positive feelings for the hostage takers long after the incident is resolved. The hostage may express some of the beliefs and attitudes of the hostage taker, may argue for leniency for the hostage takers, may refuse to testify, may establish defense funds for the hostage takers, may visit their ex-captors in prison and, occasionally, may wed a hostage taker. The hostage taker is still perceived as the victim. Debriefing the released hostage immediately upon release usually dissipates these positive feelings.

Even though the Stockholm syndrome is primarily negative (from the standpoint of the authorities), the syndrome should be allowed to develop. If nothing else, the formation of the Stockholm syndrome will help keep a hostage alive. Police negotiators also attempt to develop the Stockholm syndrome between themselves and the hostage taker. Building a relationship assists in building trust on the part of the hostage taker and assists in peacefully and successfully resolving the incident.

There are some factors which may prevent the Stockholm syndrome from developing between the hostages and hostage takers (McMains & Mullins, 1995). One, the hostage takers may distance themselves from the hostages. The hostage takers may be on the other side of the room from the hostages, may not talk to the hostages, and may ignore the hostages. The distancing may not be physical, it may be psychological. The hostage taker may continually sneer at the hostages or constantly threaten them with harm. Two, the hostage takers may keep depersonalizing the hostages. Instead of speaking to or about the hostages as persons, the hostage taker may refer to the hostages using derogatory terms, racial epitaphs, or curse word terms. Three, the hostages may be sequestered in another room, tied and gagged, or hooded. In these cases there will be no personal contact between the hostage takers and hostages, so the Stockholm syndrome will never have an opportunity to develop.

If the Stockholm syndrome is not developing, the response team can take several actions to assist in promoting the Stockholm syndrome. One, negotiators can request the names of hostages. Getting names of the hostages forces the hostage takers to recognize his victims as persons. Two, the negotiator can inquire about any injuries or illnesses among the hostages and offer medical assistance or to remove them from the situation. Psychologically, knowing someone is injured or ill more readily leads to compassion and concern for that person. Three, when inquiring about needs (i.e., food, drink, temperature, cigarettes, etc.), the negotiator should refer to everyone, not just the hostage takers. Recognizing the needs of the hostages personalizes them. Four, negotiators should not use the term "hostage." Refer to the hostages as persons or, if known, by name. Five, response teams should use the commodity of time. If nothing else is done, time alone will help promote the Stockholm syndrome. An unavoidable consequence of small group behavior in high-stress situations is that with time the group will get to know each other and become allies working together.

AFTEREFFECTS

When the terrorist operation concludes, the majority of victims will suffer some short- and/or long-term physical and psychological reactions to having been victimized (Ochberg, 1978). While this discussion will again focus on the victims of the hostage situation, it is important to realize that the victims of all types of terrorist operations are subject to experience short- and long-term reactions. The victims of the hostage situation will most likely experience some degree of post-traumatic stress disorder (PTSD; American Psychiatric Association, 1980). PTSD usually occurs when a person experiences a psychological trauma beyond the range of normal human experience.

A person who has been a hostage for a very short time (4–8 hours) can show aftereffects to the incident (Hillman, 1983). The intensity of the situation, not the duration, is most important in the development of traumatic aftereffects. Being taken hostage has been compared and likened to being a prisoner of war (Anderson, 1975). Several of the factors identified by Berger (1977) which prisoners of war experience are also shared by hostages. One, the victims are in a protracted, life-endangering situation. Two, the victims undergo a prolonged helplessness. Three, during the incident there are episodes of recurrent, terrifying events. Four, the victims undergo repeated attacks on their self-esteem and self-image.

The short-term effects which affect the victim appear in the first three to four weeks following the incident. Some of the short-term negative effects of being held hostage include tension, increased anxiety, phobias, disturbed sleep, somatic complaints (physical ailments), irritability, depression, poor concentration, and thought and/or speech preoccupation (Hauben, 1983). In addition, the victim experiences trembling hands, insomnia, exacerbation of prior physical ailments, selected memory loss or memory editing, nightmares, night sweats, startle reactions, psychosomatic ailments (perceived physical ailments), depression, paranoia, delusions, and recurrent intrusive thoughts concerning the incident (Turner & Kusy, 1987; Shaw, 1983).

Some victims have been shown to display some positive psychological aftereffects (Hauben, 1983). These positive aftereffects include heightened self-esteem, heightened enjoyment of the world around them, more intense interpersonal contacts, and improved relations with family and friends. The persons who show these positive psychological aftereffects are a small minority of victims and fall exclusively within Strentz's (1987) survivor category.

After a period of four–five weeks, many victims will still suffer from the short-term symptoms of captivity. Some of the symptoms the hostage may continue to experience include anxiety, phobic behavior, psychosomatic complaints, disturbed sleep, nightmares, and irritability. In addition, many experience other long-term effects such as deep depression, aggression, insecurity, feelings of being misunderstood, disturbed concentration, and lability (changeable, unstable, and prone to error). Some positive long-term effects have been shown by some victims (again a small minority), including a heightened self-esteem, being more attentive to the world around them, and enjoyment of the increased attention they have received.

Table 10.4.
Short- and long-term aftereffects on victims of terrorism.

	Aftereffects
Negative	*Positive*
SHORT-TERM	
Tension	Heightened self-esteem
Increased anxiety	Heightened enjoyment of the world
Phobias	More intense interpersonal relations
Disturbed sleep	Improved relations with family
Somatic complaints	
Irritability	
Depression	
Poor concentration	
Thought preoccupation	
Tremulousness	
Insomnia	
Memory loss or editing	
Nightmares	
Increased startle reaction	
Depression	
Paranoia	
Delusions	
LONG-TERM	
MOST SHORT-TERM EFFECTS	
Deep depression	Heightened self-esteem
Aggression	More attentive to surround
Insecurity	More enjoyment from life
Disturbed concentration	
Lability	

Many of the long-term effects experienced by victims of terrorism are similar to those experienced by ex-POWs, the most comprehensive and comparable data base for examining victims of terrorism. More than any other PTSD group, POWs are the most similar to victims of terrorism in the stress response, the uncontrollability of being held captive, being constantly subjected to terrifying and unpredictable events, and sense of guilt and shame at having been captured. The major difference between POWs and terrorist victims is the length of captivity. POWs have been subjected to significantly greater terms of captivity than terrorist victims.

However, in examining hostage situations, terrorist victims more closely resemble POWs than they do any other group of hostages or crime victims. Much of the following discussion comes from the research done with ex-POWs.

The PTSD reaction to captivity affects the total system of the victim (Eberly & Engdahl, 1991) and has several distinct components that affect daily functioning. There are emotional aftereffects, cognitive functioning can be impaired, behavior is affected, physical effects are manifest, and medical conditions can be elicited or exacerbated by the PTSD response. These aftereffects are intertwined with each other to produce a total systematic reaction. For example, the victim who has a great deal of unresolved anger (an emotional effect) will also display cognitive, behavioral, physical, and extant medical conditions.

Emotionally, the effects of captivity do not disappear when released. The victim may display a general degraded psychological functioning (Fairbank, Hansen, & Fitterling, 1991), psychological impairment (Sutker, Winstead, Goist, & Malow, 1986), and increased general anxiety levels (Ohry, Solomon, Neria, & Waysman, 1994; Ursano & Rundell, 1990). The victim may remain unable to relax emotionally, remain fearful of the future, and become apprehensive, tense, nervous, and experience an anxiety-like attack for no apparent reason. This general anxiety may intensify when the victim is confronted with new or unique environments. Anxiety reactions are one of the most common long-term emotional aftereffects of captivity (Tennant, Goulston, & Dent, 1986).

Anger is an emotional aftereffect experienced by many victims. Anger is directed externally against their captors, and internally for having themselves allowed to be captured, at not having done more to prevent the incident, and for not having attempted to escape, overpower the terrorists, or help resolve the incident. Related to this is a sense of insecurity over having lost personal control of their lives. All sense of personal control was taken away when victimized. Many of life's activities are now geared around retaining control of one's life and surroundings. Many refuse to be put into a situation where they do not have control.

Many victims experience emotional guilt over having let down their families, friends, coworkers, or other hostages. Phobias and paranoia are other aftereffects that plague victims. Many are terrified of the darkness, strangers, changes in the environment, and have a pronounced startle response to loud noises or sudden movement. Mr. T. G. Crews, a police officer who was an ex-POW of the Japanese, refused to work in the jail because of the perception of being confined and the fear the jail environment produced (LaForte, Marcello, & Himmel, 1994).

Severe mood swings are not an uncommon emotional aftereffect. Emotions can rapidly change, moving between extremes of severe elation, followed by a deep depression. Related to this is the aftereffect of chronic depression which can often lead to suicide. LaForte and Marcello (1993), speaking of ex-POWs of the Japanese in World War II, stated, "One ailment rarely spoken of but evident in reasons given for Lost Battalion members' deaths since 1945 is gunshot wounds." The leading cause of WWII POW deaths are accidents, homicide, and suicide (Stenger, 1992). The victim has to cope with the trauma of captivity, and the lingering ramifications of that captivity are so great they cannot live with the emotional pain it has caused (Engdahl, Speed, Eberly, & Schwartz, 1991).

Long-term cognitive effects of being victimized can include self-criticism and second-guessing. Comments like, "If only I had done so-and-so I wouldn't have been taken hostage," or "If I had only resisted more that other person would not have been killed." Such comments indicate that the guilt of having been victimized is perceived by the person as him not having done his moral duty as a contributing member of society. Psychosomatic ailments, diseases, and illnesses are common cognitive effects. There is, in fact, no physical ailment present. But, every scratch, cough, twitch, bump, bruise, and rash is endemic of a serious, debilitating, and life-threatening disease. Eventually, without psychological intervention, these psychosomatic ailments can become a self-fulfilling prophesy and the person will develop a real illness. Another common cognitive aftereffect is the inability to think and function in the world. The victim is not as good a person and not as valuable to himself, family, or society as he should be.

Behavioral aftereffects can include social and self-isolation, uncontrollable crying, an increase or decrease in aggression, poor concentration, intrusive thoughts, trouble with authority figures, an increased startle response, and alcohol and drug abuse. Behavioral aftereffects can be manifest in several ways. Unresolved emotional anger will often lead to an increase in aggression. The victim may seek out avenues in which to express this aggression. He may, for example, frequent clubs where there are numerous fights or may begin engaging in domestic violence, physically abusing his spouse or children. Cognitive tasks that should take only 10–15 minutes can take hours or days, with an impaired ability to recall the task. Intrusive thoughts about captivity are common, and once the intrusive thought is present, it will be accompanied by increased emotional and physical reactions. Many victims have difficulty taking orders from a boss, supervisor, or other authority figures. These persons have control over the victim's life.

One of the most common of all physical aftereffects is sleep disorders. Some victims cannot sleep an entire night, some sleep more than they did before the event, some sleep less, some can only catnap, some require medication, and some do not enter into stage four or only seldom engage in REM (rapid eye movement sleep). Nightmares are one of the most common of all long-term aftereffects (Goldstein, Van-Kammen, Shelly, & Miller, 1987). Nightmares are vivid dreams of the event that return the victim to the total sensory environment of captivity and include the sights, sounds, smells, tastes, and physical pains of the incident. Many nightmares revolve around a specific incident that occurred during captivity and recur every night. It is believed the nightmares help integrate the experience into the person's psyche. With time, nightmares (as with other aftereffects) become less frequent and less intense.

Flashbacks are another common aftereffect. Flashbacks are total sensory remembrances of the sensory stimuli of captivity and occur in an awakened state. They happen only in the absence of other competing external stimuli and last for only a few seconds. They are distressing to the victim because they produce a vivid memory of the incident, one the victim has been trying hard to forget. Any sensory experience can trigger a flashback: vision, sound, smell, touch, emotional feeling, etc. In general, flashbacks tend to be associated with the sensory system which has the strongest memory of the event.

Another aftereffect is withdrawal from close, personal relationships. The victim knows the emotional consequences of getting close to someone and then being placed in a situation where death is imminent. Withdrawal may also be related to feelings of guilt and failure. The victim is embarrassed by their actions in the incident and feels shamed. Sexual difficulties are related to withdrawal. Sexual relationships are the most personal of all human relationships. To keep people outside of the protective shell, victims may not engage in normal sexual practices. The victim may become impotent, may only masturbate, engage exclusively in "one-night stands," or turn to prostitutes for sexual release.

Other physical aftereffects may include eating disorders, constipation, menstrual disorders (males as well as females), weight loss, increased irritability, general somatic complaints, and increased psychophysiological complaints. Many of these aftereffects, in the short term, are normal reactions to being victimized and most can be mitigated through post-incident debriefings.

Medical aftereffects can include significantly higher occurrences of medical illnesses than the general population, nutritional disorders, neuritis, gastrointestinal disorders, and liver and genitourinary disorders. Victims may be hospitalized more than the general population and require longer stays (Hyer, Walker, Swanson, & Sperr, 1992). Eberly, Harkness, and Engdahl (1991) suggested that many social symptoms of

PTSD such as social isolation and alcohol/drug abuse may be secondary symptoms resulting from the primary symptom of stress-induced biological change.

The ordeal of being victimized by terrorists, especially in a hostage situation, may reset the nervous system to a higher resting potential level. The general homeostasis of the nervous system may become elevated because of the stresses inherent in the terrorist incident. The elevation of the nervous system responses also leads to corresponding increases in other stress response systems, such as elevated heart rate and blood pressure, impairment of cognitive functioning, decreased digestion, increased stomach acidity levels, and increased liver activity. Left unchecked and at this higher level of activity, many physiological conditions can be brought on or exacerbated, including heart disease, strokes, arteriosclerosis, liver damage, and ulcers.

Some victims will experience positive long-term aftereffects. Heightened self-esteem, heightened enjoyment of the surrounding world, encouragement of close, personal relationships, and a greater respect for life are among the more common positive aftereffects. These victims have used their ordeal to awaken to a better world and have used the terrorist incident as a rallying point to change their lives in a positive manner. There are many fewer victims that experience these positive aftereffects than ones who experience negative aftereffects. Again, most of these types of victims are survivors during the incident, not succumbers. Many of these victims also had extremely optimistic outlooks on life prior to their experience as a victim of terrorism.

Symonds (1975, 1982), in studying crime victims, has extended his findings with crime victims to the victims of terrorism. According to Symonds, the victim of terrorism goes through four phases in attempting to come to grips with having been victimized. Phase one is the shock and disbelief experienced when realizing he has been victimized. Phase two is the reality phase, where the victim comes to accept the incident. In a hostage incident, phases one and two will occur during the incident. Phase three is traumatic depression. The victim may display anger and rage at having been victimized, may show resignation and apathy about the incident and their future, may become irritable at the slightest provocation, may have a startle reaction to sudden and unexpected environmental stimuli, may have insomnia, may constantly replay the incident in their dreams, nightmares, and flashbacks, and may engage in self-recrimination at having been victimized. The dreams and nightmares of the victim may focus on the hostage taker recapturing them (Ochberg, 1978). Phase four is the resolution phase. The victim may permanently revise his value system, change attitudes about friends,

Table 10.5.

Post-traumatic stress disorder symptoms experienced by victims of terrorism.

Emotional	Cognitive	Behavioral
General degraded psychological functioning	Self-criticism	Social and self-isolation
Increased general anxiety	Second-guessing	Uncontrollable crying
Anger	Psychosomatic ailments	Aggression
Insecurity	Inability to think	Difficulty with authority figures
Guilt	Inability to function	Increased startle response
Phobias and paranoia		Alcohol or drug abuse
Severe mood swings		
Chronic depression		
Suicide		

Physical	Medical	Positive
Sleep disorders	More illnesses	Heightened self-esteem
Nightmares	Nutritional disorders	Heightened enjoyment of world
Flashbacks		
Withdrawal from personal relationships	Gastrointestinal disorders	Better relationships
Sexual difficulties	Liver and genito-urinary disorders	Greater respect for life
Eating disorders	More and longer hospitalizations	
Weight loss		
Irritability	Resetting of nervous system	
General somatic complaints		
Psychophysiological complaints		

family, and material possessions, go to extremes to avoid being victimized again (defensive alert patterns), may suffer from depression over perceived indifference by others to his plight, and may remain angry over having been victimized. The victim may also be enraged over the injustice of the incident and seek revenge on the hostage takers (Symonds, 1980).

In addition to the victims, the families of the victims could suffer adverse reactions from the incident. Just as the victims do, the families have to adapt and cope with the incident. Family members who are able to cope will seek information from the proper authorities, maintain a normal daily routine, seek diversions such as hobbies to pass the free time, affiliate with other families and friends, and keep a positive frame of mind (Hauben, 1983). Some of the short-term effects that family members may experience include heightened anxiety and tension, sleep disturbances, phobias, psychosomatic complaints, preoccupation with the incident, irritability, and depression. The long-term effects on families are similar to the long-term effects experienced by the victims.

In examining hostages of terrorists, Hauben (1983) found that 68 percent suffered from short- and long-term effects, and that 61 percent of the family members experienced similar aftereffects. Predictor variables which can influence the onset and duration of aftereffects include:

1. Age. Younger hostage takers are more likely to experience aftereffects.
2. Education. Less education is correlated with the onset of aftereffects.
3. Affiliation. Greater affiliation with other hostages reduces aftereffects.
4. Pairing. The greater amount of pairing off with another hostage was related to worsening of aftereffects.
5. Stress response. The more severe the hostage's anxiety, hyperactivity, and rigidity, the worse the aftereffects.
6. Length of captivity. The longer the duration of captivity, the worse the aftereffects.
7. Bodily functioning. The worse a victim's general bodily functioning, the worse the aftereffects.

Speed, Engdahl, Schwartz, and Eberly (1989), Sutker, Bugg, and Allain (1990), and Ursano and Rundell (1990) also reported that worse aftereffects were associated with severity of captivity, experience of torture and mistreatment, degree of biological and psychological hardship, amount of weight loss, lower pre-captivity socioeconomic status, lower rank in one's job, and lack of social supports during captivity.

In terms of the family of victims, factors associated with the appearance of aftereffects include: (1) younger age, (2) less education, (3) high stress at the beginning and end of the incident, (4) poor expectations concerning the resolution of the incident, (5) prior psychosomatic complaints, (6) allowing the incident to disturb daily routines, (7) disruption of eating patterns, (8) a high degree of pre-incident and during incident anxiety, (9) prior psychosocial problems, and (10) lower levels of cognitive and physical functioning.

Shaw (1983) reported that the perceptions of victims could influence whether or not the victims would experience aftereffects. The hostage (1) may feel guilty and embarrassment for the bad publicity the incident generated, (2) may be bothered by the trouble and expense incurred to resolve the incident or may believe they were used by the government so the government could further its own political goals, (3) may hold feelings of resentment, guilt, and doubt toward the government and government policies, (4) may deepen his resentment, guilt, and doubt if a hostage was killed by the hostage takers, and (5) may have negative perceptions of his performance during captivity. These hostages may believe they did not resist enough, try to escape, or try to overpower their captors. If the victim engages in second-guessing, aftereffects will usually appear. Second-guessing increases feelings of personal responsibility and guilt.

The symptoms experienced by victims of terrorist incidents are an all-or-none phenomenon. Unlike many other psychological conditions, aftereffects do not occur in degrees (Hillman, 1983). The victim, of example, either has a nightmare or does not have a nightmare. Depending upon the person, the frequency and duration of occurrence may differ for aftereffects. That is, the nightmares may occur nightly, once a week, or once a month. A state of depression may last for four hours, two hours, or one hour. As will be discussed, with time both the duration and frequency of aftereffects decrease.

EMOTIONAL DEBRIEFING FOR VICTIMS OF TERRORISM

Psychic trauma is defined by the *Encyclopedia of Psychology* (Eysenck, Arnold, & Meili, 1972) as "any painful individual experience, especially if that experience is associated with permanent environmental change(s). As a rule a psychic trauma involves a loss of possible motive gratification." Additionally, a traumatic event is characterized by its extraordinariness, suddenness, being overwhelming to the individual, and dangerousness (Figley, 1988). A traumatic incident is identified by having a sudden and unexpected onset, being a threat to life, involving a loss of some kind (i.e., person's sense of self), and being disruptive to one's values (Nielsen, 1984).

Most traumatic incidents have three stages (Tyhurst, 1958): impact, recoil, and adaptation. The impact stage ranges from when the victim realizes there is a threat to her well-being and ends when she no longer experiences that threat. The impact stage lasts for the duration of the incident. The recoil stage begins when the incident ends and lasts until the victim's normal life resumes. This stage is characterized by hypersensitivity where the victim seeks out support from others—family, friends, police, etc. The recoil stage may last for days or weeks following the incident. The adaptation stage begins when the victim is no longer preoccupied with the incident and returns to normal levels of functioning. When the victim has accepted the incident, she is able to talk and think about the incident without excessive emotion.

If the recoil stage of an incident lasts for more than one month and is intense enough to intervene with the victim's functioning, the victim may be suffering from post-traumatic stress disorder. As defined by the DSM–III–R (1987), PTSD is characterized by: (1) an incident outside the range of human experience, (2) has to be such that it would cause distress in most normally functioning people, (3) has to result in increased arousal, and (4) has to result in a blunting of enthusiasm for life.

Following the terrorist incident, police officers are going to be one of the first persons the victims come in contact with. Police officers need to be aware of and alert for short- and long-term symptoms, and symptoms indicating PTSD may already be or will in the future affect the victim. Police officers, being in positions of authority, as well as being the responders to terrorist incidents, can do a lot to ease the symptoms of the victims and even mitigate the later appearance of aftereffects. Police officers can debrief victims and reduce what Symonds (1975) calls "secondary wounds" many victims experience at the hands of the police or other authorities.

Depending upon the notoriety of the terrorist incident, the scene outside the situation may be more stressful, anxiety-producing, and confusing than events which occurred to the victim during the incident. Government officials, government law enforcement personnel, police officers, media members, and family and friends will all be clamoring to talk to the victims. The police officer will be one of the first who will need to talk to the victim. The police officer should spend some time outside of official questioning to help reduce the aftereffects of being victimized and to get the victim started on the road to working through the ordeal. Police officers should conduct the debriefing or interview in comfortable, familiar surroundings. The victim will be disoriented and under a great deal of stress and anxiety. By using a quiet, comfortable room (i.e., first-class passenger lounge, the waiting room in an office building, etc.) the victim will be more relaxed and receptive to the officer's assistance. All too often, the author has seen police officers attempt to debrief victims while sitting in the rear seat of a patrol vehicle with hundreds of other people around. The victim is still psychologically within the physical environment of the incident and not receptive to what the officer is saying.

The police officer should restore a sense of power to the victim as soon as possible. This can be done verbally by asking permission to speak to the victim, by asking to sit, smoke, etc., and by allowing the victim to clean up before the debriefing begins (Symonds, 1982). The officer should offer a choice of alternatives to the victim on where to hold the debriefing and allow the victim to select the debriefing site.

The victim should, before anything else is done, be given a warm reception. This "homecoming" reception should border on elation, and immediately and frequently reassure and reinforce the victim that he acted properly and survived the incident (Shaw, 1983). In addition, the victim should be isolated from the media. There are two reasons for initially isolating the victim from the media. One, the additional confusion and stress of having to respond to a frenzy of questions may only serve to worsen the aftereffects (Hauben, 1983). Two, in the weeks following the incident, when the media focuses on other stories and forgets the victim, the victim may suffer from more severe aftereffects and heightened depression by the lack of attention.

It should be realized that not all victims who are suffering from the aftereffects of the situation will overtly display symptoms. Victims who are not physically harmed may suffer more aftereffects than victims who are physically harmed (Bard & Sangrey, 1979). The unharmed victims will have more difficulty in working through the aftereffects, as other people will not believe the victim is bothered by the incident. For example, Sledge, Boydstun, and Rabe (1980) found that prisoners of war who had been injured by their captors were more likely to undergo positive changes following their internment. They termed this effect the "benefited response." Victims who have been injured by the terrorists believe they have "paid their dues" during the incident. Victims who are uninjured may feel they have let other victims down by coming through the incident unscathed. Extra care should be taken with the unharmed victim to ensure he is not suffering any aftereffects.

It should be explained to the victim that his family and friends may reject him for a short period of time following the incident. Termed "victim blaming" by Soskis and Ochberg (1982), the victim may be perceived as a loser by others. The victim of the terrorist incident is perceived as being a loser because of the nature of the situation. Also, the victim may be rejected because of Lerner's Just World Theory (Lerner, 1970, 1974). The Just World Theory states that persons need to believe in an ordered world where people get what they deserve. Undeserved harm (such as befalls a terrorist victim) threatens the belief in a just world. The person alters his belief system and will try and attribute the harm done to the victim as something the victim deserved because of the type of person the victim was. By knowing there may be a period of readjustment by family and friends, the victim may be able to better cope with the aftereffects of the terrorist incident.

The police officer should reassure the victim they acted properly when in the incident. The police officer should assure the victim he acted exactly as he should have and did the correct thing by not resisting, by helping other victims, by remaining calm, and by collecting information, etc. It should be explained to the victim that acting foolishly is not the same as using courage, strength, and rationality to cope with the situation.

The police officer should explain to the victim why the police acted the way they did. Part of the Stockholm syndrome involves the victim forming a resentment toward the police and a belief the police were partly responsible for endangering the victim's life. The police should explain why the situation was purposely extended in time, why the victims were handcuffed and treated like terrorists, why the victims were placed under guard, etc. This will help reduce both the Stockholm syndrome and any aftereffects the victim may experience. The victim will be able to get a better grasp of the entirety of the situation and be able to put her own reactions into proper perspective. Also, the officer should explain to the victim the aftereffects the victim is likely to suffer from, or why the victim is currently suffering from a particular aftereffect or set of aftereffects. The officer should be careful to ensure the victim is not given a "self-fulfilling prophecy" (i.e., experiences the aftereffect because it is expected). The officer should be careful to explain that the aftereffects do not affect every victim, and the victim may not experience some aftereffects but should be aware of what the aftereffects are. Also, by knowing what to expect, the victim may experience aftereffects to a less severe degree than they might if the aftereffects appear unexpectedly.

If the victim wants, the officer should allow the victim to ventilate their emotions. If necessary, it may even be the officer receives some verbal abuse from the victim as the victim ventilates his negative feelings toward the police, terrorists, or others involved in the incident. Along with ventilation, the officer should allow the victim to relive the situation in emotional terms. The officer should encourage the victim to verbalize the emotions experienced during the incident, as this will assist in lessening the aftereffects (Ochberg & Soskis, 1982).

The officer can ask the victim what can be done to assist other potential victims in the future or to give suggestions for establishing a victim training program to help others should they become victims. This will allow the victim to realize the positive aspects of the incident and not allow her to dwell on the negative aspects. The victim will be able to realize she can use the incident as a positive growth experience and make a useful contribution based upon her experiences. The officer may also question the victim concerning the information the terrorists gave the victim concerning the organization, philosophies of the organization, future plans, etc. The officer should explain to the victim that terrorists often feed victims false information, and this information could be used in the future to assist in preventing other operations by that organization of terrorists. In addition to allowing the victim to make a positive contribution, the victim will also realize that her perceptions of the terrorists are not entirely accurate and this may assist in defusing the Stockholm syndrome.

The police officer should keep the debriefing short. The victim will want to get home to familiar surroundings and to be left alone with his family. By dragging out and extending the debriefing, the officer only deepens the victim's resistance, distrust, and ill will toward authority figures. It is advisable for the police officer to give all of the victims a short period of time to be alone with each other. The victims will do more to work through the aftereffects on their own and with each other than the police officer or mental health professional can ever expect to do. The victim may resent the intrusion of the police officer and reject what the officer is saying because the officer "hasn't been there" and could never know what the victim is experiencing. Letting the victims form a support group is analogous to peer support teams.

The police should discuss the above issues with the families of the victims while the situation is ongoing. This will enable the families to understand and cope with some of the changes which will be evidenced on the part of the victims. If the families have an understanding of what to expect and how they can help the victims, the aftereffects will be significantly reduced. Specific suggestions for dealing with each long-term aftereffect can be offered. Thus, if the victims experience an aftereffect, the families can take preventive action to reduce the psychological severity of the aftereffect.

It is advisable for police officers to check back with victims on anniversary dates. Anniversary dates are significant dates associated with the terrorist incident. Examples might include the date one year following the onset of the incident, birthdays of the victims or of a victim who was killed during the incident, major holidays such as Christmas and New Year's Day, and trial dates of the terrorists. About two weeks prior to significant anniversary dates, aftereffects begin increasing in frequency and duration. A quick telephone call or short visit prior to anniversary dates lets the victims know they have not been forgotten and helps mitigate aftereffects.

SUMMARY

Terrorist incidents are emotionally charged and highly stressful events. Victims of those incidents are usually innocent bystanders caught in the

Table 10.6.
General guidelines for law enforcement personnel
debriefing victims of terrorism.

1. Debrief in comfortable, quiet surroundings
2. Restore a sense of power to the victim
3. Give victim a warm reception
4. Isolate victim from media
5. Explain Victim Blaming
6. Reassure victim he or she acted properly
7. Explain police response to the victim
8. Explain aftereffects the victim may experience
9. Allow victim to ventilate emotions
10. Ask about helping future victims
11. Keep debriefing short
12. Allow victims some time together
13. Discuss issues with victim's family
14. Check back with victims near anniversary date

flow of political events. The victim is caught in an event that is unexpected, sudden, life-threatening, threatening to his self-esteem, and emotionally damaging. For many victims, the stress of the incident may be so overwhelming and overpowering that the person is affected for the rest of his life. The incident can be one of those types of events that produce permanent change, usually for the worse.

Conducting an immediate debriefing for the victim can go a long way toward removing the emotional scar tissue and returning the victim to a normal life. Just as the police have a responsibility to resolve, investigate, and arrest terrorists who conduct illegal operations, the police have a responsibility to work with the victims of the terrorist operation. "To protect and serve" is not a hollow phrase seen on television and movie police shows. The victim has the perception the police failed in their first responsibility: to protect. This perception can partly be erased by fulfilling the second half of the motto: to serve. Service to the victim means far more than resolving the incident, arresting the terrorists, and going back on patrol. Service means assisting the victims to remove the emotional debris left by the incident.

Police are usually astounded and stunned when ex-victims help the terrorists, refuse to testify against their tormentors, and even visit them in prison. It should be clear that these behaviors on the part of victims are normal components of being victimized and are part of the Stockholm syndrome. Debriefing victims can help reduce the Stockholm syndrome and help the police as much as the victims. Having victims refuse to testify in court can weaken a case to the extent the terrorists are acquitted. By helping the victims, the police are helping themselves.

Some victims will be so traumatized that a debriefing will not do them any good. Even here the police officer has a responsibility to assist the victims in obtaining professional counseling. Many police departments have established victim services teams, of which one function and responsibility is to assist in emotionally debriefing victims. Members of these teams, while more thoroughly trained in emotional debriefing than most police officers, know when it is time to call in the professional counselor, and do not hesitate to do so. Most victims, however, do not require extensive counseling. A short debriefing following the incident is sufficient. Even untrained police officers can be of great assistance in these debriefings by simply following the guidelines established above.

In general, the officer should be glad there are victims to debrief. Having victims alive means the terrorists failed and did not accomplish their objectives, whether the operation was a simple bombing or a complicated hostage event. Being able to attend to victims means that, at some level, the police won and the terrorists lost.

Recognize also that victims may not be limited to civilians caught in a terrorist operation. As recently demonstrated at Oklahoma City, victims can include police officers, fire fighters, EMS personnel, other rescue personnel, and bystanders. The officer should be prepared and willing to assist these other secondary victims to the terrorist atrocity. They may be as affected as much as the primary victims.

Chapter 11

HOSTAGE TAKING

Terrorists can choose from a wide range of operations. One of the only terrorist operations open for law enforcement or government intercession is the hostage situation. In recent years, as the government has failed to change law or policy in response to terrorist operations of bombing, assassination, sabotage, etc., hostage taking has become a relatively frequent occurrence in the terrorist arsenal. As Jenkins (1985) stated, "Terrorists have added several dimensions to hostage taking: (1) hijacking airliners to make political demands, (2) seizing embassies, (3) kidnapping diplomats to gain the release of prisoners, and (4) kidnapping corporate executives to finance terrorist operations." Unlike some other forms of operations, hostage taking is an inexpensive and effective tactic for small organizations. Just a few people can have a major impact on governments (Jenkins & Wright, 1990). Increased security and intelligence gathering has made other types of operations more difficult, the number of targets available to the terrorist is virtually limitless, and military responses are not an option for governments. By taking hostages, the terrorists can command worldwide attention and gain power they otherwise could not.

The Rand Corporation reported that hostage taking is on the rise, and that hostage taking operations are lucrative for the terrorist because of the high probability of success (U.S. Government, 1975). The Rand Corporation found that upon initiating a hostage taking operation there was an 87% probability of actually taking hostages, a 79% probability of all terrorists involved in the operation escaping punishment or death, a 40% probability of all or some of the demands being met when more than safe passage or exit was demanded, a 29% probability of all terrorists' demands being met, an 83% probability of having authorities granting the terrorists an exit or safe passage to another country when this was the only demand, a 67% probability that the terrorists could still avoid capture when no demands were met, and a 100% probability of the terrorists receiving major publicity.

This data is somewhat dated and includes international terrorist incidents. No data exists following the 1975 government report, but there

435

is little question but that the numbers have significantly changed as the law enforcement and government response to hostage-taking incidents have improved. The only figure unchanged is the 100 percent probability of the incident receiving major publicity. Law enforcement has become extremely effective at dealing with terrorist hostage incidents. In the United States, the success rate of law enforcement in dealing with terrorist hostage-taking incidents as measured by hostages freed safely, terrorist demands not met, and terrorists captured following the incident is over 90 percent. Law enforcement personnel have learned the lessons of hostage negotiations through their extensive training and work with criminal and mentally disturbed hostage incidents.

Two recent and notable failures have been the Randy Weaver siege at Ruby Ridge, Idaho and the Branch Davidian incident in Waco, Texas. These two incidents serve to illustrate just how tenuous the negotiation process can be and the ever-present possibilities for failure. These two incidents, and their aftermath, made national headlines for months and still continue to be held up by the media as representing problems in government policy. What is often overlooked is that these incidents were not failures of the hostage negotiation process. They were failures of policy.

On the international level, the government is responsible for negotiating with terrorists and the success rates in these incidents are not as high. In these incidents, the government negotiates more from a policy standpoint than from a resolution standpoint. Resolution negotiations are conducted by law enforcement personnel from the area where the incident occurs. If the incident occurs in a country sympathetic to the terrorist cause, the only negotiations that take place are diplomatic negotiations. These incidents place the U.S. government in a virtual no-win situation. The government must negotiate with the terrorists and the government supporting the terrorists. All the while, American lives are in danger and there is no recourse to tactical resolutions.

This chapter will discuss terrorist hostage taking, with an emphasis on terrorist hostage taking within the United States. Government responses will be discussed since international incidents do affect the United States and does affect terrorist hostage-taking incidents that occur in the U.S. Emphasis, however, will be given to terrorist hostage taking that law enforcement can impact. The characteristics of hostage situations will be described, stages of a hostage situation explained, and variables affecting the incident discussed. Attention will be given to the relevant factors pertinent to law enforcement agencies and officers entrusted with responding to these hostage situations, including response team structure and responsibilities, crisis intervention principles, handling demands and using time, and communication strategies.

GOVERNMENT RESPONSE OPTIONS

Internationally, governments are divided on the issue of whether or not to negotiate with terrorist hostage takers. Some governments, such as the United States and Israel, have a no-negotiation, no-ransom policy, while others, including most Latin American governments, advocate a flexible response policy (Evans, 1979; Friedlander, 1983; Mickolus, 1978).

The no-ransom policy assumes all terrorists are the same and that refusing to give in to terrorist demands will deter future hostage-taking operations (Friedlander, 1983). There are several arguments used by the proponent of the no-ransom approach to support their position. One, terrorists will not keep their end of the bargain and that, once demands are met, will not release hostages and will add other demands. Once the demands are met, the terrorists may even kill the hostages. Two, agreeing to and satisfying the demands of terrorist hostage takers will only serve to increase the number of hostage incidents. Three, governments should adopt a no-ransom policy because terrorist organizations are forming an international cartel. Terrorist organizations receive funding from the same sources, meet together, help train each other, and conduct joint operations. Four, when a terrorist hostage-taking operation occurs, there is not enough time to formulate a bargaining policy. Each terrorist organization must be dealt with differently and each hostage incident has factors unique to the particular situation. Five, it is morally wrong for a government to give in to a group of terrorists. Six, many times terrorist hostage takers may demand the release of political prisoners. Seven, a no-ransom policy is one which has made the decision to sacrifice a few lives in the present for the long-term return of losing fewer lives in the future. By not ransoming, the incidents of terrorist hostage taking will decrease in the future, thus saving lives in the long run.

At the other extreme is the flexible response policy. Those advocating the flexible response argue each hostage situation has to be treated differently. Terrorist organizations are all different, they have simply adopted the same tactic to achieve their political goals (Vetter & Perlstein, 1991). Two, flexible response advocates argue that the no-ransom policy has not worked. This no-ransom policy has not deterred the terrorists and the frequency of terrorist hostage-taking operations are as high as ever, if not higher. Also, governments who have adopted this policy will eventually be forced to negotiate, thus weakening policy and sending a message to other terrorists. Three, terrorists are worried about the fate of their organization. Negotiations can be used to reassure the terrorists of the survival of organizational members and thus serve as an avenue to end the hostage situation. Four, governments have a moral responsibility to protect its citizens. By adopting a no-ransom policy and placing citizens in unnecessary jeopardy, other citizens lose respect of the government. Five, not all terrorist hostage-taking operations involve ransom demands. In fact, the granting of demands may be secondary to the true purpose of taking hostages (Wilkinson, 1974). The terrorist hostage-taking operation may be merely a means of obtaining publicity. By providing media coverage, ransom demands may be lowered and make the terrorists more likely to resolve the situation (Miller, 1978). Six, if a government adopts a no-ransom policy, this will eventually result in the government being placed in a terrorist hostage-taking situation where they are forced to negotiate. When that situation occurs and the terrorists are apt to force the situation, the government will lose face and respect by being forced to change their position. Seven, when confronted with a no-response policy, terrorists may turn from hostage-taking operations to other, more lethal operations. A flexible response policy gives the government some control over the type of operation terrorists employ.

Both sides of the argument have major weaknesses in their rationales for supporting their position. Most of these problems are fairly self-evident and will not be discussed in detail. However, the most significant weakness with the no-negotiation policy is that eventually a government will be forced into a position where it has to negotiate. Once the government violates its policy of non-negotiation, the government will be perceived as weak, non-committal, and ineffective in dealing with the terrorist problem. As defined by Friedlander (1983), a policy is "an explicit or implicit declaration of intent to act in a certain manner under prescribed circumstances, and it is designed to affect the behavior of a defined population. It refers primarily to the future and purports of affect actions not yet taken rather than to respond to deeds done." Arguments against non-negotiation reflect a basic misunderstanding of what policies are. Non-negotiation should not mean a government will not discuss issues with terrorists in an attempt to resolve the situation.

It is believed a flexible response policy is the best alternative for a government. It allows a government to keep all options open when a terrorist incident occurs and prevents the government from being placed in an untenable and undefendable position. Government policy should reflect a negotiation strategy based upon established principles of hostage negotiations. A government negotiating from the standpoint of political issues is very similar to negotiations conducted by law enforcement: the strategy and tactics are the same, techniques of negotiation are the same, and intended outcomes are the same. Neither will a willingness to negotiate send the wrong message to other terrorists.

CHARACTERISTICS OF HOSTAGE SITUATIONS

A hostage is defined by the *American Heritage Dictionary* (1980) as "a person held as a security for the fulfillment of certain terms." There are several important components of this definition. One, a person is at risk of injury or death. Without persons, there is no hostage situation. The first and foremost goal of negotiating a hostage incident is to save lives (Schlossberg, 1979). The risk of injury or death introduces a sense of the dramatic into the incident and makes the hostage incident a media attraction (Keen, 1991). Two, a hostage is a person that is held. The person is no longer free and no longer in control of his life. The person is powerless to leave. Three, the person is held for security. The hostage has certain value to the hostage taker. Four, the person is security for certain conditions or terms. To free the hostage, the hostage taker has to be given something in return. Goldaber (1979) argued there are only two factors to consider in a hostage incident: who the hostage takers are and what their demands are. McMains and Mullins (1995) said that hostage negotiations added two additional factors: what the negotiators are willing to give and what the hostage takers will give.

The process of negotiating is that of using information and power to affect behavior in circumstances of tension (Cohen, 1979). According to Cohen, conflict is an integral part of the negotiation process and involves people attempting to maximize their gains and minimize their losses. The success or failure of negotiations depend upon the attitudes of the people involved in the process. The process of negotiating is flexible and requires patience to resolve the incident. Negotiations depend upon words, not action. Negotiators must have training in crisis intervention and communication skills. They must be trained in active listening, persuasion techniques, and problem-solving skills. The purpose and objective of negotiation is to resolve conflict. Hostage takers want one thing, negotiators want another. The negotiator must resolve these differences so the terrorists believe they have won.

The most difficult job for the negotiator is to reach an agreement with the hostage taker so the hostage taker feels comfortable enough to end the incident. According to Fisher and Ury (1981), an agreement must have three elements. One, the agreement must meet the legitimate interests of all parties. There are two sides in a hostage incident. Negotiators have to consider the hostage-taker's interests and needs to successfully and peacefully resolve the incident. Two, agreements have to be reached fairly.

Negotiators cannot arbitrarily exercise their power. They have to demonstrate how a solution will benefit both sides. This does not mean granting the demands of the hostage takers. It means understanding the hostage-taker's needs and presenting new options for meeting those needs. Three, community interests must be met. Negotiators must negotiate issues, not the person raising the issues. The negotiator may despise the hostage takers, but he must ignore this personal prejudice and concentrate on the issues. The actions taken by a negotiator, especially in a high-profile incident such as a terrorist incident, are being watched by the citizens. The negotiator must gain the trust of the hostage takers and the citizens watching. Promises made and kept or not kept reflect on the public's perception and trust of the government.

Historically, the context of hostage incidents have been fourfold (Goldaber, 1983; Hassel, 1975, 1982; IACP, 1983; Miron & Goldstein, 1979; Soskis & Van Zandt, 1986). One, persons engaged in criminal activity have taken hostages to avoid capture and prosecution. Two, emotionally disturbed individuals have taken hostages as part of their illness. Three, prisoners rioting have taken hostages to obtain better living conditions. Four, terrorists have taken hostages to obtain political concessions. If negotiations are to be successful, negotiators must understand within which context the incident is occurring. The demands made by the hostage taker will be made within the context of who the hostage taker is. Demands made by a criminal will be different than those made by a terrorist. Understanding the context of the incident is the only way a negotiator can be successful.

The motivations of hostage takers are both instrumental and expressive (Miron & Goldstein, 1979). Instrumental motivations are to get a government to comply with a set of demands. Releasing terrorist prisoners, changing a law, or paying reparations are instrumental motivations. Expressive motivations are to demonstrate power. Terrorists taking hostages are demonstrating their power and strength over a society, political system, or government. Motivationally, hostage takers are on a continuum. At one end are hostage takers who stress the instrumental motivations, such as the antisocial who wants money and transportation. At the other anchor of the continuum are the emotionally disturbed who are expressing their anger, fear, or outrage over some real or perceived plight. Terrorists are toward the middle of this continuum, engaging in the activity for both instrumental (political gain) and expressive (demonstrate their power) motivations. The motivations of the hostage taker, like the context, determines the strategies and tactics of the negotiator.

Not all hostage incidents are negotiable, terrorist incidents included. In some situations, the hostage taker has no demands and does not want a peaceful solution but instead wants to commit homicide and suicide (FBI, 1991). There are certain characteristics a hostage incident must have for it to be negotiable (FBI, 1985). One, the hostage taker must have a desire to live. A negotiator cannot negotiate with a person who does not want to live. On the other hand, the desire to live is a powerful motivator. Many persons who express a desire to die actually do want to live. Of all motivations and needs, the desire to live is the strongest and most encompassing. It is incumbent upon the negotiator to find that buried motivation and negotiate from that perspective.

Two, there has to be a threat of force on the part of the response team. Without the threat of force, there is no motivation for the hostage taker to negotiate. In many international terrorist incidents, the terrorists have originated the incident or moved the hostages to a location where force was not possible. The Iranian embassy siege, TWA Flight 847, and the hostages taken in Beirut are recognizable examples. Without any force, there will be no negotiations. When force is deployed, the hostage taker has to believe the force will be used if necessary.

Three, the hostage taker has to make demands. Seen often with suicidal persons, terrorists seldom take hostages without making demands. The entire purpose of the terrorist hostage-taking operation is to gain concessions from a government. This means the terrorist must make demands. When demands are made, the negotiator has something to work with to resolve the situation. The negotiator can use time and conflict resolution techniques to bring the incident to a peaceful resolution.

Four, the hostage taker must recognize that the negotiator is a person who can hurt but is willing to help. Just like a hostage, the negotiator must be perceived as having worth to the hostage taker, both in a positive and negative sense. By manipulating helping and harm, the negotiator can become a powerful ally of the hostage taker. To reach acceptable compromise, the negotiator must become an ally of the hostage taker. It is worth reemphasizing that compromise means resolving the incident without personal harm, either to the hostages, response units, or terrorists.

Five, negotiations take time. Time is a commodity and must be used by the negotiator. Hostage takers often make demands that misuse time, such as wanting a law changed within 24 hours. Changing a law is a somewhat reasonable demand. Insisting that it be changed in 24 hours is unreasonable. It is the negotiator's responsibility to show that the time is unreasonable and get a concession on this demand. Once that concession is made, then the hostage taker is more likely to concede to other demands.

Six, a reliable channel of communications must exist between the negotiator and hostage taker. The negotiator must speak directly to the hostage taker (American Justice, 1994). Negotiators must not communicate through third parties because of the potential for misunderstanding and misinterpretation. Reliable communications also means the hostage taker and negotiator speak the same language and same dialect. Negotiating in street Spanish while the hostage taker speaks only Castillion Spanish is not communication. The negotiator must also understand the idioms and slang of the language to effectively communicate.

Seven, the situation must be contained. Both the location of the incident and communication channels have to be isolated and controlled. Hostage takers and hostages cannot be allowed the freedom to change locations. They must be controlled in an area and not allowed to move around. The reason kidnapping incidents are so difficult to resolve is that the situation is not contained. Likewise, communications must be controlled. The hostage takers cannot be allowed to establish their own forum for speaking to the news media. Containment makes the hostage taker deal with the negotiator and this gives the negotiator the advantage.

Eight, the negotiator must be able to speak with the hostage taker responsible for making decisions. The negotiator must identify the person in charge and negotiate with that person. Functionaries or representatives of the leader will not be able to make decisions but will have to relay communications to the leader. Communications will suffer, time will work against the negotiator, and conflict will not be resolved.

One may ask, why negotiate at all with terrorists? There are other options open to response units. One is an assault of the location. This tactic can produce a rapid end to the situation but is a high-risk option, both to the response units and hostages. Strentz (1979) reported that 78 percent of all hostages killed during a hostage incident are killed during an assault. Some police departments, in fact, include more officers on the assault team than necessary because they expect the first two officers to enter the location to be killed (McMains & Mullins, 1995). Another option is a sniper. The advantage is a quick kill of the hostage taker. Disadvantages include the wrong person being killed, the sniper missing, and hostage takers and hostages exchanging clothing. Also, with multiple hostage takers snipers cannot kill all in the time necessary for this solution to be effective. A third option is chemical agents. Often used with assaults, there are virtually no advantages to chemical agents and numerous negatives. Negatives can include unreliability, missing the terrorist location entirely, not being of sufficient strength to affect the hostage takers, adversely affecting hostages, adversely affecting the tactical team, and dispersing before producing the desired effects. The final and most successful option is to contain and negotiate. The negative aspects of this option are the time-consuming nature of negotiations, their being labor intensive, manpower requirements, and pre-incident preparation. The advantages are saving lives, public image, and protection from liability. Of the various options available, containment and negotiation are the most successful and reasonable options available for the terrorist hostage-taking operation.

A TYPOLOGY OF HOSTAGE SITUATIONS

Hostage-taking operations involving terrorists are more complex than hostage-taking situations involving criminals or the mentally disturbed. Criminals taking hostages are generally unplanned activities. As a general rule, the criminal hostage taker takes hostages because they were interrupted during the commission of another criminal act or as an act of passion. Examples of this type of hostage taking would include the police arriving on the scene during a robbery and the criminal taking hostages to prevent the police from entering the scene and as a method of escape, or a marital argument over child visitation rights resulting in one parent taking the child by force and then using the child as leverage to keep from getting arrested. The terrorist hostage taker is not so cavalier in the taking of hostages.

Terrorists engage in three types of hostage operations. The first type of hostage operation is the more classical operation most people would identify as a hostage incident. The taking of an airplane, its crew, and passengers would be an example of this type of operation. The great majority of terrorist hostage-taking operations of this type are planned operations. Terrorists take hostages for a purpose and these operations are designed for success, where success is defined in terms of having demands met and escaping afterwards. Very rarely do terrorists engage in unplanned hostage-taking operations. When terrorists do take hostages in an unplanned operation, it is, as with criminals, because some other operation was compromised and the lives of the hostages are used as trade for the escape of the terrorists.

Kidnappings are a second type of terrorist hostage-taking operation. One or two individuals are taken hostage by the terrorists and secreted away to some unknown location. Although terrorists do negotiate with authorities for the release of the victim, kidnappings are different from other types of hostage-taking operations in that the victim is detained in a hidden location. The negotiation process is similar to the process used in other hostage-taking situations. There are some major differences, however. One, negotiators can be more low key and consume longer amounts of time in a kidnap operation. Two, several different law enforcement individuals can serve as the negotiator. Very seldom are negotiations conducted face-to-face. Instead, negotiations may occur through the print media, letters, radio and television, and telephone. Three, and most significantly, there is no threat of force by the authorities. Because of this, the negotiator does not have the same leverage over the hostage taker as in other hostage situations and must alter negotiation strategy from a power position to more of a position of voluntary compliance. The major law enforcement effort in a kidnapping centers around finding the location of the victim. Once the victim is located, negotiations then usually proceed as in other hostage-taking situations.

The third type of terrorist hostage-taking operation is the siege. A siege operation is similar to a regular hostage-taking operation, with the major difference being that a siege operation is designed to last for a long period of time. A siege is a carefully planned operation and the terrorists have made logistical plans for remaining in the operation for a long period of time. The American embassy situation in Iran and the Hanafi Muslim takeover of three Washington D.C. buildings in March 1977 were siege operations. In a regular hostage-taking situation, the hostage takers can usually be worn down through fatigue, hunger, and thirst. This is not the case in a siege operation, as the terrorists have planned for these contingencies. The terrorist may also have made plans to deal with the loss of electricity and other necessary services. In addition, siege operations usually involve more terrorists than does a more conventional hostage-taking operation. A conventional hostage-taking operation may involve two to five terrorists. A siege operation may involve ten or twenty terrorists.

In hostage-taking operations, terrorists have taken diplomats, police officers, servicemen, businessmen, government officials, and innocent citizens as hostages (Aston, 1983). Of those, businessmen are the most likely to be kidnapped and diplomats the least likely. This makes some sense, since even in terrorist incidents many demands revolve around financial ransom. Even in the American embassy situation in Iran, one of the key demands concerned financial reparations. Police officers, servicemen, innocents, and diplomats are most often kidnapped and held in order to obtain concessions from a government. Diplomats and innocents are most likely to be taken hostage during siege operations. Sieges usually involve an embassy or government building. Although there are no data, it is believed that most of the victims of a conventional (non-kidnapping and non-siege) terrorist hostage-taking operation are innocents, people unlucky enough to be in the wrong place at the wrong time. The taking of innocent hostages has some intrinsic value for the terrorists, as governments would go farther in granting demands to assure the freedom of innocent citizens. Diplomats and service personnel would be viewed as being more expendable, as the threat of being taken hostage is a job risk for those persons. This does not imply, however, that the government would be willing to allow diplomats and service personnel to die.

Terrorist hostage takers have historically demanded political change, the release of prisoners, ransom, changes in corporate policy, and escape. Aston (1983) reported that in Western Europe, 29% of kidnappings were done for ransom, 14% for the release of prisoners, 6% for political changes, 6% for changes in corporate policy, and 33% of kidnappings resulted in no demands being made. The other 12% of kidnappings produced a combination of demands, such as ransom and release of prisoners, transfer of prisoners, and to make a public statement. In terms of siege operations, demands were 18% for safe escape, 10% for political change, 8% for the release of prisoners, 18% had a combination of demands (including escape, release of prisoners, and political change), and 46% of siege operations resulted in no demands being made.

Mickolus (1978) showed that in the time period 1968–1975, United States citizens were involved in one-third of all terrorist hostage-taking operations, but the United States government was not the recipient of demands. In most terrorist hostage-taking operations that involved U.S. citizens, the terrorists made demands on corporations or made generalistic-type demands (i.e., ransom for the safe return of hostages).

PHASE MODEL FOR HOSTAGE
SITUATIONS AND NEGOTIATIONS

The law enforcement response to a hostage situation is a three-phase response. Phase one is the initial confrontation/reaction. This phase involves the patrol officers or other officers who receive the initial call and are the first on the scene. In this phase, the officers should ensure that a hostage situation is in fact occurring, notify the commander, clear radio traffic, indicate the number of units necessary to establish the inner perimeter, instruct responding units in approach and placement, secure the area, treat and remove the wounded, remove innocent bystanders and other curiosity seekers, detain and interview witnesses, and keep the situation contained (Dalager, 1984). In some instances, the officers may make initial contact with the hostage taker, simply to assure the hostage takers that negotiators are on the way and that the demands of the hostage taker will be heard. The officer should keep the situation contained, reassure the hostage takers that their needs will be heard, and begin reducing the stress and anxiety of the hostage takers. First responders should not begin negotiations.

In terrorist hostage-taking situations, the terrorists may initiate contact with the patrol officer. Since the initial stages of a hostage-taking situation are the most dangerous, the patrol officer should be extremely careful in talking with the terrorists. The patrol officer should carefully listen to the terrorists without interruption. As stress is at its highest, the terrorists may not be comprehensible, may be threatening to immediately kill a hostage to show they mean business, and may make known their initial demands. The patrol officer should remain calm and reassure the terrorists he or she is powerless to do anything, but the authorities that can deal with the situation have been notified and are on the way. The patrol officer should use communication and stress management skills to reassure and calm the terrorists, and urge the terrorists not to act out of haste but to wait until negotiators are on the scene.

In phase two, the negotiators and special tactical teams are on the scene. Patrol officers should maintain the outer perimeter and control the crowd, traffic, and news media. The negotiations team will establish a command post in a location out of sight of the hostage takers, and members of the team will be assigned specific duties. Intelligence will begin being collected and disseminated (Bell, 1978). During the second phase, negotiations will be conducted with the hostage takers and progress made in resolving the incident.

The tactical team will establish an inner perimeter and plan for tactical operations. The tactical team will collect intelligence on the hostage takers, hostages, weapons, floor plans of the location, security devices, and other intelligence necessary for tactical operations. Contingency plans will be developed for assault operations, snipers, and chemical solutions. Typically, negotiators will not begin conversations with the hostage takers until the tactical team is deployed and comfortable with the possibility of having to tactically resolve the situation.

With a terrorist hostage situation, a second negotiating team with a separate command post, tactical team, and command staff is recommended. The secondary team should be at the scene but removed from the primary negotiating team. This secondary team should be kept informed of negotiation strategies and progress, any intelligence collected on the incident, and other relevant factors. If the incident becomes a siege or lasts for over 14–18 hours, the secondary team can step in and continue negotiations without a loss of continuity. Also, should a "breakout" occur, the secondary team can begin negotiations where the primary team left off. A breakout is the case where the terrorists move the hostages to a different location. The breakout may occur for many reasons, including a decision by the on-scene commander to allow the terrorists to move locations to preserve hostage lives, or the terrorists being mobile in an airplane, bus, train, etc., and make a self-initiated move the police are powerless to prevent.

In phase three of the incident, the negotiators establish a channel of communication with the hostage takers, the initial demands of the hostage takers are presented, and the number and condition of the hostages determined. Information gathered by the negotiator is passed on to the intelligence officer who tries to establish a profile of the hostage taker and hostages. The tactical team gathers all material and equipment needed for an assault. Negotiations progress throughout phase III until resolution is reached. Table 11.1 presents a summary of the phase response to a hostage situation.

Table 11.1.
A phase model of the hostage situation.

Phase Task	Actions
I Start of incident	Terrorists take aircraft. Passengers are used as hostages. Release flight attendant to announce demands.
I Procedures for initial police response	Seal area. Isolate aircraft on tarmac. Do not overreact. Try to make initial contact with hostage takers.
II Establish perimeter	Negotiators and tactical team relieve patrol officers. Briefing by patrol. Patrol controls traffic, crowd, and news media.
II Create command post	Find building or use mobile command post. Stay out of sight of hostage takers.
III Negotiating team	Open initial communications.
III Actions and events	Initial demands made. Determine number of hostage takers and hostages.
III Examine outside factors that exist or hinder operations, including public information	Media conducting live reports. Crowd gathering. Negotiators trying to defuse situation.
III Method of concluding incident	Terrorists release two hostages, kill one hostage. Negotiations broken off. Commander orders tactical solution to situation.
III Special equipment required	Shields, AR-15s, rope, det cord, stun grenades, tear gas, etc.

STAGES OF A HOSTAGE INCIDENT

A hostage situation is a crisis incident. Like other crises, a hostage incident has different stages, and each stage has different characteristics that require different skills to manage. The stages of a crisis have been defined by different researchers in different ways, but all agree that a crisis progresses through predictable stages (Caplan, 1964; Dalager, 1984; Tyhurst, 1986). Each stage of a crisis has unique aspects that a negotiator has to be able to recognize, for each stage of a crisis requires special skills on the part of a negotiator. Understanding the stages of a crisis is important to the on-scene commander so that he/she can evaluate progress and establish strategy for moving to the next stage of negotiations. The stages of a crisis are pre-crisis, crisis, adaptation, and resolution.

The pre-crisis stage occurs before the incident actually begins. All participants, terrorists, hostages, and law enforcement personnel are carrying on their routine functions. Stress is low, emotions are controlled, and ability to reason and make decisions is normal. The terrorists may be planning an incident and preparing the necessary materials, weapons, and supplies to conduct the operation. During the pre-crisis stage, the terrorists will move into position and begin final preparations for the incident to begin. To them, emotions are beginning to rise, stress is becoming manifest, and tension is heavy. There is not much decision making required because the plan has been established and all that is necessary to carry out the plan.

The onset of the incident is when the second stage, the crisis stage, begins. Everyday routines are interrupted, stress and tension elevates, anxiety increases, and ability to reason is low. Life seems out of control because of the high emotional content, unexpected events are occurring, and threats to life, security, and self-esteem are manifest. Basic needs are threatened and people attempt to cope with that threat by acting unpredictably (Caplan, 1961; Glasser, 1984). NOVA (1992) has defined crisis as a "cataclysm of emotions" which can range from fear to panic, anger to rage, and massive confusion resulting in a loss of decision-making ability. Even the terrorists who planned the incident are in crisis. Their emotions and stress levels are elevated because the operation is actually beginning. Even though the event has been planned, they are engaged in an activity which has unpredictable consequences, attempting to take control of people who are unpredictable and emotion-driven, and trying to regain a semblance of control over the situation. The police are in crisis because they were not expecting the event. The call has been received that a major, life-threatening event has begun.

Stress and emotions of the police are elevated because of the realization they must respond and save lives. If the police fail, people die.

During the crisis stage, emotions are manifest in certain behaviors. Actions become extreme, vocabulary has an emotional content, speech is elevated in pitch and volume, and behaviors are rapid and made without thought. Statements made have an intensity not normally used in conversation. Negotiators need to understand how emotions translate into behaviors so they can determine what skills are necessary to reduce emotions, control behaviors, and keep people from getting killed. Negotiators must listen for the intensity of communications and certain key words to assess how much emotional turmoil the person is experiencing.

The accommodation stage is often referred to as the negotiation stage, because it is during this stage of the incident that most discussion occurs. Emotions are reduced to almost pre-crisis levels and decision-making ability has increased. Stress is reduced and behavior has calmed to reasonable levels. Communications are rational, controlled, and problem-oriented. People can think, reason, and problem solve and develop, assess, and try new solutions to problems. During the accommodation stage, people have adapted to their set of circumstances and are using defense mechanisms and coping skills to deal with the situation.

The final stage of a crisis is the resolution stage. A solution has been arrived at and is being implemented. In the hostage situation, the decision to surrender has been made by the hostage takers. This stage, however, produces environmental and emotional change, so emotions and stress elevate and ability to reason declines. The negotiator's primary role is to reduce as much as possible the environmental uncertainty. The terrorist is surrendering and facing an uncertain and unpredictable future. The negotiator must reduce this uncertainty and introduce predictability. To do this, negotiators need to give explicit instructions on what the terrorist is to do and what will be happening to him at each step along the way to surrender. In addition, the negotiator should ensure that the hostage taker understands exactly what will happen and how. Many hostage incidents, though successfully resolved, have been prolonged because the hostage taker began to surrender, only to be surprised by some unexpected action on the part of the police. In these instances, the situation usually moves back to the crisis stage and has to then be brought back to resolution by the negotiator.

There are many factors which affect both the duration and severity of a crisis. One, some people are more nervous than other people. These people become more easily aroused than other people and take longer to settle down after the crisis or, in the case of a hostage incident, during the incident. Much of temperament tends to be genetic including emotionality, or intensity of reaction, impulsivity, or acting without thinking, level of activity, or total energy output, and sociability, or desire to be with others (Buss & Plomin, 1975). Since temperament tends to be constant throughout a person's life, by gathering intelligence on past behavior the negotiator can predict how the hostage taker and hostages will react at various points in the incident. With highly temperamental persons, for example, the negotiator would need to allow more time to calm down, think about alternatives, and discuss issues.

Temperament is related to personality type. Personality is a consistent way of examining, thinking about, and responding to the demands of life. Personality, in large part, defines what is threatening, how to evaluate the threat, manage the threat, and react to the threat. Antisocial personalities, which would include the majority of terrorists, see anything that may be negative to them personally as threatening. When confronted with a threat, the antisocial's first reaction is to remove the threat. Antisocials see life as a struggle for what they can get out of it, regardless of who they have to use or hurt to get ahead. Knowing the terrorist's personality type gives the negotiator the advantage of using communication and persuasion strategies geared toward that personality. With the antisocial, for example, when the negotiator provided solutions, the negotiator would have to show how those solutions are the most beneficial to the hostage taker.

The overt display of power is threatening to people. If the police show up and make it a point to display their overwhelming firepower and tactical control, the stress and emotional levels of the terrorists are going to rise and prolong the incident. The best approach is for the police to maintain a low profile. The terrorists know the police are present and what law enforcement's tactical capability is. There is no sense in artificially elevating tension.

Finally, the presence of an audience will prolong the incident. A crowd watching, bystanders, and a large media presence all play to the terrorists' desires. Non-trained persons being allowed to negotiate or talk with the hostage takers will worsen the incident, especially if it is the media that is talking with the terrorists. Every effort should be made by the police to reduce or remove the audience watching the incident. The outer perimeter should be outside the hostage-taker's vision and a media area established. The hostage-taker's avenues of communication must also be restricted, so the only person the hostage taker can talk with is the negotiator.

The terrorist hostage taker is in a crisis. The role of the hostage negotiator is to reduce the crisis and get the terrorist to surrender. As a crisis manager, the negotiator must be aware of crisis intervention principles. There are six principles of crisis intervention the negotiator must be aware of as identified by Aguilera and Messick (1978) and Hoff (1989). One, persons in crisis are not necessarily having serious emotional or mental problems. One thing many people immediately associate with terrorist behavior is "crazy." Terrorists are not crazy. They may have personality characteristics or typologies that contribute to their radical behavior, but they are not insane. The terrorist is engaging in the operation because they are in some type of crisis. It is necessary for the negotiator to identify the crisis and then resolve this crisis.

Two, crisis intervention focuses on feelings and problem solving. The person's crisis has elevated their emotions, resulted in high stress and anxiety, and has produced extreme frustration. Very often, even with terrorists, the terrorist operation is committed in response to these emotions and not well thought out. During the incident, decision making is even further impaired. It is the negotiator's responsibility to assist the person think more rationally and systematically, arrive at a solution, and then implement that solution.

Three, the crisis manager has to take an active role in managing the crisis. The hostage taker is in the situation partly because he cannot solve his own problems. The negotiator has to lead the hostage taker through the problem-solving process. This first means reducing the emotions of the hostage taker and returning stress to near normal levels. Then the negotiator can begin evaluating the problem with the hostage taker and offering realistic solutions to the problem. Also, the negotiator has to explore with the hostage taker the possible consequences of his present actions.

Four, the crisis manager must be available at all hours of the day. One of the fundamental tenets of crisis intervention is that the crisis has to be resolved while it is in the early stages of the crisis. Frequently, the reason terrorists engage in assassinations, bombings, and indiscriminant operations is that their particular crisis is not resolved. The crisis continues to build and worsen until they feel forced to commit an act. The advantage to law enforcement and the government in hostage situations is that often the terrorists' crisis is in the early stages. By intervening at that point, further harm can be prevented.

Five, crisis intervention can be effectively done by non-professionals trained in crisis management. Psychologists and other mental health professionals do not negotiate hostage situations. They are present to give advice and direction, but primary negotiators are police officers trained in the principles of crisis intervention and crisis management. The crisis manager has to be concerned about other people, has to be a good listener, able to understand people's problems, and have the ability to resolve problems. Trained police as negotiators are generally more effective than mental health professionals, as mental health professionals often carry the stigma of deep-rooted psychological problems. The terrorist especially would seriously resent a psychologist negotiating the incident because of the implications of having a mental health professional on scene.

Six, crisis management should involve a team approach. A team can more effectively assess the problem, offer solutions, better evaluate the outcomes of those solutions, and provide more resources for carrying out the solution (McMains & Mullins, 1995). Another advantage of the team approach is that it reduces stress and emotion in the response team because team members have available resources to draw upon to relieve their emotions and stress.

Table 11.2.
Summary of the principles of crisis negotiation.

Persons in crisis are not necessarily experiencing emotional or mental problems.
The focus of crisis intervention is on feelings and problem solving.
The crisis manager has to take an active role in managing the crisis.
The crisis manager must be available 24 hours per day.
Crisis intervention can be effectively accomplished by non-professionals if training in crisis management.
Crisis management is a team approach.

Hoff (1989) identified four steps crucial to the success of crisis management. One, a psychosocial assessment has to be made of the person in crisis, including the assessment of suicide or violence potential. This assessment should include an evaluation of the factors that lead up to the incident, the stage of the crisis the person is presently in, why the event is a crisis for the person, and what environmental and internal skills the hostage taker needs to have to manage the crisis. In most hostage situations, the terrorist is going to be in the early stages of the crisis, otherwise they would have engaged in a more violent activity. Negotiators need to understand why the precipitating event is a crisis. Finally, the negotiator has to make an assessment of what knowledge, skills, and abilities the hostage taker has to reduce or resolve the crisis. The negotiator might notice that the right-wing terrorist is articulate (suggesting a cognitive ability to learn), is a veteran of the military, and enjoys reading. One solution would be to suggest job training programs or more education to make the person more marketable to business.

Two, a plan to resolve the crisis has to be developed. The negotiator is responsible for reducing emotions and engaging in problem solving. The terrorist hostage taker is responsible for assessing the past, determining if that past is leading to the achievement of goals, and planning and following through on changes necessary to reach those goals. The negotiator can assist the hostage taker in making these assessments and offer solutions on how to best change, but ultimately it is the responsibility of the hostage taker. Part of the immediate plan to resolve the crisis is exploring ways to bring about political change through legitimate means, determining how that can best be done, and then providing the means to peacefully resolve the incident.

Three, the plan has to be implemented. The implementation of the surrender is dangerous to all involved. This danger can be significantly reduced by making clear to everyone what is going to occur. The perimeter police, tactical team, and negotiators have to know exactly how the terrorists are going to surrender, who is coming out first, where the weapons are, etc. The terrorists have to know what to expect when they walk out to the police. Hostages have to be instructed on what to do as they exit the scene. Not educating people to the surrender plan can increase stress, elevate emotions, and produce unnecessary danger to those involved in the incident.

Four, the crisis management plan has to be followed up on and evaluated for its effectiveness. The surrender of a hostage taker ends the crisis for the hostages and the police. In this case, follow-up refers to incident debriefing to improve the next time. Most negotiators do not follow-up with the hostage takers after the incident is resolved. The incident ends and the terrorist goes to jail. Following up, however, can provide the negotiator with valuable information that can be used beneficially in the next incident. Knowing from the hostage taker what communications were effective, what ones were ineffective, what words or statements the negotiator made that were irritating, what communications reduced stress, etc., can all assist the negotiator in the future.

During the crisis incident, the negotiator should concentrate on three major goals (NOVA, 1992). One, the negotiator has to assure the safety and security of the hostage taker. Regardless of any posturing, the hostage taker is going to feel threatened by the presence of the police. The negotiator has to continually assure the hostage taker that as long as he works with the police he is in no danger from the police. Safety needs have to be satisfied for problem solving to be effective. The negotiator has to provide security for the hostage taker. Security refers to the negotiator building trust with the hostage taker and being able to understand the hostage-taker's frustrations that lead the incident. Then the negotiator has to be perceived as an ally who is willing to assist the hostage taker resolve the frustration.

The second goal of negotiations is to allow ventilation and validation by the hostage taker. Allowing the hostage taker to ventilate and validate reduces emotions and establishes rapport between the negotiator and hostage taker. Ventilation is the process of allowing the hostage taker to tell his story in his own way and own time. Validation is the reduction of emotions by telling the story and knowing someone is listening. After prompting the hostage taker to tell his story, ventilation and validation are best accomplished by the negotiator remaining silent and actively listening to the hostage taker.

The third goal of crisis intervention is prediction and preparation. Prediction is evaluating the hostage-takers' options and is accomplished by illustrating the costs of the current solution (taking and holding hostages) and that another solution reduces costs and elevates gains. Preparation is the development of a plan for the future to implement the solution and strategies for maximizing gain and minimizing losses when carrying out that solution.

The crisis manager has much to do during the crisis and many things to attend to. The negotiator, who is the crisis manager, must recognize the stage of the incident, receive and process vast amounts of intelligence information to assist with formulating strategy for managing the crisis, actively listen and communicate with the hostage taker, all the while exploring a myriad of solutions with the hostage taker to help resolve the situation. The negotiator must filter inputs from numerous sources and always remain focused on the issue at hand (a monumental task for anyone). Because of this cognitive overload, it is critical a team approach be used.

THE HOSTAGE RESPONSE TEAM

The complexity of the hostage incident determines the police manpower response to the incident. A barricaded subject with low potential for suicide and violence may require only two or three patrol officers to maintain the perimeter and a couple of negotiators. A terrorist incident, on the other hand, may require hundreds of personnel, including two or three full teams of command personnel, negotiators, tactical units, and patrol officers. It may be necessary in the terrorist incident to employ a multi-agency response. At the Branch Davidian siege in Waco, several federal agencies were involved, a state agency, and several municipal agencies. Total, over 500 law enforcement personnel from every government level were utilized at some point during the siege.

The minimum response elements needed at a terrorist hostage situation would include: (1) a command structure to control the incident. An on-scene commander is responsible for overall command of the incident and is the primary decision maker regarding strategy to be employed. The commander is responsible for maintaining the required personnel, the well-being of the personnel, and ensuring that each element performs duties as required. (2) A negotiation unit to communicate with the hostage takers. The negotiators should be specifically trained in negotiation skills and should include several people to perform various functions related to negotiations. (3) A tactical team is needed to provide force and guarantee incident security. The tactical team is responsible for containing the hostage takers, manning the inner perimeter, conducting the assault or sniper operations, taking control of released hostages, and making the arrest of the hostage taker. (4) An intelligence element is necessary and responsible for gathering information. In a terrorist incident, intelligence-gathering responsibilities should be a team effort and include members of all response units and specialists training in intelligence gathering. (5) A security element is required to maintain an outer perimeter, control curious citizens, and handle the media. Security units are typically composed of patrol officers. (6) A media liaison. A trained officer or unit of trained officers should be responsible for periodically and continuously updating the media on any significant developments concerning the incident. This should be the only officer allowed to discuss the situation with the media, and all information to be released should be cleared through the on-scene commander. All news releases should be treated as intelligence information and disseminated to all response units involved in the situation. (7) A victim services unit should be activated and made part of the response effort. Terrorist incidents typically involve multiple hostages and last for several days or weeks. The families of hostages will be on the scene, needs attended to, and briefed on a continual basis. Personnel trained in the psychological and emotional issues of terrorist hostage incidents are needed to deal with family members concerning these issues.

Another consideration for the response units is the physical location of their command structures. Each unit should have its own command post and area to conduct its functions. The negotiators, for example, should not be located in the same location as the on-scene commander or tactical team. Doing so would only serve to interfere with the function of the negotiators. Also, all team locations should be out of sight of the hostage takers, public, and media. Each team should restrict entry to the team area to prevent unnecessary interruption and disarray in team activities. An area for rest and relaxation should be established for all response personnel. In all probability, the incident will require the rotation of on-duty personnel. Officers will need a place to eat, relax, and sleep. It is unlikely that a place for off-duty personnel can be located within the outer perimeter. Therefore, this location should be kept secret (if at all possible) or manned by patrol officers and kept off limits to non-response personnel.

The on-scene commander is the ranking officer at the scene of a hostage incident and has numerous responsibilities (NYPD, 1973). Some of these include: (1) establishing a command post in a safe area but in an area near the negotiators, tactical unit, and other response elements, (2) establishing an outer and inner perimeter, (3) designating emergency radio frequencies and having all response personnel on those channels, (4) maintaining communications with the chief or government representatives, (5) evacuation of all nonessential personnel, (6) arranging for adequate manpower to resolve the situation, (7) making tactical decisions, (8) designating a press representative and making sure the press is kept informed, and (9) maintaining the welfare of response personnel. The on-scene commander is in overall command of the operation and is responsible for controlling the incident, making final decisions, and ensuring that policies are followed.

It is critical that on-scene commanders be trained in critical incident management. Negotiators, tactical members, intelligence gatherers, patrol officers, and media relations personnel all received extensive training in managing the hostage situation. Very few on-scene commanders are afforded the same opportunity. Yet they are making some of the most critical decisions of any persons at the scene. An untrained on-scene commander is a detriment to the entire response operation.

The negotiating team is the most crucial of all response units. It is the negotiators that are responsible for communicating with the hostage takers, keeping hostages from getting harmed, dealing with the demands of the hostage takers, and peacefully resolving the incident. Negotiators should be well-trained and train together as a team (McMains, 1992). The FBI (1991) recommends a negotiating team have from two–five members. For the terrorist incident, the negotiating team should have at a minimum five persons. It may also be necessary to have a secondary negotiating team on the scene to relieve the primary negotiating team.

The responsibilities of the negotiating team include: (1) gathering intelligence concerning the hostage taker, hostages, etc., (2) developing tactics for the resolution of the incident, including negotiating strategies, reducing risk to life, etc., (3) communicating with the hostage taker, (4) recording intelligence information, (5) maintaining an up-to-date log of negotiations, (6) using and maintaining equipment, and (7) coordinating activities with the field commander and tactical team (McMains & Mullins, 1995). This myriad of activities, combined with the overwhelming nature of the terrorist incident, will dictate a minimum of five personnel be assigned to the negotiation team.

At a minimum, members of a negotiating team should include (FBI, 1991): (1) team supervisor. The supervisor is responsible for assigning team roles, communicating with the on-scene commander and other supervisors, keeping appropriate personnel on the scene, helping arrive at a negotiation strategy, and managing other aspects of team performance. (2) A primary negotiator is responsible for speaking directly to the hostage taker, employing specific verbal tactics to use with the hostage taker, controlling the hostage-taker's emotional arousal and stress levels, and collecting intelligence from the situation. (3) A secondary negotiator is needed to assist the primary negotiator in developing communication strategies, keeping a record of contacts (written and audio), communicating between the primary and other team members, and to relieve the primary negotiator if needed. (4) An intelligence officer is responsible for gathering and maintaining all intelligence of the situation. The intelligence officer must also interview family, friends, witnesses, and any hostage released. The intelligence officer is a team member but should receive specialized training in intelligence gathering. (5) A mental health consultant is responsible for evaluating the personality, emotional turmoil, and stress level of the hostage taker, monitoring stress levels of team members, recommending negotiating techniques, and consulting with team commanders. Like any other team member, the mental health consultant should receive specific training in crisis management, conflict resolution, and hostage negotiations.

Team members should be trained in all team roles and be able to function in any capacity. The different stages of the incident will stress different aspects of team functioning. In the crisis stage, intelligence collection will be a primary function, and all team members may have to assist in this function. During the accommodation stage, emphasis is on negotiating and a team member may be asked to serve as a tertiary negotiator. During resolution, team members may have to work together to debrief released hostages. The team response permits this flexible functioning so that the negotiating team can adequately manage any contingency which arises during the incident.

Tactical teams are another critical response unit at the hostage situation (Stevens & MacKenna, 1989). At the hostage situation, the tactical team has two primary responsibilities: containing the situation at one location and preparing for the use of force to resolve the incident should that be necessary (Crelinsten & Szabo, 1979; Jacobs, 1983; Maksymchuk,

1982). The tactical team implements appropriate tactics to contain the hostage takers and maintain perimeters (Biggs, 1987). If needed, the tactical team conducts reconnaissance and high-risk approaches to the hostage location. If items are delivered to the hostage taker, the tactical team has delivery responsibility. When hostages are released, the tactical team has to control the hostages until delivered to an intelligence officer. If it is necessary to negotiate face-to-face, the tactical team has the responsibility to protect, provide security for, and cover negotiators.

The tactical team and negotiating team must work closely together. Negotiators must provide intelligence information to the tactical team (Wargo, 1988), provide updates on negotiation progress and location of all parties within the situation, coordinate the release of hostages, and plan the surrender of the hostage taker. Since control of hostages and hostage takers are passed on to the tactical team as they exit the scene, negotiators must work with the tactical team to coordinate any hostage release or surrender. The tactical team will work out the tactics of the release, and the negotiator will relay this information to the hostage takers.

Like negotiators, tactical team members must be carefully selected and trained (Cole, 1989; Drouin & Adams, 1992; Mijares & Perkins, 1994). In general, the tactical team will number over ten members because of the diversity of functions the team is responsible for. The tactical team must assign members to establish and maintain perimeter security. Team members may do this or may supervise patrol officers maintaining perimeters. The tactical team should always man the inner perimeter, since this is the containment perimeter. The tactical team must have an apprehension/assault unit, responsible for approaching the location, surveilling the location, taking control of released hostages or surrendering hostage takers, and making an assault if that becomes necessary (Kaisser, 1990; Pilant, 1993). A third unit of the tactical team is one or more sniper/observer teams. Sniper/observers have two major responsibilities: providing intelligence on the location and sniping the hostage taker if necessary. Even more than the negotiators, tactical team members have to be trained in a myriad of functions (Flaherty, 1988; Kolman, 1982, Mattoons, 1987; Miller, 1979).

There must be a tactical team commander who is responsible for mobilizing the team; assigning team roles; deploying the containment team, assault team, and sniper/observer teams; maintaining contact with the on-scene commander and negotiation commander; and maintaining updated intelligence. An assault unit is one of the most dangerous activities of the tactical team and is used as a last resort (Hudson, 1989; Whittle, 1988). The assault team will need: (1) a team leader, (2) point man, (3) point cover man, (4) an observer/cover man, (5) a rear guard, and (6) marksman. One or more sniper/observer teams will have to be deployed.

Other response elements should be as well-trained as the on-scene commander, negotiators, and tactical team. The media liaison should be trained in police/media relations and communication skills. Patrol officers should receive training in first responder tactics and containment. The victim services team, who may be civilians, should receive training in incident characteristics, emotional aspects of being taken hostage, crisis management skills, and emotional debriefing issues. Exercises should be conducted using all of these response units so they learn to work together, what their responsibilities will be during an incident, and how to work effectively under a unified command structure. One of the worst things that can happen at the terrorist incident, other than having untrained personnel respond, is that trained personnel arrive on the scene without any idea of what to do or what other units are doing. This training should also involve non-police units that may be necessary on the scene. The fire department, EMS, utility company, Federal Emergency Management Teams, airport administration and Federal Aviation Administration officials, railroad employees, etc., should be included in the training so that the response to an actual incident is well-coordinated and smoothly run. Any misunderstandings, oversights, and confusion on the part of the responding units can quickly prove disastrous.

DEMANDS AND TIME

At the core of the hostage situation are demands made by the hostage takers. The issue the negotiator will have to resolve for the hostage taker in order to end the incident will be dealing with demand issues. With the terrorist hostage taker, demand issues are extremely difficult for a negotiator. Criminals make demands concerning freedom, money, no prosecution, etc. Prisoners make demands for better living conditions, return of privileges, etc. Terrorists make demands centered around government concessions and publicity (Fuselier, 1988). To effectively deal with demand issues, the negotiator must understand and be aware of how time affects the hostage incident and how the negotiator can use time as a beneficial tool.

Demands can be either instrumental or expressive (Miron & Goldstein, 1979). Instrumental demands are concrete demands, such as money, vehicles, escape, changes in laws or government, etc. Expressive demands are unstated demands and revolve around emotional issues of frustration and anger. Expressive demands may be manifest by ventilating to reduce frustration, shouting, demanding attention, or a demonstration of power. Expressive demands may not be explicitly or overtly stated by the negotiator but must be inferred by the negotiator. Before the incident can be resolved, both instrumental and expressive demands must be satisfied. A terrorist may be demanding the government change a set of laws and, at the same time, expressing frustration that the laws directly affect him negatively. In the example presented earlier, the right-wing terrorist may want the government to change affirmative action laws (instrumental demands) but is frustrated and angry by his lack of educational and job skills (expressive demands). The negotiator must be responsive to both types of demands.

To effectively deal with demand issues, the negotiator must anticipate and predict the types of demands the hostage taker will make. Being able to deal with demands requires an understanding of the hostage taker, the hostage-taker's personality, using intelligence, understanding the stressors and emotions present in the situation, and then being able to discuss demand issues and being able to reject and refuse demands.

Demands made by hostage takers have several general characteristics. One, demands will be presented in an either/or manner. Demands are presented by the hostage taker in an authoritarian manner and are not open to negotiation. The hostage taker has reached a decision on what is needed to resolve the situation and it is an open-and-shut case. Demands are accompanied by a threat of force. If the demand is not satisfied, hostages will be injured or killed. Two, the demand must be met as stated. There is no compromise in the mind of the hostage taker. Three, demands have a time limit associated with them, and the time limit itself is a demand. Usually, the time limit is set arbitrarily and has no intrinsic value to the hostage taker. Four, a consequence is associated with each demand, usually involving harm to a hostage.

Responding to demands means the negotiator should be prepared to immediately respond. The negotiator should not refuse, not say no, or not attempt to reduce the importance of the demand. All demands should initially be treated as reasonable and can be fulfilled through cooperation. If a demand is presented that is non-negotiable, it should be explained why the demand is not open to negotiation and the hostage taker encouraged to move on to other issues. Each demand presented should be negotiated separately. If the terrorist is demanding a law be changed by midnight, the negotiator should treat this demand as two different demands: a law changed and time.

The negotiator, not the hostage taker, should control conversations regarding demands. This means that the negotiator must anticipate and be prepared to meet the needs of the hostage taker. Focusing discussions on needs reduces the impact of other demands being made. With time, concentrating on need issues becomes easier, because with time need states increase. The hostage taker will want to satisfy those immediate needs, and the larger demand issues will fade to secondary status.

The negotiator can reduce the "finality" of demands by repeating them in a different and less dramatic fashion. To the hostage taker that wants legal change by midnight, the negotiator might respond by suggesting the hostage taker is dissatisfied with current political policy and would like to see future change. This shows the negotiator is willing to discuss issues and reach compromise, and that specific demands are not going to be ceded to and the hostage taker needs to rethink his position. Rephrasing suggests compromise is possible, but meeting the stated demands is not.

There are some general principles negotiators use in handling demands. One, avoid asking for demands. Do not prompt the hostage taker or provide a suggestion for something he has not thought of. Make the hostage taker present demands without assistance. Asking for demands runs the serious risk of increasing the demand list.

Two, do not offer anything not requested. The negotiator should avoid asking the hostage taker if he needs a cigarette, food, etc. The negotiator can use techniques of persuasion and suggestion to implant subtle or subconscious ideas, but should not overtly volunteer an idea for something to satisfy a need.

Three, do not give the hostage taker anything he did not ask for, and then give only enough to meet the agreement. If an agreement has been reached to provide a cigarette, give one regular-sized cigarette without matches. The agreement was for a cigarette, nothing more. If food has been agreed to, give only enough to satisfy an immediate need and the need will return in the near future. Do not give so little of a demand, however, that the hostage taker gets angry. If food has been agreed upon, one cookie indicates the negotiator is mocking the hostage taker. If giving something to satisfy a basic need, include the hostages in the agreement. If food is given, include food for the hostages.

Four, do not give anything without getting something. Make trades, not one-way concessions. A trade may involve a promise to continue talking to the negotiator, remaining calm and not verbally threatening hostages, controlling emotions, a promise not to harm hostages, or the release of a hostage. Trades are often thought of as tangible items, such as a hostage, throwing out a weapon, etc. They can be for non-tangible items as well.

Five, no demand is trivial. If the hostage taker demands a telephone call with a jailed comrade, this phone call fulfills an important need for the hostage taker. Trivializing any demand will increase frustration, elevate stress, and depreciate any trust developing between the negotiator and hostage taker. Instead, the negotiator must determine what need the demand is designed to fulfill.

Six, ignore deadlines and do not set deadlines. History has shown that even the most committed terrorist will allow deadlines to expire without harming hostages. Talk through deadlines without mentioning them in conversations. The negotiator should not set artificial deadlines on resolving the incident. Time is a commodity and is a benefit to the police. Do not destroy the advantage by artificially limiting the situation.

Seven, get sick and injured hostages out first. Any hostage that has been injured or sick should become a negotiator's immediate priority. Often a hostage taker will surrender the injured and sick if it is explained to him the disadvantage of keeping those people as hostages. Some disadvantages include extra time and attention, consequences if one dies, the energy required to watch them, and using valuable resources to treat them. By releasing those hostages, stress is reduced, emotions can be better controlled, the hostages will calm down, and added responsibility is removed from the hostage taker. Following the injured and sick, the negotiator should attempt to get children and the elderly released.

Eight, the last demand is the only important demand. The last demand made by the hostage taker is the demand that will satisfy a need. Previously made demands fade to the background of consciousness in attempting to fulfill a need. Typically, hostage takers begin the incident with grandiose demands. With time, the demands fade in importance until demand issues center around safety and security, satisfying basic need states, and fulfilling physiological needs.

Nine, assess the hostage-taker's personality type based upon demands. Different personalities make different types of demands. Schizophrenics, for example, may demand the government quit bombarding their brains with laser rays from space. Depressives may demand things to reduce their internal pain. Antisocials will demand self-gratifying items such as money or guarantees of no punishment. Inadequate personalities may center demand issues around personal recognition. Assessing personality through demand issues will assist the negotiator in arriving at alternative solutions for the hostage taker to focus on and resolve the situation.

All demands can be categorized into distinct groupings. Some of these categories are negotiable, others are not negotiable. Realize that because a demand is negotiable does not mean it is going to be granted. Negotiable demands include: (1) Food is the most requested demand made by hostage takers and is an excellent demand to use for getting hostages

Table 11.3.
General principles to use when dealing with demands made by terrorists.

1. Do not ask for demands
2. Do not offer anything not requested
3. Do not give anything not requested and then give only enough to satisfy the demand
4. Do not give anything without getting something
5. No demand is trivial
6. Ignore deadlines and do not set deadlines
7. Get the sick and injured out first
8. The last demand is the only important demand
9. Assess personality type based on demands

released. (2) Cigarettes are common demands made by hostage takers and are also vehicles for trading for hostages. (3) Drinks are negotiable demands. Drinks include water, sodas, coffee, etc. They do not include alcohol. If the hostage taker is a chronic alcoholic, the negotiator might consider providing small amounts of alcohol to reduce anxiety and prevent delirium tremens. (4) Media coverage is a common demand made by terrorists. Media coverage can be negotiated without being granted. If media coverage is granted, it should be done under the negotiator's guidance, with ground rules established with the hostage taker prior to interviews. The media should also be briefed on what is acceptable and an agreement reached to minimize live coverage of the incident until after the incident is resolved. (5) Transportation demands are often made by terrorists. In some cases, the terrorist already has a vehicle and wants an escape route. In an airplane, the demand may center on providing a pilot or refueling. (6) Money is a negotiable demand. Money issues can often be used to deflect other demands. (7) Freedom for the hostage takers is a negotiable demand.

Non-negotiable demands are ones that are not even worth spending time on. The police and usually hostage taker are aware certain demands are not going to be granted. With non-negotiable demands, the negotiator should inform the hostage taker when he makes a non-negotiable demand that the demand is not going to be negotiated. Do not mislead the hostage taker concerning non-negotiable demands. Non-negotiable demands include: (1) Weapons. The terrorists already have weapons; otherwise there would not be a hostage situation. They do not need any more weapons. (2) Drugs. An unlikely demand by terrorists, non-prescription and illicit drugs are not subject to negotiation. Prescription drugs can be negotiated. (3) Release of prisoners is not negotiable. Part of the demand package made by terrorists might include the release of comrades. This will not be allowed to happen and is not worth wasting negotiation time discussing. (4) Exchange of hostages. For many reasons, hostages cannot be exchanged. Hostage exchanges interfere with the Stockholm Syndrome, may be self-serving to the hostage takers, gives power to the hostage taker, increases stress and tension, and is not favorable to the police (Fuselier, 1986). Police officers are never exchanged for hostages for a variety of reasons (Wargo, 1989). The police officer may feel compelled to take action, the hostage taker may be given more prestige, killing the police officer produces a greater threat, and stress and pressure on the response units is elevated (Russell & Zuniga, 1986).

To deal with demands, the negotiator must effectively use time. Time is one of the most valuable tools a negotiator possesses (Lanceley, 1985; Nudell & Antokol, 1990; Schlossberg, 1979; Van Zandt, 1991). Time allows the negotiator to meet objectives and achieve strategic and tactical goals, it decreases stress and increases ability to think and problem solve, allows trust and interpersonal rapport to develop, fatigues the hostage taker, increases the probability of hostages getting released unharmed, and increases the probability that neither the police nor hostage taker get injured (Needham, 1976).

Criminal hostage incidents last an average of 12 hours (Mirabella & Trudeau, 1982). Terrorist hostage incidents will last much longer. Because of the seriousness of the incident, its impact on the public, on police functioning, and media demands, the pressure to hurry and resolve the incident will be significant. Response units must resist these pressures and spend as long as necessary to resolve the incident, even extending the time by slowing down (Goldaber, 1979). Even before negotiations begin, responding patrol officers should use time wisely and begin delaying events. The actions of the responding officers will set the tenor for all future actions of the police, so it is imperative that officers be trained in what to do when they respond to these incidents (Dolan & Fuselier, 1989; Noesner & Dolan, 1992; Sloan & Kearney, 1977). Additionally, the patrol officers are responding during the most dangerous stage of the entire incident (Culley, 1974 & 1978; Horobin, 1978; Spaulding, 1987). When negotiators open communications with the hostage takers, one of the first goals is to buy time and make time part of the response package (Gettinger, 1983).

There are many positive effects of time, but there are also drawbacks to time passing (Fuselier, 1981/1986). The positive effects of time include: (1) time increases basic need states. The negotiator has the responsibility of moving the hostage taker through these need states and fulfilling the needs as he/she does so. Fulfilling needs also means gaining concessions from the hostage taker. (2) Two, time increases the ability to process information, make decisions and solve problems, and it also decreases emotion and stress. Time allows the negotiator to move the hostage taker through the stages of a crisis. (3) Time allows the Stockholm Syndrome to develop (Fuselier, 1986). (4) The probability of a successful negotiation is increased with the passage of time. Communications can be established, decision making and problem solving can occur, solutions offered and acted upon, and the hostage taker will realize the initial solution is not the most advantageous solution. (5) Time allows for the gathering of intelligence. (6) Time gives the tactical team the opportunity to prepare, set up and prepare for a tactical solution. (7) Time gives command personnel the opportunity to get organized and professionally manage the situation. (8) Time reduces the expectations of the hostage taker. (9) Time provides increased escape opportunities for the hostages. (10) With time, the hostage taker may surrender. His cognitive expectations may change, he may come to fully realize the futility of his actions, or for any of a hundred other reasons he may just surrender.

In addition to the positive effects of time, there are several negative effects negotiators need to be aware of. (1) Time increases mental and physical exhaustion. With fatigue, impulsivity increases. The hostage taker may get frustrated and harm a hostage. The negotiator may get tired and begin offering quick and unsatisfactory solutions to the incident. The ability to make sound decisions is impaired. This is one of the primary reasons the negotiation team should set up a firm rotation schedule. McMains and Mullins (1995) suggest that negotiator teams should be rotated every 10–12 hours. (2) Time decreases the ability to think objectively. The hostage taker may engage in risky activity, take unnecessary chances, or become emotional. Response units may do likewise. (3) Time increases boredom. The hostage taker may tire of waiting and force a quick solution. The negotiator may get tired of talking to the hostage taker and not initiate negotiations.

COMMUNICATIONS IN HOSTAGE SITUATIONS

As important as the team response, management of the incident, handling demands, and time management, hostage negotiations ultimately come down to communications. The entire incident can be reduced to a two-party interaction, a negotiator talking to a hostage taker. The job of the negotiator is to convince the hostage taker to change a decision, alter strategy, and accept another course of action. In a sense, a negotiator is a salesperson attempting to get the hostage taker to "buy" something. The only avenue open to the negotiator is to employ persuasive communications to do this.

Table 11.4.
Positive and negative effects of time in a hostage situation.

Positive Effects	Negative Effects
1. Increases basic need states exhaustion	1. Increases mental and physical
2. Increases cognitive processing ability	2. Decreases objective thinking
3. Allows Stockholm syndrome to develop	3. Increases boredom
4. Increases probability of successful negotiations	
5. Helps gather intelligence	
6. Helps tactical team	
7. Helps command personnel	
8. Reduces hostage-takers' expectations	
9. Provides increased escape opportunities for hostages	
10. Helps hostage taker to surrender	

Basic Communications

There are three components to being an effective communicator. One, the negotiator must have the ability to understand what is being said to him and what he is communicating. Both the sender and receiver have to understand the communication. This means the negotiator has to communicate from the hostage-taker's point of reference (Kahneman, 1992). The reference point of the hostage taker may be cultural, religious, ethnic, educational, or motivational. Two, the communication has to achieve the desired effect. Communications have goals, and those goals have to be realized. Three, communications have to be ethical and involve trust and respect between the negotiator and hostage taker. Getting caught in a lie will destroy a negotiator's credibility and may end all negotiation attempts (Sen, 1989).

Communication is an active process that is ongoing, dynamic, fluid, and responsive to situational dynamics. Communications are also permanent. Once said, a communication cannot be retracted. Communications are interactive and allow for the exchange of information, identification of behavioral trends, development of strategy, and establishment of outcomes and solutions (Putnam & Jones, 1982). Communications are a process that consist of the source of the communication, the message being sent, the channel used to convey the message, the receiver, noise, feedback on the communication, and the context of the communication. If any of these components are absent, the communication will not be effective.

When communications are ineffective, there are usually one or more barriers present between the negotiator and hostage taker. One barrier is language. The two parties may be communicating in words that have no meaning to the other party or in a way that is unclear. Saying something like, "We are here to help you," can be interpreted in different ways. A second barrier is polarization, or using extremes to describe something. The negotiator may believe concessions from the hostage taker to be all or none, with no middle compromise positions. The hostage taker may perceive his only options to be death from a tactical assault or life imprisonment. A third barrier is simplistic generalization or "allness." The negotiator cannot believe the hostage taker is an entirely bad person, but must be able to recognize the positive qualities of the hostage taker. A fourth barrier is static evaluation, or engaging in communications that do not change as the dynamics of the hostage situation change.

The single most important thing a negotiator can do to improve communications is employ feedback (Rangarajan, 1985). The negotiator must constantly use feedback to ensure communications are accurate, negotiations are progressing forward, and that communications are being acted upon. Summarizing a communication is an active form of feedback the negotiator should constantly employ. Summarizing a communication means reiterating the important parts of the communication so there is no confusion between parties. Additionally, feedback should be provided immediately and be descriptive, not evaluative. The intent of feedback is to clarify communications, not judge.

SUMMARY

Terrorist hostage-taking operations are highly stressful and extremely dangerous for all parties involved. Terrorists are the most difficult type of hostage takers to communicate with, establish rapport with, and negotiate demands. The advantage over other types of terrorist operations is that the police have the opportunity to intercede in the operation and prevent injury or death.

The response to a hostage-taking operation takes planning, training, and coordination. Police officers cannot just show up and convince the terrorists to resolve the situation. One reason the government has been unsuccessful in resolving international incidents is partly due to faulty policy and partly due to not adhering to the basic principles of hostage negotiation. Since the 1950s, the government has held to a non-negotiation policy. When an incident occurs, the government has been forced to negotiate, usually with disastrous results. The Iranian embassy siege lasted for almost a full year before it was resolved. Then, the government was forced to grant almost all terrorist demands. The government also negotiated the release of U.S. citizens held in Beirut, bending and fracturing federal law to secure the release of those hostages.

In international hostage-taking incidents, the government usually does not follow the basic principles of hostage negotiations. In their defense, there are times the government cannot do this. In Iran, for example, there was no possible way for the government to employ force to contain the situation, nor were they able to negotiate with the leader of the terrorists. Negotiations were conducted through a government sympathetic to the terrorists. The only reason the Iranian government negotiated at all was because it was self-serving to do so.

Domestically, law enforcement agencies have a successful track record in negotiating with terrorists. These agencies have learned the basic lessons of hostage negotiations and enter into the situation with a firm plan in mind for dealing with the situation. The response effort is usually multi-agency and well-coordinated. On-scene commanders, negotiators, tactical teams, and other response personnel are well-trained and able to perform their functions with little delay or indecision.

Terrorists, as well, learn from failures. Terrorists analyze the failures and flaws from their predecessors. As a result, law enforcement response teams have to constantly adapt and adjust to deal with better prepared and more knowledgeable terrorist hostage takers. This cycle will continue as long as terrorists take hostages.

Chapter 12

THE FUTURE OF TERRORISM

Terrorists employ ambushes, assassinations, extortion, hijacking and sabotage operations to accomplish their goals. They use pistols, rifles, shotguns, and explosives. Their most powerful tool, however, is the human mind. The human mind is responsible for fear, anxiety, and dread concerning terrorists. Most people become afraid of terrorists because of their lack of knowledge concerning terrorism. Terrorists are perceived to be shadowy figures that operate in the ether of the human existence, figures that spring out of the shadows seemingly at random to bring death and destruction to the public, figures that bring chaos and uncertainty to an ordered society. William James once said, "In any contest between reason and imagination, imagination will win." Of all the tools of terrorism, imagination is the most potent, effective, and powerful. A grain of imagination can do more to change laws and political systems than a ton of explosives.

Imagination is an effective tool for the terrorist because it relies on ignorance: ignorance of who terrorists are, how terrorists operate, what terrorists' goals are, and why terrorists become terrorists. Ignorance leads to imagination. The more ignorant people are about terrorism, the more frightening terrorism becomes. Imagination, however, like terrorists, can be defeated. The key in defeating both is knowledge. The purpose of this book has been, hopefully, to provide knowledge and reduce imagination. It has examined the motivations, organizational structure, persons and organizations, strategies and tactics, and weapons of terrorists. One important issue, however, remains: what lies ahead?

Mark Twain once made a personal observation relevant to terrorism in the 1890s: "Reports of my death have been greatly exaggerated." Scholars, scribes, pundits, law enforcement, and the government have all proclaimed terrorism to be on the decline; that the 1970s left-wing radicals are in jail, the right wing is on the run from federal pressure, and international terrorists are bowing to increased hard-line U.S. government policy. Is terrorism truly on the decline or is the U.S. merely experiencing one of those common and predictable lulls in terrorist activity? It is the position of the author that terrorism is not on the

469

decline, that the lull in terrorist activity is transitory, and that terrorism will become worse than ever before in the years to come. Reports of the decline of terrorism have been greatly exaggerated.

Proclaiming terrorism to be in a decline is almost as bad as imagination. Today, terrorism presents a greater threat than it ever has. Discontent with existing political systems is at an all-time high, economic recessions are sweeping the globe, societies are in disarray and turmoil from a multitude of sources, the underprivileged are more cognizant of their rights than ever before, racial tensions are increasing exponentially, and technology is outdistancing the ability to cope with that technology. These conditions, singly and in unison, promote the use of terrorism as a form of redress. As these conditions worsen unabatedly, more and more people will reach for the extremes of the continuum of human behavior in an attempt to bring order and sanity to their position within society. These conditions also promote the operations of the terrorists, giving them more available weapons of mass destruction to bring about change.

This chapter will examine the future of terrorism at several levels. Who will be tomorrow's terrorists, who will they target, where will they operate, how will they attempt to achieve their objectives, and why will terrorism worsen? This chapter will examine the future of terrorism internationally, because the future for the United States holds hidden dangers from all parts of the world. The world of today is in all respects an international community. National borders are becoming more artificial by the day. This is true for terrorism as well. One line of evidence supporting this is the linkages between the neo-Nazis of the U.S. and Europe. Terrorist events in remote Asia will have an impact on American society and the security of American citizens. What terrorists do in South America or Africa will have an impact on the U.S. government, policy decisions, and even laws dealing with internal issues.

EUROPE

Throughout the second half of the twentieth century, Europe has experienced tremendous political change and has been a focal point for numerous world events. World War II, the rise to power of the Soviet Union, the invasions of Eastern Europe by the Soviets, the cold war and the threat of World War III, and the collapse of communism and breakup of a major world power have all combined, in one form or another, to make Europe a virtual hotbed of intrigue and a breeding ground for terrorism. In some instances, such as Belgium in the 1980s, dissatisfied government employees have actually assisted terrorists to topple the ruling regime (Jenkins, 1990). Terrorism has played a major role in many of these events and will continue to influence many aspects of European life and politics.

One of the major terrorist roles has been played by the IRA, which provides an example of how terrorism has influenced European politics. The IRA has failed to produce change in the English form of government, nor has it caused the English to leave Ireland, but they have produced change in the way England governs. Activities of the IRA have resulted in the English government passing special laws to maintain civil order, using military troops to maintain civil order and perform police functions, suspend civil liberties, and restrict movement of citizens (such as the 1993 closing of London's financial district to the public). The IRA has also produced a semi-police state in England and Ireland. The IRA has even (unwillingly) effected government procurement and military decision making when they subsidized the development of the Thompson machinegun (Bell, 1987).

Terrorism in Europe has also had an influence on United States foreign policy. The Red Army Faction (Baader-Meinhoff) has attacked U.S. and NATO facilities in Germany (including a brazen daylight rocket attack on Rhein-Main Air Force Base in Weisaben—Eva Haule, former leader of the Red Army Faction, finally went to trial in 1993 for this act), the Red Brigades (Brigate Rosse) in Italy kidnapped U.S. Army General Dozier, and France's Action Directorate has attacked U.S. business and government interests in France. In April 1986, Nezar Nawaf Hindawi bombed the La Belle Discotheque in Berlin (Sharpe, 1991). Three Americans were killed and several more injured. In response, President Reagan ordered a bombing strike on Bengazi and Tripoli, Libya. This retaliation almost resulted in the severing of relations between Spain, France, and the U.S. Although the Libyan terrorist only had hopes of attacking United States interests, his actions clearly had more dire and far-reaching consequences on U.S./European foreign policy and on the very composition of NATO (France and Spain threatened to withdraw as a result of the violation of their air space by United States war planes).

And the Soviet/East German bloc became the scapegoats. It was only natural the enemy of democracy became the "father" of all terrorists operating in Europe. Any European terrorist event became the result of orders from the Soviets/East Germans. News accounts proliferated linking the "Great Red Threat" to terrorism and few people bothered to learn the facts. While it was certainly true the Soviets and East Germans trained, helped finance and equip, and provided other technical and logistical support to terrorists, they did not order and control European terrorists.

In a similar vein, many people believe European terrorism will wane and disappear with the collapse of the Soviet Union and the reunification of Germany. Nothing could be less true. Terrorism is very much alive and thriving in Europe and will continue to do so for decades to come. Several identifiable trends have emerged and will continue into the next century.

Of these trends, it is expected that terrorists of the far left will increase their assault on the democratic institutions of Europe. The collapse of communism and the surge of new democracy has and will strengthen the growth and resolve of the neo-communist movement. Familiar organizations such as the Red Army Faction (Rote Armee Fraktion), Red Brigades, and the Action Directorate will again become strong and return to their philosophical roots—the return of communism to the world through armed struggle (Department of Justice, 1990).

One easy target for the left-wing faction will be Europe's newly formed governments (i.e., Rumania, Bulgaria, etc.) who have not yet had time to implement strong counter-terrorist units or policies, and who do not have the full support of their people. A second target will be those countries who are struggling to survive and form an identity, such as Bosnia-Herzegovina. The civil wars in these countries will provide the terrorist a ready-made army of support. Terrorists will align with all factions of these civil wars on a covert level and then seek to assist the winner in establishing the new government. Finally, established governments will fall prey to the far left as terrorists attempt to overthrow the ruling democracy in favor of a return to communism. Italy, who is besieged by internal infighting among the four major political parties (Santoro, 1987), and Germany, who is facing a myriad of problems brought on by the reunification, will be especially vulnerable to the activities of terrorists wanting to establish communist regimes.

In the former Soviet Union, it is expected the far left will intensify its attacks on the Gorbachev regime, aligning themselves with the dissident military and political factions in an attempt to reunify the Soviet states and reestablish the Soviet Union to its former position as ruler of the communist world. As the Soviets continue to be faced with a crumbling political and economic system, many of the populace will seek redemption in the rhetoric of the far left and will unite with the left to improve internal conditions (Maley, 1990). In November 1993, Gorbachev helped strengthen the far-left position by threatening limited nuclear tactical strikes against the dissident faction. Military retaliation by the government will drive people to adopt the philosophies and tactics of the far left, thus worsening the already growing problem.

One of the most active terrorist organizations in the upcoming decades will continue to be the IRA. Active since 1916, the IRA has been fighting for political and religious independence from England. Bell (1987) has reported the only thing keeping the IRA from being more destructive is their lack of sophistication with weapons systems. This lack of sophistication is primarily attributable to the fact that many members of the IRA are from the blue-collar, lower-educated social strata and thus use simple but deadly effective weapons. In the future, as support for the IRA grows, their level of sophistication will improve and their weapons will become deadlier and their attacks more frequent.

Compounding the Irish terrorism problem is the Ulster Defense Association (UDA), a Protestant, pro-British rule organization based in northern Ireland. The UDA targets pro-Irish and pro-IRA supporters. In the decade to come, the UDA will also experience rapid growth and become more violent. Many people will join with the UDA not out of political sympathy but as a counter-reaction to IRA activities. Many Irish citizens are becoming disenfranchised with the IRA and realize the government forces are not able to stop the IRA. They see the UDA as able to do that and they will allow their desperation to overcome their fear and will join the UDA. To illustrate the severity of the Irish terrorist problem, on 23 October 1993, an IRA terrorist killed himself and ten innocent people (Protestant) in a bombing attack in the Shankill district of Belfast. As a result of the attack, the UDA promised a campaign of mass murder against Irish Catholics. On 26 October 1993, the UDA began to fulfill their promise when two Catholics were killed and five others wounded in an ambush in Belfast.

Possibly the greatest threat to Europe in the coming years comes from the far right. In the 1980s and early 1990s, Europe experienced a dramatic rise in activities of the neo-Nazi movement. The rise of the "Fourth Reich," as these self-proclaimed saviors of the new Europe like to call themselves, accounted for approximately 4,500 assaults against foreigners and 17 deaths in 1992 (Mullins & Mijares, 1992, 1995). While the Nazi movement following World War II never completely died out, the reunification of Germany served as the catalyst for a resurgence in the movement. In the coming years, this movement will further strengthen and present new challenges to the European community.

Many former members of the Nazi party (including Willie Kraemer, advisor to Joseph Goebbels, and Major General Otto Remer of the Third Reich) have become active in the far-right movement and will continue to do so. These former Nazis have provided leadership, direction, and organization to the neo-Nazi movement. Until the late 1980s, the neo-Nazi movement was a loose-knit coalition of ex-punk rockers, skinheads, and other fringe personalities. Small groups of these people would get together, commit one or more hate crimes, and wait for the media to make them notorious. The involvement of former Nazi leaders into the movement has brought in the more "mainstream" neo-Nazis and pushed the fringe to a subordinate role. The ex-Nazis unified and gave guidance, solidified long-range goals, reaffirmed the basic Nazi credo, and identified targets and their vulnerabilities. Additionally, the ex-Nazi leadership has expanded the neo-Nazi movement throughout Europe, recruiting members and establishing cells in England, Spain, Italy, France, Romania, Bulgaria, and other European countries.

The reunification of Germany provided a ready-made source of expertise to the neo-Nazi movement. Many former members of Stasi, the East German secret police (many themselves ex-Nazis), have become active in the far right for ideological and political reasons (Mullins & Mijares, 1993a). They have provided technical assistance, operational leadership, intelligence information and intelligence-gathering expertise, and other terrorist instruction. The former East Germany (and to a limited extent other ex-communist bloc countries) has been an open-door shopping center for weapons acquisition. Automatic rifles, ammunition, explosive ordinance, heavy weapons, and rockets and missiles have all been acquired by the neo-Nazi movement. Some of these weapons have already been employed by the far right and many more will be in the future.

The neo-Nazi movement has received assistance and support of foreign-based terrorist organizations. The far right in the U.S. (i.e., Aryan Nations, Ku Klux Klan, American Nazi Party, among others) has assisted their European counterparts in training, finances, equipment, and other ideological and operational needs. The European neo-Nazi movement has even received assistance from the PLO (Kolinsky, 1988).

One factor which has worked against the neo-Nazi movement has been the collective memory of those Europeans who lived through the horrors of World War II and Hitler's program of racial genocide. These older Europeans know what can happen when the goals of the far right are achieved, and they are determined to not allow it to happen again. The economic and political power of these people have significantly limited the scope and activities of the far right. Unfortunately, these older Europeans are aging, dying off, and losing the strength to combat the far right. As these checks disappear, it is expected that the balance will swing in favor of the neo-Nazi movement.

In the decades to come, Europe will also experience an increase in Mideast terrorism. Of the 300-plus organizations presently active in Europe, most are Mideastern (Alexander, 1989). There are several factors which will play an important role in the increased activity of Mideastern terrorists in Europe (Pluchinsky, 1991, 1992). One, the Mideast community in Europe is rapidly growing in size. This large émigré population is not just Mideasterners dissatisfied with the strife in the Mideast, it is also filled with dissidents who see Europe as a surrogate battleground for the resolution of Mideast problems. This surrogate battleground will not be a series of isolated actions but will be a strategically and tactically coordinated series of attacks which will draw in the people and governments of Europe. Two, Europe is geographically compact with good transportation facilities. Third, the American presence in Europe is greater than in the Mideast. Thus, Europe will become the battleground to destroy the United States.

The new Single European Act (EC) will also serve to the benefit of terrorism. In 1992, the majority of Europe became "border free" (Boye, 1990). The newly opened borders will make the job of the terrorist much easier. They will be able to freely move manpower, equipment, weapons, and other resources between nations with little fear of detection. Some have predicted the EC will make the fight against terrorism easier (see Geysels, 1990, for example) because of increased cooperation of governments in establishing anti-terrorism measures, joint training and intelligence gathering, emergency contingency measures, and improved security of likely terrorist targets such as airlines and nuclear facilities. The history of Europe, however, suggests this will not occur. During the twentieth century, governments have resisted working together on far more pressing and important issues. It is unlikely European governments and law enforcement agencies will begin cooperating on the issue of terrorism. Some governments, in fact, have actively resisted the formation of the EC, and this resistance has "trickled down" to their agencies responsible for combating terrorism. One effect the EC will have on terrorism is to make it easier for terrorists to perform activities and then remove themselves to safe havens. Countries such as the Netherlands and France have always been countries of refuge for terrorists. The EC will further foster the growth of these refuges. The Netherlands, for example, has seen an increase in the number of terrorist sympathizers who provide safe houses and forged documentation and an increase in the number of hard-core activists (Vermaat, 1987). France provides a strategic staging locale and by the very fact of its permissive politics offers an open political refuge for terrorists (Moxon-Browne, 1988).

From the well-established IRA to the fledgling Fourth Reich movement, Europe is getting ready to face an explosion in terrorism. This wave of terrorism will greatly outdistance any seen in the twentieth century and last well into the twenty-first century. Neither the European community, governments, nor foreign-based interests operating in Europe will be prepared for this onslaught.

ASIA

One area of the world that has been relatively free of transnational and international terrorism has been the Far East. Many of the nations in the Far East are small, undeveloped island nations with little or no strategic value to global politics. The larger, free nations such as Japan and Australia have strong anti-terrorism policies and agencies which have helped reduce the terrorism threat. The communist nations such as China and North Korea have been under the shadow of the Soviet Union. Until recently, the Far East did not have the social or economic development necessary for terrorists to flourish. As the Pacific Rim becomes increasingly important in the coming decades, terrorism will follow these emerging political, social, and economic developments.

While communism has disappeared in Europe, it still flourishes in Asia, primarily in North Korea and China. North Korea has been involved for years in the training and supporting of terrorist organizations (primarily Mideastern). In the years ahead, North Korea will take a more active role in international and transnational terrorism. There are several attributes of North Korean society which will make it one of the leaders of Asian-based terrorism (Kim, 1988). These include an unorthodox socialistic political system. Koreans are prone to idolize leaders and systems, and it is isolated from the mainstream world, making it difficult to mount counter-terrorist attacks against. Psychologically, the people are of unquestioned dedication and loyalty, prepared to sacrifice themselves for the "cause," atheistic, and professionally trained. It is highly probable that North Korea will become a front-line participant, as trained, dedicated, and ruthless as any terrorist nation.

One other factor working in favor of North Korea becoming a force in terrorism is its position as a third-rate political power. With the demise of communism in Europe, the coming decades are primed for other countries to fill that void. North Korea has an established political system, is unable to compete in the world militarily, and has a passion that makes the nation one of the most likely candidates to make an international move. Additionally, North Korea is facing economic disaster. With an army of over 1.2 million personnel, 8,000 armored vehicles, and 1,400 combat aircraft, and the money supply from Russia cut off, North Korea must keep its people focused on outside enemies and issues. Terrorism gives North Korea the focus it needs for its people. All of the above-mentioned factors make it highly probable North Korea will become much more of a threat to world peace than even China.

Like North Korea, China will also make its terrorist presence felt. The fall of the Soviet Union has recently propelled China into world prominence as one of the final bastions of communism. Without worrying about the Soviet threat, China can now begin to turn its attention to the rest of the world, beginning in Asia. Until the collapse of Russia, most of the military and intelligence resources of China were dedicated to protecting itself from the Soviet threat. With the fall of the Soviet Union, China reestablished its priorities and its politburo developed new strategies and goals for the advancement of communism. Also, China was able to become much less isolationist and more of a global force. China, in fact, will replace Russia as the main supporter of left-wing terrorism. China has already opened and made operational several terrorist training centers, liaisoned with Mideast dictators and despots, and has made its terroristic presence felt in countries such as the Philippines, Cuba, Indonesia, and India.

Leftist terrorism will not be confined to just North Korea and China. The most notorious Far East terrorist organization has been the Japanese Red Army (*Sekigun* — headquartered in Japan). Formed as an offshoot of the Japanese Communist Party following World War II, the Japanese Red Army (JRA) recruited its hard-core activists from the All-Japan Student Federation (Zengakuran). The JRA has been involved in numerous terrorist incidents around the world, including Jakarta, Indonesia, Canada, the United States, and Western Europe. The goal of the JRA is world communism, which is to be centered in Asia. Many analysts have predicted the demise of the JRA in the coming years (Chang, 1991). Its leadership has some of the oldest members in the terrorist world, most in their fifties or sixties, and most of these are currently being held in prisons around the world. The rising prominence of the Pacific Rim region and other world events will likely prove predictions of demise incorrect. As the focus of communism entrenches itself in Asia, the JRA will find many new recruits to carry the torch of world revolution.

As the people of Asia move into the twenty-first century and attempt to catch up with the rest of the world, Asians will use terrorism to stop governmental repression. In the Philippines, for example, acts of terrorism focus on disparities between the rich and the poor and the lack of economic and social mobility (Austin, 1991). The influence of religion in conjunction with liberation theology that stresses land and tax reform, equal rights, and humane treatment will result in terrorism becoming a major influence in the Pacific regions (Wolf, 1989b). This liberation theology is akin to the basic tenets of Marxism, providing further impetus in the world of terrorism. The move toward social reform is a natural ally of the far left. As an example of how the two work together, the Huks and New People's Army in the Philippines have seen major growth since the overthrow of the Aquino regime. Their primary source of recruitment has been the rural peasantry, who, until recently, could have cared less about political ideology. This alliance and source of new manpower has made them a threat not only to the Philippine government but also to foreign interests who are helping the new government. The New People's Army (enforcement and operations are of the Philippine Communist Party) has been responsible for attacks on several U.S. military personnel, including the assassination of Colonel James N. Rowe (Dept. of Justice, 1991). The Huks have mercury poisoned pineapple crops destined for overseas shipment (Douglass & Livingston, 1984). Other countries long considered peaceful and benevolent coalitions, such as New Guinea, Malaysia, Thailand, Burma, Fiji, and Vanuatu, have all seen a significant rise in political violence and will continue to see a growth into the twenty-first century.

Increasing immigration and the growth of Muslimism will contribute to a rise in terrorism in Asia. The largest Muslim nation in the world, Indonesia, is in Asia. As in Europe, these "second-class" citizens will want equal rights and humane treatment. As governments continue to ignore their pleas, they will increasingly turn to terrorism to gain respect. As the Pacific Rim opens its arms to the world community, terrorists will use this area as a new battleground and haven from reprisal. Australia, for example, long immune from terrorism, has seen a dramatic increase in terrorist activity in the last decade and will continue to see a rise over the next several years. Australia receives 120,000–140,000 émigrés per year, about half of these from the Mideast and other areas of Asia (MacKenzie-Orr, 1991). In addition, Australia is increasing their interests in the world community, assuming a role in U.N. peacekeeping duties, and becoming a source country in the international drug trade. The Armenian Secret Army for the Liberation of Armenia and the PLO have both made inroads into Australian society and provide safe havens for terrorists.

The tentacles of the Mideast have reached Asia and will continue to strengthen in the coming decades. The Libyans have been active in recruiting and training in Asia, especially in New Caledonia and Vanuatu (Selth, 1988). The Libyans have trained and provided support to several Asian terrorist organizations, including the National Kanak Socialist Liberation Front (FLNKS), the Free Papua Movement (Organisas Papua Merdeka, or OPM), Nationalist People's Liberation Front in Sri Lanka, and also played an active role in the expulsion of Indonesia from Irian Jaya.

The twenty-first century will see a literal explosion of drug-related terrorism from Asia (Mullins, 1990c; Mullins & Becker, 1992). As increasing pressure is brought to bear on the drug cartels in Central and South

America, the focus of narcoterrorism will shift to Asia. Burma, Cambodia, Laos, Thailand, and Vietnam have long been primary sources of narcotics. Other prime growing areas include the Philippines, Malaysia, New Guinea, and other isolated islands. The ports of Hong Kong and Singapore are loosely regulated, making them ideal shipping points for drugs. Many cities in Asia are little regulated, inadequately policed, and unregulated. In short, they are an open marketplace not only for individual sales but also as wholesale distribution sites. Some governments (Cambodia, Laos, and Vietnam, for example) are actively involved in the growth, sale, and distribution of drugs. Others tacitly approve of the growth and distribution of drugs. To most others, drug usage is not an Asian problem and thus is to be ignored. As with Cuba, agents of North Korea and China are helping promote narcoterrorism by financing, acting as an intermediary, and in many other ways helping develop the Asian drug trade. Drug producers and traffickers are also using terrorist organizations to insure safe delivery of drugs and eliminate anti-drug forces.

Domestic and state terrorism will continue unabated as Asia moves into the twenty-first century. Tribal fights (i.e., the Vietnamese fighting to destroy the Montagnards, the Khmer Rouge in Cambodia, etc.) centered around racial differences will remain a significant problem in Asia. Likewise, government terrorism will worsen as the third-world nations of Asia attempt to become political and economic forces in the world. The communist regimes of Asia will continue to repress their citizens through the use of terrorism.

Asian terrorism has not historically been of worldwide concern because, until recently, acts of Asian terrorism were infrequent and isolated to a local region. However, as Asia becomes a major economic, material, industrial, resource, and economic force in the world community, its role in terrorism will also experience a corresponding growth. This will be accomplished as supporting states become more active and viable, and Asian-based international and transnational terrorism will become a world threat. This new use of domestic and state-sponsored terrorism will rival that of anywhere in the world.

AFRICA

A land of largely untapped wealth and resources, Africa remains the most underdeveloped of continents. It is a continent of extremes in terms of social development, economics, and government. It is uninhabitable and fertile, industrially progressive and mired in the tools of antiquity, rich and poor, democratic and socialistic, a land of equality and racism, justice and vigilantism. Looking into the twenty-first century, there are five general trends in terrorism which will either continue or emerge.

One, military coups will continue to be associated with terrorism. As the scene of numerous military juntas against governments for all of the twentieth century, this trend will continue well into the next century. From colonial "freedom fighters" struggling for independence from a far-removed regime to nationalist tribal fights against foreign-sponsored governments to dissatisfied Marxists fighting democracies, Africa has, and will continue to be, beset by the struggle for national identity. This fight has become the fight of the terrorist and will worsen in the years and decades to come. Few of these terrorists will make the distinction between an impoverished people who care less about a government and the forces of the government seeking to keep a nation repressed. In Liberia, the memories will linger for a long time of the leftist Charles Taylor's National Patriotic Front of Liberia attacking Harbel, a refugee farming camp, and killing over 300 impoverished refugees. In Sudan, a civil war has been raging for over 28 years between the African Christians and African Arabics (who control the government), with most of the damage inflicted upon people wholly uninvolved in the fight by the Sudanese People's Liberation Army and military forces of the government.

Two, the communist influence in Africa will continue to grow, leading to an increase in left-wing terrorism. Cuba has been present in Africa since the early 1960s, working in partnership with the Soviets. As the Soviets pull out of Africa, the Cuban presence will increase and they will become more active. In addition to filling a support role (as they have in the past), it is expected the Cubans will become more directly involved in terrorist training and operational planning assistance. It is expected that Cuban military and DGI personnel will even participate with African terrorists in terrorist operations. This is not surprising, as it parallels the pattern of Cuban intervention in Latin America. China and North Korea will become active in Africa as well, acting to aid the Cubans in promoting terrorism. China and North Korea will be particularly active in the regions of South Africa and the Horn of Africa, two particularly terrorist-vulnerable areas. The goal of China and North Korea will be the establishment of "puppet regimes" that can be used as a forum for the introduction of their political beliefs into the heart of Africa.

A third foreseeable trend is that of Africa becoming a terrorist battleground between the Mideast and Israel. Mideast terrorists have joined the African terrorist struggle for several reasons. The Mideast terrorist wants to free the Muslims living in Africa, they want to help promote communism, and Africa can be used as a staging ground for the battle against the West. Geographically, Somalia and Sudan occupy important strategic positions on the Red Sea and Suez Canal. At present, Iran is using Sudan to train anti-Egyptian Islamic terrorists. If these terrorists were to successfully overthrow the Egyptian government, the coalition of Egypt, Somalia, and Sudan could effectively act to close the Suez Canal, thus significantly impacting the transport of military fleets and oil supplies vital to the West.

In terms of state-sponsored terrorism, Africa provides a new political, economic, and religious base for the dictates of the Mideast. By expanding and establishing a larger political base, the third-world nations of the Mideast can become more of a military and political global force. Israel has entered the world of African terrorism to stop other Mideast terrorists present in Africa. Theirs is not a political fight but rather a fight for their homeland. If the Mideast terrorists can establish a foothold in Africa, the homeland of Israel is at direct threat to attack.

A fourth emerging trend in terms of African terrorism is that the corruption of governments will continue to cause widespread disease and starvation, thus forcing Africa's people to attempt to overthrow the responsible governments. In the Horn of Africa especially, it is expected that without change, this problem will become more acute as we begin to move into the twenty-first century. In Somalia, for example, over 50 percent of the children under five years of age and over 350,000 other citizens have died of starvation in the early 1990s. Terrorist bands led first to the breakdown of civil authority and ultimately to the ouster in 1991 of Dictator Mohamed Siad Barre (Caputo, 1993). Upon Barre's abdication, clans and gangs took over the country, ultimately forcing the United Nations to order military action in an attempt to save the country. In Sudan, over one million have died in the civil war and over one million others have died of starvation. In Ethiopia in 1991, the Tigray People's Liberation Army overthrew President Mengistu Haile Moriam. At present, only Eritrea is at peace, having won freedom from Ethiopia in 1991. As terrorist organizations who claim to be "fighting for the people" begin to overthrow existing corrupt regimes and replace them with their corrupt regimes, new terrorist organizations will spring up like wild grass. As the region grows poorer and starvation increases, the terrorist explosion will grow exponentially, enflaming the entire area and spreading throughout the continent.

A fifth and final emerging trend in terrorism for the continent of Africa is that the largest terrorist problem to be faced by that continent in the decades ahead is, and will continue to be, the racial unrest in South Africa and neighboring states. This is and will continue to be one of the few areas of the world where both the government and black coalitions will consistently continue to rely on terrorism in an attempt to defeat the other. The Pretoria regime will continue to rely on assassination, raids, and border incursions into neighboring states, and the financing, training, and supporting of anti-ANC and SWAPO guerrillas (Metz, 1987). The de Klerk government discovered the only effective way of dealing with the anti-apartheid forces to be reliance on terrorist tactics. Since Mandela took power and South African blacks have been acquiring rights and responsibilities, pro-apartheid proponents will increase their level of terrorism to deal with the deterioration of white power in South Africa. The white racist coalition will continue to practice the terrorist tactics learned from the de Klerk government.

On the other side of the equation, the ANC will increase their terrorist attacks on the white establishment of South Africa. The ANC will use border countries to establish sanctuaries and conduct incursive raids into South Africa (Nimer, 1990). The support from communist regimes for this effort will continue to expand. Communist states have long funded ANC and ANC-allied South African Communist Party efforts, hoping to see the white government overthrown and ultimately replaced with a black regime favorable to communist ideals. Now that the white government is no longer in power, the communists will continue their efforts to promote communism among the black community. The hope of these communists is tied partly into the radicalism of the Calvinist Dutch Reformed Church, which uses a rigid belief structure of righteousness and justice to foster a belief of physical, spiritual, and emotional separation between God's elect and the damned.

Additionally, South Africa will continue to be one of the few regions in the world where both the communist forces and free regimes work in support of terrorism. Both the communists (Cuba, the Soviets, China, North Korea, and Arab states) and democracies and democratic institutions (Sweden, Western Europe, United Methodist Church, and the World Council of Churches) support the ANC and SWAPO (Steward, 1993). Undoubtedly, the free world will continue to see the fight not as an issue of terrorism but rather as the struggle of the racially oppressed working to ease the effects of apartheid. The communist world will continue to see the support for what it is: the replacement of a government with one more accepting of communism.

As the rest of the world begins to move into the twenty-first century and Africa forges ahead to develop its resources, it will experience the pangs of growth. Unfortunately, part of that growth includes terrorism. As a continent caught in the throes of rapid development, Africa will have more trouble dealing with the terrorist threat than will other parts of the world. Terrorists have the opportunity to significantly affect the future development in Africa.

MIDEAST

The second half of the twentieth century saw the nations of the Mideast rise to world prominence. The creation of Israel, the economic benefits of large oil fields, the move to independence and nationalism, and the rise of numerous terrorist dictators, have all played a significant role in the Mideast gaining this recognition. Likewise, the second half of the twentieth century has also seen the Mideast take the lead in world terrorism, both directly and indirectly. Directly, the impact of Mideast terrorism has spread around the globe, attacking any government or group of citizens not openly supportive of their religions or style of government. Indirectly, nations of the Mideast have done more to support and sponsor terrorism than in any other continent or government in the world. In 1989, 37 percent of all world terrorist incidents occurred in the Mideast, and people of the Mideast were involved in 45 percent of international and transnational terrorist incidents (Dept. of State, 1990). Only in the Mideast do governments use terrorists to wage "war" against other nations. Unfortunately, there is no indication that Mideast terrorism will decrease in the coming years. Instead, all indications show the problem will grow in scope and severity in the coming decades.

Before describing the future of Mideast terrorism, it is important to mention that only a small minority of the Mideast community is involved in terrorist activities. Because of the frequency and severity of Mideast terrorism, many people have the perception that the terrorist issue has engulfed the entire Mideast. However, and contrary to popular belief, Mideast terrorism is not a unified whole. In fact, only a small minority of Mideast residents engage in terroristic activity. Only four states actively and openly participate in transnational and international terrorism (Iran, Iraq, Libya, and Syria; Norton, 1988), and very few others covertly support terrorism.

Internal to the region, religious terrorism will continue to grow. Muslim extremism will continue to worsen in Afghanistan, Algeria, Egypt, Lebanon, and Sudan. Historically, Islamic fundamentalists have used terrorist tactics to gain power in Algeria, Egypt, Jordan, and Tunisia and will continue to do so based upon their records of success. In fact, the Egyptian Islamic terrorist organizations al-Gamaal-Islami Ya, the Vanguards of Conquest, and Jihad have spread throughout the Middle East. Pakistan assisted Islamic extremists in planting a series of bombs (March 1993) in the financial district of Bombay, which resulted in the death of over 300 people. Islamic terrorists have also targeted government officials, Coptic Christians, and foreigners in their attempt to form an Islamic state. In Algeria, Islamic terrorists issued an ultimatum to all foreigners, warning them to leave the country or risk death. In India, Islamic Sikhs want to be freed from Hindu oppression and want an independent Punjab (renamed Khalistan; Yaeger, 1991).

Schbley (1989) has suggested this recent rise in religious terrorism is a result of geocultural immobility. That is, when a minority population's mobility is limited within a nation with low cultural pluralism, such restrictions lead to a religious resurgence and zealous behavior by the affected minorities both in regards to religion and social repression. Related to this rise in religious terrorism will also be a rise in ethnic terrorism, such as that seen in Afghanistan and in Turkey with the Armenians (Wolf, 1989a).

Two of the oldest foes in the Mideast region are the Israelis and Palestinians. If the United States is removed from the Mideast equation, the majority of terrorist incidents to date have occurred between the Israelis and Palestinians. War, terrorism, reprisal, and hatred have marked the relationship between these two since the founding of Israel in the late 1940s. State-sponsored and domestic terrorism has always been a linchpin in the relations between the two groups.

In October 1993, Israel and the Palestinians reached an historic accord that many believe will bring an end to existing hostilities between the two. At best, this peace will be temporary and may, in fact, serve to increase terrorism. Many Palestinians wanted nothing more than a homeland, which they now have, while still others want a more specific type of Palestinian homeland. George Habbash, leader of the Popular Front for the Liberation of Palestine, wants nothing less than a Marxist state. It is believed this difference in political philosophy among the Palestinians will ultimately lead to an increase in domestic terrorism, regardless of the political system eventually adopted. The death of Israel's Prime Minister Rabin may ultimately undo all peace accords and return the Mideast to what it once was: a violent torn region where terrorism was the norm of behavior, not the exception.

Many Palestinians will never be at peace with Israel. The Popular Front for the Liberation of Palestine, General Command (led by Ahmad Jabril), the Palestine Liberation Front, Al Fatah, Abu Nidal, Hamas, Palestinian Islamic Jihad, and Hezbollah have made it clear they will never accept a negotiated settlement with Israel. These organizations now view Yassir Arafat (leader of the PLO) as much of an enemy as Israel and will not rest until Israel has been destroyed (Probst, 1991). In the weeks following the peace accord, several ranking Palestinian leaders were attacked, ambushed, assassinated, and bombed in an effort to disrupt and end the settlement. As further treaties are ratified and the Palestinian homeland becomes a reality, terrorist operations of this nature will increase in frequency and severity.

Recent events, such as the Gulf War, did not only serve to establish freedom for Kuwait from Iraq but also strengthened the resolve of Mideast nations to destroy the "great interloper," the United States. Saddam Hussein has sworn to destroy the U.S., and there are many sympathetic governments in the Mideast who would be more than willing to assist. General Omar Hassan el-Bashir of Sudan, Mohammar Kaddafi of Libya, as well as the leaders of Iran and Syria, have all sworn to assist Hussein in his efforts. The Gulf War demonstrated to these governments that they cannot compete with the U.S. on the battlefield, so they will compete in the shadowy underworld of terrorism (Revell, 1991). Terrorist organizations, in fact, such as Abu Nidal, the PLO, May 15 Organization, and Hezbollah, have all been hired by Hussein and the anti-U.S. coalition to initiate and continue attacks against U.S. interests (Seger, 1991).

Indirectly, these governments will support any terrorist organization dedicated to the overthrow of the U.S. (Busby, 1990). Training camps will proliferate in the sands of the Mideast, finances will be transferred, equipment and material stolen or bought, and manpower dedicated to terrorist organizations worldwide to conduct a campaign against the U.S. As these attacks against the U.S. intensify in scope, Arab-supported terrorist networks will appear. These networks will combine the resources of several different terrorist organizations and will be supported by the governments of the Mideast, likely in cooperation with North Korea, China, and Cuba (McForan, 1987). North Korea, in fact, has been selling SCUD–C missiles to Syria. These networks will also receive expert training and support from ex-Soviet, East German, and communist bloc security services personnel. As communism fell, thousands of experts in terrorist operations suddenly found themselves displaced from government service and available on the open market (Probst, 1991). As a result, many have found their way to the Mideast. These ex-secret police bring a high degree of expertise to the world of terrorism, thus posing a greater threat than might otherwise exist.

In terms of training, financing, and material support issues, nations of the Mideast will take over the reigns from Russia and rival China, Cuba, and North Korea for producing well-trained terrorists. Training sites, safe havens, and supply depots are appearing at an alarming rate throughout the Mideast. In 1986, when President Reagan bombed Basra and Tripoli, Libya, there was a brief decline in terrorist camps. Since the U.S. military pulled out of the Mideast following the Iraq/Kuwait war, these sites have proliferated and will continue to do so well into the next century. The only possible measure which can stop the growth of these sites is direct military intervention, a responsibility no nation is ready to commit its military resources or finances to at the present time.

Along with increased activity against the West and U.S., Mideast terrorists will employ more sophisticated and deadly weapons in their war of terrorism. Hussein has prohibited U.N. inspection teams from inspecting the nuclear facilities in Iraq as he attempts to develop nuclear weapons. He has built a chemical weapons plant at Samarra (and Libya has one at Rabta), and he is developing biological agents. His plans include terrorists being given these weapons to use against the West. Pakistan and India have joined the nuclear arms race and may well use terrorists as a delivery mechanism.

CENTRAL AND SOUTH AMERICA

Central and South America is the chessboard of the world. In a group of relatively poor nations, governments rise, fall, and are replaced with certain regularity. Largely undeveloped, but rapidly attempting to catch up with the rest of the world, the Latin American countries often play Russian roulette with terrorism. As this region of the world awakes and hurries to catch the industrialized world, the people of the region have adopted the cachets of terrorism to force governments to bring the entire populous of the region into the twenty-first century, not just the few rich power brokers.

Latin America has been a hotbed of terrorist activity for years. Morris (1988) pointed out that in 1985, Latin America accounted for 42 percent of worldwide terrorist incidents and 19 percent of the terrorist organizations. As shown by Glendon (1991), Latin America is the kidnap capital of the world. Fortunately, the majority of this terrorism has been internally directed. As the region develops and international industry, financing, and community begin to move in to help develop the area, the terrorists will turn their efforts outward to affect these competing interests.

Some of the terrorist organizations in Latin America are among the largest in the world. Shining Path in Peru has almost 7,000 members. The Communist Revolutionary Armed Forces and M-19 in Colombia combined have approximately 5,000 members organized into 19 squadrons (or fronts) almost like a small army (Salavarrieta, 1989). At the height of their power, the Tupermarros in Bolivia had almost 4,000 members. As Latin America develops, these and other groups like them will unfortunately continue to gain members and grow in strength (manpower, financial, equipment, and other resources).

While the future of Latin America is bright, the threat of terrorism has the potential to grow faster and more violent there than anywhere else in the world.

This is primarily attributable to the fact that many governments in Latin America are weak despots "ripe for the plucking" by terrorists. These governments have many failings, as described by Sutton (1991). Among these, the politicos consider themselves an elite group and they provide no avenue nor mechanism for political input from the lower classes. They are incompetent, lack legitimacy among their own people, and are not respected. They are rigid, immobile, and fail to keep pace with social, industrial, and economic changes. They rely on flawed economic policies to manage their country's affairs, further impoverishing their citizens and retarding a rising Latin American standard of living. They invest the money of their country outside of the country, relying on foreign investments to drive internal economics and development. All of these factors, taken together, make these governments extremely unstable and susceptible to internal strife, the growth of terrorism, and ultimately overthrow (usually with an even less competent government). This trend will definitely continue well into the twenty-first century.

When these governments and terrorists do finally reach accord, the government will likely not know how to maintain this peace. The governments either do not know how to abide by the peace accords or, as is usually the case, do not believe they are obligated to abide by the accord. In some instances, the government sees the accord as an opportunity to eliminate the terrorists. In El Salvador, for example, rightist death squads of President Cristiani's government have assassinated over 25 leading members of the Farabundo Marti Liberation Front since a peace agreement was signed in January 1992. Regardless of the reason, treaty violations lead to a resurgence of terrorism, beginning anew a seemingly never-ending cycle of terrorism and violence. No data suggests this situation will change as Latin America moves into the next century.

As a direct corollary of the above, the civil wars which have characterized Latin America in the twentieth century will continue to feed the cause of terrorism well into the twenty-first century. From the struggles in Bolivia of the 1940s and 1950s, to the Nicaraguan and El Salvadoran situation of today, terrorists actively promote the cause of rebel fighters and teach rebels the tools and techniques of terrorism (and thus find new recruits). And they receive more than their share of external support in this endeavor. In Nicaragua, for example, almost every terrorist organization and state supporter of terrorism in the world has assisted both the Contras and Sandinistas.

As previously mentioned, most Latin American terrorism has been internally directed. Since 1980, Shining Path has killed over 20,000 Peruvians in over 12,000 attacks (McCormack, 1988). As Latin America joins the world community, these organizations will begin directing their attacks against foreigners. Shining Path has been involved in attacks on U.S. citizens, including the assassination of reporter Todd Smith in 1989. The U.S. embassy in Bolivia was bombed by the Forces of Liberation Zarate Willka (FALZU) in December 1989. The Frente Farbundo Marti De La Liberacion Nacional (FMLN) in El Salvador has repeatedly attacked U.S. interests (Dept. of Justice, 1992). These organizations see U.S. intervention as a hindrance to the development of Latin America. They see a U.S. presence as destroying and devaluating their cultural heritage. The U.S. is the imperialist aggressor, whose only purpose in Latin America is to colonize the continent and establish it as a servant to U.S. interests. They believe U.S. intervention will destroy Latin American culture, heritage, religion, and politics.

The Cuban presence, long a staple in Central America, will become more predominant throughout Latin America in the next decade. This will be due not only to Castro's use of terrorism as basic guerrilla warfare but also due to strong Cuban sentiments in the region (Fontaine, 1988). In addition to Cuban influence, other transnational terrorists will use Latin America as a home base, safe haven, and resource for manpower, supplies, and finances (Sutton, 1991). Many anti-American Mideastern and European terrorists will see Latin America as the ideal base of operations from which to conduct campaigns of terrorism against the U.S. (as an example, terrorists from Kreuzberg, Germany have been linked with Shining Path). It is close, sparsely populated, the U.S. has difficulty sending government agents after them, extradition treaties are not in place, and there is growing anti-U.S. sentiment in Central and South America. All of these factors will make Latin America attractive to the transnational terrorist.

Latin American terrorists will become more operationally and technically sophisticated in the coming decades. Morris (1988) has indicated that the Latin American terrorist has a high success rate against low security targets, but as security increases linearly, terrorist success drops exponentially. With the help of Cubans, Mideasterners, Europeans, and even Asians, the Latin American terrorist will begin to see a higher success rate and be able to conduct successful operations against high-security targets. These successes will also serve to bolster their confidence, making them more brazen in their attacks. Also, the Latin American terrorists will begin using more advanced weapons. The favorite weapons of the Latin American terrorist have been handguns. While effective against unarmed targets or in small-scale operations, they are not very effective in more advanced operations. As these terrorists receive more training, their choice of weapons will change to more deadly weapons, including rockets, high-grade explosives, and even NBC weapons. These weapons will be provided by sympathetic organizations, governments, bought on the black market, and taken from police and military arsenals.

Finally, the Latin American terrorist will become less ideologically driven and more economically driven—a rarity in the world of terrorism. Many terrorist organizations in that region of the world have become linked with drug cartels and the drug trade. Examples include the Tupac Amaru and Shining Path in Peru, the Revolutionary Armed Forces of Colombia (FARC) and April 9th Movement in Colombia (Dept. of Justice, 1989), the Manuel Rodriguez Patriotic Front in Chile, and the Sandinistas in Nicaragua. In Colombia, FARC and M-19 united with the drug lords and formed the National Terrorist Coordinator to further the goals of the drug cartels.

It was long rumored that Castro and the DGI in Cuba supported this terrorist/drug coalition as it made money for Cuba. These rumors became fact in 1989, when General Arnaldo Ochoa Sanchez and two others were tried in Cuba for being involved in drug trafficking and working to establish drug cartel/terrorist coalitions in Latin America (Lupsha, 1991). Found guilty and sentenced to die by a Castro puppet court, Sanchez clearly implicated Fidel and Raul in the coalition. Cuba relies on a healthy drug trade to provide needed economic support for Cuba and to help the destruction of the U.S. Without Russian support, Cuba will come to rely even more on successful drug-trafficking operations.

As terrorist organizations strengthen their ties with the drug cartels, they lose their ideology and change the direction of their terrorism (Inciardi, 1991). Their targets become less political and more anti-narcotic personnel. Although this does include local governments, the primary focus is U.S. law enforcement personnel and citizens. The only serious attacks on local government officials have occurred in Bolivia and Colombia. The severity of attacks in Colombia have, in fact, backfired on the terrorists. In 1990, citizens of Bogota banded together and bombed the cartel property and houses of Pablo Escobar, leader of the Medellin drug cartel. Outside of the actions in Colombia, efforts at severing this link have proved fruitless and may in the future lead to more terrorism (Moron, 1991).

THE UNITED STATES

On 26 February 1993, Omar Abdl-Rahman, El Sayyid Nosair, Moham-med Abouhalima, Abdo Mohammed Haggag, Siraj Yousif, Ahmed

Mohammed, Siddig Ibrahim Siddig Al, Fares Khallafall, Clement Rodney Hampton-El, Fadil Abdelghani, Amir Abdlgany, Tarig Elhassan, Victor Alvarez, and Mohammed A. Salameh, all members of a fanatical Egyptian Muslim sect ruled by Sheik Omar Abdel-Rahman, bombed the World Trade Center in New York City. Upon their arrest very shortly after the incident, authorities discovered plans to attack military installations, murder FBI agents, bomb the Lincoln and Holland tunnels in New York, bomb a New York federal building, and engage in hostage-taking operations to secure the release of jailed comrades.

While the bombing of the World Trade Center shocked most Americans, the country was to be stunned into disbelief less than two years later when American citizens bombed the Oklahoma City Federal Building. In 1994 and 1995, Congress ordered and held special subcommittee hearings on the actions of federal authorities in the Randy Weaver siege in Ruby Ridge, Idaho and the attack on the Branch Davidian compound outside of Waco, Texas. In general, the outcome of both these hearings suggested federal authorities had acted improperly in dealing with both incidents.

It is clear that the U.S. has entered a new era of terrorism. Historically limited to foreign operations, international and transnational terrorists now perceive the continental United States to be an integral part of the battleground against U.S. policy and the government. The World Trade Center bombing was not the first instance of foreign terrorists operating within the United States, but it was the largest and most successful. Despite claims to the contrary, domestically the far right is not dead, has not disappeared, and is not dwindling in number. The 1960s was the heyday era of the Klan, and the 1970s and 1980s for the Christian Identity movement. The 1990s have witnessed the emergence of a combining of these two philosophies in the growing militia movement. This should not suggest the Klan and Identity movement have disappeared, for clearly they have not. All factions of the far-right movement will continue to be troublesome in the years ahead. Law enforcement has come under increased public and government scrutiny in efforts to fight terrorism, and this will continue and worsen in the years to come.

One future trend that has major implications for terrorism within the United States is the growing threat of international and domestic terrorists operating on U.S. soil. Prior to the 1990s, it was extremely difficult and dangerous for foreign terrorists to enter the U.S. and conduct operations. Terrorists did not have support networks, equipment and materials were difficult to obtain, and the overall risks outweighed the possible gains. That situation began changing in the 1980s. In 1988, a member of the Japanese Red Army, Yu Kikumura, was arrested in New

Jersey. Inside his vehicle were several explosive devices he was planning on using in New York for attacks on public facilities. On 3 July 1988, a van driven by Sharon Rogers, wife of Navy Captain Will Rogers III, was bombed. Captain Rogers was commander of the *USS Vincennes,* the ship responsible for shooting down Iran Air 565 in the Persian Gulf (Buckelew, 1987). Iranian terrorists were suspected of planting the bomb as an act of retaliation for the loss of Flight 565. Also in 1988, Libyans Abdel Basset Ali al-Megrahi and Lamen Khalifa Fhimah were charged with the bombing of Pan Am 103 over Lockerbee, Scotland. Part of their motivation is believed also to be in retaliation for Flight 565. In 1993, four members of Abu Nidal living in St. Louis were arrested and charged with planning to commit terrorist bombing operations in Washington D.C. All four were naturalized U.S. citizens. For several years, members of Shining Path have actively been recruiting Hispanic gang members in Los Angeles to assist in domestic terrorism. Ricks (1988) has suggested that every major Mideast terrorist organization has an internal structure in place within the United States and are ready to begin terrorist operations at a moment's notice.

International and transnational terrorists are developing two types of organizational structures within the U.S. One type are transient cells. These cells are operational units which travel to the U.S., hit a target, and then egress the country. Of the two organizational structures, transient cells are the more difficult to intercept. These cells do all the operational planning, attack preparation, and networking at overseas locations and bases. They may be within the U.S. for less than a day. On occasion, law enforcement may gather intelligence on a terrorist support network living within the U.S. and intercept and prevent the transient cell attack. The second type of terrorist organizational structure is the sleeper cell. This cell is comprised of terrorists who have moved to the U.S., established residency, possibly gained citizenship, found employment, and are awaiting orders from their host organization (based overseas) to begin conducting operations. Both structures do require a support network in place within the U.S. Historically, proactive efforts have concentrated on transient cells, as sleeper cells were rather uncommon. This trend will reverse itself in the future, as sleeper cells become the more predominant form of international terrorism in the U.S. Also, international terrorists will become more active against people rather than structures (Hoffman, 1988). History has shown that attacks on structures are not as effective as are attacks against persons in producing fear and political change.

Domestically, the greatest threat to be faced from the far left will come from the Puerto Rican separatist movement. By the early 1990s, most

Puerto Rican terrorists had been arrested and jailed and the Puerto Rican terrorist movement had virtually ceased to exist. In 1993, Puerto Rico, in a public vote, overwhelmingly decided to remain an American territory. This vote enraged the far-left extreme element within Puerto Rico and will lead to a rebirth of Puerto Rican terrorism. This terrorism will be directed against pro-U.S. interests within Puerto Rico and the U.S. government. It is expected that Cuba will continue to be a major supporter of Puerto Rican terrorist activities (Wolf, 1989a). Cubans will provide training, equipment, and financing to the Puerto Rican separatist movement.

The far right will continue to be active and violent. Domestic right-wing organizations such as the KKK, Aryan Nations, racial and religious supremacists, neo-Nazi organizations, and the militia movement will gain strength and support. The far-right movement will continue to unify and coalesce into a nationalist movement. As in the 1980s, the far right will present the greatest threat to the United States in the coming years (Mullins, 1990a, 1990b). In the early 1990s, the far right regrouped, increased membership, and brought a new generation of terrorists into their movement: the skinheads. Once a disparate collection of unorganized and disenchanted youth, the skinhead movement now continues to grow and unify at an alarming rate (Mullins, 1993). They have been welcomed with open arms by the older vanguard of the far right and are seen as the future of white America. The established far right has provided training, instruction, equipment, finances, and motivation to the skinhead movement. Virtually every year has seen an increase in skinhead violence, a trend not likely to reverse itself in the coming years. As an example, in 1993 the FBI arrested several members of the Los Angeles Fourth Reich Skinheads who were preparing operations to begin a race war by shooting up a black church and assassinate leaders of the NAACP, Nation of Islam leader Louis Farrakhan, the Reverend Al Sharpton, and various rap artists. The skinhead movement will continue to grow much faster than efforts to prevent skinhead violence (Clarke, 1991).

The far right has historically viewed the federal (and state) government as Jewish controlled and dominated, and a government that is preventing the Second Coming of Christ. Their beliefs combined a racial and religious hatred with a misapplied Christian fundamentalism that demanded government be overthrown (Mullins, 1986, 1989, 1991a). In the mid-1990s, another motivational element has been introduced: control of the United States by the United Nations. This newly emerged militia movement combines a racial and religious fervor with a paranoia of a world dominated by the forces of communism. It was previously mentioned that the militia movement already believes large communist forces occupy America and are preparing to take over the government. The coming years will see this paranoia increase and worsen. Unfortunately, the attack on the Oklahoma City Federal Building was just a precursor of what is to come.

In dealing with the militia movement, law enforcement authorities have taken a "hands-off" approach. Primarily this policy of non-intervention has been the result of the outcomes of Ruby Ridge and Waco. Law enforcement believes their hands are tied in dealing with the militia. In Montana, several members of the Freemen have outstanding felony warrants. They have not been arrested because law enforcement authorities are afraid of another confrontation similar to Ruby Ridge and Waco. This passive policy of law enforcement will continue to serve the interests of the far-right faction, giving members an increased perception of power and strength over the government.

Four related factors will contribute to the growth of the far-right movement in the coming years. One, the recession will continue to worsen. In difficult economic times, the far right gains strength and momentum. Many people turn to the far right in a search for answers, a return to more prosperous times, and hope for a better future. Two, as the government continues to work to eliminate racial bias and discrimination, many whites will perceive a direct threat to established society. To these people, giving additional freedom to one group of people means another group (them) loses freedoms. The far right provides an alternative solution to prevent the loss of freedoms. Three, the far right believes Aryans are responsible for promoting the final race war. To the far right, the Bible has preordained that whites will win this war. Four, many believe the far right is winning the war against the government. This belief was promoted by the government's losing the sedition case against leading members in the Fort Smith, Arkansas sedition trial. Events at Ruby Ridge and Waco reinforced and strengthened this belief. To these people, the perception is that the far right is "right" and the government is wrong.

Another terrorist trend confronting the United States in the coming years is the growth of special-interest terrorism (Mullins, 1990a). The anti-abortion movement, animal rights movement, and eco-movement will all continue to grow and present terrorist problems to society. The 1990s has seen special-interest terrorism change the focus of its attacks from structures to persons. In 1993, an anti-abortionist in Florida assassinated abortion doctor Doctor David Gunn. In Boston, an anti-abortionist killed two workers at an abortion clinic in an assassination attack. Adding to the increased violence of the anti-abortion movement is the refusal of the government or federal law enforcement agencies to consider anti-abortion violence as terrorism (Wilson & Lynxwiler, 1988). The violent faction of the anti-abortionist movement is terrorism by almost any definition. The government will have to eventually recognize and treat this violence as a form of terrorism.

Animal rights activists can also be expected to continue engaging in terrorism protesting the use of animals used in research, the cosmetic industry, and the clothing industry. Animal rights terrorists will continue to attack the institutions that use animals, destroying research laboratories, animal quarantine facilities, and other businesses related to these activities. In addition, the animal rights terrorists will turn more to attacks on individuals. One common tactic employed by these activists is to attack persons wearing fur and throwing paint or other caustic substances on the garment. The failure of this type of operation to change behavior or laws will result in attacks against fur-wearing persons becoming more violent and harmful.

Eco-terrorists engage in what they refer to as "ecotage" (ecology + sabotage; Badolato, 1991). The most active eco-terrorist organizations have included Earth First!, the Evan Mecham Eco-Terrorist International Conspiracy (EMETIC), and Greenpeace. EMETIC has attacked power poles, ski lifts, and planned attacks on nuclear facilities (Dept. of Justice, 1988). Other eco-terrorists, including the Night Action Group, have likewise attacked similar targets (Dept. of Justice, 1990). In the foreseeable future, these organizations will continue to engage in terrorism to protect the environment from what they perceive to be the human destruction of the world.

In addition to the three presented special-interest terrorist issues, other special-interest organizations will use terrorism to right "injustices." One of the most rapidly growing of all special-interest terrorist movements are the anti-tax protesters, such as Posse Comitatus and Up The IRS, Inc. (Dept. of State, 1991). The tax protest movement has historically been closely allied with the far-right movement and will continue to be so. Part of the anti-tax movement philosophy centers around the illegitimacy of the federal government. They will continue to work with, associate with, and join the far-right movement.

Narco-terrorism will continue to grow in the United States. According to the Risk Assessment Information Service (RAIS), narcoterrorism is the fastest-growing form of terrorism in the United States (Quigley, 1990). The drug cartels will continue to use terrorists to assist in the production, sale, and distribution of narcotics and other drugs, to perform security functions for the drug industry, and to eliminate opponents to the drug industry. Domestic terrorists will become more actively involved in narcoterrorism for a variety of reasons. One, some will use drugs for personal pleasure. Two, involvement in the drug business can raise enormous amounts of capital in a short period of time. Three, drugs are seen as an avenue to topple American society and the U.S. government. Four, some see drug usage as promoting the coming race war and as a method of controlling the ability to fight in among the "enemy" (Mullins, 1990c).

A new form of terrorism has emerged in the U.S. in the 1990s and will continue to grow throughout the remainder of the decade: local terrorism of street gangs (Mullins & Mijares, 1993b). In all respects, terrorism has always been directed against federal systems, with a very few exceptions of terrorists directing their activities against a state's government. Gang-related terrorism takes terrorism to the local level by attempting to produce government change at the municipal level. As street gangs have strengthened in number and firepower, have consolidated neighborhood gangs, and have spread throughout the country, they have attempted to use the tactics of terrorism to force municipal change. Gang goals have included such agendas as political recognition, non-intervention in gang "turf," changes in municipal ordinances, minority aid and assistance programs, improvements in inner-city living conditions, racial issues, and narcoterrorism. The spread and size of local gangs will continue to increase and, as they mature, will become more socially conscious. As they do, they will employ the tactics of gang warfare against municipal governments.

SUMMARY

Part of the growth in terrorism as a tool of political recourse has been spurred by media coverage of terrorism. Terrorists make headline news. Their activities and atrocities are newsworthy events. As the media and public become inoculated against violence and terrorism, the terrorists will have to resort to larger and larger-scale operations to gain the same publicity. Few countries have, or will follow, the lead of Great Britain who has enacted legislation limited the news coverage of terrorist incidents (Shipler, 1988). Terrorism will increase and worsen because of the media response to terrorism. This situation will not improve nor abate in the coming years.

Larger-scale events require larger weapons. Large-scale events will be required to get media coverage, and large-scale weapons will be needed to commit large-scale events (Probst, 1991). C-4, PETN, and RDX have replaced dynamite. Guns will be replaced with missiles and rocket launchers. LAWs, TOW missiles, and SAMs will become the terrorist's weapons of the next decade. Nuclear, biological, and chemical weapons will become a part of the terrorist arsenal and an ever-increasing emerging threat for the public. Numerous NBC threats and several incidents have already occurred. Between 1966 and 1977, there were ten terrorist attacks against French nuclear installations, one attack against a French nuclear reactor in 1979, and a rocket attack against the French Creys-Malville nuclear facility in 1982. Between 1969 and 1975, U.S. nuclear facilities were targets of 240 bomb threats and 14 bombings or attempted bombings (Denton, 1987).

The possibility of terrorists obtaining nuclear weapons is not an H.G. Wells fantasy. Terrorists can obtain nuclear weapons from a variety of sources (Norman, 1978). In addition, terrorists do not have to detonate a nuclear weapon to engage in nuclear terrorism. As Alexander (1983) and Jenkins (1986) have pointed out, terrorists could use nuclear terrorism in a variety of ways, including free release in an enclosed area, stealing nuclear material and threatening free release, taking a nuclear facility hostage, or fabricating a nuclear threat. Nuclear facilities, especially those outside of the United States, are particularly vulnerable to all of these forms of nuclear terrorism (Hoenig, 1987). Finally, terrorists may be assisted by sympathetic governments (Ezeldin, 1989).

The possibility of terrorists using biological agents is a real threat. Used militarily for centuries, biological weapons open a new dimension in operations for the terrorist. In the 1980s, the Red Army Faction in Europe was discovered with a large quantity of Botullinal Toxin, one of the deadliest substances on earth (Hersh, 1968; Mullins, 1991b, 1992). Some of these agents, including deadly strains of Anthrax, are available through the mail (Mengel, 1979). Terrorists could produce biological agents resistant to any form of vaccine or human immunity against the organism. The only drawback in the use of biological agents as a terrorist weapon is controlling the spread of the agent. Today, with advances in recombinant DNA technology, and microencapsulation procedures, even this danger can be minimized.

It is most likely that terrorists will employ chemical weapons in the foreseeable future (Mullins, 1992). Terrorist regimes, such as Saddam Hussein, have already employed chemical weapons in state-sponsored terrorism. It is only a matter of time until other terrorists employ these weapons. Unlike nuclear and biological agents, chemical weapons are easy to make or obtain, easy to store, are effective agents of mass casualty (see, for example, Stephens & MacKenna, 1988), and are virtually risk-free for the terrorist in terms of self-infliction or getting caught. Chemical weapons have many benefits for the terrorist. One, they are weapons of mass casualty. Large numbers of people can be incapacitated or killed with small amounts of a chemical. Two, press coverage is guaranteed.

Three, they are simple to make and use (Joyner, 1993). In sum, they have all of the necessary advantages and virtually none of the drawbacks of other weapons, including conventional weapons.

Finally, air and maritime terrorism can be expected to increase (Ellen, 1991; Williams, 1990). These events can produce mass casualties, produce headline coverage, and, for the terrorist, result in a low probability of capture. The *Achille Lauro* incident and downing of Pan Am 103 demonstrated to terrorists worldwide the effectiveness of air and maritime terrorism.

At times, it seems we are powerless to prevent terrorism. Laws are passed, pressure is applied to supporting states, working coalitions are formed, military intervention is employed, negotiating strategies are developed, economic sanctions are imposed, covert operations are developed, and criminal sanctions are used (see, for example, Bremer, 1989; Busby, 1990; Revell, 1989). None of these strategies work. Whatever is tried, terrorists circumvent. When one type of operation becomes too costly or ineffective, the terrorist changes operation. If airplanes cannot be successfully hijacked, they will be destroyed in the air. If bombing a federal building does not produce political change, citizens will be attacked in their homes. All of the governmental edicts, treaties, coalitions, and extraditions mean little to the terrorist. The terrorist laughs in the face of these measures and continues to discriminantly and indiscriminantly kill.

So, what can be done to stop terrorism? Possibly the most effective strategy is the one that has been used the least: education. The public (and law enforcement) must be educated concerning who the terrorists are, what their goals are, and what they do, how they do it, and why they do it. The terrorist can only be stopped with knowledge. Knowledge will defeat imagination, ignorance, and fear. Knowledge will prevent the terrorist from terrorizing, nothing more, nothing less.

BIBLIOGRAPHY

Abadinsky, H. (1987). *Organized crime* (2nd Ed.). Chicago: Nelson-Hall.

Adams, J. (1986). *The financing of terror.* New York: Simon & Schuster.

Aho, J.A. (1990). *The politics of righteousness: Idaho Christian patriotism.* Seattle, Wash.: University of Washington Press.

Aho, J.A. (1994). *This thing of darkness: A sociology of the enemy.* Seattle, Wash.: University of Washington Press.

Alexander, Y. (1977). Terrorism and the media in the Near East. In Alexander, Y. & Finger, S.M. (Eds.), *Terrorism: Interdisciplinary perspectives.* New York: John Jay Press.

Alexander, Y. (1983). Terrorism and high-technology weapons. In Freedland, L.Z. & Alexander, Y. (Eds.), *Perspectives on terrorism.* Wilmington, Del.: Scholarly Resources, Inc.

Alexander, Y. (1985). Terrorism and the Soviet Union. In Merari, A. (Ed.). *On terrorism and combating terrorism.* Frederick, Maryland: University Publications of America.

Alexander, Y. (1989). The European-Middle East terrorist connection. *International Journal of Comparative and Applied Criminal Justice, 13,* 1–5.

Alexander, Y. (1993). Will terrorists use chemical weapons? In Schechterman, B. & Slann, M. (Eds.), *Violence and terrorism* (3rd Ed.). Guilford, Conn.: Dushkin Publishing Group, Inc. Reprint from *JINSA Security Affairs,* 1990, *Jun/Jul,* 10.

Alexander, Y. & Finger, S.M. (1977). Introduction. In Alexander, Y. & Finger, S.M. (Eds.), *Terrorism: Interdisciplinary perspectives.* New York: John Jay Press.

Allen, T. (1995). The buck stops here: Truman's war. Symposium at the 1945–Crucible of deliverance: Prisoners of war and the A-bomb conference sponsored by the Admiral Nimitz Museum. San Antonio, Texas (Mar.)

Almond, P. (1990). Boom times at hand for mercenary market. In Schechterman, B. & Slann, M. (Eds.), *Violence and terrorism.* Guilford, Conn.: Dushkin Publishing Group, Inc. Reprint from *Insight,* 1987, *July 6,* 36–38.

American Heritage Dictionary. (1980). New York: Houghton and Mifflin Company.

American Justice. (1994). *Hostages.* Arts and Entertainment Television Network.

American Psychiatric Association. (1980). *Diagnosis and statistical manual of mental disorders* (3rd Ed.). Washington D.C.: American Psychiatric Association.

American Psychiatric Association. (1987). *Diagnostic and statistical manual* (3rd Ed., Revised). Washington D.C.: American Psychiatric Association.

Amit, N. (1993). Diminishing the threat against terrorism. In Schechterman, B. & Slann, M. (Eds.), *Violence and terrorism* (3rd Ed.). Guilford, Conn.: Dushkin

Publishing Group, Inc. Reprint from *Israel Defense Forces Journal,* 1989, *Fall,* 8–10.

Amnesty International. (1980). *Amnesty Action, Sep.*

Anable, D. (1978). Loose net links diverse groups; No central plot. In Elliot, J.D. & Gibson, L.K. (Eds.), *Contemporary terrorism: Selected readings.* Gaithersburg, Maryland: IACP. Reprint from the *Christian Science Monitor,* 1977.

Anderson, A.G. (1979). *The business of organized crime: A Cosa Nostra family.* Stanford, CA: Hoover Institutional Press.

Anderson, R.S. (1975). Operation homecoming: Psychological observations of repatriated Vietnam prisoners of war. *Psychiatry, 38,* 65–74.

Anti-Defamation League. (1983). *Extremism on the right.* New York: Anti-Defamation League of B'nai B'rith.

Anti-Defamation League. (1985). *Computerized networks of hate.* New York: Anti-Defamation League of B'nai B'rith.

Anti-Defamation League. (1986). *Extremism targets the prisons.* New York: Anti-Defamation League of B'nai B'rith.

Anti-Defamation League. (1988). *Hate groups in America: A record of bigotry and violence.* New York: Anti-Defamation League of B'nai B'rith.

Anti-Defamation League. (1990a). *NeoNazi skinheads: A 1990 status report.* New York: Anti-Defamation League of B'nai B'rith.

Anti-Defamation League. (1990b). *Skinheads on trial.* New York: Anti-Defamation League of B'nai B'rith.

Anti-Defamation League. (1990c). *Young and violent: The growing menace of America's neo-Nazi skinheads.* New York: Anti-Defamation League of B'nai B'rith.

Anti-Defamation League. (1991a). *The KKK today: A 1991 status report.* New York: Anti-Defamation League of B'nai B'rith.

Anti-Defamation League. (1991b). *1990 Audit of Anti-Semitic incidents.* New York: Anti-Defamation League of B'nai B'rith.

Anti-Defamation League. (1993). *Young nazi killers: The rising skinhead danger.* Anti-Defamation League of B'nai B'rith.

Anti-Defamation League. (1994a). *Embattled bigots: A split in the ranks of the Holocaust denial movement.* New York: Anti-Defamation League of B'nai B'rith.

Anti-Defamation League. (1994b). *Hate crimes laws: A comprehensive guide.* New York: Anti-Defamation League of B'nai B'rith.

Anti-Defamation League. (1995a). *Research report: William L. Pierce: Novelist of hate.* New York: Anti-Defamation League of B'nai B'rith.

Anti-Defamation League. (1995b). *Research report: Dukewatch 1995.* New York: Anti-Defamation League of B'nai B'rith.

Anti-Defamation League. (1995c). *Paranoia as patriotism: Far-right influences on the militia movement.* Anti-Defamation League of B'nai B'rith.

Anti-Defamation League. (1995d). *Beyond the bombing: The militia menace grows.* New York: Anti-Defamation League of B'nai B'rith.

Anti-Defamation League. (undated). *Holocaust denial: A pocket guide.* New York: Anti-Defamation League of B'nai B'rith.

Aguilera, D.C. & Messick, J.N. (1978). *Crisis intervention: Theory and methodology.* St. Louis: C.V. Mosby Company.

Arens, M. (1986). Terrorist states. In Netanyahu, B. (Ed.), *Terrorism: How the West can win.* New York: Farrar, Straus, & Giroux.

Asa, M. (1985). Forms of state support to terrorism and the supporting states. In Merari, A. (Ed.), *On terrorism and combating terrorism.* Frederick, Maryland: University Publications of America.

Asencio, D. & Asencio, N. (1983). *Our man is inside.* Boston, Mass.: Little Brown.

Aston, C.C. (1983). Political hostage taking in Western Europe: A statistical analysis. In Freedman, L.Z. & Alexander, Y. (Eds.), *Perspectives on terrorism.* Wilmington, Del.: Scholarly Resources.

Austin, T. (1991). Toward a theory on the impact of terrorism: The Philippine scenario. *International Journal of Comparative and Applied Criminal Justice, 15,* 33–48.

Ayoob, M. (1984). Security in the Third World: The worm about to turn? *International Affairs,* 41–51.

Badolato, E.V. (1991). Environmental terrorism: A case study. *Terrorism, 14,* 237–239.

Balsiger, D.W. (1990). Narco-terrorism: "Shooting up" America. In Schechterman, B. & Slann, M. (Eds.), *Violence and terrorism.* Guilford, Conn.: Dushkin Publishing Group, Inc. Reprint from *Family Protection Scoreboard,* 1988.

Bard, M. & Sangrey, D. (1979). *The crime victim's book.* New York: Basic Books.

Barker, W.E. (1985). Linkages and co-participation in right-wing groups. Paper presented at the Academy of Criminal Justice Sciences, Las Vegas, NV (April).

Baron, R.A. & Byrne, D. (1977). *Social psychology: Understanding human interaction* (2nd Ed.). Boston: Allyn & Bacon, Inc.

Barron, J. (1974). *KGB.* New York: Bantam Books.

Bar-Zohar, M. & Haber, E. (1983). *The quest for the red prince.* New York: Morrow.

Bassiouni, M.C. (1975). *International terrorism and political crimes.* Springfield, Ill.: Charles C Thomas, Publisher.

Bassiouni, M.C. (1975). The political exception in extradition law and practice. In Bassiouni, M.C. (Ed.), *International terrorism and political crimes.* Springfield, Ill.: Charles C Thomas, Publisher.

Bayo, A. (1975). *150 questions for a guerrilla.* Colorado: Paladin Press.

Beach, E.L. (1986). *The United States Navy: A 200-year history.* Boston: Houghton Mifflin Co.

Becker, J. (1986). The centrality of the PLO. In Netanyahu, B. (Ed.), *Terrorism: How the West can win.* New York: Farrar, Straus, & Giroux.

Bell, B. (1975). *Transnational terror.* Washington D.C.: American Enterprise Institute.

Bell, J.B. (1972). Assassination international politics. *International Studies Quarterly, 16,* 78–80.

Bell, J.B. (1978a). *Assassin! The theory and practice of political violence.* New York: St. Martin's Press.

Bell, J.B. (1978b). *A time of terror.* New York: Basic Books.

Bell, J.B. (1987). Gun in politics: An analysis of Irish political conflict, 1916–1986. Rutgers, New Brunswick, NJ: Transaction Books.

Benware, P.N. (1984). *Ambassadors of Armstrongism.* Fort Washington, Penn.: Christian Literature Crusade.

Berard, S. (1985). Nuclear terrorism: More myth than reality. *Air University Review,* *36,* 30–36.

Beres, L.R. (1990). When assassination is just. In Schechterman, B. & Slann, M. (Eds.), *Violence and terrorism.* Guilford, Conn.: Dushkin Publishing Group, Inc. Reprint from *The Jerusalem Post International Edition, 1988, April.*

Berger, D.M. (1977). The survivor syndrome: A problem of nosology and treatment. *American Journal of Psychotherapy, 31,* 238–251.

Berkman, B. (1979). *Opening the prison gates: The rise of the prisoner's movement.* Lexington, Mass: Lexington Books.

Bernstein, B. (1995). The commanders in chief. Symposium at the 1945 – Crucible of deliverance: Prisoners of war and the A-bomb conference sponsored by the Admiral Nimitz Museum. San Antonio, Texas. (Mar.)

Besser, J.D. (1982). The doomsday decade. *Progress,* 46–66.

Biddle, W. (1986). It must be simple and reliable. *Discover, June,* 22–31.

Biggs, J.R. (1987). Defusing hostage situations. *Police Chief, 54,* 33–34.

Bird, K. (1995). Modern evidence and continuing controversy. Symposium at the 1945 – Crucible of deliverance: Prisoners of war and the A-bomb conference sponsored by the Admiral Nimitz Museum. San Antonio, Texas. (Mar.)

Bird, T. (1992). *American POWs of World War II: Forgotten men tell their stories.* Westport, Connecticut: Praeger.

Blumberg, M. (1986). A comparative analysis of violent left- and right-wing extremist groups in the United States. Paper presented at the American Society of Criminology, Atlanta, GA (Oct).

Bolton, C. (1984). Italian terrorism: Dead or dormant? *Journal of Defense and Diplomacy, Nov,* 39–42.

Boyce, D. (1987). Narco-terrorism. *FBI Law Enforcement Bulletin, 56,* 24–27.

Boye, I. (1990). Europe after 1992. *Police Chief, 57,* 16–17.

Bowers, R. (1987). White radicals charged with sedition. *Arkansas Gazette, April 25,* 1 & 11.

Bowers, R. (1988). Plots to poison water, stir riots alleged at trial. *Arkansas Gazette, 18 Feb,* 6A.

Bremer, L.P. III. (1989). Continuing the fight against terrorism. *Terrorism, 12,* 81–87.

Bremer, L.P. III. (1990a). Terrorism: Myths and reality. In Schechterman, B. & Slann, M. (Eds.), *Violence and terrorism.* Guilford, Conn.: Dushkin Publishing Group, Inc. Reprint from U.S. Department of State, *Current Policy #1047, 1988, Feb. 4,* 1–3.

Bremer, L.P. III. (1990b). Terrorism and the media. In Schechterman, B. & Slann, M. (Eds.), *Violence and terrorism.* Guilford, Conn.: Dushkin Publishing Group Inc. Reprint from *U.S. Department of State Current Policy #986, 1987, 25 Jun.*

Bremer, L.P. III. (1990c). Terrorism and the rule of law. In Schechterman, B. & Slann, M. (Eds.), *Violence and terrorism.* Guilford, Conn.: Dushkin Publishing Group, Inc. Reprint from *U.S. Department of State, Current Policy #947, 1987, April 23.*

Breslau, K. & Sullivan, S. (1993). Europe's new right. In Schechterman, B. & Slann, M. (Eds.), *Violence and terrorism* (3rd Ed.). Guilford, Conn.: Dushkin Publishing Group, Inc. Reprint from *Newsweek*, 1992, *April 27*, 32–34.

Broadbent, L. (1987). *Terrorism.* Law enforcement satellite training network. Kansas City: Kansas City Police Department.

Brodie, T.G. (1972). *Bombs and bombings.* Springfield, IL: Charles C Thomas, Publisher.

Brooke, J. (1993). Kidnapping and "taxes" transform guerrilla inc. In Schechterman, B. & Slann, M. (Eds.). *Violence and terrorism* (3rd Ed.). Guilford, Conn.: Dushkin Publishing Group, Inc. Reprint from *The New York Times*, 1992, *24 July*.

Brooks, D. (1993). Israel's deadly game of hide-and-seek. In Schechterman, B. & Slann, M. (Eds.). *Violence and terrorism* (3rd Ed.). Dushkin Publishing Group, Inc. Reprint from *The Wall Street Journal*, 1992, *March 19*.

Brown, D. (1972). *Bury my heart at Wounded Knee: An Indian history of the American West.* New York: Bantam.

Brown, R.M. (1975). *Strain of violence.* New York: Oxford University Press.

Buckelew, A.H. (1987). Security without constraints. *Security Management, June*, 48–54.

Burlingame, B. (1992). *Advance force Pearl Harbor: the Imperial navy's underwater assault on America.* Kailua, Hawaii: Pacific Monograph.

Burton, A. (1975). *Urban terrorism: Theory, practice and response.* New York: Plenum.

Burton, A. (1976). *Urban terrorism.* New York: Free Press.

Busby, M.D. (1991). U.S. counterterrorism policy in the 1980s and the priorities for the 1990s. *Terrorism, 13*, 7–13.

Buss, A.H. & Plomin, R.A. (1975). *A temperament theory of personality development.* London, England: John Wiley & Sons.

Butler, R.G. (undated). *The aryan warrior.* Hayden Lake, Idaho: The Aryan Nation Press.

Byrd, D. (1987). White supremacist arrested in Mexico. *Austin American Statesman, Nov 10*, D18.

Caplan, G. (1961). *An approach to community mental health.* New York: Grune and Stratton, Inc.

Caplan, G. (1964). *Principles of preventive psychiatry.* New York: Basic Books.

Caputo, R. (1993). Tragedy stalks the Horn of Africa. *National Geographic, 184*, 88–120.

Chalk, F. & Jonassohn, K. (1993). Genocide: An historical overview. In Schechterman, B. & Slann, M. (Eds.). *Violence and terrorism* (3rd Ed.). Guilford, Conn.: Dushkin Publishing Group, Inc. Reprint from *Social Education*, 1991, *55*, 92–96.

Chang, D.H. (1991). The Japanese Red Army: A case study. In Flood, S. (Ed.), *International terrorism: Policy implications.* Chicago, IL: OICJ.

Clancy, T. (1991). *The sum of all fears.* New York: G.P. Putnam and Sons.

Clark, R.C. (1980). *Technological terrorism.* Old Greenwich, Conn.: Denin-Adair.

Clarke, F.I. (1991). Hate violence in the United States. *FBI Law Enforcement Bulletin, 60*, 14–17.

Cline, R.S. & Alexander, Y. (1985). *Terrorism: The social connection.* New York: Crane, Russak & Co.

Clough, P. (1990). Proposed West German Law to tackle terrorism sparks dissent. In Schechterman, B. & Slann, M. (Eds.), *Violence and terrorism.* Guilford, Conn.: Dushkin Publishing Group, Inc. Reprint from *The Christian Science Monitor,* 1986, *Nov. 10.*

Clutterback, R. (1975). *Living with terrorism.* New York: Arlington House.

Coates, J. (1987). *Armed and dangerous: The rise of the survivalist right.* New York: Hill and Wang.

Cohen, H. (1982). *You can negotiate anything.*

Cohler, L. (1989). Republican racist: Dealing with the David Duke problem. *The New Republic, 201,* 11–14.

Cole, D. (1989). Tactical unit personnel selection in San Diego County. *The Tactical Edge, 7,* 4–6.

Coleman, J.C. (1976). *Abnormal psychology and modern life* (5th Ed.). Glenview, IL: Scott, Foresman.

Conley, J.M. (1987). *Terrorism.* Law enforcement satellite training network. Kansas City: Kansas City Police Department.

Connell, E.S. (1984). *Son of the morning star: Custer and the Little Bighorn.* New York: HarperCollins Publishers.

Cook, F.J. (1980). *The Ku Klux Klan: America's recurring nightmare.* New York: Julian Messner.

Cook, K.J. (1993). Pro-death politics: Debunking the "pro-life" agenda. In Tunnel, K. (Ed.), *Political crime in contemporary America: A critical approach.* New York: Garland Publishing Co.

Cooper, H.H.A. (1977). Terrorism and the media. In Alexander, Y. & Finger, S.M. (Eds.), *Terrorism: Interdisciplinary perspectives.* New York: John Jay Press.

Cooper, H.H.A. (1978). Close encounters of an unpleasant kind: Preliminary thoughts on the Stockholm syndrome. *Legal Medical Quarterly, 2,* 100–111.

Corddry, C.W. (1988). Poison as use alarms U.S., Israel. *The Oregonian, 28 Dec,* A7.

Cordes, B., Hoffman, B., Jenkins, B.M., Kellen, K., Moran, S., & Sater, W. (1984). *Trends in international terrorism, 1982 and 1983.* Santa Monica, CA: Rand Corporation.

Costello, J. (1981). *The Pacific war: 1941-1945.* New York: Quill.

Cox, T. (1979). *Stress.* Baltimore, Maryland: University Park Press.

Cox, T., & Mackay, C.J. (1976). A psychological model of occupational stress. Paper presented at the Medical Research Council Meeting of the Mental Health Industry, London, England (November).

Cranston, A. (1986). The nuclear terrorist state. In Netanyahu, B. (Ed.), *Terrorism: How the West can win.* New York: Farrar, Straus, & Giroux.

Crayton, J.W. (1983). Terrorism and the psychology of the self. In Freedman, L.Z. & Alexander, Y. (Eds.), *Perspectives on terrorism.* Wilmington, Del.: Scholarly Resources.

Crelinsten, R.D., Laberge-Aaltmejd, D., & Szabo, D. (1978). *Terrorism and criminal justice.* Lexington, Mass.: D.C. Heath.

Crelinsten, R.D. & Szabo, D. (1979). *Hostage taking.* Lexington, Mass.: Lexington Books.

Crenshaw, M. (1977). Defining future threats: Terrorists and nuclear proliferation.

In Alexander, Y. & Finger, S. (Eds.), *Terrorism: Interdisciplinary perspectives.* New York: John Jay.

Crenshaw, M. (1981). The causes of terrorism. *Comparative Politics, 13,* 374.

Crenshaw, M. (1983). *Terrorism, legitimacy, and power: The consequences of political violence.* Middletown, Conn.: Wesleyan University Press.

Crenshaw, M. (1985). Ideological and psychological factors in international terrorism. Defense Intelligence College Symposium Proceedings. Washington D.C.: Defense Intelligence Agency.

Cressey, D.R. (1967). The functions and structure of criminal syndicates. In *Task Force Report: Organized Crime, 25-60.* Task Force on Organized Crime. Washington D.C.: U.S. Government Printing Office.

Crotty, W.J. (1971). *Assassinations and their interpretation within the American context.* New York: Harper and Row.

Crozier, B. (1975). *Terrorist activity: International terrorism.* Hearings before the subcommittee to investigate the administration of the internal security act and other internal security laws of the committee on the judiciary. 79th Congress, 1st Session, Washington D.C.: United States Senate.

Culley, J.A. (1974). Defusing human bombs—Hostage negotiations. *FBI Law Enforcement Bulletin, October,* 10–14.

Culley, J.A. (1978). Managing the hostage situation. In Favreau, F. & Gillespie, J.E. (Eds.), *Modern police administration.* Englewood Cliffs, NJ: Prentice-Hall.

Dalager, P.D. (1984a). *Threat management operations: Hostage/barricaded, armed suspect operational guide.* College Station, TX: Texas A & M University Press.

Dalager, P.D. (1984b). *Terrorist organization and operations: A topical training guide.* College Station, TX: The Texas A & M University System.

David, B. (1985). The capability and motivation of terrorist organizations to use mass-destruction weapons. In Merari, A. (Ed.), *On terrorism and combating terrorism.* Landham, MD: University of America Press.

Davis, E.D. (1988). Combating terrorism on the corporate level: The emergence of executive protection specialists in private security. *Journal of Contemporary Criminal Justice, 4,* 241–251.

Daws, G. (1994). *Prisoners of the Japanese: POWs of World War II in the Pacific.* New York: William Morrow & Co., Inc.

Daws, G. (1995). Prisoners of the Japanese. Symposium at the 1945—Crucible of deliverance: Prisoners of war and the A-bomb conference sponsored by the Admiral Nimitz Museum. San Antonio, Texas. (Mar.)

Dawson, H.B. (1969). *The sons of liberty in New York.* New York: Arno.

Day, D. (1989). *The environmental wars: Reports from the front line.* New York: Ballantine Books.

Deakin, T.J. (1974). The legacy of Carlos Marighella. *FBI Law Enforcement Bulletin, Oct.*

Decter, M. (1975). *Liberal parents: Radical children.* New York: Coward, McCann, & Georghegan.

Defense Intelligence Agency. (1982). *Handbook on terrorism, security, and survival.* Washington D.C.: U.S. Government Printing Office.

Demaitre, E. (1973). Terrorism and the intellectuals. *Washington Star and Daily News,* *April 15.*

Denton, J. (1987). International terrorism—The nuclear dimension. *Terrorism, 9,* 113–123.

Department of the Army. (1965). *Boobytraps: FM 5-31.* Washington D.C.: Department of the Army Field Manual.

Department of the Army. (1966). *Unconventional warfare devices and techniques. TM 31-200-1.* Washington D.C.: Department of the Army Field Manual.

Department of the Army. (1969). *Improvised munitions handbook: TM 31-210.* Washington D.C.: Department of the Army Field Manual.

Department of Defense. (1983). *Report of the Department of Defense commission on Beirut International Airport terrorist act.* Washington D.C.: U.S. Government Printing Office.

Dept. of Justice. (1988). *Terrorism in the United States.* Quantico, VA: FBI—Terrorist Research and Analytical Center, Counterterrorism Section, CID.

Dept. of Justice. (1989). *Terrorism in the United States.* Quantico, VA: FBI—Terrorist Research and Analytical Center, Counterterrorism Section, CID.

Dept. of Justice. (1990). *Terrorism in the United States.* Quantico, VA: FBI—Terrorist Research and Analytical Center, Counterterrorism Section, CID.

Dept. of Justice. (1991). *Terrorism in the United States.* Quantico, VA: FBI—Terrorist Research and Analytical Center, Counterterrorism Section, CID.

Dept. of Justice. (1992). *Terrorism in the United States.* Quantico, VA: FBI—Terrorist Research and Analytical Center, Counterterrorism Section, CID.

Dept. of State. (1990). *Patterns of global terrorism: 1989.* Rockville, MD: NIJ.

Derrer, D. (1985). Terrorism. *Proceedings/Naval Review, May,* 198.

De Virgilio, J. (1991). End of an era: The destruction of the battleline at Pearl Harbor. Symposium at the Storm Unleashed conference sponsored by the National Park Service. Honolulu, Hawaii. (Dec.)

Dillon, S. (1993). Peru's rebels buck trend as troop strength grows. In Schechterman, B. & Slann, M. (Eds.), *Violence and terrorism* (3rd Ed.). Guilford, Conn.: Dushkin Publishing Group, Inc. Reprint from *The Miami Herald,* 1992, *Feb 9,* 1a, 14a.

Dimsdale, J.E. (1974). The coping behavior of Nazi concentration camp survivors. *American Journal of Psychiatry, 131,* 792–797.

Discovery. (1994). *The history of the SS.* Discovery Television Station.

Dobson, C. (1974). *Black September: Its short, violent history.* New York: Macmillan.

Dobson, C. & Payne, R. (1979). *The terrorists: Their weapons, leaders, and tactics.* New York: Facts on File.

Dobson, C. & Payne, R. (1982a). *Counterattack: The West's battle against the terrorists.* New York: Facts On File.

Dobson, C. & Payne, R. (1982b). *The terrorists: Their weapons, leaders, and tactics* (Rev. Ed.). New York: Facts on File.

Dolan, J.T. & Fuselier, G.D. (1989). A guide for first responders to hostage situations. *FBI Law Enforcement Bulletin, 58,* 9–13.

Douglas, J.D. (1984). *C.B.W.: The poor man's atomic bomb.* London, England: MacMillan.

Douglas, J.D. (1990). *Red cocaine: The drugging of America.* Dunnwoody, CA: Clarion House.

Douglass, J.D. Jr. & Livingston, N.C. (1984). *CBW: The poor man's atomic bomb.* Cambridge, Mass.: Institute for Foreign Policy Analysis.

Douglas, J.D. & Livingstone, N.C. (1987). *America the vulnerable.* Lexington, Mass.: Lexington Books.

Drouin, J. & Adams, J. (1992). Skokie's tactical intervention unit: Ready for the challenge. *Police Chief, 59,* 17–19.

Dubin, M. (1988). Fugitive from hate. *Philadelphia Enquirer.*

Dugard, J. (1973). Towards the definition of international terrorism. *American Journal of International Law, 67,* 94–100.

Duvall, R.D. & Stohl, M. (1983). Governance by terror. In Stohl, M. (Ed.), *The politics of terrorism.* New York: Marcel Dekker.

Eberly, R.E. & Engdahl, B.E. (1991). Prevalence of somatic and psychiatric disorders among former prisoners of war. *Journal of Hospital and Community Psychiatry, 42,* 807–813.

Eberly, R.E., Harkness, A.R., & Engdahl, B.E. (1991). An adaptational view of trauma response as illustrated by the prisoner of war experience. *Journal of Traumatic Stress, 4,* 363–380.

Eckstein, H. (1984). *International war.* New York: Free Press.

Ehrenfield, R. (1990). *Narco-terrorism.* New York: Basic Books.

Eitenger, L. (1982). The effects of captivity. In Ochberg, F.M. & Soskis, D.A. (Eds.). *Victims of terrorism.* Boulder, CO: Westview Press.

Elkin, M. (1990). Terrorism on TV—Who are the real hostages? In Schechterman, B. & Slann, M. (Eds.). *Violence and terrorism.* Guilford, Conn.: Dushkin Publishing Group Inc. Reprint from *Miami Jewish Tribune,* 1987, *10 Sep.,* 17–18.

Ellen, E. (1991). Maritime crime. *International Criminal Police Review, 429,* 25–29.

Elliot, J.D. & Gibson, L.K. (1978). *Contemporary terrorism: Selected readings.* Gaithersburg, Maryland: IACP.

Encyclopedia of Social Sciences. (1937). New York: Macmillan.

Engdahl, B.E., Speed, N., Eberly, R.E., & Schwartz, J. (1991). Comorbidity of psychiatric disorders and personality profiles of American World War II prisoners of war. *Journal of Nervous and Mental Disease, 179,* 181–187.

Evans, E. (1977). American policy response to international terrorism: Problems of deterrence. In Alexander, Y. & Finger, S.M. (Eds.), *Terrorism: Interdisciplinary perspectives.* New York: John Jay.

Evans, E. (1979). *Calling a truce to terror: The American response to international terrorism.* Westport, Conn.: Greenwood Press.

Everly, G. (1989). *A clinical guide to the treatment of the human stress response.* New York: Plenum Press.

Eysenck, H.J., Arnold, W., & Meili, R. (1972). *Encyclopedia of psychology.* New York: Herder & Herder.

Ezeldin, A.G. (1989). Terrorism in the 1990s: New strategies and the nuclear threat. *International Journal of Comparative and Applied Criminal Justice, 13,* 7–16.

Fairbank, J.A., Hansen, D.J., & Fitterling, J.M. (1991). Patterns of appraisal and coping across different stressor conditions among former prisoners of war with and without posttraumatic stress disorder. *Journal of Consulting and Clinical Psychology, 59,* 274–281.

FBI. (1985). Hostage Negotiations Seminar. Quantico, Virginia. February.

FBI. (1991). Advanced Hostage Negotiation Seminar. San Antonio, TX. August.

Feifer, G. (1992). *Tennozan: The battle of Okinawa and the atomic bomb.* New York: Ticknor & Fields.

Fein, R.A., Vossekuil, B., & Holden, G.A. (1995). *Threat assessment: An approach to prevent targeted violence.* Washington D.C.: National Institute of Justice.

Festinger, L. (1957). *A theory of cognitive dissonance.* Stanford, CA: Stanford University Press.

Fields, R.M. (1982). Research on the victims of terrorism. In Ochberg, F.M. & Soskis, D.A. (Eds.), *Victims of terrorism.* Boulder, CO: Westview Press.

Figley, C. (1988). Post traumatic family therapy. In Ochberg, F.M. (Ed.), *Post traumatic therapy in victims of violence.* New York: Brunner-Mazel.

Finch, P. (1983). *God, guts, and guns.* New York: Seaview Putnam.

Finger, S.M. (1990). The United Nations and international terrorism. In Schechterman, B. & Slann, M. (Eds.), *Violence and terrorism.* Guilford, Conn.: Dushkin Publishing Group, Inc. Reprint from *The Jerusalem Journal of International Relations,* 1988, *10,* 14–24.

Finn, J.E. (1993). Media coverage of political terrorism and the first amendment: Reconciling the public's right to know with public order. In Alexander, Y. & Latter, R. (Eds.), *Terrorism and the media: Dilemma for government, journalists and the public.* New York: Brassey.

Flaherty, M.J. (1988). I've got hostages. *Police Chief, 55,* 48–50.

Fleming, M. (1982). Propaganda by deed: Terrorism and anarchist theory in late nineteenth-century Europe. In Alexander, Y. & Myers, K.A. (Eds.), *Terrorism in Europe.* New York: St. Martin's Press.

Flemming, P.A., Stohl, M., & Schmid, A.P. (1988). The theoretical utility of typologies of terrorism: Lessons and opportunities. In Stohl, M. (Ed.), *The politics of terrorism.* New York: Marcel Dekker.

Flowers, B. (1976). Nuclear power and the public interest: A watchdog's view. *Bulletin of the Atomic Scientists, Dec, 27.*

Flynn, K. & Gerhard, T.G. (1989). *The silent brotherhood: Inside America's racist underground.* New York: Free Press.

Fogelson, R.M. & Rubenstein, R.E. (1969). *Mass violence in America: Affairs in the late insurrectionary states.* New York: Arno Press.

Fontaine, R.W. (1988). *Terrorism: The Cuban connection.* New York: Crane, Russak, & Co.

Ford, C.V. & Spaulding, R.C. (1973). The Pueblo incident: A comparison of factors related to coping with extreme stress. *Archives of General Psychiatry, Sep.,* 340–343.

Ford, F.L. (1985). *Political murder: From tyrannocide to terrorism.* Cambridge, Mass.: Harvard University Press.

Forrest, F.R. (1976). Nuclear terrorism and the escalation of international conflict. *Naval War College Review, 29,* 12–27.

Franck, T.M. & Lockwood, B.B. (1974). Preliminary thoughts towards an international convention on terrorism. *American Journal of International Law, 68,* 4.

Francis, S.T. (1985). *The Soviet strategy of terror.* Washington D.C.: The Heritage Foundation.

Freedman, L.Z. (1974). Terrorism: Policy, pathology, politics — Problems of the polistaraxic. *The University of Chicago Magazine, Summer,* 7–10.

Freedman, L.Z. (1983). Terrorism: Problems of the polistaraxic. In Freedman, L.Z. & Alexander, Y. (Eds.). *Perspectives on terrorism.* Wilmington, Del.: Scholarly Resources.

Friedlander, N. (1983). Hostage negotiations: Dilemmas about policy. In Freedman, L.Z. & Alexander, Y. (Eds.), *Perspectives on terrorism.* Wilmington, Del.: Scholarly Resources.

Friedlander, R.A. (1981). *Terrorism and the law: What price safety?* Gaithersburg, Maryland: IACP. *Police Chief, 51,* 59–60.

Fromkin, D. (1978). The strategy of terrorism. In Elliot, J.D. & Gibson, L.K. (Eds.). *Contemporary terrorism: Selected readings.* Gaithersburg, Maryland: IACP. Reprint from *Foreign Affairs, 53,* 684–685.

Fuselier, G.D. (1981, revised 1986). A practical overview of hostage situations. Washington D.C., Federal Bureau of Investigations: U.S. Government Printing Office. Revised from *FBI Law Enforcement Bulletin, 50.*

Fuselier, G.D. (1986). What every negotiator would like his chief to know. *FBI Law Enforcement Bulletin, 55,* 12–15.

Fuselier, G.D. (1988). Hostage negotiation consultant: Emerging role for the clinical psychologist. *Professional Psychology, 19,* 175–179.

Gallimore, T. (1991). Media compliance with voluntary press guidelines for covering terrorism. In Alexander, Y. & Picard, R. (Eds.), *In the camera's eye: News coverage of terrorist events.* New York: Brassey.

Gander, T. (1990). *Guerrilla warfare weapons: The modern underground fighter's armoury.* New York: Sterling Publishing Co., Inc.

Gates, M.E. (1987). The nuclear emergency search team. In Leventhal, P. & Alexander, Y. (Eds.), *Preventing nuclear terrorism.* Lexington, MA: Lexington Books.

Gaucher, R. (1968). *The terrorists: From Tsarist Russia to the OAS.* London: Secker and Warburg.

Gelb, N. (1984). *Less than glory.* New York: Putnam and Sons.

George, J. (1992). Extremists and the Constitution. In George, J. & Wilcox, L. (Eds.), *Nazis, communists, klansmen and others on the fringe: Political extremism in America.* Buffalo, NY: Prometheus Books.

George, J. & Wilcox, L. (1992). *Nazis, communists, klansmen and others on the fringe: Political extremism in America.* Buffalo, NY: Prometheus Books.

Georges-Abeyie, D.E. (1983). Women as terrorists. In Freedman, L.Z. & Alexander, Y. (Eds.). *Perspectives on terrorism.* Wilmington, Del.: Scholarly Resources.

Gerstein, R.S. (1983). Do terrorists have rights? In Rapoport, D.C. & Alexander, Y. (Eds.). *The morality of terrorism: Religious and secular justifications.* New York: Pergamon.

Gettinger, S. (1983). Hostage negotiators bring them out alive. *Police Magazine, 6,* 10–15.

Geysels, F. (1990). Europe from the inside. *Policing, 6,* 338–354.

Gilbert, M. (1989). *The Second World War: A complete history.* New York: Henry Holt & Co.

Gilmartin, K.M. & Gibson, R.J. (1985). Hostage negotiation: The bio-behavioral dimension. *Police Chief, 52,* 46–48.

Ginsburg, F.D. (1989). *Contested lives: The abortion debate in an American community.* Berkeley, CA: University of California Press.

Gist, T. (1990). International terrorism. In Schechterman, B. & Slann, M. (Eds.), *Violence and terrorism.* Guilford, Conn.: Dushkin Publishing Group, Inc. Reprint from *U.S. Department of State,* 1988, *May.*

Glasser, W. (1984). *Control theory.* New York: Harper and Row.

Glendon, R. (1991). International terrorism and business. In Flood, S. (Ed.), *International terrorism: Policy implications.* Chicago, IL: OICJ.

Goldaber, I. (1979). A typology of hostage takers. *The Police Chief, 46,* 21–23.

Goldaber, I. (1983). *Hostage rescue operations.* San Antonio, TX: International Chiefs of Police. September.

Goldaber, I., Pizer, H.L., Remsberg, C., Reber, J., Shaw, P., & Tilton, M.P. (1979). Hostage survival. *Assets Protection, 4,* 15–24.

Goldberg, A.J. (1986). London's Libyan embassy shootout: A case of international terrorism. In Netanyahu, B. (Ed.), *Terrorism: How the West can win.* New York: Farrar, Straus, & Giroux.

Goldstein, G., Van-Kammen, W., Shelly, C., & Miller, D.J. (1987). Survivors of imprisonment in the Pacific theater during World War II. *American Journal of Psychiatry, 144,* 1210–1213.

Goren, R. (1984). *The Soviet Union and terrorism.* London: George Allen & Unwin.

Green, L.C. (1979). The legislation of terrorism. In Alexander, Y., Carlton, D., & Wilkinson, P. (Eds.). *Terrorism in theory and practice.* Boulder, CO: Westview Press.

Green, L.C. (1985). Terrorism and its responses. *Terrorism, 8,* 33–77.

Gregor, A.J. (1983). Fascism's philosophy of violence and the concept of terror. In Rapoport, D.C. & Alexander, Y. (Eds.), *The morality of terrorism: Religious and secular justifications.* New York: Pergamon.

Greve, F. (1995). *Nerve-gas terrorists could have killed thousands if they wished.* Knight-Ridder Washington Bureau, 20 Mar.

Griffith, G.W. (1975). Biological warfare and the urban battleground. *Enforcement Journal, 14,* 4–5.

Griswold, W.S. (1972). *The night the revolution began: The Boston Tea Party.* Vermont: S. Greene.

Gross, F. (1978). Political assassination. In Livingston, M.H. (Ed.), *International terrorism in the contemporary world.* Westport, Conn.: Greenwood Press.

Gugliotta, G. & Isikoff, M. (1993). The plague off our cities. In Schechterman, B. & Slann, M. (Eds.), *Violence and terrorism* (3rd Ed.). Guilford, Conn.: Dushkin

Publishing Group, Inc. Reprint from *The Washington Post National Weekly Edition,* 1990, *20 Oct-4 Nov,* 6–7.

Gurr, T.R. (1988). Political terrorism in the United States: Historical and contemporary trends. In Stohl, M. (Ed.), *The politics of terrorism.* New York: Marcel Dekker.

Hacker, F.J. (1977). *Crusaders, criminals, crazies.* New York: Norton.

Hacker, F.J. (1983). Dialectic interrelationships of personal and political factors in terrorism. In Freedman, L.Z. & Alexander, Y. (Eds.), *Perspectives on terrorism.* Wilmington, Del.: Scholarly Resources.

Haddigan, M. (1987). Profile of 15 persons names in indictments. *Arkansas Gazette, April 25,* 1 & 11A.

Hagan, K.J. (1991). *This people's Navy: The making of American sea power.* New York: Macmillan, Inc.

Hannay, W.A. (1974). International terrorism: The need for a fresh perspective. *International Lawyer, 8,* 268–284.

Harrell, J.R. (undated). *Christian emergency defense system.* Flora, IL: Citizen Emergency Defense System.

Harris, J.W. (1987). Domestic terrorism in the 1980s. *FBI Law Enforcement Bulletin, 56,* 5–13.

Harris, R. & Paxman, J. (1982). *A higher form of killing: The secret story of chemical and biological warfare.* New York: Hill & Wang.

Harris, S.H. (1994). *Factories of death: Japanese biological warfare 1932–1945 and the American cover-up.* New York: Routledge.

Hassel, C.V. (1975). The hostage situation: Exploring the motivation and cause. *The Police Chief, September,* 55–58.

Hassel, C.V. (1982). Interactions of law enforcement and behavioral science personnel. In Ochberg, F.M. & Soskis, D.A. (Eds.), *Victims of terrorism.* Boulder, Col.: Westview Press.

Hauben, R. (1983). Hostage taking: The Dutch experience. In Freedman, L.Z. & Alexander, Y. (Eds.), *Perspectives on terrorism.* Wilmington, Del.: Scholarly Resources.

Harvey, K.D. (1991). Vanquished Americans. *Social Education, 55,* 132–134.

Herman, E.S. (1983). *The real terror network: Terrorism in fact and propaganda.* Boston: South End.

Hersh, S.M. (1968). *Chemical and biological warfare: America's hidden arsenal.* Indianapolis, Ind.: Bobbs-Merrill.

Hewitt, C. (1990). Terrorism and public opinion: A five-country comparison. *Terrorism and Political Violence, Summer,* 145–170.

Hillman, R.G. (1981). The psychopathology of being held hostage. *American Journal of Psychiatry, 138,* 1193–1197.

Hillman, R.G. (1983). The psychopathology of being held hostage. In Freedman, L.Z. & Alexander, Y. (Eds.). *Perspectives on terrorism.* Wilmington, Del.: Scholarly Resource.

Hoenig, M.M. (1987). Hidden danger: Risks of nuclear terrorism. *Terrorism, 10,* 1–21.

Hoff, L.E. (1989). *People in crisis: Understanding and helping.* Menlo Park, CA: Addison-Wesley Publishing Co.

Hoffer, E. (1951). *The true believer.* New York: Harper and Row.

Hoffman, B. (1984). *Recent trends in Palestinian terrorism.* Santa Monica, CA: Rand Corporation.

Hoffman, B. (1986). *Terrorism in the United States and the potential threat to nuclear facilities.* Santa Monica, CA: The Rand Corporation.

Hoffman, B. (1987). Terrorism in the United States in 1985. In Wilkinson, P. & Stewart, A.M. (Eds.), *Contemporary research on terrorism.* Aberdeen, UK: Aberdeen University Press.

Hoffman, B. (1988). *Recent trends and future prospects of terrorism in the United States.* Santa Monica, CA: Rand Corp.

Hoffman, B. (1993). Terrorism in the United States: Recent trends and future prospects. TVI Report 8. In Schechterman, B. & Slann, M. (Eds.), *Violence and terrorism* (3rd Ed.). Guilford, Conn.: Dushkin Publishing Group Inc. Reprint from *Recent Trends and future prospects of terrorism in the United States.* Rand Corp., 1988, Santa Monica, CA.

Hofstadter, R. & Wallace, M. (1971). *American violence.* New York: Vintage Books.

Hogg, I.V. (1978). *The complete illustrated encyclopedia of the world's firearms.* New York: A & W Publishers.

Holden, R.N. (1985). Historical and international perspectives on right-wing militancy in the United States. Paper presented at the Academy of Criminal Justice Sciences, Las Vegas, Nevada (March).

Holden, R.N. (1986a). Postmillenialism as a justification for right-wing violence. Paper presented at the Academy of Criminal Justice Sciences, Orlando, Fla. (April).

Holden, R.N. (1986b). Right-wing ideology as expressed in the writings of William P. Gale. Paper presented at the Academy of Criminal Justice Sciences, Orlando, Fla. (April).

Holden, R.N. (1986c). The Turner Diaries: The influence of Carlos Marighella on right-wing extremism. Paper presented at the American Society of Criminology, Atlanta, GA (Oct.).

Holden, R.N. (1987). Conservatism, fundamentalism and identity theology: The road to religious extremism. Paper presented at the Academy of Criminal Justice Sciences, St. Louis, MO. (March).

Holsti, O.R. (1972). *Crisis escalation war.* Montreal: McGill-Queens University Press.

Horchem, H. (1985). The development of West German terrorism after 1979: An overview. *TVI Journal, 5,* 10–16.

Horchem, H.J. (1993). The decline of the Red Army Faction. In Schechterman, B. & Slann, M. (Eds.), *Violence and terrorism* (3rd Ed.). Guilford, Conn.: Dushkin Publishing Group, Inc. Reprint from *Terrorism and Political Violence,* 1991, *3,* 61–74.

Horobin, A. (1978). Hostage taking—coping with a crisis. *Police Review, 87,* 1438–1440.

Horowitz, I.L. (1973). Political terrorism and state power. *Political and Military Sociology, Spring,* 148–150.

Horowitz, I.L. (1976). *Genocide: State power and mass murder.* New Brunswick: Transaction Books.

Hudson, R.A. (1989). Dealing with the international hostage-taker. Alternatives to reactive counterterrorist assaults. *Terrorism, 12,* 321–378.

Hueston, H.R. (1990). Battling the animal liberation front. *The Police Chief, 57,* 52–54.

Hutchinson, M.C. (1972). The concept of revolutionary terrorism. *Journal of Conflict Resolution, 16,* 383.

Hyer, L., Walker, C., Swanson, G., & Sperr, S. (1992). Validation of PTSD measures for older combat veterans. *Journal of Clinical Psychology, 48,* 579–588.

IACP. (1983). *Hostage rescue operations.* San Antonio, Texas. September.

Inciardi, J.A. (1991). Narcoterrorism: A perspective and commentary. In Kelly, R.J. & MacNamara, E.J. (Eds.), *Perspectives on deviance: Dominance, degradation and denigration.* Cincinnati, Ohio: Anderson Publishing Co.

Investigative Reports. (1995). *Biological weapons.* Arts and Entertainment television.

Irwin, J. (1980). *Prisons in turmoil.* Boston: Little, Brown.

Ivianski, Z. (1985). The blow at the center: The concept and its history. In Merari, A. (Ed.), *Terrorism and combating terrorism.* Frederick, MD: University Publications of America.

Jackson, B. (1981). *The black flag: A look back at the strange case of Nicola Sacco and Bartolomeo Vanzetti.* Boston: Routledge & Kegan Paul.

Jacobs, J. (1983). *SWAT tactics.* Boulder, CO: Paladin Press.

Jacobson, S.R. (1979). Individual and group responses to confinement in a skyjacked plane. *American Journal of Orthopsychiatry, 43,* 459–569.

Janis, I.L. (1968). Group identification under conditions of external danger. In Cartwright, D. & Zander, A. (Eds.), *Group dynamics: Research and theory* (3rd Ed.). New York: Harper & Row.

Jaszi, O. & Lewis, J.D. (1957). *Against the tyrant: The tradition and theory of tyranicade.* Glencoe, IL: Free Press.

Jenkins, B.M. (1975). *International terrorism: A new mode of conflict.* Research paper 48, California Seminar on Arms Control and Foreign Policy. Los Angeles: Crescent Publications.

Jenkins, B.M. (1978). High technology terrorism and surrogate war: The impact of new technology on low level violence. In Elliot, J.D. & Gibson, L.K. (Eds.), *Contemporary terrorism: Selected readings.* Gaithersburg, Maryland: IACP. Reprint from Rand Corporation, Santa Monica, CA (1975).

Jenkins, B.M. (1983). *New modes of conflict.* Santa Monica, CA: The Rand Corporation.

Jenkins, B.M. (1985). Future trends in international terrorism. *Proceedings of the Symposium on International Terrorism.* Washington D.C.: Defense Intelligence Agency.

Jenkins, B.M. (1986). Is nuclear terrorism plausible? In Leventhal, P. & Alexander, Y. (Eds.), *Nuclear terrorism.* New York: Pergamon Press.

Jenkins, P. (1990). Strategy of terrorism: The Belgium terrorist crisis, 1982–1986. *Terrorism, 13,* 299–309.

Jenkins, B.M. (1993). Terrorist threat to commercial aviation. In Schechterman, B. &

Slann, M. (Eds.), *Violence and terrorism* (3rd Ed.). Guilford, Conn.: Dushkin Publishing Group Inc. Reprint from *Israel Defense Forces Journal*, 1989, *Fall*, 1–12.

Jenkins, B.M., Johnsonn, J., & Ronfeldt, D. (1977). *Numbered lives: Some statistical observations from seventy-seven international hostage episodes.* Santa Monica, CA: Rand Corporation.

Jenkins, B. & Wright, R. (1990). Why hostage-taking is so popular with terrorists. In Schechterman, B., & Slann, M. (Eds.), *Violence and terrorism.* Guilford, Conn.: Dushkin Publishing Group, Inc. Reprint from *The Washington Post National Weekly Edition*, 1987, *27 July*, 23–24.

Johnpoll, B. (1977). Terrorism and the mass media in the United States. In Alexander, Y. & Finger, S.M. (Eds.), *Terrorism: Interdisciplinary perspectives.* New York: John Jay Press.

Johnson, P. (1986). The cancer of terrorism. In Netanyahu, B. (Ed.). *Terrorism: How the West can win.* New York: Farrar, Straus, & Giroux.

Jonas, G. (1984). *Vengeance: The true story of an Israeli counter-terrorist mission.* London: Collins.

Joyner, C.C. (1993). Chemoterrorism: Rethinking the reality of the threat. In Han, H.H. (Ed.), *Terrorism and political violence: Limits and possibilities of legal control.* New York: Oceana Pub. Inc.

Juergensmeyer, M. (1993). Is symbolic violence related to real violence? In Schechterman, B. & Slann, M. (Eds.), *Violence and terrorism* (3rd Ed.). Guilford, Conn.: Dushkin Publishing Group, Inc. Reprint from *Terrorism and Political Violence, 3,* 1–8.

Kaiser, N.F. (1990). The tactical incident: A total police response. *FBI Law Enforcement Bulletin, 59,* 14–18.

Kansas City Star. (1985). *Advice for extremists. April 21.*

Kaplan, A. (1978). The psychodynamics of terrorism. *Terrorism: An International Journal, 1,* 237–254.

Kedourie, E. (1986). Political terrorism in the Muslim world. In Netanyahu, B. (Ed.), *Terrorism: How the West can win.* New York: Farrar, Straus, & Giroux.

Keen, S. (1991). *Fire in the belly.* New York: Bantam Books.

Kelly, R.J. & Cook, W.J. (1995). Extremism and fundamentalism. The return to paradise. *Journal of Contemporary Criminal Justice, 11,* 14–34.

Kelly, J.R. & Rieber, R. (1992). Collateral damage on the home front: The gulf in America. *Journal of Social Distress, 1,* 1.

Kendall, W. & Moll, M. (1974). *Arson, vandalism, and violence: Law enforcement problems affecting fire departments.* National Institute for Law Enforcement and Criminal Justice. Washington D.C.: U.S. Department of Justice (LEAA).

Kidder, R.M. (1990a). Terrorists: What are they telling us? In Schechterman, B. & Slann, M. (Eds.). *Violence and terrorism.* Guilford, Conn.: Dushkin Publishing Group, Inc. Reprint from *Terrier*, 1987, *Spring*, 4–6.

Kidder, R.M. (1990b). How nations support terrorist operations around the world. In Schechterman, B. & Slann, M. (Eds.), *Violence and terrorism.* Guilford, Conn.: Dushkin Publishing Group, Inc. Reprint from *The Christian Science Monitor*, 1986, *April 14,* 13.

Kidder, R.M. (1990c). Finding a response to terrorism. In Schechterman, B. & Slann, M. (Eds.), *Violence and terrorism*. Guilford, Conn.: Dushkin Publishing Group, Inc. Reprint from *The Christian Science Monitor, 1986, Feb 20.*

Kidder, R.M. (1993). Unmasking terrorism: The terrorist mentality. In Schechterman, B. & Slann, M. (Eds.), *Violence and terrorism* (3rd Ed.). Guilford, Conn.: Dushkin Publishing Group, Inc. Reprint from *The Christian Science Monitor, May 15,* 18–19.

Kifner, J. (1974). Cinque: A dropout who has been in constant trouble. *The New York Times, May 17.*

Kim, J.T. (1988). North Korean terrorism: Trends, characteristics, and deterrence. *Terrorism, 11,* 309–322.

Kirkpatrick, J.J. (1986). The totalitarian confusion. In Netanyahu, B. (Ed.), *Terrorism: How the West can win.* New York: Farrar, Straus, & Giroux.

Klanwatch. (1993a). The white supremacist movement: 1992 at a glance. *Klanwatch Intelligence Report, 65,* 1–2.

Klanwatch. (1993b). Deadly hate violence at record levels across nation in 1992. *Intelligence Report, 65,* 1–3.

Klanwatch. (1995). Over 200 militias and support groups operate nationwide. *Klanwatch Intelligence Report, 78,* 1–3.

Knowles, G. (1976). *Bomb security guide.* Los Angeles: Security World.

Knutson, J.N. (1981). Social and psychodynamic pressures toward a negative identity: The case of an American revolutionary terrorist. In Alexander, Y. & Gleason, J.M. (Eds.), *Behavioral and quantitative perspectives on terrorism.* New York: Pergamon.

Kolinsky, E. (1988). Terrorism in West Germany. In Lodge, J. (Ed.), *The threat of terrorism.* Boulder, CO: Westview Press.

Kolman, J. (1982). *A guide to the development of special weapons and tactics teams.* Springfield, Ill.: Charles C Thomas, Publisher.

Koppel, T., Podhoretz, N., Krauthammer, C., Besancon, A., O'Sullivan, J., Schorr, D., Will, G., & Woodward, B. (1986). Terrorism and the media: A discussion. In Anzovin, S. (Ed.), *Terrorism.* New York: Wilson.

Kornbluth, J. (1987). Taking on the Klan. *San Antonio Light, Nov 8,* 1&3e.

Kort, M. (1987). Domestic terrorism: On the front line at an abortion clinic. *Ms. Magazine, XV,* 48–53.

Kren, G. & Rapoport, L. (1980). *The holocaust and the crisis of human behavior.* New York: Homes and Meier.

Krieger, D.M. (1977). What happens if? Terrorists, revolutionaries, and nuclear weapons. *The Annals of the American Academy of Political and Social Sciences, 430,* 44–57.

Kupperman, R.H. (1986). Terrorism and national security. *Terrorism: An International Journal, 8,* 255–261.

Kupperman, R. & Trent, T. (1979). *Terrorism: Threat, reality, and response.* Stanford, CA: Hoover Institute.

Ladewig, B.H., Jessee, P.O., & Strickland, M.P. (1992). Children held hostage: Mother's depressive affect and perceptions of family psychosocial functioning. *Journal of Family Issues, 13,* 65–80.

LaForte, R.S. & Marcello, R.E. (1993). *Building the Death Railway: The ordeal of American POWs in Burma, 1942-1945.* Wilmington, Delaware: Scholarly Resources Inc.

LaForte, R.S., Marcello, R.E., & Himmel, R.L. (1994). *With only the will to live:* Wilmington, Delaware: Scholarly Resources Inc.

Lanceley, F. (1985). Hostage negotiations seminar, FBI Academy, Quantico, Virginia (Feb.).

Lanza, M.L. (1986). Victims of international terrorism. *Issues in Mental Health Nursing, 8,* 95–107.

Laqueur, W. (1977). *Terrorism.* Boston: Little, Brown.

Laqueur, W. (1987). *The age of terrorism.* Boston: Little, Brown.

Lasky, M.J. (1975). Ulrike Neinhof and the Baader-Meinhoff gang. *Encounter, 44,* 9–23.

Leckie, R. (1995). *Okinawa: The last battle of World War II.* New York: Penguin Groups.

Ledeen, M.A. (1986). Soviet sponsorship: The will to disbelieve. In Netanyahu, B. (Ed.), *Terrorism: How the West can win.* New York: Farrar, Straus, & Giroux.

LeFebvre, G. (1965). *The French Revolution from its origins to 1793.* London: Routledge & Kegan Paul.

Learning Channel. (1995). *Killer virus.* Discovery Communications, Inc.: NYT Video News International, Inc.

Lerner, M.J. (1970). The desire for justice and the reactions to victims. In Macaulay, J. & Berkowitz, L. (Eds.), *Altruism and helping behavior.* New York: Academic Press.

Lerner, M.J. (1974). Social psychology of justice and interpersonal attraction. In Huston, T. (Ed.), *Perspectives on interpersonal attraction.* New York: Academic Press.

Levy, R. (1978). *Terrorism: History and profile.* College Station, TX: The Texas A & M University System.

Lewis, B. (1967). *The assassins: A radical sect in Islam.* London: Weidenfeld & Nicolson.

Lief, L. (1990). France's "terror judges": A new breed of risk taker. In Schechterman, B. & Slann, M. (Eds.), *Violence and terrorism.* Guilford, Conn.: Dushkin Publishing Group, Inc. Reprint from *The Christian Science Monitor,* 1987, *Mar 16.*

Lifton, R.J. (1986). *The Nazi doctors: Medical killing and the psychology of genocide.* New York: Basic Books.

Livingstone, N.C. (1986). Hydra of carnage. In Ralanan, U. (Ed.), *The international linkages of terrorism and other low intensity operations.* Lexington, Mass.: Lexington Books.

Livingstone, N.C. (1995). Biological nightmares. *Sea Power, April,* 85–86.

Livingstone, N.C. & Arnold, T.E. (Eds.). (1986). *Fighting back.* Lexington, Mass.: D.C. Heath.

Livingstone, N.C. & Arnold, T.E. (1986). The rise of state-sponsored terrorism. In Livingstone, N.C. & Arnold, T.E. (Eds.), *Fighting back: Winning the war against terrorism.* Lexington, Maryland: D.C. Heath.

Lodge, J. (1981). *Terrorism: A challenge to the state.* Oxford: Martin Robertson.

Lopez, G.A. (1993). Terrorism and world order. In Schechterman, B. & Slann, M.

(Eds.), *Violence and terrorism* (3rd Ed.). Guilford, Conn.: Dushkin Publishing Group, Inc. Reprint from *Whole Earth Papers*, 1983, *18*, 1–8.

Lupsha, P.A. (1991). Cuba's recent involvement in drug trafficking: The Ochoa-La Guardia cases. In Flood, S. (Ed.). *International terrorism: Policy implications.* Chicago, IL: OICJ.

Lynch, E.A. (1987). International terrorism: The search for a policy. *Terrorism: An International Journal, 9*, 1–85.

MacKenzie-Orr, M.H. (1991). Terror Australia. *Security Management, 36*, 87–90.

Maksymchuk, A.F. (1982). Strategies for hostage-taking incidents. *Police Chief, 49*, 58–65.

Madruga, L. (1974). Interview with "Urbano" (Tupamaro leader). In Kohl, J. & Litt, J. (Eds.), *Urban guerrilla warfare in Latin America.* Cambridge, Mass.: The M.I.T. Press.

Maley, R.J. (1990). Potential for terrorism within the Soviet Union in the 21st century. *Terrorism, 13*, 53–64.

Magnuson, E. (1989). An ex-klansman's win brings the G.O.P. chickens home to roost. *Time, Mar 6*, 29.

Mallin, J. (1971). *Terror and urban guerrillas.* Coral Gables, FL: University of Miami Press.

Mallin, J. (1978). Terrorism as a military weapon. In Elliot, J.D. & Gibson, L.K. (Eds.), *Contemporary terrorism: Selected readings.* Gaithersburg, Maryland: IACP. Reprint from *Air University Review, 28*, 1977.

Marchetti, V. & Marks, J. (1983). *The CIA and the cult of intelligence.* New York: Knopf.

Margolin, J. (1977). Psychological perspectives in terrorism. In Alexander, Y. & Finger, S.M. (Eds.), *Terrorism: Interdisciplinary perspectives.* New York: John Jay Press.

Martinez, D. (1991). The first shot: The *USS Ward* story. Symposium at the Storm Unleashed conference sponsored by the National Park Service. Honolulu, Hawaii. (Dec.)

Marty, M.E. (1983). Survivalism. *Christian Century, 831*, 14–21.

Maslow, A.H. (1970). *Motivation and personality* (2nd Ed.). New York: Harper and Row.

Mattoons, S. (1987). *SWAT: Training and deployment.* Boulder, CO: Paladin Press.

McCormick, G.H. (1988). Shining Path and Peruvian terrorism. In Rapoport, D.C. (Ed.), *Inside terrorist organizations.* New York: Columbia University Press.

McForan, D. (1987). *World held hostage: The war waged by international terrorism.* New York: St. Martin's Press.

McGee, J.H. (1987). Violence as communication. *Police, Nov.*, 37–39.

McMains, M.J. (1992). Psychologist's role on a hostage negotiation's team. Basic Hostage Negotiations School, SAPD, San Antonio, Texas.

McMains, M.J. & Lanceley, F. (1994, in review). The use of crisis intervention principles in hostage negotiations. III: Attitudes, communications, and treatment. *Police Chief.*

McMains, M.J. & Mullins, W.C. (1995). *Crisis negotiations: Managing critical incidents and hostage situations in law enforcement and correctional settings.* Cincinnati, Ohio: Anderson Publishing Co.

McNeil, E.B. (1970). *The psychoses.* Englewood Cliffs, NJ: Prentice-Hall.

Media Analysis Center. (1990). PLO's role in international terrorism. In Schechterman, B. & Slann, M. (Eds.), *Violence and terrorism.* Guilford, Conn.: Dushkin Publishing Group Inc. Reprint from *Contemporary Mideast Background,* 1987, *Aug 23.* Jerusalem, Israel: Media Analysis Center.

Melnichak, J.M. (1986a). American terrorists: The homegrown threat. *Police Product News, Dec.,* 24–29.

Melnichak, J.M. (1986b). Chronicle of hate: A brief history of the radical right. *The Police Marksman, Sep/Oct,* 42.

Mengel, R.W. (1979). Terrorism and new technologies of destruction: An overview of the potential risk. In Norton, A.R. & Greenberg, M.H. (Eds.), *Studies in nuclear terrorism.* Boston: G.K. Hill.

Menuez, D. (1986). "Never again!" Jewish zealots train for combat. *Penthouse, Nov,* 56–62.

Merkl, P.H. (1993). Conclusion: A new lease on life for the radical right? In Merkl, P.H. & Weinberg, L. (Eds.), *Encounters with the contemporary radical right.* Boulder, CO: Westview Press.

Merkl, P.H. & Weinberg, L. (1993). *Encounters with the contemporary radical right.* Boulder, CO: Westview Press.

Metz, S. (1987). Ideology of terrorist foreign policies in Libya and South Africa. *Conflict, 7,* 379–402.

Michel, H. (1972). *The shadow war: European resistance, 1939-1945.* New York: Harper & Row.

Mickolus, E.F. (1977). Statistical approaches to the study of terrorism. In Alexander, Y. & Finger, S.M. (Eds.), *Terrorism: Interdisciplinary perspectives.* New York: John Jay Press.

Mickolus, E.F. (1978). Negotiating for hostages: A policy dilemma. In Elliot, J.D. & Gibson, L.K. (Eds.), *Contemporary terrorism: Selected readings.* Gaithersburg, Maryland: IACP. Reprint from *Orbis,* 1976, *XIX.*

Mickolus, E.F. (1980). *Transnational terrorism: A chronology of events, 1968-1979.* Westport, Conn.: Greenwood Press.

Mickolus, E.F. (1989a). *International terrorism in the 1980s: A chronology of events.* Ames, Iowa: Iowa State University Press.

Mickolus, E.F. (1989b). *International terrorism in the 1980s: A chronology of events, Volume II: 1984-1987.* Ames, Iowa: Iowa State University Press.

Mickolus, E.F. (1993). *Terrorism, 1988-1991: A chronology of events and a selected annotated bibliography.* Westport, Conn.: Greenwood Press.

Mijares, T.C. & Perkins, D. (1994). Police liability issues: Special concerns for tactical units. *Police Liability Review, 6,* 1–9.

Milbank, D.L. (1978). International and transnational terrorism: Diagnosis and prognosis. In Elliot, J.D. & Gibson, L.K. (Eds.), *Contemporary terrorism: Selected readings.* Gaithersburg, Maryland: IACP.

Milhollin, G., Dolley, S., & Spector, L. (1991). The evidence: How Saddam planned to build a bomb. *Newsweek, 7 Oct,* 34–35.

Miller, A.H. (1978). Negotiations for hostages: Implications from the police experience. *Terrorism: An International Journal, 1,* 125–146.

Miller, A.H. (1979). Hostage negotiations. In Alexander, Y. & Kilmarx, A. (Eds.), *Political terrorism and business — The threat and response.*

Miller, A.H. (1982). Terrorism, the media, and the law: A discussion of the issues. In Miller, A.H. (Ed.), *Terrorism, the media and the law.* New York: Transnational Publishers.

Miller, A.H. (1993). Terrorism and the media: Lessons from the British experience. In Schechterman, B. & Slann, M. (Eds.), *Violence and terrorism* (3rd Ed.). Guilford, Conn.: Dushkin Publishing Group, Inc. Reprint from *The Heritage Lectures,* 1990, *Feb 15,* 1–9.

Miller, J.A. (1977). Political terrorism and insurgency: An interrogative approach. In Alexander, Y. & Finger, S.M. (Eds.), *Terrorism: Interdisciplinary perspectives.* New York: John Jay Press.

Mills, K.I. (1995). Black leaders back march despite remark. *Austin American Statesman, 16 Oct,* A8.

Mirabella, R.W. & Trudeau, J. (1982). Managing hostage negotiations. *Police Chief, 45,* 45–47.

Miron, M.S. & Goldstein, A.P. (1979). *Hostage.* New York: Pergamon Press.

Mitchell, J.G. (1983). Waiting for the apocalypse. *Audubon, March,* 18–25.

Moron, R.B. (1991). Bolivia: The psychology of the drug war. *Hemisphere, 4,* 14–16.

Morris, D. (1988). Terrorism in Latin America. In Pisan, V.S. (Ed.), *Terrorist dynamics: A geographical perspective.* Gaithersburg, MD: IACP.

Motley, J.B. (1986). Target America: The undeclared war. In Livingstone, N.C. & Arnold, T.E. (Eds.), *Fighting back: Winning the war against terrorism.* Lexington, Maryland: D.C. Heath.

Moxon-Browne, E. (1988). Terrorism in France. In Lodge, J. (Ed.), *The threat of terrorism.* Boulder, CO: Westview Press.

Mullen, R.K. (1979). Mass destruction and terrorism. In Norton, A.R. & Greenberg, M.H. (Eds.), *Studies in nuclear terrorism.* Boston, Mass.: G.K. Hill.

Mullins, W.C. (1986). Profiling the right-wing terrorist in America. Paper presented at the Society of Police and Criminal Psychology. Las Vegas, Nevada (October).

Mullins, W.C. (1987). The organizational dynamics of the terrorist organization. Paper presented at the Society of Police and Criminal Psychology. New Orlenas, LA (October).

Mullins, W.C. (1988). Stopping terrorism — The problems posed by the organizational infrastructure of terrorist organizations. *Journal of Contemporary Criminal Justice, 4,* 214–228.

Mullins, W.C. (1989). Domestic terrorism into the 1990s: The aftermath of the Ft. Smith, Arkansas sedition trial. Paper presented at the Society of Police and Criminal Psychology, Savannah, Georgia (October).

Mullins, W.C. (1990a). Terrorism in the 1990s: Predictions for the United States. *Police Chief, LVII,* 44–46.

Mullins, W.C. (1990b). Into the 1990s: Predictions of terrorism in the United States for the next decade. Paper presented at the Academy of Criminal Justice Sciences. Denver, CO (March).

Mullins, W.C. (1990c). An examination of the link between drug cartels and terrorist organizations. Paper presented at the Society of Police and Criminal Psychology. Albuquerque, NM (October).

Mullins, W.C. (1991a). A realistic examination of NBC terrorism. Paper presented at the Society of Police and Criminal Psychology. Richmond, Virginia (October).

Mullins, W.C. (1991b). The awakening of the far right: The bootsteps of hate march forward. Paper presented at the Academy of Criminal Justice Sciences. Nashville, Tennessee (March).

Mullins, W.C. (1992). An overview and analysis of nuclear, biological, and chemical terrorism: The weapons, strategies and solutions to a growing problem. *American Journal of Criminal Justice, XVI*, 95–120.

Mullins, W.C. (1993). Hate crime and the far right — Unconventional terrorism. In Tunnell, K.D. (Ed.), *Political crime in contemporary America.* New York: Garland Publishing Co.

Mullins, W.C. (1994). *1942 . . . Issue in doubt.* Austin, Texas: Eakin Press.

Mullins, W.C. (1995). Psychological effects of captivity and aftereffects of captivity on World War II POWs of the Japanese. Symposium at the 1945 — Crucible of deliverance: Prisoners of war and the A-bomb conference sponsored by the Admiral Nimitz Museum. San Antonio, Texas. (Mar.)

Mullins, W.C. & Becker, R.F. (1992). Nuclear, biological, and chemical terrorism: A new American threat. Paper presented at the Academy of Criminal Justice Sciences. Pittsburgh, PA (March).

Mullins, W.C. & Mijares, T. (1992). The new Europe and terrorism. Paper presented at the Society of Police and Criminal Psychology. Tampa, Florida (October).

Mullins, W.C. & Mijares, T. (1993a). Law enforcement and the far right: Who's really winning the war? Paper presented at the Society of Police and Criminal Psychology. New Orleans, LA (October).

Mullins, W.C. & Mijares, T. (1993b). The resurgence of terrorism in Europe. Paper presented at the Western Social Science Association. Corpus Christi, TX (April).

Mullins, W.C. & Mijares, T. (1994). Are local gangs merely a new form of terrorism? Paper presented at the Society of Police and Criminal Psychology, Madison, Wisconsin (October).

Mullins, W.C. & Mijares, T. (1995). The restructuring of Europe: Projected terrorist trends in the twenty-first century. *The Journal of Contemporary Criminal Justice, 11,* 1–3.

Murphy, S., Hay, A., & Rose, S. (1984). *No fire, no thunder: The threat of chemical and biological weapons.* New York: Monthly Review Press.

Nardini, J.E. (1952). Survival factors in American prisoners of war of the Japanese. *The American Journal of Psychiatry, 109,* 241–248.

National Advisory Commission on Civil Disorders. (1968). Task force report of the National Advisory Commission on Criminal Justice Standards and Goals in

1973. *Task force report on civil disorders.* Washington D.C.: U.S. Government Printing Office.

National Advisory Committee on Criminal Justice Standards and Goals. (1976). *Disorders and terrorism.* Washington D.C.: Law Enforcement Assistance Agency. U.S. Government Printing Office.

National Advisory Committee on Criminal Justice Standards and Goals. (1977). *Report of the task force on disorders and terrorism.* Washington D.C.: U.S. Government Printing Office.

National Commission on the Causes and Prevention of Violence. (1970). In Kirkham, J.F. (Eds.), *Assassination and political violence: A report to the national commission on the causes and prevention of violence.* New York: Bantam Books.

Neale, W.D. (1973). Terror—Oldest weapon in the arsenal. *Army, Aug.*

Needham, J.P. (1976). Research needs for hostage situations. *Military Police Law Enforcement Journal, 3,* 27–29.

Neihouse, W. (1980). *Prisoner of the jungle.* New York: Vanguard.

Nelson, A. (1986). *Terrorism: The intelligence system.* United States Defense Intelligence Agency. Unpublished.

Netanyahu, B. (1986a). Defining terrorism. In Netanyahu, B. (Ed.), *Terrorism: How the West can win.* New York: Farrar, Straus, & Giroux.

Netanyahu, B. (1986b). Terrorists and freedom fighters. In Netanyahu, B. (Ed.), *Terrorism: How the West can win.* New York: Farrar, Straus, & Giroux.

New English Bible. (1970). Cambridge, England: Oxford University Press.

Newton, M. & Newton, J.A. (1991). *Racial and religious violence in America: A chronology.* New York: Garland Publishing, Inc.

Nidal, A. (1986). The Palestinian goal justifies terrorism. In Szumski, B. (Ed.), *Terrorism: Opposing viewpoints.* St. Paul, Minn.: Greenhaven Press.

Nielsen, E. (1984). Post-shooting trauma in police work. In Reese, J. & Goldstein, H. (Eds.), *Psychological services for law enforcement.* Washington D.C.: U.S. Government Printing Office.

Nimer, B. (1990). Terrorism and Southern Africa. *Terrorism, 13,* 447–453.

Noesner, G.W. & Dolan, J.T. (1992). First responder negotiation training. *FBI Law Enforcement Bulletin, 61,* 1–4.

Nordland, R. & Wilkinson, R. (1990). Inside terror, inc. In Schechterman, B. & Slann, M. (Eds.), *Violence and terrorism.* Guilford, Conn.: Reprint from *Newsweek,* 1986, *April 7,* 25–28.

Norman, L. (1978). Our nuclear weapons sites: Next targets of terrorists? In Elliott, J.D. & Gibson, L.K. (Eds.), *Contemporary terrorism.* Gaithersburg, Maryland: IACP.

Norton, A.R. (1988). Terrorism in the Middle East. In Pisano, V.S. (Ed.), *Terrorist dynamics: A geographical perspective.* Gaithersburg, MD: IACP.

Norton, A.R. & Greenberg, M.H. (Eds.). (1979). *Studies in nuclear terrorism.* Boston: G.K. Hill.

NOVA. (1990). *Poisoned winds of war.* NOVA PBS. Boston: WGBH Television.

NOVA. (1992). *The community crisis response team training,* Fort Sam Houston, TX, April.

Nudell, M. & Antokol, N. (1990). Negotiating for life. *Security Management, 34,* 56–66.

Nunn, S. & Warner, J.W. (1987). U.S.-Soviet cooperation in countering nuclear terrorism: The role of risk reduction centers. In Leventhal, P. & Alexander, Y. (Eds.), *Preventing nuclear terrorism.* Lexington, MA: Lexington Books.

NYPD. (1973). Policies and procedures for hostage rescue. Reviewed at SAPD Hostage Negotiation Training, August 1978.

Oakley, R.B. (1985). *Combating international terrorism.* Washington D.C.: Bureau of Public Affairs, U.S. Department of State (Policy Number 667).

O'Ballance, E. (1979). *Language of violence: The blood politics of terrorism.* San Rafael, CA: Presidio Press.

Ochberg, F.M. (1978). The victims of terrorism: Psychiatric consideration. *Terrorism: An International Journal, 1,* 151.

Ochberg, F.M. (1979). Preparing for terrorist victimization. In Alexander, Y. & Kilmarx, R.A. (Eds.), *Political terrorism and business – The threat and response.* New York: Praeger.

Ochberg, F.M. (1980a). Victims of terrorism. *Journal of Clinical Psychiatry, 41,* 73–74.

Ochberg, F.M. (1980b). What is happening to the hostages in Tehran? *Psychiatric Annals, 10,* 186–189.

Ochberg, F.M. (1982). A case study: Gerard Vaders. In Ochberg, F.M. & Soskis, D.A. (Eds.), *Victims of terrorism.* Boulder, Col.: Westview Press.

Ochberg, F.M. & Soskis, D.A. (1982). Planning for the future: Means and ends. In Ochberg, F.M. & Soskis, D.A. (Eds.), *Victims of terrorism.* Boulder, CO: Westview Press.

Ohry, A., Solomon, Z., Neria, Y., & Waysman, M. (1994). The aftermath of captivity: An 18-year follow-up of Israeli POWs. *Journal of Behavioral Medicine, 20,* 27–33.

Office of the Attorney General. (1983). *Attorney General's guidelines on domestic security/terrorism investigations.* Washington D.C.: U.S. Government Printing Office.

Olin, W.R. & Born, D.G. (1983). A behavioral approach to hostage situations. *FBI Law Enforcement Bulletin, 52,* 18–24.

Oots, K.L. (1986). *A political organization approach to transnational terrorism.* Westport, Conn.: Greenwood Press.

Oots, K.L. & Wiegele, T.C. (1985). Terrorist and victim: Psychiatric and physiological approaches from a social science perspective. *Terrorism, 8,* 1–32.

O'Sullivan, J. (1986). Deny them publicity. In Netanyahu, B. (Ed.), *Terrorism: How the West can win.* New York: Farrar, Straus, & Giroux.

Padover, S.K. (1943). Patterns of assassination in occupied territory. *Public Opinion Quarterly, 7,* 680.

Papanikolas, Z. (1982). *Buried unsung: Louis Tikas and the Ludlow massacre.* Salt Lake City, Utah: University of Utah.

Parry, A. (1976). *Terrorism: From Robespierre to Arafat.* New York: Vanguard Press.

Paust, J.J. (1977). A definitional focus. In Alexander, Y. & Finger, S.M. (Eds.), *Terrorism: Interdisciplinary perspectives.* New York: John Jay Press.

Pierre, A.J. (1978). The politics of international terrorism. In Elliot, J.D. & Gibson, L.K. (Eds.), *Contemporary terrorism: Selected readings.* Gaithersburg, Maryland: IACP. Reprint from *Orbis, XIX,* 1976.

Pilant, L. (1993). Less-than-lethal weapons: New solutions for law enforcement. *IACP Executive Brief.* Washington D.C.: International Association of Chiefs of Police.

Pluchinsky, D. (1982). Political terrorism in western Europe: Some themes and variations. In Alexander, Y. & Meyers, K.A. (Eds.), *Terrorism in Europe.* New York: St. Martin's Press.

Pluchinsky, D.A. (1991). Middle eastern terrorism in Europe: Trends and prospects. *Terrorism, 14,* 67–76.

Pluchinsky, D.A. (1992). Academic research on European terrorist developments: Pleas from a government terrorist analyst. *Studies in Conflict and Terrorism, 15,* 13–23.

Poland, J.M. (1988). *Understanding terrorism: Groups, strategies, and responses.* Englewood Cliffs, NJ: Prentice-Hall.

Pollack, M. (1990). The selling of terrorism: Profit from a lucrative export. In Schechterman, B. & Slann, M. (Eds.), *Violence and terrorism.* Guilford, Conn.: Dushkin Publishing Group, Inc. Reprint from *Insight,* 1987, *July 20,* 30–33.

Polmar, N. (1995). Operation Downfall: How many more would have been killed? Symposium at the 1945–Crucible of deliverance: Prisoners of war and the A-bomb conference sponsored by the Admiral Nimitz Museum. San Antonio, Texas. (Mar.)

Polmar, N. & Allen, T.B. (1991). *World war II: America at war: 1941-1945.* New York: Random House.

Pomerantz, S.L. (1987). The FBI and terrorism. *FBI Law Enforcement Bulletin, 56,* 15–23.

Popkin, J. (1993). Bombs over America. In Schechterman, B. & Slann, M. (Eds.), *Violence and terrorism* (3rd Ed.). Guilford, Conn.: Dushkin Publishing Group, Inc. Reprint from *U.S. News and World Report,* 1991, *29 July,* 18–20.

Post, J.M. (1984). Notes on a psychodynamic theory of terrorist behavior. *Terrorism: An International Journal, 7,* 241–256.

Powell, W. (1971). *The anarchist cookbook.* Secaucus, NJ: Lyle Stuart.

Prange, G.W., Goldstein, D., & Dillon, K. (1981). *At dawn we slept: The untold story of Pearl Harbor.* New York: Penguin Books.

Prange, G.W., Goldstein, D., & Dillon, K. (1988). *December 7, 1941: The day the Japanese attacked Pearl Harbor.* New York: Warner Books.

Preston, R. (1994). *The hot zone.* New York: Random House.

Probst, P. (1991). Future trends: Some observations. *Terrorism, 14,* 233–236.

Quigley, R.C. (1990). Terror marches on. *Security Management, 35,* 31–32.

Quarles, C.L. (1988). Kidnapped: Surviving the ordeal. *Security Management, 32,* 40–44.

Rahe, R.H. & Geneder, E. (1983). Adaptation to and recovery from captivity stress. *Military Medicine, 148,* 577–585.

Randall, W.P. (1965). *The Ku Klux Klan: A century of infamy.* New York: Chilton Books.

Rapoport, D.C. (1977). The politics of atrocity. In Alexander, Y. & Finger, S.M. (Eds.), *Terrorism: Interdisciplinary perspectives.* New York: John Jay Press.

Rapoport, D.C. (1988). Messianic sanctions for terror. *Comparative Politics, 20,* 195–213.

Rapoport, D.C. & Alexander, Y. (1983). *The morality of terrorism: Religious and secular justifications.* New York: Pergamon.

Reif, L.L. (1986). Women in Latin American guerrilla movements. *Comparative Politics, 18,* 147–169.

Revell, D.B. (1987). Terrorism today. *FBI Law Enforcement Bulletin, 56,* 1–4.

Revell, O.B. (1989). International terrorism in the United States. *Police Chief, 26,* 16–22.

Revell, O.B. (1991). Terrorism: Implications of the Gulf War. *Police Chief, 58,* 47–50.

Revell, O.B. (1993). Terrorism. In Schechterman, B. & Slann, M. (Eds.), *Violence and terrorism* (3rd Ed.). Guilford, Conn.: Dushkin Publishing Group, Inc. Reprint from *Terrorism,* 1991, *14,* 134–144.

Richardson, L.D. (1985). Surviving captivity: A hundred days. In Jenkins, B.M. (Ed.), *Terrorism and personal protection.* Stoneham, Mass.: Butterworth.

Ricks, B.A. (1988). Future domestic and international terrorism. The FBI perspective. *Terrorism, 11,* 538–541.

Risks International Inc. (1979). *Regional risk assessment: Latin America.* Alexandria, VA: Risks International Inc.

Risks International. (1985). *Terrorism: 1970–1984.* Alexandria, VA: Risks International, Inc.

Robinson, J.P. (1977). *Chemical weapons for NATO? A framework for considering policy options.* In Meselson, M. (Ed.), Chemical weapons and chemical arms control. Boston: Carnegie Endowment for International Peace.

Rodriguez, M.L. (1986). Unique considerations of a local government in a free society in developing a strategy for the prevention of international terrorism. Paper presented at the Academy of Criminal Justice Sciences, Orlando, FL (April).

Rosen, B. (1993). The media dilemma and terrorism. In Alexander, Y. & Latter, R. (Eds.), *Terrorism and the media: Dilemma for government, journalists and the public.* New York: Brassey.

Rosenblum, D.M. (1978). Nuclear terror. In Elliott, J.D. & Gibson, L.K. (Eds.), *Contemporary terrorism.* Gaithersburg, Maryland: IACP.

Rosenbaum, J.H. & Sederberg, P. (1976). *Vigilante politics.* Philadelphia, Penn.: University of Pennsylvania Press.

Rosewicz, B. & Seib, G.F. (1990). Aside from being a movement, the PLO is a financial giant. In Schechterman, B. & Slann, M. (Eds.), *Violence and terrorism.* Guilford, Conn.: Dushkin Publishing Group, Inc. Reprint from *The Wall Street Journal,* 1986, *July 21.*

Ross, J.I. (1993a). Structural causes of oppositional political terrorism: Towards a causal model. *Journal of Peace Research, 30,* 317–329.

Ross, J.I. (1993b). Research on contemporary oppositional political terrorism in the United States: Merits, drawbacks, and suggestions for improvement. In Tunnell, K.D. (Ed.), *Political crime in contemporary America: A critical approach.* New York: Garland Publishing Inc.

Ross, J.I. (1995). The relationship between domestic protest and oppositional political terrorism in connection with the Gulf Conflict. *Journal of Contemporary Criminal Justice, 11,* 35–51.

Ross, J.I. & Gurr, T.R. (1989). Why terrorism subsides: A comparative study of Canada and the United States. *The Journal of Comparative Politics, July,* 21.

Rostow, W.W. (1991). Introduction: Prelude to war. Symposium at the Storm Unleashed conference sponsored by the National Park Service. Honolulu, Hawaii. (Dec.)

Rubenstein, A. (1981). *Soviet foreign policy since World War II.* Cambridge, Mass.: Winthrop.

Rummel, R. (1966). Dimensions of conflict behavior within nations, 1946–1959. *Journal of Conflict Resolution, 10,* 65–73.

Rummel, R.J. (1990). War isn't this century's biggest killer. In Schechterman, B. & Slann, M. (Eds.), *Violence and terrorism.* Guilford, Conn.: Dushkin Publishing Group, Inc. Reprint from *The Wall Street Journal,* 1986, *July 7.*

Russell, C. (1985). Kidnapping as a terrorist tactic. In Jenkins, B.M. (Ed.), *Terrorism and personal protection.* Stoneham, Mass.: Butterworth Publishers.

Russell, F. (1986). *Sacco and Vanzetti: The case resolved.* New York: Harper and Row.

Russell, C.A. & Miller, B.H. (1978). Profile of a terrorist. In Elliot, J.D. & Gibson, L.K. (Eds.), *Contemporary terrorism: Selected readings.* Gaithersburg, Maryland: IACP. Reprint from *Terrorism: An International Journal, 1,* 1977.

Russell, H.E. & Zuniga, R. (1986). Special stress factors in hostage/barricaded situations when the perpetrator is a police officer. In Reese, J. & Goldstein, H.A. (Eds.), *Psychological services for law enforcement.* Washington D.C.: U.S. Government Printing Office.

Salavarrieta, A.P. (1989). Terrorism in Columbia. In Buckwalter, J.R. (Ed.), *International terrorism: The decade ahead.* Chicago, IL: OICJ.

Salerno, R. & Tompkins, J.S. (1969). *The crime confederation.* Garden City, NY: Doubleday.

Sandler, T., Enders, W. & Lapan, H.E. (1993). Economic analysis can help fight international terrorism. In Schechterman, B. & Slann, M. (Eds.), *Violence and terrorism* (3rd Ed.). Guilford, Conn.: Dushkin Publishing Group, Inc. Reprint from *Challenge,* 1991, *Jan/Feb,* 10–17.

Santoro, K. (1987). Italian attitudes and responses to terrorism. *Terrorism, 10,* 289–310.

Sapp, A.D. (1985). Basic ideologies of right-wing extremist groups in America. Paper presented at the Academy of Criminal Justice Sciences, Las Vegas, Nevada (April).

Sapp, A.D. (1986a). Rationalization for domestic violence: An analysis of The Secret Army . . . Wenn Alle Bruder Schweigen. Paper presented at the Academy of Criminal Justice Sciences, Orlando, Fla. (April).

Sapp, A.D. (1986b). The Nehemiah Township Charter: Applied right-wing ideology. Paper presented at the Academy of Criminal Justice Sciences, Orlando, Fla. (April).

Sapp, A.D. (1986c). A philosophy of terrorism as expressed in The Turner Diaries. Paper presented at the American Society of Criminology, Atlanta, GA. (October).

Sapp, A.D. (1987). Organizational linkages of right-wing extremist groups. Paper presented at the Academy of Criminal Justice Sciences, St. Louis, MO. (April).

Saxon, K. (1986). *The poor man's James Bond* (2nd Ed.). Harrison, AR: Atlan Formularies.

Scarce, R. (1990). *Ecowarriors: Understanding the radical environmental movement.* Chicago: Noble Press, Inc.

Schbley, A.H. (1989). Resurgent religious terrorism: A study of some of the Lebanese Shi'i contemporary terrorism. *Terrorism, 12,* 213–247.

Schechterman, B. (1990a). Religious fanaticism as a factor in political violence. In Schechterman, B. & Slann, M. (Eds.), *Violence and terrorism.* Guilford, Conn.: Dushkin Publishing Group, Inc. Reprint from *International Freedom Foundation,* 1986, *1,* 1–6.

Schechterman, B. (1990b). U.S. Government organizations to counter terrorism. In Schechterman, B. & Slann, M. (Eds.), *Violence and terrorism.* Guilford, Conn.: Dushkin Publishing Group, Inc.

Schechterman, B. & McGuinn, B.R. (1990). Linkages between Sunni and Shi'i radical fundamentalist organizations: A new variable in recent middle eastern politics? In Schechterman, B. & Slann, M. (Eds.). *Violence and terrorism.* Dushkin Publishing Group, Inc. Reprint from The Political Chronicle, 1989, *1.*

Schelling, T.C. (1976). Who will have the bomb? *International Security, 1,* 77–91.

Schlossberg, H. (1979). Hostage negotiations. Presentation at the Texas Department of Public Safety's Terrorism School, Austin, Texas.

Schmid, A.P. (1983). *Political terrorism: A research guide to concepts, theories, data bases and literature.* Amsterdam: North Holland Publishing Co.

Schmid, A.P. (1985). Goals and objectives of international terrorism. *Defense Intelligence College Symposium Proceedings.* Washington D.C.: Defense Intelligence Agency.

Schmid, A.P. & de Graaf, J. (1982). *Violence as communication: Insurgent terrorism and the western news media.* Beverly Hills, CA: Sage.

Schreiber, M. (1973). An after action report of terrorist activities, 20th Olympic games, Munich, West Germany. Reviewed at FBI Hostage Negotiation Seminar, Feb. 1985.

Schreiber, J. (1978). *The ultimate weapon: Terrorists and world order.* New York: William Morrow.

Scott, A. (1970). *Insurgency.* Chapel Hill, NC: University of North Carolina Press.

Scotti, A.J. (1986). *Executive safety and international terrorism.* Englewood Cliffs, NJ: Prentice-Hall.

Scruton, R. (1982). *A dictionary of political thought.* New York: Hill & Wang.

Secretary General. (1972). *U.S. Doc. A/C.6/418.* Washington D.C.: U.S. Government Printing Office.

Sederberg, P.C. (1993a). Explaining terrorism. Terrorism: Contending themes in contemporary research. In Schechterman, B. & Slann, M. (Eds.), *Violence and terrorism* (3rd Ed.). Guilford, Conn.: Dushkin Publishing Group, Inc. Reprint from Sederberg, P.C. (Ed.), *Annual review of conflict knowledge.* New York: Garland Publishing.

Sederburg, P.C. (1993b). Responses to terrorism. In Schechterman, B. & Slann, M. (Eds.), *Violence and terrorism* (3rd Ed.). Guilford, Conn.: Dushkin Publishing

Group, Inc. Reprint from *Terrorism: Contending themes in contemporary research*, 1991.

Sederberg, P.C. (1994). *Fires within: Political violence and revolutionary change*. New York: HarperCollins College Pub.

Segal, D. (1986). Middle-east menace. *Police Product News, Dec.*, 38–44.

Segal, J., Hunter, E.J., & Segal, Z. (1976). Universal consequences of captivity: Stress reactions among divergent populations of prisoners of war and their families. *International Social Science Journal, 28*, 593–609.

Seger, K.A. (1991). Is America next? *Security Management, 35*, 30–32.

Selth, A. (1988). *Against every human law: The terrorist threat to diplomacy*. Rushcutters Bay, Australia: Australian National Press.

Selye, H. (1956). *The stress of life*. New York: McGraw-Hill.

Shagmar, M. (1986). An international convention against terrorism. In Netanyahu, B. (Ed.), *Terrorism: How the West can win*. New York: Farrar, Straus, & Giroux.

Sharpe, H.F. Jr. (1991). Bombing of the La Belle Discotheque: Anatomy of a terrorist incident. In Flood, S. (Ed.), *International terrorism: Policy implications*. Chicago, IL: OICJ.

Shaw, E. (1983). Political hostages: Sanction and recovery process. In Freedman, L.Z. & Alexander, Y. (Eds.), *Perspectives on terrorism*. Wilmington, Del.: Scholarly Resources.

Sherrod, R. (1993). *Tarawa: The story of a battle*. Fredericksburg, TX: Admiral Nimitz Foundation.

Shipler, D.K. (1988). Future domestic and international terrorism: The media perspective. *Terrorism, 11*, 543–545.

Shultz, G.P. (1986). The challenge to the democracies. In Netanyahu, B. (Ed.), *Terrorism: How the West can win*. New York: Farrar, Straus, & Giroux.

Siegel, R.K. (1984). Hostage hallucination: Visual imagery induced by isolation and life threatening stress. *Journal of Nervous and Mental Disease, 172*, 264–272.

Silberman, C. (1980). *Criminal justice, criminal violence*. New York: Vintage Books.

Siljander, R.P. (1980). *Terrorist attacks: A protective service guide for executives, body-guards and policemen*. Springfield, IL: Charles C Thomas, Publisher.

Simon, J.D. (1994). *The terrorist trap: America's experience with terrorism*. Bloomington, Ind.: Indiana University Press.

Simon, R.I. & Blum, R.A. (1987). After the terrorist incident: Psychotherapeutic treatment of former hostages. *American Journal of Psychotherapy, 41*, 194–200.

Singh, B. (1977). An overview. In Alexander, Y. & Finger, S.M. (Eds.), *Terrorism: Interdisciplinary perspectives*. New York: John Jay Press.

Slann, M. (1993). The state as terrorist. In Schechterman, B. & Slann, M. (Eds.), *Violence and terrorism* (3rd Ed.). Guilford, Conn.: Dushkin Publishing Group, Inc.

Sledge, W.H., Boydstun, J.A., & Rabe, A.J. (1980). Self-concept changes related to war captivity. *Archives of General Psychiatry, 37*, 430–443.

Sloan, S. (1987). *Beating international terrorism: An action strategy for preemption and punishment*. Maxwell Air Force Base, Ala.: Air University Press.

Sloan, S. & Kearney, R. (1977). An analysis of a simulated terrorist incident. *Police Chief, 22,* 57–59.

Smart, I.M.H. (1978). The power of terror. In Elliot, J.D. & Gibson, L.K. (Eds.), *Contemporary terrorism: Selected readings.* Gaithersburg, Maryland: IACP. Reprint from *International Journal, XXX,* 1975.

Smith, B.L. (1994). *Terrorism in America: Pipe bombs and pipe dreams.* Albany, NY: State University of New York Press.

Smith, D. (1982). Ideology and the ethics of economic crime control. In Elliston, F. & Bowie, N. (Eds.), *Ethics, public policy, and criminal justice.* Cambridge, Mass.: Oelgeschlager, Gunn and Hein.

Snow, D.A. & Machalek, R. (1982). On the presumed fragility of unconventional beliefs. *Journal for the Scientific Study of Religion, 21,* 15–26.

Snyder, L.L. (1989). *Encyclopedia of the Third Reich.* New York: Paragon House.

Sobel, L.A. (1975). *Political terrorism.* New York: Facts on File.

Sofaer, A. (1986). Terrorism and the law. *Foreign Affairs, 64,* 901–922.

Soskis, D.A. & Ochberg, F.M. (1982). Concepts of terrorist victimization. In Ochberg, F.M. & Soskis, D.A. (Eds.), *Victims of terrorism.* Boulder, CO: Westview Press.

Spaulding, W.G. (1987). The longest hour: the first response to terrorist incidents. *Law Enforcement Technology, Jul/Aug,* 26.

Spaulding, R.C. & Ford, C.V. (1972). The Pueblo incident: Psychological reactions to the stresses of imprisonment and repatriation. *American Journal of Psychiatry, 129,* 17–26.

Spector, L.S. (1985). *The nuclear nations.* New York: Vintage Books.

Speed, N., Engdahl, B., Schwartz, J., & Eberly, R. (1989). Posttraumatic stress disorder as a consequence of the POW experience. *Journal of Nervous and Mental Disease, 177,* 147–153.

Staff. (1972). Russia: In the dark ages of psychiatry. *The Economist, Jul 8,* London, England.

Staff. (1987). Racist radio makes Utah debate. *San Antonio Light, Dec. 6,* 5A.

Steinberg, G. (1993). Hidden threat. In Schechterman, B. & Slann, M. (Eds.), *Violence and terrorism* (3rd Ed.). Guilford, Conn.: Dushkin Publishing Group, Inc. Reprint from *The Jerusalem Post Weekly English Edition,* 1992, *15 Feb.*

Steinhoff, P.G. (1976). Portrait of a terrorist: An interview with Kozo O. Kamoto. *Asian Survey, XVI,* 835.

Stephan, M. (1973). *Vulnerability of total petroleum systems.* Washington D.C.: Department of the Interior.

Stephens, D. & Mackenna, D. (1988). Next tool for terrorists. *Security Management, 32,* 26–32.

Sterling, C. (1982). *The terror network.* New York: Berkley Pub.

Sterling, C. (1986). Unraveling the riddle. In Netanyahu, B. (Ed.), *Terrorism: How the West can win.* New York: Farrar, Straus, & Giroux.

Stevens, J.W. & MacKenna, D.W. (1989). Assignment and coordination of tactical units. *FBI Law Enforcement Bulletin, 58,* 2–9.

Stevenson, W. (1976). *90 minutes at Entebbe.* New York: Bantam.

Steward, D. (1993). Terrorism and revolutionary violence: A view from South

Africa. In Han, H.H. (Ed.), *Terrorism and political violence: Limits and possibilities of legal control.* New York: Oceana Pub. Inc.

Stewart, R.C. (1980). *Identification and investigation of organized criminal activity.* Houston, TX: National College of District Attorneys.

Stimson, E. (1986). *Christianity today, Aug,* 30–31.

Stinson, J. (1987). Domestic terrorism in the United States. *The Police Chief, Sep,* 62–69.

Stinson, J. (1993). Domestic terrorism in the United States. In Schechterman, B. & Slann, M. (Eds.), *Violence and terrorism* (3rd Ed.). Guilford, Conn.: Dushkin Publishing Group, Inc. Reprinted from *Police Chief,* 1987, *Sep,* 62–69.

Stoffel, J.P. (1972). *Explosives and homemade bombs.* Springfield, IL: Charles C Thomas, Publisher.

Stohl, M. (1985). States, terrorism, and state terrorism: The role of the superpowers. *Proceedings of the symposium on international terrorism.* Washington D.C.: Defense Intelligence Agency.

Stone, J. (1990). The ballad of the greenbean beret. In Schechterman, B. & Slann, M. (Eds.), *Violence and terrorism.* Guilford, Conn.: Dushkin Publishing Group, Inc. Reprint from *Discover,* 1988, *Dec.,* 80–83.

Strentz, T. (1979). Law enforcement policies and ego defenses of the hostage. *FBI Law Enforcement Bulletin, 48,* 1–12.

Strentz, T. (1982). The Stockholm syndrome: Law enforcement policy and hostage behavior. In Ochberg, F.M. & Soskis, D.A. (Eds.), *Victims of terrorism.* Boulder, CO: Westview Press.

Strentz, T. (1987). Preparing the person with high potential for victimization as a hostage. In Turner, J.T. (Ed.), *Violence in the medical care setting: A survival guide.* Rockville, Maryland: Aspen Press.

Strentz, T. (1987). A hostage psychological survival guide. *FBI Law Enforcement Bulletin, Nov,* 1–8.

Strentz, T. (1987). *Terrorism.* Law Enforcement Satellite Training Network. Kansas City, Kansas: Kansas City Police Department.

Strentz, T. (1988). A terrorist psychosocial profile, past and present. *FBI Law Enforcement Bulletin, 57,* 13–19.

Strentz, T. (1990). Radical right vs. radical left: Terrorist theory and threat. *Police Chief, Aug,* 70–75.

Strentz, T. & Auerbach, S.M. (1988). Adjustment to the stress of simulated captivity: Effects of emotion-focused versus problem-focused preparation on hostages differing in locus of control. *Journal of Personality and Social Psychology, 55,* 652–660.

Suall, I. & Lowe, D. (1987). Special report. The hate movement today: A chronicle of violence and disarray. *Terrorism, 10,* 345–364.

Sullivan, C. (1990). New extremists exceed "Jim Crowism" of KKK. In Schechterman, B. & Slann, M. (Eds.), *Violence and terrorism.* Guilford, Conn.: Dushkin Publishing Group, Inc. Reprint from *The Christian Science Monitor,* 1987, *Jan 12.*

Sutker, P.B., Bugg, F., & Allain, A.N. (1990). Person and situation correlates of posttraumatic stress disorder among POW survivors. *Psychological Reports, 66,* 912–914.

Sutker, P.B., Winstead, D.K., Goist, K.C., & Malow, R.M. (1986). Psychopathology subtypes and symptom correlates among former prisoners of war. *Journal of Psychopathology and Behavioral Assessment, 8,* 89–101.

Sutton, J.R. (1991). Future of terrorism in Latin America. In Flood, S. (Ed.), *International terrorism: Policy implications.* Chicago, IL: OICJ.

Symes, L. & Clement, T. (1972). *Rebel America: The story of social revolt in the United States.* New York: De Capo Press.

Symonds, M. (1975). Victims of violence: Psychological effects and aftereffects. *American Journal of Psychoanalysis, 35,* 19–26.

Symonds, M. (1980). The "second injury" to victims. *Evaluation and Change, Special Issue,* 36–38.

Symonds, M. (1982). Victim responses to terror: Understanding and treatment. In Ochberg, F.M. & Soskis, D.A. (Eds.), *Victims of terrorism.* Boulder, CO: Westview Press.

Symonds, M. (1983). Victimization and rehabilitative treatment. In Eichelman, B., Soskis, D., & Reid, W. (Eds.), *Terrorism: Interdisciplinary perspectives.* Washington D.C.: American Psychiatric Association.

Task Force on Organized Crime. (1976). *Organized crime.* Washington D.C.: U.S. Government Printing Office.

Teller, E. (1995). Keynote address. Symposium at the 1945 — Crucible of deliverance: Prisoners of war and the A-bomb conference sponsored by the Admiral Nimitz Museum. San Antonio, Texas. (Mar.)

Tennant, C., Goulston, K., & Dent, O. (1986). Clinical psychiatric illnesses in prisoners of war of the Japanese: Forty years after release. *Psychological Medicine, 16,* 833–839.

Texas Department of Public Safety. (1985). *Texas criminal laws.* Austin, TX: Department of Public Safety.

Thatcher, G. & Aeppel, T. (1989). How Iraq got way to wage chemical war. *The Oregonian, 25 Jan,* A7.

Thomas, G. (1989). *Journey into madness.* New York: Bantam Books.

Thompson, L.B. (1989). *Low-intensity conflict: The pattern of warfare in the modern world.* Lexington, Mass.: D.C. Heath.

Thornton, T.P. (1964). Terror as a weapon of political agitation. In Eckstein, H. (Ed.), *Internal war.* New York: Free Press.

Tinklenberg, J. (1982). Coping with terrorist victimization. In Ochberg, F.M. & Soskis, D.A. (Eds.), *Victims of terrorism.* Boulder, CO: Westview Press.

Toch, H. (1969). *Violent men.* Chicago: Aldine.

Trick, M.M. (1976). Chronology of incidents of terroristic, quasi-terroristic, and political violence in the United States: January 1965 to March 1976. National Advisory Committee on Criminal Justice Standards and Goals. *Disorders and terrorism: Report of the task force on disorders and terrorism.* Washington D.C.: Law Enforcement Assistance Administration, Department of Justice.

Trujillo, S.G. (1993). Peru's Maoist drug dealers. In Schechterman, B. & Slann, M.

(Eds.), *Violence and terrorism* (3rd Ed.). Guilford, Conn.: Dushkin Publishing Group, Inc. Reprint from *The New York Times,* 1992, *8 April.*

Tucker, R.C. (1974). *Stalin as a revolutionary, 1879–1929: A study in history and personality.* New York: Norton.

Tuohy, W. (1989). State owned company tied to Libyan plant. *The Oregonian, 25 Jan,* A7.

Turco, R.M. (1987). Psychiatric contributions to the understanding of international terrorism. *International Journal of Offender Therapy and Comparative Criminology, 31,* 153–161.

Turner, J.T. & Kusy, V. (1987). Summary of psychotraumatology and victimology: How did we miss each other? Paper presented at the International Conference on Victimology, San Francisco, Cal. (July).

Turner, S. (1993). 10 steps against terror. In Schechterman, B. & Slann, M. (Eds.), *Violence and terrorism* (3rd Ed.). Guilford, Conn.: Dushkin Publishing Group, Inc. Reprint from *World Monitor,* 1991, *July,* 46–50.

Tyhurst, J.S. (1958). The role of transition states—including disasters—in mental illness. In *Proceedings of Symposium on Prevention and Social Psychiatry.* Washington D.C.: U.S. Government Printing Office.

Tyhurst, J.S. (1986). The role of transition states—including disasters—in mental illness. In *Proceedings of Symposium on Preventive and Social Psychiatry.* Washington D.C.: U.S. Government Printing Office.

Ulam, A.B. (1973). *Stalin: The man and his era.* New York: Viking Press.

Unnamed. (1993). Columbia's bloodstained peace. In Schechterman, B. & Slann, M. (Eds.), *Violence and terrorism* (3rd Ed.). Guilford, Conn.: Dushkin Publishing Group, Inc. Reprint from *The Economist,* 1992, *6 Jun,* 41–42.

Ursano, R.J. & Rundell, J.R. (1990). The prisoner of war. *Military Medicine, 155,* 176–180.

USAF Operations Plan 208-85. (1985). *Protection against terrorist activity.* Maxwell AFB, AL: Department of the Air Force ROTC (ATC).

U.S. Air Force. (1985). *U.S. Air Force special operations school.* Florida.

U.S. Bureau of Alcohol, Tobacco and Firearms. (1983). *Explosive incidents in 1982.* Washington D.C.: U.S. Government Printing Office.

U.S. Congress, Senate Committee on the Judiciary. (1975). *Terrorist activity: Hostage defense measures.* Hearings before a Subcommittee to Investigate the Administration of the Internal Security Act and other Internal Security Laws, Part 5, 94th Congress, First Session, 265.

U.S. Department of State. (1983). *Terrorist bombings.* Washington D.C.: U.S. Government Printing Office.

U.S. Department of State. (1985). *Patterns of global terrorism: 1984.* Washington D.C.: U.S. Government Printing Office.

U.S. Department of Transportation, Federal Aviation Administration. (1985). *Explosions aboard aircraft.* Washington D.C.: U.S. Government Printing Office.

U.S. Government. (1975). *Terroristic activity—International terrorism.* Hearings before the subcommittee to investigate the administration of the international security act and other internal security laws of the Committee on the Judiciary. United

States Senate, Ninety-Fourth Congress, First Session, Part 4, May 14. Washington D.C.: U.S. Government Printing Office.

Vaksburg, A. (1991). *The Soviet mafia.* New York: St. Martin's Press.

Van den Haag, E. (1972). *Political violence and civil disobedience.* New York: Harper & Row.

Van Gelder, A.P. & Schlatter, H. (1972). *History of the explosives industry in America.* New York: Arno Press.

Van Zandt, C.R. (1991). Hostage situations: Separating negotiation and command duties. *FBI Law Enforcement Bulletin, 60,* 18–19.

Vermaat, J.A.E. (1987). Terrorist sympathizers in the Netherlands. *Terrorism, 10,* 329–335.

Verrengia, J.B. (1995). Gas used in Tokyo is plentiful: U.S. as well as volatile nations own weapons filled with sarin. *Rocky Mountain News, 21 Mar,* 26A.

Vetter, H.J. & Perlstein, G.R. (1991). *Perspectives on terrorism.* Pacific Grove, CA: Brooks/Cole.

Wald, C. (1985). *Atlas of the North American Indian.* New York: Facts on File.

Walker, J.L. (1971). *The human cost of communism in China.* Washington D.C.: U.S. Government Printing Office.

Walter, E.V. (1969). *Terror and resistance: A study of political violence.* London: Oxford University Press.

Wardlaw, G. (1982). *Political terrorism: Theory, tactics, and countermeasures.* Cambridge: Cambridge University Press.

Wardlaw, G. (1985). State response to international terrorism: Some cautionary comments. *Proceedings of the Symposium on International Terrorism.* Washington D.C.: Defense Intelligence Agency.

Wargo, M.G. (1988). The tactical use of negotiators. *The Tactical Edge, 6,* 39–40.

Wardlaw, G. (1989). *Political terrorism.* New York: Cambridge University Press.

Waterman, C. (1990). Religious fervor makes terrorists tougher to handle. In Schechterman, B. & Slann, M. (Eds.), *Violence and terrorism.* Guilford, Conn.: Dushkin Publishing Group, Inc. Reprint from *The Christian Science Monitor,* 1985, *June 27,* 9–11.

Watson, R., Walcott, J., Barry, J., Clifton, T., & Marshall, R. (1986). Kaddafi's crusade. *Newsweek, Nov 10,* 20–24.

Waxman, S. (1993). The new sound of hate. In Schechterman, B. & Slann, M. (Eds.), *Violence and terrorism* (3rd Ed.). Guilford, Conn.: Dushkin Publishing Group, Inc. Reprint from *The Washington Post,* 1992, *12 July,* G1 & G4.

Webster, W.H. (1986). Fighting terrorism in the United States. In Netanyahu, B. (Ed.), *Terrorism: How the West can win.* New York: Farrar, Straus, & Giroux.

Wege, C.A. (1993). The Abu Nidal Organization. In Schechterman, B. & Slann, M. (Eds.), *Violence and terrorism* (3rd Ed.). Guilford, Conn.: Dushkin Publishing Group, Inc. Reprint from *Terrorism,* 1992, *14,* 59–66.

Weinberg, L. (1993). The American radical right: Exit, voice and violence. In Merkl, P. & Weinberg, L. (Eds.), *Encounters with the radical contemporary radical right.* Boulder, CO: Westview Press.

Weinberg, L. & Eubank, W.L. (1987). Italian women terrorists. *Terrorism: An International Journal, 9,* 241–262.

Wheal, E.A., Pope, S., & Taylor, J. (1989). *Encyclopedia of the Second World War.* Secaucus, NJ: Castle Books.

Welch, M.F. (1984). Applied typology and victimology in the hostage negotiation process. *Journal of Crime and Justice, 7,* 63–86.

Wesselius, C.L. & DeSarno, J.V. (1983). The anatomy of a hostage situation. *Behavioral Science and the Law, 1,* 33–45.

White, J.R. (1986). *Holy war: Terrorism as a theological construct.* Gaithersburg, MD: IACP.

White, J.R. (1991). *Terrorism: An introduction.* Pacific Grove, CA: Brooks/Cole.

Whittle, R.A. (1988). Hostage negotiations: A situational motivational approach for police response. In Palmiotto, M.J. (Ed.), *Critical issues in criminal investigations* (2nd Ed.).

Wiggins, M.E. (1985). Rationale and justification for right-wing terrorism: A politicosocial analysis of The Turner Diaries. Paper presented at the American Society of Criminology. Atlanta, GA. (October).

Wiggins, M.E. (1986a). An extremist right-wing group and domestic terrorism. Paper presented at the Academy of Criminal Justice Sciences. Orlando, Fla. (April).

Wiggins, M.E. (1986b). The Turner Diaries: Blueprint for right-wing extremist violence. Paper presented at the Academy of Criminal Justice Sciences. Orlando, Fla. (April).

Wiggins, M.E. (1986c). A descriptive profile of criminal activities of a right-wing extremist group. Paper presented at the Society of Police and Criminal Psychology. Little Rock, Ark. (October).

Wiggins, M.E. (1987). Preparing for war: Right-wing paramilitary training. Paper presented at the Academy of Criminal Justice Sciences. St. Louis, MO. (April).

Wilcox, L. (1992). What is extremism? Style and tactics matter more than goals. In George, J. & Wilcox, L. (Eds.), *Nazis, communists, klansmen and others on the fringe: Political extremism in America.* Buffalo, NY: Prometheus Books.

Williams, D.F. Jr. (1990). The skull and crossbones still flies. *Police Chief, Sep,* 47–49.

Wilkinson, P. (1974). *Political terrorism.* New York: Wiley.

Wilkinson, P. (1977). *Terrorism and the liberal state.* London: MacMillan.

Wilkinson, P. (1983). *The new fascists* (Rev. Ed.). London: Pan Books.

Wilkinson, P. (1986a). *Terrorism and the liberal state.* New York: New York University Press.

Wilkinson, P. (1986b). Trends in international terrorism and the American response. In *Terrorism and international order.* London: Routledge & Kegan Paul.

Wilkinson, P. (1983). *The new fascists* (Rev. Ed.). London: Pan Books.

Williams, D.F. Jr. (1990). Terrorism in the 90s: The skull and crossbones still flies. *Police Chief, 57,* 47–50.

Willrich, M. & Taylor, T.B. (1979). Nuclear theft: Risks and safeguards. In Norton, A.R. & Greenberg, M.H. (Eds.), *Studies in nuclear terrorism.* Boston: G.K. Hill.

Wilson, J.Q. (1973). *Political organizations.* New York: Basic Books.

Wilson, M. & Lynxwiler, J. (1988). Abortion clinic violence as terrorism. *Terrorism, 11*, 26–273.

WMAQ. (1985). *The dragons of God.* News documentary (Feb.). Chicago, IL: WMAQ Television.

Wolfe, B.D. (1965). *Marxism: One hundred years in the life of a doctrine.* New York: Dial Press.

Wolf, J.B. (1978a). Controlling political terrorism in a free society. In Elliot, J.D. & Gibson, L.K. (Eds.), *Contemporary terrorism: Selected readings.* Gaithersburg, Maryland: IACP. Reprint from *Orbis, 19,* 1976.

Wolf, J.B. (1978b). Organization and management practice of urban terrorist groups. *Terrorism: An International Journal, 1,* 169–186.

Wolf, J.B. (1981). *Fear of fear: A survey of terrorist operations and controls in open societies.* New York: Plenum Press.

Wolf, J.B. (1989a). State-directed terrorist squads. In Wolf, J.B. (Ed.), *Antiterrorist initiatives.* New York: Plenum Press.

Wolf, J.B. (1989b). Terrorism in the Pacific regions. In Wolf, J.B. (Ed.), *Antiterrorist initiatives.* New York: Plenum Press.

Woodruff, P.B. (1991). In Hall, R.C. (Ed.), *Lighting over Bougainville: The Yamamoto mission reconsidered.* Washington D.C.: Smithsonian Institute Press.

World Press Review. (1985). *"Born" in the U.S.: Terrorist training in the South, Sep,* 39–40.

Wurth, D.E. (1985). The proper function and use of the private sector bodyguard. In Jenkins, B.M. (Ed.), *Terrorism and personal protection.* Stoneham, Mass.: Butterworth Publishers.

Yeager, C. (1986). Terrorism: Who? Why? What is to be done? *Omega Focus Series, 1.* Boulder, Col.: Omega Group Ltd.

Yaeger, C.H. (1991). Sikh terrorism in the struggle for Khakistan. *Terrorism, 14,* 221–231.

Yost, G. (1985). *Spy-tech.* New York: Facts on File.

Zawodny, J.M. (1978). Internal organizational problems and the sources of tensions of terrorist movements as catalysts of violence. *Terrorism: An International Journal, 1,* 277–285.

Zawodny, J.K. (1983). Infrastructures of terrorist organizations. In Freedman, L.Z. & Alexander, Y. (Eds.), *Perspectives on terrorism.* Wilmington, Del.: Scholarly Resources.

Zimmermann, T. & Cooperman, A. (1995). The Russian connection. *U.S. News and World Report, 119,* 59–67.

Zobel, H.B. (1970). *The Boston massacre.* New York: Norton.

INDEX